FOUNDATIONS OF THE SEVENTH-DAY ADVENTIST MESSAGE AND MISSION

FOUNDATIONS OF THE SEVENTH-DAY ADVENTIST MESSAGE AND MISSION

by

P. Gerard Damsteegt, Dr. Theol.

William B. Eerdmans Publishing Company
Grand Rapids, Michigan

Second printing, September 1978

Library of Congress Cataloging in Publication Data
Damsteegt, P   Gerard.
   Foundations of the Seventh-day Adventist message
and mission.
   Bibliography: p. 314.
   Includes index.
   1. Seventh-day Adventists. I. Title. II. United States—
Religion—19th century.
BX6121.D35   286.7'3   76-56799
ISBN 0-8028-1698-3

To
my Mother
and to
Leon and Dolores

Contents

Acknowledgments

It is with a deep sense of indebtedness and gratitude that I reflect on my academic training. It would be impossible to mention all those who have influenced me during these formative years. While expressing my thanks to all who, in some way or another, assisted me in my education, I shall refer only to the most significant influences.

This study is the result of many converging influences from theological studies in England, the United States, the Netherlands, and Switzerland. My interest in the theological significance of the missionary nature of the church has been stimulated by Dr. Gottfried Oosterwal, and his encouragement was a major factor in the decision to pursue my theological studies at the Free University of Amsterdam. I am thankful for the insights I received during my study there, being especially grateful for the opportunity to study under Dr. J. Verkuyl whose dynamic personality and Christo-centric theology have greatly enlarged my understanding of the relevance of the Gospel of Jesus Christ for contemporary society. His openness of spirit in dealing with those of a different persuasion, his respect for the human personality, and his never ceasing concern for peace, reconciliation, and righteousness were a stimulating example of a life which maintained a rare balance between doctrine and practice. I express also my appreciation to Dr. J. van den Berg for his careful reading of the manuscript and his valuable advice, and to Dr. G. C. Berkouwer who, through his lectures and books, has made me aware of the importance of historical-theological studies.

Through Prof. J. Verkuyl's encouragement I attended the Graduate School of Ecumenical Studies, Céligny, Switzerland, held under the auspices of the World Council of Churches and the University of Geneva. The lectures and research there contributed considerably to the selection of the subject matter of the study. Discussions and interviews with various officials of the World Council of Churches such as Dr. Hans-Rudi Weber, Dr. W. A. Visser 't Hooft, Dr. Lukas Vischer, Dr. Konrad Raiser, and Dr. W. Hollenweger were of great value and confirmed the necessity of my present research.

I also express my thanks to the administration of Andrews University and its theological faculty for their cooperation while engaged in the research and writing of this subject. Discussions with Dr. C. Mervyn Maxwell,

Dr. Sakae Kubo, Dr. Gerhard F. Hasel, Dr. Hans K. La Rondelle, and Rolf J. Pöhler and their encouragement and constructive suggestions have proved to be very beneficial.

The major share of my research was done through the Andrews University Archives and the Ellen G. White Research Center, Berrien Springs, Michigan. Use was also made of the Orrin Roe Jenks Memorial Collection of Adventual Materials, Aurora College, Aurora, Illinois; the Seventh Day Baptist Historical Society, Plainfield, New Jersey; the Second Adventist Collection of the American Antiquarian Society, Worcester, Massachusetts; the Library of Congress, Washington, D.C.; and the Ellen G. White Estate, Takoma Park, Washington, D.C. I am grateful for the aid rendered by those in charge, in particular the invaluable assistance provided by Elder Arthur L. White, Mrs. Hedwig Jemison, Mrs. Louise F. Dederen, Mrs. Doris K. Colby, and Rev. Albert N. Rogers.

I am very much indebted to Dr. Sakae Kubo regarding matters dealing with the form of the footnotes, to Dr. Leona G. Running, Dr. C. Mervyn Maxwell, Mrs. Victor H. Campbell, Miss Diana Stevens, Miss Laurel A. Nelson, Mrs. James M. Crawford, and Alan Crandall for the proofreading and/or editing, and to Mrs. James Campbell for the typing of the manuscript.

Furthermore I would like to express my gratitude to Leon and Dolores Slikkers for their generous financial support. Without their assistance the completion of this research would have taken several more years.

The publication of the research was made possible through the much appreciated cooperation of the Netherlands Organization for the Advancement of Pure Research.

I am also thankful to my mother whose spiritual, moral, and financial support during my life has been an indispensable influence and strength.

The greatest source of inspiration was the Lord Jesus Christ who through His abundant love and grace provided me with the necessary strength, perseverance, patience, and insight to complete my research.

With the increasing network of communications, in many parts of the world action between members of the human race has intensified. These interhuman relations have led to a desire and search for mutual understanding through dialogue. Such communication has taken place among Christians as well as between Christians and persons of other religions. To discover the depth of faith of those who have different religious convictions, an openness of spirit and a thorough knowledge of their religious self-image is indispensable.

With this in mind we have attempted to arrive at an understanding of the origins and basic structure of the theology which has motivated the Seventh-day Adventist Church for more than a century, making it one of the most widespread Protestant churches. The study, which is limited to a descriptive historical-theological and missiological approach, has penetrated into the Seventh-day Adventist self-understanding through an analysis of their use of Scripture. Without analyzing the original Scriptural basis of Seventh-day Adventism it is impossible to grasp fully the significance of its missionary nature. This was very well brought out by Dr. Paul Schwarzenau in his evaluation of a dialogue with certain Seventh-day Adventists in Europe. He observed that "prior to and underlying every particular church doctrine, however objectively it may be based on biblical exegesis and theological argument, are experiences of faith which have left an indelible mark on that doctrine and are the source which consciously or unconsciously determines the questions, inquiries and teachings of the church in question." He illustrated his point by drawing a parallel between Luther's experience and the 1844 Adventist experience, stating that "the living resonance of the Protestant 'Scripture principle' rests on the fact that Luther had earlier experienced in the depths of despair the converting power of the Gospel. . . . And it is very much to the point that Adventist doctrine is rooted in and derives strength from an event which Adventists later referred to as 'the great disappointment' (October 22, 1844)." He concluded with a most relevant observation for any dialogue among Christians that "the full truth of a church's doctrine is therefore not yet grasped so long as, in its details or as a whole, we see it in isolation from such events and as mere doctrine."[1] The present study, therefore, has investigated in the light of the Adventist experience the origin and significance of methods of Bible interpretation by Seventh-day Adventists; the development of their ecclesiology, soteriology, and apocalyptic-eschatology; their self-understanding of the role they play in the history of the Christian church and salvation history; their views on inter-church relations; their concepts on truth and revelation; and their approach to others. The investigation also deals with the fundamental questions of the influence of the general hermeneutical tradition of 19th-century evangelical Protestantism, why Adventism did not disintegrate after the failure of the Millerite predictions of Christ's return but resulted in the successful development of Seventh-day Adventism, and the Millerite contribution to Seventh-day Adventist eschatology. All these factors are of relevance for an understanding of their present theology of mission, the basic structure of which was formed in the first decades after 1844. In 1874 its basic structure had progressed so much that believers began a gradual expansion on a worldwide scale. Post-1874 developments, which are beyond the scope of this inquiry, resulted in a more Christocentric mission theology with a greater non-apocalyptic thrust. The fact, however, that its basic theological framework has generally remained unchanged makes this research of great relevance for an understanding of contemporary Seventh-day Adventism. This study endeavors to contribute to an in-depth understanding of Seventh-day Adventists and to lead to improved relations between them and persons of other persuasions.

As far as possible use has been made of primary source material, including leading Millerite publications and all available Sabbatarian Adventist and Seventh-day Adventist publications. Books, pamphlets, published reports, sermons, periodical articles, published and unpublished letters, and manuscripts have been used as sources. Non-contemporary material has only been used to elucidate developmental trends without contradicting contemporary source material. Footnotes entail secondary sources providing the reader with further explanatory background in areas on question and biographic information on the major personalities quoted. Source material was selected on the basis of its qualitative and quantitative nature and its relevance in understanding the development of the theology of mission in its historical and contemporary perspective.

Part One deals with the immediate origins of the Seventh-day Adventist theology of mission and limits itself to the early 19th-century religious climate in the U.S.A. when millennialism flourished and an interconfessional movement emerged. William Miller, one of the foremost premillennialists during the first half of the 19th century, was its great inspirational force stressing the imminence of Christ's personal return. It was out of this movement that the Seventh-day Adventist Church gradually arose. In the foot-

1 Paul Schwarzenau in *So Much in Common* . . . , 1973, pp. 106, 107 (*Ecumenical Review*, April 1972, pp. 201, 202).

notes of Part One frequently reference has been made to publications by some of the most authoritative Seventh-day Adventists indicating the continuity of theological ideas between them and the Millerites. Part Two discusses the post-1844 theological developments till 1874. This early period is of great importance because during it the distinctive and basic characteristics of Seventh-day Adventism were formulated.

The theological concepts which lay behind the missionary consciousness of the Adventists formed within their hermeneutical framework a coherent unifying theological system which determined almost all their mission endeavors. This fact led to the use of the term "theology of mission" in this study. During the period under consideration one has to realize, however, that their theology of mission was a dynamic concept which gradually deepened and took on a more permanent structure. Thus this study can be called: Toward the Seventh-day Adventist theology of mission. The term "mission" and its derivatives used in this study include both the traditional meaning of missions — converting men of other faiths to Christianity — and the meaning of evangelism — calling back those who have apostatized or are gradually backsliding, thus signifying any activity in regard to man's salvation. Depending on the historical context, the scope of "mission" refers to either the population of the U.S.A. or that of the whole inhabited world.

The name "Millerites" has been used to designate Adventists in the U.S.A. who accepted many of Miller's expositions on the imminence of the Second Advent. The fact that the Millerites split up into different groups after 1844 makes it advisable to substitute the term "Adventists." The terms "Sabbatarian Adventists" and "Seventh-day Adventists" have been employed to indicate one of these groups which soon made the observance of the Sabbath a part of its faith, the latter term (abbreviated SDA) applying after their organization as the Seventh-day Adventist Church, in 1863.

Regarding the technical nature of the study, as far as possible the orthography of the sources has been honored. In general the chapter arrangement is chronological. However, chapters V and VI cover the same time period, each dealing with a different but complementary aspect of the emerging theology. It was necessary to make chapter V substantially larger than any other chapter in order to incorporate the many facets of the basic structure of the theology of mission. Within the footnotes, whenever a manuscript, letter, article or series of articles has been reprinted in a pamphlet or book, that source is indicated between parentheses to facilitate its accessibility to the reader. In some cases these reprints reproduce only sections of a primary source; other times the title of the reprint differs from the title of the article or articles. Unless otherwise indicated, Scriptural references are taken from the King James Version. The abbreviation *ibid.* refers to the last reference in the preceding footnote. It was virtually impossible to include in the bibliography all sources used for the preparation of this study or referred to in the footnotes, so the sources for the selective bibliography have been chosen on the basis of their importance and/or their frequent use in the actual writing. The bibliography also lists the primary source locations.

Part One

The Origins of the Seventh-day Adventist Theology of Mission

As general background this chapter first provides an introductory survey of some of the major characteristics of the religious situation in the U.S.A. during the first half of the 19th century which led to the rise of an interconfessional movement out of which the SDA emerged. This period has been described in the light of two successive historical phases characterized by their dominant features as an "era of good feeling" and an "era of controversy," indicating a change in the mood of the nation which provided an ideal climate for the development of Adventism. The major part of the chapter describes the major theological and missiological factors that brought about this movement and which are basic to an understanding of the formation of the SDA theology of mission.

A. *The Religious Situation in the United States During the Early Part of the 19th Century.*

1. *General characteristics.*

At the turn of the 19th century American Christianity was predominantly Protestant. In its character the Puritan-Pietist-Evangelical strains were more prominent than in Europe.[1] Only a small section of the population was officially associated with a church at the time of Independence even though the colonies had experienced the Great Awakening in the 18th century.[2] With the adoption of the Constitution a unique feature was introduced in the newly formed nation: the official separation of Church and State. The new Constitution declared that "no religious test shall ever be required as a

---

1 Kenneth S. Latourette, *Christianity in a Revolutionary Age. . .*, Vol. III: *Nineteenth Century Outside Europe. . .*, 1961, p. 4.

2 In 1800 estimates of the percentage of the population holding membership in the churches was 6.9; in 1840, 14.5; in 1850, 15.5; in 1900, 35.7 (Herman C. Weber, ed., *Yearbook of American Churches, 1933,* p. 299). Cf. Latourette, *Christianity,* III, 12; Franklin H. Littell, *From State Church to Pluralism. . .,* 1962, pp. 48, 49; Robert T. Handy, *A Christian America: Protestant Hopes and Historical Realities,* 1971, p. 27. The form of membership was on a voluntary basis and not compulsory by State Law. It should be noticed that the congregations were generally considerably larger than the actual membership (*ibid.,* pp. 27, 28). Regarding the value of these statistics, see Winthrop S. Hudson, *Religion in America,* 2nd ed., 1973, pp. 129, 130.

qualification to any office of public trust under the United States."[3] The first part of the First Amendment to the Constitution elaborated this further by forbidding the government to issue any law "respecting an establishment of religion or prohibiting the free exercise thereof."[4] Religious pluralism, a desire to avoid a State Church situation, and the influence of European rationalism and deism were among the major factors that contributed to the formulation of the principle of religious freedom in the Constitution.[5] The effect of the Constitution was that it made church organizations no longer dependent on the State for survival and growth but on their own resources and voluntary membership.[6] Its adoption together with increasing immigration stimulated a further development of religious plurality. The result, according to Kenneth Scott Latourette, was that by 1914 "nearly every kind of Christianity found anywhere else in the world was present."[7]

This religious plurality was an important reason for general weakness of the churches as compared with their position in Europe. The Roman Catholics were in a minority, the Orthodox were very small, Lutherans were less prominent than in Europe, the Episcopalians were only socially important and far less represented than in England, Presbyterians were much weaker than in Scotland, and the Reformed represented but a faint reflection of their position in the Netherlands and Switzerland. The Methodists and Baptists, however, who were minorities in England, together made up more than half of the Protestants.[8]

The 19th century was a time of unprecedented geographical expansion for both the nation and the churches. It was during this period that a powerful nationalistic spirit arose, which influenced the development of the missionary movement. The expansion of the U.S.A. differed significantly from that of the European powers. Generally, it was a westward movement into neighboring territories thinly populated by Indians. The Louisiana Purchase from France under Jefferson greatly extended the territory of the nation. Many Americans felt that their Manifest Destiny was: "the conquest

3   Article VI of the Constitution of the U.S.A.
4   First Amendment of the Constitution of the U.S.A.
5   Leo Pfeffer, *Church, State, and Freedom*, rev. ed., 1967, pp. 92, 93; Anson P. Stokes, *Church and State in the United States*, I, 1950, chaps. 3, 5, 8; Latourette, *Christianity*, III, 9. Cf. Jerald C. Brauer, *Protestantism in America*, rev. ed., 1965, pp. 74-88; Handy, *Christian America*, pp. 3-26; Littell, *State Church*, pp. 29-52. Other contributing factors mentioned by Pfeffer were the English Act of Toleration of 1689, the lack of church affiliation of most Americans, the rise of commercial intercourse, the exigencies of the Revolutionary War, the Williams-Penn tradition and the success of their experiments, the writings of Locke, the social contract theory, and the Great Awakening (*Church, State, and Freedom*, pp. 92-104). Cf. Latourette, *Christianity*, III, 9.
6   See e.g., Handy, *Christian America*, pp. 3, 30.
7   Latourette, *Christianity*, III, 10.
8   *Ibid.*, p. 11. On the growth of Methodists and Baptists, see Sydney E. Ahlstrom, *A Religious History of the American People*, 1972, pp. 436-39, 441-44. For approximate memberships of the major churches during the 19th century, see Edwin S. Gaustad, *Historical Atlas of Religion in America*, 1962, pp. 40, 110.

4

of the entire continent, that one day the standard of the Republic would fly over that gigantic sweep of territory which plunged westward to greet the ocean."[9] With the accession of Florida, Texas, Oregon, and California this ideal was realized. It was "perhaps the most optimistic period" in American history.[10] To the American Indians, however, the westward move of the white settlers signified one of the most pessimistic periods in their history. In fact, there seemed to be a disparity between the ideals expressed in the Declaration of Independence that "all men were created free and equal" and in the treatment of the native population. Under the presidency of Andrew Jackson (1828-36) it became the federal policy to remove all Indians to the western side of the Mississippi in order to vacate potentially prosperous lands for the westward-moving white settlers. The resettlement of the Indians took place relentlessly with much suffering and the cost of many lives.[11]

In the early 19th century the Industrial Revolution made its initial impact on the country. An accompaniment of this Revolution, together with the territorial expansion, was an enormous growth of population caused by a high birth rate, a reduced death rate, and a tidal wave of immigrants. From 1790 to 1860 the population increased eight times, from nearly four million to more than 31 million. The immigrants, mainly from Europe, were attracted by the demand for unskilled labor in the mines, factories, railway building, and by the vacant lands in the West. There was also the dream of life in a free nation where land was cheap, salaries relatively high, and opportunities unlimited. Furthermore, immigration was prompted by adverse economic conditions and unfavorable political and social developments in Europe.[12] During the 19th century there was a strong increase of Roman Catholic immigrants. In the period of 1790-1840 the population of the nation increased by less than 4½ times; the Catholics increased nearly 19 times.[13] By 1850 they had become the largest single church in America.[14] The accelerating speed of Catholic immigration inevitably created fear and tension among many Protestants who conceived of the U.S.A. as a Protestant nation. It was felt that the near monopoly of the Protestant churches was threatened by a church known for its authoritarian government and persecuting policies. In the decade following 1825 at least 5,000 Irish Roman Catholics entered the country each year. They not only brought with them their Old World customs, but their progress in

9 Clifton E. Olmstead, *History of Religion in the United States*, 1960, p. 264.

10 *Ibid.*

11 Angie Debo, *A History of the Indians of the United States*, 1970, pp. 101-17; Robert F. Berkhofer, Jr., *Salvation and the Savage: An Analysis of Protestant Missions and American Indian Response, 1787-1862*, 1965, p. 2. Cf. Gaustad, ed., *The Rise of Adventism...*, 1974, p. xiv.

12 Olmstead, *United States*, pp. 321, 322; Latourette, *Christianity*, III, 7. Cf. Ahlstrom, *American People*, p. 516.

13 H. Shelton Smith, Robert T. Handy, and Lefferts A. Loetscher, *American Christianity*, II, 1963, p. 6.

14 Ahlstrom, *American People*, pp. 513, 527.

Americanization was very slow, arousing fears as to the foreign nature of the Roman Catholic Church — a fear that was strengthened when several Roman Catholic missionary societies were founded in Europe to promote the propagation of the Roman Catholic missionary work in America.[15] There was a resurgence of the anti-Catholic tradition of the colonial fathers, who in turn had received their ideas from the Reformation literature — especially from 16th- and 17th-century England. A flood of anti-Catholic publications supported this "no-popery" crusade.[16] Feelings ran so high that a Catholic convent was burned in 1834. The Protestant opposition developed into a national issue. In 1837 the Native American Party was formed, which had as one of its main aims to curtail immigration. No doubt this side of Protestantism together with its earnest profession of concern for freedom sounded rather hollow to those outside that segment of society.[17]

Another important element in American Christianity was the impact of millennialism on the American self-consciousness. The early New England Puritans had seen their settlements as God's new Israel, a "wilderness Zion." During the American Revolution the place of the nation in God's plan was often stressed,[18] the Revolution itself being interpreted as one of the greatest events since the Reformation. Frequently from the pulpits the view was presented that it was the destiny of the newly formed Republic to lead the world to millennial glory.[19]

Various factors contributed to the popularization of this version of America's destiny. First, there was a Protestant view of history held among many Christians which rested partly on the usual Protestant interpretation of a papal apostasy and the Reformation renewal of the church, and partly on the conviction that the British kingdoms harbored a people chosen by God for unusual service in advancing God's plan for humanity. This view was modified and applied to the American scene, causing many to consider the nation the "American Israel with all its implications of special election, vocation and guidance,"[20] while justifying the rapidly increasing expansion

15   Cf. Olmstead, *United States*, pp. 323-26.

16   Ray A. Billington, *The Protestant Crusade, 1800-1860*, 1938, pp. 1-52. Cf. Jerome L. Clark, *1844*, I, 1968, pp. 203-76. In 1829 the English Catholic Emancipation Bill provoked a large increase of anti-Catholic literature which had also its impact on the U.S.A. (Ahlstrom, *American People*, p. 559).

17   Handy, *Christian America*, p. 58.

18   H. S. Smith, *et al.*, *American Christianity*, II, 4.

19   The thought was expressed that as the nations would increasingly adopt the American "wisdom, liberty, and happiness," knowledge and religion would be diffused throughout the earth, and mankind would be prepared "for the universal REIGN of the SON OF GOD in the glories of the latter day" (Benjamin Trumbull, *A Sermon Delivered at North-Haven, December 11, 1783*, cited by J. F. Maclear, "The Republic and the Millennium," in *The Religion of the Republic*, ed. by Elwyn A. Smith, 1971, p. 185). Cf. Handy, *Christian America*, pp. 33, 34.

20   Maclear, "Republic," p. 188. Cf. William Haller, *Elect Nation: The Meaning and Relevance of Foxe's Book of Martyrs*, 1963, pp. 52, 53, 224-50; Ernest L. Tuveson, *Redeemer Nation: The Idea of America's Millennial Role*, 1968, pp. 137-75; Ernest R. Sandeen, *The Roots of Fundamentalism: British and American Millenarianism 1800-1930*, 1970, p. 43; James A. De Jong, *As the Waters Cover the Sea: Millennial Expectations in the Rise of Anglo-American Missions 1640-1810*, 1970, pp. 51, 29-33.

of the new nation. Secondly, during the 18th century there was a growing millennial expectation in evangelical circles; the main emphasis was on postmillennialism — a view which expected the Second Advent of Christ not at the beginning but at the end of the millennial age. The millennial blessing to be enjoyed by the church was often seen to be realized by human means of propagating the gospel in the power of the Spirit. Among the factors which contributed to the acceptance of this idea were the influence from Britain through Protestant immigrants, literature, and personal contacts and its proclamation in the U.S.A. by Jonathan Edwards and his followers. Especially were the religious awakenings of the 1730s-40s occasions for widespread acceptance of this view.[21] It also found its way into popular works of Moses Lowman, Thomas Scott, Adam Clarke, and David Bogue. Thus, many undoubtedly expected some kind of glorious state of history, achieved by progressive stages.[22] Thirdly, through revivalistic preaching the millennium became the object of intense speculation and anticipation. The dawn of the millennium seemed imminent. Edwards perceived signs of the coming millennium in the New England converts. Thomas Prince saw the French and Indian wars as "opening a way to enlighten the utmost regions of America" preparatory to the millennial reign.[23] When the age of reform and benevolence arrived, the millennial role of America became a generally accepted idea among the clergy, and the American achievement was seen as "God's handiwork, and American history was evolving into the millennium of Christ."[24] Those ideas seemed to be confirmed by the fact that every day more and more Europeans came to America who considered it a land of opportunity and the hope of the world, in contrast to European reactionism and authoritarianism after the French Revolution.

In American Christianity there were other theological and philosophical forces that provided a willing support for the postmillennial view of the present establishment of the Kingdom of God. The culture in America was becoming more and more democratic with a growing emphasis upon the dignity and worth of man, a concept advocated by Unitarianism, Universalism, the natural rights philosophy, and Jeffersonian individualism. At the same time the burgeoning Methodist denominations proclaimed the Arminian view of God's infinite love and mercy for all sinful men and reasoned that if God's plan of salvation included all men, then everyone ought to have the opportunity to accept it. There was an increasing shift of emphasis

21 *Ibid.,* pp. 81-83, 119, 120; Maclear, "Republic," pp. 189, 190; LeRoy E. Froom, *PFF,* II, 1948, pp. 640, 649-54; III, 1946, p. 254. Cf. Tuveson, *Redeemer Nation,* pp. 26-73. The eschatology of Daniel Whitby had English antecedents so that the widely held conclusion that he was the father of postmillennialism is inaccurate (De Jong, *Millennial Expectations,* pp. 16-29, 36-40, 81-84. Cf. Peter Toon, ed., *Puritans, the Millennium and the Future of Israel,* 1970. For some of the origins of postmillennialism among English-speaking people, see Toon, "The Latter-Day Glory," in *ibid.,* pp. 22-41.

22 Maclear, "Republic," p. 189.

23 Thomas Prince, *Six Sermons,* 1785, cited in Maclear, "Republic," p. 190.

24 *Ibid.*

away from God's sovereign initiative.[25] The growing man-centeredness was further stimulated by the process of nation building that was going on at that time. The people were occupying an increasingly vast area and developing successfully its resources, and their interest in doing seemed to be greater than in reflecting. Latourette characterized the type of Christianity at this time as "activism."[26]

The new spirit of nationalism, the millennial consciousness, the spirit of activism based on a strong emphasis on man's initiative, and a realization of God's mercy and love for mankind made a definite impact upon the churches. If the American society was to be won to Christianity, the churches would have to develop a strong missionary program. Many regarded such a program as "the means whereby the West, the nation, and ultimately the world might be redeemed from the disastrous effects of immorality, skepticism and materialism."[27] The most immediate concern was the conversion of the U.S.A., which was an enormous task. The missionary efforts were concentrated in three areas: One was the winning of the partially secularized among the descendants of immigrants who had come to the country in the colonial period, another effort concerned persons of other religions — the Indians and Negroes, and the third effort was aimed at the 19th-century immigrants.[28] Various missionary societies were established, the most important being the American Home Missionary Society, founded in 1826, which was formed by individuals from various churches. However, most denominations realized that the distinctive tenets of their faith could not be maintained in the new regions under this kind of non-ecclesiastical control. The strong competitive spirit between denominational and non-denominational organizations had as its result that the purely denominational mission board became standard.[29] The motivations that prompted the rise of the home-missionary movement were also a powerful force in the development of foreign missions. Stirring reports by English missionaries as well as tales of exotic life in the Orient by New England seamen and tourists contributed to the increasing interest in missions. In 1810 the American Board of Commissioners for Foreign Missions was formed.[30]

2. Era of good feeling.

25 H. S. Smith, *et al., American Christianity,* II, 8; Olmstead, *United States,* p. 265. Cf. William G. Mcloughlin, "Revivalism," in Gaustad, *Adventism,* p. 142.

26 Latourette, *Christianity,* III, 13. Reference was made to the lay character of Protestant American Christianity (*ibid.*).

27 Olmstead, *United States,* p. 265.

28 Latourette, *Christianity,* III, 16-83.

29 H. S. Smith, *et al., American Christianity,* II, 3, 4. Cf. William W. Sweet, *Religion in the Development of American Culture 1765-1840,* 1952, pp. 263-81.

30 Olmstead, *United States,* pp. 280-83. On the anti-mission sentiment, see *infra,* p. 12, n. 46.

In national politics the "era of good feeling" or the "early national period" started with the inauguration of George Washington as president in 1789 and ended when Andrew Jackson, a hero of the masses, became president in 1829. For American Christianity it was also an "era of good feeling." Although aspects of anxiety and insecurity could be perceived,[31] the optimistic postmillennial view of the future of society was popular, and the vision of America as a redemptive instrument strengthened the activism of evangelical Protestantism. There seemed to be a strong determination by many churches to keep the Republic a Christian nation even though there was a separation between Church and State. The prospect of a millennial perfection to be established through the Christianization of society by voluntary human endeavor reinforced and sustained evangelical revivals.[32] Lyman Beecher argued that if we only pray and wait upon the Lord, He will not come.[33] Of a similar nature was the view of president Eliphalet Nott of Union College: the millennium was at the door and would be "introduced BY HUMAN EXERTIONS."[34] As far as the commencement of the millennium was concerned Timothy Dwight, president of Yale College, thought he could perceive its "dawn" in 1812.[35] The strategy of many Protestants concerning the Christianization of society was to increase the strength of their churches and influence the Republic through reform and benevolence societies. These were voluntary societies, whose membership often was on an interconfessional basis, and were used by various churches as a "useful bridge across the gap between church and civilization" which had been widened by religious freedom and pluralism.[36]

Apart from the association of millennial views with the triumph of Christian civilization, a number of other forces were responsible for the reform and benevolence movements. One of them was the success of British evangelical and reform societies which inspired similar developments in America. Then, as a result of the Enlightenment, there was a humanitarian concern which had already created an atmosphere favorable to benevolence activity. Serious interest was aroused in the cause of peace and temperance. Furthermore, the changes in theology favored an emphasis on man's freedom, while minimizing man's total depravity, and stressing human effort for self-improvement. It was felt that the improvement of society depended much on what man himself would accomplish. Then there was a general atmosphere of optimism. A new nation had been born, devoting itself to the cause of liberty and equality for all, and it was thought that these high ideals could be realized. Finally, there was the aspect of revivalism that, together

31   Cf. Sandeen, "Millennialism," in Gaustad, *Adventism*, pp. 107-9, 114, 115; *infra*, p. 11.
32   Handy, *Christian America*, pp. 35, 36.
33   Maclear, "Republic," p. 191.
34   Eliphalet Nott, *A Sermon Preached before the General Assembly of the Presbyterian Church . . . May 19, 1806*, cited by Froom, *PFF*, IV, 1954, p. 60.
35   Timothy Dwight, *A Discourse in Two Parts, Delivered Aug. 20, 1812. . .*, 1812, pp. 29, 30. Cf. Maclear, "Republic," p. 196.
36   Handy, *Christian America*, pp. 42-44.

with the other factors, gave the reform and benevolence movement its power and purpose.[37]

This wave of revivalism began with the Second Great Awakening or Great Revival and increased in intensity after 1826 when Charles G. Finney had started his preaching and great revivals swept through the country. In 1830 he moved away from an exclusive stress on personal conversion, and developed a close relationship between revivalism and benevolent action, an approach which made him more acceptable in the eastern part of the country. The remaking of society in the light of the establishment of the kingdom of God was considered as important as converting people and building churches. This union of revivalism and reform contributed greatly to the growth of the benevolence movement. As the century progressed, the interest of Protestantism in temperance, peace, prison reform, poor relief, proper Sunday observance, education, abolition of slavery, and many other moral and social problems grew steadily until social reform became the absorbing passion of many Christians who embraced revivalism.[38]

In the context of this revivalism and millennial expectation the increase in the consumption of alcohol[39] was seen by many Christians as a threat to the furtherance of the Christianization of society. Thus a temperance movement was launched which resulted in the founding of the American Temperance Society (1826). In 1836 the American Temperance Union was established on a platform of total abstinence. Large groups of people favored prohibition and conversion methods were used to fight intemperance. Most of the major denominations endorsed the temperance movement whose influence later on was manifested in State prohibition legislation.[40] Another area for reform was the decline in the strict observance of Sunday, especially on the frontier. In 1828 the General Union for Promoting the Observance of the Christian Sabbath was organized. Later, as a result of the Sunday reform revival of 1843, the American and Foreign Sabbath Union was established.[41] Other issues the evangelical reform hoped to correct were various practices not conducive to Christian morality such as dueling, theater going, card playing, dancing, and prostitution. In 1834 the American Female Moral Reform Society and the Young Men's Moral Reform Society were founded.[42] Furthermore, peace societies were organized by

37 H. S. Smith, et al., American Christianity, II, 10-17; Brauer, Protestantism, pp. 148-50. Cf. Ahlstrom, American People, pp. 422-28.

38 H. S. Smith, et al., American Christianity, I, 522-25; II, 12-14. Cf. Olmstead, United States, pp. 348, 349, 359.

39 Alice F. Tyler, Freedom's Ferment. . . , 1944, pp. 312, 313.

40 H. S. Smith, et al., American Christianity, II, p. 15; Handy, Christian America, pp. 51, 52; Ahlstrom, American People, p. 426. Cf. Clark, 1844, II, 199-244.

41 Olmstead, United States, pp. 355-57. An important reason for the Sunday reform revival was that many Protestants were agitated in 1810 when Congress passed a law that post offices should be open and mail carried on Sunday. Various societies were formed to crusade for maintaining Sunday observance (Handy, Christian America, pp. 48-51).

42 Cf. H. S. Smith, et al., American Christianity, I, 525, 552, 553; II, 15-17; Olmstead, United States, pp. 287, 291, 337, 369. Cf. Ahlstrom, American People, pp. 425, 426; Clark, 1844, II, 346-51.

10

several states in 1815 with the American Peace Society being organized in 1828. Education was another important concern of the benevolence movement and in 1815 the American Education Society was established. The opinion was generally held that an increase in number and quality of educational institutions would contribute to the Christianization of the world. Protestants contributed considerably to the development of public school systems for primary and elementary education, but it was believed that higher education should remain under private denominational sponsorship. The benevolence societies also supported humanitarian movements in aiding the handicapped and helpless, giving attention to education of the deaf and blind, and the care of the insane. Abolition of slavery was also championed, with the American Anti-Slavery Society being formed in 1833. With the previously mentioned wave of missionary enthusiasm sweeping the country, in 1816 the American Bible Society was established, in 1825 the American Tract Society, and in 1824 the American Sunday School Union.[43]

This period also witnessed the rise of a number of utopian communal movements with members dedicating themselves to the establishment of an ideal order along religious lines. Almost all of these held to a literal interpretation of the Bible and were pietistic in their emphasis. Usually, however, they adhered to collective ownership of property and put into practice various principles which were advocated by the reform movements. Although their numbers and influence were not large, they generally represented the concern for moral fervor and reform in American religious life. Some of the better known were the Shakers (officially known as the Millennial Church or the United Society of Believers), the Rappites, the Amana Society or Community of True Inspiration, the Hopedale Community, the Brook Farm Community, and the Oneida Community.[44]

3. Era of controversy.

During the 1830s the "era of good feeling" gradually gave way to an "era of controversy"[45] with rapidly increasing threats to the popular postmillennial views and the success of the benevolence movement.

First, there was the development of "sectionalism." The survival and identity of the Republic were brought into question by sectional animosities between the various States. Rising tension over slavery, States' rights, and the anti-Roman Catholic nativism divided many in the country. While mil-

43 Andrews L. Drummond, *Story of American Protestantism*, 1950, p. 212. Cf. Clark, *1844*, II, 13-133, 280-329; III, 17-53, 74-138.

44 See e.g., John H. Noyes, *History of American Socialism*, 1961, *passim;* Olmstead, *United States*, pp. 338-43; Brauer, *Protestantism*, pp. 151-60; Tyler, *Freedom's Ferment*, pp. 121-25, 130-32, 140-95. Cf. Ahlstrom, *American People*, pp. 492-501; Robert V. Hine, "Communitarianism," in Gaustad, *Adventism*, pp. 70-76; Sweet, *American Culture*, pp. 291-305; Clark, *1844*, II, 139-96.

45 One has to realize that these descriptions only indicate the dominant character of these periods. Therefore allowance should be made for some overlapping and continuation of specific trends.

lennial dreams stimulated the Northern abolitionists, the Southerners saw the preservation of slavery and the limiting of the power of government as their main interest. Although revivals continued, anti-slavery eclipsed other reforms and divided the churches.[46]

Secondly, the glorious millennial dream cooled off through the devastating effects of the financial depression of 1837,[47] hindering the effectiveness of the benevolence societies. The spirit of the movement was no longer that of confidence and it became evident that the earlier bright hopes were not to be fulfilled so easily.[48]

Furthermore, revivalism had increased the individualism of the people. Much seemed to depend upon the personal decision of the individual. Non-conformity was both acceptable and desirable, and the quest for truth became paramount. Thus, the whole revivalistic impulse tended to create a fruitful atmosphere out of which not only extremist and perfectionistic ideas could develop, but also new churches and religious movements.[49] During the 1830s an extremist, "ultraist" party appeared in many of the societies,[50] growing out of the intensity of revivalism that was connected with the reform movement. The revivalists had claimed that their work was done under guidance of the Holy Spirit and their assurance was strengthened by their expectancy of an imminent millennium. Because of this, many societies suffered inner dissensions between absolutists and moderates which divided the churches. In general the rise of perfectionism was one of the clearest expressions of ultraism. Where revivalism had reached its height there was a development of belief in the possibility that Christians could live perfect, sanctified lives. Some types of perfectionism were radical; others moved toward antinomianism.[51] The frontier in particular was a place where discontent could reign, extremism could develop, and utopian societies could experiment. The rural areas of New England,

46 Maclear, "Republic," p. 201. Cf. Brauer, Protestantism, pp. 124, 174-84. For British influences on the anti-slavery sentiment, see ibid., pp. 169-77. After 1820 there arose among the Baptists and the Disciples of Christ an anti-mission movement dividing many churches (Olmstead, United States, pp. 271-74; Sweet, American Culture, pp. 272-75; Brauer, Protestantism, pp. 145, 146).

47 Reuben E. E. Harkness, "Social Origins of the Millerite Movement," Ph.D. dissertation, 1927, pp. 111-16, 121, 130.

48 Whitney R. Cross, The Burned-over District: The Social and Intellectual History of Enthusiastic Religion in Western New York, 1800-1850, 1950, pp. 215, 268, 271, 273, 317, 318. Cf. David M. Ludlum, Social Ferment in Vermont 1791-1850, 1939, pp. 62, 76.

49 Brauer traced the origin of dissension and schism within the Protestant churches to the Second Great Awakening (Protestantism, pp. 117-32). Cf. W. S. Hudson, "A Time of Religious Ferment," in Gaustad, Adventism, pp. 1-17. For anti-denominational trends, see Clark, 1844, I, 182-201.

50 Cf. Cross, Burned-over District, pp. 198, 199, 211-39; Ahlstrom, American People, p. 475. Regarding ultraism Cross said: "The stage of religious emotionalism immediately preceding heterodoxy was that which contemporaries called ultraism. An amorphous thing in an intellectual sense, it can scarcely be considered a system of belief. It is better described as a combination of activities, personalities, and attitudes creating a condition of society which could foster experimental doctrines" (Burned-over District, p. 173). Cf. Ludlum, Social Ferment, p. 55.

51 H. S. Smith, et al., American Christianity, II, 16.

Pennsylvania, and the Middle West harbored many dissident groups. One of the most conducive places for the rise of new religious movements was in central and western New York State. This area was called "the Burned-over District" because it had been swept over so often by the fires of revivalism. This region witnessed within two decades the rise of Mormonism, Adventism, and Spiritualism.[52]

Finally, during the early part of the 19th century among evangelical Christians there was an increasing emphasis on the study of Bible passages which alluded to the Second Advent — the parousia. First, the emphasis on eschatology, which was stimulated by the events of the French Revolution,[53] took place in Europe; later it arose in America.[54] Many participating in these studies became convinced that Christ's return and the Day of Judgment were imminent and would inaugurate the millennium — a view designated as premillennialism. Consequently, these individuals strongly opposed the current postmillennial views.[55] The principal exponent of premillennialism in America during this period was William Miller (1782-1849). He was born in Pittsfield, Massachusetts, just following the Revolutionary War in which his father was a captain. Eldest in a family of sixteen children, he was reared in a religious atmosphere in Low Hampton, in northeastern New York State. During his youth he satisfied his thirst for knowledge largely through self-study. He came to be considered unusually well read, self-educated, and conspicuously methodical in all his ways. After marriage he lived for a few years in Poultney, Vermont, where at times he served as deputy sheriff and justice of the peace. Through his friendship with various prominent citizens who were deists Miller gave up his religious convictions and became a deist. In the war between the U.S.A. and Britain (1812-14) he served as lieutenant and captain, which seems to have disillusioned him about his deistic principles as he began to realize the sinful nature of man. When he left the army and began to work as a farmer he devoted more time to existential questions regarding man's predicament. During this quest for a deeper significance of life he attended the Baptist Church regularly, though he was not a member. In 1816, while publicly reading a sermon on Is. 53, Miller experienced conversion and joined this church. Challenged by his deist friends, he began an intensive study of the Bible so that he might

52   *Ibid.,* pp. 17, 18; Olmstead, *United States,* pp. 334-46; Cross, *Burned-over District,* pp. 3, 4. Regarding the millennial views of the Early Mormons, the Shakers, John Humphry Noyes, leader of the Oneida community, and William Miller, see Sandeen, *Fundamentalism,* pp. 47-54.

53   Commenting on the significance of the French Revolution Sandeen said: "That political cataclysm broke with such force upon Europeans and Americans that no image but an apocalyptic one seemed to give adequate expression to the drama and panoramic sweep of those events" ("Millennialism," pp. 107, 108). This Revolution was seen to upset the idea of the gradual development of history (*ibid.,* p. 108).

54   On the European revival, see Froom, *PFF,* III, 263-751; on the American, *ibid.,* IV, 15-426. Cf. Sandeen, *Fundamentalism,* pp. 3-58; Oliver W. Elsbree, *The Rise of the Missionary Spirit in America 1790-1815,* 1928, pp. 122, 123.

55   On the millennial polemic, see Froom, *PFF,* IV, chaps, 15, 16, 18, 19. For the millennial tradition in the U.S.A. (1800-45), see Sandeen, *Fundamentalism,* pp. 42-58.

justify his decision to accept the Christian faith.[56] On the basis of a two-year investigation, he concluded that, according to Scripture, the Second Advent was premillennial instead of postmillennial[57] and within his lifetime, indicating there could be no world conversion before Christ's return at the beginning of the millennium.[58] Miller continued the study of the Bible until, as the result of an invitation, he made his first public appearance in 1831 when there was already some excitement in the various Protestant churches over the imminence of the parousia.[59] From that time onward until 1844, he lectured wherever he had a chance. In 1831 Miller prepared a series of eight articles for a Baptist weekly, the *Vermont Telegraph*, which were published during 1832-33.[60] In 1833 these articles were incorporated in a pamphlet entitled *Evidences from Scripture and History of the Second Coming of Christ About the Year A.D. 1843, and of His Personal Reign of 1000 Years.* During the same year he was provided by the Baptists with a license to preach. From 1834 onward he devoted all his time to the proclamation of the Second Advent. In 1836 his lectures were published in a book which was reprinted and enlarged several times,[61] and received nation-wide publicity.

In many churches Miller gained numerous followers who became known as the "Millerites." This interconfessional movement[62] swelled into a

56   See Sylvester Bliss, *Memoirs of William Miller. . . ,* 1853, pp. 1-70; Francis D. Nichol, *The Midnight Cry. . . ,* 1844, pp. 17-33; Froom, *PFF,* IV, 455-62. Cf. David L. Rowe, "Thunder and Trumpets: The Millerite Movement . . . ," Ph.D. dissertation, 1974, pp. 10-27.

57   Generally premillennialists had a pessimistic view on the condition of society and man's attempts to improve it. They felt that only the cataclysmic return of Christ could bring about the perfect society of the millennium. Postmillennialists were optimistic about the human ability to gradually transform the secular world into an ideal society in which the principles of the kingdom of God would triumph.

58   William Miller, MS, Sept. 5, 1822. Cf. Miller, *Wm. Miller's Apology and Defense,* 1845, pp. 7, 8, 11. Cross stated that Miller's view was no startling novelty but that "his chronology merely elaborated and refined the kind of calculations his contemporaries had long been making but became more dramatic because it was more exact, and because the predicted event was more startling" (*Burned-over District,* p. 291). To Sandeen predictions like those of Miller were "quite common among historicist premillenarians in both Britain and the United States" (*Fundamentalism,* p. 52). For a comparison between the two countries, see Sandeen, "Millennialism," pp. 110, 111.

59   Sandeen, *Fundamentalism,* pp. 49, 57, 58. There was a simultaneous increased interest in Britain (*ibid.,* pp. 57, 58).

60   See *Vermont Telegraph* (Brandon, Vt.), Nov. 6, 1832-March 12, 1833.

61   Froom, *PFF,* IV, 476-519; "Miller, William," *SDAE,* 1966, p. 788.

62   The Millerites were of the following persuasions: "Protestant, Episcopal, Methodist Episcopal, Methodist Protestant, Primitive Methodist, Wesleyan Methodist, Close Communion Baptist, and Open Communion Baptist, Calvinists and Arminians, Baptists, Presbyterians, Old and New School Congregationalists, Old and New School Lutherans, Dutch Reformed, etc., etc." ([Josiah Litch], "RPA," in *ASR,* May 1844, p. 90). E. N. Dick's study of 174 Millerite lecturers indicated that 44.3 were Methodists, 27 Baptists, 9 Congregationalists, 8 Christians, 7 Presbyterians, 2 Episcopalians, 1.5 Dutch Reformed, 0.6 Lutherans, and 0.6 Friends ("The Adventist Crisis of 1843-1844," Ph.D. dissertation, 1930, pp. 232, 233). On the church affiliation of prominent participants, see David T. Arthur, "Come Out of Babylon: A Study of Millerite Separatism and Denominationalism, 1840-1865," Ph.D. dissertation, 1970, p. 14. See also *infra,* pp. 48, 49.

crusade which reached a climax in the years 1843 and 1844. In North America about 200 ministers accepted Miller's views and "Advent congregations" were established which had a total number of approximately 50,000 believers.[63] Some of the most influential personalities in this movement were Joshua V. Himes,[64] a minister of the Massachusetts Christian Conference, Josiah Litch,[65] a minister and member of the New England Methodist Episcopalian Conference, Dr. Henry Dana Ward,[66] a prominent Episcopalian clergyman, Charles Fitch,[67] a minister of the Congregational Church and the Presbyterian Church, Apollos Hale,[68] a Methodist minister, and Sylvester Bliss,[69] a Congregationalist. For some, Miller's prediction must have implied an instant utopia, especially after the financial depression which prevailed throughout the nation; for others, who were disillusioned with the movements of the 1830s, the premillennial ideas of Miller offered

63   Miller, *Apology*, p. 22. Cf. Joseph Bates, "Incidents in My Past Life," No. 51, *YI*, May 1863, p. 34 (*The Autobiography . . .* , 1868, p. 294); James White, *Life Incidents . . .* , 1868, p. 236; Ellen G. White, *GC*, 1888, p. 376. Unless indicated otherwise the 1888 ed. of *GC* has been used.

64   Joshua Vaughan Himes (1805-95) was a minister, reformer and the major publicist, promoter and organizer of the Millerite movement. First he learned a trade. Later he experienced conversion. He felt a call to the ministry. A reformer by nature, he opposed liquor traffic and was an assistant to William Lloyd Garrison in his fight against slavery. Himes' Chardon Street Chapel in Boston became the headquarters for all kinds of reform meetings. In 1839 he invited Miller to speak in his church. Immediately after he was convicted of the correctness of Miller's teachings, he began to organize the movement more effectively. He launched several periodicals among which were the *ST* and *MC*. He also introduced Miller into the large cities and took a leading role in the organization of camp meetings and General Conferences for Second Advent believers. See also Arthur, "Joshua V. Himes and the Cause of Adventism, 1839-1845," M.A. thesis (University of Chicago), 1963.

65   Josiah Litch (1809-86) was a minister and reformer. He participated in the temperance and abolition movements. After his conversion he joined the Methodist Episcopal Church. Through the study of Miller's lectures he became one of the first Methodist ministers to advocate Miller's views. He was editor of several Millerite periodicals and published books on prophetic interpretation. Several of his ideas were adopted by the Sabbatarian Adventists.

66   Henry Dana Ward (1797-1884) graduated from Harvard. As a reformer he was known in the Anti-Masonic movement. After that he embraced the cause of Adventism. He published several books. One of them, *Glad Tidings "For the Kingdom of Heaven Is at Hand,"* 1838, was a study on millennialism which reached conclusions somewhat similar to Miller's. He was chosen as chairman of the first General Conference of Second Advent believers, Boston, 1840. However, owing to his opposition against the setting of a definite time he receded into the background.

67   Charles Fitch (1805-October 14, 1844) studied at Brown University, Providence, R.I. He became first a minister of a Congregational church, then a minister of a Presbyterian church. He was editor of a Millerite periodical. Fitch could be considered as one of the most aggressive and successful Millerite leaders and preachers. Together with Apollos Hale he designed *A Chronological Chart of the Visions of Daniel & John*. See Appendix IV.

68   Apollos Hale was associate editor of the *ST*. His argumentation on prophetic subject matters was concise and scholarly. He was noted for his clarity and logic and wrote many articles, pamphlets and books.

69   Sylvester Bliss (1814-63) received a liberal education and became a member of the Historical Society of Boston. This background caused him to be very careful in citing historical sources and various authorities. This made him one of the ablest of the Millerite editors and apologists. He frequently engaged in polemical writing in which he critically examined and analyzed the positions of opponents. He was one of the editors of the *ST*.

a way out of the religious ultraism which had failed to redeem civilization.[70] Still others saw in his prediction a culmination of their desires for the "blessed hope" and deliverance from an evil world.

In summarizing the religious situation at the beginning of the 19th century in the U.S.A. one could say that it provided a climate conducive to the development of new religious movements. There was a relative weakness of the major churches, a religious plurality and the constitutionally guaranteed freedom of religion which stimulated individual religious expression independent from the larger churches. The democratizing of the American culture, the Second Great Awakening, and further revivalism contributed also to increasing religious individualism. New movements developed from the larger Protestant bodies. With the passing of the era of benevolence, schism and controversy began to reign. The financial depression of 1837, disillusionment with the millennial dreams, and a fast growing Roman Catholicism created feelings of insecurity and discontentment. It was in such an environment that Adventists successfully developed as one of various new religious movements.

B. The Millerite Apocalyptic-Eschatological Motives for Mission.

This section discusses Miller's hermeneutical principles without which it is impossible to understand the biblical motives underlying the mission thrust of the Millerite movement. In the exposition of the motives for mission references to these principles will be made. This study has been confined to apocalyptic-eschatological motives because these were overwhelmingly dominant in the Millerite literature. The concept of "the time of the end" provided a general motivation for Millerites based on the theological significance of certain historical incidents, while concepts such as the time of the Second Advent, the Midnight Cry, and the Judgment Hour message characterized their specific mission motivation. Several of these concepts were also prevalent in the circle of evangelical Christianity. However, it was especially the view of an imminent premillennial parousia associated with a definite time setting that made the following apocalyptic views an integral part of the Millerite mission thrust.

1. Hermeneutical principles.

The two major published sources enumerating Miller's hermeneutical principles are the introduction to his lectures and a letter he wrote regarding principles of biblical interpretation. The introduction to his lectures

---

70 Cross, *Burned-over District*, pp. 277, 278, 320; Sweet, *American Culture*, p. 306. Cf. Henry Morris in Bliss, *Review of Morris' "Modern Chiliasm . . . ,"* 1842, pp. 162, 163; Harkness, "Millerite Movement," pp. 134-36; Sandeen, "Millennialism," pp 115, 116; Rowe, "Millerite Movement," pp. 37, 55, 64.

discussed especially the principles of interpreting apocalyptic-eschatology, which he considered as predictive prophecy. In 1840, however, one of Miller's letters summarizing his rules of hermeneutic was published.[71] These rules came to be known as "Miller's Rules of Bible Interpretation."[72] The major part of the following discussion is based on these rules as they were published by Apollos Hale (see Appendix I).[73]

In general Miller's hermeneutical principles were a part of the Protestant hermeneutical tradition which can be traced back to the primitive church.[74] His hermeneutic was based on the presuppositions of the *sola scriptura* principle and the unity and self-authentication of Scripture.[75] The first four hermeneutical rules dealt with general rules of interpretation. Miller indicated that the Christian canon provided the context for interpretation and that Scripture can be understood[76] (Rule I). He advocated the hermeneutical rule that Scripture is its own expositor,[77] and based it on the concept of the Bible as an ultimate norm[78] (Rule III). The principle of the analogy of Scripture and its application to a particular subject he frequently used as a means to understand Scripture (Rule IV).[79] As to its application he stressed that the importance of "every word" had to be taken into consideration (Rules II, IV). Not only a word but also a sentence had its importance: "Let

71 Miller, "Letters. No. 5," *ST,* May 15, 1840, pp. 25, 26.

72 Miller's letter was published in a schematic arrangement in Miller, *Views of the Prophecies and Prophetic Chronology Selected from Manuscripts of William Miller . . . ,* 1841, ed. by Joshua V. Himes, pp. 20-24. These rules were also published in England ("Rules of Interpretation," *SAH,* March 26, 1844, pp. 9, 10).

73 In 1843 these hermeneutical principles, with the exception of one, were published by Hale in a rearranged form which provided a more systematic sequence (A. Hale, *SAM,* 1843, pp. 103-6; Appendix I). The rearrangement could have been done by Miller or Hale. The rule which was omitted read: "Nothing revealed in the scripture can or will be hid from those who ask in faith, not wavering." Textual evidence: Deut. 29:29; Mt. 10:26, 27; 1 Cor. 2:10; Phil. 3:15; Is. 45:11; Mt. 21:22; Jn. 14:13, 14; 15:7; James 1:5, 6; 1 Jn. 5:13-15 (Miller, *Views,* p. 20). The fact that this rule can be considered as being implied in the first rule of Hale's arrangement may explain the reason for its omission (cf. Appendix I). For an essay on the heremeneutic employed by Miller and early SDA, see Don F. Neufeld, "Bible Interpretation in the Advent Movement" in *A Symposium on Biblical Hermeneutics,* ed. by Gordon M. Hyde, 1974, pp. 109-25.

74 Cf. Sandeen, "Millennialism," pp. 111-13; Froom, *PFF,* I, II, III, IV.

75 Hale, *SAM,* pp. 103, 106. Cf. E. G. White, *SG,* I, 1858, p. 117; E. G. White, *GC,* pp. d, 204 (*GC,* 1950, pp. vi, 204, 205); E. G. White, MS 24, 1886 (*SM,* I, 1958, pp. 20, 21); Letter, E. G. White to S. N. Haskell, No. 53, 1900 (*SM,* I, 21, 22).

76 Cf. the Reformation doctrine of the *claritas sacrae Scripturae.* Miller's assertion ought to be seen in the polemic against contemporaries who stated that the books of Daniel and Revelation could not be understood. Cf. E. G. White, *TM,* 1923, p. 113.

77 Cf. the Reformation concept of *sacra Scriptura sui ipsius interpres.* This functions as a basic principle in SDA hermeneutics. Cf. E. G. White, "Search the Scriptures," *RH,* Oct. 9, 1883, p. 625 (*Counsels on Sabbath School Work,* 1938, p. 42); E. G. White, *GC,* p. 521; E. G. White, *Ed,* 1903, p. 190.

78 Cf. E. G. White, *GC,* pp. d, 193 (*GC,* 1950, pp. vii, 193); E. G. White, "The Value of Bible Study," *RH,* July 17, 1888, p. 449 (*FE,* 1923, p. 126); E. G. White, *T,* VI, 1900, p. 402; E. G. White, *The Ministry of Healing,* 1905, p. 462.

79 Cf. Hale, *SAM,* pp. 64-66; E. G. White, "Search the Scriptures," p. 625 (*Our High Calling,* 1961, p. 205; *Sabbath School Work,* pp. 42, 43); E. G. White, "Value of Bible Study," p. 450 (*FE,* p. 127); E. G. White, "The Science of Salvation the First of Sciences," *RH,* Dec. 1, 1891, p. 737 (*FE,* p. 187); E. G. White, *Ed,* p. 190.

17

every word have its own scriptural meaning, every sentence its proper bearing, and have no contradiction, and your theory will and must of necessity be correct."[80] He also suggested that when all scriptural passages related to a particular subject were brought together, each word and sentence should have "its proper bearing and force in the grand whole."[81]

The remaining rules were predominantly concerned with principles of interpreting apocalyptic-eschatology. This, according to Miller, included visions, symbols, and parables, and had prophetic significance. He referred to existing prophetic parallels which were complements to each other requiring integration to achieve their full understanding[82] (Rule V). This rule led to the important question: Do the words of Scripture have a literal or nonliteral sense? Miller's hermeneutic gave preference to a literal interpretation of a word as long as it contextually made "good sense." But, if its literal meaning violated "the simple laws of nature" the word had to be interpreted in a figurative sense (Rule VII).[83]

Miller devoted special attention to interpreting symbols. According to him, symbols always had a "figurative meaning," explaining that, when used in prophecy, symbols could have, for example, the following significance: mountains, meaning governments; beasts, kingdoms; waters, people; lamp, Word of God; day, year[84] (Rule VIII). However, he acknowledged that symbols had also a "metaphorical meaning" which signified "some peculiar quality of the thing prophecied of — by the most prominent feature or quality of the figure used, as *beasts;* if a *lion,* power and rule; if a *leopard,* celerity; if a *bear* voracious; [if] an *ox,* submissive."[85] He, therefore, remarked that "almost all figures used in prophecy have their literal and metaphorical meaning; as *beasts* denote, literally, a kingdom; so metaphorically good and bad, as the case may be, to be understood by the subject in connection."[86] The meaning of symbols could be obtained through the use of the principle of analogy of Scripture and the "good sense" idea within the context of the canon (Rule IX).[87] He recognized the importance of the

80 Miller, *ESH,* 1836, p. 5.
81 *Ibid.*
82 Miller, *ESH,* 1836, pp. 4, 5. Cf. E. G. White, *TM,* pp. 114, 115, 117.
83 Cf. E. G. White, *GC,* p. 599.
84 Although Miller had been exposed to Bible commentaries he seems to have arrived at his major interpretations by using mainly the Bible with its marginal references and Cruden's *Concordance* (Hale, *SAM,* p. 66; Miller, *Views,* p. 11; Bliss, *Miller,* p. 69). It should also be remembered that Miller grew up in a religious climate in which there was a growing influence of apocalyptic millenarianism. Cf. Sandeen, "Millennialism," pp. 109, 110.
85 Miller, *ESH,* 1836, pp. 3, 4.
86 *Ibid.,* p. 4. Cf. *ibid.,* 1833, p. 3 (*ST,* April 1, 1841, p. 1). Most of the 1833 publication was reprinted with some modifications in a series of installments in *ST,* April 1, 1841—Oct. 1, 1841.
87 Cf. Rules I, II, III. Miller illustrated the application of the principle of analogy of Scripture to symbols as follows: "To understand the literal meaning of figures used in prophecy, I have pursued the following method — say I find the word *'beast,'* I follow that word through all the prophets, and find in Daniel 7:17, it is explained to mean 'kings or kingdoms.' Again I find the word *'bird or fowl,'* and in Isaiah 46:11, it is used meaning a conqueror or warrior, to wit, Cyrus. Also in Ezekiel 39:4-9, denotes armies or conquerors" (*ESH,* 1833, p. 3 [*ST,* April 1, 1841, p. 1]). Cf. Hale, *SAM,* p. 66.

immediate context by indicating that because of different contextual situations a particular symbol could have different significances;[88] especially, reference was made to the various symbolic meanings of the word "day" (Rule XI). Frequently Miller and most of his contemporaries[89] made use of the so-called "year-day" principle which had been employed by interpreters for many centuries[90] as a key to determine the time element in symbolic prophecy. This principle indicated that a prophetic day stood symbolically for a literal solar year, a prophetic month for 30 literal years, and a prophetic year for 360 literal years. On the basis of the analogy-of-Scripture principle, the biblical evidence for this approach was found in Num. 14:34, Ezek. 4:6, and the fulfillment of the 70 weeks of Dan. 9.[91] Parables, Miller said, should be interpreted like symbols through the application of the analogy-of-Scripture principle to a particular subject within the context of the canon (Rule XI).[92]

In determining the fulfillment of prophecies he employed the hermeneutical principle that symbols were not to be fulfilled in a figurative manner but stood for a historical reality. For example, the symbols in the books of Daniel and Revelation were seen to depict the history of God's people from the time of their inception till the end of the world. Thus Miller might be classified with the "historicists" — a term used by some scholars to designate this hermeneutic.[93] Miller's procedure in discovering the predicted event was first to determine the meaning of the symbol, then to locate a historical event which would literally fulfill "every word" of the passage (Rule XII).[94] This approach to symbolic prophecy, which will be designated by the term "historicization," did not originate with Miller but had deep roots in the Christian tradition.[95]

In prophetic interpretation Miller also used the principle of typology,

88 Cf. E. G. White, MS 24, 1886 (SM, I, 20).
89 M. Stuart, Hints on the Interpretation of Prophecy, 1842, p. 74.
90 See Froom for a survey of the use of the year-day principle by: (1) American expositors, 1798-1844, PFF, IV, 396-401; (2) 19th-century European expositors, ibid., III, 743, 744; (3) post-Reformation expositors, ibid., II, 784-87; (4) Reformation expositors, ibid., pp. 528-31; (5) pre-Reformation expositors, ibid., p. 156; (6) early Medieval expositors, ibid., I, 1950, pp. 894-97; (7) early Church expositors, ibid., pp. 164, 457; (8) Jewish expositors till the Reformation era, ibid., pp. 175, 176, 203; II, 194.
91 Miller, ESH, 1833, p. 11 (ST, April 15, 1841, p. 10). Cf. Editorial, "Day For a Year — Length of a Year," MC, Jan. 20, 1843, p. 12; "Year-Day Principle," SDAE, p. 1440. Later J. H. Waggoner pointed out that Gen. 7:11, 24 and 8:4 demonstrated a 30-day monthly cycle (The Nature and Obligation of the Sabbath of the Fourth Commandment . . . , 1857, p. 51).
92 Cf. Rules IV, IX.
93 See e.g., Froom, PFF, I-IV; Sandeen, Fundamentalism, pp. 50-52; D. Guthrie, et al., eds., The New Bible Commentary: Revised, 1970, p. 1279; Merrill C. Tenney, ed., The Zondervan Pictorial Encyclopedia of the Bible, V, 1975, pp. 95, 96.
94 Miller's position that biblical references regarding the parousia would have a literal fulfillment was based on the idea that predictive prophecy had two focal points: the First and Second Advent of Christ. Owing to the fact that the prophecies regarding the First Advent had been literally fulfilled, he concluded from analogous reasoning that the predictions relating to the parousia also had to be fulfilled in a literal manner (ESH, 1833, pp. 4, 5 [ST, April 1, 1841, p. 1]).
95 See e.g., Froom, PFF, I, II; Toon, "Introduction" and "The Latter-Day Glory" in Puritans, pp. 8-41.

employing it to bring out the fuller import of a text. He rationalized such methodology through the following reasoning:

> Prophecy is sometimes typical, that is, partially fulfilled in one event, but completely only in the last. Such was the prophecy concerning Isaac, partly fulfilled in him, wholly so in Christ; likewise the prophecies concerning the Jewish captivity in Babylon, and their return, are only partly accomplished in the history of those events; the description of these things in the prophets, are so august and magnificent, that if only applicable to the Jews' return, the exposition would be weak, inefficient and barren. Therefore I humbly believe, that the exact fulfillment can only be looked for in the captivity of the church, destruction of mystical Babylon, and final glorification of the saints in the new Jerusalem state.[96]

In this context he pointed to the intimate relationship between the Old and New Testament, particularly referring to a continuity of symbolism between these two books.[97]

Miller's final and most important hermeneutical rule was that the interpreter of Scripture must have a faith that would not question or doubt "any part of God's word" (Rule XIII).[98] It was his conviction that the biblical motives for his mission efforts rested solidly on these principles of interpretation. It will be seen that the following motives, which were the results of this hermeneutic, indeed framed the basic pillars of the Advent or Millerite movement.

2. The "time of the end."

> But thou, O Daniel, shut up the words, and seal the book, even to the time of the end: many shall run to and fro, and knowledge shall be increased. Dan. 12:4.

The expression "the time of the end" was taken from Dan. 12:4, 9 and characterized all missionary motives of the Millerites. It was frequently used in the polemic against postmillennialists. In describing the era in which he was living, Miller wrote in 1831 that they were "almost on the threshold of Eternity when the Gospel dispensation is closing up"; this was "the last state of the Church militant."[99]

The Millerite concept of "the time of the end" was determined by use of a historicist hermeneutic which interpreted a number of transpiring historical events during the 18th and 19th centuries as fulfillment of Bible prophecy.

---

96 Miller, *ESH*, 1883, pp. 5, 6 (*ST*, April 1, 1841, p. 1); cf. E. G. White, *The Captivity and Restoration of Israel* [*The Story of Prophets and Kings*], 1917, p. 731 regarding the fuller sense of Old Testament predictive prophecy. Cf. E. G. White, *TM*, pp. 114, 117.

97 Miller, *ESH*, 1833, p. 6 (*ST*, April 1, 1841, p. 1). Here he said: "About every prophecy spoken by Christ, and his apostles may be found in the old testament, in part, and represented by figures, which were familiar to the writers and readers of those times." Cf. E. G. White, *T,* VI, 392; E. G. White, *COL*, 1900, pp. 128, 133; E. G. White, *TM,* pp. 114-17.

98 Cf. E. G. White, *TC*, No. 33, 1889, pp. 231-34 (*T*, V, 1889, pp. 703-6), E. G. White, MS 24, 1886 (*SM*, I, 20).

99 Miller, MSVT, No. 8, c. 1831, pp. 1, 2.

To some Millerites this concept signified a point of time, others felt it was a period of time. Miller himself said that the "time of the end" meant the end of the power of the pope "to tread on the Church by his civil authority, or reign over the kings of the earth, and to dispose of lands for gain."[100] Papal power came to an end during the French Revolution when, "in the beginning of the year 1798, on the fifteenth of February, a French general, Berthier, entered Rome with a French army without resistance, deposed the Pope, abolished the Papal government and erected the republic of Italy."[101] Other Millerites, although adhering to the principal event of 1798, expanded this concept. Some years later Josiah Litch wrote that the time of the end had begun at the time of the unsealing of the book of Daniel in 1798.[102] By this he meant that in that year the significance of the time element of "a time and times and the dividing of time" (Dan. 7:25) became clear. Litch stated that the time of the end was "not a single point of time, but a period, extending from 1798 to the end itself."[103]

The next section deals with the Millerite theological interpretation of historical events such as the captivity of the pope, cosmic phenomena, and the decline of the Ottoman empire which were basic to their understanding of the time of the end.

a. The end of the 1260 days.

The approach to the different apocalyptic passages in Daniel and Revelation was based upon the idea held by a long tradition of historicist interpreters[104] that these passages represented a symbolic prophetic time-sequence parallelism,[105] covering approximately the same period in history. Each prophecy explained this period in different symbolic imagery and was complementary to the others. Thus, the image of Dan. 2 was seen as a symbolic picture of salvation-historical events covering the time from the sixth century B.C. to the Second Advent; Dan. 7, 8, 11, 12 were thought to cover the same historical territory, and taken together they seemed to complement and confirm each other. Similar symbolic prophetic parallelism was found in Revelation, describing in symbols the history of the Christian church till the restoration of all things. During the time of the Millerites, many other evangelical Christians held somewhat similar views on prophecy.[106]

William Miller, when applying his hermeneutic, noticed in the various

100 Miller, *ESH*, 1836, p. 74.
101 *Ibid.* In 1798 the little book of Rev. 10 was opened (Miller, "Chronological Chart of the World," *ST*, May 1, 1841, p. 20).
102 J. Litch, "Discussion between Litch and Jones," *ST*, July 15, 1840, p. 59. Cf. E. G. White, *GC*, p. 356.
103 Litch, "Discussion," p. 59.
104 See Froom, *PFF*, I, II, III, IV.
105 Cf. Appendix I, Rule V.
106 For a survey of non-Millerite interpreters, 1798-1844, see *ibid.*, IV, 396-401. SDA have identified this method as a continuous-historical, historical, or historicist view of prophecy; see "Daniel, Interpretation of," *SDAE*, p. 325; "Historical (Historicist) View of Prophecy," *ibid.*, p. 524.

apocalyptic passages a recurring theme of controversy between the people of God and their enemies. In his analysis of the persecuting powers of God's people throughout the ages he developed the concept of the two abominations, defined as paganism (the first abomination) symbolizing the persecuting force outside the church, and the papacy (the second abomination) representing the persecuting power within the church.[107] It was the motif of the two abominations that characterized most of his following prophetic interpretations.

The image of Dan. 2 Miller interpreted as a "prophecy of the four kingdoms which would arise in the world, from that same time, until the end of all earthly kingdoms."[108] The golden head of the image was a symbol of the "Chaldean kingdom under Nebuchadnezzar," the breast and arms denoted the "Mede and Persian kingdom which began [with] Cyrus after the destruction of the Babylonish kingdom," the belly and thighs represented the "Grecian monarchy," the legs and feet of the image indicated the Roman empire, and the kingdom of Christ was signified by the stone that destroyed the image and filled the whole earth.[109] In a later publication his interpretation of the "Roman Kingdom," iron-clay phase, reflected the two-abominations motif. Thus he could refer to the mixture of the iron and clay

107 Miller, *ESH*, 1836, pp. 50, 51. Here he said: "We learn that there are two abominations spoken of by Daniel. The first is the Pagan mode of worship which was performed by the sacrificing of beasts upon altars, similar to the Jewish rites, and by which means the nations around Jerusalem drew away many of the Jews into idolatry, and brought down the heavy judgments of God upon idolatrous Israel; and God permitted his people to be led into captivity and persecuted by the very nations that they, the Jews, had been so fond of copying after in their mode of worship. Therefore was the sanctuary and place of worship at Jerusalem trodden down by Pagan worshippers, and the altars erected by the command of God and according to the pattern and form which God had prescribed were broken down, and more fashionable altars of the heathen erected in their room. Thus were the commands of God disobeyed, his laws perverted, his people enslaved, the sanctuary trodden down, and the temple polluted, until at last God took away the Jewish rites and ceremonies, instituted new forms, new laws, and set up the gospel kingdom in the world.

"This for a season was kept pure from the worldly sanctuaries and policy of satan. But satan, an arch enemy, found his Pagan abominations could have but little or no effect to draw the followers of Christ into idolatry, for they believed the bloody rites and sacrifices had their fulfillment in Christ. Therefore, in order to carry the war into the Christian camp, [he] suffers the daily sacrifice abomination to be taken out of the way and sets up Papacy which is more congenial to the Christian mode of worship in its outside forms and ceremonies, but retaining all the hateful qualities of the former. He persuades them to erect images to some or all of the dear apostles, and even to Christ, and Mary the mother of God. He then flatters them that the church is infallible. . . . He then clothes them with power to make laws and to dispense with those which God had made. . . . This was satan's master piece, and as Daniel says, 'He would think to change times and laws and they should be given into his hand for a time, times and an half; but they shall take away his dominion to consume and destroy it unto the end' [7:25,26]." Cf. e.g., J. N. Andrews, "The Sanctuary," *RH*, Jan. 6, 1853, p. 129 (*The Sanctuary and Twenty-Three Hundred Days*, 1853, pp. 24-26); J. White, "Our Faith and Hope . . . ," *RH*, Feb. 15, 1870, pp. 57-59 (*Sermons on the Coming and Kingdom of Our Lord Jesus Christ . . .* , 1870, pp. 108, 116, 117, 122-25). See also E. G. White's use of the term "paganism" in *SP*, IV, 1884, pp. 39, 43, 51, 52, 55, 57, 276.

108 Miller, *ESH*, 1833, p. 7 (*ST*, April 15, 1841, p. 9).

109 *Ibid.;* Miller, MSVT, No. 1, p. 1. Cf. "Daniel's Testimony," *ST*, May 10, 1843, pp. 79, 80.

in the feet and toes of the image as "pagan" and "papal" Rome "both 'mixing themselves with the seed of man,' [2:43] that is uniting church and state, ecclesiastical and civil, in government."[110]

Miller interpreted the "four great beasts" of Dan. 7 similarly. The lion stood for Babylon, the bear for the Medo-Persian kingdom, the leopard for the Grecian kingdom under Alexander, and the fourth beast represented the Roman empire. In the interpretation of the fourth beast the two-abominations motif was again manifested. The ten horns of this beast, which were compared with the ten toes of the image, alluded to "the ten kingdoms, in which the Western or Roman Empire was divided about A.D. 476 by the Goths, Huns, and Vandals."[111] The ten kingdoms he considered to be "England, France, Spain, Portugal, Germany, Austria, Prussia, Ravenna, Lombardy, and Rome."[112] Josiah Litch felt, however, that the ten horns signified the Huns, Ostrogoths, Visigoths, Franks, Vandals, Suevi and Alans, the Burgundians, the Heruli and "Rugii or Thuringi," the Saxons and Angles, and the Lombards.[113] The little horn was interpreted by Miller, as was done by many other evangelical Protestants,[114] as the papal power which arose among these ten kingdoms. Litch designated the three horns that were plucked up as the Heruli, Ostrogoths, and Vandals.[115] According to Miller they represented Ravenna, Lombardy, and Rome and were called the "states of the Church" by the pope's authority.[116] The reign of papal

110 Miller, ESH, 1836, p. 40. Cf. Litch, "Historical Prophecy," MC, Aug. 10, 1843, p. 195; E. G. White, MS 63, 1899 (SDABC, IV, 1955, pp. 1168, 1169).

111 Miller, ESH, 1833, p. 9 (ST, April 15, 1841, p. 9). Many expositors dated the division of the Western empire into 10 kingdoms from A.D. 356 to 483.

112 Miller, ESH, 1833 as revised in ST, April 15, 1841, p. 10; Miller, ESH, 1836, p. 42 mentioned Naples and Tuscany instead of Germany and Prussia, citing Edward Irving as authority. In ESH, 1833, p. 10 he stated: "The principle [sic] kingdoms were France, Spain, Italy, Germany, Great Britain — the lesser kingdoms authors disagree in — but Dr. [John] Gill names Portugal, Scotland, Poland, Denmark, and Sweden."

113 Litch, "Discussion," p. 57. Cf. Appendix IV. Similar views were held by William Hales, George S. Faber, George Storrs, and the bishops Edward Chandler, Thomas Newton, and William Lloyd. In general Machiavelli's Florentine History, chap. 1 was referred to as the earliest authority. J. White's exposition on Daniel depended heavily on Storrs. Cf. Storrs, "Exposition of Nebuchadnezzar's Dream," MC, Jan. 6, 1843, p. [2] (The Bible Examiner: Containing Various Prophetic Expositions, 1843, p. 7) with [J. White], "Exposition of Daniel II, 31-34: or Nebuchadnezzar's Dream," RH, Oct. 31, 1854, p. 93 (The Four Universal Monarchies . . . , 1855, p. 7); [J. White], The Prophecy of Daniel . . . , 1859, p. 7; J. White, "Faith and Hope," RH, Feb. 1, 1870, p. 41 (Sermons, pp. 69, 70).

114 For a survey of European commentators of the Reformation and post-Reformation era, see Froom, PFF, II, 528-31, 784-87; on 17th- and 18th-century American expositors, ibid., II, 252; on 19th-century European expositors, ibid., p. 744; on Miller's contemporaries, 1798-1844, ibid., IV, 396.

115 Litch, "Discussion," p. 57. Cf. Appendix IV; Storrs, "Exposition of Daniel, 7th Chapter, or Vision of the Four Beasts," MC, Jan. 6, 1843, p. [12] (Examiner, pp. 23, 24); [J. White], "Exposition of Daniel VII: or the Vision of the Four Beasts," RH, Nov. 14, 1854, p. 109 (Universal Monarchies, pp. 31, 32); J. White, "Faith and Hope," RH, Feb. 8, 1870, p. 50 (Sermons, pp. 101, 102). Litch based this on E. Gibson, The History of the Decline and Fall of the Roman Empire.

116 Miller, ESH, 1833, as revised in ST, April 15, 1841, p. 10. In 1831 he saw the three horns as France, Italy, and Germany which were given to Charlemagne by the power of the pope (MSVT, No. 1, p. 3); ESH, 1833, p. 9 mentioned Spain, Italy and Germany.

Rome, which was to be destroyed at Christ's return, was given in 7:25 as "a time and times and the dividing of times." Miller's application of the year-day principle to this expression resulted in the following calculation: "time" was considered as one prophetic year, or 360 prophetic days; "times" as 2 prophetic years, or 720 prophetic days; "dividing of time" as a half prophetic year, or 180 prophetic days. The sum total amounted to 1260 prophetic days or 1260 literal years.[117] The 1260-year period began in 538 when he thought Justinian, the emperor of the Eastern empire, made the bishop of Rome universal bishop.[118] According to Litch, 538 saw the lifting of the Ostrogoth's siege of Rome and their overthrow by Justinian's General Belisarius, resulting in the restoration of the city of Rome to the emperor and contributing to the rise of papal authority.[119] The end of the 1260 years' reign of the little horn Miller calculated as 1798 when during the French Revolution "the pope lost his power to tread the Church underfoot, and to reign over the kings of the earth."[120]

Another prophetic parallelism, related to the 1260-day period and interpreted in the context of the second abomination, was found in Rev. 11:2, 3; 12:6, 14; 13:5. In 11:2, 3 it was stated that "the court which is without the temple . . . is given unto the Gentiles: and the holy city shall they tread underfoot forty and two months. And I will give power unto my two witnesses, and they shall prophesy a thousand two hundred and three score days, clothed in sackcloth." The two witnesses Miller believed to be the Scriptures with its two covenants or testaments.[121] The court was seen as the Christian church, trodden down for forty-two months or 1260 prophetic days which, according to the year-day principle, signified 1260 actual years. During this period, the Scriptures prophesied while in sackcloth. Again, Miller applied it to the period 538 to 1798, during which the Christian church was persecuted by the Roman Catholic Church and the reading of Scripture by laymen was suppressed.[122] The next prophetic parallel covering the same period was seen in 12:6, "the woman fled into the wilderness, where she hath a place prepared of God, that they should feed her there a thousand two hundred and threescore days." Miller identified the

117 *Ibid.*, p. 11 (*ST*, April 15, 1841, p. 10). This interpretation had been followed for many centuries (Froom, *PFF*, I, 894; II, 156, 528, 784; III, 252, 744; IV, 392, 396).

118 Letter, Miller to T. Hendryx, Aug. 9, 1831. Litch placed Justinian's decree declaring the Bishop of Rome the head of all the churches in 533 (*PE*, I, 1842, pp. 85-87).

119 Litch, *SCC*, 1838, pp. 89, 111, 114, 139, 162. Cf. Hale, *SAM*, pp. 85-91; Froom, *PFF*, II, 784; III, 744; IV, 396, 846; E. G. White, *SP*, IV, 57; E. G. White, *GC*, pp. 54, 266, 439.

120 Letter, Miller to Hendryx, Aug. 9, 1831. Cf. Hale, *SAM*, pp. 91-93; Froom, *PFF*, II, 731-82; III, 744; IV, 396, 846; E. G. White, *GC*, pp. 266, 439. Sandeen called the dethroning of the pope in 1798 a "prophetic Rosetta Stone" (*Fundamentalism*, p. 7; "Millennialism," p. 108).

121 Miller, *ESH*, 1833, pp. 44, 45 (*ST*, Sept. 1, 1841, p. 82). For the Christian tradition of this view, see Froom, *PFF*, II, 530, 787; III, 745; IV, 399, 849. Cf. E. G. White, *SP*, IV, 188-90.

122 Miller, *ESH*, 1833, pp. 43-48 (*ST*, Sept. 1, 1841, p. 82); Miller, "A Dissertation on Prophetic Chronology," in *The First Report of the General Conference of Christians . . . ,* 1841, p. 91. Cf. Froom, *PFF*, II, 787; III, 253; IV, 399, 849; E. G. White, *SP*, IV, 188, 190.

woman as the church, cared for by God during the 1260 days. The designated period was again from 538 till 1798 "during which time, the true church, or those who believed in Jesus Christ, and would not bow down and worship Papacy, were not permitted any civil rights, under any of the governments composing the Roman kingdom."[123] The last parallel passage was placed in the context of a beast which emerged out of the sea (13:1). In his early period this imagery signified to Miller the development of the papacy.[124] The blasphemous acts of the beast and the forty-two months duration of its power (13:5, 6) were interpreted as symbols of the blasphemous claims of the papacy and its period of domination during "forty-two prophetic months, which is 1260 years" from 538 to 1798.[125]

Thus, it was obvious that the year 1798 was of special significance to those who accepted this method of apocalyptic interpretation. The recent events of the French Revolution in relation to the Roman Catholic Church were seen as the fulfillment of Dan. 12:4. The time of the end had arrived, for the apocalyptic passages had been unsealed, and their significance had become clear.

b. Cosmic signs.

During the last decades of the 18th century and the early decades of the 19th century, certain phenomena occurred in nature that were interpreted by various evangelical Christians as signs of the approaching end of the world. Several Millerites had identified "the great tribulation" of Mt. 24:21 as the church suffering under the persecution of pagan and papal Rome,[126] the two abominations. The Reformation they recognized as the instrument to shorten the days of this tribulation (Mt. 24:27).[127] Then their minds had been directed to the cosmic signs of Mt. 24:29 which were to take place after the tribulation. The sudden darkening of the sun and full moon in a section of the eastern part of the North American continent on May 19,

123   Miller, ESH, 1833, p. 51 (ST, Oct. 1, 1841, p. 97). Cf. E. G. White, SP, IV, 57, 58. For the Christian tradition of this view, see Froom, PFF, I, 897; II, 531, 787; IV, 394, 399, 849.
124   Miller, ESH, 1833, p. 32 (ST, July 15, 1841, p. 57). Here he said: "By sea I understand the Roman government, or fourth kingdom in Daniel's vision, and it denotes wicked nations, 'for the wicked are like a troubled sea;' by the beast we must understand the Papal power, or little horn." Miller saw in Rev. 13 a view of Antichrist in his political (13:1-10) and ecclesiastical (13:11-18) aspects (ibid.). Later on he defined these different dimensions more specifically as the first beast or pagan Rome and the image beast or papal Rome (ESH, 1836, p. 56). See infra, p. 39, n. 197. Cf. Litch, PE, I, 95, 96; Appendix IV.
125   Miller, ESH, 1833, p. 32 (ST, July 15, 1841, p. 57). Cf. Litch, PE, I, 97, 104, 105; E. G. White, SP, IV, 57, 276. For centuries commentators interpreted this beast and the 42 months in a somewhat similar way; see Froom, PFF, II, 531, 787; III, 253, 745; IV, 394, 399.
126   Joel Spaulding, "Exposition on Matt. XXIV," ST, Sept. 14, 1842, p. 185; [Litch], "The 24th of Matthew," MC, Aug. 17, 1843, p. 202; Bliss, An Exposition of the Twenty Fourth of Matthew . . . , 1843, pp. 42-44. Cf. E. G. White, GC, p. 393. Miller discussed this in the context of the fall of Jerusalem which he saw as a type of the end of the world (A Familiar Exposition of the Twenty-Fourth Chapter of Matthew . . . , 1842, pp. 18, 19).
127   Spaulding, "Matt. XXIV," p. 185; [Litch], "Matthew," p. 202; Bliss, Matthew, p. 44. Cf. E. G. White, GC, p. 267. Miller referred to the shortening of the siege of Jerusalem (Matthew, p. 21).

1780 was seen as a fulfillment of Mt. 24:29, Rev. 6:12, and Joel 2:31. In America many had interpreted this event as a sign of the Second Advent, later literature referring to the day as the "Dark Day of May 19, 1780."[128] The next sign to be expected, according to Mt. 24:29 and Rev. 6:13, was that of the falling of the stars. When the most spectacular meteoric shower on record occurred over the Western Hemisphere on November 15, 1833, it was seen as the fulfillment of these texts.[129] Such events, coupled in at least one editorial with the Lisbon earthquake of 1755,[130] were frequently mentioned in Millerite literature. During the year 1843 the most brilliant comet of the century appeared and an increase in celestial phenomena was reported in the newspapers.[131] These phenomena were another indication to believers that they were living in the time of the end. Miller himself, however, seemed to favor a nonliteral interpretation of these signs.[132]

c. The fall of the Turkish or Ottoman empire.

The events that occurred on August 11, 1841 were an important boost to

128 Spaulding, "Matt. XXIV," p. 185; Editorial, "The Sign of the Son of Man in Heaven," *ST*, Oct. 11, 1843, p. 59; Litch, *PE*, I, 151-55; II, 235; Bliss, *Matthew*, pp. 46, 47; Editorial, "Exposition of the 24th Chapter of Saint Matthew," *SAH*, April 2, 1844, p. 23; Henry Jones, *Modern Phenomena of the Heavens . . .* , 1843, pp. 13-17. Cf. E. G. White, *GC*, pp. 305-8; Froom, *PFF*, III, 147, 208, 212, 233, 253, 259; IV, 53, 54, 290-92, 586, 1144, 1217.

129 Spaulding, "Matt. XXIV," pp. 185, 186; Editorial, "Signs," pp. 62, 63; Litch, *PE*, I, 154, 155; II, 235-39; Bliss, *Matthew*, pp. 47-59; Editorial, "24th of Matthew," *SAH*, April 9, 1844, p. 30; Jones, *Phenomena*, pp. 21-30. Cf. E. G. White, *GC*, pp. 333, 334; Froom, *PFF*, IV, 145, 146, 289-300, 569, 586, 1210-20.

130 Editorial, "The Sixth Seal," *ST*, Oct. 11, 1843, p. 46. Regarding the Lisbon earthquake it was said that "the greatest earthquake of which we have an account in modern history, occurred on the 1st of November, 1755, and extended to every quarter of the globe. It was felt in Europe, Asia, Africa, and America — from Greenland on the north, to the extreme south" (*ibid.*). Cf. L. D. Fleming, "Earthquakes," *MC*, March 21, 1844, p. 285; "The Sixth Seal," *Blackwood's Mag.*, repr. in *AH*, Sept. 18, 1844, p. 54; E. G. White, *GC*, pp. 304, 305; Froom, *PFF*, II, 640, 674-76; III, 147, 187-93, 251, 253, 258; IV, 53. As far as possible the full surname of the author with his initials will be given instead of only the initials indicating the authorship of articles, omitting the use of brackets. In this instance L.D.F. has been changed to L. D. Fleming.

131 Jones, *Phenomena*, pp. 15-19, 31-43; Nichol, *Midnight Cry*, p. 145. Bates stated that in 1843 Millerites were considered as "the most fortunate people in the world, for they had signs in the heavens to help prove their doctrine" (Life," No. 47, *YI*, Nov. 1862, p. 81 [*Autobiography*, p. 274]). Henry Jones indicated that the aurora borealis was a modern phenomenon which could be interpreted as a fulfillment of the signs of Joel 2:30 announcing the approach of the Day of the Lord (*Phenomena*, pp. 2-12). Cf. Rowe, "Millerite Movement," pp. 58, 59.

132 The darkening of the sun signified to Miller that "the moral sun — the gospel — which is the means of light to the church, should become obscured." Its historical realization he saw in the persecution of the church "from the destruction of Jerusalem until A.D. 312, when Constantine put a stop to persecution, and began to bring in these abominable heresies, which finally ended in the rise of Antichrist, the clothing of the witnesses in sackcloth, and the driving out of the church into the wilderness" (*Matthew*, p. 25). The darkening of the moon meant that "the church should not spread her light. She would flee into the wilderness, where she would be fed twelve hundred and sixty years; the same length of time the two witnesses were clothed in sackcloth, or the sun was darkened" (*ibid.*). The falling of the stars he saw as a reference to "the ministers of the gospel (lesser lights in the moral heavens) falling from the purity of the gospel into anti-christian abominations" (*ibid.*). Cf. Litch, *SCC*, pp. 140-43. Miller's lecture on the signs of the times listed 25 signs but not one of them referred to cosmic phenomena (*ESH*, 1836, pp. 213-33).

the missionary enthusiasm of the Millerite movement. The significance of this date was based on the historicist view of the seven trumpets of Rev. 8 and 9. According to Litch the sounding of the seven trumpets symbolized "the instrumentalities by which the Roman empire was to be overthrown and subverted, and finally ruined."[133] He indicated that under the first four trumpets (Rev. 8) the western part of the Roman empire fell, under the fifth and sixth trumpet (Rev. 9) "the eastern empire was crushed," and finally under the seventh trumpet "great Babylon entire will sink to rise no more at all."[134] Many of Litch's contemporaries applied the fifth and sixth trumpet to Muhammadanism, or Islam, and the Ottoman empire arising out of that religious system.[135] In Rev. 9:3, 5, 10 the Turkish empire was symbolized as locusts commissioned to torment men for five months or 150 prophetic days, representing 150 actual years according to the year-day principle. Litch accepted the idea that the Ottoman empire was to torment the "Greek empire." The crucial question was the precise time when the tormenting began. Litch's authority for his answer was Edward Gibbon's *History of the Decline and Fall of the Roman Empire,* according to which the Ottoman Turks first entered the territory of Nicomedia and attacked the Greeks on July 27, 1299.[136] From this, Litch inferred that the 150 years would finish in 1449 when the fifth trumpet would end and the sixth begin to sound (9:13), and indicated that from 1299 to 1449 the Turks were continually tormenting the Greeks by wars without conquering them. The events related to the succession of the Greek throne in Constantinople in 1449 were interpreted as the fulfillment of the 150 years. In that year the Greek emperor died and left the throne to his brother, Deacozes. But before Deacozes dared ascend the throne, he sent ambassadors to Anereth, the Turkish Sultan, to request his permission. Thus, according to Litch, his independence was gone before the fall of the city in 1453 and the "Turkish nations were therefore loosed by divine command."[137]

The sixth trumpet of Rev. 9 depicted the conquest and killing done by the Ottoman empire. The duration of the supremacy of this power was "an hour, and a day, and a month, and a year" (9:15). The actual time was again found by using the year-day principle. An hour was 15 days; a day, one year; a month, 30 years; and a year, 360 literal years, the whole amounting to 391 years and 15 days. Thus, to Litch the completion of the sixth trumpet, or the end of the Ottoman supremacy, should occur "150 years" and "391 years and 15 days" after July 27, 1299, that is, precisely on August 11, 1840. To

133 Litch, *PE,* II, 132, 133. Cf. [Litch], *The Sounding of the Seven Trumpets of Revelation VIII and IX,* ed. by J. White, 1859, pp. 1, 2.

134 Litch, *PE,* II, 133. Cf. [Litch], *Seven Trumpets,* p. 2. For his exposition of Rev. 8 and 9 Litch followed closely Alexander Keith, *The Signs of the Times . . . ,* I, 1832, pp. 222-355.

135 For a survey of views on Rev. 8 and 9 by American commentators, 1798-1844, see Froom, *PFF,* IV, 398; on 19th-century European commentators, *ibid.,* III, 745.

136 See Gibbon, *Decline and Fall of the Roman Empire,* ed. J. B. Bury, VII, 1900, p. 24.

137 Litch, "Fall of the Ottoman Power in Constantinople," *ST,* Aug. 1, 1840, p. 70.

this conclusion he arrived about two weeks before the expected event.[138]

Several months later another article by Litch on the Eastern question appeared in which he claimed that the latest political developments were a confirmation of his prediction. The Sultan of the empire had been engaged in a quarrel with Mehemet Ali, Pasha of Egypt. The Pasha rebelled against the Sultan, declared his independence, and conquered a large part of the Ottoman empire and fleet. This aroused the Western European powers, who wanted to restore the balance of power. A conference was held in London on July 15, 1840 and an ultimatum was drawn up demanding the Pasha to return part of his conquests and the Sultan's fleet. Rifaat Bey, the Sultan's envoy, was sent to Alexandria to communicate the ultimatum to the Pasha. Litch felt that the end of the prophetic period of Rev. 9:15 and the end of the supremacy of the Sultan were inseparably connected with the ultimatum of the great powers to Mehemet Ali. As long as the decision of that conference remained in the hands of Rifaat Bey, the Sultan maintained his independence. But when the ultimatum had been passed into the Pasha's hands, the question of war or peace was beyond the Sultan's control. This happened, Litch said, when "Rifaat Bey arrived at Alexandria on the 11th of August and threw the decision of the affair into the hands of Mehemet Ali. And from that time it was out of the sultan's power to control the affairs. It lay with Mehemet Ali to say whether there should be war or peace."[139] According to Litch, this was the conclusion of the sixth trumpet, and since the 11th of August the Ottoman power in Constantinople had been "entirely under the dictation of the great christian powers of Europe."[140] He concluded his remarks by stressing the urgency of the times:

> I am entirely satisfied that on the 11th of August, 1840, *The Ottoman power according to previous calculation* DEPARTED TO RETURN NO MORE. I can now say with utmost confidence, "The second woe is past and behold the third

138 *Ibid.* Here he added, "Allowing the first period, 150 years to have been exactly fulfilled before Deacozes ascended the throne by permission of the Turks, and that the 391 years 15 days commenced at the close of the first period, it will end on the 11th of August, 1840, when the Ottoman power in Constantinople may be expected to be broken. And this, I believe, will be found to be the case." Cf. Editorial, "Plan of Calculating the Prophetic Periods," *SAH,* April 23, 1844, p. 45; E. G. White, *GC,* pp. 334, 335. However, Litch added that there could be a calculation error of a few months ("Ottoman Power," p. 70). Already in 1838 he predicted this event to be in "A.D. 1840, some time in the month of August" (*SCC,* p. 157). Cf. E. G. White, *GC,* p. 334. Miller's earliest position was 1843 (Letter, Miller to Hendryx, Aug. 9, 1831). Later, he adopted 1839 (MSVT, No. 5, p. 13; *ESH,* 1836, pp. 93-97). Finally, he accepted Gibbon's chronology (Editorial Remark, *ST,* Aug. 16, 1841, p. 73).

139 Litch, "The Nations," *ST,* Feb. 1, 1841, p. 162; Litch, "Fall of the Ottoman Power," *ST,* Jan. 1, 1842, pp. 147, 148. Later he stated more precisely that the ultimatum was officially put into the power of Mehemet Ali and was disposed of by his order to place the Turkish government steamer with the Turkish envoy under quarantine on the 11th of August, 1841 ("The Three Wo [sic] Trumpets," *Great Crisis,* Aug. 4, 1842, in *ST,* Sept. 7, 1842, p. 182).

140 Litch, "Nations," p. 162. Cf. E. G. White, *GC,* p. 335. She called Litch's prediction a "remarkable fulfillment of prophecy" (*ibid.,* p. 334).

28

woe cometh quickly [Rev. 11:14]." *"Blessed is he that watcheth and keepeth his garments lest he walk naked and they see his shame* [16:15]."[141]

Litch's most complete exposition of the Eastern question was published more than a year later. From additional evidence[142] he concluded that on the same 11th of August the Sultan applied in Constantinople to the ambassadors of the major powers for information in case the Pasha should reject the ultimatum. The requested information was not given, on the basis that provision had already been made. Litch reacted by asking, "Where was the sultan's independence that day? GONE. Who had the supremacy of the Ottoman empire in their hands? *The great powers.*"[143]

This interpretation of Rev. 9 contributed considerably to the awareness of the time of the end because they thought that one of the last signs of the times had taken place. An editorial comment on Litch's findings stated that if the Ottoman supremacy had departed, then the end of the world was imminent.[144] Litch's prediction was a great stimulus to the missionary zeal of the Millerite movement. Years later a participant commented that it was to "the advent movement what the power of steam is on the machinery of the railroad locomotive. So from the 11th day of August, 1840, the advent cause and message, or angel, careered on its way with *greater power than ever before.*"[145]

3. The time of the Second Advent.

In the first half of the 19th century in America and Europe there was among historicists a gradual shift of interest from Dan. 7 and the 1260 days to Dan. 8, leading to an upsurge of Second Advent expectancy throughout Christendom. The focal point of their attention was the "two thousand and three hundred days" (Dan. 8:14), which was interpreted by many Protestant commentators with the year-day principle.[146] The reason for this shift in prophetic interest seems to have been that they were satisfied with the view

141 Litch, "Nations," p. 162. As historical evidence he used extracts from the *Moniteur Ottoman,* Aug. 22, 1840 and the *London Morning Chronicle,* Sept. 18, 1840 *(ibid.).*
142 Extract from a Letter of a Correspondent of the *London Chronicle,* dated Constantinople, Aug. 12, 1840 cited in "Arrival of the Britannia!" *ST,* Oct. 1, 1840, pp. 101, 102. The article included contemporary interpretations of the fall of Turkey which Litch saw as further evidence for his position. See also Isaac C. Wellcome, *History of the Second Advent Message . . . ,* 1874, pp. 132-40.
143 Litch, "Trumpets," p. 182.
144 Editorial, "The Fall of the Ottoman Power," *ST,* Jan. 1, 1842, p. 149.
145 Hiram Edson, *The Time of the End . . . ,* 1849, p. 8. Cf. [Litch], "RPA," pp. 59, 60; Bates, "Life," No. 43, *YI,* July 1862, p. 50 *(Autobiography,* p. 258); J. White, *Life,* p. 128; E. G. White, *GC,* p. 335. This progress was also due to the contribution of Himes, who joined the movement in 1840 and became its principal organizer. J. N. Andrews stated that with the fulfillment of this prophecy "a demonstration of the truthfulness of the mode of calculation respecting the prophetic times was given to the world" ("TAR," *RH,* Feb. 6, 1855, p. 169 [*TAR,* 1855, p. 22]). Cf. E. G. White, *GC,* p. 335. In *SP,* IV, 222 she dated the Second Advent movement from 1840.
146 John Dowling, *An Exposition of the Prophecies . . . ,* 1840, p. 71.

that the 1260 days had been fulfilled sometime during the French Revolution, while the end of the 2300 days was to be expected in the immediate future.[147]

Contemporary commentators who considered Dan. 8:14 as predictive prophecy but did not apply the year-day principle to the 2300 days interpreted this period as literal days fulfilled in the persecution of the Jews by Antiochus IV, Epiphanes.[148] Most contemporary American and European historicists, however, were convinced that this period began sometime between 457 and 453 B.C. and would end between A.D. 1843 and 1847.[149] The application of the year-day principle generally resulted in two major interpretations of the little horn (8:9-14): (1) Pagan and papal Rome; (2) Muhammadanism (Islam).[150] Yet, many historicists looked to the end of the 2300 days as the inauguration of some significant event such as the cleansing or purification of the church, the restoration of true worship, the destruction of antichrist or papacy, the liberation of Palestine or Jerusalem from the Muslims, the dissolution of Islam, the fall of Turkey, the beginning of the millennium, the establishment of the kingdom, the Day of Judgment, or the Second Advent.[151]

Postmillennialists generally expected the establishment of a millennial kingdom and a gradual conversion of the world for 1000 years, at the end of which Christ would return.[152] Litch designated such persons as "Millenists."[153] Premillennialists, however, looked for Christ's coming at the beginning of His millennial reign on earth with His saints. Litch distinguished two categories of premillennialists, Adventists (Millerites)[154] and Millenarians, their major distinctions being that

> the Millennarians [sic] believe in the premillennial advent of Christ, and his personal reign for a thousand years before the consummation or the end of the present world, and creation of the new heavens and earth, and the descent of the New Jerusalem. While the Adventists believe in the end of the world or age, the destruction of the wicked, the dissolution of the earth, the renovation of nature, and the descent of New Jerusalem will be at the beginning of the thousand years. The Millennarians believe in the return of the Jews, as such, either before, at, or after the advent of Christ, to Palestine, to possess that land a thousand years, while the Adventists believe that all the return of the Jews to that country, will be the return of all pious Jews who have ever lived, to the inheritance of the new earth, in their resurrection state.

147 Froom, *PFF,* IV, 204-25.
148 See *infra,* pp. 63-76.
149 *Ibid.,* IV, 301-29, 404.
150 *Ibid.,* pp. 397, 405.
151 *Ibid.,* pp. 397, 404. Cf. Sandeen, *Fundamentalism,* p. 52.
152 See *infra,* pp. 59-64.
153 [Litch], "RPA," p. 47.
154 See *supra,* p. xv, *infra,* p. 91.

The *Millennarians* believe a part of the heathen world will be left on the earth, to multiply and increase, during the one thousand years, and to be converted and governed by the glorified saints during that period; while the *Adventists* believe that when the Son of Man shall come in his glory, then he shall be seated on the throne of his glory, and before him shall be gathered all nations, and he shall separate them one from the other, as a shepherd divideth his sheep from the goats. . . . They cannot see any probation for any nation, either Jew or Gentile, after the Son of Man comes in his glory, and takes out his own saints from among all nations.[155]

To Millerite Adventists there was no distinction between the general character of the millennium and the eternal glory except for some events around the resurrection and judgment of the righteous at the beginning of the millennium and the resurrection and judgment of the wicked at the end of the millennium.[156]

a. The sanctuary of Dan. 8:14.

Then I heard one saint speaking, and another saint said unto that certain saint which spoke, How long shall be the vision concerning the daily sacrifice, and the transgression of desolation to give both the sanctuary and the host to be trodden under foot? And he said to me, Unto two thousand and three hundred days; then shall the sanctuary be cleansed. Dan. 8:13, 14.

The center of Millerite missionary motivation lay in their position on Dan. 8. The vision described in this chapter was considered to be another

155 *Ibid.,* pp. 47, 48. He added that "the *Millennarians* believe that the saints must have mortal men in a state of probation, for a thousand years, as their subjects, in order for them to reign as kings; for, say they, how can they reign without subjects? To which the *Adventists* reply, If it is necessary for them to have such subjects for a thousand years in order to reign, by the same rule they must have them *eternally;* for '*they shall reign forever and ever.*' Rev. xxii:5. And again it is replied, Adam had dominion given him, but not a dominion over man. It was a 'dominion over all the earth,' and all its creatures [Gen. 1:28]. So also the kingdom Christ will give to the saints when he comes in his glory, is 'the Kingdom prepared for them from the foundation of the world [Mt. 25:34].' Just the dominion which Adam had, will belong to the saints." For the difference between Adventists and Millenarians, see also Miller, "An Address to the Second Advent Conference . . . ," *ST,* Nov. 1, 1841, pp. 114, 115; Wellcome, *Second Advent Message,* pp. 169-71. Several scholars do not seem to make such a distinction but simply classify the Millerites as Millenarians (e.g., Timothy L. Smith, "Social Reform: Some Reflections on Causation and Consequence," in Gaustad, *Adventism,* p. 20; Sandeen, *Fundamentalism,* p. 53).
156 See Wellcome, *Second Advent Message,* pp. 170, 171; Miller, *Views,* pp. 33-35. Miller's view on the millennium was the following: The millennium would be inaugurated by: (1) The parousia; (2) the resurrection of the righteous dead and the translation of the living ones; (3) the encounter between the living and resurrected saints and the Lord in the air; (4) the judgment of the saints and the marriage between the church and Christ; (5) the destruction of the wicked; (6) the cleansing of the earth with fire; (7) the banishment of the devil, the evil spirits, and the souls of the wicked; (8) the return of Christ and His saints to the new and cleansed earth, the inheritance of the saints, which is full of God's glory. The millennium would be terminated by: (1) The gathering of the saints into the holy city on earth; (2) the resurrection of the wicked; (3) the loosening of the devil to deceive the wicked and prepare them for a battle against the saints; (4) the judgment of the wicked by the saints and their second death in the lake of fire; (5) the possession of the earth by the saints forever *(ibid.).* See also Miller, "Second Advent Conference," p. 115; *infra,* p. 64, n. 49.

element in the series of prophetic passages covering approximately the same time period as Dan. 2 and 7, its different symbolism being considered as a confirming complement. The ram and goat in the vision were identified within the chapter itself as "the kings of Media and Persia" and "the king of Grecia." Miller interpreted the great horn of 8:21 as Alexander the Great, whose conquest of the Persian empire was considered fulfilling the goat's victory over the ram (8:5-7). The breaking of the goat's great horn and its being replaced by four other horns (8:8, 22) was seen as the death of Alexander at the height of his power and a subsequent division of the empire by his principal generals into four parts. The little horn, which was generally interpreted as coming out of one of the four horns,[157] was identified in the context of the two abominations as a persecuting power against God's people and represented two different successive powers in history. The first persecuting phase of the little horn (8:9-11) was identified by Miller with the Roman empire which made Macedonia, the first of the four divisions of the Greek empire, a Roman province. From there the Roman empire extended itself toward the South, the East, and the pleasant land, Palestine (8:9). Dan. 8:10, 11 pictured the struggle between the Jews and the Romans. The specific actions of the little horn against "the prince of the host" and the system of worship so that "the daily sacrifice was taken away, and the place of his sanctuary was cast down" (8:11) he interpreted as the actions of the Roman empire which "would magnify itself even against Christ the prince of his people, and be the instrument of destroying the Jewish ceremonial law, and finally Jerusalem itself, the place of Christ's sanctuary."[158]

In Dan. 8:12 Miller saw the emergence of the second persecuting phase of the little horn which followed the persecution under the Roman empire and was identified with the period of the little horn of Dan. 7. This verse, he said, signified "the Papal power or abomination that maketh desolate, by reason of departing from the truth and leading off an host with them; they cast out and trampled on the true followers of Christ, and practiced and prospered in their iniquity."[159] Dan. 8:24-26 and 2 Thes. 2:4 were also applied in this context. Because the second dimension of the little horn of Dan. 8 was interpreted as the papacy, the sanctuary against which the little

157 Though in 1842 Miller remarked about the origin of the little horn that it "rose up out of one of the four winds of heaven" (*Matthew*, p. 17). Cf. Miller, *ESH*, 1836, p. 45.

158 Miller, *ESH*, 1833, p. 14 (*ST*, May 1, 1841, pp. 17, 18). Cf. Miller, MSVT, No. 1, pp. 4-7; Editorial, "The 'Four Great Beasts,'" *SAH*, May 7, 1844, p. 62. Regarding Dan. 8:10 Miller said: "By the *host of heaven*, we can only understand the people of God, the Jews; by the stars, I understand rulers, such as kings, high priests or sanhedrim, which was fulfilled by the Romans depriving the Jews of their right to appoint their own kings, or high priests, and taking away from the 70 elders or sanhedrim the power of life or death over the Jews themselves; the Romans trampling on their authority, claiming and exercising all the power, which the Jewish laws only give to their own rulers" (*ESH*, 1833, p. 13 [*ST*, May 1, 1841, p. 17]). In his early period he associated the daily sacrifice (8:13) with "the completion of the typical priesthood, or seventy weeks" (*ibid.*, p. 15 [*ST*, May 1, 1841, p. 25]).

159 *Ibid.*, p. 14 (*ST*, May 1, 1841, p. 18).

horn had directed its activities was given a meaning that was relevant for both phases of the persecution period.

The dual significance of the sanctuary was of vital importance for the understanding of why Millerites believed that Christ's coming was imminent. Because of the pagan and papal dimensions of the little horn, it was impossible to interpret the sanctuary against which its activities were directed as the Jewish sanctuary in Jerusalem, for such a view had no relevance for the papal dimension. Miller, therefore, viewed the sanctuary of Dan. 8:14, which was to be "cleansed" or "justified," as the church, "the people of God in all the World, and among all nations."[160] Dan. 8:13 he interpreted in the context of the two abominations, remarking that the "daily sacrifice" referred to "the completion of the typical priesthood, or seventy weeks; the other [transgression of desolation] to the sufferings of the people of God, under the abominations of the fourth kingdom, both pagan and papal, when they should be trodden under foot, until Christ should be revealed in his glory."[161] A few years later Miller seemed to have harmonized his exposition of the "daily sacrifice" of 8:13 with the daily-sacrifice exposition of 12:11 in the context of the two-abominations motif.[162] In a similar context he explained the expression "the sanctuary and the host" (8:13): In the light of the first abomination the "sanctuary" was seen as "the temple at Jerusalem and those who worship therein, which was trodden under foot by the Pagan kingdoms of the world, since the days of Daniel"; in reference to the second abomination the "host" was identified as "the people who worship in the outer court, and fitly represents the Christian church [Rev. 11:2, 3]."[163] The sanctuary of 8:14 Miller interpreted as "the true sanctuary which God has built of lively stones to his own acceptance, through Christ, of which the temple at Jerusalem was but a type."[164] Regarding its cleansing or justification, he stated that "when that New Jerusalem is perfected, then shall we be cleansed and justified" and added that "the spiritual sanctuary will not be cleansed until Christ's second coming, and then all Israel shall be raised, judged and justified in his

160 Miller, MSVT, No. 2, pp. 4, 5. Cf. Miller, ESH, 1833, p. 15 (ST, May 15, 1841, p. 25).

161 Ibid.

162 Ibid., 1836, p. 37. To Miller the term "daily sacrifice" had been interpreted "by some to mean the Jewish rites and ceremonies; and by others the Pagan rites and sacrifices" because of the close resemblance between the Jewish sacrificial system and that of paganism. He concluded, however, that this term in 8:13 because of its context could not be considered as referring to the Jewish sacrificial system. He indicated that this term signified "Pagan and Papal rites, for it stands coupled with 'the abomination of desolation,' and performs the same acts, such as are ascribed to the Papal abomination, 'To give both the sanctuary and host to be trodden under foot' " (ibid.). Thus he stated that "the 'daily sacrifice' means Pagan rites and sacrifices, and the transgression of desolation, the Papal, and both together shall tread under foot the 'sanctuary and host' " (ibid.). In this manner the term "daily sacrifice" became a part of the two-abominations motif. Cf. Litch, PE, II, 82; supra, p. 22, n. 107.

163 Miller, ESH, 1836, pp. 37, 38.

164 Ibid., p. 38. In relation to the "true sanctuary" of 8:14 "the temple at Jerusalem was only a shadow" (Miller, Miller's Reply to Stuart's Hints . . . , 1842, p. 31).

sight."[165] Separate from this cleansing of the sanctuary, he distinguished a cleansing of the earth by fire when Christ returns.[166]

In his most extensive exposition of the sanctuary, published in 1842, Miller indicated that the word "sanctuary" could mean: (1) Jesus Christ (Is. 8:14; Ezek. 10:16); (2) heaven (Ps. 102:19, 20:2); (3) Judah (Ps. 114:2); (4) the temple of Jerusalem (1 Chron. 22:19; Ex. 25:8); (5) the holy of holies (1 Chron. 28:10; Rev. 4:6); (6) the earth (Is. 60:13; 1 Kings 8:27; Rev. 5:10; Rev. 20:6; Mt. 6:20; Ps. 82:8; Rev. 11:15; Ps. 96:6-13); (7) the saints (1 Cor. 3:16-17; 2 Cor. 6:16; Eph. 2:21-22).[167] The question of which sanctuary was meant in Dan. 8:14 was intimately related to the question of its *cleansing.* With this in mind Miller analyzed the seven different meanings of the word "sanctuary," showing that it could not be Christ, for He was not impure, or heaven, for that was not unclean; it could not be literal Judah, for that was cut off and was no more a nation; it could not be the temple nor the holy of holies in the temple of Jerusalem, for they were destroyed. He concluded that only two things could be called a sanctuary: "the EARTH and the CHURCH: when these are cleansed, then, and not until then, will the entire Sanctuary of God be cleansed and *justified* (as it reads in the margin)."[168] The earth, he felt, would be cleansed by fire when the Lord should come, and at that time the saints would be cleansed or justified, adding that "the whole church will then be cleansed from all uncleanness, and presented without spot or wrinkle [Eph. 5:27], and will then be clothed with fine linen, clean and white [Rev. 19:8]. . . . *'Then shall the sanctuary be cleansed,'* when the will of God is done in earth as in heaven."[169] Thus by expanding the concept of the sanctuary, he unified his previous separate cleansings of the church and the earth. This seems to have become the predominant view among the Millerites.[170]

Hale arrived at a different interpretation of the sanctuary. According to him, the sanctuary was the promised land, for "the sanctuary here spoken of must be capable of being *'trodden under foot',* and of being *'cleansed',* and . . . of being cleansed *at the coming of Christ and the resurrection of the righteous dead.*"[171] In this context the cleansing of the sanctuary meant "1. Its purifi-

---

165 Miller, *ESH,* 1836, p. 38. In 1831 he described the cleansing of the sanctuary as the "complete redemption from sin, both soul and body, after the resurrection, when Christ comes the second time, 'without sin unto salvation' [Heb. 9:28]" (Letter, Miller to Andrus, Feb. 15, 1831).

166 Miller referred to Rev. 20:9, 10; 2 Pet. 3:7-12 (MSVT, No. 7, p. 6). Cf. Miller, *Dissertations on the True Inheritance of the Saints . . . ,* 1842, p. 25.

167 Miller, "Cleansing of the Sanctuary," *ST,* April 6, 1842, p. 1.

168 *Ibid.*

169 *Ibid.,* p. 2.

170 Application of the sanctuary to the earth enabled Miller to use Dan. 8:14 in combatting postmillennial views. This view seems to be stressed so much "that many later writers, when recounting Miller's understanding of the sanctuary, spoke only of his application of this symbol to the earth" (Robert Haddock, "A History of the Doctrine of the Sanctuary in the Advent Movement 1800-1905," B.D. thesis, 1970, p. 84). Cf. J. White, *Sketches of the Christian Life and Public Labors of William Miller,* 1875, p. 7; E. G. White, *SP,* IV, 258.

171 Hale, *SAM,* p. 46. Cf. R. Winter, "A Lecture on the Cleansing of the Sanctuary," *SAII,* April 16, 1844, p. 39.

cation from the wicked agents of its desolation, and, 2. The removal of the curse which is upon it, at the termination of its predicted desolation. Isa. 1:27, 28; 49:13-17, 19."[172]

There were others who referred to the sanctuary as a place of worship. They reasoned that under the Jewish dispensation it meant the tabernacle, the temple, and Jerusalem itself, but under the Christian dispensation the place of worship was not restricted to a particular place. It was the world itself. Thus, the earth had to be purified.[173]

Although there was some difference as to the meaning of the sanctuary of Dan. 8:14 and its cleansing, those divergences did not seem to interfere with the importance of the time of the cleansing at the end of the 2300 days. Furthermore, it seems that whether the Millerites interpreted the sanctuary as the church, the promised land of Palestine, or the earth, they were united on the fact that either cleansing of the sanctuary could only take place at the end of the world.[174]

This view became an important argument in the hands of believers to combat the popular postmillennial views. Litch formulated the contemporary polemic in an "Address to the Clergy," remarking that the issue was whether the "termination of the 2300 days of Dan. 8:14 will introduce a temporal millennium, and the literal restoration of the Jews 'or' the establishment of a glorious and everlasting kingdom of God on earth, at the resurrection of the just."[175]

b. The end of the "two thousand and three hundred days."

There were quite a few of Miller's contemporaries who had attempted to determine the time of the sanctuary cleansing of Dan. 8:14.[176] The earliest expositors were to be found in Europe; later Americans followed their example. Like many other Christians[177] Miller assumed that the prophecy of the 70 weeks of Dan. 9:24-27 provided the key for determining the commencement of the sanctuary cleansing of 8:14: The 70 weeks and the

---

172 Hale, *SAM*, p. 15. Cf. George Storrs, "Then Shall the Sanctuary Be Cleansed," *MC*, April 25, 1844, pp. 321-23.

173 Cf. "Letter of David Bernard, on the Second Coming of Christ," *ST*, March 1, 1843, p. 191. In 1840 Litch interpreted the sanctuary of Dan. 8:14 as the "Christian Church" on the basis of Heb. 8:2 ("Mr. Litch's Reply to Rev. Ethan Smith . . . ," *ST*, May 1, 1840, p. 18). Litch rejected the idea that the cleansing of the sanctuary signified the purification of the earth by fire. Instead of the word "cleansing," he used the marginal reading "justification." He preferred, however, George Bush's use of the term "vindication." This idea was not endorsed by the *ST*. At the end of the 2300 years, just before the Resurrection, Litch expected the vindication of the sanctuary, which meant "that Jerusalem will be vindicated, or proved innocent, or justified, by the punishment of her destroyer. . . . God will vindicate *Jerusalem*, by the destruction of *Rome*" ("Babylon's Fall — the Sanctuary Cleansed," *ST*, July 26, 1843, p. 165). Cf. Litch, "Daniel's Vision of Four Beasts," *MC*, Aug. 10, 1843, p. 197.

174 Editorial, "Then Shall the Sanctuary Be Cleansed," *ST*, Oct. 25, 1843, pp. 76, 77.

175 Litch, "Address to the Clergy," *ST*, Jan. 1, 1842, p. 151. Cf. Miller, *ESH*, 1836, p. 22.

176 Froom, *PFF*, III, 263-751; IV, 15-426.

177 For a survey of pre-1844 usage of Dan. 9 as a key for Dan. 8, see *ibid.*, pp. 226-48, 405.

2300 days shared the same starting point.[178] The year 457 B.C. was accepted as the time when the commandment to restore and to rebuild Jerusalem was issued (Dan. 9:25).[179] His presupposition was that the 70 weeks or 490 prophetic days terminated at the time of the crucifixion of Christ. Miller dated this event in A.D. 33.[180] Thus, it seemed that there were exactly 490 years between 457 B.C. and A.D. 33. Having determined this, Miller proceeded by stating, "take 457 from 2300 years, and you leave us A.D. 1843 when the vision will end, and the sanctuary shall be cleansed. Or take 490, which is the 70 weeks, from 2300, and it will leave us 1810 after Christ's crucifixion; and then by adding the life of Christ which is 33 years we make the same, 1843, as before."[181] As a result the hopes of many were directed to the year 1843 as the year of the Second Advent.

Miller hesitated to confine himself to a specific date. His caution was reflected in the title of his popular lecture book, *Evidences from Scripture and History of the Second Coming of Christ; About the year 1843*. Others were even more cautious. At the First General Conference of Advent believers in Boston, 1840, there was no general agreement in regard to fixing the year of Christ's coming, though all felt that the coming was "nigh at hand."[182] In 1841 Dr. Henry D. Ward wrote to Miller: "I think you wrong in urging the matter of the date; but I honor your zeal, your fidelity, your learning, your industry."[183] He wrote also to the *Signs of the Times,* asking them to publish his views against a definite time setting, for "it is not for you to *know* the

178   Miller based the relation between Dan. 8 and 9 on the following inferences: (1) The angel Gabriel was commanded to make Daniel understand the vision (8:16); (2) although the angel instructed Daniel, he did not explain when the 2300 days began; (3) therefore, the return of Gabriel in Dan. 9 was considered as a further explanation of 8:14; (4) the term "vision" in 9:21, 23, 24 was interpreted as a reference to the vision of Dan. 8 (*ESH*, 1833, p. 16 [*ST*, May 15, 1841, p. 25]). Cf. Miller, MSVT, No. 2, pp. 2-4; E. G. White, *GC*, p. 325. Another evidence was found in the rendering of the word "determined" (9:24) as "cut off" or "separated." This suggested that the 70 weeks were "cut off" from the period of 2300 days or the 490 years from the 2300 years. The logical conclusion was to let the two periods commence together (Hale, *SAM*, pp. 55, 56; Litch, *PE*, I, 133; cf. E. G. White, *GC*, p. 326).
179   Miller, MSVT, No. 2, p. 4; Letter, Miller to Hendryx, Aug. 9, 1831.
180   Miller, *ESH*, 1833, p. 18 (*ST*, May 15, 1841, p. 26). James Ferguson (1710-76), a Scottish astronomer, seems to be the chief authority for this Crucifixion date. The "Extract from Ferguson's Astronomy" in Miller, *Views*, pp. 244-48 was from J. Ferguson, *The Works of James Ferguson* ... , I, 1823, pp. 332-36. The A.D. 33 tradition was traced back to Roger Bacon (William Hales, *A New Analysis of Chronology* ... , I, 2nd ed. rev., 1830, p. 99). Dan. 9:27 was interpreted by Miller as the preaching of the Gospel for 7 years: Both John and Christ preached 3½ years (*ESH*, 1833, p. 17 [*ST*, May 15, 1841, p. 26]). Others advocated a period of 7 years for Christ's ministry (Litch, *PE*, II, 39-42; Hale, *SAM*, pp. 25, 26).
181   Miller, MSVT, No. 2, p. 4. Cf. Miller, *ESH*, 1833, p. 18 (*ST*, May 15, 1841, p. 25); Letter, Miller to Hendryx, Aug. 9, 1831; Miller, *ESH*, 1836, pp. 47-49; Sandeen, *Fundamentalism*, p. 52. An earlier position was that he thought the period began in the 20th year of Artaxerxes (margin of Dan. 9:24) which he dated "about 455 years before Christ," leading to 1845 as the final date, though he made allowance for Christ's coming between 1843 and 1847 (Letter, Miller to Andrus, Feb. 15, 1831). His earliest position was "on or before 1843" (MS, 1822). The Septuagint reading of 2400 was rejected (Litch, *PE*, I, 115).
182   "The General Conference," *ST*, Nov. 1, 1840, p. 116.
183   Letter, H. D. Ward to Miller, Oct. 29, 1841.

time, or *the seasons,* which the Father has put in His own power [Acts 1:7]."[184]

Up until 1842 the adherence to a definite time for the parousia was still an open question, but as the year 1843 approached, there was in the mission motivation of those who accepted the doctrine of an imminent Second Advent an increasing emphasis on time. From then on the "non-timeists" receded into the background. At the Boston Second Advent Conference (May 24, 1842) the time element came definitely to the front, and it was resolved "that in the opinion of this conference, there are most serious and important reasons for believing that God has revealed the time of the end of the world and that that time is 1843."[185] The emphasis on a definite time was also defended on the grounds that it produced results.[186] The preaching of the date 1843 had stirred the churches. This would have been unlikely if there had not been anything definite about the time of Christ's return.[187] Two months before the year 1843 began, one of the major Millerite papers still cautioned against the setting of a definite hour, day, or month:

> The editors . . . *solemnly* PROTEST against the setting of the hour, day, or month, of the end of the world. There are various events, the anniversaries of which, within the year, may be the end of all things, but we have never fixed on any particular day. Different individuals have fixed upon several different days, and it has gone forth to the world that we have fixed the day. This has only been done by individuals upon their own responsibility, and contrary to our knowledge. Neither does Mr. Miller or the principal lecturers look to any particular time in 1843. That, we are willing to leave in the hands of God, and will endeavor to be ready whenever he may come.[188]

On January 1, 1843 Miller wrote a fourteen-point synopsis of his views in which he became more specific on the time by determining the limits of the year 1843. He wrote: "I am fully convinced that sometime between March 21st, 1843, and March 21st, 1844, according to Jewish mode of computation of time, Christ will come and bring all His saints with Him; and that

184 Ward, "MS, Nov. 15th, 1841," *ST,* Dec. 1, 1841, p. 136. Cf. Arthur, "Babylon," p. 29. To those who argued against the calculation of the parousia on the basis of Mt. 24:36 Miller remarked: "I would then immediately examine the context in which it was found, and I saw at once, that in the same connection we are informed how we may know when it is nigh, even at the doors: consequently that text could not teach that we could know nothing of the time of that event" (*Apology,* pp. 13, 14). Cf. E. G. White, *GC,* pp. 359, 360, 370-72. One of the reasons why Miller stated "about the year 1843" was that he recognized that no man could know the day or the hour of Christ's return (*Apology,* p. 25).

185 Editorial, "Boston Second Advent Conference," *ST,* June 1, 1842, p. 69. Cf. Arthur, "Babylon," pp. 31-33. Arthur stated that this conference had the effect of making Millerites out of Adventists (*ibid.,* p. 33).

186 "Midnight Cry," *ST,* June 15, 1842, p. 84. A similar rationale was used for the revival techniques or "measures" during the Second Awakening revivals.

187 *Ibid.*

188 Editorial, "Messrs. Editors," *ST,* Nov. 9, 1842, p. 61. Cf. Editorial, "The Time of the End," *ST,* Jan. 4, 1843, p. 121.

then he will reward every man as his work shall be."[189] This statement was followed by fifteen different biblical proofs[190] that seemed to point to 1843 as the year of the Second Advent and the end of the world.

c. The year of the resurrection.

> And from the time that the daily sacrifice shall be taken away, and the abomination that maketh desolate set up, there shall be a thousand two hundred and ninety days. Blessed is he that waiteth, and cometh to the thousand three hundred and five and thirty days. Dan. 12:11, 12.

Another frequently used passage which seemed to verify the above mentioned date of 1843 was Dan. 12:11, 12. Characteristic for the interpretation of these texts was the significance of the "taking away of the daily sacrifice."[191] Miller's interpretation of this text was based on the hermeneutical principle of the analogy of Scripture. He made a comparison between Dan. 12:11, 21 and 2 Thes. 2:7, "for the mystery of iniquity doth already work: only he who now letteth [hinders] will let [hinder], until he be taken out of the way." As other commentators had done for centuries, he identified the mystery of iniquity as papal Rome while the hindering power in the development of the papacy was interpreted as paganism.[192] Through analogous reasoning Miller concluded that the daily sacrifice also signified paganism which gave way to papal Rome.[193] The application of this view to Dan. 12:11 had as a result that the term "daily sacrifice" generally was interpreted by Millerites as the "daily sacrifice abomination" or first abomination and was represented as paganism in general or pagan Rome more

---

189   Miller, "Synopsis of Miller's Views," *ST*, Jan. 25, 1843, p. 147. According to Miller, he was forced to change to this position. He declared that he believed that "the periods would terminate in 1843, *if* there were no mistake in my calculation; but that I could not say the end might not come even before that time, and that they should be continually prepared. In 1842, some of my brethren preached with great positiveness the exact year, and censured me for putting in an IF. The public press had also published that I had fixed upon a definite day, the 23rd of April, for the Lord's Advent. Therefore in December of that year, as I could see no error in my reckoning, I published my belief, that sometime between March 21st, 1843, and March 21st, 1844, the Lord would come" (*Apology*, p. 24). However, it seems that in 1839 Miller already had this concept of the Jewish year ([Litch], "RPA," p. 73).

190   In this study only those arguments have been selected which continue to have relevance in the SDA theology of mission. For arguments such as the period of bondage of God's people during the 2520 years of the time of the Gentiles (677 B.C.-A.D. 1843), the 6000 years of the age of the earth, the 2450 years of the Jubilee of Jubilees (607 B.C.-A.D. 1843) and others, see Miller, "Synopsis," pp. 147, 148. Cf. Appendix IV.

191   Hale's evaluation of contemporary views of the "daily sacrifice": "Upon the meaning of this very ambiguous term, there are but two, or at the farthest, three opinions. The older and more prevalent opinion applies to the Jewish worship; a few apply it, in a secondary or figurative sense, to the true Christian worship of which the Jewish was typical; recently it has been applied, and I think it will be seen to be the true application, to Paganism" (*SAM*, p. 63). The interpretation of this term as the daily or continual mediation of Christ was an exception among Millerites (see, "The Daily," *MC*, Oct. 4, 1843, p. 52).

192   For the papacy interpretation, see Froom, *PFF*, I, 895; II, 157, 530, 786; III, 253, 743; IV, 393, 397. For the paganism interpretation, see *ibid.*, I, 457, 895; II, 530; IV, 393, 397.

193   Hale, *SAM*, p. 66. See *supra*, p. 22, n. 107.

specifically.[194] The "abomination that maketh desolate" was seen as the last abomination, or specifically papal Rome. Thus, Dan. 12:11 indicated that the paganism of the Roman empire would be taken away, and papal Rome would be set up.

To determine the period of the 1290 days a starting point had to be found. Miller's rendering of Dan. 12:11, together with the year-day principle, provided a point of contact with the period of the 1260 years. He understood the text to mean that "from the taking away cf the first abomination, which may be properly called '*the daily sacrifice of abomination,*' to the end of the last abomination that maketh desolate, should be 1290 years."[195] The termination of the last abomination, papal Rome, had already been established on the basis of the 1260 days.[196] Thus, the termination dates for the 1260 and 1290 days were identical — 1798. By subtracting 1290 from 1798 Miller came to 508 as the commencement of the 1290 years,[197] when the daily abomination, pagan Rome, was taken away. He concluded that the difference between the 1290 years and 1260 years was a period of thirty years between the time that pagan Rome was destroyed in 508 and papal Rome was set up in 538.[198]

In determining the meaning of Dan. 12:12 Miller identified "blessed is he that waiteth and cometh" with "blessed and holy is he that hath part in the first resurrection" of Rev. 20:6, leading him to conclude that Dan. 12:12

194   Miller, MSVT, No. 3, pp. 2, 3; Miller, *ESH,* 1833, pp. 24, 25 (*ST,* June 15, 1841, p. 41); Miller, *ESH,* 1833, pp. 30, 31 (*ST,* July 1, 1841, p. 49).

195   *Ibid.,* p. 30 (*ST,* July 1, 1841, p. 50).

196   See *supra,* pp. 24, 25.

197   Another method by which he determined the year 508 was based on the presupposition that Rev. 13:18 indicated the length of the reign of pagan Rome. The first beast of Rev. 13 was identified with the abomination of pagan Rome, the second beast with the papal abomination. The application of the number 666 of Rev. 13:18 to the first beast meant to Miller a period of 666 years for the duration of pagan Rome. For the beginning of the abomination of pagan Rome he found the year 158 B.C. when it became connected with the Jews by a league that ended the besieging of Jerusalem by the Greeks under Bachides and forced them out of Judea (1 Macc. 8; 9:70-72 and Josephus' *Antiquities,* B, XII, chap. 10, section 6 were given as evidence); see MSVT, No. 2, pp. 6, 7, No. 3, pp. 1, 2; *ESH,* 1836, p. 61; *ibid.,* 1833, pp. 22, 23, 26 (*ST,* June 1, 1841, p. 34). The end of the pagan abomination he found by adding 666 to 158 B.C. which led to the year A.D. 508. Litch applied 666 to the Roman empire because the Greek letters which spelled "the Latin Kingdom," ἡ λατίνη βασιλεία, amounted to 666 (*SCC,* pp. 183, 184).

198   According to Miller, the Roman empire disintegrated about 476 and the barbarian invasions established ten kingdoms within the Western empire. These kingdoms were ruled by pagan kings who offered human sacrifices to their deities. However, by 508 the last of these kings was baptized and paganism ceased in the empire (*ESH,* 1836, pp. 61, 62). To Litch the paganism of Rome disappeared in 508 and the Roman government then became a professed Christian government (*SCC,* p. 184). Furthermore, the first papal war took place against the church (Litch, "Trumpets," p. 182); and Vitalian, a Gothic chieftain, with an army of Huns and Bulgarians, declared themselves the champions of the Catholic faith and ended the pagan sacrifices at Rome (Storrs, "Exposition of Matthew, XXIV, Chap.," *Bible Examiner,* n.d., p. 1 (*Examiner,* p. 113), repr. in *MC,* Jan. 27, 1843, p. 12). That year also saw the election of Arthur as monarch of Britain, the last of the kingdoms to be Christianized, who favored the Christian cause from the commencement of his public life ([Hale], "Letter of Dr. Pond," *ST,* Dec. 14, 1842, p. 99). Cf. [Hale], "Dr. Pond," *ST,* Dec. 14 and 21, 1842, pp. 98, 99, 108, 109; E. G. White, *SP,* IV, 57.

referred to the Resurrection, which would take place at the end of the 1335 prophetic days (years). Assuming that the 1290 days and 1335 days both began in 508, Miller concluded that the Resurrection would occur in 1843[199] — a confirmation of his previous conclusions that Dan. 8:14 pointed to 1843 as the year of the parousia and final destruction of the world by fire.

The interpretation of the sanctuary of Dan. 8:14 and of the various time calculations pointing to 1843 for Christ's return to earth was the core of the Millerite theology of mission, without which the movement would never have come into existence. The Second Advent seemed to be within sight and the cry "Behold the bridegroom cometh; go ye out to meet him" was heard throughout Christendom.

4. The "Midnight Cry."

> And at midnight there was a cry made, Behold, the bridegroom cometh; go ye out to meet him. Mt. 25:6.

The expression "the Midnight Cry" had been derived from the parable of the ten virgins (Mt. 25:1-13) in Jesus' eschatological discourse and was seen by Millerites as the symbol of their missionary activity. This parable was historicized[200] by applying it specifically to the contemporary setting of the Advent movement. Its eschatological dimension came to be perceived as a present reality. The kingdom of heaven in the parable was interpreted by Miller as the "gospel day or circle of God's government under the gospel dispensation" (Mt. 3:1, 2; Lk. 16:16); the ten virgins as "mankind in general, in a probationary state," including both Jews and Gentiles (Is. 52:1-5); the five wise virgins as "the believers in God, or the children of the kingdom" (Ps. 45:13, 14; Lam. 2:13); the five foolish virgins as the "unbelieving class of mankind, while in this probationary state under the means of grace" (Is. 47:1; Jer. 46:11); the lamps as a "figure of the word of God" (Ps. 119:105; Prov. 6:23); the oil as a "representation or emblem of faith, as oil produces light by burning, so does faith in exercise by the fire of love produce more light and gives comfort in adversity, hope in darkness, love for the coming bridegroom" (Songs 1:2; 1 Jn. 2:27).[201] Furthermore, he identified the vessels with the "persons or mind that believes or disbelieves in the word of God" (1 Thes. 4:4; 2 Tim. 2:21) and the bridegroom with Christ (Is. 62:5; Mt. 9:15).[202] The marriage he saw as the time when Christ shall come the

199   Miller, *ESH*, 1833, p. 30 (*ST*, July 1, 1841, p. 50). Because some accepted as the end of the 1290 years, Feb. 10, 1798, when the French captured Rome, and others Feb. 15, 1798, when the papal government was abolished and the Roman Republic was established, these dates were considered as the end of the 1335 years in 1843 ([Litch], "RPA," p. 73). See *infra*, p. 86.

200   Appendix I, Rules IX, XII; *supra*, p. 19.

201   Miller, *ESH*, 1838, pp. 228-30. Cf. "Mr. Miller," *Maine Wesleyan Journ.*, repr. in *ST*, May 15, 1840, p. 32; Litch, *PE*, I, 162-70. The *ESH*, 1838 ed., has been used because different copies of the 1836 ed. show irregularities in pagination on this section.

202   Miller, *ESH*, 1838, p. 230.

second time to this earth to present the church as His bride to the Father and marry her so that she will be forever with Him in the New Jerusalem (Rev. 19:7-9; 21:2-4).[203]

The Midnight Cry (Mt. 25:6) Miller defined as "the watchmen, or some of them, who by the word of God discover the time as revealed, and immediately give the warning voice, 'Behold the bridegroom cometh, go ye out to meet him.' "[204] This fulfillment he saw being accomplished in the current widespread preaching on the imminence of the Second Advent based on the exposition of the 2300 days: "This has been fulfilled in a most remarkable manner. One or two on every quarter of the globe have proclaimed the news, and agree in the time. [Joseph] Wolff, of Asia; [Edward] Irving, late of England; [Archibald] Mason of Scotland; [William C.] Davis of South Carolina; and quite a number in this region, are, or have been giving the cry."[205]

Miller identified the Midnight Cry of the parable with the loud voice of the angel of Rev. 14:9 who was "giving due notice to the world of the near approach of the judgment day."[206] However, the Midnight Cry was more frequently identified by others with the loud voice of the angel of Rev. 14:6, 7 who was "flying thro' the midst of heaven and proclaiming the hour of his judgment come."[207] Joshua V. Himes, chief promoter and organizer of the Millerite missionary efforts, saw in the Midnight Cry a symbol for their activities in the time of the end.[208] The cry symbolized very aptly the sense of urgency of their mission and provided, according to Himes, the only answer to the objections against the personal return of Christ in 1843.[209]

The timeliness of the Midnight Cry was especially seen in the fact that the cry was made at midnight while all the virgins slept. According to Miller, this sleeping condition was shown in the apathy and ignorance on the subject of Christ's return at the time of His coming. Evaluating the contemporary situation, he commented: "Can we not bear witness that this has been the true state of the church for a number of years past? The writers on the

203 *Ibid.*, p. 231.
204 *Ibid.*
205 *Ibid.*, pp. 231, 232. Cf. Froom, *PFF*, IV, 404. Joseph Wolff (1795-1862) was a Jewish Christian missionary and linguist. He became known throughout the world because of his trips to Asia. He proclaimed the parousia to be in 1847. Edward Irving (1792-1834) was a Scottish Presbyterian minister in London. Especially during 1826-32 he preached on the imminent Second Advent in both England and Scotland. William C. Davis (1760-1831) was a Presbyterian minister and founder of an independent Presbyterian church in South Carolina. He was one of the first in the U.S.A. to begin the 70 weeks and 2300 days synchronously. The commencement of the temporal millennium he expected about 1847. Archibald Mason (1753-1831) was a Scottish Presbyterian minister who was influenced by W. C. Davis. In 1820 he dated the 2300 days from 457 B.C. till A.D. 1843. See Froom, *PFF*, III, 396-404, 461-81, 514-26; IV, 211-23.
206 Miller, "Miller's Lectures — No. 1," *ST*, July 1, 1840, p. 50. Rev. 14:10, 11 he saw as a description of the wrath of God which would take place after the parousia (*ibid.*).
207 Editorial, "Does the Bible Shroud the Coming[?]," *ST*, Nov. 16, 1842, p. 68.
208 Himes, "Our Work," *ST*, Aug. 2, 1841, p. 68.
209 Himes, "The Crisis Has Come!" *ST*, Aug. 3, 1842, p. 140.

word of God have adopted in their creeds, that there would be a temporal millennium before Christ would come."[210]

In the parable the proclamation of the Midnight Cry aroused the virgins to trim their lamps (Mt. 25:7). Miller saw this fulfilled in contemporary events. In the translation and distribution of the Bible he saw that "the world for a number of years have been trimming their lamps, and the wise and the foolish have been engaged in translating the word of God into almost every language known unto us upon the earth . . . and we are informed that part if not all of the word of God is now given to all nations in their own language."[211] All societies for moral reform and Bible societies appeared to Miller also as fulfilling the parable, whether organized through the agency of the church, or through "political men, men of the world, the great men, merchants of the earth and those who trade in ships; all who live under the influence of the gospel, the 'kingdom of heaven,' have been engaged in the work."[212] Tract societies, too, which had been established to remove prejudice against the Bible and to explain biblical truths, were considered a part of the trimming of lamps, "harbingers of light, the forerunners of the Bible."[213] Missionary societies were especially clear fulfillments of the awakening of the virgins:

> See [said Miller] the missionary spirit extending from east to west and from north to south, warming the breast of the philanthropist, giving life and vigour to the cold hearted moralist, and animating and enlivening the social circle of the pious devotee. Every nation, from India to Oregon, from Kamskatka to New Zealand, have been visited by these wise servants (as we hope) of the cross, proclaiming "the acceptable *year* of the Lord, and the *day* of vengeance of our God," carrying the lamp, the word of God in their hands, and oil, faith in God, in their hearts.[214]

The "Sabbath schools and Bible classes" were to Miller also an indication of the trimming of the lamps, especially of those of the youth.[215] Finally, he saw in the current temperance societies one of the last attempts of the virgins to awaken the people to the Midnight Cry. His argument was that in previous decades drinking was a real problem, its dangers were not realized, and people were totally unprepared to accept the Midnight Cry. He remarked:

> Therefore, in order that men might be in a suitable frame of mind to receive

---

210   Miller, *ESH*, 1838, p. 236. Cf. C., "Midnight Cry," p. 84.

211   Miller, *ESH*, 1838, p. 237. Cf. *ibid.*, p. 232. He said: "Mr. Judson tells us that it has been translated into one hundred and fifty languages within thirty years. That is, three times the number of all the translations known to us before" (*ibid.*, p. 237). Adoniram Judson (1788-1850) was a well-known American Baptist missionary to Burma.

212   *Ibid.*, p. 238. Here he said: "Thirty years past, more than three fourths of the families in what we call Christian lands were without the lamp of life, and now nearly all [have been] supplied."

213   *Ibid.*, p. 240.

214   *Ibid.*, pp. 238, 239.

215   *Ibid.*, p. 239.

42

instruction at the close of this dispensation, and be in a situation to listen to the midnight cry, God ordered the virgins, and they arose and trimmed their lamps, and in all human probability thousands who would have met a drunkard's grave if this society had not arose [*sic*], are now watching, with their lamps trimmed and burning, ready to meet the bridegroom at his coming.[216]

The reaction of the public to the Midnight Cry Miller viewed as a division between the foolish and the wise virgins,[217] the culmination of which would take place when the "door was shut" (Mt. 25:10). This closed door signified to Miller the "closing up of the mediatorial kingdom, and finishing the gospel period"[218] when the time of grace and mercy for the world was expected to end some time before Christ's return, a view he supported with Rev. 10:5-7:

> And the angel which I saw stand upon the sea and upon the earth lifted up his hand to heaven, and sware by him that liveth for ever and ever ... that there should be time no longer: But in the days of the voice of the seventh angel, when he shall begin to sound, the mystery of God should be finished, as he hath declared to his servants the prophets.

Identifying the angel who swore that "there should be time no longer" as Christ,[219] Miller commented that it pointed to the moment when

> the gospel or mediatorial time should cease. No more time for mercy, no more Spirit to strive with you, sinner, no more means of grace, no more repentance with life, no more hopes for heaven, for Jesus has sworn by himself, because he could swear by no greater, that your day of probation "should be no longer." For "he that is filthy shall be filthy still" [Rev. 22:11]. The bridegroom has come and shut to the door.[220]

The time that this event would take place Miller saw "in the days of the voice of the seventh angel," after the sixth trumpet — the fall of the Ottoman empire — would have been fulfilled. Then, he said, "will the seventh trump and last woe begin, under which the kingdoms of the earth, and the anti-christian beast will be destroyed, the powers of darkness chained, the world cleansed and the church purified."[221] No wonder that in 1840 the subject of the shut door drew the attention of many Millerites. The issue of the *Signs of the Times* which published Litch's prediction of the exact date of the fall of the Ottoman empire included the opinion that at that event

---

216 *Ibid.*, pp. 240, 241.
217 C., "Midnight Cry," p. 84.
218 Miller, *ESH*, 1838, p. 230. Here Lk. 13:25-28 was seen as a similar event.
219 *Ibid.*, 1836, p. 97. Cf. E. G. White, MS 59, 1900 (*SDABC*, VII, 1957, p. 971).
220 Miller, *ESH*, 1836, p. 97.
221 *Ibid.* Cf. Litch on Rev. 10:6: "This scene is to take place immediately after the end of the three hundred and ninety-one years and fifteen days, or the drying up of the great river Euphrates. There shall be no more mercy; for in the days of the seventh angel, when he shall begin to sound, the mystery of God shall be finished. The great mystery of salvation by faith shall be ended, and the year of his redeemed will come" (*SCC*, pp. 158, 159).

probation would close.[222] Commenting on the same event, Litch said, "there is no certainty that the day of grace will be continued for one hour" after the empire had fallen.[223] However, on the basis of Rev. 11:14, "The second woe is past; and behold, the third woe cometh quickly," he refused to define a specific date for the close of probation in absolute terms. He stated that "when any one can prove to me satisfactory how long a period '*quickly*' is . . . I will tell them how long the day of grace will last."[224] It seems that Miller also thought that the door of mercy would close in the month of August 1840.[225] However, in September 1840 Miller commented that he could not say positively when the door would be shut, for he did not know how much time might be included in the words "when the seventh trump begins to sound" and he added "that the seventh trump has begun to sound I have little or no doubt; and how long *beginning* to sound may last, whether one month, six months, or a year, I cannot tell."[226]

Thus to many Millerites the door of the parable of Mt. 25 became a symbol of the door of mercy, the closing of which was interpreted in the light of Rev. 10:5-7 and Rev. 22:11 as signifying the finishing of the "mystery of God," the preaching of the gospel to the world. Although this solemn and final moment could take place any time after the fall of the Ottoman empire, the subject receded into the background until it became of great importance in 1844.

The parable of Mt. 25 was considered by the Millerites as a present reality predicted by Jesus Himself. Yet, there were some slight differences in the interpretation. While Miller applied the parable to the general widespread expectation of the Second Advent, others historicized the parable more in the light of the specific experience of the Millerites. This was done especially during the years 1843 and 1844 when the realization that they were proclaiming the Midnight Cry to awaken the sleeping virgins, provided one of the major motivations in their theology of mission. At that time, most Millerites came to see their missionary activity as a fulfillment of a part of salvation history predicted in Christ's eschatological discourse and the Apocalypse of John.

222 [Himes], "The Closing Up of the Day of Grace," *ST,* Aug. 1, 1840, p. 69 (Miller, *Views,* p. 252). Because the fall of the empire was also identified with the end of the sixth vial (Rev. 16:12-16), the expression "It is done" under the following seventh vial was applied to the end of the time of grace; Mt. 25:10-12 and Rev. 22:11 were used in the context of the end of the mystery of God or dispensation of grace *(ibid.).* Previous to the Millerites many interpreters had applied the sixth vial to the Turkish empire (Froom, *PFF,* II, 531, 656, 716; III, 106, 139, 345, 352, 354, 371, 403, 404, 457, 528, 536, 539, 627, 628; IV, 394, 401).

223 Litch, "Events to Succeed the Second Woe," *ST,* Aug. 1, 1840, p. 70.

224 *Ibid.* Litch saw the time element of Rev. 8:1 as the period after the close of probation when "the judgment or trial" would proceed to the living before the parousia *(PE,* I, 53).

225 Litch, "Second Woe," p. 70.

226 Miller, "Miller's Letters — No. 8," *ST,* Sept. 1, 1840, p. 81 *(Views,* p. 239). Here he interpreted the mystery of God more precisely in the context of Eph. 3:4-9 as the gospel that was preached to the Gentiles. He concluded that "time shall be no longer" meant the end of gospel time, and "the mystery of God shall be finished" signified, therefore, that the preaching of the gospel to the world would be completed.

5. The Judgment Hour message.

> And I saw another angel fly in the midst of heaven, having the everlasting gospel to preach unto them that dwell on the earth, and to every nation, and kindred, and tongue, and people, Saying with a loud voice, Fear God, and give glory to him; for the hour of his judgment is come: and worship him that made heaven, and earth, and the sea, and the fountains of waters. Rev. 14:6, 7.

In the early beginnings of the Millerite movement, through historicist hermeneutic this apocalyptic passage was more considered a sign of the times than a strong motive for mission. Miller believed that he was living in the time "when the angel having the everlasting Gospel to preach, is flying through the midst of heaven and God by his holy spirit is accomplishing the last great work on earth."[227] Litch interpreted the angel as the "missionary angel, which has so swiftly flown through the earth for the last forty years, scattering light and life in all his path. These extraordinary efforts commenced about the time of the fall of popery, 1798, and have been gaining strength and influence from that to the present time."[228] The proclamation of "the hour of his judgment is come" he identified with the judgment scene in Dan. 7:9, 10 when the dominion of the beast was to be taken away and given to the saints. This judgment he considered a past event, associated with the judgment on the papacy under the French Revolution.[229] Miller recognized also the missionary nature of this first angel of Rev. 14, which signified "the sending out of Missionaries and Bibles into every part of the world, which began about 1798."[230] However, he identified Rev. 14:6 more specifically with the spreading of the gospel so that "those who hear and believe may and will be harvested for eternal life," while Rev. 14:7 "contains the new song, sung by those that are brought in by the gospel."[231] Since the 18th century the association of this angel with the contemporary missionary movement was quite common.[232]

When the time came closer to the judgment year of 1843, the passage of Rev. 14:6, 7 took its place in the Millerite missionary thrust, becoming an effective argument in the polemic against postmillennialism. The phrase "the hour of his judgment is come" was interpreted as referring to the Day of Judgment and emphasis shifted from Rev. 14:6 to Rev. 14:7. For example, Ward said:

> The flying angel carries the gospel to all nations, *for a warning* to them that dwell on the face of the earth. The angel does not say, "Give glory to God for the time of this world's conversion is come!" — although this is the idea the God of this world contrives to infuse into the hearts of the Lord's people. . . .

227 Miller, MSVT, No. 8, p. 2.
228 Litch, *SCC*, p. 186. Cf. John Hooper, " 'The Second Advent,' " *ST*, June 15, 1840, p. 44.
229 Litch, *SCC*, pp. 144, 186.
230 Miller, "Lectures — No. 1," p. 50.
231 *Ibid.*
232 See e.g., Froom, *PFF*, IV, 89, 91, 92, 139, 197, 259, 357.

> But this is the word of the flying angel, uttered with a loud voice, saying, "Fear God, and give glory to him; for the hour of his judgment is come."[233]

The message of the angel he interpreted as "the doctrine of the judgment to come."[234] "The hour of his judgment" soon came to be considered an indispensable aspect of the "everlasting gospel,"[235] and its fulfillment was discerned in the Judgment Hour message then being preached. Thus, it was in the context of the contemporary polemical situation that the message of the first angel of Rev. 14 was historicized and considered as a symbolic representation of the Millerite missionary experience.

The preaching of such a message just before the expected Day of Judgment in 1843 was recognized as timely and as an evidence of the Midnight Cry.[236] This was understandable because it was only when the cry "Behold the bridegroom cometh" had been interpreted as a present reality in the Millerite experience and was placed in the judgment-hour setting, that both the parable of Mt. 25:1-13 and the judgment-hour angel became such a strong eschatological motivation for the Millerite mission.

C. The Millerite Attitudes to Other Churches.

> And there followed another angel saying, Babylon is fallen, is fallen, that great city, because she made all nations drink of the wine of the wrath of her fornication. Rev. 14:8.

This section describes the general Millerite ecclesiological self-understanding in relation to the Roman Catholic Church and the Protestant churches before 1843 and their attempts to function as an interconfessional movement. Their relation to the various ecclesiastical organizations was interrelated to their historicist interpretation of the term "Babylon" and the seven churches of Revelation. From its beginnings Millerism was an interconfessional movement with its aim to arouse the churches regarding Christ's imminent return. It was only when the missionary activity of the individual Millerites in their respective churches resulted in strong opposition, antagonism, and hostility that separatism became inevitable.

1. The Roman Catholic Church.

In common with many other Protestants who employed historicist hermeneutic,[237] the Millerites identified the Roman Catholic Church with

---

233 Ward, "To the Conference of Christians . . . ," *ST*, Jan. 1, 1842, p. 146. Cf. E. G. White, *SG*, I, 132, 134; E. G. White, *SP*, IV, 222; Froom, *PFF*, IV, 139, 197, 201.

234 Ward, "Conference," p. 146. In 1840 Miller considered the third angel of Rev. 14:9 as the judgment proclamation (*supra*, p. 41).

235 C. B., "Hour of the Judgment Come," *ST*, Aug. 24, 1842, p. 162. Cf. [Litch], "RPA," pp. 86, 87.

236 Editorial. "Does the Bible Shroud the Coming[?]," p. 68. See *supra*, p. 41.

237 Cf. Froom, *PFF*, IV, 114, 121, 122, 124, 148, 150, 189, 248, 259, 280, 342, 353.

Babylon, especially during the early years of their movement. There was a strong anti-Roman Catholic sentiment throughout the U.S.A., so that scriptural interpretations unfavorable to this church were readily accepted by many. The fall of Babylon as stated in Rev. 14:8 was seen by Litch as the fall of Rome caused by the French.[238] Miller declared that this text "shows the downfall of the papal power; or mystical Babylon, which was fulfilled in 1798, when she lost her power to rule over the kings of the earth."[239] Its final destruction was expected in the immediate future.[240] Although the Roman Catholic Church frequently was denounced in Millerite publications, the adherents to this faith who accepted the premillennial doctrine of the Second Advent were welcomed in the movement.[241]

2. The Protestant churches.

The Millerite ecclesiology was strongly affected by the historicist interpretation of the seven churches of Rev. 2 and 3. In harmony with a long tradition of Protestant commentators[242] Miller stated that these seven churches "describe the spirit and qualities of the several periods of the Christian church."[243] The church of Ephesus (2:1-7) he identified as the church of the apostolic age, the church of Smyrna (2:8-11) as the church under the persecution of the Roman empire from the first century until the year 312, the church of Pergamos (2:12-17) as the worldly church from the time of Constantine to the rise of the papacy (312-538), the church of Thyatira (2:18-29) as the church in the wilderness persecuted by the papacy (538-10th century), the Sardis church (3:1-6) as the church of the "Waldenses, Valdenses, &c" (10th century — Reformation), and the Philadelphian church (3:7-13) with the church of the Reformation (Reformation — about 1798).[244] Miller considered himself living in the time of the last period of the Christian church, the Laodicean church (3:14-22), which began about 1798 and would last until 1843 "when this dispensation will close, and the books be opened, the hypocrites will be spued out of the church and the sanctuary cleansed."[245] Laodicea Miller evaluated as the Protestant churches of his day

---

238 Litch, SCC, p. 186. C. B. interpreted the fall of Babylon in Rev. 18 as the future fall of Rome ("Judgment," p. 162).

239 Miller, "Lectures — No. 1," p. 50.

240 Litch interpreted the cleansing of the sanctuary as the destruction of Rome ("Babylon's Fall," p. 166). See supra, p. 35, n. 173.

241 Editorial, "Our Course," ST, Nov. 15, 1840, p. 126. Ward called for unity around the message of Rev. 14:6, 7 and said: "Some men are Roman Catholic, some are Protestants: let them be Catholics or Protestants, only looking for the coming of the Lord according to his word" ("Conference," pp. 146, 147).

242 For the tradition that the 7 churches symbolically represented 7 successive historical periods of the Christian era, see Froom, PFF, II, 397, 514, 530, 585, 655, 678, 679, 785; III, 224, 483, 505, 580, 698; IV, 206.

243 Miller, ESH, 1836, p. 101.

244 Ibid., pp. 101-20.

245 Ibid., p. 124.

enjoying peace in and among the kingdoms of the earth, enjoying all the privileges of citizens without persecution, making great and many improvements in her worldly concerns, rich in this world's goods, having at her command many millions of funds, and almost swaying the destinies of the world; great, learned and rich men enlisting under her banners, controlling the fashions, customs and laws of the day, swaying a mighty influence over the education of our youth, and giving a general tone to the literature of the world, increasing her demands for power, establishing bishoprics, presbyteries, national and state conventions, conferences, councils, associations, consociations, societies innumerable: and all these controlled almost exclusively by her clergy.[246]

Others did not stress the power and influence of Protestantism, but pointed to its division as manifested in "the hundreds of the sectarian or broken fragments of her body."[247] From here it was only one step further to associate the multiplicity of divisions and dissensions, which created such a confusion and strife among Christians, with the term "Babylon."[248] The identification of the Protestant churches with Babylon was not a new concept developed by some Millerites but had already been expounded by individuals in England and America in the 18th century.[249] This view, however, was not common among Millerites during the early years of their movement. Up until 1842 the general idea was held of the Roman Catholic Church as Babylon.

Besides the criticism of the quest for power and sectarianism, the Protestant churches were also attacked for heresy and their adherence to creeds above the Bible. The Millerites had a high regard for the primitive church and the Reformers, but they felt the churches of the Reformation had departed from the Scriptures, especially in their interpretation of the millennium.[250] Eschewing postmillennialism, the Millerites considered it their main objective "to revive and restore this ancient faith" of the premillennial coming of Christ and "to renew the ancient landmarks."[251]

3. Interconfessionalism.

Although the Millerites strongly criticized the Roman Catholic Church and Protestant churches, they had no intention at first of starting a separate religious organization. In 1840 at the First General Conference they stated explicitly regarding their mission objectives that

246 *Ibid.*, pp. 124, 125.
247 J., "Our Object," *ST*, March 15, 1841, p. 189.
248 Recommended Letter, *ST*, Feb. 1, 1841, p. 167. Cf. J., "Second Advent Just at Hand. No. II," *ST*, Feb. 15, 1841, p. 176; Editorial, "Second Advent Conference," *ST*, July 15, 1841, p. 61; E. S. Holland, "Extract of a Letter," *ST*, Dec. 1, 1840, p. 136.
249 See e.g., David Hartley, *Observations on Man, His Frame, His Duty, and His Expectations*, II, 1749, pp. 370, 371; Samuel Hopkins, *Treatise of the Millennium . . .*, 1793, p. 11; Froom, *PFF*, IV, 767-70.
250 "General Conference," p. 116.
251 Ward, "Circular," in *Report of the General Conference*, p. 20.

we have no purpose to distract the churches with any new inventions, or to get to ourselves a name by starting another sect among the followers of the Lamb. We neither condemn, nor rudely assail, others of a faith different from our own nor dictate in matters of conscience for our brethren, nor seek to demolish their organizations, nor build new ones of our own; but simply to express our convictions like Christians, with the reasons for entertaining them which have persuaded us to understand the word and promises, the prophecies and the gospel, of our Lord, as the first Christians, the primitive ages of the church, and the profoundly learned and intelligent reformers, have unanimously done, in the faith and hope that the Lord will "come quickly," "in his glory" to fulfill all his promises in the resurrection of the dead.[252]

In view of the implications of the Midnight Cry, it was their aim to warn their "fellow Christians of all sects and denominations, to trim their lamps, and be in readiness for the coming of the bridegroom."[253]

Without separating themselves from their respective churches, Christians from different churches participated in the Millerite movement, which seemed to have affected almost all churches.[254] The leaders of the movement gave those who accepted Miller's views the advice not to sever their connection with the various churches but to "remain as they are," and to "seek rather to purify, and prepare the elect for the coming of the Lord, when Babylon will fall, and God will make all things new."[255] Prejudicial attitudes had to be avoided, and there was no sympathy with "those who sow discord among brethren, who withdraw from the fellowship of the churches, who rail at the office of the ministry, and triumph in the exposure of the errors of a secular apostate church, and who count themselves holier than others, or wiser than their fellows."[256] Thus, one could read in their publications that "the right hand of our Christian fellowship and union" was offered to "all disciples of our common Lord, of every sect and denomination."[257]

Among the Millerites there seemed to be no fundamental difference as to the ground of man's salvation. However, due to the interconfessional nature of the movement there was a difference in emphasis so that some believers referred to the mercy of Christ while others mentioned the fear of God or stressed the justice or righteousness of God. The ground of man's salvation was seen in the work of Christ and human response, a response not limited merely to acceptance of the mercy and love of Christ but including also the necessity of accepting Millerite apocalyptic-eschatology.

252 Ibid., pp. 20, 21. Cf. Miller, Apology, p. 23.
253 [Himes], "Day of Grace," p. 69.
254 Editorial, "Our Course," p. 126; Editorial, "Our Duty," ST, Nov. 30, 1842, p. 86. See supra, p. 14, n. 62.
255 Editorial, "Our Course," p. 127.
256 Ibid., pp. 126, 127. Cf. Miller, Apology, p. 23; Himes, et al., "To the Public," ST, May 10, 1843, pp. 74, 75.
257 Editorial, "Our Course," p. 126. For the irenical tendencies of the Millerite movement, see Konrad F. Mueller, Die Frühgeschichte der Siebenten-tags Adventisten . . . , 1969, pp. 56-58, 88-93.

Initially little attention was given to the question of the atonement, so that on this aspect the Millerites reflected their respective church traditions. This situation changed in 1843-44 when they gave more attention to the termination of Christ's high-priestly ministry. At that time no reference was made to the traditional doctrine that the atonement happened once and for all on the cross, but the concept began to be emphasized that the atonement was the continual process of Christ's ministry in heaven.[258] According to Miller, the death and sacrifice of Christ were "only preparatory steps" to the atonement made by His "life and intercession in heaven."[259]

D. The Millerite Concept of World Mission.

1. The interpretation of Mt. 24:14.

> And this gospel of the kingdom shall be preached in all the world for a witness unto all nations; and then shall the end come. Mt. 24:14.

The concept of world mission among the Millerites was strongly determined by their interpretation of Mt. 24:14. There was no doubt in the mind of Miller that this prediction had been accomplished as one of the signs of the time of the end. As evidence for this opinion, he said that the

> Bible [was] translated into more than 200 different languages; missionaries [were] sent among all the nations known to us on the globe, and reformation [was] succeeding reformation in every town, nook or corner in this land. The gospel has now spread over the four quarters of the globe. It began in Asia. In the apostles' day, that quarter was full of light. From thence it went into Africa; and, for a number of centuries, Africa stretched out her hands unto God. Europe, too, has had a long visitation of gospel blessings; and now America, the last quarter of the globe, is reaping a harvest of souls for the last day. The gospel, like the sun, arose in the east, and will set in the west.[260]

In commenting on Mt. 24:14 John Hooper,[261] an English Adventist, had already stated a decade earlier that a comparison between the map of the world and reports of different missionary and Bible societies would make it difficult "to place our finger on one spot of the globe where the glorious

258   See e.g., Letter, Miller to Himes, ST, May 17, 1843, p. 85; C. B. Hotchkiss, "Termination of Prophetic Periods," MC, Sept. 21, 1843, p. 39; G. W. Peavey, "Behold the Bridegroom Cometh!" MC, Sept. 12, 1844, p. 103; Editorial, "The Types," MC, Oct. 11, 1844, p. 117; Hale, "Letter to N. N. Whiting," AH, Oct. 16, 1844, 2nd ed., pp. 82, 83; infra, pp. 95, 96. See also James Macknight, A New Literal Translation . . . of All the Apostolic Epistles, 1835 on Heb. 9:28.

259   Letter, Miller to Holmes, WMC, Dec. 21, 1844, p. 26.

260   Miller, "A Lecture on the Signs of the Present Times," ST, March 20, 1840, p. 4. Cf. Miller, ESH, 1838, pp. 237-43.

261   John Hooper was a rector in the Church of England and author of a number of works on predictive prophecy and the imminent parousia. He terminated the 2300 days in 1847. See Froom, PFF, III, 564-70.

gospel ... has not been sent!"[262] The rapidity and the universality of the proclamation of the gospel were seen as unparalleled in history, and he remarked that "more has been effected in this way during the last five and thirty years, than since the introduction of the Christian era."[263] It was during the time of the French Revolution that the church was aroused from her lethargy and became actively involved in the missionary enterprise.[264] This global missionary awakening, Hooper said, was a clear fulfillment of Rev. 14:6.[265] Other Christians also associated the universality of the proclamation of this first angel of Rev. 14, which was identified as the contemporary missionary movement,[266] with the accomplishment of Mt. 24:14. Some also saw this missionary activity predicted in the phrase "many shall run to and fro, and knowledge shall be increased" (Dan. 12:4). Miller alluded to it by saying that "we live when 'many (missionaries) shall run to and fro, and knowledge (of the word of God) shall be increased.' "[267]

In 1842 Miller expressed himself even more specifically in his interpretation of Mt. 24:14 by elaborating on the term "witness" so that the fulfillment of the text could be convincingly harmonized with a return of Christ in 1843. He remarked that "the text does not tell us that the gospel shall be preached in all the world at one time, or that all men would believe it; but as a 'witness among all nations.' "[268] Reasoning along similar lines Joel Spaulding, a Millerite lecturer, explained the accomplishment of this text through the idea that in the apostolic age Asia and parts of Europe and Africa received the gospel; in the fourth century Africa was completely reached, and after that, Europe, North and South America, and the Pacific. This led him to conclude that the gospel "has, as it appears, gone round the world and touched on shore on every land."[269]

Litch dealt with this text even more specifically by relating it to the

262 John Hooper, " 'Second Advent,' " p. 44. For a detailed description on the missionary situation, see Litch, *PE,* I, 147-49.
263 Hooper, " 'Second Advent,' " p. 44.
264 *Ibid.* Miller had explained this by the rise of the two witnesses (Rev. 11:11, 12) during the French Revolution: "We have seen their [Old and New Testament] rise in 1798 and stand upon their feet (their own intrinsic merit). We have seen them at the close of the last century ascend up into heaven ... by means of the Bible societies and their agents, transmitted into all nations, translated into every language" (MSVT, No. 8, p. 3). Cf. E. G. White, *GC,* pp. 287, 288; Froom, *PFF,* III, 293, 389, 546; IV, 196, 341.
265 Hooper, " 'Second Advent,' " p. 44.
266 Cf. Froom, *PFF,* III, 370-72, 412, 438, 613; IV, 89, 91, 92, 139; 192, 197, 201, 259, 358, 1091.
267 Miller, MSVT, No. 8, p. 2. Cf. Miller, "Signs," p. 5; *infra,* p. 200, n. 263; L. D. Fleming, *A Synopsis of the Second Coming of Christ, About A.D. 1843,* 3rd ed., rev., 1842, p. 63.
268 Miller, *Matthew,* p. 15. Cf. Spaulding, "Matt. XXIV," p. 185.
269 *Ibid.* Miller stated: "Mosheim, in his Church History, tells us that in the fourth century Africa was enlightened by the gospel, as much as Asia had been in the first century; and we know that every part of Europe and America has in these last times been favored with the gospel light" (*Matthew,* p. 15). Cf. Bliss, *Matthew,* p. 15; Editorial, "The Gospel of the Kingdom," *SAH,* May 7, 1844, p. 64. Several works of Johann L. von Mosheim (1694-1755), the German Lutheran Church historian, had been translated into English during the first half of the 19th century.

Millerite mission of proclaiming the Judgment Hour message. In focusing his attention on the interpretation of the phrase "this gospel of the kingdom," he posed the question whether "this gospel" referred to the ordinary proclamation of the gospel truth or to a general proclamation of Christ's coming. Then he argued that the ordinary gospel proclamation to the world of Lk. 2:11, "To you is born in the city of David, a Savior, which is Christ the Lord"[270] was accomplished in the apostolic age. At Pentecost it reached men from every nation under heaven and thus was carried abroad by these men. This, he felt, was affirmed by Paul who said that "the gospel" was "preached to every creature which is under heaven" (Col. 1:23). However, the gospel of Mt. 24:14 "proclaims 'THE HOUR OF HIS JUDGMENT IS COME' Rev. xiv:7. This last, is *the everlasting glad tidings* of the kingdom or reign of Christ. It is to be proclaimed by the *flight* of the *messenger* or *angel* who bears it to every kindred, nation, tongue, and people. When this is accomplished, 'then shall the end come.' "[271] Then Litch proceeded to show that the *news* of Christ's coming in 1843 had gone to the various parts of the world. Therefore, he concluded that it was not necessary that this message had to be preached to everyone, but the *news* throughout the world that such a truth was preached was a sufficient proclamation to fulfill the prediction of Mt. 24:14. Reasoning from analogy, he said:

> If it was sufficient in the days of the apostles, it is now. That it was then is clear from Acts xix.8-10. Where Paul preached as taught in Ephesus two years and three months, so that all they in Asia, both Jews and Greeks, heard the word of Jesus. They could not all have heard a sermon, but they heard the sound of the gospel. In this sense I have no doubt but the gospel of the kingdom is preached in all the world.[272]

An attempt was made to harmonize the fact that the Midnight Cry and the Judgment Hour message were preached most generally in North America, less frequently in Europe, and the least in the rest of the world, with the fulfillment of Mt. 24:14. It was suggested that God had always sent His warnings to His people before significant events occurred which would affect them. On this basis it was reasoned that the greatest manifestations of the signs of the times were given in places where God had the greatest number of followers. There where He had fewer followers the sounds of warning were feebler. Because the object was to warn the people of God, it was not necessary that the world should be equally warned. Reference was made to the fact that when Christ came to make atonement for sins He came to that part of the world where "religion shone with the greatest lustre, however dark its brightness was; while only the sound of his mighty works was heard in other places."[273] It was reasoned from analogy that the signs of the times would be most general in those parts of the world where

270 Litch, "This Gospel of the Kingdom," *ST*, Nov. 15, 1843, p. 109.
271 *Ibid.*
272 *Ibid.* Support was found in contemporary views (Litch, *PE*, I, 147-49).
273 Editorial, "The World Has Had the Midnight Cry," *ST*, Sept. 20, 1843, p. 36.

there was the greatest proportion of true Christians. In other places with few Christians the evidence of the Lord's coming would be less distinct, while in countries with no Christians there might be no evidence at all.

> Thus, New England, being the most pious portion of the earth, would naturally be the theatre of the darkening of the sun and moon, and the falling of the stars. . . . The testimony of the fulfillment of these events has however gone into all the earth. The proclamation of the coming of Christ has also been the most effectually proclaimed here, while that sound has gone into all lands.[274]

After New England came Europe as the place where the Christian religion was best known. There, however, the gospel light was darkened and "the heresies of Puseyism, Romanism, Neology, Rationalism, Transcendentalism, and Infidelity" had almost removed "the candle-stick of the true gospel" from its place.[275] Signs, similar to those in the U.S.A. but less significant, had occurred in Europe, and the nearness of the Second Advent had been preached by Joseph Wolff in Asia. Such argumentation led to the conclusion that "the world has had the Midnight Cry, as much as we could expect from the analogy from other events, and in proportion to the prevalence of true Christianity in the various parts of the earth."[276]

2. The extent of the Millerite world mission.

Although the Millerites did not think the Advent message had to be preached to every individual, their concept of world missions was that they thought it necessary to send their publications to every reachable Christian community on earth so that the news of the message would reach those unaware of the imminence of Christ's coming. Therefore, the Millerites did everything to increase their publications, giving them a circulation as wide as possible.

Miller's lectures were frequently reprinted with slight additions and minor revisions. When in 1840 Himes joined Miller, the publishing work became of major importance in their mission efforts.[277] On March 20, 1840, Himes issued the first Millerite periodical, *Signs of the Times,* which endured as the leading representative periodical of the movement. Originally a bimonthly, after April 1842 it was published as a weekly.

At the First General Conference of Second Advent believers held at Boston (October 14-15, 1840) it was proposed that the printed report of the conference be sent to

> 1. The Theological Seminaries of the land. 2. The ministers of the gospel who are willing to examine the subject. 3. The members of Christ's body —

---

274   *Ibid.* For similar argumentation as to the preaching of Rev. 14:6-12, see Bates, *SAWH,* 1847, p. 27.
275   Editorial, "Midnight Cry," p. 36.
276   *Ibid.*
277   See [Litch], "RPA," pp. 57-73.

and the world, to as great an extent as our means will allow. 4. We shall send them to foreign lands. (1) To our friends in Great Britain, whom we shall get to assist us in this good work. (2) To the missionaries of the cross in all the world, so far as we can get access to them.[278]

During the Bangor Second Advent Conference (July 12-19, 1841) some of the participants were engaged in missionary work on the various ships lying in the harbor of Bangor, Maine. Himes mentioned that "a number of our brethren being furnished with several thousand papers and tracts, on the subject of Christ's second coming, visited every vessel, and supplied them."[279] By the use of this method in other ports also, Millerite publications received world-wide distribution,[280] so that in the following year Himes could report that most Millerite works had been "sent to all the Missionary stations that we know of on the globe. They have been sent also to many parts of Europe, Asia, Africa, and also to the Islands of the Ocean."[281]

On November 17, 1842 another influential periodical, the *Midnight Cry,* was published in New York. First, it was a daily paper with 10,000 copies an issue; after December 17, 1842 it became a weekly publication.[282] During 1842 Fitch and Hale had produced *A Chronological Chart of the Visions of Daniel & John* (Appendix IV) so that the prophetic positions on the year 1843 could be presented more effectively. This chart, called the 1843 Chart, was widely used and became the standard chart among Millerites.

One of the most detailed accounts on the global distribution of Millerite publications came from Litch:

> Within the last three years, there have been sent from our office in this city [Boston], second advent publications to nearly all the English and American missionary stations on the earth. They have been sent to China; to Burma; to Hindostan; to the East Indies; to Persia, Egypt, Palestine, Syria, Asia Minor, Greece, Constantinople; into Africa, the W. India Islands of the Pacific; the Indian missions both sides of the Rocky Mountains. They have also been scattered broadcast all over these States, and in the Canadas, Nova Scotia, New Brunswick, &c.[283]

It was not surprising that because of such a missionary activity the Millerites concluded that the Midnight Cry and the Judgment Hour message,

---

278 "General Conference," p. 113. Several months later, the conference report, which included the Millerite position, was sent to "the Mission at Calcutta, Madras, Bombay, Ceylon, Burma, Siam, Oroomiah, Persia, Jerusalem, Sandwich Islands, and Oregon" (Editorial, "Reports," *ST,* Feb. 15, 1841, p. 173). Later it was reported that "the 2,000 copies of the Report which have been scattered broadcast *through the world* will continue to exert their influence until time shall be no more" (Editorial, "Second Advent Conference," p. 61).

279 Himes, "Editorial Correspondence, No. II," *ST,* July 27, 1842, p. 132.

280 Editorial, "The Expectation of the Second Advent in 1843," *ST,* Jan. 4, 1843, p 128.

281 Himes, "Crisis," p. 140.

282 Initially it was published to advertise Miller's first meetings in New York. For a survey of Millerite periodicals, see Froom, *PFF,* IV, 621-41.

283 Litch, *PE,* I, 166, 167.

which were seen as the proclamation of "the everlasting gospel" (Rev. 14:6) or "this gospel of the kingdom" (Mt. 24:14), had been spread throughout all the world when the year 1843 had arrived. In that year one could read the firm belief that the "advent publications have been sent by the hundred thousand broadcast all over the world, to the islands of the sea, and to every missionary station on the globe. They have been scattered over land and ocean, and the sailors who came into port testify that the coming of Christ is a subject of conversation all over the world."[284] At the same time the leading periodicals the *Signs of the Times* and the *Midnight Cry* published testimonies and letters received from individuals of the various parts of the world who expected the Second Advent in 1843.[285] All this confirmed the Millerite opinion that Mt. 24:14 had been fulfilled.

E. Summary.

The background for the origins of the SDA was the political, social, and religious climate of the U.S.A. during the first half of the 19th century, a context conducive to the development of new religious movements. In this climate in which postmillennialism was prevalent, a very active interconfessional movement emerged around William Miller, the major exponent of premillennialism at that time. To the followers of Miller, the Millerites, the only hope for this world was the personal return of Christ inaugurating the millennium. The missionary consciousness of the Millerites must be placed in the context of their conviction that they were living in the time of the end of the world. On the basis of historicist hermeneutical principles the time of the end was associated with the captivity of the pope in 1798. Several cosmic phenomena and certain events in the decline of the Ottoman empire, indicating its dependence on the Christian powers of Europe, were

284 Editorial, "Error Must Be So Proved," *ST*, July 19, 1843, p. 156. Cf. [Litch], "RPA," pp. 86, 87.

285 For examples of Millerite work or contacts in England, see "Robert Winter — Cause in London," *ST*, Feb. 1, 1843, p. 158; Editorial, "The Cause in England," *MC*, May 18, 1843, p. 65; Elizabeth Lloyd, "A Call from London," *ST*, Aug. 16, 1843, p. 189; Edward Routon, "Letter from London," *ST*, Oct. 18, 1843, pp. 66, 67; Editorial, "The Cry from Europe," *ST*, Oct. 25, 1843, p. 77; Winter, "The Cause in England," *ST*, Nov. 15, 1843, pp. 109, 110; Winter, "Extract of a Letter from England," *ST*, Dec. 27, 1843, p. 157; Joseph Curry, "Letter from England," *ST*, Dec. 27, 1843, p. 157; Editorial, "The English Mission," *ST*, Jan. 24, 1844, p. 192; in Canada, Columbus Greene, "The Cause in Canada," *ST*, April 5, 1843, p. 40; Daniel Campbell and Dayton F. Reed, "Letter from Upper Canada," *ST*, April 19, 1843, p. 51; William Stewart, "Letter from Canada," *MC*, Nov. 16, 1843; in Norway, Editorial, *MC*, Sept. 21, 1843, p. 37; in the Sandwich Islands, Editorial, "The Midnight Cry at the Sandwich Islands," *ST*, Oct. 4, 1843, pp. 54, 55; in South America, Litch, "Gospel of the Kingdom," p. 109; in Holland, Editorial, "The Cry in Holland," *MC*, June 6, 1844, p. 373 (here reference was made to H. Henzepeter who wrote two pamphlets on the end of the world which were published in 1831 and 1841); H. Hentypeter [Henzepeter], "A Voice from Holland," *MC*, July 11, 1844, p. 415 (here he indicated his position as "Keeper of the Royal Museum at the Hague." The 1816-74 Correspondence Index of the Mauritshuis, the Hague, pp. 3, 7, stated that from 1824 until his death in 1845 he was door-keeper of the Mauritshuis and caretaker of its picture museum).

considered further confirmation for their identification of the time of the end. The central thrust of the Millerite motives for mission was based on Dan. 8:14. Owing to their understanding of the sanctuary, their premillennial views, and the application of historicist hermeneutic it was concluded that this text predicted the end of the world and the return of Christ in 1843, followed immediately by the establishment of the millennium. This date was confirmed by various other time calculations.

Other concepts which provided additional thrust for the Millerite missionary enterprise were the Midnight Cry and the Judgment Hour message. The Midnight Cry of the parable of the ten virgins was interpreted as a present reality and a symbol of the contemporary widespread proclamation of the Second Advent and was closely associated with the Judgment Hour message of Rev. 14:6, 7. Both of these thrusts contributed to the Millerite self-understanding as an important movement in the history of salvation.

Being generally an interconfessional movement among Protestants, Millerism initially adhered to the Protestant view of the Roman Catholic Church as Babylon and had a high regard for the primitive church and the Reformers. However, the spiritual condition of the Protestant churches of their day was strongly criticized for sectarianism, heresies, and thirst for power.

As a result of the predominant apocalyptic-eschatological motives for mission the Millerites felt an urgent responsibility to proclaim on a world-wide scope the news of the imminent Second Advent and judgment. They did not think it necessary that this message be given to every individual but only as a witness to all nations. When the year 1843 approached they were generally convinced that their world-wide mission was currently being accomplished, so that the end of the present world and Christ's return could be expected at any time.

The idealistic aim of reforming the churches on the subject of the Second Advent was soon put to the test. At first Miller's prophetic exposition created widespread interest, but it was not long before their emphasis on the time of the end, Christ's personal return "about 1843," the Midnight Cry, and the Judgment Hour message, together with their polemic against postmillennialists and their criticism of the Roman Catholic and Protestant churches, resulted in opposition. Although many of Miller's interpretations were criticized, the discussion here will be confined to the opposition directed against the central theme of his theology of mission: The imminent premillennial Second Advent and conflagration of the earth based on Dan. 8:14 and the time calculations associated with it.

One of the most crucial issues in the theological controversy was the significance of the little horn of Dan. 8, of which there were three major interpretations at that time.[1] As pointed out above, the Millerites and some non-Millerite commentators, employing historicist hermeneutic, interpreted the little horn as the pagan and papal phases of Rome. Among the opponents of the Millerites who held a different view regarding the little horn were both historicists and those reflecting historical-critical trends. The first group of opponents (historicists) were evangelical Christians,[2] who, in general, recognized that the prediction in Dan. 8:14 pointed to a significant event in the history of mankind. But mainly due to their millenarian views,[3] which were influenced by British millenarian thinking, they differed with the Millerites as to the nature of the predicted event. The second group of opponents, who did not so interpret Dan. 8, may be described as those who tended toward a historical-critical approach in the U.S.A. in so far as they seem to have taken into account some of the findings of European rationalistic theology.[4] But although they interpreted Dan. 8 in the context of Jewish history, they still considered it predictive prophecy. In general the first group of opponents interpreted the little horn as Muhammadanism, or Islam, while the second group identified it with Antiochus IV, Epiphanes.

---

1   Cf. Dowling, *Prophecies,* pp. 59-61.
2   See *supra,* p. 19.
3   See *supra,* pp. 30, 31.
4   Cf. N. N. Whiting, *Origin, Nature, and Influence of Neology,* 1844.

The major part of the discussion will be devoted to the Antiochus Epiphanes view, for the reason that though it did not dominate the American theological scene, it was considered by the Millerites as a most effective instrument to prejudice people against their views and hence was widely discussed in their literature.[5]

A. The Millerites versus non-Millerite historicists.

Among the historicists who advocated Muhammadanism, or Islam, as the little horn of Dan. 8, it was probably David Campbell,[6] an evangelical clergyman, who received the most attention from the Millerites. Although he was considered a millenarian,[7] he was allowed to express some of his views in the *Signs of the Times*. In the little horn of Dan. 8 he saw an evil religious power in contrast to a normal horn which represented a political power. This religious power, according to him, could signify nothing else than "the Mahomedan [*sic*] delusion" because it arose from Syria, which was one of Alexander's four kingdoms out of which the little horn emerged (8:9).[8] He indicated that Syria, as the great center of its operations, "embraced 'the pleasant land,' the Jewish 'sanctuary' which was to be 'cast down,' and afterwards 'cleansed.' Syria contained also a part of the Christian 'host,' part of which [it] was to 'cast down,' and whose 'daily sacrifice' was to be 'taken away.' "[9] Syria, therefore, was "one of the horns of the goat, and the identical one from which the 'little horn' of Mohamedanism [*sic*] arose."[10] The geographical progress of the little horn (8:9) Campbell identified with the progress of Islam, for it had, he said, "ever prevailed 'towards the south,' in Egypt and many parts of Africa, 'towards the east,' in India and Persia, 'and towards the pleasant land,' Palestine of course, also Syria and Turkey, further on."[11] The taking away of the daily sacrifice he interpreted as the conversion of the Christian churches into mosques by Muham-

---

5 Regarding the effectiveness of the major expositors of the Antiochus interpretation the following comment was made:
" '*Dowling* has slain his *thousands*,
And *Stuart* his *tens of thousands*,
But *Great 'Doctor Chase' excels all the hosts of the Lord!*'
And its propriety could not be questioned for no slaughter, by human or superhuman agency in the ranks of Israel or their enemies, ever exceeded the slaughter which may be fairly described to these modern heroes" (Hale, "The Review," *ASR,* May 1844, p. 144). Cf. Litch, *Refutation of "Dowling's Reply to Miller . . . ,"* 1842, pp. iii, iv.
6 The procedure has been followed to use the name "Campbell" instead of the incorrect spelling of "Cambell" in the *ST.*
7 Miller, "Lectures — No. 1," p. 51. Campbell's views were associated with those of his contemporaries, Ethan Smith and Phelps (*ibid.;* Miller, "Mr. Miller's Reply to Campbell, Smith and Others . . . ," *ST,* March 20, 1840, p. 1).
8 [David Campbell], "Mr. Campbell's Reply to Mr. Miller . . ," *ST,* April 13, 1840, p. 9.
9 *Ibid.*
10 *Ibid.*
11 *Ibid.,* p. 10.

madanism,[12] resulting in mass apostasy among "nominal christians" and a persecution of "real christians and ministers" which "fulfilled the prediction, that 'he cast down some of the host, and of the stars to the ground, and stamped on them [8:10].' "[13] The relation between Islam and the magnification of the little horn against Christ as "the prince of the host" (8:11) he saw fulfilled in the fact that Muhammad and his followers considered "Christ to be a prophet, but deem Mohamed his superior."[14] On the basis of the year-day principle he terminated the 2300 days in 1843 when the power of the Ottoman empire and Islam would end, the Jews would return to Palestine, and a great progression of society would begin.[15]

Miller rejected this view of the little horn. Some of his objections were based on the observation that the little horn was to come out of one of the four kingdoms into which Alexander's empire was divided (8:9). These kingdoms, he insisted, had become Roman provinces between 148 and 30 B.C. so that the little horn must have come into existence "before Christ, instead of 622 years after Christ, when Mahomet [sic] arose."[16] It was also pointed out that the little horn, symbolized as "a king of fierce countenance" (8:23), should emerge in "the latter time" of the four kingdoms of Alexander's empire "when the Jews are come to the height of their transgression."[17] This provided another argument that the little horn was Rome, "for Mahomet did not exist until 550 years after the Jews were destroyed for their transgressions."[18] Another objection, according to Miller, was that Campbell's interpretation violated the unity between Dan. 7 and 8.[19] Litch remarked that the practice by such historicists to interpret the little horn in

12 Ibid., pp. 9, 10. He added: "This expression, of taking away the 'daily sacrifice,' is repeatedly used in reference to the Latin church as well as the Greek, and with equal propriety. The suppression of pure Christian worship in these great sections of the nominal Christian Church, and the establishment of popish image worship in the western and Mohamedan worship in the eastern branch, was indeed the taking away of the 'daily sacrifice,' and the 'setting up the abomination of desolation' " (ibid., p. 10).

13 Ibid. On Dan. 8:12 he commented: "Had not the 'host' or the Christian churches in the east, become sadly degenerate and corrupt, an opposing host, like the Arabian imposture, could never have gained a permanent foothold in that country. The success of error was 'by reason of transgression' in the Christian church" (ibid., p. 9).

14 Ibid.

15 Campbell, "Chronology of Revelation," ST, May 1, 1840, p. 20; Campbell, "Mr. Campbell on the Return of the Jews," ST, June 15, 1840, pp. 41, 42; Miller, "Campbell, Smith and Others," p. 1 (Views, p. 176). Cf. Aaron Kinne, An Explanation of the Principal Types . . . , 1814, pp. 145-47, 366, 367.

16 Miller, "Campbell, Smith and Others," p. 1 (Views, p. 173). Litch remarked that the papacy and not Muhammadanism emerged out of one of the four kingdoms ("Ethan Smith," ST, May 1, 1840, pp. 17, 18). Regarding the papacy he said that "the clergy did not exercise any civil power until it was conferred on them by the Greek emperors; and the bishop of Rome was finally constituted head of all the churches by a Greek emperor [Justinian]; and Rome itself, was conquered, and the pope put in possession of it, by the same emperor [A.D. 538]" (ibid., p. 18). Cf. Litch, Address to the Public . . . , 1842, pp. 78-80.

17 Miller, "Campbell, Smith and Others," p. 1 (Views, p. 174).

18 Ibid.

19 Miller, "Mr. Miller's Reply to Mr. Campbell," ST, June 1, 1840, pp. 34, 35 (Views, pp. 232, 233).

59

Dan. 7 as the papacy and the little horn in Dan. 8 as Islam violated the hermeneutical principle of time-sequence parallelism.[20]

The view that the Jews would return at the end of the 2300 days was strongly opposed by Millerites. Miller reminded his opponents that Christ had broken down the wall of partition between Jews and Gentiles, and emphasized that the only future restoration for both groups was a spiritual one achieved through conversion to Jesus Christ.[21] As for Old Testament references to a return of the Jews to Palestine, he stated that these passages were written "before the Jews were restored from Babylon, and had their literal fulfillment in that event."[22] In those instances where such had not been completely realized to the Jews prior to the cross, they would be fulfilled to spiritual Israel under the new covenant.[23] Furthermore, Miller found the concept of a millennium on earth before Christ's return incongruous with Dan. 7:9-13, 21, 22; Lk. 17:26-30; Mk. 13:23-29; 1 Thes. 4:14-18; 5:1-4; 2 Thes. 2:7-10 and Rev. 14:14-20.[24]

In 1842 Richard C. Shimeall,[25] an Episcopalian minister and a millenarian, who advocated a premillennial Second Advent followed by a "period of millenial [sic] blessedness of the saved nations in the flesh," published a work in which the little horn was also designated as "the Mohamedan [sic] imposture."[26] The termination of the 2300 days he dated in 1847 when "the

20 Litch, "Ethan Smith," p. 17. This parallelism he based on the following rule: "Having once clearly fixed the meaning of a prophetic symbol and applied it to a particular case, never change its meaning, to accommodate another passage. If that passage cannot be explained without [altering its meaning], let it go unexplained (see Faber on Prophecies)" (ibid.).

21 Miller, "Letter From Mr. Miller, No. 3," ST, April 15, 1840, pp. 14, 15 (Views, pp. 225-29). Some textual evidence used was Acts 10:34, 35; Rom. 3:1-9; 10:12; Gal. 6:15; Eph. 1:10; 2:12, 16. Since apostolic times the special time for the Jews had passed and the period for the Gentiles had arrived (Rom. 1:16, 17; 2:7-11, 28, 29) (ibid., p. 14 [Views, pp. 226, 227]). Quoting Gal. 3:28, 29, Litch said: "The Jews, therefore, as such, are not God's Israel to whom the promise was made; but true Christians are. The Jews will never be restored to literal Canaan, but all the elect of Christ, at his coming, will be gathered from the four winds into the heavenly Canaan, and the new Jerusalem" ("The Restoration of the Jews," ST, Aug. 15, 1840, p. 77). Cf. Ward, "The Restoration of Israel," ST, Sept. 1, 1840, p. 86.

22 Miller, "Letter, No. 3," p. 15 (Views, p. 229).

23 Ibid. His hermeneutic he described as follows: "If you will examine your Bibles you will find every prophecy which could not be fulfilled literally, have a direct allusion to the new covenant, and cannot be fulfilled under the old. There Israel, Judah, and my people, are to be understood [as] spiritual Israel &c. as in Isa. xi.10, 12.... The 11th verse speaks of the gathering of the remnant of his people. The 10th and 12th verses show that it is under the new covenant. Also Jer. xxxii.37, 40.... Verses 36th and 37th speak of their gathering out of Babylon, 38th and 40th show plain that it is under the new covenant" (ibid. [Views, pp. 229, 230]). Ward stated that "all the literal promises of a restoration were made during and previous to the Babylonish captivity of the natural seed, and were fulfilled in their return from that captivity; but the spiritual sense of these promises remains to be fulfilled in the restoration of the true Israel from the captivity of 'this evil world,' Babylon the Great, to the liberty of the sons of God in the resurrection of the dead" ("Restoration," p. 86).

24 Miller, "Campbell," p. 35 (Views, pp. 232-35). Cf. "General Conference," p. 116.

25 Richard C. Shimeall (1803-74) was a graduate of the Episcopal General Theological Seminary in New York City. Then he became a minister. He had a thorough knowledge of Greek and Oriental languages and he adopted views of British millenarians. See Froom, PFF, IV, 370-74.

26 Richard C. Shimeall, Age of the World ..., 1842, pp. 252, 357. Is. 2:1-5; 65:1-11 and Mic. 4 described the situation after the parousia (ibid., p. 357).

Lord Jehovah will appear for the restoration and re-establishment in Palestine of the seed of Abraham."[27] The end of this period would also signify "the overthrow of the last Anti-Christ" which included "ALL the persecuting Anti-Christian powers — the *Pagan,* the *Papal,* the Mahometan [*sic*], and the Infidel."[28]

The following year William C. Brownlee, D.D.,[29] a minister of the Dutch Reformed Church and a millenarian, also interpreted the termination of Dan. 8:14 in the context of the Jews. In his polemic against Millerism he stated that the end of the 2300 days would bring " 'the cleansing of the sanctuary,' long trodden under foot, and 'the putting an end to the desolations of the afflicted,' and 'peeled remnants' of the house of Judah, and Israel. The prophet is predicting deliverances to the Hebrews, NOT the end of the world!"[30] Some of the imminent events he expected were: (1) The destruction of the antichrists of Rome and Constantinople; (2) the return of the Jews to Palestine and their conversion; (3) the proclamation of the gospel to the whole world and the conversion of the Gentiles; (4) the spiritual reign of Christ during the millennium.[31]

During this year (1843), another millenarian, Samuel F. Jarvis, D.D., LL.D.,[32] Professor of Biblical Literature at the Episcopalian General Theological Seminary in New York City, also associated the completion of Dan. 8:14 with the return and conversion of the Jewish nation.[33] He rejected Miller's assumed connection between Dan. 8 and 9, concluding that it was impossible to determine the beginning of the 2300 days except by

---

27   *Ibid.,* pp. 241, 278, 310, 333, 334, 353, 354.

28   *Ibid.,* p. 254.

29   William C. Brownlee (1784-1860) was born in Scotland, studied theology at the University of Glasgow, and began to work as a minister. Then he emigrated to the U.S.A. He became well known for his opposition to Roman Catholicism, and also opposed Unitarianism and Universalism. He edited several journals and wrote various books. For his criticism on Millerism, see Froom, *PFF,* IV, 744, 745; W. C. Brownlee, *The Roman Catholic Religion Viewed in the Light of Prophecy and History* . . . , 1843, Appendix III.

30   *Ibid.,* pp. 100, 101. He saw the years 1764, 1783, 1842 or 1843, 1856, 1866, and 1868 as possibilities for the termination of the 2300 days (*ibid.*). Cf. Nathaniel Folsom and John Truair, *A Dissertation on the Second Coming* . . . , 1840, pp. 65-72. Here Dan. 8:14; 12:12 were terminated in 1864, Dan. 12:11 in 1819, while the little horn was associated with Justinian (*ibid.*).

31   Brownlee, *Catholic Religion,* p. 102. He anticipated that "all mankind shall be regenerated, — in the universal spiritual resurrection" which pointed to "the golden age of the Christian Church" (*ibid.,* pp. 71, 72).

32   Samuel F. Jarvis (1786-1851) was a graduate of Yale College. He became a minister for the Episcopalian Church. For several years he did research in the major libraries of Europe for his major work, *A Complete History of the Christian Church.* He died before it was completed. However, portions of it were published.

33   S. F. Jarvis, *Two Discourses on Prophecy with an Appendix in Which Mr. Miller's Scheme, Concerning Our Lord's Advent Is Considered and Refuted,* 1843, pp. 45, 46. Regarding the end of Dan. 8:14 he said: "The Jewish nation ceasing to rebel, will cease to be trampled under foot. The sanctuary which their rebellion caused to be desolate and trampled under foot, shall be expiated or purified. The Jews converted to the Christian faith will be restored as a body-politic; and a new temple expiated and purified will again represent the only great oblation; not as before with the blood of slain beasts, but with the unbloody symbols which Christ himself appointed" (*ibid.*).

counting backward — whenever it should occur — from "the conversion of the Jews and their restoration to their own land."[34]

In 1844 George Bush,[35] Professor of Hebrew and Oriental Literature at New York City University — an exceptional exegete who placed the millennium in the past (5th-15th century, A.D.)[36] — wrote Miller that his usage of the year-day principle was "sustained by the soundest exegesis, as well as fortified by the high names of [Joseph] Mede, Sir I. Newton, Bishop [Thomas] Newton, [William] Kirby, [Thomas] Scott, [Alexander] Keith, and a host of others who have long since come to *substantially* your conclusion on this head."[37] Miller's mistake, according to Bush, was not in his "*chronology*" but in "*the nature of the events*" which are to occur when those periods have expired."[38] In Bush's opinion mankind had "arrived at a momentous era of the world, and that the expiration of these periods is to introduce, by *gradual steps,* a new order of things, intellectual, political and moral."[39] Regarding the time sequence between the fourth kingdom and the establishment of the everlasting kingdom (Dan. 7:27), Bush remarked that "the plain import of the passage is, that the one power should be *gradually* abolished, and the other *gradually* introduced."[40] Thus, he said, "the great event before the world is not its *physical conflagration,* but its moral regeneration."[41]

The idea of gradual moral regeneration was strongly criticized by William Miller. The concept, he said, was incongruous with the testimony of Dan. 7 in which verse 11 pictures a "sudden destruction by *fire,"* verse 13 suggests Christ's return, verse 25 provides "an allusion to the sudden destruction of the fourth kingdom," and verse 26 shows "a judgment setting, and a taking away [of] the fourth kingdom first, not wearing away."[42] A Millerite editorial stated that the concept of a gradual introduction of the kingdom of God

34 *Ibid.,* p. 49. *Cf. ibid.,* pp. 47, 48.

35 George Bush (1796-1859) studied theology at Princeton and became a minister of the Presbyterian church for several years. After his appointment at the New York University he entered upon a literary career which won for him the reputation of profound scholarly ability. He was also instructor in Sacred Literature at Union Theological Seminary. A number of O.T. commentaries, a Hebrew grammar, and various other works were published by him. Later he became a Swedenborgian.

36 George Bush, *The Millennium of the Apocalypse,* 1842, 2nd ed., pp. 101, 102, 189, 190. He said that the end of the millennium would "nearly coincide with the establishment of the Turkish power in Western Asia in consequence of the capture of Constantinople, A.D. 1453" (*ibid.,* pp. 101, 102).

37 Bush, "Prof. Bush to Wm. Miller," in *Reasons for Rejecting Mr. Miller's Views on the Advent . . . ,* 1844, p. 6.

38 *Ibid.,* pp. 7, 11.

39 *Ibid.,* p. 11.

40 *Ibid.,* p. 13.

41 *Ibid.,* p. 11. He added: "Although there is doubtless a sense in which Christ may be said to come, in connection with the passing away of the Fourth Empire, and of the Ottoman power, and his kingdom to be illustriously established, yet that will be found to be a *spiritual coming* in the power of his gospel, in the ample outpouring of his spirit, and the glorious administration of his Providence. This is the common and prevailing belief of Christendom, and I have no doubt the true one" (*ibid.,* p. 12).

42 Miller, "Mr. Miller's Reply to Prof. Bush," in *Miller's Views,* pp. 25, 26.

on earth was in contradiction to Peter's testimony regarding the judgment of the present earth (2 Pet. 3:5-10) at the Second Advent (2 Tim. 4:1) when the Resurrection would take place (1 Thes. 4:16). Bush's concept was also seen to be in conflict with Daniel's testimony on the nature of the judgment (Dan. 2:34, 35, 44, 45; 7:9, 10, 13, 14).[43]

B. The Millerites versus those reflecting historical-critical trends.

The hermeneutical principles of those tending toward a historical-critical approach to the apocalyptic-eschatology of Scripture while affirming the predictive nature of prophecy were seen by the Millerites as a very effective means in counteracting their historicist hermeneutic. This was the reason why this approach was extensively discussed and attacked. Among those who employed such a critical approach against Miller's interpretations and who stirred the strongest Millerite reaction were John Dowling, A.M.,[44] a Baptist minister, Moses Stuart,[45] a Congregationalist professor at Andover Theological Seminary, Nathaniel Colver,[46] a Baptist minister, and Irah Chase, D.D.,[47] Professor of Ecclesiastical History at Newton Theological Institute. Most of those employing this kind of hermeneutic also advocated a postmillennial future for Christianity.[48] Litch designated these individuals

43 Editorial, "Both Sides, Prof. Bush to Wm. Miller," *AH,* March 13, 1844, p. 42.

44 John Dowling (1807-78) was an English immigrant of Church of England parentage. At the age of 17 he joined the Baptist Church. Four years later he taught Greek, Hebrew, Latin and French. Later he accepted a call to the ministry and became a well-known Baptist clergyman in New York City.

45 Moses Stuart (1780-1852) was a minister and a scholar in Biblical studies. He studied theology under President Timothy Dwight at Yale College. He served for some time as a minister. From 1810 till 1848 he was professor of Sacred Literature at Andover. His life was one of incessant labor and devoted chiefly to Biblical literature and principles of exegesis.

46 Nathaniel Colver (1794-1870) was a Baptist clergyman. He had a natural oratorical ability and was a vigorous champion of reform. He was recognized as a very able advocate of abolition and functioned as an agent of the American Anti-Slavery Society. He was one of the founders of the Divinity School of the University of Chicago.

47 Irah Chase (1793-1864) studied at Andover Theological Seminary and entered into the Baptist ministry. For a short time he studied at the Universities of Halle and Göttingen. From 1825 till 1845 he was professor at Newton Theological Institute. His main interest was in the scientific study of the Bible. He wrote many articles of a historical and theological character and published several books.

48 For Dowling's view, see Dowling, *Prophecies,* pp. 166-81. He said: "The doctrine I hold in relation to the millenium [*sic*], and for which I think I am indebted to the Bible is — that the reign of Christ on earth will not be a personal but a spiritual reign; that it will be preceded by the overthrow of Popery, Mahomedanism [*sic*], Paganism, and all false systems; that it will consist in the universal prevalence of righteousness and true holiness, throughout the whole world; that during its continuance, war, rapine, robbery, and oppression, shall be unknown; there shall be nothing to hurt or destroy, and universal love shall govern the actions of all mankind; that this glorious age shall pass away and be succeeded by a brief but dreadful period of wickedness, after which the Lord Jesus shall be revealed from Heaven with his mighty angels, in flaming fire, taking vengeance on them that know not God, and that obey not the gospel of our Lord Jesus Christ" (*ibid.,* pp. 167, 168; cf. *ibid.,* p. 172). The Millerites questioned this view as follows: (1) How could there be a period of a 1000 years of happiness if the conditions of Dan. 7:21, 22 continue till the last judgment? (2) On the basis of Rev. 20 "how

as "Millenists." According to him the major distinction between Millerite Adventists and Millenists was that *"Adventists* believe in a pre-millennial and personal advent of Christ from heaven, to glorify his saints and to take vengeance on his foes, while the *Millenists* believe in the universal spiritual reign of Christ a thousand years, before his second personal advent."[49]

When in 1840 Dowling published his critique on the idea of Christ's coming in 1843, Miller considered it one of the most subtle attacks ever launched against his views.[50] Generally, Dowling employed the historicist hermeneutic to apocalyptic-eschatology,[51] but he made an exception of Dan. 8. His rationale for making this exception was based on his conviction that the year-day principle could not be applied to the expression "two thousand and three hundred days" because the literal rendering was not "days" but *"evening-mornings."*[52] This, he said, indicated that Dan. 8:14 referred to a

---

can we have a Millenium [*sic*] *before* the first Resurrection, at which time, Paul informs us, Christ will come. 1 Thess. iv.16"; (3) "If all the people are righteous during the thousand years' glorious reign, before the coming of Christ, *Where will they get this army of the wicked,* that are to succeed, and triumph for a season?" (4) How could this "brief and dreadful period of wickedness" be the fruits of the millennium (Editorial, "Dowling's Reply to Miller," *ST,* July 1, 1840, p. 53)? For Stuart's view, see Stuart, *Prophecy,* pp. 126-133, 140, 141. Stuart's millennium was a long indefinite time period which could be designated as "the thousand years of triumph to the church" (*ibid.,* pp. 126, 132). He said that "during the millennial period, when many of the present causes of abridging and destroying human life shall cease, and the means of subsistence be greatly increased, that the world will support some twenty or more times as many people as it now does . . . and that the predominant part of these, during all that period, will be Christians" (*ibid.,* p. 127). Miller's criticism was that "a period of great prosperity and glory to the church" was in contradiction to Jesus' words in Mt. 13:40-42; 24:38, 39 (*Stuart's Hints,* pp. 58, 59). Bliss' objections were based on Mt. 7:13, 14; 24:14 and Dan. 7:21, 22 ("Review of Prof. Stuart's Hints on Prophecy," No. VII, *ST,* Nov. 2, 1842, pp. 50, 51). For other opponents of Miller in this category, see Otis A. Skinner, *The Theory of William Miller . . . ,* 1840, p. 145; Enoch Pond, *A Review of the Second Advent Publications,* 3rd ed., 1843, pp. 35-37, 48, 59, 60; Bliss, *Morris' "Chiliasm,"* pp. 7-63, 120-44. It was the opinion of the Universalist ministers Otis A. Skinner and Thomas Whittemore that the parousia, which was seen to be spiritual and not personal, had already taken place at the fall of Jerusalem in A.D. 70 (Skinner, *Miller,* pp. 5-59; Thomas Whittemore, "A Sermon on the Scriptural Sense of the Phrase, 'End of the World,' " in Skinner, *Miller,* pp. 153-79). Another Universalist, John M. Austin, dated the end of the 2300 years at the siege of Jerusalem ("Brief Review of William Miller's Destruction of the World," Skinner, *Miller,* pp. 206-10).

49   Litch, "RPA," p. 47. See *supra,* pp. 30, 31. Miller said that "the millennium is a state of personal and glorious and immortal reign on the new earth, or this earth cleansed by fire, as it was once by water, and it will be a new dispensation; new heavens and new earth" (*ESII,* 1836, p. 27). It was also described as "the personal reign of Jesus with his people . . . . the glorious reign after the resurrection of the righteous, and before the resurrection of the wicked" (*ibid.,* p. 22). See also *ibid.,* pp. 26-35; *supra,* p. 31, n. 156. Cf. Wellcome, *Second Advent Message,* pp. 170, 171. The major difference between this view of the millennium and that of the SDA was that during the millennium the saints were in heaven and not on the earth (Appendix II and III). The views of E. G. Harmon seemed to have contributed to this modification. See e.g., E. G. White [E. G. Harmon], "RSA," pp. 15, 16.

50   Miller, "Mr. Miller's Reply to Dowling," No. 2, *ST,* Aug. 15, 1840, p. 74 (*Views,* pp. 187, 188). Cf. Litch, *Refutation,* pp. iii, iv, 7, 8.

51   The time concepts in Dan. 7:25; 12:7; Rev. 11:2, 3; 12:6, 14, 13:3 Dowling applied, like the Millerites, to the Roman Catholic Church (*Prophecies,* pp. 114, 115). The 1260 days he dated from A.D. 755-2015, when the millennium was to begin (*ibid.,* pp. 131, 132). Cf. Skinner, *Miller,* pp. 92-98.

52   Dowling, *Prophecies,* p. 72. Cf. regarding the year-day principle, Skinner, *Miller,* pp.

period of natural days, not years, and thus could not be related to the time concepts of Dan. 9.[53] The term "evening-mornings" he saw as a reference to the Jewish sacrificial system which led to an interpretation of the symbolism of Dan. 8 in the context of Jewish history. He associated the "2300 evenings and mornings" with "the number of daily burnt offerings," which, counting "both morning and evening sacrifices,"[54] pointed to a period of 1150 days or three years and 55 days, during which the Jewish sanctuary would be polluted and the daily sacrifice taken away.[55] Relying on historical information found in other commentators, Dowling interpreted the little horn as the person responsible for these actions, Antiochus IV, Epiphanes.[56] In support of this view he provided the following data on the desecration of the sanctuary: (1) On the 15th day of Casleu, a month he equated with December 168 B.C., the image of Jupiter Olympus was erected by Antiochus in the temple of Jerusalem (1 Macc. 1:54); (2) ten days later sacrifices were offered to this idol (1 Macc. 1:59); (3) three years later, on the 25th of Casleu, the temple was purified and dedicated anew to the worship of the God of Israel by Judas Maccabaeus (1 Macc. 4:52), exactly three years after the idolatrous sacrifices began.[57] In an attempt to harmonize the difference between these three years and his interpretation of the 2300 days as three years and 55 days, Dowling pointed out that although "we are not informed by any historian exactly how many days elapsed between the time when Athenaeus stopped the daily sacrifices, and the 25th of the month Casleu," it could be conjectured that this time lapse was "exactly 55 days."[58] This meant that the Jewish daily sacrifices had been interrupted for a period of 1150 days.[59] The sudden death of Antiochus he interpreted in the context of Dan. 8:25 as a divine judgment.[60]

66-72, 114, 115; Nathaniel S. Folsom, *Critical and Historical Interpretation of the Prophecies of Daniel*, 1842, pp. 84, 85.

53   For a discontinuity between Dan. 8 and 9, see Dowling, *Prophecies*, pp. 87, 88, 91-95. Cf. Skinner, *Miller*, pp. 64, 65; Folsom, *Daniel*, pp. 166, 167.

54   Dowling, *Prophecies*, p. 73.

55   *Ibid.*, pp. 73, 74, 77. Cf. Skinner, *Miller*, p. 72; Irah Chase, *Remarks on the Book of Daniel . . .*, 1844, pp. 58-60. The 2300 days Chase interpreted by Dan. 7:25 on the assumption that the little horns were identical (*ibid.*, p. 61). Furthermore, it was felt that in relation to "the idea of a gradual progress of events" the number 1150 corresponded with 1290 and 1335 (*ibid.*, p. 62). Dowling seemed to be influenced by J. Jahn, Professor of Oriental Languages and Biblical Archeology at the University of Vienna (Whiting, *Neology*, pp. 12, 24, 47).

56   Dowling, *Prophecies*, pp. 59, 63, 66, 67.

57   *Ibid.*, pp. 76-78.

58   *Ibid.*, p. 77. Cf. Nathaniel Colver, *The Prophecy of Daniel, Literally Fulfilled . . .*, 1843, p. 34; Chase, *Daniel*, pp. 62, 69, 71, 72, 80.

59   To Dowling the 1150 days best agreed with the historical evidence, though he felt that in the polemics with Millerism it did not make much difference whether one advocated the figure of 2300 or 1150. He said that those who favored the period of 2300 days reckoned from the beginning of the conflict between Jews and Antiochus "which was rather over six years before the cleansing of the sanctuary by Judas Maccabaeus" (*Prophecies*, p. 75). To Skinner the 1150 days referred to "the desolation of the temple, and the removal of the morning and evening sacrifice by Antiochus," while the 2300 days indicated "the time of the defection of the Jewish people" which was reckoned "from the defection procured by Menelaus the High priest, to the time the sanctuary was cleansed" (*Miller*, p. 72).

60   Dowling, *Prophecies*, pp. 67-70.

The Millerites strongly criticized Dowling's views. One of their arguments was that the application of the year-day principle to Dan. 8 harmonized both with the internal structure of the chapter, and with a consistent approach to apocalyptic Scriptures, and also provided an exact time period supportable by historical evidence. Both Miller and Litch pointed out that according to Daniel's question, "How long shall be the vision . . . ?" (8:13), the reply in the next verse not only pertained to the attack of the little horn on the sanctuary but referred to the whole of Daniel's vision, including events related to the Persian and Greek empires.[61] To Litch the 2300 days included both the pagan and papal abominations,[62] which is impossible if 8:14 signified a period of 1150 natural days. Miller criticized Dowling's inconsistency in applying the year-day principle to 9:25-27; 12:11, 12 and not to 8:14, pointing out: (1) It destroyed the harmony between Dan. 8 and 9 which was based on the time references; (2) it destroyed the harmony between Dan. 8 and 12 which was founded on the idea that the daily sacrifice of 8:13 and that of 12:11 were identical.[63] Litch added that the fact that the original rendering of Dan. 8:14 was not "days" was no valid reason for not applying the year-day principle, for there were other passages in which the term "day" was not used but to which this hermeneutical principle was applied, such as "time and times and the dividing of time" (Dan. 7:25), "time, times, and an half" (Dan. 12:7), and "forty and two months" (Rev. 11:2; 13:5).[64] He remarked further that there was no historical evidence available for an exact period of 2300 literal days.[65] Therefore, on the basis of historicist hermeneutic the Millerites felt it necessary to look for another interpretation which would fulfill the prophetic time in every detail. The only interpretation which, according to the Millerites, could satisfy this requirement was the one achieved by employment of the year-day principle.

Still another argument used by Miller against Dowling was that the Antiochus view violated the concept of prophetic time-sequence parallelism in Daniel, according to which the fourth beast of Dan. 7, which was interpreted as Rome in its pagan and papal phases, had to be identified with the little horn of Dan. 8 and not with Antiochus Epiphanes.[66] Litch brought out

---

61 Miller, "Mr. Miller's Review of Dowling," *ST*, Aug. 1, 1840, p. 67 (*Views*, p. 184); Litch, *Refutation*, p. 34. Cf. Miller, *Stuart's Hints*, pp. 17, 22; Bliss, "Stuart," No. IV, *ST*, Oct. 12, 1842, p. 25; [Hale], "Letter of Dr. Pond," *ST*, Nov. 9, 1842, p. 57; Austin, "William Miller," pp. 206-10.

62 Litch, *Refutation*, p. 54.

63 Miller, "Dowling," No. 2, p. 74 (*Views*, p. 190). Regarding the relation between Dan. 8 and 9, see Litch, *Refutation*, pp. 56-62. Cf. Miller, *Stuart's Hints*, pp. 23, 28, 29; [Hale], "Dr. Pond," pp. 57, 58; Elijah Shaw, *Christ's Second Coming*, 1843, pp. 31, 32; Chase, *Daniel*, p. 73. Regarding the term "daily sacrifice," Litch remarked that the word "sacrifice" was supplied and did not occur in the original. This was to him sufficient evidence to state that the term "daily" could not be used to indicate Jewish daily sacrifices (*Refutation*, pp. 42-44, 53. Cf. "Is Antiochus Epiphanes the Hero of Daniel's Prophecy?" *ST*, Extra, Dec. 21, 1842, p. 2).

64 Litch, *Refutation*, p. 41.

65 *Ibid.*, pp. 34, 35.

66 Miller, "Dowling, No. 2," p. 74.

that the Antiochus view was difficult to harmonize with the exegesis of Dan. 8:8, 9 because Antiochus was a king of Syria, one of the four kingdoms (horns) of the Greek empire, and was not another horn coming out of one of these kingdoms. In fact, neither the rise nor the fall of Antiochus affected the continuation of Syria as a kingdom.[67] Later, in the context of the four dynasties which succeeded Alexander and were represented by the four horns, "one for Egypt, one for Syria, one for Macedonia, and one for Thrace and Bithinia" (8:8), he observed that "Antiochus Epiphanes was but *one* of *twenty-six* individuals, who constituted the Syrian horn. Could he, at the *same* time, be *another* remarkable horn?"[68] Finally, the expression "for at the time of the end shall be the vision" (8:17) indicated to Litch that Dan. 8 had relevance for the time after 1798,[69] proving again that it could not apply to Antiochus.[70]

In 1842 Moses Stuart published *Hints on the Interpretation of Prophecy* which was directed against historicist hermeneutic. In contrast with Dowling, Stuart did not employ historicist hermeneutical principles to any apocalyptic passages, rendering himself less vulnerable to the charge of inconsistency. He concentrated his critique on three areas: (1) The dual nature of predictive prophecy; (2) the mystical sense of a prophecy, which could never be understood until the event intended had transpired; (3) the year-day principle. The first two areas dealt mainly with a discussion of principles of prophetic interpretation. His arguments against the dual application of prophecy ought to be placed against the background that at that time many commentators thought that the apocalyptic passages of Daniel had been fulfilled in one sense in the conflict between the Jews and Antiochus Epiphanus but in a larger sense in the history of the Christian church.[71] The dual nature of prophecy was, according to Stuart, contrary to the laws of the interpretation of language.[72] He argued that although the Bible was a unique book, it should be subjected to the common laws of interpretation to which other books are subjected.[73] He pointed out that one of the greatest difficulties with the dual sense of prophecy was that there was no standard by which to evaluate it;[74] everyone, therefore, ought,

---

67 Litch, *Refutation*, pp. 33, 34. Bliss said that the little horn was to come out of one of the four horns "whereas Antiochus was one of the four horns, and therefore could not be the fifth horn" ("Stuart," No. IV, p. 25). Cf. Bliss, *Inconsistencies of Colver's Literal Fulfilment of Daniel's Prophecy*, 1843, p. 32.

68 "Antiochus Epiphanes," p. 1.

69 See *supra*, p. 21.

70 Litch, *Refutation*, pp. 44, 45. Cf. "Antiochus Epiphanes," p. 1.

71 Ward, "Prof. Stuart's Hints on Prophecy," No. II, *ST*, Sept. 7, 1842, p. 183. Cf. Campbell, "Miller," p. 100.

72 Stuart, *Prophecy*, pp. 13, 14. Cf. Chase, *Daniel*, pp. 40-43. He did not accept the idea that "*Antiochus Epiphanes was a type of Antichrist*, and that what is predicted of him . . . was fulfilled *partly in him*, and will be fulfilled, *entirely in Antichrist*" (*ibid.*, p. 40). Cf. Folsom, *Daniel*, pp. 86, 87.

73 Stuart, *Prophecy*, pp. 14-17.

74 *Ibid.*, pp. 18, 19.

he said, to follow the general laws of exegesis.[75] Consonant with this conviction, Stuart rejected the year-day principle on the basis that Num. 14:34, Ezek. 4:5, 6, and Dan. 9:24-27 were so non-apocalyptic in character that the analogy-of-Scripture principle could not be applied.[76] It was his conviction that the time designations in Daniel and Revelation could satisfactorily be solved on *"the common ground of grammatico-historical exegesis,"* making historicist hermeneutic unnecessary.[77]

The application of this approach to Dan. 7 led Stuart to conclude that the fourth beast was "the divided Grecian dominion which succeeded the reign of Alexander the Great."[78] The little horn he identified with Antiochus Epiphanes.[79] The duration of the persecution under the little horn (7:25; 12:7) he interpreted as a period of three and a half years, signifying the *general nature* of the period of persecution[80] during which "Antiochus had complete possession and control of every thing in and around Jerusalem and the temple,"[81] whereas the *exact* period of the persecution was 1290 days (12:11), thirty days longer than the general period.[82] The 1290 days began from the time that "Apollonius captured Jerusalem in the latter part of May, B.C. 168" and ended when "Judas Maccabaeus expurgated the temple and restored the rites."[83] He assumed that the 1335 days (12:12) began with the 1290 days but terminated at the death of Antiochus, "some time in February of the year 164, B.C."[84] Thus Stuart interpreted the little horn much as Dowling did, with the difference that Dowling designated the persecution period (8:14) as 1150 days while Stuart preferred 2300 days,[85] beginning with the magnification of the little horn against the "prince of the host"

75   *Ibid.,* pp. 44, 84. In order to avoid confusion he stated that the interpreter of Scripture should only confine his work to discover the intention of the original author (*ibid.,* p. 42).

76   *Ibid.,* pp. 74-82. Cf. Skinner, *Miller,* pp. 114, 115; Cosmopolite, *Miller Overthrown: or The False Prophet Confounded,* 1840, pp. 26, 27; Shaw, *Second Coming,* p. 31; Folsom, *Daniel,* p. 85.

77   Stuart, *Prophecy,* p. 82. Cf. *ibid.,* p. 42.

78   *Ibid.,* p. 83. Cf. Folsom, *Daniel,* p. 106; Chase, *Daniel,* pp. 19-24.

79   Stuart, *Prophecy,* pp. 83, 84. Cf. Chase, *Daniel,* p. 26. Stuart supported his argument through analogous reasoning from the characteristics of the little horn of Dan. 8 (*Prophecy,* 2nd ed., 1842, pp. 87, 88). On the assumption that the little horns were identical, Chase determined the nature of the little horn of Dan. 7 by the one of Dan. 8 (*Daniel,* pp. 39, 48). Later, however, he interpreted the time element of 8:14 by 7:25 (*ibid.,* pp. 61, 62).

80   Stuart, *Prophecy,* p. 88.

81   *Ibid.,* p. 85. Cf. Folsom, *Daniel,* pp. 128-30.

82   Stuart, *Prophecy,* pp. 88-90. Cf. Folsom, *Daniel,* pp. 224, 225.

83   Stuart, *Prophecy,* pp. 89-91. An anti-Millerite publication by a Roman Catholic dated the 1290 days "from the time the fire should be taken from the temple, *until* the time that Antiochus should set up the abomination that maketh desolate, or image, in the holy place" (Cosmopolite, *Miller,* p. 82). Shaw identified the 1290 days as a definite period which he equated with the "time, times and a half" (Dan. 12:7). This time period was dated from "the time Apollonius took away the daily sacrifice early in June 168, to the time that Judas Maccabeus cleansed the sanctuary the last of 165 B.C." (*Second Coming,* p. 34). Folsom seemed to favor a period "from the setting up of the abomination of desolation to the building of the wall, and chambers and gates [1 Macc. 4:57-60]" (*Daniel,* pp. 225, 226).

84   Stuart, *Prophecy,* p. 92. Cf. Folsom, *Daniel,* p. 226. The phrase "blessed is he that waiteth . . . " (Dan. 12:12) was seen as a reference to the experience of the Jews "who lived to see such a day of deliverance" (Stuart, *Prophecy,* p. 92). Cf. Colver, *Daniel,* p. 37.

85   Stuart, *Prophecy,* pp. 93-95.

(8:11, interpreted as the murder of the high priest Onias III in 171 B.C.), and terminating with the restoration of the sanctuary (or temple).[86] The 2300 days of persecution Stuart considered to be a period of which the first part consisted of "frequent and long-continued interruptions of active oppression," while the 1260, 1290, and 1335 days he saw as periods of persecution with "no interruptions of the tyrannical and overbearing power of Antiochus."[87]

There was probably no one whose views received as much attention and criticism among the Millerites as Moses Stuart. In general they agreed with him on the first two areas of his critique. Miller remarked that his views were "the most Christian, candid, and reasonable arguments that I have ever met with, from any source whatever."[88] He agreed that "there is no double meaning to the words in the prophecies of the Old and New Testament."[89] He strongly cautioned, however, against the view that time elements in symbolic prophecy could not be symbolic,[90] explaining that God had some very good reasons for not always revealing the future in a plain literal sense, citing as samples Mt. 11:25; Lk. 8:10; 10:21; Dan. 12:10; 1 Thes. 5:3, 4; and Ps. 78:2.[91] Miller's overall impression was that Stuart's principles of interpretation were good. His major criticism concerned some of Stuart's applications of his principles in which Miller could see "neither reason nor common sense."[92]

Unlike Miller, Henry Ward criticized Stuart's view of the dual nature of prophecy and the subjection of Scripture to similar methods of interpretation as other books in order to prevent a dual or mystical interpretation. Said Ward: "We do not say that a rule of interpretation should be adopted for the Bible which is not common to other books; but rather that the Bible, together with every other book, ought to be interpreted in harmony with itself, and on principles recognized by the author in the volume of his works."[93] For example, he pointed out, the frequent practice of New Tes-

86 Ibid., p. 96. Cf. Shaw, Second Coming, pp. 29-32; Folsom, Daniel, pp. 81-83. To Dr. Pond from the Theological Institute, Bangor, Maine, the 2300 days were "the precise time during which 'the daily sacrifice was taken away' by Antiochus, and the place of 'the sanctuary was cast down'" (Second Advent Publications, p. 10). The possibility of 2300 weeks (44 years) was also considered, for it seemed to be 44 years after the angel's conversation that "the decree is . . . given to rebuild Jerusalem, to purify the sanctuary, and restore the true worship" (Cosmopolite, Miller, p. 30).

87 Stuart, Prophecy, p. 98. He added that at "the very close" of the 1335 days there was an interruption of persecution.

88 Miller, Stuart's Hints, pp. 5, 6.

89 Ibid., p. 7.

90 Ibid., p. 31.

91 Ibid., pp. 37-40.

92 Ibid., p. 8.

93 Ward, "Prof. Stuart's Hints on Prophecy," No. 1, ST, Aug. 31, 1842, p. 176. He added: "In reading Milton, it is fair to use a method of interpreting some obscure passages, which method Milton has himself used in another part of his works, to interpret a similar passage: so a prophetical obscurity in one part of the Bible may well be explained on a principle used in another part of the Bible, to explain a similar prophetical obscurity. The New Testament does frequently put a new, a mystical, or a double sense on the language of a text of the Old Testament; and this leads the student of the Bible to the knowledge of a Bible rule of interpretation."

tament writers to give new interpretations to the language of the Old Testament through the typological principle justifies use of the same hermeneutical practice today.[94] In commenting on Stuart's denial that many prophecies are mystical, and explicable only by the fulfillment of the predicted event itself, Ward pointed to prophecies regarding Christ's first Advent which had been very imperfectly understood until the predicted event had taken place.[95]

The application of Stuart's hermeneutic to the interpretation of the little horn of Dan. 7 on the basis of his "grammatico-historical exegesis" was strongly criticized by the Millerites. Miller remarked that Stuart's approach failed to deal with the specific manner in which the little horn arose (7:8, 19, 20).[96] If Antiochus was the little horn, he should have emerged from among ten kingdoms, three of which he would have subdued. In reality there was, according to Miller, not a great difference between the Syrian kingdom and the other kingdoms of the divided empire of Alexander: "All arose in the same manner, all made war on each other, and each in turn succeeded in its warlike enterprises. Neither one of them was able to subdue all the other three."[97] It was the opinion of Sylvester Bliss, the junior editor of the *Signs of the Times,* that this interpretation did not recognize the principle of time-sequence parallelism between Dan. 2 and 7. Arguing from this principle, the fourth beast of Dan. 7 could not signify the divided empire of Alexander but had to be interpreted, like the iron legs of Dan. 2, as Rome.[98] In reference to the death of Antiochus, Miller stated that this event differed sharply from the biblical account that "the beast was slain, and his body destroyed and given to the burning flame" (7:11).[99]

According to the Millerites, another problem for Stuart was the reconciliation of Antiochus with Dan. 7:21, 22. Charles Fitch called on Stuart to provide evidence that Antiochus "either did, or does, or will make war with the saints and prevail against them, until the Ancient of days comes, and judgment is given to the saints of the Most High, and the time come[s] that the saints possess the kingdom."[100] Stuart's answer was that Fitch had been mistaken in applying the judgment (7:10, 22) and the dominion given to the saints (7:22) to the last judgment and the millennial dominion of the church instead of the judgment and punishment of Antiochus.[101] According to Stuart, the Messianic kingdom, as described in 7:13, 14, 27, had no connection with 7:10, 22 and would find its fulfillment after a certain time interval. Although the context seemed to indicate that the Messianic dominion would immediately follow the destruction of the kingdom of Antiochus, he

94   Ibid.
95   Ibid.
96   Miller, *Stuart's Hints,* p. 34.
97   Ibid., pp. 9, 34.
98   Bliss, "Stuart," No. III, *ST,* Oct. 5, 1842, p. 17.
99   Miller, *Stuart's Hints,* p. 35.
100 Fitch, "Letters to Moses Stuart," *ST,* Aug. 24, 1842, p. 164.
101 Stuart, *Prophecy,* 2nd ed., p. 87.

said that such a conclusion was not necessary because in this particular instance Daniel was not directly concerned with chronological sequence.[102] Miller of course, convinced that Daniel *was* concerned with chronology,[103] rejected Stuart on this point, urging that the kingdom which the saints would possess (7:18, 22) was not the kingdom of Judas Maccabaeus but nothing less than the everlasting kingdom of 7:27.[104] He insisted that contextual evidence clearly supported the view that 7:10, 22 referred to the last judgment.[105]

Stuart's interpretation of Dan. 8 received a criticism similar to that launched against Dowling's view of the chapter. In addition, Miller argued that the pollution of the sanctuary did not end with the death of Antiochus, as Stuart had suggested, pointing to the fact that it was "twenty years or more after the death of Antiochus, [that] Simon, the high priest, drove out the heathen who had polluted the sanctuary and the holy place; 1 Maccab. xiv. 36."[106] Bliss stated that "the Prince of princes" (8:25) against whom the little horn acted was the Messiah, which implied that the little horn could not be Antiochus, for he died before Christ was born.[107] Two additional arguments were brought out in an article in the *Signs of the Times*. The first said that it was contrary to the history of the progressive development of world powers to state that the Medo-Persian power was called "great" (8:4), the Greek empire designated as "very great" (8:8), and Antiochus characterized as "exceeding great" (8:9). Because Antiochus was obliged to pay tribute to the Romans, there was no question that Rome was the exceeding great power of 8:9.[108] The second argument pointed out that the conquests of the Roman empire, not those of Antiochus, fulfilled the geographical progressions of 8:9.[109]

Regarding Stuart's view of Dan. 12, Miller commented that contextual evidence (especially 12:1-3, 10) pointed to the resurrection of the dead, and hence could not refer to the death of Antiochus.[110]

The absence in Stuart's presentation of "exact" historical evidence for the fulfillment of the time prophecies was used by Millerites as a major argument against his whole method for interpreting apocalyptic-eschatology.[111] In harmony with Miller's hermeneutical rules, Bliss stated that each prediction had to be fulfilled "to the very letter, both in respect to manner and to

---

102   *Ibid.*, p. 88.
103   Miller, *Stuart's Hints*, pp. 74, 75.
104   *Ibid.*, pp. 9, 10, 72, 73.
105   *Ibid.*, pp. 70, 71.
106   *Ibid.*, p. 24. He added that even in the time of Christ the sanctuary was polluted (Mt. 21:13).
107   Bliss, "Stuart," No. IV, p. 25.
108   "Antiochus Epiphanes," p. 1. It was indicated that the power of Antiochus, instead of becoming stronger, became weaker toward the end of his life (*ibid.*, p. 2).
109   *Ibid.*, p. 1.
110   Miller, *Stuart's Hints*, pp. 13-16, 29, 30, 42, 43. Cf. Bliss, "Stuart," No. III, pp. 17, 18.
111   Cf. *ibid.*

time; or it will be necessary to look for a farther fulfillment."[112] Defending the historicist's use of the year-day principle, he remarked that "we only claim that a day is used as a figure of a year, where it cannot be shown that the prediction was fulfilled in literal days; and also where it was *impossible* that they should have been so fulfilled."[113] In support, the Millerites used against Stuart, Bush's argument that chronological periods attached to symbolic prophecies must also be interpreted symbolically: The use of the year-day principle in Ezekiel and Numbers as a tool for interpreting Daniel and the Apocalypse Bush justified on the basis that the prophetic symbolism of these passages in Ezekiel and Numbers was a "miniature symbolization," or model in miniature, revealing a prophetic nature quite similar to — and not different from — that of Daniel and Revelation.[114] The difference between the Millerite historicist hermeneutic and Stuart's approach was, according to Bliss, that on the one hand

> we have not only shown that the time was accurately fulfilled, but also that the history of those fulfilments accorded perfectly in all the particular minutia, with the respective predictions. On the other hand, it is claimed that those periods were fulfilled in literal days, while it cannot be shown that a single period was fulfilled in the given number of days; or that the particulars of the prophecy accorded with the fulfilment.[115]

In 1843 Nathaniel Colver published three sermons criticizing the Millerite position. His interpretation of Dan. 8 and 12, basically similar to that of Stuart, varied somewhat in the historical data applied to the prophetic time periods. The 2300 days he related to the beginning of the apostasy among the Jews as described in 1 Macc. This apostasy, Colver said, took

112 Bliss, "Stuart," No. II, *ST*, Sept. 28, 1842, p. 9.
113 *Ibid.*
114 Bush, "Prophetic Designations of Time," *AH*, March 6, 1844, p. 34. Here he said: "The grand principle into which the usage of employing a day for a year is to be resolved, is that of *miniature symbolization*. As the *events* are thus economically reduced, the *periods* are to be reduced in the same relative proportion. What that proportion is, we cannot positively determine without some antecedent information touching the *rate* or scale of reduction." To him this information was given in Ezek. 4:5, 6 and Num. 14:34. Regarding Ezek. 4 he said that "Ezekiel was commanded to 'lie on his left side 390 days, that so he might bear the iniquity of the house of Israel.' This was a typical action constituting a symbolical prophecy, and so far as its chronological support is concerned, Jehovah himself adds, 'I have appointed *each day for a year.*' Ezekiel is in this transaction a *miniature hieroglyphic* of Israel; a man, of a nation. Hence as the man represented the nation in miniature, so the 390 days represented the period of 390 years in miniature." As to Num. 14 he stated that "the twelve selected spies jointly constituted a *miniature symbol* of the entire nation. Accordingly, the predicted term of the national wanderings was analogously represented in miniature also." Bush concluded that these examples "are to be considered as merely giving us a clue to a general principle of interpretation. Here are two or three striking examples of predictions constructed on the plan of *miniature symbolic representation* in which the involved periods of time are reduced to a scale proportioned to that of the events themselves. What then more natural or more legitimate, than that when we meet with other prophecies, constructed on precisely the same principle, we should interpret their chronological periods by the same rule?" (*ibid.*).
115 Bliss, "Stuart," No. VI, *ST*, Oct. 26, 1842, p. 47. The timing of the flood, the Exodus, the sojourn of Israel in the wilderness, the Babylonian captivity and Dan. 9:24-27 were to him evidences that God worked with "statistical exactness" (*ibid.*, pp. 46, 47).

place "some time previous to the first invasion of Egypt by Antiochus, on his return from which he entered Jerusalem; which gives it a date of something more than six years preceding the cleansing of the sanctuary," leading to the conclusion that this "gives us the '2300 days,' covering the whole apostasy and subversion."[116] The commencement of the 1290 days he determined on the basis of 1 Macc., which to him provided the evidence that the taking away of the daily sacrifice, the pollution of the sanctuary, the setting up of altars, groves, chapels of idols, and the sacrifices of swine flesh and other unclean animals were performed "at least six months before the setting up of 'the abomination of desolation' upon the altar in the temple."[117] This period he added to the three years and ten days (1 Macc. 1:58; 4:52), giving him the 1290 days of persecution under Antiochus.[118] Although Colver stated that there was no exact historical information as to "the *precise date* of the death of Antiochus, or the *precise time* when the news of it took effect upon the affairs of the Jews," he felt that sufficient evidence was available on which to assume that it was "more than probable" that the end of the 1335 days occurred at that event.[119] Colver presented a more fully developed exposition of Dan. 12 than Stuart. The standing up of Michael (12:1) he paraphrased as "the cleansing of the sanctuary, by the victorious arms of the Michael-sustained host of Judas Maccabaeus."[120] The "time of trouble such as never was since there was a nation" (12:1) he described as the warfare between the Jews and Antiochus' allies covering the period between the cleansing of the sanctuary (end of 1290 days) and the termination of this oppression caused by the news of Antiochus' death (end of 1335 days).[121]

Unlike Stuart, Colver saw a sharp difference between the little horn of Dan. 7 and the one of Dan. 8. In his analysis of the difference between these horns as to their origin, rise, character, work, and final end, he indicated that the little horn of Dan. 7 was not Antiochus, but Nero.[122] The period of persecution (7:25) he defined as Nero's persecution of the Christians during a period of "between three and four years."[123]

The response to Colver's position was provided by Bliss in one of the most elaborate Millerite polemics against the Antiochus interpretation. Objections to the Antiochus view which had not been mentioned before included: (1) A hermeneutical objection from Sir Isaac Newton that "a horn

---

116 Colver, *Daniel,* p. 35.
117 *Ibid.,* p. 34.
118 *Ibid.*
119 *Ibid.,* p. 36. He said that "the distance the news [Judas' victory] had to travel to reach him [Antiochus] at Ecbatana, and the subsequent account of his death, leave us little reason to doubt the accuracy of the angel, in fixing the time at *forty-five days*" (*ibid.,* p. 37).
120 *Ibid.,* p. 36. Cf. Cosmopolite, *Miller,* pp. 71, 72.
121 Colver, *Daniel,* p. 36. Dan. 12:9 he interpreted to mean that the events described in this predictive prophecy did not concern Daniel personally but that it would be "useful to those for whose benefit it is intended," namely to the Jews living in the time of the oppression by Antiochus (*ibid.,* p. 38).
122 *Ibid.,* pp. 40-50.
123 *Ibid.,* p. 48.

of a beast is never taken for a single person: it always signifies a *new* kingdom; and the kingdom of Antiochus was an *old* one";[124] (2) according to 8:23, the little horn was to rise "in the *latter* time" of the kingdoms of the four horns. Antiochus, however, was "the *eighth* in the Syrian line of kings, which numbered *twenty-five*, and he therefore could not be in the *latter time* of that kingdom";[125] (3) the little horn was to cast down the place of the sanctuary (8:11), something which was not accomplished by Antiochus but by the Romans during the destruction of Jerusalem in 70 A.D. as had been pointed out in 9:26, "And the people of the prince that shall come shall destroy the city and the sanctuary."[126] Bliss rejected also the interpretation of Nero.[127] Like other Millerite reactions against Dowling and Stuart, one of his major criticisms was that although Colver claimed to have shown that the time periods in Daniel had been fulfilled in literal days, he provided no exact historical evidence but only conjectures suggested by assumed applications of the 2300, 1260, 1290 and 1335 days.[128] Such an approach Bliss regarded as unacceptable, especially when, according to Millerites, the application of the year-day principle was verifiable by precise historical facts.

In 1844 Irah Chase wrote a work which was primarily devoted to the fulfillment of the apocalyptic passages of Daniel by Antiochus Epiphanes. Compared with Dowling, Stuart, and Colver, Chase's presentation brought out additional information regarding the development of the little horn of Dan. 7 but differed from the others as far as the time periods were concerned. Stating that the little horns of Dan. 7 and 8 are identical, he argued: "The little horn in Dan. 8:9, arises from one of the branches of the Greek empire, and indicates Antiochus Epiphanes, the little horn in the parallel passage, Dan. 7:8, must arise from the same source, and indicate the same individual; that is, it must arise from the Greek empire."[129] He concluded that "the empire indicated by the fourth beast must be the Greek and not the Roman."[130] The Greek empire he exclusively associated with the dynasty of Seleucus.[131] The ten horns of this beast (7:7, 8, 24) he did not interpret as kingdoms[132] but as "kings or aspirants to the crown of that dynasty before Antiochus Epiphanes ascended the throne."[133] The three horns he identified with "the usurper Heliodorus [royal treasurer], the aspirant Ptolemy [nephew of Seleucus Philopator], and Demetrius [son of

124 Bliss, *Colver's Fulfilment*, p. 32.
125 *Ibid.*
126 *Ibid.*, p. 35.
127 *Ibid.*, pp. 28-31.
128 *Ibid.*, pp. 11-21.
129 Chase, *Daniel*, p. 39. Cf. *ibid.*, pp. 23, 48; Folsom, *Daniel*, pp. 105, 106.
130 Chase, *Daniel*, pp. 40, 41.
131 *Ibid.*, pp. 17-24.
132 In general historicists employed the hermeneutical principle that the ten horns and the little horn of Dan. 7, and the four horns and the little horn of Dan. 8, symbolized kingdoms. Those tending toward historical-criticism identified the ten horns of Dan. 7 and the little horns of Dan. 7 and 8 as kings but the four horns of Dan. 8 as kingdoms. Cf. *ibid.*, pp. 36-38.
133 *Ibid.*, pp. 24, 25. He provided the following list which consisted of seven Seleucid

Seleucus Philopator] the legitimate heir" who "all stood in the way of Antiochus Epiphanes."[134]

In his time calculations Chase interpreted Dan. 8:14, like Dowling, as "two thousand and three hundred times of sacrifice, evening and morning," signifying 1150 days.[135] On the assumption that the little horns of Dan. 7 and 8 were identical, he interpreted "time and times and the dividing of time" (7:25) in the light of 8:14 as an equivalent of 1150 days.[136] Although admitting that precise historical evidence about its beginning was lacking, he dated this period, during which both the sanctuary and the Jewish people were to be trodden down, "from the taking away of the daily sacrifice to its restoration."[137] He stated that the 1150, 1290, and 1335 days had the same starting point. The 1290 days, which he described as "a more definite statement" of 12:7 — "a time, times, and a half" — terminated with the death of Antiochus, 140 days after the restoration.[138] According to Chase, forty-five days later, at the termination of the 1335 days, the news of Antiochus' death reached the Jews.[139]

Apollos Hale rejected Chase's view that the rise of the little horn of Dan. 7 had been fulfilled in the person of Antiochus Epiphanes, who had seven kings as his predecessors and eliminated three pretenders to the throne. According to him, the account of the origin of the little horn clearly provided a different picture because *"'it* [fourth beast] *had ten horns,'* and *'the little horn came up* AMONG *them,'*[7:8] implying their existence all at one time. Before this little horn *'three of the first horns were plucked up by the roots.'* "[140] In Hale's opinion the interpretation was equally plain: *"The fourth beast is the fourth kingdom upon earth, and the ten horns are ten kings that shall arise, and another shall rise after them, and he shall subdue* THREE

---

kings and three pretenders of Antiochus Epiphanes: (1) Seleucus I, Nicator, founder of the dynasty (312 B.C.); (2) Antiochus I, Soter (279-260); (3) Antiochus II, Theos (260-245); (4) Seleucus II, Callinicus (245-226); (5) Selucus III, Ceraunus (225-223); (6) Antiochus III, the Great (223-187); (7) Seleucus IV, Philopator (186-175); (8) Heliodorus; (9) Ptolemy IV, Philometor (King of Egypt); (10) Demetrius I, Soter (son of Seleucus, Philopator) (*ibid.,* p. 25). Cf. Folsom, *Daniel,* p. 107. For a discussion on the various historical-critical attempts to identify the 10 horns in relation to Antiochus, see *ibid.,* pp. 106-13. According to Folsom the "ten horns denoted ten kings, or *races* of kings, which began after Alexander's death." The Seleucid dynasty was interpreted as the little horn (*ibid.,* pp. 109-13, 126).

134 Chase, *Daniel,* pp. 25, 26. Cf. *ibid.,* p. 36. Folsom suggested "three of Alexander's immediate successors, who are explicably mentioned as kings, viz. Antigonus, Lysimachus, and Demetrius" who were subdued by Seleucus I (*Daniel,* pp. 101, 102).

135 Chase, *Daniel,* pp. 57, 59, 60.

136 *Ibid.,* pp. 61, 62. Cf. *supra,* p. 65.

137 *Ibid.,* pp. 62, 69, 80.

138 *Ibid.,* pp. 80, 81. He stated: "The events recorded in the fifth chapter of the first book of Maccabees, as occurring between the restoration of the daily sacrifice and his death, would seem to require a period of, at least, 140 days, or somewhat more than four months" (*ibid.,* p. 81).

139 *Ibid.,* pp. 82, 83. The fact that it took 45 days for this news to reach the Jews was attributed to bad travel facilities and the possibility that Antiochus' death might have been concealed for some time (*ibid.*).

140 Hale, "Review," p. 131.

KINGS" (7:24).[141] Furthermore, he saw in Chase's argumentation various unanswered problems:

> If the fourth kingdom, represented by the fourth beast, consisted of the *four divisions* of Alexander's kingdom, why should the horns or kings be confined to *one* division of his kingdom [Seleucan dynasty]? If that *one* division is the fourth kingdom, did the little horn come up *among* the ten horns or kings, specified by Dr. Chase, (granting the "usurpers and aspirants," by which only he can make out the number, were kings) any more than he come up among the *twenty-three,* or more kings of the same dynasty?[142]

Chase's hermeneutic identifying the three throne pretenders with horns or kings was also questioned. Finally, Hale found it problematic that after the judgment was executed on Antiochus by the Ancient of Days, which according to Chase took place with the destruction of the beast (7:9-11), the Seleucan dynasty continued to exist for more than a hundred years.[143]

In 1844, due to a growing opposition and a polarization of positions between Millerites and other Christians, various Millerites associated the above described historical-critical trends with the term "Neology" as other evangelical Christians had done before. Regarding the views of Stuart and Chase, Millerites remarked that "one of the most alarming features of the present state of the churches, is, the railroad speed with which many of the most prominent divines are leaving the OLD LANDMARKS, and taking *Neological ground.*"[144] Colver and Dowling were also accused of Neology.[145] According to Nathan N. Whiting, D.D.,[146] a Baptist scholar and Millerite lecturer and editor, the term "Neology" could be equated with "Rationalism" and had once been applied to "the *actual* creed of a large portion of the members of the German church, who profess a nominal adhesion to the Augsburgh Confession of Faith, while they reject its fundamental principles" and maintain positions in contradiction to it.[147] Now the term was described as "New Theology — departing from the old established principles of Biblical interpretation, and leaving the faith once delivered to the saints, *for new doctrine,*"[148] which had adopted "views on the prophecies

---

141 *Ibid.*

142 *Ibid.,* pp. 131, 132.

143 *Ibid.,* p. 132.

144 Editorial, "The Neology of the Church," *AH,* April 3, 1844, p. 68. Cf. Editorial, "A Specimen of Elder Shaw's Neology," *AH,* April 24, 1844, p. 93; [Himes], "New Publication," *AH,* March 13, 1844, p. 48; Whiting, *Neology,* pp. 33-39.

145 *Ibid.,* p. 47.

146 Nathan N. Whiting (1794-1872) studied theology at Union College when Eliphalet Nott was president. He became a minister, scholar, and linguist (especially in Greek and Hebrew). He provided a translation of the N.T. under the auspices of the Baptist Church. This was called *The Good News of Our Lord Jesus, the Anointed; from the Critical Greek Text of Tittman,* 1842. He was one of the Millerite leaders opposed to time setting.

147 Whiting, *Neology,* p. 3. He attributed the reason for its German origin to the fact that "the German church was a national establishment." Through this Church State relationship the "magistracy," who preferred "high *literary* qualifications" above "*vital piety,*" had an influence on the church's affairs which resulted in "the admission of unconverted men into religious offices" (*ibid.,* pp. 4, 5).

148 Editorial, "Neology," *AH,* May 1, 1844, p. 100.

in accordance with the philosophies of Germany and France."[149] It is evident that the Millerites had no sympathy with the hermeneutics employed by those who tended toward historical criticism.

C. Summary.

Underlying the theological controversy between the Millerites and other Christians was a question of the principles of hermeneutic and their application. The opponents of the Millerites can be classified as including both historicists and others who reflected historical-critical trends. In regard to the crucial issue of the interpretation of the little horn of Dan. 8, the majority of opponents who employed historicist hermeneutics identified the horn as Islam, while those who tended toward a historical-critical approach advocated Antiochus IV, Epiphanes as the fulfillment.

The Millerites rejected the view of Islam because it appeared to violate the historicist hermeneutical principles, and also because there existed no precise agreement between the symbolism of the biblical passage and the historical facts of the origin and rise of that religion. They criticized the Antiochus view because the historical data of the life of Antiochus also were difficult to harmonize with the exegesis of Dan. 8. It violated, they said, the prophetic time-sequence parallelism of Daniel and could provide no exact historical evidence for a period of persecution identifiable by the 2300 days of Dan. 8:14.

In this controversy the Millerites argued that the historicist interpretation of the little horn as the pagan and papal phases of Rome, the persecuting power of God's people, was most consistent with available historical data. They especially emphasized that only the application of the year-day principle as a key to the interpretation of time periods in apocalyptic eschatology provided an exact time period for which there existed accurate historical evidence.

---

149   Editorial, "Backing Out," *AH*, Feb. 21, 1844, p. 20. Cf. Whiting, *Neology*, pp. 1-33; Editorial, "The Methodists Also on the Road to German Neology," *AH*, April 10, 1844, p. 76.

This chapter will show how increasing opposition led the Millerites to develop a new ecclesiological self-understanding, one which ultimately led to their separation from the churches and the creation of a new religious body. Further study will also be given to developments in their understanding of time calculations, partly because they were perennially a primary motivation for the Millerite mission to warn mankind, and partly because — due to a new understanding of the Midnight Cry — they climaxed in a special missionary movement of paramount importance to the formation of the SDA theology of mission.

A. Attitudes to Other Churches.

The closer the year 1843 approached, the greater the Millerite missionary endeavors became and the stronger the opposition and antagonism grew. As early as 1841 there was a report of a mob that attempted to break up a meeting of a lecturer who preached on the Midnight Cry.[1] The next year some opponents accused the Millerites of ultraism,[2] several churches took official action against members who sympathized with or adhered to Miller's ideas, and many churches closed their doors against Millerite lecturers.[3] In an article, "The Crisis has Come!" Himes indicated that the situation, once favorable, had changed and that "the opposition have at length begun to put forth their energies to crush the advocates of the midnight cry, and to hush the voice of alarm to the slumbering virgins."[4] To a number of Millerites it seemed that the church and the world had combined to overthrow their beliefs and that "Orthodox and Heterodox, Universalists and Calvinists, Unitarians and Infidels, Methodists and Baptists, Drunkards, Swearers and Gamblers, of every grade, are all 'hail fellows well met,' if they can only overthrow 'Miller' and 'millerism.' "[5]

1   T. M. Preble, "A Mob," *ST,* Jan. 15, 1841, p. 159. See Rowe, "Millerite Movement," pp. 213, 214 on the use of violence against Millerites.

2   D., "More Ultraism," *ST,* July 20, 1842, p. 126. See *supra,* p. 12.

3   Cf. "Look at Facts," *Day Star,* repr. in*ST,* Oct. 19, 1842, p. 34; E. G. White,*SG,* II, 1860, pp. 21-25.

4   Himes, "Crisis," p. 140. For a view of the various forms of opposition against Millerites in non-Millerite literature, see Rowe, "Millerite Movement," pp. 189-213.

5   Editorial, " 'Made Friends,' " *ST,* Oct. 5, 1842, p. 20. On the Millerite attitude to secular and religious institutions, see Rowe, "Millerite Movement," pp. 157-88.

In spite of this strong anti-Millerite sentiment, the official position of the leaders of the movement just before 1843 was that — except in the face of actual "persecution" — Millerites should stay in their respective churches to fulfill their task of warning their fellow church members.[6]

Previous to 1843 Millerite ecclesiology portrayed the Roman Catholic Church as Babylon and Protestant churches as fulfilling the Laodicean church of Rev. 3, the last period of the Christian church. Faults criticized in Protestantism varied from clerical dominance to heresy and, especially, to "sectarianism," an aspect which led some Millerites, rather loosely, to associate the Protestant churches also with the term "Babylon" (confusion).[7]

1. Separation from Babylon.

> And he cried mightily with a strong voice, saying, Babylon the great is fallen, is fallen, and is become the habitation of devils, and the hold of every foul spirit, and a cage of every unclean and hateful bird. . . . And I heard another voice from heaven, saying, Come out of her, my people, that ye be not partakers of her sins, and that ye receive not of her plagues. Rev. 18:2, 4.

As anti-Millerite sentiment in the Protestant churches developed rapidly in the year 1843, and large numbers of Millerites began to be disfellowshiped, the concept that Protestantism as well as Roman Catholicism constituted Babylon was formulated into a careful theology and the cry arose, "Babylon is fallen. Come out of her, my people." Charles Fitch's sermon, *Come Out of Her, My People,* set the pace.

Fitch had by now become one of the Millerite leaders. In the first section of his sermon he defined Babylon as antichrist[8] and explained that anyone who opposes the "PERSONAL REIGN of Jesus Christ over this world on David's throne, is ANTICHRIST."[9] His criterion established, he identified antichrist as the entire Roman Catholic Church, for "when the papacy came into power, they concluded to have Christ reign, not personally, but spiritually, and hence the Pope entered into the stead of Christ, and undertook to rule the world for him — claiming to be God's vicegerent on earth."[10] According to Fitch, the Catholics wished to retain their power so they would be "opposed to Christ's coming to establish a personal reign."[11] But, he went on, Protestants also were opposed to Christ's personal reign, for they had rejected this doctrine and "turned away their ears to the groundless fable of a spiritual reign of Christ, during what is called a temporal millenium [*sic*] when they expect all the world will be converted; and each sect is expecting at that time to have the predominant influence."[12] To Fitch

6 Editorial, "Our Duty," p. 86.
7 See *supra,* p. 48.
8 Fitch, *"Come Out of Her, My People": A Sermon,* p. 5 (repr. in *MC,* Sept. 21, 1843, pp. 33-36).
9 Fitch, *Come Out,* p. 9.
10 *Ibid.*
11 *Ibid.*
12 *Ibid.,* p. 11.

the conclusion was inescapable that the Protestant churches also belonged to the category of antichrist,[13] and especially so in view of the opposition of the "Christian sects" to Christ's personal return during the Jewish sacred year of 1843. "The professed Christian world," said he, "Catholic and Protestant, are Antichrist."[14]

The second section of Fitch's sermon dealt with the fall of Babylon as expressed in Rev. 18:2. It was obvious to him that the language of the text applied to the Roman Catholic Church; but he pointed out that the language characterized also the Protestant churches in view of their spirit of oppression (pro-slavery), their pride, and their desire for power and wealth.[15]

In the third section Fitch took a step of far-reaching consequence for the interconfessionalism of the Millerite movement. Referring to the call, "Come out of her, my people" (Rev. 18:4), he spelled out its implications as follows:

> To come out of Babylon is to be converted to the true scriptural doctrine of the personal coming and the kingdom of Christ; to receive the truth on this subject with all readiness of mind, as you find it plainly written out on the pages of the Bible; to love Christ's appearing, and rejoice in it, and fully and faithfully to avow to the world your unshrinking belief in God's word touching this momentous subject, and to do all in your power to open the eyes of others, and influence them to a similar course, that they may be ready to meet their Lord.[16]

Then Fitch made the appeal, "If you are a Christian, *come out of Babylon*! If you intend to be found a Christian when Christ appears, *come out of Babylon*, and come out NOW!"[17]

In the last section of his sermon he discussed the consequences of refusing to come out of Babylon, consequences which he summarized in his final appeal: "Come out of Babylon or perish."[18]

Published and widely distributed, this sermon became very influential. It is not surprising that many Millerites saw in Fitch's exposition a biblical explanation for the hostility of their environment and a theological argument for separation. To many it also implied that although ultimately the mercy of Christ was the ground of man's salvation, separation from fallen

---

13   *Ibid.*, p. 13.
14   *Ibid.*, p. 15.
15   *Ibid.*, pp. 16, 17.
16   *Ibid.*, p. 18. Only the third section was repr. in *ST*, Sept. 13, 1843, p. 27, so that the editors avoided giving wider circulation to Fitch's definition of Babylon with which they did not agree (Arthur, "Babylon," p. 66).
17   Fitch, *Come Out*, p. 19. In his call the clergy were also included (*ibid.*, p. 21). Cf. "Letter from T. M. Preble," *ST*, Sept. 20, 1843, p. 39; "Letter from Brother Boutelle," *ST*, Oct. 18, 1843, p. 65; J. Marsh, "Elder J. Marsh's Resignation as One of the Editors of the Christian Palladium" (Organ of the Christian Church), *ST*, Nov. 29, 1843, p. 127; F. G. Brown, "Coming out of the Churches," *ST*, Jan. 10, 1844, p. 175; D. Plumb, "Babylon," *MC*, Feb. 1, 1844, pp. 218, 219; Brown, "Reasons for Withdrawing from the Church,"*AH*, March 27, 1844, pp. 58, 59.
18   Fitch, *Come Out*, p. 24.

Babylon before the close of human probation was an indispensable response on the part of those who loved Christ's appearing. It was therefore felt that those who would not separate themselves from the churches did not love Christ and could not be saved. Such argumentation was for many sufficient for severing their connection with their churches. Thus, it was only after the Midnight Cry and the Judgment Hour message had been rejected by the other churches and after a reaction had started to counteract Millerite mission efforts, that the cry "Babylon is fallen, Come out of her, my people" became vocal as a part of their theology of mission.[19]

Not all Millerite leaders supported Fitch's ideas. Some considered it their only business to proclaim the Midnight Cry and not to interfere with the question of church membership, an individual matter respecting which "every person must be his own judge."[20] Only during the late summer of 1844 did the Millerite leaders support separation with any degree of unanimity.[21] A similar attitude to the separation from the churches was taken by a number of British Adventists who seemed to have been influenced by the Millerites.[22]

The view of the relation of the Roman Catholic and Protestant churches to Babylon was also developed in the context of Rev. 17:5, "And upon her forehead was a name written, MYSTERY, BABYLON THE GREAT, THE MOTHER OF HARLOTS AND ABOMINATIONS OF THE EARTH." At the Second Advent Conference in Boston (January 28, 1844) Miller seems to have commented on this text saying, "If the Roman church was the mother of harlots, then her daughters must be the harlots: and therefore that portion of the Protestant churches that imitate and partake of the spirit of the old mother must be the daughters referred to."[23] Miller confessed that he had always advised believers to stay in their churches, "but God had ordered it otherwise."[24] (Incidentally, others besides the Millerites had

19 In 1844 there appeared a periodical entitled *Babylon the Great is Fallen* (Froom, *PFF*, IV, 625, 772).

20 Editorial Comment in "Letter from Boutelle," p. 65.

21 Himes, "Editorial Correspondence," *AH*, Sept. 18, 1844, p. 53. Here Himes stated that there was still some disagreement as to what constituted Babylon. Contemporary sources show that the definitions of Babylon in such general terms as antichrist and Satan's kingdom, and the fall of Babylon as the "end of the world, when Satan's supremacy shall cease at the coming of Christ" (Bliss, "The Downfall of Great Babylon," *ASR*, May 1844, pp. 112-20) do not reflect the general Millerite position but indicate the more moderate view among some of the leaders. Cf. [Marsh], "Come Out of Babylon!" *VT*, Sept. 11, 1844, p. 127 (*RH*, Dec. 9, 1851, p. 58); Bates, *SAWH*, p. 18. For an Advent Christian evaluation of Millerite separatism in the period 1843-44, see Arthur, "Babylon," pp. 42-83; Arthur, "Millerism," in Gaustad, *Adventism*, pp. 162-70. Later Miller deplored the results of Fitch's views and said that "it prejudiced many against us so that they would not listen to the truth" as well as that "it created a deep feeling of hostility between Adventists and those who did not embrace the doctrine" (Miller, *Apology*, p. 25). For clerical reactions, see Editorial, "Persecution," *AH*, March 6, 1844, pp. 36, 37. On reasons for hostility, see Arthur, "Babylon," pp. 36-40.

22 Editorial, "Come Out of Her, My People," *SAH*, April 2, 1844, pp. 19-21.

23 Editorial, "The Conference," *AH*, Feb. 14, 1844, p. 9. Cf. Himes, "Editorial Correspondence," p. 53; Editorial, "Coming Out of Babylon," *VT*, April 27, 1844, pp. 46, 47; E. G. White, *SP*, IV, 233; E. G. White, *GC*, pp. 382, 383.

24 Editorial, "Conference," p. 9. It is probable that Miller allowed for a voluntary separa-

earlier designated the Protestant churches as the daughters of Babylon.[25])
This view was refined by Joseph Marsh, editor of the Millerite periodical
the *Voice of Truth,* as follows:

> There can be no question but that the "woman" is symbolical of the *church,*
> and as she is called *Babylon,* there can be no dispute but that the church is
> Babylon. What church? We can make no distinction no farther than the figure
> will justify. It is a *mother* and her *daughters* — a family of harlots [Rev. 17:5].
> We admit the *mother* represents the Catholic Church the eldest member of the
> family; and we believe her *daughters* symbolize the Protestant sects. If they do
> not, pray what do they represent? . . . We can see no resemblance between
> the *"mother,"* a *unit,* and a *"great city* [Rev. 17:18]."* But the *"whole family"*
> most strictly represents that city. Take the whole and the figure is perfect;
> leave out the *children* and it is imperfect.[26]

In view of the prevailing opposition, Babylon's "oppressive" dimension
was especially stressed in the identification of the Protestant churches as a
part of Babylon. However, the other dimension of Babylon, "confusion,"
was also stressed. It was worked out in a typological relationship between
Babel of Gen. 11 and Babylon of the Apocalypse and analyzed against the
historical development of the Christian church:

> The church commenced building her a tower and a city, under the influence
> of Catholicism. God confounded her language and scattered her; or different
> sects have sprung up; each has built a tower, and attempted to build up a city;
> they too have been confounded and scattered. Hence the work of tower
> building, confounding and scattering, has gone on until perfect "confusion"
> reigns throughout christendom. The great city is complete; and reaching far
> above its many towers is seen the one first reared by the "mother" of the city.
> And upon *her* tower the name of the city is properly inscribed, MYSTERY,
> BABYLON THE GREAT, THE MOTHER OF HARLOTS, AND
> ABOMINATIONS OF THE EARTH. It is inscribed upon the "mother's"
> tower, because as in the case of Babel, the type, "THERE" the works of
> confounding, and from "THENCE" the scattering commenced.[27]

A more church-centered approach in defining Babylon, which united the
aspects of oppression and confusion, was provided by George Storrs.[28] He

---

tion from the churches. However, he did not support the growing preoccupation of many
believers with a call for separatism on the basis of Fitch's exposition of Rev. 18:4. He doubted
the correctness of this interpretation and was concerned that this would divert the attention
from the real issue of proclaiming the Midnight Cry (Letter, Miller to Galusha, April 5, 1844).
For his difficult dilemma whether or not to support separatism, see Letter, Miller to Himes,
AH, May 1, 1844, p. 9.

25   David Simpson, *A Plea for Religion . . . ,* 1824, pp. 211, 212, 439, 440; Elias Smith, *A
Discourse: . . . Nebuchadnezzar's Dream,* 1803, p. 22. Here E. Smith characterized the daughters
of the mother of harlots as those churches which had been "unscripturally connected with the
civil power." He alluded especially to the Church of England and the early American churches
of the colonists.

26   [Marsh], "Babylon," p. 128 (*RH,* Dec. 9, 1851, p. 58).

27   *Ibid.*

28   George Storrs (1796-1879) joined the Congregational Church at the age of 19. Later he

82

reasoned that in the Old Testament, Babylon was the principal oppressor of God's people; in the New Testament it designated the agents who oppress the church of God. In order to identify contemporary Babylon he first defined the true church of God as "that loving unbroken band of believers in any one place, city or town 'who were' of one heart and of one soul" (Acts 4:32) and were characterized by the oneness of Jn. 17:21, 22.[29] Everything that hindered or destroyed this situation he identified as Babylon; that is to say, as

> all these sects, whether Roman Catholics or Protestants, that go to work to divide and bring in "confusion" to the oneness of that Church. And how is this done? It is done by the manufacturing of creeds, whether written or oral, and endeavoring to organize a party; the test of fellowship being now, not love to God and each other, but assent to these creeds. . . . Now look for the loving Church of God; where is it? All is "confusion" — rent and torn into as many parties as there are agents of sects to carry on the Babylonish work. Instead of the Church of God, a loving, united, brotherly body, delighting to meet each other, you now have Baptists, Methodists, Presbyterians, &c., &c., down to the end of the list of divisions; and the so called churches are each making war on the other, not because they do not live as holy as themselves, but because their *creeds differ;* and hence "confusion" or *Babylon* is truly their name.[30]

It was these Babylonian agencies, according to Storrs, that prevented and opposed the witness of the doctrine of the Second Advent in 1843. Those participating in these oppressive activities were "the *old mother,* and all her children; who are known by the family likeness, a domineering, lordly spirit: a spirit to suppress a free search after truth, and a free expression of our conviction of what is truth."[31] Such arguments left Storrs no alternative but to endorse Fitch's conclusion, "Come out of her, my people." At the same time, he warned his readers not to organize another church, for "no church can be organized by man's invention but what it becomes Babylon the *moment it is organized.* The Lord organizes his own church by the strong bonds of love."[32]

The separation of the Millerites from their respective churches did not take place without criticism. In defense of it, Marsh remarked, "I am aware that by some this will be called ultraism, come-outism, or some other ism;

---

became a Methodist and felt the call to the preaching ministry. Because of opposition against his anti-slavery activities he withdrew from the Methodist ministry. In 1842 he came under the influence of the Millerites and began to participate in their movement. He was one of the most vigorous advocates of the Seventh Month movement but one of the first to reject it after the second disappointment. His study on the biblical nature of man led him to accept the doctrine of conditional immortality. Fitch accepted his views but Miller and Litch opposed them. Conditionalism was also accepted by SDA. See Appendix II, Principles XIX-XXI, XXIV; Appendix III, 9-12, 21.

29 Storrs, "Come Out of Her, My People," *MC*, Feb. 15, 1844, p. 237.
30 *Ibid.*
31 *Ibid.,* pp. 237, 238.
32 *Ibid.,* p. 238.

but what of that? we should not seek to please men, but God."[33]

2. The Philadelphian church.

Generally, the Millerites considered themselves to be living in the Laodicean state of the church. When they still belonged to their respective churches, they felt it their mission to reform their churches on the doctrine of the 1843 Second Advent. But when, as we have seen, Millerites left the churches and held separate meetings, the Laodicean church came to be considered the nominal church which Christ had spewed out of His mouth (Rev. 3:15),[34] and the interconfessional movement became crystallized as a new and independent religious group.

One of the earliest attempts to discover a biblical explanation for the recent experience of the new religious community was made in 1844 by J. Weston, a Millerite lecturer, and was based on a new interpretation of the seven churches of Revelation.[35] He accepted Miller's interpretation of the churches Ephesus, Smyrna, and Pergamos, but Thyatira he dated from 538 until 1798, and Sardis from 1798 to "the time [that] the Midnight Cry developed the true state of the nominal church."[36] Sardis, he said, heard the Midnight Cry but rejected it except for "the few names which have not defiled their garments, in the Sardis church, [who] come out at God's command, and constitute the Philadelphia church. And the remainder of the Sardis church, after Philadelphia is separated from them, make up the Laodicean church, which is rejected of Christ at his appearing."[37] This new ecclesiological self-understanding, which identified the Millerites with the Philadelphian church, was intimately related to their personal experience. It grew in importance after 1844 and continued to affect relationships with other churches for many years.

B. The "Year 1843."

1. Time calculations.

When the year 1843 arrived, the Millerite missionary thrust became stronger than ever, for this was the year of the termination of several time prophecies,[38] the year of Christ's personal return, and the last chance for the church and the world to accept the truth. The Millerites were unani-

---

33 "Letter from Bro. Joseph Marsh," *ST*, Jan. 3, 1844, p. 166. Cf. Fitch, *Come Out*, p. 11; Shaw, *Second Coming*, p. 55; Arthur, "Babylon," p. 72. Ingemar Lindén applied the criticism of ultraism to the Seventh Month movement (*Biblicism Apocalyptik Utopi* . . . , 1971, pp. 56-59).

34 Brown, "Withdrawing from the Church," p. 59.

35 See *supra*, p. 47.

36 J. Weston, "The Seven Churches," *AH*, July 3, 1844, p. 174.

37 *Ibid.* Cf. Editorial, "An Open Door," *MC*, June 22, 1843, p. 127; H. H. Gross, "The Times and the Seasons," *WMC*, Feb. 7, 1845, p. 51.

38 See Appendix IV.

mous that "the year 1843" was the year of the Second Advent. Some, however, expected Christ to come within the regular Gregorian calendar year (January 1 to December 31, 1843),[39] whereas Miller himself anticipated this event sometime between March 21, 1843 and March 21, 1844. Miller assumed that the "Jewish mode of computation of time" was based on the reckoning from the vernal equinox of 1843 to the vernal equinox of 1844.[40] Later in the year 1843, when calculation of the Jewish year was further analyzed, it was discovered that there were two methods for determining the Jewish year. One method, Rabbinical reckoning, regulated the "commencement of the year by astronomical calculations," and commenced it with "the first day of the new moon nearest the vernal equinox when the sun is in Aries."[41] According to this method, the Jewish year of 1843 commenced on April 1, 1843 and terminated on March 20, 1844,[42] a period which fell within the limits of Miller's year. The other method was the Karaite reckoning and was derived from the Karaite Jews, a small group who "still adhere to the letter of the Mosaic law, and commence [the year] with the new moon nearest the barley harvest in Judea ... which is one moon later than the Rabinical [sic] year."[43] The Karaites stressed Lev. 23:10, 11, which required the Jews to bring a sheaf of the first fruits of their harvest to the priest as a wave offering on the 16th of the first month, a ceremony which, quite obviously, could only be observed when the barley harvest was ripe in Judea. On this basis, the Karaite Jewish year 1843 commenced on April 29, 1843 and terminated on April 17, 1844.[44] The Millerites also learned that most Jews followed the Rabbinical reckoning because it was more practical to calculate the year by astronomical calculations related to the vernal equinox than by the ripening of the barley harvest in Judea.[45]

During the year 1843 various dates were looked upon with different degrees of interest as possibilities for Christ's return, but there was no unanimity of opinion on any one of them. The earliest of these dates were associated with the termination of the 1335 days of Dan. 12:12.[46] The 1335

39 Editorial, "Fundamental Principles, on Which the Second Advent Cause Is Based," *ST,* May 3, 1843, p. 68. Cf. Editorial, "The New Year," *ST,* Jan. 3, 1844, p. 164. Later on, this position was changed to the Jewish year (Editorial, "Fundamental Principles," *ST,* Nov. 29, 1843, p. 121).
40 Miller, "Synopsis of Miller's Views," p. 147. Cf. Editorial, "The Vernal Equinox," *AH,* April 3, 1844, p. 68. Miller's year was an equinoctial solar year.
41 Editorial, "Chronology," *ST,* June 21, 1843, p. 123.
42 Editorial, "The Midst of the Week," *ST,* Dec. 5, 1843, p. 134; Editorial "Chronology," p. 123. Later, the end of the Rabbinical Jewish year of 1843 was terminated on March 18, 1844 ([Hale], "The Tenth Day of the Seventh Month," *AH,* Sept. 25, 1844, p. 60). Cf. Nathan Daboll, *The New England Almanac . . . ,* 1844, p. 7; Editorial, "The Jewish Year," *MC,* Oct. 11, 1844, p. 117.
43 Editorial, "Chronology," p. 123; Lev. 23:5, 10-21. Cf. Editorial, "Midst of the Week," pp. 133-35.
44 Editorial, "Chronology," p. 123; Daboll, *Almanac,* 1844, p. 8; [Hale], "Seventh Month," p. 60.
45 Editorial, "Chronology," p. 123; Editorial, "Midst of the Week," p. 134.
46 See *supra,* p. 40, n. 199.

days were considered by many Millerites as extending exactly 45 years beyond the termination of the 1290 days of Dan. 12:11, a date to be identified by either one of two events during the French Revolution. The earliest of these events was the capture of Rome on February 10, 1798 by the French army under General Berthier. The other event took place on February 15, 1798, and indicated "the abolition of the papal government and the erection of the Roman Republic."[47] Thus, the 1335 days were regarded as extending to either February 10 or February 15, 1843. As these dates approached, "the expectation with many was on tip-toe, fully believing that the great day of the Lord would then break upon the world."[48]

The second group of dates set by various Millerites was associated with the termination of the 2300 days of Dan. 8:14, an event taken to be precisely 1810 years after the termination of the 70 weeks of Dan. 9:24-27.[49] Many placed the termination of the 70 weeks at the crucifixion of Christ, others, at Ascension or Pentecost; further, there were two schools of thought on the exact date of the Crucifixion, resulting in two sets of dates for the Ascension and Pentecost.

The earliest date for the Crucifixion which drew much attention was the 3rd of April in the year A.D. 33 "when many supposed the 70 weeks expired."[50] James Ferguson's astronomical calculations formed the basis for this date, making it 1810 years to April 3rd, 1843.[51] Those adhering to this opinion thought that the calendar change in 1752, when the British dominions adopted the Gregorian calendar, had no effect on calculations based on the original date.[52] Consequently, in contrast to others who will be discussed below, they would not accept the 14th of April as the date of Christ's death as had been indicated by the Gregorian liturgical calendar of 1843. When Christ failed to appear in April, some among this group pointed to the possibility that the 70 weeks terminated at Christ's ascension, and thought "the 2300 days would expire the middle of May, so that on the anniversary of the ascension of our Lord [May 14], the saints may ascend to meet him in the air."[53] Bliss,

47 [Litch], "RPA," p. 73.
48 *Ibid.,* pp. 73, 74.
49 See *supra,* p. 36.
50 [Bliss], "The End of the Prophetic Periods," *ST,* April 5, 1843, p. 34.
51 *Ibid.* See *supra,* p. 36, n. 180.
52 Bliss in arguing for the 3rd of April date stated that "the difference between Old Style and New Style, was 11 days, which was caused by an addition of 11 minutes to each year, the year being 11 minutes too long, from the time of Julius Caesar. In the last century, this gradual variation had amounted to 11 days, from about the time of the Christian era, so that events that occurred on the 3rd of April in the time of Christ, were made to fall on the 23rd of March, 11 days previous; and what was then the 3rd of April should have been the 14th. To reconcile this discrepancy, in 1752, the 11 days which had been thus added since about the time of the crucifixion, were left out of the calendar; so that what would fall on the 23rd of March, Old Style, was carried forward to the 3rd of April, the same as it would have been had no such variation of 11 minutes each year been made, and therefore the anniversary of events which took place before the variation of 11 days was made, will fall on the same days of the month N.S. after the variation made since the events, is rectified" (*ibid.*). Cf. Editorial, "Time of the End," p. 121.
53 [Bliss], "Prophetic Periods," p. 34.

86

a leading advocate of the April 3rd date for the Crucifixion, favored the Feast of Pentecost. He stated that as the Crucifixion was "April 3rd, A.D. 33 and the 70 weeks seem to have terminated within 50 days after, the 2300 days which extend to the coming of Christ, 1810 years from the 70 weeks, seem to terminate by the 23rd of May, 1843, by which time the righteous have reason to expect to meet their Lord in the air."[54]

Most Millerites, however, advocated the dates for Crucifixion, Ascension, and Pentecost as found on the Gregorian calendar. Litch said: "The 14th of April was a point of time anticipated with the deepest solicitude by many. They had the fullest confidence that it would not pass without bringing the expected crises."[55] When the time passed they looked toward another possible date and continued their missionary activity "with greater zeal than ever," being convinced that their hopes would be fulfilled during the rest of the year.[56] Others looked forward to "the season of Ascension or Feast of Pentecost as being the most likely time for the Advent,"[57]

54 Ibid. The date of May 23 was supported by an unusual interpretation of the 1335 days of Dan. 12:12. The termination of these days signified, according to Bliss, the date the righteous would stand on the new earth. To determine this he associated the termination of the 1290 days of Dan. 12:11 with the phrase "at the time of the end shall the king of the South push at him" (Dan. 11:40). This text symbolized an aspect of the war between Egypt and Napoleon in 1798. The 1290 days were "to extend to the time Egypt [king of the South] should push at Buonaparte, which was the first day of July 1798. The 1335 days extend 45 years after that time, and would therefore terminate on the first of next July; and which from the termination of the 2300 days by the 23rd of May, would be inclusive just forty days. At that time, therefore, the righteous have reason to expect to stand in their lot on the new earth, to shine as the brightness of the firmament, forever, even forever and ever" (ibid., p. 35). In this argument the period of 40 days played an important role, as was indicated by the various O.T. references as to the significance of the figure 40 (ibid.). After the failure of this prediction, it was suggested that the end of the 1335 days was to take place sometime during the 45th anniversary of the period between July 2, 1798 and Feb. 27, 1799 when Napoleon was in Egypt and the king of the South pushed at him (Editorial, "Reply to Brother Turner," ST, July 12, 1843, p. 148).

55 [Litch], "RPA," p. 76. Cf. "Letter from Brother H. B. Skinner," ST, May 31, 1843, p. 99. The passover feast of 1843 also pointed to the typological significance of the deliverance of God's people from Egypt ([Litch], "RPA," p. 74). The fact that the Rabbinical passover fell on April 14th may have given additional importance to this date (Editorial, "Midst of the Week," p. 134).

56 [Litch], "RPA," p. 76.

57 Ibid. According to the liturgical calendar the dates for the Ascension and Pentecost were May 25 and June 4, 1843 (Daboll, Almanac, 1843, pp. 9, 10). In 1844 Litch reaffirmed his previous conviction that the 2300 days terminated with "the anniversary of the ascension" in the spring of 1843 ("Where Are We?," AH, April 17, 1844, p. 87). This argument was based on the idea that the termination of the 70 weeks was determined by the beginning of Christ's priestly ministry in heaven. He remarked that "the last event which was to take place in the 70 weeks, was the anointing of the MOST HOLY, or literally, the HOLY of HOLIES, the Sanctum Sanctorum [Dan. 9:24]." He said: "This anointing [of the earthly sanctuary — Ex. 30:25-31; Lev. 8:10-13] took place immediately previous to and preparatory for the presentation of the blood of the sin offering in the holy place. That ark built by Moses, was a perfect pattern of the tabernacle in heaven, whither Christ is for us entered with his blood as the sin offering, which he shed without the camp. See Heb. 7th to the 10th chapters. What, therefore, Moses and the High Priest did in the pattern, Christ our prophet and priest did in the true tabernacle, heaven itself. That must have been anointed immediately after his ascension into heaven, and before the Pentecost, because the peaceful answer then came, the evidence that he

related not to the third but to the 14th of April.[58]

The next time setting that attracted the attention of Millerites was based on the typological significance of the Jewish ceremonial feasts and was introduced by Miller himself. He pointed out that one "will find all the ceremonies of the typical law that were observed in the first month [Abib or Nisan], or vernal equinox, had their fulfillment in Christ's first advent and sufferings, but all the feasts and ceremonies in the seventh month [Tishri], or autumnal equinox, can only have their fulfillment at his second advent."[59] Some of his arguments were: (1) "The sanctuary, and worshippers, and all appertaining to it, were cleansed on the seventh month tenth to seventeenth day" (Lev. 16:29-34); (2) "the atonement was made on the tenth day seventh month, and this is certainly typical of the atonement Christ is now making for us" (Lev. 16:1-34; Heb. 9:1-28); (3) "when the high priest came out of the holy of holies after making the atonement, he blessed the people. Lev. ix.22, 23; 2 Sam. vi.18. So will our great High Priest. Heb. ix.28. This was on the seventh month tenth day"[60]; (4) the Feast of Tabernacles (Lev. 23:34) was a type of the great day when "Jesus' voice will call forth the righteous dead" (Jn. 5:28, 29; 1 Thes. 4:16).[61] Owing to this reasoning, which explained Dan. 8:14 in the light of Leviticus and Hebrews, he did not expect Christ's coming until after the autumnal equinox. At this stage of the Millerite experience the seventh month of the Jewish year was most likely determined by the Rabbinical reckoning, yielding as limits for this month September 24 and October 24, 1843.[62] One additional reason why this period was looked upon with great interest was that the Jewish Civil Year ended in the month of October.[63] Miller's idea on the antitypical significance of the seventh month was so well appreciated by at least one correspondent that a letter appeared in *Signs of the Times* stating that "father Miller's seventh month will bring the end."[64] When the "autumnal equinox approached, the expectations of many were raised, that the Lord would come at the season of the Feast of Tabernacles."[65]

---

prevailed before the Mercy Seat" (*ibid.*). Cf. Litch, "Discussion," *ST*, Sept. 15, 1840, p. 89. Here he said that "it was 'the Holy of Holies,' 'Heaven itself,' which the Holy of Holies in the tabernacle was a type, which was consecrated [anointed] for us by the sacrifice of Christ, and his appearing there with his own blood for us." (Brackets his.) Cf. Hotchkiss, "Prophetic Periods," p. 39. Miller associated Dan. 9:24 with the entrance of Christ into the holy of holies (*ESH*, 1833, p. 16 [*ST*, May 15, 1841, p. 25]).

58 During this period, non Millerite sources mentioned April 23, 1843 as the Millerite date for the parousia. This was strongly refuted by the Millerites and it was indicated that this rumor originated with the *New York Sun* and even aroused the expectancy for the Second Advent on that specific date in Chile ([Litch], "RPA," p. 87; Litch, "Gospel of the Kingdom," p. 109).

59 Letter, Miller to Himes, *ST*, May 17, 1843, p. 85. This was written "because some were looking to definite days in the *Spring*" (Miller, *Apology*, p. 25).

60 For similar typology, see Macknight, *Apostolic Epistles*, on Heb. 9:28, and John Bunyan, *Solomon's Temple Spiritualized* . . . , 1814, p. 177 (Editorial, "Types," p. 117).

61 Letter, Miller to Himes, *ST*, May 17, 1843, p. 85.

62 Editorial, "Midst of the Week," p. 134.

63 Editorial, "Our Position," *AH*, April 24, 1844, p. 93; [Litch], "RPA," p. 121.

64 "Letter from Bro. H. A. Chittenden," *ST*, Aug. 23, 1843, p. 3.

65 [Litch], "RPA," p. 77. Cf. [Hale], "Seventh Month," *AH*, Sept. 18, 1844, p. 52.

The Millerite leadership rejected the idea of a 1847 return of Christ. Those advocating this date doubted the generally held view of the Crucifixion at the termination of the 70 weeks and interpreted the phrase "in the midst of the week he shall cause the sacrifice and oblation to cease" (Dan. 9:27) as meaning that Christ died in the middle of the 70th week. The 70 weeks would then terminate "3½ years after the crucifixion, with the vision of Peter, when he was shown that the wall between Jew and Gentile was broken down, and Cornelius converted. This is the view of Wolff and others, who are looking to 1847 as the end of the 2300 days, and the end of the world."[66]

2. Calculation adjustments.

During 1843, as a result of careful analysis of the prophetic time calculations, several adjustments were introduced which were gradually accepted. The first correction may be designated the "full year" concept. It was discovered that it was a mistake to calculate the period between 457 B.C. and A.D. 1843 by simply adding the figures together as if they were cardinal numbers. They are ordinal numbers, not separated by a zero year, so that only one year separates 1 B.C. from A.D. 1. It was therefore recognized that in order

> to make out 2300 full years, it is necessary that there should be 457 full years, B.C. and 1843 full years after Christ. It is evident that from a given point in the year 1 B.C., to the same point A.D. 1, would be but one entire year. Upon the same principle, from a given point in the year 457 B.C. to the same point A.D. 1843, would be but 2299 entire years; it is *minus* one year of 2300 full years. . . . If, therefore, the 2300 years began at a given point in the year 457 B.C. they will not end till the same point is reached A.D. 1844.[67]

The second correction was related to the correct year for the parousia. Miller's "Jewish year" from March 21, 1843 to March 21, 1844 was at first quite generally accepted among his followers. Gradually, however, as attention was called to different Jewish reckonings, the general trend of discussion favored the Karaite reckoning above the Rabbinical as being more biblical. Acceptance of the Karaite reckoning led them to the correction of

66 [Bliss], "Prophetic Periods," p. 35. This was advocated by Silar Hawley, Jr., a Millerite lecturer ("Is It Not So?" *ST*, Dec. 5 and 20, 1843, pp. 130-32, 145-49). For an editorial reaction, see "Midst of the Week," pp. 132, 133. The editorial stated that the phrase "in the midst" (Dan. 9:27) besides "middle" had several other meanings so that one could conclude that "the crucifixion might have been in the middle of the week, near the middle, at the end, or only somewhere near the end, so far as criticism on this phrase can fix it" (*ibid.,* p. 133). Litch tried to show that the termination of the 2300 days depended on the strong chonological support for the year A.D. 26-27 as the end of the 69th week and not on the time when the Crucifixion occurred ("The Vulgar Era," *ST*, Dec. 20, 1843, pp. 150-52. Cf. Editorial, "Watch Meeting," *ST*, Jan. 3, 1844, p. 168). For a survey of non-Millerite interpreters on the termination of Dan. 8:14 in 1847, see Froom, *PFF*, IV, 404. Cf. Rev. J. L. Wilson, D.D., "When Shall the Sanctuary Be Cleansed?" *ST*, Jan. 31, 1844, pp. 194, 195.

67 Editorial, "Chronology," p. 123. Cf. Hotchkiss, "The 2300 Days," *MC*, Aug. 22, 1844, p. 49; E. G. White, *SG*, I, 137, 138, 153.

the date for the Crucifixion, because Ferguson, heretofore the Millerite's chief authority on the Crucifixion date, had used the Rabbinical reckoning in determining it.[68] On the basis that the Jewish Passover, according to Rabbinical reckoning, was kept on the day of the first full moon after the vernal equinox and that Christ was crucified on a Friday, Ferguson dated the Crucifixion in the year A.D. 33. According to the Karaite reckoning, however, the Passover was kept at the next full moon one month later, with the result that it could not also fall on a Friday in A.D. 33, making that year an impossible one for the Crucifixion.[69] In this light the view of Dr. William Hales,[70] an Irish clergyman and chronologist, who determined the year of the Crucifixion as A.D. 31 on the basis of historical accounts about the darkening of the sun,[71] came to be generally accepted. Hale placed the Crucifixion in the middle of the 70th week (Dan. 9:27), making the end of the week fall in A.D. 34.[72] His interpretation became especially acceptable because it fitted into the shift of emphasis from the year 1843 to the year 1844 that was going on at that time.

In the winter of 1843-44 the last correction was introduced by Samuel S. Snow.[73] His calculations were based on the assumption that the decree "to restore and to build Jerusalem" (Dan. 9:25) had been issued toward the latter part of 457 B.C. and that the 69th week (Dan. 9:25), according to the "full year" concept, terminated in the autumn of A.D. 27 when Jesus began His ministry as the Messiah.[74] He concluded that

> if, then, the 69 weeks ended in the autumn of A.D. 27, when may we expect the 2300 days to end? The answer is plain. Deduct 483 from 2300, and the remainder is 1817. So many years remained to be fulfilled in the autumn of

68 Editorial, "Turner," p. 149; Hale, "Watchman's Last Warning," AH, April 10, 1844, p. 77.

69 Editorial, "Midst of the Week," pp. 133, 134. The article stated that the astronomical calculation of the first full moon after the vernal equinox could not be considered as absolute evidence for the determination of the exact day of the Jewish Passover because the 14th of Abib was dated at the 14th day after the "appearance" of the moon: "The changing of the moon early or late in the day, would make one day's difference in the time of its appearance" (ibid.). Cf. Hale, "Watchman's Last Warning," p. 77; Editorial, "The Jewish Year," AH, March 20, 1844, pp. 52, 53.

70 William Hales (1747-1831) held during a part of his life a professorship of Oriental Languages at Trinity College in Dublin, Ireland.

71 Hales, A New Analysis of Chronology . . . , II, 1811, p. 564 (cf. Hales, New Analysis, I, 1830, pp. 98-100; III); Editorial, "Midst of the Week," p. 136. On the basis of an early Christian tradition Hales interpreted the unique darkening of the sun as a supernatural event (ibid.; Hales, New Chronology, III, 1830, pp. 230, 231). Cf. E. G. White, SP, III, 1878, pp. 163, 164.

72 Editorial, "Midst of the Week," p. 135.

73 Samuel S. Snow (1806-70) became a Christian at the age of 17 and joined the Congregational Church. After experiencing a period of skepticism he regained his faith through a careful study of Miller's Lectures and other writings on the Second Advent. He began to proclaim the imminence of the parousia. In 1843 he became a Millerite lecturer. He was considered as the initiator of the Seventh Month movement.

74 Letter, Samuel S. Snow to Southard, MC, Feb. 22, 1844, p. 243. Cf. Hales, New Chronology, I, 1830, p. 97. Sixty-nine prophetic weeks are 483 prophetic days or 483 literal years. By taking 457 B.C. as commencement, the termination of this period was A.D. 27.

A.D. 27. Then add to that date, these 1817 years, and we see it brings us to the autumn of A.D. 1844.[75]

Calculations depending on the year of the Resurrection (Dan. 12:11, 12) Snow also adjusted to the year 1844;[76] but although he published his views prior to the spring of 1844, they were not accepted widely until some time after the first disappointment.

3. The first disappointment.

The Gregorian calendar year 1843 passed without the hopes of many at the beginning of that year having been fulfilled.[77] However, because Miller's year and the other Jewish years had not ended, expectations of an imminent return of Christ remained high and missionary activity did not slow down. Announcements of conferences were introduced with the phrase "providence permitting" or "if time continue."[78] Furthermore, the name of the major periodical, the *Signs of the Times*, was changed because

> the advent of the Lord being "at the door" we "herald" its approach with joy. As this paper was in fact the first Herald of the Advent cause as proclaimed by Mr. Miller, and his friends, we now adopt the appropriate title "THE ADVENT HERALD, *and Signs of the Times*." We shall "herald" the Bridegroom's approach by the prophetic word, as God shall give us light, and note the "signs of the times," which show the event at hand.[79]

Just before the disappointment in the spring of 1844, the editors of the *Advent Herald* adopted the name "Adventists" as a suitable name for those participating in the Millerite movement. The rationale for it was as follows:

> Convenience and propriety demand that we should have a name that will convey to the world as true an idea of our position as distinct from that of our opponents, as may be. We have no particular objection to being called "Millerites," the current name applied to us by those who are in the habit of using nicknames, in speaking of their neighbors; but there are many of our number who do not believe with Mr. Miller in several important particulars. It is also his special wish that we should not be distinguished by that appellation. "Believers in the coming of Christ at hand" — which would express the true idea, is quite too long. *Adventists*, the personal advent (or coming) of our Lord Jesus Christ being understood, is both convenient and proper. Its convenience is sufficiently apparent. It is also proper, because it marks the real ground of

75 Letter, Snow to Southard, p. 243.
76 *Ibid.*, pp. 243, 244. Here he began the 1290 days in A.D. 509 and terminated them in 1799, which led him to conclude that the 1335 days also terminated in the autumn of 1844 (*ibid.*, p. 244). Cf. Snow, "Prophetic Chronology," *AH*, Aug. 14, 1844, p. 15; A. Flavell, "The 1290 and 1335 days," *MC*, Oct. 12, 1844, p. 123. Later SDA interpreted Dan. 12:11 again with the 508 and 1843 dates (see *infra*, pp. 169, 170).
77 Editorial, "New Year," p. 164.
78 Cf. Himes, "Second Advent Conference in Boston," *ST*, Jan. 24, 1844, p. 190; Editorial, "Conference in New York," *ST*, Jan. 24, 1844, p. 192.
79 Editorial, "Next Volume," *ST*, Jan. 31, 1844, p. 200.

difference between us and the great body of our opponents.[80]

Although the Karaite reckoning which indicated the end of the Jewish year at the new moon on April 17, 1844, was favored in the major Millerite periodicals,[81] the majority of believers looked to March 21, 1844 as the time for Christ's return. Outside the Millerite movement March 21 was well known and there was "a very general expectation of an entire overthrow of the whole system of Adventism" on that date.[82] Immediately after it passed, Miller wrote that "the time, as I have calculated it, is now filled up; and I expect every moment to see the Savior descend from heaven. I have now nothing to look for but this glorious hope."[83] The disappointment was very real and acknowledged by many (including Miller), who frankly confessed their error.[84] Yet, many remained faithful to the imminent expectancy of Christ's return, and the leaders could state that "our faith is unwavering respecting the reality of those events being already to burst upon us at any moment. And this we can never give up."[85] Not only Millerites, but also the English "Millerites" experienced a disappointment when the Second Advent did not occur in the spring of 1844.[86]

Various reasons explain the fact that the faith of many remained strong. First, although the majority of Millerites were convinced that the Second Advent would take place during the year 1843, there were various opinions on the specific date. Millerite periodicals warned strongly against the setting of a specific date; yet, so great was the freedom of expression, that articles were printed advocating the specific times. This diversity of opinion prevented an over-confidence on the definite time element. Secondly, various time adjustments were introduced which, although not generally accepted during 1843, avoided a too explicit position. Among these, as we have seen, were: (1) The discussion on the Rabbinical versus Karaite reckoning and their influence on the calculation of the Crucifixion, which in turn created some uncertainty about the validity of the end of the 70 weeks as a norm for the termination of the 2300 days; (2) the introduction of the "full year"

80   Hale, "Adventists," *AH,* March 20, 1844, p. 53. Miller claimed that the name Adventists originated with the Millerites ("The Albany Conference," *AH,* June 4, 1845, p. 130). On the use of the name in this study, see *supra,* p. xv.
81   Editorial, "Jewish Year," pp. 52, 53; Editorial, "Vernal Equinox," p. 68; Editorial, "Our Position," p. 93. This position was also stated in one of the earliest Sabbatarian Adventist historical accounts (Bates, *SAWH,* p. 15). Cf. Daboll, *Almanac,* 1844, p. 8. March 21, 1844 was the termination of Miller's vernal equinoctial year which became identified in the mind of many as the Rabbinical year ([Litch], "RPA," p. 79). Later historical works by SDA mention only March 21, 1843 as the first disappointment; see J. White, *Life,* pp. 141, 154; J. N. Loughborough, *The Great Second Advent Movement: Its Rise and Progress,* 1905, p. 150; M. Ellsworth Olsen, *A History of the Origin and Progress of Seventh-day Adventists,* 1925, p. 147. Bates' *Autobiography,* p. 294, favored April 17, 1844.
82   [Litch], "RPA," p. 79.
83   Letter, Miller to Himes, *AH,* April 10, 1844, p. 77.
84   Editorial, "Will You Give It Up Now?" *AH,* April 17, 1844, p. 85; Editorial, "Our Position," p. 92; Miller, "To Second Advent Believers" in Bliss, *Miller,* p. 256.
85   Editorial, "Give It Up Now?" p. 85.
86   Cf. Editorial, "Fundamental Principles . . . ," *SAH,* March 26, 1844, p. 9; Winter, "A Word to Those Who Think the Time Has Passed," *SAH,* April 2, 1844, p. 21; *supra,* p. 81.

concept, which led to a shift of emphasis from the year 1843 to the year 1844. Finally, there was Miller's allusion some weeks before March 21, 1844, to a possible delay: "If Christ comes, as we expect, we will sing the song of victory soon; if not, we will watch, and pray, and preach until he comes, for soon our time, and all prophetic days, will have been fulfilled."[87]

C. The Climax of Millerite Missionary Activity.

1. The "10th day of the seventh month."

Not long after the first disappointment, the Millerites found an explanation that helped maintain their faith in the imminent Second Advent through their interpretation of Hab. 2:3 which suggested a delay:

> "For the vision is yet for an appointed time, but at the end" [of the prophetic periods] "it shall speak and not lie; though it tarry," [beyond their apparent termination] "wait for it; because" [when they are fulfilled] "it will surely come, it will not tarry."[88]

When after the disappointment various Millerites renounced their former convictions, the faithful ones interpreted the delay as a means of purifying the Advent believers so that they were "enabled to know who would have loved to have the Lord come."[89] They called the period after March 21, 1843 the *tarrying time* "when the Bridegroom tarries — Matt. xxv.5, to which the kingdom of heaven should be likened when 'that evil servant [there having been an apparent failure in the time] shall say in his heart, My Lord delayeth his coming.'"[90] This period was also designated as the "little while" (Heb. 10:37), the "quickly" (Rev. 11:14), the "waiting time" (Heb. 2:1, 4), and the "day" (Heb. 10:25).[91]

Immediately following the spring disappointment missionary activity was reduced, but the Midnight Cry and Judgment Hour message continued to be preached but without the emphasis on a definite time period. The missionary thrust was now to induce people to live "in continual readiness and constant expectation of the Lord's coming."[92]

After some months, a time setting expounded by Snow aroused the attention of many Millerites. Already in February 1844, on the basis that the 69th week (Dan. 9:27) terminated in the fall of A.D. 27, he reckoned that the Second Advent would take place in the autumn of 1844.[93] In May

---

87   Miller, "Mr. Miller at Washington," *AH,* March 6, 1844, p. 39.
88   Editorial, "Fundamental Principles," *AH,* April 24, 1844, p. 92. (Brackets his.) Cf. E. G. White, *SG,* I, 138, 153; *ibid.,* IV, 1864, pp. 241, 242. A similar rationale was used in 1843 (Editorial, "If the Vision Tarry, Wait for It," *ST,* Aug. 9, 1843, p. 180).
89   Editorial, "Who Would Love To See the Lord[?]" *AH,* April 17, 1844, p. 86.
90   Editorial, "Our Position," p. 93. (Brackets his.)
91   Himes, "The Gilmanton Feast," *AH,* July 17, 1844, p. 190.
92   Editorial, "Our Position As To Time . . . ," *ASR,* May 1844, p. 125.
93   See *supra,* p. 91. Cf. Snow, "Prophetic Chronology," p. 15. Snow began to propagate his new insights in Jan. 1844 (Letter, Snow to Southard, *MC,* June 27, 1844, p. 397).

1844 Snow calculated the end of the 2300 days in the autumn of 1844 because of his view that the Crucifixion occurred in the middle of the 70th week in the spring of A.D. 31 and the 70th week terminated in the autumn of A.D. 34.[94]

It was in August, 1844, that Snow issued a periodical, the *True Midnight Cry,* for the specific purpose of proclaiming this message. In his exposition Snow assumed that the commencement of the 2300 days and the 70 weeks had to be dated from the time of "the *promulgation and execution*" of the decree (Dan. 9:25) in Judea and not from the time that the decree was first issued.[95] The time of the execution of the decree he found as follows:

> From Ezra vii.8, 9 we learn that Ezra began to go up [to Jerusalem] on the first day of the first month, and arrived at Jerusalem on the first day of the fifth month, in the 7th year of Artaxerxes, B.C. 457. Having arrived at Jerusalem, he appointed magistrates and judges, and restored the Jewish Commonwealth, under the protection of the king of Persia, as he was fully authorized to do by the decree of Artaxerxes. This necessarily required some little time, and brings us to the point when, the restoring having been effected, the building of the street and wall commenced. The 70 weeks are divided into three parts: 7 weeks, 62 weeks, and 1 week — see Dan. ix.25. The connection shows that the 7 weeks were allotted for the building of the street and wall. They therefore commenced when they began to build, in the autumn of B.C. 457; from that point, 2300 years reach to the autumn of A.D. 1844.[96]

Another method of verifying this calculation Snow based on the relation between the date of the Crucifixion and the termination of the 70 weeks. The termination of the 69th week he placed at the time of "the manifestation of the Messiah" when "Jesus began the proclamation of the gospel in Galilee, in the autumn of A.D. 27."[97] Three and a half years later, in the middle of the 70th week (Dan. 9:27), "Jesus caused the sacrifice and the oblation to cease by offering himself as a Lamb, without spot, to God upon the cross."[98] Snow accepted Dr. Hales' view that the Crucifixion occurred in the spring of A.D. 31 and stated that it was confirmed by the Karaite

94 Snow, "Dear Brethren of the Advent Faith," *MC,* May 2, 1844, p. 353 [335]. Here he determined the year A.D. 31 on the dating of the reign of Tiberius, the ministry of John the Baptist, and Christ's ministry of 3½ years. Cf. Snow, "Prophetic Chronology," *MC,* Sept. 19, 1844, p. 87.

95 Snow, *TMC,* Aug. 22, 1844, p. [2]. For an extensive study on the significance of the decrees of Cyrus, Darius I, and Artaxerxes for "the going forth of the commandment to restore and to build Jerusalem" (Dan. 9:25), see Andrews, *The Commandment to Restore and to Build Jerusalem,* 1865.

96 Snow, *TMC,* p. [2]. Cf. E. G. White, *GC,* pp. 327, 398, 399. For a recent scholarly study by two SDA which advocated the year 457 B.C. for Ezra's journey in the 7th regnal year of Artaxerxes, see Siegfried H. Horn and Lynn H. Wood, *The Chronology of Ezra 7,* 2nd ed., rev., 1970.

97 Snow, *TMC,* p. [3]. Snow added that Jesus Himself told the Jewish nation when the period of 69 weeks had terminated by proclaiming, "The time is fulfilled" (Mk. 1:14, 15; Mt. 4:12, 17; Acts 10:37). Cf. E. G. White, *GC,* p. 327.

98 Snow, *TMC,* p. [3]. Cf. E. G. White, *GC,* pp. 327, 328.

reckoning.[99] The covenant of Dan. 9:27 he identified with "the new covenant, i.e. the gospel" while its confirmation signified its establishment "on a *firm foundation*" during the 70th week, when "the covenant was *confirmed* half a week by Christ, and the other half by his apostles."[100] The termination of the 70th week occurred in the autumn of A.D. 34 when Paul was converted and became the last apostolic witness to confirm the covenant.[101] From the end of the 70th week he arrived at the autumn of 1844:

> As Jesus Christ was crucified in the midst or middle of the week, and the day of the Passover, which was the fourteenth day of the first month, it follows that the week began in the 7th month of A.D. 27, and ended in the 7th month of A.D. 34. . . . And from the 7th month of A.D. 34, 1810 years extended to the 7th month of A.D. 1844.[102]

Although these calculations indicated the season in which the Second Advent would take place, the exact date was determined by Snow through the typological argument which had been expounded by Miller more than a year before. Miller had shown that the Jewish feasts were types that were to be fulfilled by Christ at both His First and Second Advent.[103] According to Snow, the vernal types which had been fulfilled at the First Advent were: (1) The Passover with its antitype in the death of Christ as the Passover Lamb (1 Cor. 5:7); (2) the offering of the first fruits of the harvest on the morning after the Sabbath (Lev. 23:6, 7, 10, 11) with its antitype in the resurrection of Christ as the first fruits from the dead (1 Cor. 15:20-23); (3) the Feast of Weeks (Lev. 23:15, 16), seen as the anniversary of the Lord's descent on Mount Sinai at the giving of the Law, with its antitype in the descent of the Holy Spirit at Pentecost.[104] However, the autumnal types which were observed in the seventh month of the Jewish year never had their fulfillment in the antitype. The only explanation for this he found in the assumption that they were to be fulfilled at the Second Advent. It was the type of the Day of Atonement, Yom Kippur, which led Snow to the calculation of the exact date of Christ's return, stating that on the Day of Atonement, the 10th day of the seventh month,

> the high priest went into the most holy place of the tabernacle, presenting the blood of the victim before the mercy seat, after which on the *same day* he came out and blessed the waiting congregation of Israel. See Lev. ix.7, 22, 23, 24, and Lev. 16th chap.; Heb. v.1-6, and ix.1-12, 27, 28. Now the *important point* in this type is the *completion* of the reconciliation at the *coming* of the high priest *out of* the holy place. The high priest was a type of Jesus our High Priest; the most holy place, a type of heaven itself; and the coming out of the high

99 Snow, *TMC*, p. [3].
100 *Ibid.*
101 *Ibid.*, p. [4]. Cf. E. G. White, *GC*, p. 328.
102 Snow, *TMC*, p. [4].
103 See *supra*, p. 88.
104 *Ibid.* On the typological significance of the Mosaic institutions, see [Hale], "Seventh Month," pp. 52, 53, 60-62; Editorial, "Behold! the Bridegroom Cometh!" *AH*, Oct. 9, 1844, pp. 78, 79.

priest a type of the coming of Jesus the second time to bless his waiting people. As this was on the tenth day of the 7th month [Karaite reckoning], so on that day Jesus will certainly come, because not a *single point* of the law is to fail. *All must be fulfilled.*[105]

It was a rather general belief that Christ, as the antitypical High Priest, had entered into the most holy place of the heavenly sanctuary after His ascension to perform His intercessory work. The Millerites concluded that, after the completion of this ministry, Christ would come out of the most holy place to bless His people, just as, according to their exegesis, the high priest of the earthly sanctuary did after having completed his atoning ministry, on the 10th day of the seventh month.[106]

2. The "True Midnight Cry."

For months Snow's calculations aroused but little attention. At the Exeter camp meeting (August 12-17, 1844), however, his exact date for Christ's return stirred many Millerites with an enormous enthusiasm, bringing their missionary endeavor to a peak. Their response as a whole came quickly to be known as the Seventh Month movement.[107] Although the Millerite leaders recognized some value in Snow's position, they were skeptical about the renewed emphasis on time and pointed out that "in view of our Savior's assurance, that we know not 'the day or the hour,' or as some read it, no man 'maketh it known,' we should hesitate before we should feel authorized to attempt to 'make known' the very day."[108] Some weeks before the expected event, however, the leaders joined the Seventh Month movement and allowed Snow's views to be printed in the major Millerite periodicals and gave their full support.[109] After Snow's influence on the British "Millerites" they also paid attention to the subject of the 10th day of the seventh month.[110]

This enthusiastic revival of missionary enterprise was interpreted as the

105   Snow, *TMC*, p. [4]. Cf. Hotchkiss, "Prophetic Periods," pp. 38, 39; Peavey, "The Seventh Month," *MC*, Sept. 12, 1844, p. 75; Peavey, "Bridegroom," p. 103; Storrs, " 'Go Ye Out To Meet Him,' " *Bible Examiner*, Sept. 24, 1844, p. [1]; Editorial, "Bridegroom," p. 79; Editorial, "Types," pp. 116, 117; Miller, "Bro. Miller's Letter on the Seventh Month," *MC*, Oct. 12, 1844, p. 122; Hale, "Whiting," pp. 82, 83; Editorial, "Address to the Public," *AH*, Nov. 13, 1844, pp. 109, 110. The Feast of Tabernacles, which began on the 15th day of the 7th month (Lev. 23:34-43), Snow interpreted as "a type of the marriage supper of the Lamb; which will be celebrated in the New Jerusalem, the tabernacle of God which is to be with men" (*TMC*, p. [4]).

106   See *supra*, p. 80, n. 60. The idea that Christ would enter the holy place on the antitypical Day of Atonement was dismissed (Hale, "Whiting," p. 83).

107   Bliss, "The Seventh Month Movement . . . ," *ASR*, Jan. 1845, p. 267.

108   Editorial, "The Exeter Campmeeting," *AH*, Aug. 21, 1844, p. 20. On Litch's scepticism of Snow's views, see "The Seventh Month," *AH*, Aug. 21, 1844, p. 21; "The Deliverance — the Seventh Month," *AH*, Sept. 11, 1844, pp. 46, 47.

109   Miller, "Miller's Letter," p. 121; Himes, "The Time of the Advent," *AH*, Oct. 9, 1844, p. 80, Litch, "Bro. Litch on the Seventh Month," *AH*, Oct. 16, 1844, 2nd ed., p. 81. Whiting remained doubtful as to the exact date (Hale, "Whiting," pp. 81-83).

110   Editorial, "The Seventh Month," *Advent Harbinger and Midnight Alarm* [Aug. ? 1844], pp. 7, 8. Cf. *supra*, p. 81.

exact fulfillment of the parable of the ten virgins of Mt. 25 and was identified as the True Midnight Cry. According to Storrs, the previously proclaimed Midnight Cry was "but the *alarm*. NOW THE REAL ONE IS SOUNDING: and Oh, how solemn the hour."[111] He interpreted the ten virgins of the parable not any more as symbolizing mankind in general as Miller had done,[112] but as "the professed believers in the advent in '1843.' "[113] After the first disappointment, he felt that the virgins entered the tarrying time because they all slumbered and slept on the subject of the exact time of the Second Advent, but the True Midnight Cry aroused them at midnight so that the believers in the imminent return of Christ began searching their Bibles to verify the validity of the new insight into the exact date of the parousia.[114]

Storrs pointed out that the parable provided the chronology of the tarrying time and the explanation for the True Midnight Cry of the Seventh Month movement. The tarrying time, he argued, would last for half a year,

> because, our Lord says "at mid-night," while the Bridegroom tarried. This vision was for "2300 evening mornings," or days. An "evening," or night is half of one of those prophetic days, and is therefore six months. That is the whole length of the tarrying time. The present strong cry of time commenced about the middle of July, and has spread with great rapidity and power, and is attended with a demonstration of the Spirit, such as I never witnessed when the cry was "1843." It is now literally, "go ye out to meet him."[115]

Thus, the time element "at midnight" (Mt. 25:6) was interpreted in the context of the 2300 days of Dan. 8:14 and the year-day principle. The commencement of the tarrying time he dated in "March or April" 1844 and the termination of the 10th of the seventh month as not "farther off than October 22 or 23: it may be sooner."[116] Storrs stated that the True Mid-

---

111 Storrs, " 'Go Ye Out,' " p. [1]. Storrs' exposition on Mt. 25 was repr. in the major Millerite periodicals.
112 See *supra*, p. 40.
113 Storrs, " 'Go Ye Out,' " p. [2].
114 Storrs, "The Lord's Chronology," *MC*, Oct. 3, 1844, p. 102.
115 Storrs, " 'Go Ye Out,' " p. [2]. Cf. Editorial, "The Advent Herald," *AH*, Oct. 30, 1844, p. 93; J. White, *Life*, p. 165; E. G. White, *SG*, IV, 248; E. G. White, *GC*, pp. 398, 426-28. According to Bates, Snow gave the True Midnight Cry in the Tabernacle in Boston about July 20, 1844. Then it was presented at a camp meeting in Concord, New Hampshire, about the first of August before it was presented at Exeter *(SAWH*, p. 30).
116 Storrs, " 'Go Ye Out,' " p. [2]. To clear the uncertainty about the exact dating of the 10th day of the 7th month on the Gregorian calendar, Hale published Oct. 22, 1844 as the Jewish Day of Atonement according to Karaite reckoning ("Seventh Month," p. 60). Although the editor of the *Midnight Cry* suggested Oct. 23, 1844 (Editorial, "Jewish Year," p. 117), the periodical also published articles favoring Oct. 22 for the parousia. There was also the suggestion that the event could take place between Oct. 22 and 24 (Editorial, "Time at Jerusalem," *MC*, Oct. 19, 1844, p. 132). In the last issue before the expected event, Oct. 22 was favored (Himes, "Disturbances at the Tabernacle," *MC*, Oct. 19, 1844, p. 136). Because of circumstances due to variations of the moon and the ripening of the harvest by which the Karaite year was determined, it could sometimes occur that the Karaite and the Rabbinical year commenced with the same new moon. This resulted in the idea that there was even a possibility that the 7th month could commence with the new moon in Sept. 1844 (Peavey, "Seventh Month," p. 75). Cf. Editorial, "The Seventh Month," *AH*, Sept. 11, 1844, p. 45.

night Cry commenced "at midnight" in the middle of the tarrying time in "the latter part of July," when

> God put this cry into the hearts of some of his servants, and they saw, from the Bible, that God had given the chronology of the tarrying time, and its length. There it is, in the 25th of Mat. — "At midnight there was a cry made, BEHOLD THE BRIDEGROOM COMETH; GO YE OUT TO MEET HIM." Here we are — the last warning is now sounding!![117]

It was the historicization of the parable of Mt. 25 that gave the Millerites the conviction that they fulfilled a vital part in the consummation of the history of salvation. The self-identification of those participating in the Seventh Month movement with the virgins in the parable explains in large measure why the imminence of Christ's coming did not paralyze their missionary activity. In the parable the sleeping virgins were awakened through the proclamation of the midnight cry regarding the coming of the Bridegroom. To those preaching the True Midnight Cry this indicated that, with their message of the definite time for the coming of the Bridegroom, they had the responsibility of awakening the sleeping virgins. It was especially this self-understanding of being participants in a prophetic movement that transformed their fervent eschatological expectations into a zealous missionary enthusiasm. Thus Storrs could report that this last warning progressed during September 1844 "with the rapidity of lightning."[118] Regarding its effects on believers he stated:

> Where this cry gets hold of the heart, farmers leave their farms, with their crops standing, to go out and sound the alarm — and mechanics their shops. There is a strong crying with tears, and a consecration of all to God, such as I never witnessed. There is a confidence in this truth such as was never felt in the previous cry, in the same degree; and a weeping or melting glory in it that passes all understanding except to those who have felt it.[119]

During this time even "tobacco and snuff boxes, and pipes" were sacrificed, their use being considered "an idle and sinful habit" that neither benefited the body nor glorified God.[120]

It does not seem that they envisaged a world-wide proclamation of the True Midnight Cry (the time being so short), but many did as much as possible to warn others. The main thrust and purpose of this last mission of warning, according to Storrs, was to wake up the sleeping virgins — those who had been believers in the Advent message in 1843.[121] In regard to man's salvation the general feeling among participants in the Seventh Month movement seems to be that those who loved Christ and His appearing would demonstrate the fact by accepting the message of the imminent

117 Storrs, " 'Go Ye Out,' " p. [2].
118 Storrs, "Lord's Chronology," p. 102.
119 Storrs, " 'Go Ye Out,' " p. [2].
120 Bates, *SLG,* 1849, p. 67.
121 Storrs, " 'Go Ye Out,' " p. [1].

personal return of Christ and separate themselves from fallen Babylon before the door of probation would close and the destiny of human lives be fixed forever.

3. The second or great disappointment.

Shortly before the expected event nearly all Millerites participated in the proclamation of the True Midnight Cry of the Seventh Month movement, and it was stated that "the time has been almost universally received by all the Adventists."[122] Miller anticipated that probationary time for mankind would terminate a few days before October 22, stating, "I am strong in my opinion that the next [October 13] will be the last Lord's day sinners will ever have in probation and within ten or fifteen days from thence, they will see him, whom they have hated and despised."[123] On the 16th of October, the editors of the *Advent Herald* expressed the following sentiments:

> We feel that we have arrived at a most solemn and momentous crisis; and from the light we have, we are shut up to the conviction that the tenth day of the seventh month must usher in the glorious appearing of the great God and our Savior Jesus Christ. We therefore feel that our work is now finished, and that all we have to do is to go out to meet the Bridegroom, and to trim our lamps accordingly. . . . Now we feel that our controversies are all over, that the battle has been fought, and our warfare ended. And now we wish to humble ourselves under the mighty hand of God that we may be accepted at his coming.[124]

When Tuesday, October 22, passed, the Millerites experienced a very great disappointment that could be best described by those who experienced it. Hiram Edson, a Millerite with Methodist background, said:

> Our expectations were raised high, and thus we looked for our coming Lord until the clock tolled 12 at midnight. The day had then passed and our disappointment became a certainty. Our fondest hopes and expectations were blasted, and such a spirit of weeping came over us as I never experienced before. It seemed that the loss of all earthly friends could have been no comparison. We wept, and wept, till the day dawn. I mused in my own heart, saying, My advent experience has been the richest and brightest of all my Christian experiences. If this had proved a failure, what was the rest of my Christian experience worth? Has the Bible proved a failure? Is there no God, no heaven, no golden home city, no paradise? Is all this but a cunningly devised fable? Is there no reality to our fondest hope and expectation of these things? And thus we had something to grieve and weep over, if all our fond hopes were lost.[125]

122   Editorial, "The Meetings at the Tabernacle," *AH,* Oct. 16, 1844, p. 88.
123   Miller, "Seventh Month," p. 122. Cf. Bates, *SAWH,* pp. 40, 41.
124   Editorial, "To Our Readers," *AH,* Oct. 16, 1844, p. 88.
125   Edson, MS (Incomplete), Experience in the Advent Movement, n.d., pp. 8, 9. Cf. J. White, *Life,* pp. 180-82.

Some Millerites renounced their beliefs and either returned to their former churches or rejected the Christian faith altogether. However, many of those who had separated themselves from the churches remained faithful, waiting for the return of Christ which could occur any moment. Now most of their attention was directed toward encouraging one another and looking for signs which would indicate the inauguration of the Second Advent.

D. Summary.

During the 1843-44 period a shift took place in the ecclesiology of the Millerites. The concept of Babylon came to be theologically formulated in relation to both the Roman Catholic Church and the Protestant churches. The rejection of the proclamation of the Midnight Cry, the Judgment Hour message, and the fast growing anti-Millerite sentiment among Protestants led to the conclusion that their churches had not only become a part of Babylon but that the fall of Babylon was a present reality. This added a new dimension to the Millerite mission proclamation: the call to God's people to separate themselves from Babylon.

In this crisis period various attempts were made to discover the precise date for Christ's return, and various dating systems were employed in determining both the limits of the year 1843 and the specific time within that year when the Second Advent was to occur. A number of time settings were made during that year. The failure of a time setting did not diminish the hopes and missionary zeal of most Millerites because they were convinced that the Second Advent had to take place within 1843. Every failure brought them closer to the parousia, implying that the next time setting could be looked upon with greater expectation than the previous ones. These expectations were translated into an active mission to warn others of the coming events because they realized their responsibility for the salvation of mankind. Thus these time settings played an important part in the missionary activity. When finally the end of the year 1843 passed without the appearance of Christ Millerites experienced a general disappointment. For some their mission outreach slowed down. Further adjustments of time calculations and a study of the cleansing of the sanctuary in the light of the typological implications of the Old Testament Day of Atonement for Christ's high-priestly ministry led to the most important time-setting movement — the Seventh Month movement — which predicted the Second Advent to occur on October 22, 1844, the 10th day of the seventh month of the Jewish Karaite year. This movement, which brought about a great revival of missionary enthusiasm, was identified as the True Midnight Cry and interpreted as the fulfillment of the parable of the ten virgins. Stimulated by convincing arguments, the Millerites went forth in a final attempt to proclaim their message of warning. When Christ did not return at the predicted time, the second or great disappointment was a reality.

Part Two

The Formation of the Seventh-day Adventist
Theology of Mission

In this chapter the aftermath of the second or great disappointment will be discussed in the context of the early development of the Sabbatarian Adventists. From 1845 onward the majority of Adventists began to interpret this Disappointment[1] as another failure in their time calculations. However, for a minority the mistake was not in the time setting but in the prediction of the nature of the event which was to take place on October 22, 1844. From this minority the Sabbatarian Adventists emerged. Therefore special attention will be given to attempts by this group in their search for a biblical rationale for the Disappointment which would vindicate the Seventh Month movement as a vital event in the history of salvation. Furthermore it will be shown how Sabbatarian Adventists integrated the Sabbath doctrine into their 1844 experience, an integration responsible for the unique relation between the Sabbath and the imminent parousia in their theology of mission. Developments in ecclesiological self-understanding gave Sabbatarian Adventists a self-identity which justified their mission among other Adventists. The chapter concludes with a description of the gradual missiological development from a position which confined the outreach to Adventists, toward a view that Sabbatarian Adventists had a future mission to non-Adventists who had not yet rejected the doctrine of the imminent Second Advent. Some of the most influential Sabbatarian Adventists were James White,[2] his wife Ellen G. White[3] (nee Ellen G. Harmon),

1 From now on the term "Disappointment" refers exclusively to the second or great disappointment.

2 James Springer White (1821-1881), who was largely a self-made man, was recognized as one of the most outstanding leaders among Sabbatarian Adventists and SDA. When he joined the Millerite movement White began a preaching ministry. In the beginning of 1845 he became acquainted with Ellen G. Harmon and was married on August 30, 1846. During the autumn of that year they began to observe the Sabbath. In 1849 he began a publishing work. He founded various periodicals such as *PT* (1849), *AdR* (1850), *RH* (1850), and *YI* (1852). As long as he lived White was the leading influence in the *RH* and most of the time he functioned as either editor or corresponding editor. He wrote many articles and a number of pamphlets. Furthermore he wrote or edited several books and produced charts. In the 1850s he took the lead in urging organization among the Sabbatarian Adventists. This culminated in the formation of a General Conference of SDA in 1863. For a number of years he served as the president of the General Conference. See *SDAE*, pp. 1419-25.

3 Ellen Gould White (1827-1915) was one of the most influential personalities among Sabbatarian Adventists and SDA. At the age of 12 she was baptized by immersion and joined the Methodist Church. In 1843 she and her parents were disfellowshiped because they had accepted Miller's teachings. After the Disappointment she received what she and some other

Joseph Bates,[4] Hiram Edson,[5] and John N. Andrews.[6]

A. *The Vindication of the Seventh Month Movement.*

The Adventists were deeply disappointed that Jesus did not return at the end of the prophetic time calculations. Although some of them rejected the Advent movement altogether immediately after the passing of the expected time, the hopes of many continued to be strong, and there was for awhile a constant state of expectancy that Christ would return at any time.

This great disappointment was interpreted as another and "more searching test" than the first disappointment, and it was seen to be destined to purify the believers.[7] An analogy was drawn with the experience of Jonah in Nineveh. In the Jonah experience an explanation was found which "justified the preaching of *time,* although the event did not occur as predicted."[8] It was pointed out that "we have done the will of God in thus sounding the alarm, as we believe that Jonah did when he entered into Nineveh."[9] Another analogy which brought comfort was found in the experience of Abraham when he was going to offer Isaac on Mount Moriah. On the basis of typology it was argued that

> no one will say that Abraham was mistaken in believing that he was to slay his son; but God chose this very way to test his faith. Even so do we believe that

Adventists identified as revelations from God. In this they recognized the revival of the biblical gift of prophecy which was designated as "Spirit of Prophecy." As a result the Sabbatarian Adventists considered her statements on spiritual matters to be of great authority. In the theological and organizational developments as well as in the establishment of a publishing work, a medical missionary work, and a mission on a world-wide scope, she had a decisive and guiding influence. She was an extremely prolific writer of letters, manuscripts, articles, pamphlets, and books. Besides this she also traveled extensively through several continents giving lectures and counsel on spiritual matters. See *SDAE,* pp. 1406-14.

4   Joseph Bates (1792-1872) was a former sea captain, a Millerite preacher, and one of the principal leaders of the Sabbatarian Adventists. He was involved in the Temperance movement before he became an active participant in the Millerite movement. After the Disappointment he read an article on the seventh-day Sabbath by T. M. Preble and decided to observe that day as the biblical day of rest. He was instrumental in convincing J. White, E. G. White, and H. Edson to accept the Sabbath.

5   Hiram Edson (1806-82) was an Adventist with a Methodist background. He seemed to be responsible for the earliest biblical rationale for the Disappointment, which stressed the validity of the Seventh Month movement in context of a change in Christ's high-priestly ministry. This view was further developed by his protégé O. R. L. Crosier and published in the *DD* and *DS* in 1846. It became the standard view among SDA.

6   John N. Andrews (1829-83) was one of the principal leaders of the SDA. In 1846 he accepted the Sabbath doctrine. He was one of the major contributors to the formation of their doctrines, a prolific writer, and one of their best scholars. He functioned both as editor and corresponding editor of the *RH.* In 1874 he became their first American-born missionary to Europe.

7   Editorial, "Address to the Public," *AH,* Nov. 13, 1844, p. 109. Later the necessity was recognized of a spiritual regeneration through the "furnace of affliction" (Editorial, "The Body of Christ," *DS,* June 13, 1846, p. 9). Cf. E. G. White, *SG,* I, 148, 157.

8   Editorial, "Public," p. 109. Cf. E. G. White, *SP,* IV, 254.

9   Editorial, "Public," p. 109.

God permitted the preaching of this last time for the same purpose respecting his children now, to test their faith. And we should have sinned none the less, had we desired in our hearts to delay the Lord's coming, than Abraham would, had he withheld his son. God has brought us to mount Moriah, and he will deliver us, or provide for us a lamb.[10]

Furthermore a typological significance was seen in the experience of the disciples who participated in the triumphal entry of Jesus, which was a fulfillment of prophecy (Mt. 21:1-11), but who were utterly disappointed at His crucifixion. J. B. Cook,[11] an Adventist lecturer and a former Baptist minister, stated that the disciples "were disappointed, because they misconceived his design in fulfilling that predicted event. The prophecy was however, *just* as *really fulfilled,* as if they had correctly conceived God's purposes, and realized their expectations."[12] Through typological argumentation he pointed out that

> the mistake was of precisely the same nature with that of the Holy Twelve, and others, Mat. 21:4. They overlooked the events which were to intervene between that prophetic fulfillment and the Kingdom. They mistook our Lord's design in that fulfillment. *It was however a fulfillment.* So in our case precisely, God's will was done.[13]

Cook's argument was influenced by his philosophy of divine providence which said that God did not guide His people "into their mistakes, but He employs them, *notwithstanding their mistakes.* He verifies His promises to them in spite of all their weaknesses, and gradually brings them to 'understand,' both his word and Providence."[14]

Hiram Edson, who became a pioneer among the Sabbatarian Adventists, interpreted the Disappointment in the context of Rev. 10:8-10, stating that "the seventh angel had begun to sound; we had eaten the little book; it had been sweet in our mouths, and it had now become bitter in our belly, embittering our whole being."[15]

Interpretations of the Disappointment in the context of a shut door and

---

10 *Ibid.*

11 John B. Cook (1804-74) advocated the validity of the Seventh Month movement and the idea of a shut door in 1844. Immediately after the Disappointment he published together with J. D. Pickands a periodical, the *Voice of the Fourth Angel.* In 1846 he joined the Sabbatarian Adventists and for some time he advocated the Sabbath. But after 1849 he became one of their opponents.

12 [J. B. Cook], "The Doctrine of Providence," *AT,* March 1846, p. 4.

13 [Cook], "Providence," p. 5. Cf. E. G. White, *SG,* IV, 253, 254; E. G. White, *GC,* pp. 351, 352, 404, 405.

14 [Cook], "The Necessity and Certainty of Divine Guidance," *AT,* March 1846, p. 6. He added that "the Apostles exhibited their full share of human infirmity, by misconceiving the purposes of Jesus, though they were honored, to fulfill the prophecies concerning his first Advent. They were 'willing to do his will;' therefore they were guided 'into all truth.' They did understand as the unfolding purpose of Jehovah was gradually opened to their minds. In every instance their weakness, as well as ignorance was overruled to fulfill scripture. . . . So with the 2d Advent people, God has led them in 'His way,' at every turn, and in every trial they fulfill scripture."

15 Edson, MS, pp. 9, 10.

Christ's high-priestly ministry[16] provided an additional reason why the Second Advent did not take place on the 10th day of the seventh month, 1844. Later, Sabbatarian Adventists pointed to the fact that the seventh-day Sabbath had to be restored before the return of Christ could occur.

1. The immediate soteriological-missiological consequences of the Disappointment.

> And while they went to buy, the bridegroom came; and they that were ready went in with him to the marriage: and the door was shut. Afterward came also the other virgins, saying, Lord, Lord, open to us. But he answered and said, Verily I say unto you, I know you not. Mt. 25:10-12.

Immediately after the Disappointment there was among nearly all Adventists a feeling that the door of Mt. 25:10, which had been identified as the door of mercy for the churches and the world, had been shut forever on the 10th day of the seventh month, 1844. For a short period of time this "extreme" shut-door concept, which excluded the possibility of salvation for all who had not participated in the Seventh Month movement and separated themselves from the churches,[17] brought nearly all missionary efforts of Adventists among non-Adventists to a complete stop. Some weeks after the Disappointment Miller wrote:

> We have done our work in warning sinners, and in trying to awake a formal church. God in his providence had shut the door; we can only stir one another up to be *patient;* and be diligent to make our calling and election sure. We are now living in the time specified by Malachi iii:18, also Daniel xii:10, Rev. xxii:10-12. In this passage we cannot help but see that a little while before Christ should come, there would be a separation between the just and unjust, the righteous and wicked, between those who love his appearing and those who hate it. And never since the days of the apostles has there been such a division line drawn, as was drawn about the 10th or 23rd day of the 7th Jewish month.[18]

The reaction of society in general against the Adventists was to them evidence of the correctness of their shut-door views. Miller described this reaction as follows:

> The amount of scoffing and mocking at the present time, is beyond any

16 See *infra*, pp. 115-32.
17 See *supra*, pp. 96-98. The shut-door question was especially related to the message of the Seventh Month movement. Because the Seventh Month movement mainly affected the North American continent, the discussion on the shut-door idea pertained especially to that part of the world. Therefore hardly any reference was made regarding the conditions for salvation in areas outside North America. However, one can conjecture that, according to many Millerites, salvation was within the reach of those who had accepted their Second Advent doctrine because it had been distributed through literature on a world-wide scope. Those who had rejected that message were considered lost.
18 Letter, Miller to Himes, *AH*, Dec. 11, 1844, p. 142. Cf. Letter, Brown to Bliss, *AH*, Dec. 11, 1844, p. 139. For an elaborate statement on Miller's reasons for a shut door, see Letter, Miller to Bliss, *AH*, Feb. 12, 1845, pp. 2, 3. Later he denied his shut-door convictions (Letter, Miller to Brother, *MW*, March 20, 1845, pp. 91, 92). Cf. *supra*, pp. 43, 44.

calculation. We can hardly pass a man, professor or non-professor, but what he scoffingly inquires "You have not gone up," or "God cannot burn the world," &c., ridiculing the Bible itself, and blaspheming the word and power of God. And yet ministers and moral editors wink at it. And some of them are performing the same, to the no small joy of the most depraved characters in [the] community.[19]

The reaction of Adventists who rejected the Advent movement immediately after the Disappointment was no less hostile than that of society at large, causing Miller to question whether this group had not "sinned against the Holy Ghost."[20]

In the January issue of the *Advent Mirror*, which was devoted to a new interpretation of the coming of the Bridegroom as a rationale for the Disappointment, the editors Apollos Hale and Joseph Turner[21] saw the shut-door concept confirmed by the contemporary religious situation.[22] At this time Turner advocated also the view that Christ's atonement had been completed on October 22, 1844.[23] The attitude of both editors toward the possibility of new conversions must be interpreted against the contemporary polemic among Adventists regarding the validity of the Seventh Month movement. Toward the end of 1844 various Adventists began to question the correctness of the Seventh Month movement and the idea of the shut door on the basis of rumors regarding new conversions.[24] It was therefore no surprise that in general the acceptance of the idea of new converts was

19 Letter, Miller to Himes, *AH,* Dec. 11, 1844, p. 142. Cf. Letter, Wm. Gage to Enoch Jacobs, *DS,* Sept. 20, 1845, p. 27. In 1845 J. White summarized the public reaction in the State of Maine: "We have been brought before magistrates — publically whipped — put in the jail — workhouse, and families torn asunder — all to prevent us from following the Lamb: but to no effect" (Letter, J. White to Jacobs, *DS,* Sept. 6, 1845, p. 17). Cf. C., " 'In Prison,' " *HI,* April 17, 1845, p. 3.

20 Letter, Miller to I. E. Jones, *AH,* Dec. 25, 1844, p. 154. Cf. Letter, Miller to J. O. Orr, Dec. 13, 1844.

21 Joseph Turner was a Millerite preacher. After the Disappointment he seemed to be co-editor of the *HI.* At first he had cordial relations with E. G. Harmon and her family but when he became involved in fanaticism the friendship was terminated and he became her opponent (E. G. White, *SG,* II, 49, 50, 62, 63, 67, 68).

22 They remarked that "it is confessed, by those who could never be suspected of any desire to favor our position, that there has not been such a time of religious indifference for many years. It may be shown from a large number of facts that the last cases of spiritual interest among the professed churches were the result, directly or indirectly of the Advent doctrine; that where that doctrine has been avowedly opposed, and its believers silenced, spiritual death has followed, our enemies being judges. And we do not know of a single case of noticeable religious interest but where the doctrine is received, or at least not opposed; and these cases are so limited in their extent and number, that they can form no objection to the supposition that the door is shut, but rather go to confirm it" (A. Hale and J. Turner, "Has Not the Savior Come as the Bridegroom?" *Advent Mirror,* Jan. 1845, p. [3]). Some historians from the Advent Christian tradition have argued that the shut-door concept originated with Turner and Hale (Wellcome, *Second Advent Message,* p. 397; Arthur, "After the Great Disappointment: To Albany and Beyond," *Adventist Heritage,* Jan. 1974, p. 6). However, as has been shown above, this concept existed already for some time before it was more extensively worked out by Hale and Turner.

23 Letter, Turner, *HI,* Jan. 24, 1845, cited in Wellcome, *Second Advent Message,* p. 398.

24 See *infra,* p. 113.

equated with the rejection of the validity of the Seventh Month movement and the shut-door concept. In describing the attitudes of Adventists who reported new conversions, J. D. Pickands, a fervent supporter of the Seventh Month movement, said that these individuals were "already deeply committed in opposition" to the new interpretations which affirmed the divine guidance of this movement. According to him, Adventists were faced with the difficult dilemma either "to deny the reality of sound conversions, as reported by our brethren, or to deny the whole history of Adventism."[25] It is in this light that the rejection of reports about new conversions by Hale and Turner has to be interpreted. Their shut-door concept, which was associated with "the closing of the door of mercy," was defined on the basis of the *rejection of truth* and signified "the exclusion from all farther access to saving mercy, those who have rejected its offers during their time of proba-tion."[26] As a result they denied the possibility of genuine conversions among "sinners," though "changes that may appear to be conversions may take place."[27] This they supported through the following reasoning:

> As it is a fundamental principle in the economy of heaven that "it is ac-cepted according to what a man hath" [2 Cor. 8:12], we know that at the closing of the door of mercy, all who fear God and work righteousness, according to the light they have, must be embraced by the arms of his mercy; though as the measure of light they have differs, the apparent form of their character must differ. And there may be changes in the form of their charac-ter, which we might call conversions, though it would imply no change in their inward character before God. That such may be found for whom we should labor, there can be no doubt; and in fact, it is with such a class only, few indeed is their number, that our labors are in any sense successful.[28]

This group seemed to consist of God's children outside of the Adventists and formed the limits of their mission efforts, "but to think of laboring to convert the great mass of the world at such a time, would be as idle as it would have been for the Israelites, when they were down by the Red sea, to have turned about to convert the Egyptians."[29]

However, the fact that Christ had not yet returned led many to the conclusion that the door of mercy was still open, so that the shut door had to be placed in the future. From this time onward Adventists entered into a

25 Letter, J. D. Pickands to Snow, *JS,* June 19, 1845, p. 120.
26 Hale and Turner, "Bridegroom," pp. [3, 4]: E. G. White's first vision also defined the shut-door concept in the context of rejection of truth, but no mention was made of those who had not rejected the Midnight Cry (*infra,* pp. 112, 149, 150).
27 *Ibid.,* p. [4].
28 *Ibid.* Cf. Hale, "Has the Bridegroom Come?" *AH,* March 5, 1845, p. 26. Except for this quotation little is known as to whether they saw as the ground of salvation the mercy of Christ, or the fear of God and the working of righteousness. The interconfessional nature of Adven-tism and the absence of sufficient data prohibit the making of generalizations. However, one thing was clear to them: Those who had rejected the Seventh Month movement did not have the fear of God but had rejected truth and the mercy of Christ so that they were beyond the possibility of salvation.
29 Hale and Turner, "Bridegroom," p. [3].

period of confusion as to the interpretation of the meaning of the shut door.

The periodical which most stoutly affirmed the validity of the Seventh Month movement and published correspondence of several Adventists who later became Sabbatarian Adventists was the *Day-Star*.[30] This periodical published a variety of shut-door views, which seems to indicate that it was possible to believe in the correctness of the Seventh Month movement without necessarily holding to shut-door views as originally advocated by Miller, Hale and Turner. Soon after the Disappointment its editor, Enoch Jacobs, a former Methodist minister, opposed the idea of proclaiming the end of human probation, or that Christ had left the mediatorial throne, because this was unbiblical.[31] He stated that he always should feel it his duty "to point the *enquiring penitent* to Christ" but added that "now especially, do I believe it our duty to *comfort God's people*."[32] Several months later Jacobs concluded from the condition among Adventists and their absence of missionary zeal for sinners that the time described in Rev. 22:11, 12 had arrived.[33] This implied, according to him, that the "ceasing of labor for an 'apostate church and dying world' a 'little while' before our mortal career is done, is not only a duty imposed upon those that 'are alive and remain,' but a process or exercise through which every child of God is called."[34] His shut-door concept, however, was not an extreme one, for he added that Rev. 22:11, 12 did not exclude the possibility of people changing "their character, IF they make use of the means *provided*."[35] Thus he still could accept an invitation from individuals who did not make any profession of religion to lecture in a place where the Second Advent had never been presented. In commenting on this meeting he said that "if God has any children in that place I doubt not that that occasion will bring them out where they will be 'discerned.' "[36] The door of Mt. 25:10 Jacobs defined as the door of the "Kingdom of heaven" and not as the door of mercy.[37] He also interpreted it as "this gospel of the kingdom" (Mt. 24:14) or "the

30   The *Day-Star*, called the *Western Midnight Cry* before Feb. 18, 1845, was for some time representative of some of the theological positions among Sabbatarian Adventists until the middle of 1846, when it started to advocate various views of the Shakers. Other periodicals which affirmed the validity of the 1844 movement were the *Jubilee Standard*, the *Hope of Israel*, the *Hope Within the Veil*, the *Voice of the Shepherd*, the *Advent Testimony*, and the *True Day Star*. In 1845 the *Voice of Truth* occupied a position between these periodicals and the *Advent Herald*.

31   [Enoch Jacobs], "The Time," *WMC*, Nov. 29, 1844, p. 20. Cf. Editorial, "Matthew 24th and 25th Chapters," *WMC*, May 11, 1844, p. 67; [Jacobs], "The Door of Matt. 25:10 Is Shut," *DS*, June 24, 1845, p. 26; Letter, O.R.L. Crosier to Pearson, *HI*, April 17, 1845, p. [4]. F. B. Hahn, a friend of Crosier and Edson, had similar ideas (Editorial, "A Mistake Corrected," *VT*, July 2, 1845, p. 368).

32   [Jacobs], "Time," p. 20. At this time it seems that he had not yet fully accepted the new interpretation of Mt. 25:1-10 ([Jacobs], Remarks on Letter from Charles Burlingham, *DS*, Feb. 25, 1845, p. 8).

33   [Jacobs], "Rev. 22:11, 12," *DS*, April 29, 1845, pp. 46-48.

34   *Ibid.*, p. 47.

35   Jacobs, "Is the Door Shut?" *DS*, May 20, 1845, p. 8.

36   [Jacobs], "Visit to Kentucky," *DS*, May 27, 1845, p. 11. One of his lectures was also attended by a congregation of the Disciples of Christ (*ibid.*).

37   [Jacobs], "Door of Matt. 25:10," pp. 26, 27.

everlasting gospel" (Rev. 14:6), which was the proclamation immediately preceding the establishing of the kingdom, which led him to conclude that "the truths concerning the Kingdom are *its door.*"[38] He further indicated that in the early 1840s the Lord opened the "effectual door" to the world so that the proclamation of the coming kingdom gained access to the people and millions of Second Advent publications were scattered on a world-wide scope. He felt that this successful missionary enterprise was a fulfillment of the words to the Philadelphian church in Rev. 3:8: "I have set before thee an *open door,* and *no man* CAN SHUT IT."[39] He added, however, that after October 22, 1844 the Adventists learned from experience that further mission efforts were unsuccessful because "there was no more access to the people — no more openings for proclaiming the 'original ground of the Advent faith.' 'THE DOOR WAS SHUT'!"[40] This understanding of the shut door was a reason that the door of Mt. 25:10 was also called the "door of access."[41] As a theological reason behind the shutting of the door Jacobs pointed to a change in Christ's ministry.[42] The possibility of individual conversions, he said, had to be left in the hands of God.[43] Cook, who joined the Sabbatarian Adventists for a while in 1846, stated emphatically that the door had been shut against those who had rejected the Advent truths. However, he felt that mercy was still available so that "honest souls, to whose minds these truths have not been fairly presented, may yet receive them."[44] He added that Christ had not left His mediatorial throne and had never pleaded for sinners in general, but still mediated as He had always done "for those *only* that commit their cause to him."[45] Soon after this Cook baptized several persons[46] and through his influence a few others were persuaded to leave the Baptist Church.[47] After having visited various

38 *Ibid.,* p. 27.
39 *Ibid.,* pp. 27, 28.
40 *Ibid.,* p. 28. Cf. Wm. B. Elliott, "The Door Is Shut, and We Know It," *JS,* May 22, 1845, pp. 81, 82; Letter, Otis Nichols to Miller, April 20, 1846. Here Nichols stated that "the message to the church and the world" of Rev. 14:7 had ended in the autumn of 1844, "for there has not been any effect produced on the church or world by preaching the gospel of the kingdom and judgment since that time." Regarding the accessibility in 1850, see E. G. White, "Notes of Travel," *RH,* Nov. 20, 1883, p. 721.
41 [Jacobs], "Door of Matt. 25:10," p. 28. Cf. [Jacobs], "The Two Covenants," *DS,* Sept. 27, 1845, p. 32; Letter, Cook to Jacobs, *DS,* July 8, 1845, p. 36; Letter, Pickands to Jacobs, *DS,* Sept. 20, 1845, p. 25.
42 [Jacobs], "Door of Matt. 25:10," p. 28. Reference was also made to Lk. 13:25.
43 *Ibid.*
44 Cook, "Bro. J. B. Cook," *WMC,* Jan. 30, 1845, p. 46.
45 *Ibid.* Cf. Letter, Crosier to Pearson, p. [4]. Although "the last call of mercy to the world" had been completed, Crosier denied that Christ had "left the mercy seat" because this was located in the "Holiest of all" of the heavenly sanctuary into which He had entered to perform "the final atonement" for His people (*ibid.*).
46 Letter, N. M. Catlin to Jacobs, *DS,* April 15, 1845, p. 40; Letter, Cook to Jacobs, *DS,* June 24, 1845, p. 26. Little information is available regarding those who were baptized. Most of these may have been Adventists who had not yet experienced baptism by immersion (*ibid.*; Letter, J. W. to Brother, *DS,* Feb. 18, 1845, p. 2; Letter, Pickands to Jacobs, *DS,* Sept. 27, 1845, p. 33). Some, however, could have been sinners who experienced conversion after the Disappointment (Letter, Catlin to Jacobs, p. 40).
47 Letter, E. S. Willard to Jacobs, *DS,* June 3, 1845, p. 16.

groups of Adventists who affirmed the validity of the 1844 movement, he observed that different individuals expressed themselves differently regarding the shut door.[48] Cook's shut-door view was that "the great and effectual door that God had opened for proclaiming the 'Everlasting Gospel' " (Rev. 14:6), the "door of access" to the world, was closed.[49] He remarked that "our sympathies now belong to Jesus — His truth and His people. . . . Now it is not my duty, nor yours to run about giving invitations among those who have rejected the call."[50] Yet at the same time he would attend a Baptist church service and afterward give a Bible study to the preacher.[51] This indicated that his shut-door concept was not an extreme one and allowed for an outreach to non-Adventists who had not rejected the Advent doctrine. Later, however, he compared the contemporary situation of the Adventists with that of Noah after the animals were in the ark.[52] Pickands argued that the door of Rev. 3:8 was the "door of access" which shut out the world and the churches from the Second Advent doctrine in the autumn of 1844, while the door of Mt. 25:10 would shut out the foolish virgins at the Second Advent.[53] One correspondent suggested that in October 1844 the door of Mt. 25:10 was shut to the "foolish virgins" who had rejected the new interpretation of the coming of the Bridegroom[54] but not to "the nominal professors of the different churches" and "unbelievers who made no profession of religion" in as far as they had not "sinned away their day of grace."[55] To another correspondent new baptisms were evidence that "God's administration of grace for the salvation of sinners, is yet extended!"[56] In 1846 the *Day-Star* published the first vision[57] of E. G. Har-

---

48 Letter, Cook to Jacobs, *DS*, June 24, 1845, p. 26.

49 Cook, "Extracts from a Discourse by J. B. Cook," *DS*, July 8, 1845, p. 36; Letter, Cook to Jacobs, *DS*, July 8, 1845, p. 36.

50 *Ibid.*

51 Letter, Daniel Ashton to Jacobs, *DS*, July 29, 1845, p. 47. The fact that this individual agreed to examine the subject presented by Cook might suggest that he had not fully investigated the Advent doctrine as set forth by Adventists (see *ibid.*).

52 [Cook], "Providence," p. 4; [Cook], "Divine Guidance," p. 7. Cf. [Cook], "Shut Door," *AT*, April 1846, p. 15.

53 Letter, Pickands to Jacobs, *DS*, Sept. 20, 1845, p. 25.

54 See *infra*, pp. 117-22.

55 Letter, L. Drew to Jacobs, *DS*, Jan. 10, 1846, p. 13. Several years later he became a Sabbatarian Adventist ([J. White], "Meetings at Wheeler and Catlin," *RH*, July 8, 1852, p. 40).

56 Letter, Catlin to Jacobs, p. 40. For other arguments against the shut door, see Letter, E. Holmes to Jacobs, *DS*, June 17, 1845, p. 22.

57 The majority of Adventists had no confidence in visions. However, to some of those who believed in the correctness of the Seventh Month movement E. G. Harmon's visions functioned as a confirmation of their beliefs. When she became a part of the Sabbatarian Adventists many of this group considered her visions as being from God. Regarding the biblical rationale for these visions and their role she said: "I recommend to you, dear reader, the word of God as the rule of your faith and practice. By that Word we are to be judged. God has, in that Word, promised to give visions in the *'last days'*; not for a new rule of faith, but for the comfort of his people, and to correct those who err from bible truth" (E. G. White, *CEV*, 1851, p. 64 [*EW*, 1945, p. 78]). Cf. E. G. White, "To Those Who Are Receiving the Seal of the Living God" (Broadside), Jan. 31, 1849 (*SM*, I, 40). Later SDA views on the major role of her visions could be stated as follows: (1) Assisting and confirming theological developments after

mon.[58] It seems that immediately after the Disappointment she held for a short time, "in common with the advent body, that the door of mercy was then for ever closed to the world."[59] However, before she received her first vision in December 1844, she "had given up the midnight-cry, and shut door, as being in the past."[60] It was through this vision that she became convinced of the validity of the Seventh Month movement and that there was a shut door on October 22, 1844.[61] Her shut-door view that was published pertained *to Adventists who had rejected the Midnight Cry*[62] and also *to the wicked world.*[63]

The *Day-Star* also printed articles advocating the "extreme" shut-door position.[64] One of them criticized the idea of some Adventists that, because of the refusal to accept truth, the church and the world had been rejected "as a whole" with the exception only of some parts of the world on the basis that "all have not had the same light that some have."[65] This writer then proceeded to argue that such a shut-door concept was incorrect because it was based on the rejection of truth and not on the completion of Christ's atonement on October 22, 1844. He insisted that "if the door is shut, it is done by finishing the atonement, on the 10th day of the 7th month, and if the atonement is not finished, then the door is not shut, and all who come to Christ, in any land, may yet be saved."[66] This writer also implied that the mystery of God was finished.[67]

1844; (2) assisting in solving current problems and guiding future developments; (3) providing a lesser light in order to achieve a better understanding of the greater light of Scripture. See Arthur L. White, *Ellen G. White: Messenger to the Remnant,* 1969, pp. 27-51; Froom, *PFF,* IV, 964-1016.

58 Contextual references to events and publications previous to her marriage will be indicated by the name E. G. Harmon; those after her marriage by E. G. White.

59 E. G. White, MS 4, 1883 (*SM,* I, 63); Letter, E. G. White to Loughborough, No. 2, 1874 (*SM,* I, 74).

60 J. White, ed., *WLF,* 1847, p. 22. Cf. E. G. White to Bates, No. 3, 1847.

61 J. White, *WLF,* p. 22; Letter, E. G. White to Bates, No. 3, 1847. Cf. E. G. White, MS 4, 1883 (*SM,* I, 63).

62 From now on the term "Midnight Cry" signifies the True Midnight Cry of the Seventh Month movement. The equating of these expressions with each other became the practice among those who affirmed the validity of this movement.

63 Letter, E. G. Harmon to Jacobs, *DS,* Jan. 24, 1846, p. 31. See *infra,* pp. 133, n. 176; 149, 150. This vision was also published on April 6, 1846, as part of a broadside "To the Little Remnant Scattered Abroad" and under the title "To the Remnant Scattered Abroad" in *WLF,* pp. 14-16. All further references to it will be indicated by the abbreviation "RSA" because this source is easily available in a facsimile reproduction of *WLF.* Owing to the fact that this vision was received before her marriage while *WLF* was published after this event, the authorship of "RSA" will be stated as E. G. White [E. G. Harmon].

64 Cf. Letter, Brown to Editor, *HI,* repr. in *DS,* April 15, 1845, p. 34; Letter, Emily C. Clemons to Editor, *JS,* repr. in *DS,* April 15, 1845, p. 35; Snow, "Behold He Cometh!!" *JS,* repr. in *DS,* April 22, 1845, p. 41; C. S. Minor, " 'The Harvest Is Past,' " *JS,* repr. in *DS,* April 22, 1845, p. 42.

65 "To the Believers Scattered Abroad," *HI,* repr. in *DS,* March 25, 1845, p. 23.

66 *Ibid.* Cf. Letter, Brown to Jacobs, p. 34; Snow, "Behold He Cometh!!" p. 41; Minor, " 'Harvest,' " p. 42. Those who had been included in this atonement were supposed to be secure of salvation if they had not committed any willful sins since the Disappointment (Letter, Clemons to Editor, p. 35; Letter, Peavey to Snow and Matthias, *JS,* April 24, 1845, p. 55).

67 "To the Believers Scattered Abroad," p. 21. Cf. Minor, " 'Harvest,' " p. 42.

According to other Adventists, the new interest in the Advent message and rumors of new conversions were evidence that probation for mankind had not yet been closed. In December 1844 an editorial in the *Advent Herald* stated: "The Tide Turning — Already our friends are sending in new subscribers" and "we are happy to know that the efforts of our enemies to destroy us have gained the sympathy of many who had been indifferent, have made us many new friends, and greatly strengthened our old ones."[68]

At the Low Hampton Conference of Adventists (December 28, 29, 1844) Himes urged three aspects of future missionary activity: (1) Comforting the saints who are still looking for the kingdom at hand; (2) arousing the professed Christian world once more to prepare for the Advent; (3) fully and freely proclaiming salvation to lost and perishing sinners.[69] A few weeks later the Advent press was again in operation, and Himes declared, "I am more and more convinced that the door of salvation is open wide, and that we are to 'preach the Gospel of the Kingdom to all the world,' in the faith that sinners may and will be converted, until the *end comes*."[70] In response to reports about new conversions[71] and pressure of some of his colleagues[72] Miller became gradually less dogmatic on the extreme shut-door concept and after the Jewish Karaite year 1844 had passed he gave it up[73] and returned to his original view of the Midnight Cry.[74]

However, new interpretations of the Disappointment, relating it to Christ's heavenly ministry, seemed to some to confirm the validity of the Seventh Month movement and some kind of a shut-door concept, and created a strong controversy — even fanaticism — among Adventists.

At the end of April 1845 at Albany, New York, a conference of Adventists was called together by Himes[75] with the object of ending the confusion and division. Miller commented, "It need not be replied that it was convened to deliberate respecting, and if possible to extricate ourselves from the anarchy and confusion of BABYLON in which we had so unexpectedly

---

68   Editorial, *AH*, Dec. 11, 1844, p. 141. Cf. Marsh, "Door of Mercy," *VT*, Feb. 26, 1845, pp. 18, 19.

69   Editorial, "Low-Hampton Conference," *AH*, Jan. 15, 1845, p. 182.

70   Himes, "Meetings in New London, Ct," *AH*, Feb. 5, 1845, p. 205. Cf. "Mutual Conference of Adventists at Albany," *AH*, May 14, 1845, p. 107.

71   See e.g., Letter, Bliss to Miller, Feb. 11, 1845; Letter, J. H. Shipman to Miller, Feb. 28, 1845; "Extract from a Letter Written by Bro. Samuel Chapman," *MW*, March 13, 1845, pp. 87, 88.

72   See e. g., Letter, Bliss to Miller, Feb. 11, 1845; Letter, Himes, March 12 and 29, 1845. Cf. Rowe, "Millerite Movement," pp. 274-76.

73   Cf. Letter, Miller to Himes, *MC*, Dec. 5, 1844, pp. 179, 180; Letter, Miller to Himes, *AH*, Dec. 11, 1844, p. 142; Letter, Miller to Bliss, *AH*, Feb. 12, 1845, p. 3; Letter, Miller to Wrightson and Others, March 20, 1845; "Letter from Bro. Miller," *MW*, March 20, 1845, pp. 91, 92; Himes, "Editorial Correspondence," *AH*, April 9, 1845, p. 68; "Mutual Conference," p. 107; Editorial, "Anniversary Week in Boston," *AH*, June 4, 1845, p. 132; Miller, *Apology*, p. 28.

74   Himes, "Editorial Correspondence," *AH*, April 9, 1845, p. 68. Cf. Litch, "The Ten Virgins," *AH*, May 21, 1845, p. 120. See *supra*, pp. 40-43.

75   Letter, T. Wrightson to Miller, March 18, 1845.

found ourselves."[76] At the Albany Conference, chaired by Miller, it was decided to reject all new theological interpretations which had been developed since the Disappointment.[77] Thus the conference refused to accept the newly developed views which recognized the special significance of the Seventh Month movement in salvation history.

The Albany Conference was not very successful in uniting the believers. Some months later Hale was able to distinguish four major classes of Adventists: (1) Those who deplored or even condemned their past Advent experience and were strongly opposed to any further time calculations; (2) those who expressed confidence in the former calculations and felt that the predicted events had taken place; (3) those whose confidence had been shaken by the Disappointment so that they were now afflicted with doubt; (4) those who continued setting time, building their calculations upon anything they could find.[78] Hale's own position and that of the Adventist leaders in general may be described as a modified form of the fourth group. Convinced that the period of 2300 days had not yet expired, they continued to look with much caution for a new date for the Second Advent.[79] The basic difference between the second and fourth group was that the former affirmed that the 2300 days had indeed ended on October 22, 1844, while the latter considered their fulfillment still in the future, — leading them to continue setting time for decades.[80] It is on the second group, which became a minority without much influence among other Adventists after the

76 Miller, "The Albany Conference," *AH,* June 4, 1845, p. 129. On the contemporary confusion, see Letter, I. E. Jones to Miller, Feb. 15, 1845; Letter, T. M. Preble to Bliss, *AH,* March 12, 1845, p. 40; Letter, J. F. Wardwell to Crosier, *DD,* April 16, 1847, p. 10.

77 "Mutual Conference," p. 107. It was resolved "that we can have no sympathy or fellowship with those things which have only a show of wisdom in will-worship and neglecting of the body, after the commandments and doctrines of men. That we have no fellowship with any of the *new tests* as conditions of salvation, in addition to repentance toward God, and faith in our Lord Jesus Christ, and a looking for and loving his appearing. That we have no fellowship for Jewish fables and commandments of men, that turn from the truth, or for any of the distinctive characteristics of modern Judaism. And that the act of promiscuous feet-washing and the salutation kiss, as practiced by some professing Adventists *as religious* ceremonies, sitting on the floor as an act of voluntary humility, shaving the head to humble one's self, and acting like children in understanding, are not only unscriptural, but subversive, — if persevered in, — of purity and morality" (*ibid.*).

78 Hale, "Editorial Correspondence," *AH,* Sept. 10, 1845, p. 40. In 1847 the situation among the Adventists seemed to be even more confused. An editorial stated, "are there not 'Albany Conference' Adventists, 'Hartford Convention' Adventists, and Anti-conference Adventists? Seventh day, first day, and every day Adventists? Workers and no workers? Shut-door, open-door, feetwashers? 'Whole truth,' and 'apostate' Adventists? Baptist, Methodist, Calvinist, Episcopal, Congregational and Presbyterian Adventists?" (Editorial, "The Advent Question," *AH,* Nov. 27, 1847, p. 133). On the confusion among certain Adventists in 1847, see Letter, Wardwell to Crosier, p. 10.

79 See e.g., Letter, Miller to Himes, Nov. 15, 1845. Storrs belonged to the first group. Fitch died a few days before the Disappointment.

80 For some time after the Disappointment the second group also engaged in time settings. The fundamental difference was that theirs was based on the validity of Oct. 22, 1844 as the end of the 2300 days. However, they felt there were additional time predictions which would reach beyond the 2300 days and would provide the exact date of the parousia. See *infra,* p. 156, n. 303.

Albany Conference, that attention will be focused here, for out of it emerged the SDA theology of mission. From these groups there arose in time the following major bodies: Evangelical Adventists, SDA, Advent Christians, Life and Advent Union, and "Age-to-come" Adventists.[81]

Adventists in Hale's second group, which acknowledged the validity of the Seventh Month movement and the fulfillment of the time calculations, had in their search for a new interpretation of the Disappointment two major problems to solve: (1) What was the coming of the Bridegroom if the parable of Mt. 25:1-10 had its fulfillment in the Seventh Month movement and the coming of the Bridegroom did not signify the Second Advent? (2) What was the meaning of the cleansing of the sanctuary of Dan. 8:14 if the 2300 days had terminated on October 22, 1844? In the search for a biblical solution to these two problems the subject of Christ's high-priestly ministry in the heavenly sanctuary seemed to provide a key. The result was a development of two new interpretations: The coming of the Bridegroom (Mt. 25:10) signified Christ's coming to the most holy place in the heavenly sanctuary on October 22, 1844, and the cleansing of the sanctuary of Dan. 8:14 indicated the nature of Christ's ministry after that date. After the completion of this ministry it was thought that He would return to earth. Although both of these new interpretations could be described in an integrated way, the method followed below is to treat them as distinct (though related) as was generally done in the primary source material of 1845-46.

2. The sanctuary theology.

From 1845-49 the second group mentioned above gradually declined in numbers. Although they were united on the validity of the Seventh Month movement, they were divided as to the significance of October 22, 1844 in salvation history. About the middle of 1845 Cook described his experience among this group:

> The prevailing, nay almost universal conviction of the brethren is that the Lord has been leading us. . . . Different individuals express themselves differently relative to the Midnight Cry, — the shutting of the door, and the sounding of the 7th trumpet, yet the prevailing sentiment seems to have come from the same source, — our experience as molded by God's word.[82]

---

81 Evangelical Adventists disappeared in the beginning of the 20th century. The Life and Advent Union united with the Advent Christian Church in 1964 while the Primitive Advent Christian Church recently separated from it. "Age-to-come" Adventists were nationally organized as the Churches of God in Jesus Christ (1888), and as the Church of God of the Abrahamic Faith (1921). Their current name is Church of God General Conference, Oregon, Illinois. Sabbatarian Adventists who did not accept the adoption of the name SDA, the subsequent organization into the SDA Church (1863), and the authority of E. G. White, formed themselves into the Church of God (Adventist). As a result of a 1933 schism, there are presently two bodies: The Church of God (Seventh Day), Denver, Colo., and the Church of God (Seventh Day) in Salem, West Virginia.

82 Letter, Cook to Jacobs, *DS*, June 24, 1845, p. 26. Cf. Letter, Jones to Miller, Feb. 15, 1845.

A survey of the divergence of opinion on some of the contemporary issues discussed immediately after the Disappointment provides ample evidence of the heterogeneous structure of this group. As has been noticed above, interpretations of the expression "the door was shut" (Mt. 25:10) were as follows: (1) The "extreme" position that the door of mercy was closed to all who had not participated in the Seventh Month movement. The underlying assumption here was that their non-participation in this movement was based on either their rejection of the Second Advent proclamation or on the completion of the atonement on October 22, 1844, or both; (2) the view that the door of mercy was closed to all who had consciously rejected the Advent truth. Those who had not participated in the 1844 movement because they were ignorant of its significance but who had lived up to such light as they had could still join the Adventists; (3) the position which rejected the use of the term "door of mercy" as being unbiblical; (4) the concept that the door of the kingdom or the door of access to the people was closed because missionary activity had no practical results.

The ministry of Christ on and after October 22, 1844, was also subject to a variety of opinions: (1) After the completion of the atonement on October 22, Christ came out of the most holy place of heaven and went as the Bridegroom to the Ancient of Days to the marriage to receive the kingdom;[83] (2) before coming to the marriage Christ terminated His daily ministrations on October 22, entered into the "holiest of all" to make an atonement, and came out of that place on the same day;[84] (3) the atonement on the antitypical Day of Atonement was not completed on October 22, but would continue for some time;[85] (4) the atonement began after October 22, when Jesus entered into the holy of holies;[86] (5) the return of Christ was spiritual, not personal, and had already taken place in the hearts of the saints.[87]

83 Letter, Pickands to Marsh, VT, Feb. 12, 1845, p. 12. On the completion of the atonement, see e.g., Letter, Turner, p. 398; Letter, Snow to Marsh, VT, April 16, 1845, p. 20; Letter, J. White to Jacobs, DS, Sept. 20, 1845, p. 26.

84 Letter, Peavey to Snow and Matthias, p. 55. This atonement covered all unknown sins committed by those who had received pardon on Oct. 22, 1844 (ibid.). Peavey, " 'Unto Two Thousand and Three Hundred Days . . . ,' " JS, Aug. 7, 1845, p. 166. Cf. Clemons, "Letter from Sister Clemons," JS, April 17, 1845, p. 42.

85 Cf. Letter, Crosier to Pearson, p. [4]; Letter, Crosier to Jacobs, DS, Oct. 11, 1845, p. 51; Letter, Crosier to Jacobs, DS, Nov. 15, 1845, p. 23. Crosier, "The Law of Moses," DS, Extra, Feb. 7, 1846, pp. 37-44.

86 Cf. Letter, Jones to Miller, Feb. 15, 1845; Editorial, " 'The Hope within the Veil,' " JS, July 3, 1845, pp. 132, 133; Snow, "Remarks," JS, June 5, 1845, p. 102; Editorial, "Hope of Israel," VT, May 14, 1845, p. 56. Editorial, "Where is Christ?" VT, March 5, 1845, p. 26.

87 Orlando Squires, "Where Is Heaven?" VS, March 1845, p. 4; Squires, "The Body of Moses," VS, March 1845, p. 5; Solomon Fenton, "The Coming of Christ," VS, March 1845, p. 6; Fenton, "Why Stand Ye Gazing Up into Heaven?" VS, March 1845, p. 8. Cf. M. Williamson, "Trodden under Foot," VT, April 2, 1845, pp. 1, 2. Adherents to this view were called by the others of the second group "mystics" and "spiritualizers" (Editorial, "Doctrine of the Mystics," JS, July 10, 1845, p. 140; Editorial, " 'Beware of False Prophets,' " JS, June 26, 1845, pp. 124, 125; Letter, Eli Curtis to Snow, JS, June 26, 1845, p. 127; Bates, SAWH, p. 79). J. White called it "spiritualism" ("Brother Miller's Dream," PT, May 1850, p. 74 [Brother Miller's Dream, 1850, p. 7]).

As to the sealing (Rev. 7:1-4), some felt that it had been completed on October 22,[88] while others suggested that it was a present process or imminent reality.[89] In regard to the judgment some of the following views were expressed: (1) The "judiciary" phase or the "sitting of judgment" had been accomplished because the antitypical Day of Atonement was also a day of judgment through which the fate of mankind had been decided;[90] (2) the "judiciary" phase of the judgment was a present reality and preceded the "executive" phase of the judgment;[91] (3) the judgment was imminent.[92]

From now on the development of the SDA theology of mission will be traced from this heterogeneous group of Adventists who all affirmed the prophetic role of the Seventh Month movement.

a. The Bridegroom theme.

One of the earliest interpretations of the Disappointment which endorsed the validity of the Seventh Month movement and the October 22, 1844, time calculations seems to have come from Hiram Edson. On the very day following the Disappointment he felt impressed, after prayer, that a mistake had been made in the *manner* in which the Adventists had expected Christ to come as the Bridegroom, but not in the predicted *time*. He stated:

> After breakfast I said to one of my brethren, "Let us go and see, and encourage some of our brn [brethren]." We started, and while passing through a large field I was stopped about midway of the field. Heaven seemed open to my view, and I saw distinctly and clearly that instead of our High Priest coming out of the Most Holy of the heavenly sanctuary to come to this earth on the tenth day of the seventh month, at the end of the 2300 days, that He for the first time entered on that day the second apartment of that sanctuary; and that He had a work to perform in the Most Holy before coming to this earth. That he came to the marriage at that time; in other words, to the Ancient of days to receive a kingdom, dominion, and glory; and we must wait for his return *from the wedding.*[93]

88   Letter, Edson to Snow, *JS,* May 29, 1845, p. 91; Letter, Wm. J. Greenleaf to Jacobs, *DS,* June 3, 1845, p. 14; Snow, "The Confederacy," *JS,* June 12, 1845, p. 109. Cf. Hotchkiss, "The Revelation of Jesus Christ," *VS,* Sept. 1845, pp. 26, 27. In Maine, during the summer of 1844, various Millerites believed that the sealing process was a present reality (Editorial, "Advent Herald," p. 93; *infra,* p. 150, n. 273).

89   H. B. Woodcock, "The True Millennium," *WMC,* Dec. 30, 1844, p. 31; Letter, Nichols to Miller, April 20, 1846. Cf. Letter, E. G. Harmon to Jacobs, *DS,* March 14, 1846, p. 7.

90   [Jacobs], "Time," pp. 19, 20; Peavey, " 'The Hour of His Judgment Is Come,' " *JS,* June 19, 1845, p. 114.

91   See *infra,* p. 118, n. 96.

92   Gross, "Times and Seasons," pp. 50, 51; J. White, *WLF,* p. 24.

93   Edson, MS, p. 9. Cf. Letter, T. Greer Clayton to Miller, Oct. 26, 1844; Letter, Edson to Snow, p. 91. For accounts of the Edson experience, see H. M. Kelley, "The Spirit of 1844," *RH,* June 23, 1921, p. 5; Loughborough, "The Second Advent Movement — No. 8," *RH,* Sept. 15, 1921, p. 5; W. A. Spicer, "A Meeting with O. R. L. Crosier," *RH,* March 29, 1945, p. 5. Although Edson's MS is an autobiographical source, it has been used because to SDA it represents the classical illustration of the interpretation of the Disappointment. As such, it is a valuable source for understanding the SDA self-image. This source does not contradict 1845 source material, though it is possible that the MS reflects later influences. For Edson's pre-Disappointment supernatural experiences, see MS, pp. 5-7.

In Edson's interpretation, the sanctuary of Dan. 8:14 was seen to be the heavenly sanctuary and not the earth or the church. He blamed "modern orthodoxy" for the interpretation of Mt. 25:10 which held "that the coming of the Bridegroom to the marriage would be fulfilled in the personal second advent of Christ to this earth."[94] The coming of the Bridegroom to the marriage he placed in the context of Dan. 7:13, 14 and related it to the coming of Christ as the High Priest to the second apartment of the heavenly sanctuary. Thus, according to Edson, on the 10th day of the seventh month, 1844, Christ came to the "marriage," that is, to His reception of the kingdom, dominion, and glory. The time of the parousia he interpreted in the context of Lk. 12:36, which calls on believers to wait until Christ returns from the marriage. For awhile he anticipated the Second Advent in 1845.[95]

An editorial by Jacobs in the *Western Midnight Cry,* December 1844, alluded to the coming of Christ in the setting of the judgment and made a distinction between a pre-Advent judgment and an executive judgment at the time of the Second Advent.[96]

One of the most extensive early treatments of the Bridegroom theme appeared in the first and only issue of the *Advent Mirror,* January 1845. According to its editors, Hale and Turner, the parable of Mt. 25:1-13 had to be interpreted in a "spiritual or figurative sense."[97] The current issue, they said, was whether Christ was represented in Mt. 25:10 as the Bridegroom coming as the "King of glory" to the earth or as the Bridegroom coming to the marriage in heaven. They resolved the issue by alluding to the heavenly marriage of the Lamb. From Rev. 21:9-14 they inferred that the bride was the "great city, the holy Jerusalem,"[98] citing as collaborative evidence the typological relationship between Gal. 4:26 and Ezek. 16: "What Old Jerusalem was to the Church under the old covenant, that the New Jerusalem is to be, to the Church under the new covenant in its perfected state. As Jehovah declares that he married the old Jerusalem, Ezekiel xvi.,

94 *Ibid.,* p. 8.
95 Letter, Edson to Snow, pp. 90, 91.
96 The article stated that "1st. There are certain brethren who believe that Christ did in some 'sense,' come on 'the tenth day,' 'more than he has come since or for centuries previous.' 2d. They argue that Christ did on the 'tenth day,' 'come' from his 'Father's throne,' to his 'judgment seat,' where he is now sitting in judgment on our world, Ex. 28:15, 29, 30; Num. 27:18-21; Ex. 30:10; Lev. 16:29-31; Lev. 23:29, 31; Heb. 4:14-16; 5:8; 9:6-12, 19-26; Lev. 9:22-24; Acts 3:19-21. Whether the judgment has yet set upon the 'living,' they do not pretend to say. 3d. They give us further evidence, that the judgment must set before Christ personally appears to 'execute judgment.' Rev. 11:15-18; 20:12; Matt. 5:25; Dan. 7:9, 10; Ezek. 21:30; Isa. 11:3, 4; Ps. 98:8, 9; 50:3-5; 82:8; 96:11-13; 76:8; 2:7-9; Rev. 4:1-6; 20:11; 14:14; I Thess. 4:16, 17" ([Jacobs], "Intolerance," *WMC,* Dec. 30, 1844, p. 30). Cf. [Jacobs], "Time," pp. 19, 20; Hale, "Has the Bridegroom Come?" *AH,* Feb. 26, 1845, p. 18; Snow, " 'And the Door Was Shut,' " *JS,* April 24, 1845, p. 53; "The Judgment Dispensation," *DS,* June 6, 1846, p. 4. For Millerite views on a pre-Advent judgment, see Litch, *PE,* I, 50, 51, 53; Hale, *Herald of the Bridegroom* . . . , 1843, p. 22; Editorial, "Advent Herald," p. 93.
97 Hale and Turner, "Bridegroom," p. [2]. Turner wrote Miller that the mistake had been that no distinction was made "between Christ as the Bridegroom, and Christ the King of glory" (Letter, Turner to Miller, Jan. 20, 1845). Cf. Letter, Turner to Miller, Feb. 7, 1845; Letter, Clemons to Miller, Feb. 17, 1845.
98 Hale and Turner, "Bridegroom," p. [1].

so the Son of God is to be married to the new Jerusalem."[99] On the basis of Mt. 22:8-14 they said that the believers were the guests at the marriage of the Lamb. Their conclusion was that the marriage had to take place *before* Christ would come as the King of glory to this earth and that His actual return was symbolized by His return *from the wedding* (Lk. 12:35-37). The marriage they defined as the inauguration of Christ as King of glory, at which occasion He would receive His "kingdom, city and throne,"[100] and as "the actual investment of Christ with 'the throne.' "[101] Therefore, they said, the coming of the Bridegroom (Mt. 25:10) denoted "that change in his [Christ's] heavenly state, in which he comes to the Ancient of Days to receive dominion, and glory, which we know must take place before he can come in his glory."[102]

Because Adventists were guests at the heavenly marriage, the editors suggested that the believers were "now in the guest-chamber, where all depends on our keeping our garments,"[103] indicating an intimate relationship between the change in Christ's work in heaven and a change in the believers' responsibility on earth:

> The coming of the bridegroom would point out some change of work or office, on the part of our Lord, in the invisible world; and the going in with him a corresponding change on the part of his true people. With him it is within the veil — where he has gone to prepare a place for us; with them it is outside the veil where they are to wait and keep themselves ready till they pass in to the marriage supper.[104]

In February and March of 1845 Hale published two articles on the same subject in which he provided a hermeneutical foundation for the new interpretation of Mt. 25:10 aimed at harmonizing the various passages regarding Christ's marriage. He indicated that in the historicization of the parable of Mt. 25 Miller's rules (IX, X, XI)[105] had not been applied consistently but the new interpretation had eliminated this inaccuracy by a more precise application of the principles of analogy of Scripture and of "good sense."[106] Hale also stressed the necessity of a preparatory work to be done in the city in connection with the inauguration of Christ as King on His throne. This preparatory work he explained in the light of Christ's atoning ministry for the purification of the "true tabernacle" (Heb. 8:2; 9:23) which was iden-

---

99 *Ibid.* The prevailing opinion that the church is the bride and the marriage the reception of the church was rejected. The testimony of Revelation was taken as normative for the new covenant times so that Paul's allusions to the church as the bride were only seen as allegorical. It was stated that "under the old covenant God is the husband, 'Jerusalem,' 'the land,' or country is the wife, and the church are the children. Hos. i; Ezek. xvi, xxiii, xxiv: 15-27; Gal. iv: 25: Under the new covenant, Christ the husband, the New Jerusalem the wife, and believers the children. Gal. iv:26-31" (*ibid.,* p. [2]). See also J. White, *Life,* pp. 202-4.
100 Hale and Turner, "Bridegroom," pp. [1], [3].
101 *Ibid.,* p. [3].
102 *Ibid.,* p. [1].
103 *Ibid.,* p. [2].
104 *Ibid.,* p. [3].
105 See Appendix I.
106 Hale, "Has the Bridegroom Come?" pp. 18, 19.

tified with the "heavenly Jerusalem" (Rev. 21:2, 3).[107] This work of purification, however, should not be identified with the sanctuary cleansing of Dan. 8:14, but was to precede that process.[108]

For awhile even Miller was impressed by the various aspects of the Bridegroom theme as presented by Hale and Turner. In a letter to Marsh he admitted that Mt. 25:10 could not refer to the Second Advent, this event being referred to in Lk. 12:36, but affirmed that Christ had come in the sense spoken of in Mt. 25:10.[109] After the Albany Conference, however, he gave up this view.

In January of 1846 the *Day-Star* published E. G. Harmon's December 1844 vision which depicted a place in heaven similar to the most holy place of the earthly sanctuary and described it in the context of Heb. 9:3-5 and the marriage supper of the Lamb,[110] which suggested the physical reality of a heavenly sanctuary. In March 1846 the *Day-Star* published another vision of E. G. Harmon received in February 1845, picturing the coming of the Bridegroom to the marriage, a view also held by Edson, Hale, and Turner. It described a transition in the ministry of Christ in the heavenly sanctuary. Jesus, as the Intercessor for His people, was seen sitting on a throne with the Father in the holy place of the sanctuary. Both then left this throne and entered into the most holy place where Jesus as "a great High Priest," standing before the place where the Father sat, would receive the Kingdom (Dan. 7:13, 14).[111] The commission given to the Adventists was to keep

107   Hale, "Has the Bridegroom Come?" p. 27. He said: "We do not suppose there is any bride to 'make herself ready' [Rev. 19:7]; but that this figurative expression denotes some important preparatory work, in case of the city, in connection with its becoming 'the throne of the Lord.' And what that work is it is not difficult to determine. The 'holy city' is called also 'the tabernacle of God' — Rev. xxi. Christ is 'the minister of the true tabernacle which the Lord pitched and not man' — Heb. viii. 2. The typical tabernacle had to be 'purified;' and Paul tells us the true tabernacle must also be purified: — 'It was therefore necessary that the patterns of things in heaven should be purified with these; (the blood of calves and of goats,) but *the heavenly things themselves* with better sacrifices than these.' — Heb. ix.23. The typical work of 'atonement for the holy sanctuary, and for the tabernacle of the congregation, and the altar;' as well as for 'the priests and for all the people of the congregation,' was on the tenth day of the seventh month. — Lev. xvi.29, 33. And when that work of atonement for 'the heavenly things themselves' shall have been accomplished by Christ, then we suppose that preparation denoted in the figure, will have been effected: — what had been hitherto the tabernacle of our Great High Priest is 'ready' to become his throne" (*ibid.*). Hale concluded his view of this preparatory work in the context of Rev. 19:8; 7:14 and Heb. 9:12 with the remark that "the holy city — the heavenly Jerusalem — is indebted to the same atoning blood for her purity, that the saints are indebted to for theirs" (*ibid.*). No further comment was made on the nature of this atonement which was currently going on in heaven as a preparation and purification of the New Jerusalem. Some months later, however, Hale repudiated the Bridegroom theme (Editorial, "Anniversary Week in Boston," *AH*, June 11, 1845, p. 138).

108   Hale, "Has the Bridegroom Come?" p. 27; Hale, "End of the Prophetic Periods," *AH*, March 12, 1845, pp. 38, 39.

109   Letter, Miller to Marsh, *VT* [Feb. 19, 1845], repr. in *DS*, March 11, 1845, p. 13.

110   E. G. White [E. G. Harmon], "RSA," p. 16. For the reality of the heavenly sanctuary, see also E. G. White, *SG*, I, 161; E. G. White, *SP*, IV, 260, 261.

111   On this transition Nichols commented: "The Ancient of days, did change his place where Jesus was sitting at his right hand, to the throne of judgment in the Holy of holies and did sit. Dan. 7:9" (Letter, Nichols to Miller, April 20, 1846). Later E. G. White said that Dan. 7:13; 8:14; Mal. 3:1; and Mt. 25:10 were representations of the same event (*GC*, p. 426).

their "garments spotless," for in "a little while" Christ would "return from the wedding" to His followers (Lk. 12:36). Adventists who had been deceived, were ignorant of the view of the coming of the Bridegroom and were described as being under the influence of Satan.[112]

Because these ideas had been communicated in a vision, they were accepted by some Adventists as a confirmation by God of the correctness of the Bridegroom theme and the Seventh Month movement. However, though Ellen Harmon's revelations seem to have been "well known, and much talked about at that time,"[113] most Adventists remained rather skeptical of visions.[114]

Although the Bridegroom theme enabled Adventists to adhere to the validity of the Seventh Month movement and the contemporary shut-door opinions, gradually it was rejected by most of them. They preferred to explain the Disappointment as an error in the *time* calculations and not as a mistake in the *manner* they had expected Christ to come. One of their main arguments for rejecting the interpretation of Mt. 25:10, that Christ as the Bridegroom had come to the Ancient of Days and that the door was shut, was that it was considered as a departure from the traditional view that this text symbolized the Second Advent. Opposing the new interpretations, Himes stated that "the recent movement, relating to the coming of the Bridegroom, and the shutting of the door of salvation, consequent on the cry of the seventh month we believe to be an error."[115] After the Albany Conference Miller criticized those advocating the Bridegroom theme as "spiritualizers" because he thought they had renounced "the *personal* appearing of Christ."[116] A strong controversy developed between those accepting the Bridegroom theme and a shut door, and those who rejected it. According to Eli Curtis, who had accepted this new view, there was "no other prophecy than that of the parable of the ten virgins" which caused so much opposition and division among Adventists.[117] Toward the end of

---

112 Letter, E. G. Harmon to Jacobs, *DS*, March 14, 1846, p. 7 (*EW*, pp. 54-56). Cf. Letter, E. G. White to Bates, No. 3, 1847. On April 6, 1846 the vision was published as part of a broadside "To the Little Remant Scattered Abroad." She denied she had any knowledge of the Bridegroom theme previous to the vision (Letter, E. G. White to Bates, No. 3, 1847).

113 Miles Grant, " 'Visions and Prophecies,' " *WC*, July 1, 1874, p. 50 (*The True Sabbath . . .*, 1874, p. 68).

114 Regarding E. G. White [E. G. Harmon], see e.g., Editorial, "Topsham, Me," *AH*, April 30, 1845, pp. 94, 95; Letter, M. L. Clark to Himes, *AH*, May 14, 1850, p. 111; A. N. Seymour, "Delusion — E. White's Visions," *AHBA*, March 26, 1853, p. 323 (cf. E. G. White, "Dear Brethren and Sisters," *RH*, April 14, 1853, p. 192). Regarding other manifestations, see Storrs, "Note from Brother Storrs," *MC*, Oct. 31, 1844, p. 138; Editorial, "Vision of C. R. Gorgas," *MC*, Oct. 31, 1844, pp. 143, 144; Letter, Jones to Miller, Nov. 23, 1844; Letter, Himes to Miller, March 12 and 29, 1845. In 1845 in Portland J. and C. H. Pearson published *The Christian Experience of William E. Foy Together with the Two Visions He Received in the Months of Jan. and Feb. 1842* as an encouragement and comfort to the Adventists.

115 Himes, "A Word to the Advent Brethren," *MW*, April 3, 1845, p. 112. Cf. Letter, Himes to Miller, March 12 and 29, 1845; Miller, *Apology*, p. 28.

116 Letter, Miller to Himes, *AH*, May 6, 1846, p. 99. Cf. Letter, Bliss to Miller, Feb. 11, 1845.

117 Letter, Curtis to Snow, *JS*, June 19, 1845, p. 116. Cf. Snow, "Visit to Philadelphia," *JS*, April 3, 1845, p. 28.

1845 a correspondent of the *Advent Herald* stated: "I view the Bridegroom-come-theory, as the leading error of the dread train that has scattered 'fire-brands, arrows, and death' in our ranks."[118] For Sabbatarian Adventists, however, the Bridegroom theme was seen as one of the strongest evidences of the genuineness of the Advent experience.

b. New dimensions in soteriology.

After the Disappointment various Adventists restudied the subject of the sanctuary and its cleansing (Dan. 8:14) in an attempt to harmonize it with their time calculations and the delay of the Second Advent. Through a new interpretation of Dan. 8:14 new concepts of soteriology were developed. One of the earliest new interpretations was provided by Edson, who pointed out that Christ did not *come out* of the most holy place of the heavenly sanctuary as generally had been expected, but that He *entered* for the first time into the second apartment to perform a special work — the reception of the kingdom, dominion, and glory.[119] In February 1845 a corresponding view seems to have been known in Boston.[120] About the same time, E. G. Harmon received her Bridegroom vision with a similar content in Exeter, Maine.[121] Soon after this two Adventist periodicals, the *Hope within the Veil* and the *Hope of Israel,* which were published in Portland, Maine, where E. G. Harmon had related her views, began to circulate similar concepts and carried their influence as far as New York State and Ohio.[122] The *Hope within the Veil* seems to have advocated the position that the two apartments of the tabernacle represented "two dispensations, or two divisions of the covenant," and that Jesus had entered into the "holy of holies" to begin His atonement on October 22, 1844.[123] The *Hope of Israel* said that now Adventists were "in the marriage, in the holiest with Jesus."[124] In April 1845 it published an article by Owen R. L. Crosier,[125] who was a friend of Edson's and a Sabbatarian Adventist for a

118 Letter, Clemons to Himes, *AH,* Dec. 31, 1845, p. 163. Cf. A. Mussey, "Confession and Exhortation," *AH,* Nov. 5, 1845, p. 99. I. E. Jones said that "Turner's views since adopted by . . . Hale, have done more to distruct [*sic*] us than all the rest together" (Letter, Jones to Miller, Feb. 15, 1845).

119 Edson, MS, p. 9. See *supra,* pp. 95, 96. Some time later he indicated that the "dispensation of the fullness of times" had arrived. This time was described in the context of Christ's present ministry as " 'the times of restitution of all things,' and the time of blotting out of sins, when the 'refreshing shall come from the presence of the Lord,' and the time of the Covenant, when He 'shall take away their sins;' Rom. viii.23; xi.25-27; Eph. i.14; iv.30; Acts iii.19-21" (Letter, Edson to Snow, p. 91). See *infra,* pp. 130, 131. Cf. Letter, Clemons to Editor, p. 35.

120 Letter, Jones to Miller, Feb. 15, 1845.

121 Letter, E. G. Harmon to Jacobs, *DS,* March 14, 1846, p. 7 (*EW,* pp. 54-56). See *supra,* pp. 117, 118, 121.

122 Unfortunately hardly any copies of these periodicals seem to be in existence. Some data on their positions, however, could be obtained from critical evaluations in other contemporary Adventist periodicals.

123 Snow, "Remarks," p. 102; Editorial, " 'Hope within the Veil,' " pp. 132, 133.

124 Editorial, "Hope of Israel," p. 56.

125 Owen R. L. Crosier (1820-1913) was a Millerite lay preacher. He was editor of the *DD,* a post-Disappointment periodical. In 1846 he published a treatise which synthesized and

short time, claiming that the antitypical Day of Atonement was not to be finished in one literal day but would continue for a year.[126] Crosier remarked that "the last call of mercy to the world" was completed in the fall of 1844 and that on the 10th day of the seventh month Jesus had entered "upon the office of bridegroom as the final atonement for his people. . . . Our great High Priest is now making the atonement for his whole Israel."[127] The idea that Christ had "*left* the mercy seat, and hence that all access by prayer is cut off," he rejected, stating that "the mercy seat is in the Holiest of all. . . . So that *he has approached directly to the mercy seat.*" With reference to Heb. 10:19-27 he pointed out that "here Paul teaches us that *now* we have *liberty* (margin) to enter into the *holiest* by the blood of Jesus who is the High Priest over the *house of God.*"[128] In September 1845 Otis Nichols,[129] who seems to have been familiar with the Bridegroom vision, employed the analogy-of-Scripture principle to the subject of the sanctuary and concluded that "the 10th of the 7th month is a landmark and a glorious light for us to look back upon" because at that time the Bridegroom "suddenly came to his temple, Mal. 3:1, which 'was opened in heaven,' [Rev. 11:19] after the 7th angel began to sound, Lev. 16:33, Heb. 9:3-4 to finish the atonement for the people, and cleansing of the Sanctuary, Heb. 9:23."[130]

In March 1845 Hale had explained the delay of the Second Advent by referring to a purification (Heb. 8, 9; Lev. 16) of the heavenly Jerusalem — the true tabernacle and antitype of the earthly tabernacle — a process which he designated as "atonement" and believed must be accomplished before Christ's return.[131] Around this time a view was published which tried by typology to harmonize the Levitical high-priestly ministry with the completion of Christ's atoning ministry on the antitypical Day of Atonement. It was concluded that prior to October 22, 1844 Christ, as man's advocate, fulfilled the antitype of the Jewish high priest in his daily ministry, but that on the 10th day of the seventh month Jesus as the antitype of the "dead and living goat" (Lev. 16) *entered* into "the Holy place, or inner court . . . and shut the door" to make the atonement. On the same day that the atonement was completed (October 22, 1844) He *came out* of that place as the Bride-

---

further developed contemporary thinking on a rationale of the Disappointment in the context of Christ's high-priestly ministry. This treatise became the basis of the SDA sanctuary theology. In 1846 he accepted the Sabbath but soon repudiated it together with his sanctuary position.

126   Letter, Crosier to Pearson, p. [4]. This year was dated from the spring of 1844 to the spring of 1845 (*ibid.*). Cf. Crosier, "Prophetic Day and Hour," *VT*, April 9, 1845, p. 15.

127   Letter, Crosier to Pearson, p. [4].

128   *Ibid.*

129   Otis Nichols (1798-1876) was one of the first Adventists to accept Bates' Sabbath teaching and E. G. Harmon's visions. He published prophetic charts used by Sabbatarian Adventists.

130   Letter, Nichols to Jacobs, *DS*, Sept. 27, 1845, p. 34. Cf. Snow, "The Laodicean Church," *JS*, June 19, 1845, p. 117. On Mal. 3:1, see E. G. White, *GC*, pp. 424, 426.

131   Hale, "Has the Bridegroom Come?" p. 27. See *supra*, p. 120, n. 107.

groom to receive His kingdom. Since that day His work as Mediator and High Priest was confined to God's people.[132] Later G. W. Peavey, a strong defender of the Seventh Month movement, stated that Christ had "closed the work typified by the daily ministrations previous to the 10th day of the 7th month, and on that day went into the holiest of all, presenting his blood once for all for those who had accepted of his mediation at that time."[133] He interpreted Dan. 8:14 in the context of Heb. 9:23, 24 and Lev. 16:16 and concluded that the "heavenly things" needed purification with Christ's blood because of the "uncleanness of the children of Israel." According to him, both the cleansing of the sanctuary and the termination of the atonement occurred on October 22, 1844.[134] It was through the influence of Turner that Snow had accepted the Bridegroom theme and the idea that the atonement was finished.[135] Now Snow interpreted the sanctuary of Dan. 8:14 as the Lord's dwelling place — Zion, or the heavenly Jerusalem, which was "the *inheritance* of our Lord and his people." Its justification, he said, was to be achieved "by the *atonement or reconciliation.*" Employing typological reasoning he stated that like the type in Lev. 16, "so also in the antitype, the 'HOLY SANCTUARY,' i.e. Zion or Jerusalem must receive the atonement or reconciling on *the same day,* and thus be *pardoned* or 'JUSTIFIED.'" After its completion at the end of the 2300 days Is. 40:1, 2 had a "binding force upon God's ministers."[136]

In the search for a new interpretation of their former predictions, a current controversy among those affirming the validity of the Seventh Month movement, whether or not Christ's atoning ministry in heaven had been finished since the autumn of 1844, was of specific missiological significance. In October 1845 Crosier again pointed out that the atonement had *not* been completed,[137] stating that "the brethren do not search it [atonement] close enough. It is not yet finished; but we are in the Antitype of the tenth day of Atonement."[138] In February 1846, already familiar with many of the above mentioned positions, he published an extensive treatise on the cleansing of the sanctuary of Dan. 8:14 in the light of Christ's *continuing* atoning ministry in the heavenly sanctuary. This treatise, "The

132   "To the Believers Scattered Abroad," p. 23.
133   Letter, Peavey to Snow and Matthias, p. 55.
134   Peavey, " 'Two Thousand and Three Hundred Days,' " p. 166. The application of typological argumentation to the sanctuary of Dan. 8:14 was based on Heb. 9:23, 24. He said: "Here we learn that the antitype of the most holy place on earth is the presence of God: there, then, is the antitype of the mercy-seat, &c.; there Jesus was 'set on the right hand of the throne of the Majesty in the heavens,' as our intercessor. We also learn that it was necessary that those patterns should be purified in this manner; but the heavenly things, — the substance with better sacrifices, the blood of Jesus himself' (*ibid.*).
135   Letter, Snow to Marsh, p. 20.
136   Snow, "Prophetic Chronology," *JS,* May 22, 1845, p. 85.
137   In Sept. 1845, J. White also stated that the atonement had ended at the end of the 2300 days (Letter, J. White to Jacobs, *DS,* Sept. 20, 1845, p. 26).
138   Letter, Crosier to Jacobs, *DS,* Oct. 11, 1845, p. 51. The duration of the antitypical Day of Atonement, he remarked, was "not one literal day nor year, but must be *many* years" (Letter, Crosier to Jacobs, *DS,* Nov. 15, 1845, p. 23).

Law of Moses," was quickly recommended by E. G. White[139] and became of vital significance in the development of the SDA theology of mission.

This article, while affirming that "righteousness comes not by the Law, but by faith in the promises [of God]," advocated the relevance of the law of Moses for the period after the Disappointment.[140] Crosier started out by modifying the Seventh Month movement position regarding the typological significance of the vernal Jewish festivals.[141] The complete fulfillment of these festivals, he said, did not take place at a point of time at the first Advent; the incarnation of Christ was only the beginning of their antitypical fulfillment which was to be completed after many years at the end of the "gospel dispensation," at the Second Advent. Reasoning from analogy, he stated that the complete fulfillment of the autumnal Jewish festivals, in particular of Yom Kippur (Lev. 23:26-32), would also cover "a dispensation of *many years.*"[142] In his opinion the antitype of the Day of Atonement, a time of restoration, would cover a period from the "end of the 2300 days" till the end of the millennium, when redemptive history would be complete.

Before discussing this period of restoration Crosier dealt with the interpretation of the sanctuary of Dan. 8:14 and the typological implications of the Old Testament sanctuary ministry to the priestly ministry of Christ. His interpretation rejected the previously held general opinion that at the end of the 2300 days Christ would come out of the most holy place of the heavenly sanctuary to the earth after completing the atonement in that place.[143] Instead, interpreting Dan. 8:14 in the context of Christ's high-priestly ministry, he spoke of two phases of that ministry, one beginning at His ascension, when Christ entered the holy place of the heavenly sanctuary, and a second beginning on October 22, 1844, when Christ for the first time entered the most holy place.

The biblical rationale for his interpretation he predominantly based on two hermeneutical principles: The analogy of Scripture and typology. Through the former he analyzed scriptural references on the subject of the sanctuary and its services, through the latter the relationship between the Levitical priestly ministry in the earthly sanctuary and the priestly ministry of Christ in the heavenly sanctuary.[144] These hermeneutical principles led

139   She said: "The Lord shew [*sic*] me in vision, more than one year ago, that Brother Crosier had the true light, on the cleansing of the Sanctuary, &c; and that it was his will, that Brother C. should write out the view which he gave us in the Day-Star, Extra, February 7, 1846. I feel fully authorized by the Lord, to recommend that Extra, to every saint" (Letter, E. G. White to Curtis, *WLF,* p. 12). SDA have usually interpreted this statement to mean that Crosier's presentation was not without mistakes, but that his major typological argumentation was correct. Reprints of the article omitted the aspects which they felt to be inaccurate.

140   Crosier, "Law of Moses," p. 37. His basic arguments underlying this article were stated earlier in Letter, Crosier to Jacobs, *DS,* Nov. 15, 1845, p. 23.

141   See *supra,* pp. 88, 95.

142   Crosier, "Law of Moses," p. 37. Cf. Letter, Crosier to Jacobs, *DS,* Nov. 15, 1845, p. 23.

143   See *supra,* pp. 95, 96.

144   Crosier analyzed the priesthood of Christ in the context of the priesthoods of both Melchisedec and Aaron. His conclusion was that Christ *"fulfills both the Priesthood of Melchisedec and Aaron.* In some respects the priesthood of Christ resembles that of Melchisedec; and in

Crosier to interpret the true tabernacle or sanctuary of the new covenant in which Christ ministers (Heb. 8:1, 2, 6) as a literal heavenly sanctuary. He associated it with the New Jerusalem, "like the Sanctuary of the first covenant was with Old Jerusalem."[145]

When interpreting Dan. 8:14 he introduced, in addition to the above hermeneutic, another principle which could broadly be described as follows: Old Testament prophetic symbolism ought to be interpreted in a New Testament new-covenant sense if these prophecies refer to a historical period after the Crucifixion. This principle led him to interpret the sanctuary of Dan. 8:14 as the heavenly sanctuary of the new covenant. He stated that "the Sanctuary to be cleansed at the end of the 2300 days is also the *Sanctuary* of the new covenant, for the vision of the treading down and cleansing, is after the crucifixion."[146]

---

others that of Aaron or Levi" ("Law of Moses," p. 39). Regarding the Levitical priesthood, he said, "there is a resemblance in every instance, but Christ's is superior to Levi's" (*ibid.*).

145 *Ibid.*, p. 38.

146 *Ibid.* On the casting down of the sanctuary of Dan. 8:11 he commented that "this casting down was in the days and by the means of the Roman power; therefore the Sanctuary of this text was not the Earth, nor Palestine, because the former was cast down at the fall, more than 4000 years, and the latter at the captivity, more than 700 years previous to the event of this passage, and neither by Roman agency. The Sanctuary cast down is his against whom Rome magnified himself, which was the Prince of the host, Jesus Christ; and Paul teaches that his Sanctuary is in heaven. Again, Dan. 11:30, 31, 'For the ships of Chittim shall come against him; therefore shall he be grieved and return, and have indignation [the staff to chastise] against the holy covenant [Christianity,] so shall he do; he shall even return and have intelligence with them [priest and bishops] that forsake the holy covenant. And arms (civil and religious) shall stand on his part, and they [Rome and those that forsake the holy covenant] shall pollute the Sanctuary of strength.' What was this that Rome and the apostles of Christianity should jointly pollute? This combination was formed against the 'holy covenant' and it was the Sanctuary of that covenant they polluted; which they could do as well as to pollute the name of God; Jer. 34:16; Ezek. 20; Mal. 1:7. This was the same as profaning or blaspheming his name. In this sense this 'politico-religious' beast polluted the Sanctuary (Rev. 13:6) and cast it down from its place in heaven (Ps. 102:19; Jer. 17:12; Heb. 8:1, 2) when they called Rome the holy city (Rev. 21:2) and enstalled the Pope there with the titles, 'Lord God the Pope,' 'Holy Father,' 'Head of the Church,' &c., and there, in the counterfeit 'temple of God' he professes to do what Jesus actually does in his Sanctuary; 2 Thes. 2:1-8. The Sanctuary had been trodden under foot (Dan. 8:13) the same as the Son of God has; Heb. 10:29" (*ibid.*). (Brackets his.) Cf. Bates, *The Opening Heavens . . . ,* 1846, p. 32; U. Smith, "The Sanctuary," *RH,* March 28, 1854, p. 78 (*The 2300 Days and the Sanctuary,* 1854, p. 22); Andrews, "The Opening of the Temple in Heaven," *RH,* April 6, 1869, p. 115. In another article Crosier criticized Miller's interpretation of the daily sacrifice in Daniel. He stated that Miller had violated his hermeneutical rule that "Scripture must be its own expositor." Explaining his new insights he said: "When first mentioned in Daniel, ch. 8:11, it is so introduced as to make it positively certain that it belonged originally to Christ. No construction of the prepositions in that verse can, as we see, apply it to Rome. . . . Again, it should be noticed that God's people, under the Gospel dispensation, were punished for their 'transgression against the Daily Sacrifice,' v. 12, (margin) — the ancient Daily Sacrifice was a Jewish institution — this, its antitype, must be a Christian institution." Referring to Litch's description of the beginning of "the first Papal war" (*PE,* II, 78-87) — A.D. 508 — Crosier stated that its achievement was "the *suppression* in the church of the doctrine, that *Christ* 'WAS CRUCIFIED FOR US.' This was the Daily Sacrifice they took away, Dan. 11:31, and the direct object was, 'to *set up* the abomination that maketh desolate,' the Papacy, ch. 12.11, (margin,) with its human merit, intercessions and institutions in the place of Christ's. Now we see plainly, that the Daily Sacrifice was taken *from* Christ *by* the little horn, ch. 8.11" ([Crosier], Remarks to Weston, *DD,* March 19, 1847, p. 2). Cf. "Daily," p. 52. This change in interpretation did not affect the time calculations of Dan. 12:11, 12 but helped "rather [to] facilitate" one's understanding of them ([Crosier], Remarks, p. 2).

Then he proceeded to the central issue of his presentation: The typological relevance of the Levitical atonement to Christ's high-priestly ministry in heaven. In doing this he referred to the various aspects of the atonement in the Old Testament sanctuary service:

> The atonement which the priest made for the people in connection with their daily ministration was different from that made on the tenth day of the 7th month. In making the former they went no further than in the Holy; but to make the latter they entered the Holy of Holies — The former was made for individual cases, the latter for the whole nation of Israel collectively — The former was made for the *forgiveness of sins,* the latter for *blotting them out* — the former could be made at any time, the latter only on the tenth day of the seventh month. Hence the former may be called the daily atonement and the latter the yearly, or the former the individual, and the latter the national atonement.[147]

This distinction between the forgiveness of sins and the blotting out of sins was one of the major aspects of his argumentation. In the context of Lev. 16 he stated that "the whole nation having had their sins previously forgiven by the atonement made in the Holy, now assemble about their Sanctuary, while the High Priest . . . enters the Holy of Holies to make an atonement *to cleanse them,* that they may be *clean* from all their sins before the Lord, ver. 30."[148]

The antitype of the Levitical priesthood was fulfilled in Christ's priestly ministry in the heavenly sanctuary, the true tabernacle (Heb. 8, 9). According to Crosier, the heavenly sanctuary, like the earthly, had two apartments, not one apartment as other Christians seemed to believe. Earlier, Edson and E. G. Harmon had already pointed to this division in the heavenly sanctuary. Crosier found scriptural support in Heb. 9:8; 10:19. Referring to the Douai-Rheims Bible[149] he said that "the word in ch. 9:8, 10:19, is Hagion, 'of the Holies,' instead of 'holiest of all' [KJV]; and shows that the blood of Christ is the way or means by which he, as our High Priest, was to enter both apartments of the heavenly tabernacle."[150] Thus, to be consis-

---

147 Crosier, "Law of Moses," p. 40.
148 *Ibid.*
149 See e.g., *The Holy Bible, Translated from the Latin Vulgate . . . ,* rev. and cor., 1816. Other Bible translations in which the Book of Hebrews was referred to as evidence for the concept of a divided heavenly sanctuary were: (1) Macknight, *Apostolic Epistles;* (2) George Campbell, James Macknight, and Philip Doddridge, *The Sacred Writings of the Apostles and Evangelists of Jesus Christ, Commonly Styled the New Testament,* 1826. (The Book of Hebrews had been translated by Macknight.)
150 Crosier, "Law of Moses," p. 41. Later Andrews stated that "Paul plainly states that 'the holy places [plural] made with hands' 'are the figures [plural] of the true.' And that the tabernacle, and its vessels, are 'patterns of things in the heavens.' Heb. ix, 23, 24. This is direct evidence that, in the greater and more perfect tabernacle, there are two holy places, even as in the 'figure,' 'example' or 'pattern.' . . . The Apostle actually uses the word holies, [plural] in speaking of the heavenly sanctuary. The expression 'holiest of all,' in Heb. ix, 8; x, 19, has been supposed by some to prove that Christ began to minister in the most holy place at his ascension. But the expression is not '*hagia hagion,*' holy of holies, as in chapter ix, 3; but is simply '*hagion,*' holies. It is the same word that is rendered sanctuary in Heb. viii, 2. In each of

tent with the typological relationship between the Levitical priestly ministry and that of Christ, Crosier understood the heavenly sanctuary to be divided into two different sections, reflecting two distinct phases of Christ's atonement: the atonement of forgiveness of sins in the first apartment and the atonement of the blotting out of sins in the second. He stated that Christ's atoning ministry did not commence on the cross but after His ascension when He entered the first apartment of the heavenly sanctuary to begin the antitypical daily ministration.[151] His atoning ministry would be completed with "blotting out of sin with all its direful effects" during the antitypical Day of Atonement.[152] Crosier found New Testament evidence for two phases in Christ's heavenly atonement in Peter's appeal on the day of Pentecost: "Repent ye therefore; and be converted, that your sins may be blotted out when the times of refreshing shall come from the presence of the Lord" (Acts 3:19). He interpreted this text as a statement of two successive chronological periods in which repentance and conversion pertained to Christ's daily atoning ministry in the first apartment of the heavenly sanctuary, and the *blotting out of sins* to His atoning ministry that would cleanse both the sanctuary and God's people during the antitypical Day of Atonement commencing on the 10th day of the seventh month 1844:[153]

> The atonement of the Gospel dispensation is the antitype of that made by the priests in their daily service, and that prepared for and made necessary the yearly atonement, and *cleansed* the Sanctuary and the people from all their

these three texts, [Heb. viii, 2; ix, 8; x, 19] Macknight renders the word, 'holy places.' The Doway Bible renders it 'the holies.' And thus we learn that the heavenly sanctuary consists of two 'holy places'" ("Sanctuary," *RH,* Feb. 3, 1853, p. 145 [*Sanctuary,* p. 53]). (Brackets his.) Thus the view that after His ascension Christ entered into the most holy place of the heavenly sanctuary was seen as unscriptural. Cf. E. G. White, *Christ in His Sanctuary,* 1969, pp. 11-13. The expression, "a figure for the time then present, in which were offered both gifts and sacrifices" (Heb. 9:9), E. G. White applied to the whole earthly sanctuary, not merely its holy place (*SP,* IV, 260).

151 Crosier, "Law of Moses," p. 41. Miller had similar views on the relation of the cross to atonement *(supra,* p. 50). Crosier supported this view with the following arguments: "1. If the atonement was made on Calvary, by whom was it made? The making of the atonement is the work of a Priest; but who officiated on Calvary? Roman soldiers and wicked Jews. 2. The *slaying* of the victim was not making the atonement; the sinner slew the victim, Lev. 4:1-4, 13-15, &c., after that the Priest took the blood and made the atonement. Lev. 4:5-12, 16-21. 3. Christ was the appointed High Priest to make the atonement, and he certainly could not have acted in that capacity till after his resurrection, and we have no record of his doing anything on earth after his resurrection, which could be called the atonement. 4. The atonement was made in the Sanctuary, but Calvary was not such a place. 5. He could not, according to Heb. 8:4, make the atonement while on earth. 'If he were on earth, he should not be a Priest.' The Levitical was the earthly priesthood, the Divine, the heavenly. 6. Therefore, he did not begin the work of making the atonement, whatever the nature of that work may be, till after his ascension, when by his own blood he entered his heavenly Sanctuary for us" ("Law of Moses," p. 41). Rom. 5:11 was interpreted to indicate "a present possession of the atonement at the time the apostle wrote; but by no means proves that the entire atonement was then in the past" *(ibid.).* Cf. *infra,* pp. 174, 175.

152 *Ibid.,* p. 42.

153 *Ibid.,* pp. 41, 42. Cf. Letter, Clemons to Editor, p. 35; Snow, " 'Door was Shut,' " p. 54; Letter, Edson to Snow, p. 91; E. G. White, *SP,* IV, 308, 309; E. G. White, *GC,* pp. 485, 612.

sins. It appears like certainty, that the antitypes of the daily ministration of priests and the vernal types stretch through the Gospel Dispensation; as that composed but part of the atonement and antitypes, we have good reason to believe that the remaining antitype, the autumnal, and the remainder of the atonement, the yearly, will be fulfilled on the same principle as to time and occupy a period or dispensation of at least 1000 years.[154]

Crosier rejected the common contemporary view that Christ entered into the holy of holies after His ascension.[155]

Christ's cleansing of the heavenly sanctuary (Dan. 8:14) before the Resurrection,[156] Crosier identified with the removal of the moral uncleanness which had defiled it. The sanctuary, he said, could only be "defiled by mortals through his [Christ's] agency, and for them cleansed by the same agency."[157] The cleansing he interpreted in the context of the *reconciliation* of the "things on earth" with the "things in heaven" (Col. 1:19, 20), the preparation of a place for the believers (Jn. 14:2, 3), and the *purification* of the heavenly sanctuary (Heb. 9:23).[158] On the necessity of the purification mentioned in Heb. 9:23 he remarked:

> The necessity of cleansing the heavenly things, is induced by the atonement being made therein by the blood of Christ for the remission or forgiveness of sins and purifying of our consciences. And almost all things are by the law purged with blood. The patterns were purified "every year" (ver. 25) with the blood of bulls and goats; but in the antitype of that yearly expiation the heavenly things themselves must be purified with the blood of the better sacrifice of Christ himself once offered. This reconciles the "things in heaven" (Col. 1:20) and cleanses the Sanctuary of the new Covenant, Dan. 8:14.[159]

Crosier opposed the common interpretation of the scapegoat (Lev. 16:8,

154 Crosier, "Law of Moses," p. 42. The Gospel dispensation was terminated at the Resurrection while the antitype of Yom Kippur would last till the restoration of all things (*ibid.*, p. 44). He stated that "the antitype of the legal tenth day, the Dispensation of the fulness of times, must begin long enough before the 1000 years of Rev. 20: to give time for the cleansing of the Sanctuary, and the antitype of confessing and putting the sins on the head of the scape-goat" (*ibid.*, p. 43). Not all aspects of Crosier's views on the dispensation of the fulness of times or "the age to come" received the endorsement of the Sabbatarian Adventist leadership, so that their reprints of his treatise appear without these disputed sections. Cf. *infra*, p. 132.

155 *Ibid.*, p. 41.

156 It seems that at this time he held the view that the Resurrection (end of the 1335 days) would occur in the spring of 1847. The cleansing of the sanctuary was to be completed before that time ([Crosier], "The Advent This Spring," *DD*, April 2, 1847, p. 7).

157 Crosier, "Law of Moses," p. 42. Some months earlier Crosier stated that "the Sanctuary of the New Covenant, to be cleansed at the end of the 2300 days, was not the church nor the earth, but the New Jerusalem, and that the 'Sanctuary and Host' are [also to be cleansed], that the *Host* is the temple of the *Holy Ghost,* but the *Sanctuary* the temple of *Christ.* . . . That Christ, after he has finished the atonement in which he will have redeemed his entire kingdom — the Capitol, New Jerusalem, in cleansing it, the Sanctuary — the subjects by raising his saints from their graves — and the territory, by purifying the earth, will, *as the Son of David according to the flesh,* inherit his father David's throne, in the New Jerusalem forever" (Letter, Crosier to Marsh, *VT,* Oct. 29, 1845, p. 505).

158 Crosier, "Law of Moses," p. 43.

159 *Ibid.*

10, 20-22) as a symbol of Christ and insisted, instead, that it was a type of Satan.[160] After the cleansing of the sanctuary but before the beginning of the millennium "the antitype of confessing and putting the sins on the head of the scapegoat" would take place.[161]

The antitypical Day of Atonement he identified with "the dispensation of the fulness of the times"[162] in which the Father "might gather together in one all things in Christ, both which are in heaven, and which are on earth" (Eph. 1:10). During this dispensation "the different and sundered parts of the kingdom, Capitol and King 'in heaven,' the subjects and territory 'on earth,' are to be redeemed or gathered again into one kingdom under one 'Head,' of the Son of David."[163] This period he also named an "age to come," an age of repairs, and a time of restitution and restoration.[164] Said he, "This is the period of inheritance and follows that of heirship, the dispensation of grace, ch. 3:2, 6 [Eph.]."[165] During this period of restoration — "blotting out of sin with all its direful effects" — the following major events would occur: (1) The cleansing of the sanctuary of Dan. 8:14; (2) the

160 *Ibid.* His arguments were: "1st, That goat was not sent away till after the High Priest had *made an end* of cleansing the Sanctuary, Lev. 16:20, 21; hence, that event cannot meet its antitype till after the end of the 2300 days. 2nd, It was sent away from Israel into the wilderness, a land not inhabited, to receive them. If our blessed Saviour is its anti-type, He also must be sent away, not his body alone, but soul and body, for the goat was sent away alive, from, not to nor into, his people; neither into heaven, for that is not a wilderness or land not inhabited. 3d, It received and retained all the iniquities of Israel; but when Christ appears the second time He will be 'without sin.' 4th, The goat received the iniquities from the hands of the priest and he *sent it away.* As Christ is the Priest, the goat must be something else besides himself and which he can *send away.* 5th, This was one of two goats chosen for that day, one was the Lord's and offered for a sin-offering; but the other was not called the Lord's, neither offered as a sacrifice. Its only office was to receive the iniquities for the priest after he had cleansed the Sanctuary for them, and bear them into a land not inhabited, leaving the Sanctuary, priest and people behind and free from their iniquities. Lev. 16:7-10, 22. 6th, The Hebrew name of the scape-goat, as will be seen from the margin of ver. 8, is 'Azazel.' On this verse, Wm. Jenks in his Comp. Com. [*The Comprehensive Commentary on the Holy Bible . . . ,* 1835] has the following remarks: 'Scape-goat. See diff. opin. in Bochart. Spencer, after the *oldest* opinion of the Hebrews and Christians, thinks Azazel is the name of the devil; and so Rosemire [Rosenmüller], whom see. The Syriac has Azzael [*sic*], the angel (Strong one) who revolted.' 7th, At the appearing of Christ, as taught from Rev. 20: Satan is to be bound and cast into the bottomless pit, which act and place are significantly symbolized by the ancient High Priest sending the scape-goat into a separate and uninhabited wilderness. 8th, Thus we have [in] the Scripture the definition of the name in two ancient languages both spoken at the same time, & the oldest opinion of the Christians in favor of regarding the scape-goat as a type of *Satan*" ("Law of Moses," p. 43). Cf. E. G. White, *SP,* IV, 266.

161 Crosier, "Law of Moses," p. 43. Cf. Letter, Crosier to Jacobs, *DS,* Nov. 15, 1845, p. 23.

162 Various Adventists used this term to designate the period following the Disappointment: Editorial, "The Types," p. 117; Letter, Pickands to Marsh, p. 12; Letter, Edson to Snow, p. 91.

163 Crosier, "Law of Moses," p. 42.

164 *Ibid.* He identified " 'the age to come' with 'the times of restitution,' *'Apokatastasis,* restoration of any thing to its former state, hence, the introduction of a new and better era;' and 'the times of refreshing,' *'Anapsuxis,* refreshing coolness after heat, recreation, rest.' " He said: "The identity of 'the times of restitution' with 'The Dispensation of the fulness of times,' Eph. 1:10, is also apparent" (*ibid.*). Cf. Letter, Edson to Snow, p. 91.

165 Crosier, "Law of Moses," p. 42.

marriage between Christ and the New Jerusalem; (3) the transference of sin to the scapegoat; (4) Christ's return; (5) the cleansing of God's people; (6) the millennium.[166] Although the dispensation of the fulness of the times began in the fall of 1844, the Gospel dispensation or dispensation of grace did not end at that time. The expression "there should be time no more" (Rev. 10:6) could not refer to the Second Advent, according to Crosier, for after this oath came the commission to prophesy again (Rev. 10:11).[167] He pointed to Rev. 10:6, 7 for a description of "the *manner* in which time should close."[168] The "days" in Rev. 10:7 indicated "a short *period* of time, in which not only the 7th angel begins to sound, but the mystery of God is finished. Thus we see that the mystery is finished, not in a *point,* but in a *period,* and while the mystery is finishing, the 7th angel is beginning to sound."[169] In other words,

> as the Dispensation of the fulness of times begins with the 7th trumpet, and the Gos. Dis. reaches to the resurrection, it is manifest that the Dis. of the fulness of times, begins before the Gos. Dis. ends. — There is a short period of overlapping or running together of the two Dispensations, in which the peculiarities of both mingle like the twilight, minglings of light and darkness.[170]

These statements indicate that Crosier's shut-door view was not of an extreme nature, for he advocated a *continuation* of the atonement process, the Gospel dispensation, and the mystery of God[171] after October 22, 1844.

Besides providing an explanation for the Disappointment, a major soteriological contribution of Crosier's treatise was that it pointed out that the atonement was not yet finished.

Some months later Crosier expanded his view of the cleansing of the

166 *Ibid.,* pp. 42-44. Although the validity of the Bridegroom theme was recognized, he did not fully integrate it into the sanctuary theology (cf. *ibid.,* pp. 42, 44). Cf. Letter, Crosier to Jacobs, *DS,* Oct. 11, 1845, p. 51. Earlier, however, he stated that Christ had entered "upon the office of bridegroom or the final atonement for his people" since the autumn of 1844 (Letter, Crosier to Pearson, p. [4]). Cf. E. G. White, *SG,* I, 162, 163.

167 Crosier, "Law of Moses," p. 44.

168 *Ibid.*

169 *Ibid.* He defined the mystery of God (Rev. 10:6) on the basis of Eph. 6:19, Col. 1:27, and Eph. 2:4-6 as the dispensation of the grace of God or the Gospel dispensation (*ibid.*). To Bates the mystery of God was finished in a point of time (*SAWH,* pp. 42, 43).

170 Crosier, "Law of Moses," p. 44. Some months earlier he posed the question: "Did not the legal Covenant overlap the Covenant of grace 7 years, the last week of the 70? and will not the Covenant of grace overlap the 'Dispensation of the fulness of times' a corresponding length of time?" (Letter, Crosier to Jacobs, *DS,* Nov. 15, 1845, p. 23). However, in the present article he saw "no evidence that the latter must be of the same *length* of the former" ("Law of Moses," p. 44). Other source material seems to indicate that at this time he held the view that the Resurrection (end of the 1335 days) would take place in the spring of 1847 ([Crosier], Remarks, p. 2; [Crosier], "Advent This Spring," p. 7). This implied also the termination of the Gospel dispensation.

171 He indicated that the Gospel dispensation was "the period of *hope* and *heirship*" which implied that as long as "we hope the mystery is not finished." Thus it was concluded that "the mystery of God will *end* with the mysterious change from mortal to immortality; 1 Cor. 15:51-54" ("Law of Moses," p. 44). See *infra,* p. 157.

sanctuary, making it apply to both the sanctuary in heaven and the church on earth:

> Many seem not to have discovered that there is a literal and a spiritual temple — the literal being the Sanctuary in New Jerusalem (literal city), and the spiritual the church — the literal occupied by Jesus Christ, our King and Priest, Jno. 14:2, Heb. 8:2, 9:11; the spiritual by the Holy Ghost, I Cor. 3:17; 6:19; Eph. 2:20-22. Between these two there is a perfect concert of action; as Christ "prepares the *place*" the Spirit does the people. When he came to his temple, the sanctuary, to cleanse it; the Spirit commenced the special cleansing of the people, Mal. 3:1-13.[172]

Crosier's interpretation of the antitypical Day of Atonement shed additional light on the nature of the pre-Advent judgment.[173] It was also in harmony with the view of the conditional immortality of man — a doctrine which had been advocated by some Millerites and came to be one of the SDA teachings.[174]

Soon other Sabbatarian Adventists limited Crosier's view on the duration of the antitypical Day of Atonement to Jesus' cleansing ministry in the sanctuary before His return. The time of the blotting out of sins of the living believers was closely associated with the sanctuary cleansing and seen as a present or imminent event.[175]

3. Evaluation of the Seventh Month movement.

The sanctuary theology provided an explanation of the Disappointment and interpreted the event as an important factor in God's plan of redemption. A number of Adventists saw the importance of the Seventh Month movement not only confirmed by their personal experience but also by the first two visions of E. G. Harmon. The vision of December 1844 pictured

172 Letter, Crosier to Jacobs, *DS,* April 18, 1846, p. 31. Cf. Bates, *Opening Heavens,* p. 31.

173 Wardwell commented on Dan. 12:13: "And when I speak of Daniel standing in his lot in the judgment, I would be understood as saying, that when our great High Priest entered the Most Holy Place with the names of all Israel inscribed upon his breastplate, Daniel was judged worthy or unworthy to be thus borne before the Father. This is what I understand by the dead standing before God in the judgment" (Letter, Wardwell to Crosier, p. 10). Regarding the breastplate of judgment, see Peavey, "'Hour of His Judgment,'" p. 114; Crosier, "Law of Moses," p. 40. See *supra,* p. 118, n. 96. The view of a pre-Advent judgment was only gradually adopted by J. White (J. White, *WLF,* p. 24; J. White, "The Day of Judgment," *AdR,* Sept. 1850, pp. 49, 50; [J. White], "The Seventh Angel . . . ," *RH,* March 7, 1854, p. 52; J. White, "The Judgment," *RH,* Jan. 29, 1857, p. 100).

174 See Appendix II and III. Conditional immortality was introduced into the Millerite movement by Storrs. It was also accepted by Fitch. Early publications of J. White and E. G. White reflect a similar view on the nature of man. They were also annihilationists (J. White, *WLF,* pp. 3, 11, 12, 24). Cf. Froom, *The Conditionalist Faith of Our Fathers . . . ,* II, 1965, pp. 300-14, 671-79.

175 See e.g., Bates, *SLG,* pp. 20, 38; E. G. White, "DBS," *PT,* Sept. 1849, p. 32 (*EW,* p. 48); Edson, "An Appeal to the Laodicean Church," *AdR,* Extra, Sept. 1850, pp. 3, 14; Bates, "The Laodicean Church," *RH,* Nov. 1850, p. 8; Bates, *TAS,* 1850, pp. 11, 15. Cf. E. G. White, *SP,* IV, 309; E. G. White, *GC,* pp. 422, 483-86.

the validity of the Midnight Cry of the Seventh Month movement and an 1844 shut door.[176] The immediate results of the vision was that she and about 60 other believers in Portland, Maine, "acknowledged their 7th month experience to be the work of God."[177]

In February 1845 E. G. Harmon received another vision in which the Midnight Cry again was symbolized as a great light from Christ. It pictured a throne in the first apartment of the heavenly sanctuary with two groups of people before it. One group was bowed down and represented the Adventists; the other stood uninterested and careless, symbolizing the church and the world. Then an exceeding bright light passed from the Father to Christ and waved over the individuals before the throne. Many opposed this great light and came out from under it; a few accepted it and bowed down with the little praying company. Then Jesus went as the Bridegroom to the wedding in the second apartment, where He officiated as High Priest before the Father. Those who by faith followed the change of Christ's ministry were blessed but those who, being deceived, did not know of the change came under the influence of Satan.[178] Thus, like Edson, E. G. Harmon placed the coming of the Bridegroom to the wedding in the setting of Christ's high-priestly ministry.

In 1847 one of the earliest extensive historical evaluations of the Millerite movement was written by Joseph Bates, an active participant who accepted the Sabbath in 1845. He strongly stressed the validity of both the Millerite movement in general and the Midnight Cry of the Seventh Month movement as phases in salvation history.[179] Similar views were found in later Sabbatarian Adventist publications. During this time Miller had a dream[180] which J. White interpreted as being of divine origin and con-

---

176 E. G. White [E. G. Harmon], "RSA," p. 14. She said: I saw "a straight and narrow path, cast up high above the world. On this path the Advent people were traveling to the City, which was at the farther end of the path. They had a bright light set up behind them at the first end of the path, which an angel told me was the Midnight Cry. This light shone all along the path, and gave light for their feet so they might not stumble. And if they kept their eyes fixed on Jesus, who was just before them, leading them to the City, they were safe. But some grew weary, and they said the City was a great way off, and they expected to have entered it before. Then Jesus would encourage them by raising his glorious right arm, and from his arm came a glorious light which waved over the Advent band, and they shouted Hallelujah! Others rashly denied the light behind them, and said that it was not God that had led them out so far. The light behind them went out which left their feet in perfect darkness, and they stumbled and got their eyes off the mark and lost sight of Jesus, and fell off the path down in the dark and wicked world below. It was just as impossible for them to get on the path again & go to the City, as all the wicked world which God had rejected" (ibid.). Cf. Letter, J. White to Jacobs, DS, Sept. 6, 1845, p. 17. For her first autobiographical account on the Advent movement and the Seventh Month movement in the context of salvation history, see SG, I, 133-73.

177 J. White, WLF, p. 22.

178 Letter, E. G. Harmon to Jacobs, DS, March 14, 1846, p. 7 (EW, pp. 54-56).

179 Bates, SAWH, pp. 6-16, 30-33.

180 Letter, Miller to Himes, AH, Jan. 8, 1848, p. 182 (CEV, 2nd ed., 1882, pp. 70, 71 [EW, pp. 81-83]). In 1826 Miller had a dream which was not published until after his death ("A Dream," AH, Feb. 2, 1850, pp. 2, 3). David Arnold interpreted this as another confirmation of the Advent movement ("Dream of William Miller," RH, Extra, c. 1851).

firmed his confidence in the prophetic significance of the past Advent experience.[181]

The majority of Adventists, however, gradually lost confidence in the new interpretations which emphasized the validity of the Seventh Month movement. This was especially evident after the Albany Conference in the spring of 1845, held after the termination of the Jewish Karaite year. During the summer of 1845 Miller remarked that

> some are disposed to lay stress on the seventh month movement which is not warranted by the Word. . . .
> I have no confidence in any of the new theories that have grown out of that movement, viz., that Christ then came as the Bridegroom, that the door of mercy was closed, that there is no salvation for sinners, that the seventh trumpet then sounded, or that it was a fulfillment of prophecy in any sense.[182]

Miller, according to Himes, returned to his original view of the Midnight Cry as set forth in his lecture, "The Ten Virgins," which Himes also considered as the correct interpretation.[183] Until his death in December 1849, Miller expressed confidence in the divine guidance of the Advent movement of the 1840s and felt that some minor error in the calculations would explain the Disappointment.

4. Summary.

One of the most important problems which confronted Adventists after October 22, 1844, was how to evaluate and interpret the Seventh Month movement and the Disappointment. Initially the general opinion was that the Midnight Cry of the parable of Mt. 25 had met its fulfillment in the Seventh Month movement and that the Second Advent would take place at any time. The immediate soteriological and missiological consequences of the Disappointment were that Adventists thought their mission had been completed and the door of mercy closed against the churches and the world which had rejected the Advent proclamation of Christ's imminent personal return. They also felt that their shut-door views were confirmed by the hostile reaction of the public after the Disappointment. As time continued and the Second Coming still tarried, Adventists entered a period of controversy which destroyed their unity. The majority of the approximately 50,000 Adventists lost confidence in the validity of the Seventh Month movement and all shut-door ideas. A gradually diminishing minority, from which the Sabbatarian Adventists arose, continued to express their belief

---

181 [J. White], "Miller's Dream," pp. 73-75 (*Miller's Dream*). Cf. Arnold, "Dream of Miller."

182 Miller, *Apology*, p. 28. See *supra*, pp. 40-43. Himes said that "the *Cry* that was then made, was a *part* of the general cry, and not the *only*, and *final* one" (Editorial, "A Word to the Advent Brethren," *MW*, April 3, 1845, p. 112). Cf. Letter, B. Matthias to Miller, *JS*, April 24, 1845, p. 56. Lindén designated the Seventh Month movement as the ultraistic stage of the Millerite movement (*Biblicism*, p. 57). Cf. *supra*, pp. 78, 83.

183 See *supra*, p. 113.

that no mistake had been made in the time calculations of the Seventh Month movement, but only in the prediction of the event to take place at the end of the 2300 days. They explained their error as an incorrect application of some of Miller's hermeneutical principles. The major questions which confronted them were that if the parable of the ten virgins had its fulfillment in the Seventh Month movement, what was the significance of the coming of the Bridegroom and that of the cleansing of the sanctuary of Dan. 8:14? To solve these questions the sanctuary theology was developed dealing with the nature of Christ's heavenly ministry. Within the context of the sanctuary theology a variety of views emerged, contributing to the heterogeneous character of this minority. On the basis of a more consistent application of Miller's hermeneutical principles, the early Sabbatarian Adventists concluded that the coming of the Bridegroom signified Christ's coming to the marriage in the heavenly sanctuary on October 22, 1844, while Dan. 8:14 announced the beginning of Christ's high-priestly ministry on the antitypical Day of Atonement. When these two aspects of Christ's final ministry were completed, they expected the Second Advent to take place. Because of the fact that this interpretation presupposed the validity of the Seventh Month movement, its vindication became of crucial importance for Sabbatarian Adventists.

Most Adventists considered the new interpretation to be a spiritualization of the Advent expectancy; Sabbatarian Adventists, however, denied this charge. Those who did not accept the sanctuary theology but still adhered to the validity of the Seventh Month movement did advocate a spiritual return of Christ and not a personal one. Sabbatarian Adventists designated such interpretation as spiritualism.

B. The Formation of the Third Angel's Message.

> And the third angel followed them, saying with a loud voice, If any man worship the beast and his image, and receive his mark in his forehead, or in his hand, the same shall drink of the wine of the wrath of God, which is poured out without mixture into the cup of his indignation; and he shall be tormented with fire and brimstone in the presence of the holy angels, and in the presence of the Lamb: And the smoke of their torment ascendeth up forever and ever: and they have no rest day nor night, who worship the beast and his image, and whosoever receiveth the mark of his name. Here is the patience of the saints: here are they that keep the commandments of God, and the faith of Jesus. Rev. 14:9-12.

It was predominantly through the influence of the Seventh Day Baptists that in 1844 the attention of a number of Adventists was directed to the subject of the continued obligation of the observance of the seventh-day Sabbath of the fourth commandment of the Decalogue. After the Disappointment various Adventists began to observe this day as the biblical day for worship. These Adventists, here called Sabbatarian Adventists, gradually developed a biblical rationale for the contemporary emphasis on this day of worship by associating the Sabbath[184] with the idea of a restoration of all biblical principles before Christ's return, with the sanctuary theology, and especially with the third angel's message. In this way the Sabbath doctrine became integrated into the Advent experience. The following discussion will deal with the origin of the revival of the Sabbath during the 1840s, its influence on the Adventists, its incorporation into the Advent experience, and its contribution to the Sabbatarian Adventist theology of mission.

1. The Seventh-day Sabbath reform movement.

The Sunday reform revival[185] in 1843 created a great concern among the Seventh Day Baptists[186] who feared new Sunday law legislation. This concern resulted in resolutions by the 1843 and 1844 General Conferences of Seventh Day Baptists to set apart a day of fasting and prayer on November 1, 1843 and on January 1, 1845 for divine intervention and restoration of the Sabbath.[187] To arouse the attention of other Christians resolutions were passed to send one address to the Baptists[188] and another to all evangelical denominations in the U.S.A., urging them to investigate the importance of the Sabbath doctrine.[189] The Millerites were also approached but they generally felt that either this doctrine was irrelevant or Jewish.

As early as 1841 one could find a reference to the Sabbath in Millerite literature. This was made by James A. Begg,[190] a Scottish Sabbatarian millenarian, who wrote that, besides his preoccupation with the Advent movement, he had to "work on the continued obligation of the Seventh Day, as the Christian Sabbath."[191] One year later a letter pertaining to the Sabbath question was disposed within an editorial remark that Millerites wished "to have no controversy with the 'Seventh Day Baptists.' "[192]

184   All references to the seventh-day Sabbath are indicated by the term "Sabbath."
185   See supra, p. 10.
186   Seventh Day Baptists are Baptists who observe the seventh-day Sabbath, the Saturday, as the biblical day of rest. The Sabbath seems to have been introduced in America by Stephen Mumford, a British Seventh Day Baptist immigrant. The first American Seventh Day Baptist Church was organized at Newport, R.I., in 1671. By 1843 churches had been established in New York State, New Jersey, Rhode Island, Connecticut and Virginia. The reported membership at the 1843 General Conference was 6077 (Seventh Day Baptists, Manual of the Seventh Day Baptists . . . , 1858, pp. 39, 51-53).
187   Seventh Day Baptists, Seventh Day Baptist Anniversaries . . . , 1843, p. 9; [George B. Utter], "Our Anniversaries," Sabbath Recorder, Sept. 19, 1844, p. 50.
188   See e.g., An Address to the Baptists of the United States, on the Observance of the Sabbath: From the Seventh Day Baptist General Conference, 3rd ed., 1843.
189   Seventh Day Baptists, Anniversaries, p. 8; Seventh Day Baptists, Minutes of the General Conference, 1844, p. 10.
190   James A. Begg (1800-68) was brought up in the Reformed Presbyterian Church of Scotland. Influenced by the current revival of British millenarianism he became an expositor of prophecy. In 1832 he began observing the Sabbath. He wrote several articles for the ST.
191   J. A. Begg, "Letter from Scotland," ST, April 1, 1841, p. 3.
192   Editorial, "To Correspondents," ST, April 6, 1842, p. 5.

In 1844 the Seventh Day Baptists were more successful. The *Midnight Cry* observed that "many persons have their minds deeply exercised respecting a supposed obligation to observe the *seventh day*."[193] After a lengthy discussion the editor stated that

> we feel borne irresistibly to the conclusion that *there is no particular portion of time which Christians are required by law to set apart, as holy time.* If the Scriptures, and the considerations presented, do not convince our readers of this, then we think there is another conclusion to which they must come, viz., *The particular portion of time which God requires us to observe as holy, is the seventh day of the week,* that is, Saturday.[194]

In the next issue of the *Midnight Cry* the discussion was concluded with the remark that "we love the seventh-day brethren and sisters, but we think they are trying to mend the old broken Jewish yoke, and put it on their necks, instead of standing fast in the liberty wherewith Christ makes free."[195]

It was through Rachel Oakes, a Seventh Day Baptist, that the Sabbath was introduced to a group of Millerite Adventists in Washington, New Hampshire, in the winter of 1843-44. As a result, Fredrick Wheeler, a Methodist Adventist circuit rider, and various members of this group became the first Sabbatarian Adventists in North America in the spring of 1844.[196] Later in that year, the Sabbath was accepted by another clergyman, Thomas M. Preble, a Free-Will Baptist Adventist, who soon began publishing his new convictions.[197] Much of his exposition included Seventh Day Baptist arguments for Sabbath observance, such as the continuing validity of the Decalogue for Christians and the Sabbath as an everlasting sign between God and His people. The responsibility of changing the day of worship from Saturday to Sunday was attributed to the Roman Catholic Church. From historical data Preble inferred, "Thus we see Dan. vii:25 fulfilled, the 'little horn' changing 'times and laws.' Therefore, it appears to me that all who keep the first day of the week for '*the Sabbath*,' are *Pope's*

193 Editorial, " 'The Lord's Day,' " *MC,* Sept. 5, 1844, p. 68.

194 Editorial, " 'Lord's Day,' " p. 69.

195 Editorial, "The 'Lord's Day,' " *MC,* Sept. 12, 1844, p. 77. The article recommended discontinuing the use of "the word 'Sabbath' to the first day of the week. If we all habitually use the only Scriptural name for it, — 'The Lord's Day,' — the name would awaken the associations which ought to be connected with it, and we see not how any one could devote it to secular pursuits, while the thought, 'it is the Lord's day' was constantly before his mind" (*ibid.*). For a Seventh Day Baptist response to these articles, see [Utter], "Perpetuity of the Sabbath," *Sabbath Recorder,* Sept. 26, 1844, p. 54; T., "The Midnight Cry," *Sabbath Recorder,* Oct. 10, 1844, p. 62.

196 It was not until 1850 that these individuals accepted the third angel's message (Letter, Fredrick Wheeler, *RH,* Dec. 1850, p. 16; J. White, "A Sketch of the Rise and Progress of the Present Truth," *RH,* Dec. 31, 1857, p. 61).

197 Froom, *PFF,* I, 941-52. Preble accepted the Sabbath in 1844. He was probably the first Adventist in the U.S.A. to advocate the Sabbath in print. His exposition was first published in the *HI,* Feb. 28, 1845, and re-issued in a special pamphlet. He discontinued Sabbath observance in 1847, later opposing it.

Sunday Keepers!! and God's SABBATH BREAKERS!!!"[198]

Preble's plea for Sabbath observance aroused the interest of Bates, Edson, and others. Bates influenced James and Ellen G. White to accept the Sabbath.[199] However, the editor of the *Day-Star* designated the Sabbath as a type or shadow with no claims on Christians;[200] nevertheless, the periodical published various accounts of Adventists who had begun observing the Sabbath.[201] A nucleus of Sabbatarian Adventists was formed[202] who developed a doctrine of the Sabbath which was intimately related to their Advent experience.

2. The Sabbath and the Advent experience.

During the formative years of the Sabbatarian Adventists the Sabbath was integrated into the Advent experience through three closely related themes: (1) The restoration of all biblical principles before the Second Coming; (2) the sanctuary theology; (3) the third angel's message.

a. The restoration theme.

The first ones to associate the Sabbath with the Advent experience were Preble[203] and Bates. In 1846 Bates, in addressing himself to Adventists, pointed to the necessity of the restoration of the Sabbath before the Second Advent. He said: "I understand that the *seventh* day Sabbath is not the *least* one, among ALL things that are to be restored before the second advent of Jesus Christ, seeing that the Imperial and Papal power of Rome, since the

---

198   T. M. Preble, *A Tract, Showing That the Seventh Day Should Be Observed as the Sabbath . . .*, 1845, p. 10. Cf. Preble, "The Sabbath," *HI*, Feb. 28, 1845 in *RH*, Aug. 23, 1870, p. 74. This view was a standard historicist interpretation among Seventh Day Baptists; Froom, *PFF*, IV, 908, 911, 913, 916, 920.

199   After E. G. White commenced to observe the Sabbath in the autumn of 1846 she received a vision in reference to it (Letter, E. G. White to Loughborough, No. 2, 1874 [A. L. White, *Ellen G. White*, p. 34]).

200   [Jacobs], "The Sabbath," *DS*, Aug. 11 and 18, 1845, pp. 3-7.

201   Letter, George W. Jones to Jacobs, *DS*, Aug. 25, 1845, p. 10; Letter, C. Main to Jacobs, *DS*, Aug. 25, 1845, p. 12; Letter, A Little Child to Jacobs, *DS*, Oct. 3, 1845, p. 39; Letter, Henry Emmons to Jacobs, *DS*, Oct. 25, 1845, p. 6; Letter, Stephen Pratt to Jacobs, *DS*, Nov. 1, 1845, p. 13; Letter, D. B. Gibbs to Jacobs, *DS*, Nov. 22, 1845, p. 31; Letter, Oren Wetherbee to Jacobs, *DS*, Jan. 24, 1846, p. 30; Letter, Cook to Jacobs, *DS*, March 7, 1846, p. 3.

202   From the Disappointment till 1846 Adventists in different States accepted the Sabbath. As a result of strong opposition and confusion "many of those who embraced the Sabbath gave it up" ([J. White], "A Brief Sketch of the Past," *RH*, May 6, 1852, p. 5).

203   Preble alluded to the general Millerite understanding that the Sabbath was a sign of "the seventh thousand years" which were supposed to have begun after 1843 when the 6000 years of earth's history seems to have ended. He argued that his "practice" should agree with his "theory" which implied the observance of "the seventh day" as a "sign" ("The Sabbath," *VT*, Aug. 27, 1845, p. 433). Cf. Preble, *Sabbath*, pp. 5, 6. See Miller, *A Lecture on the Typical Sabbaths and Great Jubilee*, 1842, pp. 22-27. Cf. [Jacobs], "Sabbath," p. 3. Preble also said that "if the Sabbath is 'a sign to the children of Israel for-ever [Ex. 31:17];' how can the *sign* cease, till the thing *signified* by it is realized? And if we are a part of the true Israel, as we claim to be, how could 'Israel' before Christ, keep the *seventh* day, and 'Israel' since Christ keep the *first* day; and yet *each* be a sign of the *same thing*?" ("Sabbath," p. 433).

days of the Apostles have changed the seventh day Sabbath to the first day of the week!"[204] During the same year, Cook associated the Sabbath with the idea that "Elijah is to *restore all things'* [Mt. 17:11]."[205] In 1847 Bates developed the restoration theme in the setting of a final conflict:

> The keeping of the seventh day Sabbath has been made void by the working of Satan, and is to be restored as one of the *all* things spoken of by all the holy prophets since the world began, before Jesus can come, is evident. See Acts iii:20, 21. "And they that shall be of THEE shall *build the old waste places — thou shalt raise up the foundation of many generations,* and thou shalt be called the REPAIRER *of the breach, the* RESTORER *of paths to dwell in."* Is. 58:12. The two following verses show that keeping or restoring the Sabbath is the special work. Jesus says, "they shall be called great in the kingdom of heaven, that *do* and *teach* the commandments." [Mt. 5:19] That there will yet be a mighty struggle about the restoring and keeping the seventh day Sabbath, that will test every soul that enters the gates of the city, cannot be disputed. It is evident the Devil is making war on all such. See Rev. 12:17.[206]

Both James and E. G. White endorsed the restoration theme but placed it in the context of a preparatory work to escape God's final wrath.[207] Later the theme was integrated into the third angel's message through the Elijah motif.[208]

b. The Sabbath and the sanctuary theology.

The sanctuary theology of Edson, E. G. White, and Crosier facilitated the acceptance of the Sabbath doctrine and the third angel's message. A point of contact between the heavenly sanctuary and the Sabbath was seen in Rev. 11:19. Bates commented that

> God in a peculiar manner, to instruct his honest, confiding children, shows them spiritually under the sounding of the seventh Angel, the ark of his testament after the temple of God was opened in heaven xi:19. These are the ten commandments. Here then I understand is where the spirit made an indelible impression to search the scriptures for the TESTIMONY of God.[209]

Edson had already discussed the Sabbath with friends before Bates ap-

---

204 Bates, *SSP,* 1846, p. 2. Cf. Letter, Main to Jacobs, p. 12. For a more extensive treatment of Dan. 7:25, see Bates, *SSP,* 1846, pp. 41, 42. The introduction of the practice of feetwashing (Jn. 13:1-17) in association with the celebration of the Lord's supper was seen as another aspect of a restoration of worship. Cf. Pickands to Jacobs, *DS,* Sept. 25, 1845, p. 33.

205 Letter, Cook to Jacobs, *DS,* March 7, 1846, p. 3. Referring to Sunday observance he urged people to "throw off the *last rag* of 'the mother of harlots' [Rev. 17:5]" (Cook, "The Sabbath," *AT,* April 1846, p. 12). Some Adventists identified Snow with Elijah in the context of Mal. 4:5 (*True Day Star,* Dec. 29, 1845). In reacting against those who anticipated the coming of Elijah, Miller said that Mal. 4:5, 6 had been fulfilled in Jesus Christ, the antitypical Elijah, at the first Advent ("Elijah the Prophet," *AH,* Feb. 5, 1845, pp. 201-3).

206 Bates, *SSP* [2nd ed., rev. and enl.], 1847, p. 60. Cf. E. G. White, *LS,* 1915, p. 96.

207 [J. White], "Repairing the Breach in the Law of God," *PT,* Sept. 1849, pp. 25, 28, 29; E. G. White, *CEV,* pp. 52, 53 (*EW,* p. 65).

208 See *infra,* pp. 250-53.

209 Bates, *SSP,* 1847, p. [iii]. Cf. Hale, *Bridegroom,* p. 28.

proached him on this subject. Alluding to the preparatory function of the sanctuary doctrine Edson stated that from his "understanding of the opening of the tabernacle of the *testimony* in heaven, and the seeing of the ark of his testimony [Rev. 11:19], and the few lines I had seen from the pen of T. M. Preble, I had been looking at the subject of the seventh day — Sabbath."[210] Thus it was felt that Rev. 11:19 was an indication that the heavenly sanctuary, like the earthly sanctuary, contained an ark with the Decalogue in the most holy place. This typology provided an argument for the perpetuity of the Decalogue. The April 3, 1847, heavenly-sanctuary view of E. G. White supported this interpretation.[211] In 1849 she revealed that through the change in Jesus' high-priestly ministry the attention of God's people had been directed to the most holy place, resulting in a deeper understanding of the relevance of the Decalogue. Because of this additional light, she said that they were "being tested on the Sabbath question";[212] in fact, it was not until after the Disappointment that the Sabbath became a test for God's people.[213] Thus the Sabbath doctrine was incorporated into the sanctuary theology and, being a test, it achieved major importance in the emerging theology of mission.

c. The Sabbath and the third angel's message.

The special message affirming the validity of the Seventh Month movement and proclaiming the restoration of the Sabbath as a test, in the context of the imminent Second Advent and God's wrath, was the message of the third angel of Rev. 14. Bates was one of the first to associate the Sabbath with Rev. 14:9-11 as the third angel's message. The fact that some Adventists began to observe the Sabbath he saw as a consequence of the Disappointment and another sign of the times. Adopting a position held by some that the third angel of Rev. 14 had terminated its mission at the Disappointment,[214] Bates pointed out that Rev. 14:12, "Here is the patience of the saints: here are they that keep the commandments of God, and the faith of Jesus" was the result of the third angel's message. The difference be-

210   Edson, MS, p. 10.
211   Letter, E. G. White to Bates, April 7, 1847 in *WLF*, pp. 18, 19 (*EW*, pp. 32, 33). Cf. [J. White], "The Law of God, or the Ten Commandments," *PT*, July 1849, p. 4; E. G. White, *SP*, IV, 273.
212   E. G. White, "DBS," *PT*, Aug. 1849, p. 21 (*EW*, p. 42).
213   *Ibid.* (*EW*, pp. 42, 43). Here she said that "the present test on the Sabbath could not come, until the mediation of Jesus in the Holy Place was finished, and he had passed within the second vail; therefore, Christians, who fell asleep before the door was opened to the Most Holy, when the midnight cry was finished, at the seventh month 1844; and [who] had not kept the true Sabbath, now rest in hope; for they had not the light and the test on the Sabbath, which we now have, since that door was opened."
214   Cook and Pickands had published the *Voice of the Fourth Angel*, which stated that the mission of the first three angels of Rev. 14 had been fulfilled. Cf. Editorial, "Voice of the Fourth Angel," *WMC*, Dec. 21, 1844, p. 28; Woodcock, "True Millennium," p. 32; Pickands, "Our Position and Present Duty," *Voice of the Fourth Angel*, repr. in *VT*, Jan. 8, 1845, p. 197; Letter, Turner to Snow, *JS*, July 10, 1845, p. 137; [Crosier], "Advent This Spring," p. 7; Bates, *SAWH*, pp. 20, 23-25, 27.

tween Rev. 14:9-11 and Rev. 14:12, he said, was that they represented two successive, not concurrent, phases in the Advent experience: The Disappointment was the end of the proclamation of the third angel and the beginning of the period of Rev. 14:12.[215] He argued that the angels of Rev. 14:6-11 brought about a company of individuals who observed the Sabbath:

> In the xiv ch. Rev. 6-11, he [John] saw three angels following each other in succession: first one preaching the everlasting gospel (second advent doctrine); 2nd, announcing the fall of Babylon; 3d, calling God's people out of her by showing the awful destruction that awaited all such as did not obey. He sees the separation and cries out, "Here is the patience of the Saints, here are they that keep the *commandments* of God and the faith of Jesus. . . ." Now it seems to me that the seventh day Sabbath is more clearly included in these commandments, than thou shalt not steal, nor kill, nor commit adultery, for it is the only one that was written at the creation or in the *beginning*.[216]

In 1847 Bates became even more specific and indicated that the cry of the third angel had produced a number of Adventists "in their patience, (or trying time,) keeping the commandments of God and the faith or testimony of Jesus."[217] The fact, he said, "such a people [who keep the Decalogue] can be found on the earth as described in the 12v. [Rev. 14] and have been uniting in companies for the last two years, on the commandments of God and faith or testimony of Jesus, is indisputable and clear. I say here then is demonstrated proof that Babylon has fallen."[218] The "faith of Jesus" (Rev. 14:12), he suggested, was synonymous with the "testimony of Jesus" (Rev. 12:17), and identified in the context of Mt. 28:19, 20. It was also substituted for the Mosaic laws after they had been "nailed to the cross."[219] Bates was one of the first to equate the observance of Sunday as the Sabbath or holy day with "a mark of the beast" (Rev. 14:9).[220]

J. White, however, disagreed with Bates' interpretation of the third angel's message. The mission of the third angel to Adventists, he said, did not end in 1844 but commenced in the "patient waiting time" *after* the 1844 Disappointment when various Adventists began observing the Sabbath. The view that Rev. 14:9-11 was concurrent with Rev. 14:12 was based on his definition of the third angel's message:

---

215 Bates, *SSP*, 1846, p. 24. Cf. Letter, Wm. Evans to Snow, *JS*, May 22, 1845, p. 87.

216 Bates, *SSP*, 1846, p. 24. Cf. Litch, "Cleansing of the Sanctuary," *MC*, June 22, 1843, p. 127. Regarding Rev. 14:12, see Letter, Cook to Jacobs, *DS*, March 7, 1846, p. 3. Bates identified Rev. 14:9-11 with Rev. 18:4 as the third angel's message (*SAWH*, pp. 23, 24, 68). Cf. Editorial, "Come Out," pp. 20, 21; Letter, Hotchkiss to Marsh, *VT*, Feb. 5, 1845, p. 7. In 1847 Bates indicated that the third angel showed "the curse that befell all such as 'worship the beast or his image, or *receive his mark*,' that is, if they go back again [to Babylon]" (*SSP*, 1847, p. 58).

217 *Ibid.* Cf. Bates, *SAWH*, pp. 68, 69.

218 Bates, *SSP*, 1847, pp. 58, 59.

219 *Ibid.*, p. 52. Another definition he gave was that the faith of Jesus signified His "teachings or testimony at his first advent, except the Revelation after his ascension" (*SAWH*, p. 71).

220 Bates, *SSP*, 1847, p. 59.

The third angel's message was, and still is, a WARNING to the saints to "hold fast," and not go back, and "receive" the marks which the virgin band got rid of, during the second angel's cry.

And has not the true message for God's people, since the 7th month 1844, been just such a warning? It certainly has. I cannot agree with those who make two messages of the cry, "Babylon the great is fallen," and the voice, "Come out of her my people," for every sermon that was printed, or preached on this subject, contained them both in one message. The 12th verse [Rev. 14] reads, "Here is the patience of the saints: here are they that keep the commandments of God," etc. Where did you see them, John? Why, *"here"* during this third angel. As the patient waiting time has been since the 7th month 1844, and as the class that keep the Sabbath, etc. have appeared since that time: it is plain that we live in the time of the third angel's message.[221]

Soon this view was also accepted by Bates.[222]

Thus it seemed that Rev. 14:12 most aptly portrayed the place of Sabbatarian Adventists ("here are they that keep the commandments of God") in the final period of salvation history ("the patience of the saints" or "the patient waiting time").[223] From 1847 onward the test was gradually incorporated in the mission of the third angel so that it was said that "the third angel proclaiming the commandments of God and the faith of Jesus, represents the people who receive this message, and raise the voice of warning."[224] The interpretation of Rev. 14:12 was another example of how the Sabbath doctrine was integrated into the Advent experience.

During these formative years the relationship between the sanctuary theology and the third angel's message could be described as follows: Both had their roots in the Advent movement and affirmed the validity of the Seventh Month movement and the Decalogue. The sanctuary theology, however, drew attention to the significance of the Decalogue in the context of Rev. 11:19, while the third angel's message pointed to the importance of the commandments of God in the setting of Rev. 14:12. It was especially the preparatory function of the sanctuary theology for the acceptance of the Sabbath that brought about a close association between Christ's ministry and the third angel's message. This close relation was acknowledged by Eli Curtis, publisher of the *Girdle of Truth, and Advent Review,*[225] when in

221 J. White, *WLF,* p. 11. Cf. Letter, B. B. Hill to Snow, *JS,* June 5, 1845, p. 100.

222 Cf. Bates, *SAWH,* pp. 20, 23-25, 27 with Bates, "Second Advent Way Marks . . . ," rev. ed., *AdR,* Nov. 1850, pp. 66-68.

223 J. White, *WLF,* p. 11; Bates, *SAWH,* p. 59. Edson said: "We are now emphatically in the time of 'the patience of the saints,' Rev. 14:12. Let us not forget that here in this time of the patience of the saints, 'are they that keep the commandments of God and the faith of Jesus,' Rev. 14:12, ch. 12:17" (Letter, Edson to Crosier, *DD,* April 2, 1847, p. 8).

224 E. G. White, *LS,* p. 96. Edson remarked that Rev. 14:12 was "a part of the third angel's message" (*Time of the End,* p. 20). Cf. [J. White], "Miller's Dream," p. 75 (*Miller's Dream,* p. 9); [Samuel W. Rhodes], *A Pictorial Illustration of the Visions of Daniel & John . . . ,* 1850. Further references will indicate it as the *1850 Chart.*

225 Curtis' publication also contained the visions of the Midnight Cry and the New Earth (cf. E. G. White, *SG,* II, 52-55). His remarks and treatment of the visions seem to indicate that he had not fully accepted her views. Cf. Letter, E. G. White to Curtis, p. 12. The break between E. G. White and Curtis came in 1850 (E. G. White, "Eli Curtis," *PT,* May 1850, p. 80).

1848 he referred to E. G. White's April 1847 sanctuary view as a divine revelation of the "the nature of the message, and work, of the Third Angel [Rev. 14:9]."[226]

3. The sealing message.

Differences of interpretation on various aspects relating to the Sabbath and Advent experience led, in 1848, to a series of conferences aimed at achieving more uniformity.[227] It was pointed out that the believers must "unite upon the third angel's message," which they did.[228] At the last conference (November 1848) new insights were gained in regard to the sealing of God's people,[229] stressing the importance of the Sabbath and the third angel's message in the Sabbatarian Adventist theology of mission.

In January 1849, E. G. White identified the Sabbath with the "seal of the living God" (Rev. 7:2)[230] and Bates explained that this interpretation was based on identifying the Sabbath as a sign (Ex. 31:13, 17) with a seal. A sign, he said, "signifies subscribe, represent, notify, mark. This being the significance of a sign, it is the same as seal."[231] To illustrate his point he referred to procedures used in making up a sales contract: First, such a contract had to be written, then signed and sealed, and finally delivered. Reasoning from analogy, Bates said that if God's law would be observed "then we have the sign of the Sabbath, and [are] ready to be sealed, and then delivered by the voice of God from the time of trouble."[232] This view of the sealing process he saw confirmed by Paul's remark about Abraham, " 'and he received the sign of circumcision, a seal of the righteousness of the faith which he had,' &c., Rom. iv:11."[233] He concluded that "the sign shows that the seal must follow, and as there is no other truth which God has given his servants that is to be a sign between him and them but the keeping [of] his Sabbath, then 'a seal of the living God' is the Sabbath."[234]

226 [Curtis], Remarks, *GT,* Extra, Jan. 20, 1848, p. [4]. (Brackets his.)
227 See Froom, *PFF,* IV, 1021-27. On the importance of the year 1848, see [J. White], "Miller's Dream," p. 75 (*Miller's Dream,* p. 9); Edson, "Appeal," p. 6; Arnold, "Dream of Miller," p. 12; [J. White], "Sketch of the Past," p. 5; J. White, "Present Truth," p. 61. Cf. E. G. White, "They Sleep in Jesus," *RH,* April 21, 1868, p. 297.
228 E. G. White, *SG,* II, 1860, p. 99. Regarding these conferences J. White stated: "Here the work of uniting the brethren on the great truths connected with the message of the third angel commenced" ("Sketch of the Past," p. 5).
229 In 1847 reference to a future sealing was made by J. White (*WLF,* p. 3) and Bates (Bates, *Vindication of the Sabbath,* cited in *SLG,* p. 12; J. White, *Life,* p. 269). It seems that as a result of the Nov. 1848 sealing view of E. G. White (Bates, *SLG,* pp. 24-26) Bates and J. White began to stress the sealing as a present reality (*infra,* p. 145).
230 E. G. White, MS 3, 1849; E. G. White, "To Those Who Are Receiving the Seal of the Living God" (Broadside), Jan. 31, 1849. Cf. Bates, *SLG,* p. 17.
231 *Ibid.,* p. 23. Cf. [J. White], "The Sabbath a Perpetual Weekly Memorial," *PT,* July 1849, pp. 2, 3.
232 Bates, *SLG,* p. 24.
233 *Ibid.*
234 *Ibid.* He referred to E. G. White who seemed to have said that "the Sabbath is the seal, because it's the greatest and last truth, and continues forever" (*ibid.,* p. 26). See *ibid.,* pp. 24-26 for this Nov. 1848 view of E. G. White.

The sealing itself Bates described as "to *close, settle, confirm, ratify,* make sure between two parties forever,"[235] indicating that

> the parties are God, Jesus Christ, and the Holy Ghost, with 144,000 men and women on the earth, witnessed by all the holy angels in heaven. When the 144,000 on the earth, individually, keep God's Holy Sabbath according to the commandment, see the example in Luke xxiii:56, and decalogue, Exo. xx:8-10, then the sign of that Sabbath is manifest, and this sign will be a seal of their righteous act and faith, as circumcision was to faithful Abraham, Rom. iv:11, and the act ratified, by their being 'sealed by the holy spirit of promise unto the day of *redemption*' [Eph. 4:30].[236]

In the context of the sealing angel of Rev. 7:2 Bates further developed J. White's 1847 reference[237] regarding the typological implications of Ezek. 9 for the time just before Christ's return. Bates related the activities of Ezek. 9:2-4, picturing a man, clothed in linen with a writing case in his hand who was commanded to go through the city of Jerusalem to put a mark upon the foreheads of the righteous, to those of the sealing angel of Rev. 7:2.[238] In another Old Testament reference, "Bind up the testimony, seal the law among my disciples" (Is. 8:16) he saw a prophecy of the sealing message with implications for the remnant described in Rev. 12:17, who "keep the commandments of God, and have the testimony of Jesus Christ."[239]

There was some discussion about Bates' interpretation of the "four angels standing on the four corners of the earth" (Rev. 7:1) and "the angel ascending from the east, having the seal of the living God" (Rev. 7:2). He maintained that the four angels, or messengers, symbolized the four world powers, Great Britain, France, Russia, and the U.S.A.; the sealing angel depicted the experience of "the Sabbath keepers ascending with the Sabbath, 'the seal of the living God.' "[240] Because of strong opposition from fellow believers he interpreted the angels of Rev. 7:1, 2 as literal angels.[241] By this time (1849) the Sabbath had become solidly entrenched in the apocalyptic-eschatology of the Sabbatarian Adventists by relating it to Dan. 7:25, Rev. 7:2, and Rev. 14:9, 12.

235 *Ibid.,* p. 35.
236 *Ibid.,* pp. 35, 36. The 1848 revolutions in Europe were for Bates an indication that both the time of trouble and the sealing time had begun (*ibid.,* pp. 26, 40, 46-49). E. G. White denied that the time of trouble had already started, although she saw that the angels of Rev. 7:1 "had started on their mission to let them [four winds] go," but intervention by Jesus for the sake of "the remnant that were not all sealed" cancelled their mission ("DBS," pp. 22, 23 [*EW,* pp. 36, 38]). However, she affirmed that the sealing time had commenced (*ibid.,* pp. 21, 22 [*EW,* pp. 42, 43]).
237 J. White, *WLF,* p. 3. The marking of the doorposts of the houses of the Israelites by blood before the firstborn of the Egyptians were slain (Ex. 12) was interpreted as a type of the apocalyptic sealing of the saints (*ibid.*).
238 Bates, *SLG,* pp. 4, 28, 41-45. Cf. [J. White], "Repairing the Breach," p. 26; E. G. White, *SG,* I, 197.
239 Bates, *SLG,* pp. 54-56.
240 *Ibid.,* pp. 4, 17, 33-35. Others had also alluded to these four world powers; see Hale, *Bridegroom,* p. 18; Editorial, "The Watchman's Warning," *SAH,* April 16, 1844, p. 35; Editorial, "The Holy Alliance," *DS,* July 1, 1845, p. 31.
241 Editorial, "Not So," *RH,* Dec. 23, 1851, p. 72. Bates indicated this change in his *Synopsis of the Seal,* May 1849 (*ibid.*).

The logical consequence of interpreting the Sabbath as "the seal of the living God" was to call the third angel's message, with its emphasis on the commandments of God (Rev. 14:12), the sealing message. Although Bates had referred to a relation between Rev. 7:2 and Rev. 14:6-12, it was E. G. White who used the term "present, sealing truth" in the context of an exposition on the third angel's message.[242] In more explicit terms J. White expressed himself about "the sealing, separating message — the cutting message of the 3rd angel of Rev. 14 chapter. This 3rd angel bears, in its flight, the sealing mark, the Sabbath, to the saints, while it reaps the awful doom of those who receive the opposite mark, — the first day of the week."[243] The sealing message, being equated with "present truth," was a sign of the times indicating that the believers were living in the "sealing time,"[244] which was to last until the end of Christ's sanctuary ministry when God's Sabbath-observing people would be sealed with the seal of the living God for protection against the "burning wrath of God, in the seven last plagues."[245] At the completion of the sealing all the sins of the believers were considered to have been blotted out.[246] No one, however, could receive the seal without having an experiential knowledge of self-denial and suffering for Christ. In 1850, therefore, in referring to individuals who had recently accepted the present truth, E. G. White pointed out that they "would have to know what it was to suffer for Christ's sake. That they would have trials to pass through that would be keen and cutting, in order that they may be purified, and fitted through suffering to receive the seal of the living God."[247] This indicated that the sealing was not only a present but also an imminent future reality: During the present sealing time the believers were being, or about to be, sealed; while at any time Christ could finish His heavenly ministry, which would indicate the completion of the sealing.[248] It was not until several years later, when the Second Advent had lost

242   E. G. White, "DBS," p. 21 (*EW*, p. 43). Cf. E. G. White, "DBS," p. 32; J. White, "TAM," *PT*, April 1850, p. 68 (*TAM*, 1850, p. 11). Here he alluded to the sanctifying influence of the sealing truth.

243   Letter, J. White to Bowles, Nov. 8, 1849. Cf. Bates, *SLG*, p. 133. In 1845 the sealing was already considered by some as a present reality (Editorial, "Holy Alliance," p. 31; Letter, George W. Jones to Jacobs, *DS*, Aug. 25, 1845, p. 10; Letter, Cook to Jacobs, *DS*, Nov. 22, 1845, p. 31).

244   For the present reality of the sealing, see e.g., the title of Bates' book *SLG; ibid.,* pp. 26, 34, 40; E. G. White, "DBS," pp. 21-23 (*EW*, pp. 42, 43).

245   *Ibid.,* pp. 21, 22 (*EW*, p. 44). For the future reality of the sealing, see E. G. White, "DBS," p. 32. The importance of the sealing was stressed because "those only who have the seal of the living God, will be sheltered from the storm of wrath, that will soon fall on the heads of those who have rejected the truth" (*ibid.*). Cf. Bates, *SLG*, p. 69.

246   *Ibid.,* p. 38; E. G. White, "DBS," p. 32 (*EW*, p. 48).

247   E. G. White, *CEV*, pp. 54, 55 (*EW*, p. 67).

248   The apocalyptic sealing had present and future soteriological significance so that E. G. White could say on the one hand that "when Jesus leaves the Sanctuary, then he that is holy and righteous, will be holy and righteous still [Rev. 22:11]; for all their sins will then be blotted out, and they will be sealed with the seal of the living God [Rev. 7]" (E. G. White, "DBS," p. 32 [*EW*, p. 48], while on the other hand it was stated that a particular individual who had gone through the traumatic experience of the Disappointment but who had just died was considered as being sealed (Letter, E. G. White to Hastings, No. 10, 1850 [*SM*, II, 1958, p. 263]). Cf. E. G. White, "DBS," p. 23. This last act suggested that those who had accepted in faith the

some of its urgency, that the sealing process was more carefully analyzed.[249]

4. Summary.

The Seventh-day Sabbath reform movement had called the attention of Adventists to the Sabbath doctrine causing some of them to observe the Sabbath. Initially the theological arguments used in support of Sabbath observance were somewhat similar to those employed by Seventh Day Baptists, emphasizing the validity of all precepts of the Decalogue for Christians, the significance of the Sabbath as a sign between God and His people, and the responsibility of the Roman Catholic Church for changing the day of worship in Christendom. Soon, however, these Sabbatarian Adventists began to associate the Sabbath with their Advent experience. First, the Sabbath was connected with the idea that in the post-1844 period all biblical principles had to be restored among God's people before the Second Advent could take place. Secondly, the sanctuary theology was considered to facilitate an acceptance of the Sabbath and indicated its special relevance after 1844 by focusing the attention of believers on the central role of the Decalogue in Christ's high-priestly ministry in the most holy place of the heavenly sanctuary. Thirdly, the third angel's message, being closely associated with the restoration theme and theology, was responsible for the important position of the Sabbath doctrine. Because this message stressed the vital significance of obedience to God's commandments in contrast to loyalties to other powers, the phenomenon of Sabbath observance after 1844 came to be an integral part of the Advent experience. As a result of identifying the Sabbath with the seal of the living God — a protection against God's wrath — the third angel's message came to be called the sealing message, or present truth. The sealing time was considered to be a present and imminent future reality, and would terminate at the completion of Christ's sanctuary ministry.

The importance of the third angel's message was its concise formulation of the emerging theology of mission uniting the two principal elements of the raison d'être of Sabbatarian Adventists: (1) The proclamation of the validity of their past Advent experience as an important phase in salvation history; (2) the proclamation of the restoration of the Sabbath to prepare God's people for the day of His wrath. It was at this stage of the development of the third angel's message that E. G. White stated, "We have the truth. We know it."[250]

---

present sealing truth before they died were assured of salvation as long as they remained faithful. Cf. Letter, E. G. White to Haskell and Irwin, No. 207, 1899 (*SDABC,* VII, p. 982); E. G. White, MS 173, 1902 (*SDABC,* IV, p. 1161). During the early years of the Sabbatarian Adventist movement the general understanding of the sealing was placed in the context of the apocalyptic sealing, which did include soteriological aspects but did not differentiate or analyze them in terms of a sealing process as was done later on.

249 See *infra,* pp. 211, 212.

250 Letter, E. G. White to the Hastingses, No. 18 (Jan. 11), 1850.

C. The Ecclesiological Self-understanding.

The ecclesiological self-understanding of the Sabbatarian Adventists was a consistent extension of the Millerite views during the crisis of 1843-44.[251] The "organized churches" were considered to be Babylon.[252] J. White remarked that "the fall of Babylon commenced in the spring of '43 when the churches all around, began to fall into a cold state, and was complete on the 7th month '44, when the last faint ray of hope was taken up from a wicked world and church."[253] In 1849 he compiled and edited a hymnal which included a hymn on the proclamation of the fall of Babylon referring to her "poisonous creeds" as an argument for separatism.[254] According to Bates, the observance of the Sabbath by Adventists, as indicated in Rev. 14:12, was "demonstrated proof that Babylon has fallen."[255]

Adventists who remained faithful to their Advent beliefs after the Disappointment were designated as God's people[256] and called the "remnant," the "little remnant," the "scattered remnant," the "little flock" (Lk. 12:32), or the "scattered flock."[257] Adventists who rejected the Advent movement were called "the synagogue of Satan" (Rev. 3:9).[258]

The rejection of the validity of the Seventh Month movement and the Sabbath doctrine by the majority of Adventists contributed to a development in the Sabbatarian ecclesiology. J. White denounced the "unfaithful ones," stating that "since the 7th month 1844, the 'rebellious house' of Israel, have been removing the 'landmarks,' and writing, and proclaiming false visions; but we all know that it has been the work of man, and not of God."[259]

---

251   See *supra*, pp. 78-84.
252   Letter, J. White to Jacobs, *DS*, Sept. 20, 1845, p. 26; Bates, *SAWH*, pp. 17-23. Bates stated that "*mystery Babylon*, the antertype of literal Babylon, which signifies confusion and mixture, represents the organized Churches of all descriptions, divided into three parts, Rev. xvi:19, viz: Roman, Greek and Protestant" (*SAWH*, p. 24). Cf. Letter, H. L. Smith to Jacobs, *DS*, April 22, 1845, p. 44. Bates said that the cry of Rev. 18:4 was directed to the Protestant churches and not to the Roman Catholic Church, for God's people "*departed* from her certainly 300 years ago" (*SAWH*, p. 27).
253   Letter, J. White to Jacobs, *DS*, Sept. 20, 1845, p. 26.
254   [J. White, ed. and comp.], *Hymns for God's Peculiar People* . . . , 1849, p. 4. The theology in this hymn suggests a Sabbatarian Adventist composer.
255   Bates, *SSP*, 1847, p. 59.
256   E. G. White, *CEV*, p. 63 (*EW*, p. 76). Cf. E. G. White, *SG*, II, 58, 64.
257   See e.g., Letter, J. White to Jacobs, *DS*, Sept. 6, 1845, p. 17; J. White, *WLF*, p. 1; E. G. White, "DBS," p. 23 (*EW*, p. 38); *ibid.*, p. 32 (*EW*, p. 47); [J. White], Introduction, *PT*, July 1849, p. 1.
258   Letter, J. White to Jacobs, *DS*, Sept. 6, 1845, p. 17; E. G. White [E. G. Harmon], "RSA," p. 15; Letter, E. G. White to Curtis, p. 12. In identifying themselves with the Philadelphian church (Rev. 3:7-13), this term was of particular relevance. Cf. J. White, "The Philadelphia Church," *RH*, Oct. 30, 1856, p. 205.
259   J. White, *WLF*, p. 5. Bates stated: "Hosea says the Princes of Judea were like those that remove the bound [*sic*] v. 10. The spiritual leaders in Israel remove the bound, and make sad the heart of the humble seeker. This has been done undoubtedly since the days of the going out of Egypt, but never in so general and in such a particular manner as within the last thirty months. Hence the pressing necessity for God's people to set their hearts toward the

E. G. White designated them as "nominal Adventists."[260] In her April 1847 vision the Sabbath was used as a criterion to indicate the ecclesiological distinctiveness of the Sabbatarian Adventists. She stated that "the holy Sabbath is, and will be, the separating wall between the true Israel of God and unbelievers"[261] but warned against exclusivism, for "God had children, who do not see and keep the Sabbath. They had not rejected the light on it."[262] These people were among the nominal Adventists and in the churches of Babylon, and would accept the Sabbath doctrine and unite with Sabbatarians in the future.[263]

One of the earliest statements that applied the term "church" to Sabbatarian Adventists came from E. G. White, who, in January 1849, addressed a manuscript to "the church of God who keep the Sabbath — the seal of the living God."[264]

Bates and others symbolized the churches from which Adventists had separated themselves as the Sardis Church (Rev. 3:1-6). The Sabbatarian Adventists he identified with the Philadelphian church (Rev. 3:7-13) and the "nominal Adventists" with the Laodicean state of the church (Rev. 3:14-22).[265]

Thus, the ecclesiological self-understanding of the believers developed around three concentric circles: The inner circle represented the true Israel of God, the Philadelphian church, which observed the Sabbath; the second signified God's people among the "nominal Adventists" and in the churches, who had not rejected the Sabbath doctrine and were unaware of its implications; the outer circle embraced the remaining "nominal Adventists" and church people, who had rejected the Sabbath doctrine as binding for Christians, and equated them with unbelievers. The future prospects were a unification of all God's people with Sabbatarian Adventists resulting in a final conflict between them and unbelievers.

---

highway which they went, and look well to, and remember their *way marks* and *high heaps*, or as Jesus taught those in the Philadelphi [*sic*] church 'to hold fast that which they had'" (*SAWH*, pp. 5, 6).

260   Letter, E. G. White to Bates, *WLF*, p. 19 (*EW*, p. 33).

261   *Ibid*. For the true Israel concept, see Letter, Turner to Snow, p. 137; Letter, Nichols to Jacobs, p. 34; Letter, Main to Jacobs, p. 12; Preble, "Sabbath," p. 433.

262   Letter, E. G. White to Bates, *WLF*, p. 19 (*EW*, p. 33).

263   *Ibid*. When this process of assimilation has taken place a tension would have developed between the Sabbatarian Adventists on the one hand and the rest of Christianity on the other hand. This would result in a "time of trouble" during which Sabbatarian Adventists would be persecuted. The end of this conflict would be solved through the parousia bringing the deliverance (*ibid*., pp. 19, 20 [*EW*, pp. 33-35]).

264   E. G. White, MS 3, 1849.

265   Bates, *SAWH*, pp. 34-35. The Albany conference of May 1845 was seen by some as the starting point of the Laodicean church. Cf. Letter, E. L. H. Chamberlain to Jacobs, *DS*, Aug. 11, 1845, p. 22; Edson, *Time of the End*, p. 24. Cf. Letter, Turner to Snow, pp. 137, 138. When in 1845 the spirit of "brotherhood" was broken among Adventists, they were identified by some as the Laodicean church (Letter, Hill to Snow, p. 100; Snow, "The Laodicean Church," *JS*, June 12 and 19, 1845, pp. 108, 117). Snow alluded to the relevance of the name Laodicea ("judging of the people") under the present pre-Advent judgment (*ibid*., p. 117).

D. The Concept of Mission.

The idea of the termination of human probation at the completion of the Midnight Cry of the Seventh Month movement was responsible for an absence of mission activities among non-Adventists after the Disappointment. During 1845-49, especially through the influence of E. G. White, the minds of the believers were gradually taken away from the extreme shut-door view and prepared for future missionary outreach. To facilitate the analysis of this period, a chronological treatment is given of all contemporary and harmonizing non-contemporary source material on the views of E. G. White, which is followed by a discussion of other Sabbatarian Adventists.

1. The views of E. G. White.[266]

The Midnight Cry vision (December 1844) and the Bridegroom vision (February 1845) convinced a number of Adventists who had already given up the idea of a shut door that it was shut in the autumn of 1844.[267] The Midnight Cry vision indicated that the door was shut for two classes of individuals: (1) Adventists who had accepted the Midnight Cry but afterward renounced it as a delusion;[268] (2) "all the wicked world which God had rejected."[269] The wording of this vision, appearing first in a letter written with no intent of its publication,[270] could well have been interpreted as supporting a shut-door concept which excluded all mankind from God's mercy except those who adhered to the validity of the Midnight Cry of the

266 There were two major traditions of interpreting E. G. White's position on the shut door. One tradition, consisting of eyewitness accounts by SDA, affirmed the view that she did not adhere to the extreme shut-door view after the Bridegroom vision of Feb. 1845. The witnesses were J. White, Mrs. Marion C. Truesdail, Ira Abbey, and John Y. Wilcox (Loughborough, "Response," RH, Sept. 25, 1866, p. 134; Loughborough, Second Advent Movement, pp. 222-24; George I. Butler, "Advent Experience. — No. 9," RH, April 7, 1885, p. 217). Cf. Butler's account of 21 witnesses (ibid.). The other tradition, frequently cited by non-SDA, stated that she advocated the extreme shut-door view for a number of years. The witnesses were I. C. Wellcome, Israel Damman, John Megquier, Mrs. L. S. Burdick (formerly Mrs. John Howell), and Crosier. Their testimony pertained to the period 1845-48. At the time of their testimony they were very critical of SDA. See Grant, True Sabbath, pp. 69-75; Wellcome, Second Advent Message, p. 397; D. M. Canright, Seventh-Day Adventism Renounced, 1889, 2nd ed., pp. 143, 144; L. R. Conradi, Ist Frau E. G. White die Prophetin der Endgemeinde?, 193?, p. 29. This tradition assumed that during 1844-51 there was only one shut-door concept in existence, namely the extreme one, which advocated that the door of mercy was forever closed to the world or to sinners in general, whether or not truth had been rejected.

267 J. White, WLF, p. 22; Letter, E. G. White to Bates, No. 3, 1847. For her views prior to Dec. 1844, see supra, p. 112.

268 E. G. White [E. G. Harmon], "RSA," p. 14. This class was also identified with the synagogue of Satan in Rev. 3:9 (ibid., p. 15; cf. Letter, J. White to Jacobs, DS, Sept. 6, 1845, p. 17). E. G. White stated that "this class were professed Adventists, who had fallen away, and 'crucified to themselves the Son of God afresh, and put him to an open shame' [Heb. 6:6]" (Letter, E. G. White to Curtis, p. 12).

269 E. G. White [E. G. Harmon], "RSA," p. 14.

270 Letter, E. G. Harmon to Jacobs, DS, March 14, 1846, p. 7.

Seventh Month movement.[271] Such interpretation was possible on the basis of the following presuppositions: (1) That all who had not accepted the Midnight Cry had rejected the Advent proclamation, thus symbolizing the wicked world; (2) that the Seventh Month movement had caused a final separation between the righteous and wicked whether or not each individual had consciously rejected the Advent message. Later, in a response to her critics, E. G. White denied that this was the correct interpretation of the vision. As a result of further light[272] on the shut door she defined the term "all the wicked world" more precisely as being "the wicked of the world who having rejected the light, had been rejected of God,"[273] adding that "no reference is made to those who had not seen the light, and therefore were not guilty of its rejection."[274] The shut door, according to her, pertained to those who had rejected the Holy Spirit and placed themselves beyond reach of divine mercy.[275]

In February 1845, on her first journey east, E. G. Harmon received the Bridegroom vision[276] — the first vision with missiological aspects. It in-

271 For the tradition of this interpretation, see Letter, Nichols to Miller, April 20, 1846; B. F. Snook and Wm. H. Brinkerhoff, *The Visions of E. G. White, Not of God*, 1886, pp. 4, 5; H. E. Carver, *Mrs. E. G. White's Claims to Divine Inspiration Examined*, 1870, pp. 50, 51; Wellcome, *Second Advent Message*, p. 397; Grant, *True Sabbath*, pp. 68-75. Cf. Canright, *Seventh-day Adventism*, p. 145; Conradi, *E. G. White*, pp. 21, 22; Lindén, *Biblicism*, p. 78 (Letter, Lindén to A. L. White, Sept. 3, 1971, p. 8). Curtis' publication of this vision omitted the shut-door statement (*GT*, Extra, Jan. 20, 1848, p. [1]). One of the reasons why he omitted this statement could be that either he himself saw in it the extreme shut-door concept, or he felt that the statement was likely to be interpreted as an extreme shut-door view. One of the reasons for its omission in E. G. White's *CEV* (cf. E. G. White [E. G. Harmon], "RSA," p. 12 with *CEV*, p. 10 [*EW*, p. 15]) could well have been to avoid an extreme shut-door interpretation which, to E. G. White, was not the correct meaning of the statement (MS 4, 1883 [*SM*, I, 62-64]). At a time when mission work among non-Adventists was in its early stages it seemed important to E. G. White as she prepared the materials for her first book that the wording of the vision should correctly convey the understanding and intent of its author. This would lead her to eliminate any expressions which might give support to misinterpretations of the intent of the visions. See E. G. White, "Experience and Views," *RH*, Extra, July 21, 1851, p. [2]. For other reasons of omission, see A. L. White, "Ellen G. White and the Shut Door Question," Unpublished MS, 1971, pp. 33-37.
272 E. G. White, MS 4, 1883 (*SM*, I, 63). Here she said that "it was the light given me of God that corrected our error." The reference to "the light" seems to be an allusion to all her visions on this subject and should not be confined to her first vision. Cf. Loughborough, "Response," p. 134.
273 E. G. White, MS 4, 1883 (*SM*, I, 64). If J. White's autobiographical account as reported by Loughborough is correct, then she might not have been aware of the full significance of this interpretation until after her Bridegroom vision of Feb. 1845 ("Response," p. 134). Nichol, who accepted estimates by Miller and early SDA that there were approximately 50,000 Millerites in 1844 (*supra*, p. 15, n. 63), saw an open-door allusion in the vision, for it mentioned that there would be 144,000 believers living on earth at the time of the parousia (*Ellen G. White and Her Critics*, 1951, pp. 239-41). Non-Adventist estimates of the number of Miller's followers vary from 30,000 to 1,000,000 (Froom, *PFF*, IV, 686; "The Late William Miller," *New York Tribune*, Dec. 29, 1849, quoted in "Notices of Mr. Miller's Death," *AH*, Feb. 16, 1850, p. 20). In 1845 some Adventists thought that the 144,000 were already a present reality (Letter, Greenleaf to Jacobs, *DS*, June 3, 1845, p. 14; Snow, "Confederacy," p. 109; Letter, Cook to Jacobs, *DS*, Nov. 22, 1845, p. 31).
274 E. G. White, MS 4, 1883 (*SM*, I, 64)
275 *Ibid.*
276 E. G. White, *SG*, II, 35-39; Letter, E. G. White to Bates, No. 3, 1847; Letter, E. G.

cluded both open- and shut-door implications[277] and pictured the Bride-groom coming to the marriage (Mt. 25:10) in the context of the change in Christ's high-priestly ministry.[278] Acceptance of this view led various Adventists to conclude that the door of Mt. 25:10 had also been shut.[279] An open-door implication, calling attention to further mission work, appeared in a non-contemporary source. It stated that "there was a great work to be done in the world for those who had not the light and rejected it," signifying that the contemporary shut-door situation was only of a temporary nature.[280] In 1845 this progressive view was not understood by believers, some criticizing her strongly,[281] which might explain why it was not pub-

---

White to Loughborough (*SM*, I, 74). It seems that this vision was repeated later on — which may explain its chronological place in *EW* (Loughborough, "Response," p. 134).

277 Letter, E. G. White to Loughborough (*SM*, I, 74); Loughborough, "Response," p. 134.

278 Letter, E. G. Harmon to Jacobs, *DS*, March 14, 1846, p. 7 (*EW*, pp. 54-56).

279 Letter, E. G. White to Bates, No. 3, 1847. Although the vision did not mention the term "shut door," this concept was reflected in the "careless multitude" who had not received the light of the Advent doctrine in 1844 and were said to be "left in perfect darkness" after the change in Christ's ministry. Those who had accepted the light of the Advent doctrine but who still approached Christ in the first apartment of the heavenly sanctuary because "they did not know that Jesus had left it" were described as being under the influence of Satan (Letter, E. G. Harmon to Jacobs, *DS*, March 14, 1846, p. 7 [*EW*, pp. 55, 56]). Commenting on this last group, Lindén concluded that the possibility "of salvation no longer existed for those people" (Lindén, *Biblicism*, p. 80; Letter, Lindén to A. L. White, p. 7). However, he failed to notice that it was because of ignorance that these individuals became subject to demonic influences. "Satan's object was to keep them deceived," which still implied the possibility of a change for the better (Letter, E. G. Harmon to Jacobs, *DS*, March 14, 1846, p. 7 [*EW*, p. 56]. Here Lindén reflects the tradition of former SDA like Carver and Canright. See Carver, *E. G. White*, pp. 59, 60; Canright, *Seventh-day Adventism*, p. 146. Cf. William Sheldon, "The Visions and Theories of the Prophetess Ellen G. White . . . ," *Voice of the West . . .* , Jan. 1, 1867, p. 52.

280 Letter, E. G. White to Loughborough (*SM*, I, 74). Cf. Loughborough, "Response," p. 134; Truesdail in Butler, "Advent Experience. — No. 9," p. 217. Another autobiographical source seemed to indicate that in the same year she revealed to Washington Morse that the nature of this "great work," which implied "bringing sinners to repentance and salvation," consisted of a wider proclamation of the judgment warning and the testing of people with "greater light." As reason for this she wrote that "the mercy of God" had given the world some more time to prepare for the parousia (E. G. White, "Mrs. Ellen G. White," *Signs of the Times*, May 4, 1876, p. 165 [*LS*, p. 78]. Cf. E. G. White, *SG*, II, 46). In comparing this account with contemporary sources of the group to which E. G. Harmon belonged, one might conclude that the language she used was quite advanced for 1845. Some sources, however, seem to indicate that the first contacts between E. G. White and Washington Morse did not occur until the summer of 1850 (Washington Morse, "Items of Advent Experience During the Past Fifty Years. — No. 4," *RH*, Oct. 16, 1888, p. 642; J. White, "Our Tour East," *AdR*, No. 1, Aug. 1850, p. 14; A. L. White, "Memorandum Concerning Washington Morse," Jan. 21, 1975). The nature of E. G. White's counsel to Morse could fit the situation in 1850. The fact that she described this experience for the first time in 1876, and because the description of the condition of Morse after the Disappointment could very well be placed in 1845, might have been a reason why this incident was located in 1845. This did not pose a serious problem for E. G. White because she never claimed infallible accuracy for her purely biographical accounts (*SG*, II, iii, iv; cf. E. G. White, MS 107, 1909 in *SM*, I, 37-39; A. L. White, "Morse"). From this one should be careful not to conclude that her 1874 and 1883 statements regarding the shut door were unreliable. The criterion for the reliability of later biographical materials should be whether or not they contradict contemporary source material. Both the 1874 and 1883 statements seem to be in harmony with contemporary sources. It is interesting to notice that she never used her experience with Morse as an argument against her critics.

281 E. G. White stated that "our brethren could not understand this with our faith in the

lished at the time. It is possible that in 1845 or 1846 she also received a vision of an expanding mission picturing an increasing number of believers as "jets of light in the world."[282] Up until this time the future mission task was not clearly defined in contemporary sources.

The first reference that more specifically described the future mission among non-Adventists appeared in an 1847 publication when the Seventh-day Sabbath Reform movement had made some headway among Adventists. In this publication, which included a reprint of the Midnight Cry vision, E. G. White affirmed that there was a shut door in 1844[283] while at the same time revealing through her April 3, 1847 vision that God still had followers in the churches of fallen Babylon.[284] In the future when the Sabbath doctrine would be proclaimed "more fully" these individuals would unite with the Sabbatarian Adventists.[285] This vision supported the above non-contemporary data that the present absence of mission among non-Adventists was of a temporary nature.[286] This indicates that her shut-door

---

immediate appearing of Christ. Some accused me of saying, My Lord delayeth his coming; especially the fanatical ones" (Letter, E. G. White to Loughborough [SM, I, 74]). Cf. Loughborough, "Response," p. 134. J. White remarked, according to Loughborough, that "she did not at first distinctly understand what this open door meant," because it was contrary to the faith of the Adventists and her previous opinions (ibid.).

282   E. G. White, "Serving God Fervently," RH, July 26, 1887, p. 466. If her statement that this vision was received in her "very girlhood" (ibid.) signified the period before her marriage, then the vision must be dated earlier than Aug. 30, 1846. It could be that both this vision and the Bridegroom vision occurred on her "first journey east" (Feb. 1845) and brought out the great work still to be done (cf. Letter, E. G. White to Loughborough [SM, I, 74]).

283   Letter, E. G. White to Curtis, p. 12. For the nature of this shut door, see Lk. 13:25. Cf. supra, p. 151, n. 279.

284   Letter, E. G. White to Bates, WLF, p. 19 (EW, p. 33). Whenever the term "church" or "churches" is used in early Sabbatarian Adventist literature as an opposing force, it signifies the church organizations in fallen Babylon. Cf. Bates, SSP, 1847, p. 59; Bates, SAWH, pp. 20-22; J. White, "TAM," pp. 65, 66 (TAM, pp. 2, 4, 5).

285   Letter, E. G. White to Bates, WLF, p. 19 (EW, p. 33).

286   In an autobiographical statement E. G. White stated that through the visions her original idea "that the door of mercy was then [after the Disappointment] forever closed to the world" was changed into a shut-door concept which was limited to certain classes of people. She referred to the following biblical parallels to illustrate this: "There was a shut door in Noah's day. There was at that time a withdrawal of the Spirit of God from the sinful race that perished in the waters of the flood. God Himself gave the shut-door message to Noah: 'My spirit shall not always strive with man, for that he also is flesh: yet his days shall be an hundred and twenty years' [Gen. 6:3]. There was a shut door in the days of Abraham. Mercy ceased to plead with the inhabitants of Sodom, and all but Lot, with his wife and two daughters, were consumed by the fire sent down from heaven. There was a shut door in Christ's day. The Son of God declared to the unbelieving Jews of that generation, 'Your house is left unto you desolate' [Mt. 23:38]. Looking down the stream of time to the last days, the same infinite power proclaimed through John, 'These things saith he that is holy, he that is true, he that hath the key of David, he that openeth, and no man shutteth; and shutteth, and no man openeth' [Rev. 3:7]. I was shown in vision, and I still believe, that there was a shut door in 1844. All who saw the light of the first and second angels' messages, and rejected that light, were left in darkness. And those who accepted it and received the Holy Spirit which attended the proclamation of the message from heaven, and who afterward renounced their faith and pronounced their experience a delusion, thereby rejected the Spirit of God, and it no longer pleaded with them" (MS 4, 1883 [SM, I, 63]). Cf. Letter, E. G. White to Loughborough (SM, I, 74).

concept was of a somewhat different nature than the previously mentioned views of Miller, Hale and Turner.[287]

At the last of a series of conferences among Sabbatarian Adventists (November 1848) E. G. White received a vision regarding "the proclamation of the sealing message" and the necessity of publishing their newly developed views.[288] Bates recorded some of the phrases she spoke and published them as part of a publication in January 1849. According to him she said that the believers had had the shut door and that the time had arrived for the Sabbath as the sealing truth.[289] Regarding this truth she remarked that "it commenced from the rising of the sun, keeps on its course like the sun, but it never sets" which seems to imply a reference to a future global influence of the Sabbath.[290] This view probably influenced Bates to conclude that the Sabbath had to be proclaimed to individuals who lived in Europe and Asia.[291] Later E. G. White mentioned that she also saw the future impact of the publication of the sealing truth as "streams of light that went clear around the world."[292]

When the year 1849 arrived, a new theological framework for mission had been developed in the form of the third angel's message (sealing message), which included the proclamation of the validity of the past Advent experience and the Sabbath doctrine. But preoccupation with the theological implications of the shut door of Mt. 25:10 was still a reason to prevent mission among non-Adventists. E. G. White's March 1849 vision removed these theological objections by placing the shut-door concept in the perspective of the change of Christ's ministry in 1844. She paraphrased Rev. 3:7, 8 by stating "that Jesus had shut the door in the Holy Place, and no man can open it; and that he had opened the door in the Most Holy, and no man can shut it,"[293] and inaugurated a gradual development away from the shut door of Mt. 25:10. At that time the phrase, "the Sabbath and the shut door" was frequently used to identify the specific theological position of Sabbatarian Adventists.[294] The vision confirmed the close inter-relationship between "the Sabbath and the shut door" and integrated it into the third angel's message in a sanctuary setting. She stated that

> the commandments of God, and the testimony of Jesus Christ, relating to the shut door, could not be separated, and that the time for the commandments of

287 See *supra*, pp. 106-8.
288 E. G. White, *LS*, p. 125.
289 Bates, *SLG*, p. 26. Cf. Bates, *TAS*, p. 16.
290 Bates, *SLG*, p. 25.
291 *Ibid.*, pp. 35, 62.
292 E. G. White, *LS*, p. 125. Cf. Bates, *SLG*, pp. 25, 26.
293 E. G. White, "DBS," p. 21 (*EW*, p. 42). In 1854 E. G. White commented that "the application of Rev. iii:7, 8 to the Heavenly Sanctuary and Christ's ministry was entirely new to me" (*SCEV*, 1854, p. 4 [*EW*, p. 86]). A few months earlier Bates had applied the term "open door" in referring to Rev. 11:19 and the raising of the veil between the holy and most holy place of the heavenly sanctuary in 1844 (*SLG*, pp. 19, 20).
294 Letter, J. White to the Hastingses, Aug. 26, 1848; Letter, J. White to the Hastingses, Oct. 2, 1848; Bates, *SLG*, p. 65.

God to shine out, with all their importance, and for God's people to be tried on the Sabbath truth, was when the door was opened in the Most Holy Place of the Heavenly Sanctuary, where the Ark is, containing the ten commandments. This door was not opened, until the mediation of Jesus was finished in the Holy Place of the Sanctuary in 1844. Then Jesus rose up, and shut the door in the Holy Place, and opened the door in the Most Holy, and passed within the second vail, where he now stands by the Ark; and where the faith of Israel now reaches.[295]

Thus when in 1844 the door of the first apartment of the heavenly sanctuary was closed, the door of the second apartment was opened, and attention came to be focused on the ark, the Decalogue and the Sabbath. From that time onward the people of God were going to be tested on the Sabbath doctrine. The vision therefore set the stage for the Sabbatarian Adventist mission of the third angel's message: the proclamation of the Sabbath doctrine in the context of the past Advent experience to test God's people.[296]

The vision further reaffirmed the views of her first vision regarding the limitation of salvation for those who had rejected truth. In the context of current revivals among non-Adventists and Adventists she described a shut-door view which pertained to the following persons: (1) Non-Adventist ministers "who have rejected the truth"; (2) "some professed Adventists who had rejected the present truth"; (3) their new converts who "appeared to have been really converted" but "if their hearts could be seen, they would appear as black as ever."[297] As evidence she referred to the fact that there was no more "the travel [travail] of soul for sinners as used to be . . . for the time for their salvation is past."[298]

---

295   E. G. White, "DBS," p. 21 (*EW*, p. 42). The phrase "the commandments of God and the testimony of Jesus Christ" (Rev. 12:17) in the vision was used interchangeably with Rev. 14:12 as the central theme of the third angel's message. Thus, both texts summarized the basic thrust of the third angel ([J. White], "Repairing the Breach," p. 28; Bates, *SAWH*, pp. 69, 71; Bates, *SSP*, 1847, p. 52). Since the Disappointment, according to E. G. White, the Sabbath had become a special test (*supra*, p. 140, n. 213).

296   In the light of the April 1847 vision God's people were also within the various non-Adventist church organizations (Letter, E. G. White to Bates, *WLF*, p. 19 [*EW*, p. 33]) so that the Sabbatarian Adventist mission work would eventually embrace the whole of Christianity.

297   E. G. White, "DBS," p. 22 (*EW*, pp. 43-45). In this context the term "truth" seems to refer to the Advent doctrine of 1844, while the term "present truth" designates the biblical rationale for the Disappointment in the context of the sanctuary theology and the third angel's message. The term "present truth" was an allusion to 2 Pet. 1:12, "Wherefore, I will not be negligent to put you always in remembrance of these things, though ye know them, and be established in the present truth." J. White defined this term as follows: "In Peter's time there was present truth, or truth applicable to that present time. The Church has ever had a present truth. The present truth now, is that which shows present duty, and the right position for us who are about to witness the time of trouble, such as never was" (Introduction, *PT*, July 1849, p. 1). Already in 1845 the term "present truth" had been used among Adventists (Letter, Nichols to Jacobs, p. 34; Letter, Cook to Jacobs, *DS*, Nov. 22, 1845, p. 31).

298   E. G. White, "DBS," p. 22 (*EW*, p. 45). One reason for the omission of the negative description of the inner condition of new converts in 1851 (cf. *ibid.*, with *CEV*, 27 [*EW*, p. 45]) might have been to avoid an interpretation of the omitted phrase which was not intended by

In summarizing the missiological significance of the visions one could conclude that: (1) At first the shut-door concept was defined as referring to all who had rejected the Advent doctrine; (2) then the visions indicated that some of God's people were still in the churches, and would, after being reached successfully through future missionary efforts, separate themselves from Babylon; (3) and finally there was a shift away from a shut-door concept which referred to a limitation of salvation for certain individuals to one in the setting of the sanctuary theology. These developments prepared the minds of Sabbatarian Adventists gradually for a new mission.

2. Shut-door modifications.

When immediately after the Disappointment Edson interpreted this event as a fulfillment of John's bitter experience of eating the little book (Rev. 10:9, 10), his attention was drawn to the phrase, 'Thou must prophesy again" (Rev. 10:11),[299] though he did not realize its significance at that time. In January 1845 J. White received "light on the shut door"[300] and began lecturing on the Bridegroom theme.[301] He probably was aware of the views of Hale and Turner which advocated a shut door for all who had rejected the truth but allowing mission activity among the very few who were not yet fully acquainted with the Advent doctrine and were living in accordance with the light received.[302] This awareness together with his support for

---

E. G. White, namely that there was a shut door for sinners in general. In a time when mission work began to develop such an interpretation could only delay the progress. E. G. White's explanatory statement in 1854 seems to be an indication that some still had difficulty with the understanding of the vision. She commented that this view on revivals or "false reformations" related "more particularly to those who have heard and rejected the light of the Advent doctrine. They are given over to strong delusions. Such will not have 'the travail of soul for sinners' as formerly. Having rejected the Advent, and being given over to the delusions of Satan, 'the time for their salvation is past'" (SCEV, p. 4 [EW, p. 45]). U. Smith referred the word "their" primarily to the word "ministers," presumably in the context of non-Adventists ("Objections to the Visions," RH, Jan. 21, 1862, p. 63). Nichol took a similar position but then especially in the context of Spiritualism (Ellen G. White, pp. 225-28) Lindén applied the word "their" primarily to new converts as a result of the current revivals and reformations through the activity of "nominal Adventist" ministers of the Albany group (Biblicism, pp. 76, 77 [Letter, Lindén to A. L. White, pp. 4, 5]). See also Snook and Brinkerhoff, E. G. White, pp. 6, 7; Carver, E. G. White, pp. 51-55; Grant, " 'Visions and Prophecies,' " WC, July 22, 1874, p. 62; Conradi, E. G. White, pp. 25, 26. Contextual evidence seems to favor a harmonization of the views of Smith, Nichol, and Lindén so that the word "their" indicated ministers and preachers as well as their professed new converts in the contextual setting of revivals outside of the Sabbatarian Adventist community, whether it be among non-Adventists or Adventists. Therefore the final paragraph of the account of this vision in the PT ought to be interpreted as a concluding statement regarding the whole subject matter instead of a reference to just one sentence or section.

299 Edson, MS, p. 10. Cf. Letter, Matthias to Miller, p. 56; Gross, "Times and Seasons," p. 51; Henry Stevens, "Exposition of Revelation Tenth Chapter," VT, Sept. 24, 1845, p. 463.

300 Letter, J. White to Jacobs, DS, Sept. 20, 1845, p. 26. Cf. Letter, Turner to Miller, Jan. 20, 1845. He might also have become familiar with the Midnight Cry vision (E. G. White, SG, II, 35-38).

301 Letter, I. Damman to Snow, JS, June 5, 1845, p. 104.

302 For others who allowed limited mission in a shut-door context, see supra, pp. 108-12.

another time-setting movement[303] predicting Christ's return on the 10th day of the seventh month 1845, and his knowledge of the February 1845 vision, may have caused him to do some mission work in 1845 among those who had not yet received a full understanding of the Advent doctrine.[304] Such an attitude was in harmony with several contemporary views which indicated that one could affirm the validity of the Seventh Month movement while rejecting the idea of the closing of the door of mercy to everyone outside this movement after the autumn of 1844.[305] Toward the end of the 1845 time-setting movement J. White stated that "the atonement ended" in October 1844 when the year of the redeemed began and "the last faint ray of hope was taken up from a wicked world and church."[306] A belief in the completion of the atonement, however, did not automatically rule out all mission work.[307] After the passing of the seventh month of 1845 White became more specific and pointed out that "Jerusalem's conquest is accomplished," indicating that his task was no longer "to combat with opponents but in meekness and love give each one of the household [Adventists] his portion of meat in due season."[308] Although he did not clearly define his shut-door view, the fact that he saw no possibility for the salvation of "a wicked world and church" and "opponents" seems to indicate that these people were excluded from God's mercy because of their rejection of the Advent doctrine.

303   Letter, J. White to Jacobs, *DS*, Sept. 20, 1845, pp. 25, 26. For the difference between the major types of time settings after the Disappointment, see *supra*, p. 114. To J. White the "waiting, watching time" was only one year which he divided into four watches. He remarked that "the watches are 3 months each: The first commencing on the 10th [of the 7th month, 1844], reached to January [1845], when we got light on the shut door. The second brought us to the *Passover* (Midnight, or midway in this watching night). The third brought us to the supposed end of the 1335 days in July, since which we have been *in* the morning watch. . . . Three have passed, and there is but four. All who see this light will receive a certainty that before the 10th day of the 7th month 1845, our King will come, and we will watch, and like Noah, know the day (Rev. 3:3)" (*ibid.*). Cf. W. Thayer, "The Watches," *DS*, July 8, 1845, pp. 34, 35; Editorial, "The Watches," *DS*, July 15, 1845, pp. 38-40; Letter, R. G. Bunting to Jacobs, *DS*, Sept. 6, 1845, p. 18. Many expected the parousia at that predicted time (Editorial, "The Meetings," *DS*, Nov. 1, 1845, p. 14; J. White, *WLF*, p. 22). For other exact time settings, see e.g., Letter, Miller to Himes, *AH*, Nov. 27, 1844, p. 128; Letter, Crosier to Pearson, p. [4]; Letter, Edson to Snow, pp. 90, 91; Letter, Nichols to Jacobs, p. 34; Edson, *Time of the End*, pp. 13, 15; Bates, *TAS*, pp. 10, 11. Cf. [J. White] "Our Present Work," *RH*, Aug. 19, 1851, p. 13. E. G. White stated that time "will never again be a test" ("DBS," *PT*, Nov. 1850, p. 86). Cf. E. G. White, *CEV*, 1882, p. 64 (*EW*, p. 75). For a number of decades the term "this generation" (Mt. 24:34) was employed to stress the imminence of the parousia. See e.g., Nichols, "This Generation . . ." *RH*, Nov. 18, 1858, p. 204; Loughborough, "This Generation," *RH*, March 25, 1862, p. 135; Bates, "The Second Advent," *RH*, May 7, 1867, p. 254; J. White, "Present Truth and Present Conflicts. . . ," *RH*, Nov. 29, 1870, p. 188. Cf. Edson, *Time of the End*, p. 13. Later E. G. White applied "this generation" to those who saw the signs of the darkening of the sun and moon, and the falling of the stars (*The Desire of Ages*, 1898, p. 632).
304   Cf. Loughborough, "Response," p. 134.
305   See *supra*, pp. 109-12.
306   Letter, J. White to Jacobs, *DS*, Sept. 20, 1845, p. 26. Cf. Letter, J. White to Jacobs, *DS*, Oct. 11, 1845, p. 47.
307   See *supra*, pp. 107, 108.
308   Letter, J. White to Jacobs, *DS*, Jan. 24, 1846, p. 25. Cf. Peavey, " 'Hour of His Judgment,' " p. 114; Peavey, " 'Two Thousand and Three Hundred Days,' " p. 116.

Crosier's sanctuary treatise of 1846 referred not only to a continuation of atonement after 1844 but also to the existence of a period of transition from the Gospel dispensation to the next dispensation.[309] He said that this transition time was partly characterized by the text, "Thou must prophesy again" (Rev. 10:11), "whatever the nature of this prophesying may be."[310] Although his position on the shut door was not clearly defined because of his transition period and the absence of the term "shut door,"[311] an analysis of his use of the term "open door" may provide some insight. Crosier's remark that "the Philadelphia church, having 'an open door' [Rev. 3:8] gave the Midnight Cry"[312] seems to suggest that he adhered to a door-of-access concept. Adventists who advocated this kind of shut door referred to the period before the Disappointment when the Millerites, the Philadelphian church, proclaimed the Midnight Cry as a period of great access to the people — as having an open door—, in contrast to the impossibility of gaining access after October 22, 1844.[313] It is worthy of notice that his friend and associate Franklin B. Hahn, M.D.,[314] who was a Sabbatarian Adventist for several years, earlier objected to the use of the expression the "door of mercy being closed against sinners" because it was unscriptural.[315]

By 1847 J. White had accepted the concept of the continuation of Christ's atonement.[316] In the same publication which carried E. G. White's April 1847 vision on the future mission among God's people in the churches, he wrote that

> from the ascension, to the shutting of the door, Oct. 1844, Jesus stood with wide-spread arms of love, and mercy; ready to receive, and plead the cause of every sinner, who would come to God by him.
>
> On the 10th day of the 7th month, 1844, he passed into the Holy of Holies, where he has since been a merciful "high priest over the house of God."[317]

309 See *supra*, p. 131. At that time he expected the Gospel dispensation to end in the spring of 1847 ([Crosier], Remarks, p. 2).
310 Crosier, "Law of Moses," pp. 43, 44.
311 In 1853, however, after he had given up his sanctuary view, Crosier stated that the article was written "for the express purpose of explaining and proving the doctrine of the *'shut door'*" ("Inquiry — the Sanctuary, &c.," *AHBA*, March 5, 1853, p. 301). It was J. White's opinion that the article "no more goes to prove a shut door than it does an open door" ("The Sanctuary," *RH*, March 17, 1853, p. 176). Later Crosier denied that the article supported the shut-door concept (Autobiography, *The Daily Messenger* [Canandaigua, N.Y.], Nov. 22, 1923, p. 22).
312 Crosier, "Law of Moses," p. 44.
313 Cf. Jacobs, "Door of Matt. 25:10," pp. 27, 28; Elliott, "Door Is Shut," pp. 81, 82. See *supra*, pp. 110, 111.
314 Franklin B. Hahn was a physician who joined Crosier and Edson in their study of Christ's high-priestly ministry.
315 Editorial, "Mistake Corrected," p. 368. Cf. Letter, Crosier to Pearson, p. [4]. It should also be noticed that Crosier appreciated the *VT*, which did not favor the extreme shut-door position in 1845 (Crosier, "Prophetic Day," p. 15).
316 J. White, *WLF*, p. 9. Cf. Bates, *SAWH*, p. 60.
317 J. White, *WLF*, p. 2. Cf. "To the Believers Scattered Abroad," p. 23; Letter, Nichols to Miller, April 20, 1846. As textual evidence for the condition after Oct. 1844, J. White cited Is. 59:16, "And he saw that there was no man, and wondered that there was no *intercessor*" (*WLF*, p. 2).

J. White's view of Jesus' mercy could only be in harmony with her vision if His ministry over the "house of God" included God's people outside of the faithful Adventists. If not, it would contradict the vision. This is true also of Bates' 1847 statement that E. G. White's visions were to comfort and strengthen God's " 'scattered,' 'torn,' and 'peeled people,' since the closing up of our work for the world in October 1844."[318] In the same year, however, Bates denied that the "door of mercy" was closed because such terminology was unscriptural.[319] The shut doors of Mt. 25:10 and Lk. 13:25 he explained in the context of Christ — the open door of the Philadelphian church (Jn. 10:7, 9; 14:6; Rev. 3:7, 8),[320] and attributed the closing of Paul's door of access to the Gentiles (1 Cor. 16:9) to the 1844 change in His ministry.[321] When he still believed that the three angels' messages had completed their mission,[322] Bates remarked that in the autumn of 1844 "ended our last work in warning the world; and our labor ceased. Why? Because the messages ceased, and left us entirely destitute of labor."[323] Although he desired the salvation of non-Adventists, he was bound by a theological understanding of the shut door which made further mission work unbiblical.[324] He therefore had to reject the rumors of new conversions from the "Babylonian revivals," seeing as his only task the reclaiming of backsliders among Adventists.[325]

There were various reasons for the reluctance to engage in mission activity among non-Adventists: (1) A preoccupation with the idea that the shut door of Mt. 25:10 referred to a limitation of God's mercy for non-Adventists; (2) the absence of a new theology of mission during the first few years after 1844, making it difficult to proclaim a relevant message which would arrest the attention of non-Adventists; (3) the incompatibility of future mission with the idea of an imminent Second Advent; (4) the difficulty of gaining access to non-Adventists because of their great prejudice toward Adventism.[326]

In 1848 Eli Curtis, who was a Sabbatarian Adventist at this time, published a poem on the sanctuary and shut door which designated the period

318 Bates, "Remarks," *WLF*, p. 21. To him the fact that the mystery of God (Rev. 10:7) was finished implied that "there is no more mediation for the world" (*SAWH*, p. 38). Already in the spring of 1845 he said, "the door is shut — not half or three-quarters of the way — but effectually" (Letter, Bates to Snow, *JS*, May 29, 1845, p. 90).

319 Bates, *SAWH*, p. 68. He added: "I have no desire nor wish in my soul to see my worst enemy lost. I think I have made it manifest for the last twenty years, and am still willing to do what I can to save those that will help themselves. But I am perfectly sensible that it cannot [*sic*] be done only in God's appointed way."

320 *Ibid.*, pp. 65, 66.

321 *Ibid.*, pp. 67, 68.

322 See *supra*, p. 141.

323 *Ibid.* This statement was placed in the context of the mystery of God which was supposed to be finished in 1844 (*ibid.*, pp. 42, 43).

324 *Ibid.*, pp. 52, 53, 68.

325 *Ibid.*, p. 53.

326 For the last reason, see E. G. White, "Travel," p. 377. Cf. Editorial, "Door of Matt. 25:10," p. 28.

after the Disappointment as "the gleaning time" (Is. 17:6)[327] and placed the closing of probation in the future.[328] His shut-door concept was related to the door of access and explained as the "great effectual door" (1 Cor. 16:9) which "seems to have been closed more than three years since; as our experience *very plainly* teaches, but *not* the door of mercy!"[329]

During this year the term "shut door" was applied by J. White in a broader framework than the limitation of salvation for certain people. Although he still stated that "Jesus had left his mediatorial throne,"[330] he remarked that "the principal points on which we dwell as present truth are the 7th Day Sabbath and Shut Door. In this we wish to honor God's most holy institution and also acknowledge the work of God in our Second Advent experience."[331] It showed that the shut door was not confined to the idea of limited mercy for certain people, but included the Advent experience as a part of salvation history. In fact the contemporary theological position or the "present truth" could be summarized under the heading of "the Sabbath and shut door,"[332] which was nothing less than a paraphrase of the interrelationship of the central theme of the third angel's message indicated by the phrase "the commandments of God and the testimony or faith of Jesus." In 1849 both J. White and Edson referred to the present truth as the Sabbath doctrine and the Advent experience.[333]

In 1849 Sabbatarian Adventists continued emphasizing shut-door views, though various statements were made to embrace within divine mercy certain categories of non-Adventists. The publication, which included E. G. White's reference implying a global influence of the sealing truth, contained a modification of Bates's previous shut-door concept. In considering who would constitute the 144,000 (Rev. 7:1-8; 14:1-5, Midnight Cry vision), he suggested that one part was to be made up of those Adventists who participated in "the advent messages" of Rev. 14:6-13 and observed the Sabbath,

327 Poem, *GT*, Extra, Jan. 20, 1848, p. [3]. Cf. Edson, "Appeal," pp. 2, 3.
328 Poem, p. [3]. A section of this poem (brackets his) read:
Our "Great High Priest" hath entered in,
To "the most holy place:" [1 *Kings* 8:6]
Until "He comes out as King of Kings," [*Rev.* 19:16]
Sinners may obtain his grace.

For tho' the Master of the house arose, [*Lu.* 13:25]
In the fall of forty four;
Yet probation will not fully close,
Till He comes out, and shuts the door [*Matt.* 25:10].
329 Editorial Comment, *GT*, Extra, Jan. 20, 1848, p. [3]. The periodical contained the Midnight Cry vision from which the shut-door statement had been omitted.
330 Letter, J. White to the Hastingses, Aug. 26, 1848. Cf. Letter, E. G. White to Bates, No. 3, 1847. This could be a reference to the throne in the first apartment of the heavenly sanctuary, see *supra*, p. 121.
331 Letter, J. White to the Hastingses, Oct. 2, 1848.
332 *Ibid.;* Letter, J. White to the Hastingses, Aug. 26, 1848; Bates, *SLG*, p. 65. Cf. Bates, *TAS*, p. 16.
333 [J. White], "Repairing the Breach," p. 28; Edson, "Beloved Brethren, Scattered Abroad —," *PT*, Dec. 1849, p. 34.

while the other part consisted of "those who do not yet, so well understand the advent doctrine, but are endeavoring to serve God with their whole hearts, and are willing, and will receive this covenant [the Decalogue] and Sabbath as soon as they hear it explained."[334] Because the term "advent doctrine" was generally used by believers as a reference to the doctrine of the Seventh Month movement,[335] the second group represented God's people who had some understanding of Christ's return but had not, like Adventists in North America, participated in the movement. Commenting on the extensiveness of the mission of the sealing message, Bates said that "the United States certainly will have it. England and Russia both have colonies on this continent. England will surely have it. France is but twenty-one miles from Great Britain. This is in the future, and can all, for what I see, be fulfilled."[336] He even thought that some of the 144,000 would come from Asia, from an area east of the river Euphrates.[337]

David Arnold, another Sabbatarian Adventist pioneer, advocated a shut-door concept[338] in which divine mercy was extended to individuals who had passed the "line of accountability" after the Disappointment because "as they were then [on October 22] in a state of INNOCENCY, they were entitled to a record upon the breastplate of judgment as much as those who had sinned and received pardon; and are therefore subjects of the present intercession of our great high priest."[339] Although his concept referred to the existence of an "open door" (Rev. 3:8) for non-Adventist children,[340] he rejected the possibility of conversions among those who were accountable for their actions in 1844 but had not accepted the Advent doctrine. Conversions from this group he disqualified on the basis of Hos. 5:6, 7 and described them as "strange children" who were "converted to the religion of the various sects, but not to God, and the high standard of the Bible."[341]

334 Bates, *SLG*, pp. 60-62.

335 See e.g., Bates, *SAWH*, p. 28; J. White, "Voice of the Fourth Angel," *AdR*, No. 2, Aug. 1850, p. 6; Letter, E. G. White to the Collinses, No. 4, 1850.

336 Bates, *SLG*, p. 35.

337 *Ibid.*, p. 62. Here he said: "I think the evidence is pretty clear that a part of the 144,000 will come from the east; the river Euphrates will be dried up for them to cross over at the pouring out of the sixth seal, in 'THE GREAT DAY OF THE LORD.' Esdras xiii:40-47. Isa. xi:15, 16. Rev. xvi:12."

338 Arnold's shut-door concept of Mt. 25:10 referred to the closing of the door of the first apartment of the heavenly sanctuary by Christ (Rev. 3:7) and a corresponding change in His relation to the world, leaving the present generation who were accountable for their actions in 1844 without mercy because there was no Intercessor any more in the first apartment (Arnold, "The Shut Door Explained," *PT*, Dec. 1849, pp. 43-45). Cf. Arnold, "Daniel's Visions, the 2300 Days, and the Shut Door," *PT*, March 1850, pp. 60, 63.

339 Arnold, "Shut Door," p. 45. Regarding the breastplate of judgment, see Bates, *SLG*, p. 20; *supra*, pp. 118, n. 96; 132, n. 173.

340 Arnold, "Shut Door," p. 45. The use of Rev. 3:7, 8 indicated the influence of E. G. White (*supra*, pp. 153,154).

341 *Ibid.*, p. 46. Cf. Hotchkiss, "Reformations," *VT*, March 26, 1845, p. 47 (*DS*, April 15, 1845, p. 39); Bates, *SAWH*, pp. 52, 79; [J. White], "Miller's Dream," p. 74 (*Miller's Dream*, p. 6); E. G. White, "DBS," *PT*, March 1850, p. 64; E. G. White, *SG*, II, 123.

J. White, while adhering to a shut-door view,[342] expected extensive mission work among non-Adventists when he pointed out that "the Sabbath truth is yet to ring through the land, as the Advent never has."[343]

These views of an expanding mission were influenced by the following factors: (1) The views of E. G. White referring to a future mission work among non-Adventists; (2) the immense task for Sabbatarian Adventists, who numbered only "about one hundred" in 1849,[344] to reach their mission goal of 144,000 before Christ's imminent return. The scarcity of source material with open-door allusions in 1849, however, was evidence that the implications of the visions had not yet been fully understood, but suggestions to include certain groups of non-Adventists in the intercessory work of Christ indicated that the shut-door concept of some of the leaders had undergone a modification, preparing the way for a gradual shift toward an open-door position in mission.[345]

From the account presented above, one could infer that the shut-door views had paralyzed the activities of Sabbatarian Adventists, but in reality the situation was different. J. White interpreted the period from 1844 till 1848 as "the scattering time" of Ezek. 34[346] when the leaders of the Advent movement had been "scattering the flock since 1844, by opposing the present truth,"[347] but indicated that since the spring of 1848 the "work of uniting the brethren on the great truths connected with the message of the

---

342   Cf. J. White, "TAM," pp. 65, 66 (*TAM*, pp. 3, 5).

343   Letter, J. White to Bowles, Nov. 8, 1849.

344   J. White, "The Cause," *RH*, July 23, 1857, p. 93.

345   Through a selective use of facts Lindén proposed the thesis that E. G. White's visions reflected the "heretical" shut-door concept of Hale and Turner according to which salvation in principle was no longer possible for the world (Lindén, *Biblicism*, pp. 75, 76, 84; Letter, Lindén to A. L. White, pp. 4, 11). To prove his thesis he made an exclusive use of contemporary source material. The most important arguments he selected were: The Midnight Cry vision; the Bridegroom vision, the March 1849 vision; Letter, E. G. White to Bates, July 13, 1847; the omissions in reprints of visions in *CEV;* and a June 29, 1851 vision at Camden which was never recognized as genuine by SDA (see *supra*, pp. 149-51, 154; *infra*, p. 276). He omitted, however, important contemporary data such as the future mission aspect in the April 1847 vision and the new shut-door concept in the context of the sanctuary theology in the March 1849 vision which contributed significantly to the development of a new theology of mission. Cf. E. G. White's views with the shut-door criterion of Hale and Turner (*supra*, p. 108). The fact that Lindén designated the shut-door concept as heretical inevitably affected his objectivity and the conclusion of his study. A similar attitude could be discovered in the publications by Carver and Canright. For the tradition of critics who suggested the genuineness of the "Camden vision," see "The Camden Vision," attributed to E. G. White by R. R. Chapin; Snook and Brinkerhoff, *E. G. White*, pp. 6, 7; Carver, *E. G. White*, pp. 31-33, 56-58; Grant, " 'Visions and Prophecies,' " *WC*, Jan. 27, 1875, p. 62; Canright, *Life of Mrs. E. G. White*, 1919, p. 150. E. G. White did not acknowledge its genuineness. However, Carver attempted to show the opposite (*E. G. White*, pp. 31-33). E. G. White's attitude can be understood through the fact that little is known about the origin of the vision. No contemporary evidence seems to be available, while the historical data provided by her critics as to the time and place of the vision were inaccurate.

346   [J. White], "Repairing the Breach," p. 28. Cf. Edson, "Beloved Brethren," p. 34; E. G. White, "DBS," p. 86 (*EW*, p. 74).

347   [J. White], "Repairing the Breach," p. 28. During that time the opposition against the Sabbath doctrine was quite successful ([J. White], "Sketch of the Past," p. 5).

third angel commenced—."[348] The 1844-48 period can be described as a time of intensive search for a new interpretation of the events associated with the termination of the time calculations, while at the same time vigorous efforts were made to convince Adventists of the validity of the Seventh Month movement. Only when this search, which placed the Millerite motives for mission in a framework of post-1844 theological developments, had been achieved in 1848 could the mission of the Sabbatarian Adventists be in any way successful. Already in 1849, when their first periodical *The Present Truth* was published and widely distributed among Adventists,[349] J. White stated that "the gathering time has come, and the sheep are beginning to hear the cheering voice of the true Shepherd, in the commandments of God, and the testimony of Jesus, as they are being more fully proclaimed. The message will go, the sheep will be gathered into the present truth."[350] At the same time, E. G. White urged believers "to rescue souls from the coming storm of wrath."[351] From that time onward, various Sabbatarian Adventists were actively engaged in spreading the present truth predominantly among other Adventists. Early in 1850 E. G. White commented on the result of these missionary activities that "souls are coming out upon the truth all around here. They are those who have not heard the Advent doctrine and some of them are those who went forth to meet the Bridegroom in 1844, but since that time have been deceived by false shepherds."[352] About this time J. White published the first Sabbatarian Adventist hymnal[353] which included a hymn on the "Fall of Babylon" with the phrase "Come 'my people' and forsake her," implying the presence of God's people within fallen Babylon and a mission call for separation.[354] These developments indicated that the shut-door concept at that time was of such a nature that it allowed for successful missionary work among both Adventists and non-Adventists.

From 1850 onward there was a further modification of the shut-door concept. Due to the successful mission praxis among non-Adventists the concept of an open door was stressed. However, the idea of a shut door in

348   *Ibid.* On the importance of 1848, see *supra,* p. 143.
349   Letter, J. White to Bowles, Oct. 17, 1849.
350   [J. White], "Repairing the Breach," p. 28. Cf. Edson, "Beloved Brethren," p. 34; J. N. Andrews, "Dear Brethren and Sisters," *PT,* Dec. 1849, p. 39; E. G. White, "DBS," p. 86 (*EW,* p. 74).
351   E. G. White, "DBS," p. 32 (*EW,* p. 48).
352   Letter, E. G. White to the Collinses, No. 4, Feb. 10, 1850.
353   Although the hymnal was dated 1849, it seems to have been published early in 1850. Cf. *PT,* Dec. 1849, p. 47 with Letter, E. G. White to the Collinses, No. 4, 1850.
354   [J. White], *Hymns,* p. 42. This phrase seems to have been the result of J. White's editing of a previously published hymn (cf. D. M. Millard and J. Badger, *Hymns and Spiritual Songs . . . for the Use of Christians,* 9th ed., 1842, p. 400). Another hymn which dealt with the "Second Advent History" seems to indicate that for those who worshiped the beast or his image "mercy *now* no longer pleads" ([J. White], *Hymns,* p. 4). In the hymnbook publications *Hymns for Second Advent Believers Who Observe the Sabbath of the Lord,* 1852, p. 19 and *Hymns for Those Who Keep the Commandments of God, and Faith of Jesus,* 1855, p. 321; 1861, p. 360 the word "now" did not any more appear in italics. Later hymnbooks omitted this hymn.

1844 was retained in the SDA view of salvation history. Developments in the interpretation of Mt. 25:1-11 and the understanding of the shut door in relation to the mission praxis during the period of 1850-74 will be discussed in Chapter VI.

3. Summary.

The Disappointment practically terminated all mission efforts of Adventists because of their general understanding that the door of mercy was closed for humanity with the completion of the Midnight Cry of the Seventh Month movement. When time continued and the Second Advent did not take place, the Bridegroom theme, hostile reactions of the public, and difficulties in getting attention of non-Adventists due to prejudicial attitudes, provided sufficient arguments for the early Sabbatarian Adventists to accept the validity of the Seventh Month movement and the idea that the door was shut. There existed a number of shut-door concepts, some of which allowed mission activity on a very limited scale, others being more restrictive. But whatever shut-door concept was advocated, there were no significant results in converting non-Adventists during the 1845-1849 period. The gradual change in the meaning of the shut door among Sabbatarian Adventists could be attributed to the influence of E. G. White's views on a successful mission in the future. In general it can be said that first the shut-door views excluded salvation for all who had rejected the Advent doctrine, then the concept was enlarged to embrace God's activities in the Advent experience, and at last it extended the possibility of salvation to other categories of individuals besides Adventists. Although these individuals were to be the target of a new mission outreach, it was not until 1850 that the new mission efforts had success.

E. Summary.

In this chapter the early development of the Sabbatarian Adventist theology of mission has been described in the context of interaction between theological interpretations of the Disappointment and an agitation for the observance of the Sabbath. The new developments were the result of a further study of Christ's heavenly ministry and created a sanctuary theology which provided an explanation for the delay of Christ's return, vindicated the Midnight Cry of the Seventh Month movement, and opened up new dimensions in eschatology and soteriology. One aspect of the sanctuary theology, dealing with Christ's role as the Bridegroom, made it possible to continue believing that the parable of the ten virgins had its fulfillment in the Midnight Cry. Another aspect was concerned with Christ's function as High Priest and made it possible to affirm the termination of the 2300 days on October 22, 1844, indicating that the expected event was not the Second

Advent but an inauguration of the antitypical Day of Atonement.

During the new theological developments the validity of the observance of the Sabbath for Christians was a subject of discussion among Adventists. It was especially those who had accepted the sanctuary theology who saw the relevance of the Sabbath because this theology stressed the important role of the Decalogue in Christ's post-Disappointment ministry which facilitated the acceptance of the Sabbath doctrine.

Both Christ's ministry after the Disappointment and the Sabbath doctrine provided a rationale for why Christ had not returned in 1844: Christ had to complete His atoning ministry in heaven and a restoration of the Sabbath had to take place among God's people on earth before the Second Advent would occur. This explanation indicated to Sabbatarian Adventists the interrelationship between the Sabbath, the Advent experience, and the Second Coming. The third angel's message was the special message which integrated the restoration of the Sabbath into the Advent experience and became the central thrust of their theology of mission. The Sabbath was a criterion in their ecclesiology, determining the true Israel of God, the Remnant, and separating them from all other Adventists for a unique mission.

During most of the period under consideration the Sabbatarian Adventists devoted much of their time persuading other Adventists not to deny the past Advent experience but to accept the new understanding of Christ's heavenly ministry and the Sabbath doctrine as the explanation of the Disappointment. One can discover a gradual shift in the understanding of the shut-door concept which prepared the minds of believers for a future mission among non-Adventists. From the contemporary sources one is forced to admit that the views of E. G. White had a profound influence on the new theological interpretations as well as the emerging missionary consciousness, making doubtful that without her influence the early Sabbatarian Adventists would have survived this period of turmoil.

During the decades following 1850, the new Sabbatarian Adventist theology was further developed and later incorporated by SDA[1] into a system of doctrines which became a vital and integral part of their theology of mission. The apocalyptic-eschatological aspects of this theology, indicated by the three angels' messages with its focus on the third angel's message, were central in their mission proclamation to prepare mankind for the Second Advent. Too, their ecclesiology became a vital element of the mission thrust. Gradually, however, there was a development of various non-apocalyptic aspects in the mission theology, but they played a minor role until 1874. In this chapter the treatment of the three angels' messages is arranged according to their numerical sequence, not to their importance.

A. *The First Angel's Message.*

The three angels' messages (Rev. 14:6-12) were considered intimately related to events transpiring around the change in Christ's high-priestly ministry in 1844. The first angel, however, was specifically associated with Christ's pre-Advent judgment and the atonement.

The question of atonement was of special missiological significance because since 1850 the mission efforts resulted in conversions among non-Adventists while there was not yet a theological formulation of the sanctuary theology allowing for pardon or forgiveness of sins during the antitypical Day of Atonement.

1. *Christ's high-priestly ministry.*

a. The pre-Advent judgment and God's people.

In 1850, as a result of the sanctuary theology, Christ's heavenly ministry in the most holy place was seen as consisting of two tasks: (1) The cleansing of the sanctuary associated with the blotting out of sins; (2) the reception of His kingdom.[2] By this time Crosier's idea of a continued atonement during

---

1 For the difference between the term Sabbatarian Adventists and SDA, see *supra*, p. xv.
2 See e.g., J. White, "The Sanctuary, 2300 Days, and the Shut Door," *PT*, May 1850, p. 76; Bates, "Laodicean Church," p. 8; Bates, "Midnight Cry in the Past," *RH*, Dec. 1850, p. 22; J. White, "The Parable, Matthew XXV, 1-12," *RH*, June 9, 1851, p. 101 (*The Parable . . .* [1851], pp. 15, 16).

the post-Disappointment period had been accepted and Bates referred to this period as "the great day of atonement."[3] When the idea of the "hour of his judgment" (Rev. 14:7), which had been interpreted by Millerites as a reference to the Day of Judgment, was applied to the post-1844 period, the foundation was laid for the concept of a pre-Advent judgment. The relevance of the term "hour of his judgment" became clear through a consistent application of the typological principle to the functions of the high priest under the Old Covenant and those of Christ as High Priest under the New Covenant. As had earlier been done,[4] Bates applied Ex. 28:29, "And Aaron shall bear the names of the children of Israel in the breastplate of judgment upon his heart, when he goeth in unto the holy place for a memorial before the Lord continually," to Christ's high-priestly ministry implying that "he like his pattern in the type, entered the Most Holy Place, bearing upon his breastplate of Judgment the twelve tribes of the House of Israel. See Exo. xxviii.29, and Rev. vii.4."[5] He remarked that in harmony with Dan. 7:9, 10, 13 and Rev. 14:6, 7 both the Father and the Son had moved to the second apartment of the heavenly sanctuary "to set [sic] in judgment."[6] There, according to Bates, Christ as the Bridegroom, High Priest, Mediator and crowned King of Israel stood before the Father "advocating the cause of all presented on his breastplate of judgment. As Daniel sees it, the judgment is now set and the books open."[7] The Father, he said, was the judge who was "to decide who is, and who is not worthy to enter the gates of the holy city."[8] Both Bates and J. White saw the "day of judgment" as being distinct from "the hour of judgment."[9] J. White differed from Bates in the fact that to White the judgment testimony of the first angel "could only signify, that the period had come for this generation to be tested by the second advent truth."[10] There was a participation of believers in this judgment trial before the close of probation, he said, because "they bear the cutting truths of God's word, which separates the wheat and tares . . . but the work of judging to be done in the great day of judgment, and executing the 'judgment written' is the work of immortal saints."[11] The fact that in 1854 J. White also used the term "breast plate of judgment" was no evidence of a shift to a pre-Advent judgment.[12]

In 1854 J. White acknowledged a kind of judgment going on under the present sounding of the seventh angel (Rev. 11:15-18), but he indicated

3 Bates, "Midnight Cry," p. 22. Later, R. F. Cottrell stated that the first angel "announces the commencement of a period called, 'the hour of judgment' " ("Faith in Prophecy," *RH,* Sept. 3, 1867, p. 177).

4 See *supra,* p. 132, n. 173.

5 Bates, *TAS,* p. 9. Cf. Edson, "Appeal," p. 3.

6 Bates, *TAS,* p. 10.

7 *Ibid.* Cf. Bates, "New Testament Testimony," *RH,* Dec. 1850, p. 13.

8 Bates, *TAS,* p. 10.

9 *Ibid.;* J. White, "Day of Judgment," pp. 49, 50. Uncertainty about these terms was indicated by the remark that "some have contended that the day of judgment was prior to the second advent. This view is certainly without foundation in the word of God" (*ibid.,* p. 49).

10 *Ibid.*

11 *Ibid.,* pp. 49, 50.

12 J. White, "Parable," p. 102 (*Parable,* p. 17).

that this was distinct from the Day of Judgment, stating "that judgment has begun at the house of God, that this is, in a certain sense, a period of judgment and decision, we freely admit; but *the* judgment, *the day* of judgment, *the time* of the dead that they should be judged, is, evidently, in the future."[13]

In 1855 Uriah Smith[14] defined more clearly the pre-Advent judgment. On the basis of Dan. 7:10 and Rev. 20:12 he concluded that "a record is kept of the acts of all men; and from that record, their reward is given them according to their deserts."[15] The judgment of these records as indicated by 1 Pet. 4:17 and 1 Tim. 5:24, he said, "must begin at the house of God," inferring that it had to be of "the same nature and can refer to no other work than the closing up of the ministration of the heavenly Sanctuary, hence that work must embrace the examination of individual character."[16] He felt, therefore, that the judgment was a vital part of Christ's sanctuary ministry, and indicated that "the lives of the children of God, not only those who are living, but all who have ever lived, whose names are written in the Lamb's book of life, will during this time pass in the final review before that great tribunal."[17]

Finally, in 1857 J. White had completely accepted the idea of a pre-Advent judgment and affirmed that "the 2300 days . . . reached to the cleansing of the Sanctuary, or to the great day of atonement in which the sins of all who shall have part in the first resurrection will be blotted out."[18] Like his colleagues, he interpreted 1 Pet. 4:17, 18 as a prophetic statement referring to the last period of God's church during the time of the cleansing of the sanctuary. 1 Tim. 5:24 he read as follows: "Some men's sins [the righteous] are open before hand, going before to judgment, and some men [the wicked] they follow after," which he paraphrased by saying "some men lay open, or confess their sins, and they go to judgment while Jesus' blood can blot them out, and the sins be remembered no more; while sins unconfessed, and unrepented of, will stand against the sinner in that great day of judgment of 1000 years."[19] Additional support he found in 1 Pet. 4:5-7 which showed that "the investigative judgment of the saints, dead and living, takes place prior to the second coming of Christ."[20] This may have been one of the earliest uses of the well-known term of "investigative judgment" used among SDA to distinguish the judgment of God's people

---

13   [J. White], "Seventh Angel," p. 52.
14   Uriah Smith (1832-1903) was a prolific writer, being editor of the *RH* for many years. One of the most influential publications on SDA prophetic teaching was his exposition of Daniel and Revelation. This was a good example of his ability to synthesize the thoughts of his fellow believers and other commentators into a coherent framework.
15   Smith, "The Cleansing of the Sanctuary," *RH*, Oct. 2, 1855, pp. 52, 53.
16   *Ibid.*, p. 53.
17   *Ibid.*
18   J. White, "Judgment," p. 100.
19   *Ibid.* (Brackets his.) The "great day of judgment of 1000 years" signified to him the millennium. Cf. J. White, *WLF*, p. 24.
20   J. White, "Judgment," p. 100.

before Christ's return from the judgment at or after the Second Advent. At first, E. G. White employed the term "judgment"[21] for the pre-Advent judgment but later she also used the term "investigative judgment."[22] R. F. Cottrell[23] referred to the term "judicial judgment" which he differentiated from "the executive judgment at his coming, when his *reward* is with him 'to *give* to every man' according to the decisions of the judgment in the heavenly Sanctuary, previously made."[24]

It was thought that the judgment of God's people, which had begun on October 22, 1844, would first deal with the righteous dead, then with the righteous living.[25] The judgment of the living was obviously considered as a very important occasion for which the Sabbatarian Adventists should be fully prepared. The Laodicean message (Rev. 3:14-20),[26] according to J. White, was "a special call to the remnant," directing the attention of believers to a work of preparation for the imminent judgment of the living so that their sins would be blotted out before the completion of Christ's sanctuary ministry. Their salvation depended on a total obedience to this counsel.[27]

b. The pre-Advent judgment and the 1335 days.

Additional evidence for a pre-Advent judgment was seen in the passage: "Blessed is he that waiteth, and cometh to the thousand three hundred and five and thirty days. But go thou [Daniel] thy way till the end be, for thou shalt rest, and stand in thy lot at the end of the days" (Dan. 12:12, 13). Soon after the Disappointment references were made to Daniel standing in his lot in the judgment[28] but it was not until much later that this text was employed by J. White as evidence for a pre-Advent judgment. He stated that

> in the great day of atonement for the blotting out of sins of all of every age, the cases of patriarchs and prophets, and sleeping saints of all past ages will come up in judgment, the books will be opened, and they will be judged according to the things written in the books. It is thus, at the end of the 1335 days, [Dan. xii, 13,] that DANIEL STANDS IN HIS LOT.[29]

An analysis of the Hebrew word from which the word "lot" was translated and its use in Scripture led White to conclude that "Daniel does not stand in

---

21   E. G. White, *SG*, I, 198.
22   See e.g., E. G. White, *SP*, IV, 266, 307-15. Cf. E. G. White, *GC*, pp. 352, 422-29, 479-91.
23   Roswell F. Cottrell (1814-92) was an early Sabbatarian Adventist. Born in a Seventh Day Baptist family, he accepted the third angel's message and propagated it as a writer, poet, and minister. For some time he was corresponding editor of the *RH*.
24   Cottrell, "Unity of the Remnant Church," *RH*, March 10, 1859, p. 125 (*Unity of the Church*, 1859, p. 14).
25   See e.g., E. G. White, *SG*, I, 198.
26   In 1856 there was a shift in the ecclesiological self-understanding from the Philadelphian church to the Laodicean church. See *infra*, pp. 244-48.
27   J. White, "Judgment," pp. 100, 101. Cf. E. Everts, " 'Be Zealous and Repent,' " *RH*, Jan. 8, 1857, p. 75; Letter, Albert Stone to Smith, *RH*, Jan. 29, 1857, p. 101.
28   See *supra*, p. 132, n. 173.
29   J. White, "Judgment," p. 100. (Brackets his.)

the 'lot of his inheritance,' as it has been expressed, at the end of the 1335 days, but he stands in his lot in the decisions of the judgment of the righteous dead."[30]

The view was further developed by various others. Smith's presentation in 1871 was one of the clearest, stating that Daniel stood in his lot

> in the person of his Advocate, our great High Priest, as he [Christ] presents the cases of the righteous for acceptance to his Father. The word here translated lot, does not mean a piece of real estate, a lot of land, but the decisions of chance, or determinations of Providence. At the end of the days, the lot, so to speak, was to be cast. In other words, a determination was to be made in reference to those who should be accounted worthy of a possession in the heavenly inheritance. And when Daniel's case comes up for examination, he is found righteous, he stands, a place is assigned him in the heavenly Canaan. Does not the language of the psalmist have reference to this time, when he says, Ps. 1:5, "The ungodly shall not stand in the Judgment?"[31]

Already in 1850 E. G. White had written that "the 1335 days were ended,"[32] without specifying the time of their completion. J. White thought the evidence was "conclusive that the 1335 days ended with the 2300, with the Midnight Cry in 1844."[33] He felt he could not assign a later date thinking that no prophetic periods were to extend beyond October 22, 1844 because of the expression "that there should be time no longer" (Rev. 10:6).[34] He concluded, therefore, that "the judgment of the righteous dead commenced at that time, and has been progressing more than twelve years."[35]

Not everyone agreed that the 1335 days had terminated in 1844. A few years later Smith made an attempt to preserve the Millerite chronology on the relationship between the commencement of the 1290 days of Dan. 12:11 and the 1335 days[36] so that both periods would commence in 508 A.D. with the termination of the 1290 days in 1798 and the 1335 days in 1843.[37]

30 *Ibid.* Cf. E. G. White, *GC,* p. 488.
31 Smith, "Thoughts on the Book of Daniel," *RH,* July 18, 1871, p. 37 (*Thoughts . . . on the Book of Daniel,* 1873, pp. 370, 371). Cf. Edson, "Daniel Standing in His Lot," *RH,* July 30, 1857, p. 101. In this context he defined the cleansing of the sanctuary as "the canceling and atoning for and blotting out and putting away the errors and sins of the whole Israel of God, and that this would be the judging or judgment of the house of God; or in other words, it would be the time when all Israel would stand in their lot, when all Israel should be judged and acquitted and divine providence would determine and award to them eternal life" (*ibid.*).
32 Letter, E. G. White to the Church in Hastings' House, No. 28, 1850.
33 J. White, "Judgment," p. 100. For his earlier position, see *supra,* p. 132, n. 173. For arguments on the end of the 1335 days, see *supra,* pp. 39, 40.
34 *Ibid.* The millennium was not considered as a prophetic time period (*ibid.*). E. G. White said: "Prophetic time closed in 1844" (*SG,* I, 148). Cf. E. G. White, MS 59, 1900 (*SDABC,* VII, 971).
35 J. White, "Judgment," p. 100.
36 See *supra,* pp. 39, 40; [Smith], "Synopsis of the Present Truth," No. 12, *RH,* Jan. 28, 1858, pp. 92, 93; [Smith], "The 1335 Days," *RH,* Feb. 27, 1866, p. 100; [Smith], "The Daily and Abomination of Desolation," *RH,* April 3, 1866, p. 139.
37 [Smith], "Synopsis," No. 12, pp. 92, 93. Cf. *supra,* pp. 39, 40.

Because of the fact that the 2300 days ended in 1844, the question arose as to the "blessing" that was to mark the termination of the 1335 days in 1843. Smith placed the "blessing" in the setting of "the great proclamation of the near coming of Christ," stating that

> the new and stirring doctrine of the setting up of God's kingdom, was shaking the world. New life was being imparted to the people of God. . . . A Spirit of revival was awakened, unknown since the days of the Great Reformation. And thousands can testify to the blessing they received, and the infinite gratitude of heart with which they hailed, the newly-risen and glorious light.[38]

Later he paraphrased the "blessing" by pointing out that "about the year 1843, there was a grand culmination of all the light that had been shed on prophetic subjects up to that time. The proclamation went forth in power."[39]

Thus, in order to harmonize Dan. 12:11-13 with Christ's ministry after 1844, the passage was interpreted in the light of the pre-Advent judgment while retaining the Millerite calculation of terminating the 1335 days in 1843. This interpretation of Dan. 12:13 affirmed the idea of a pre-Advent judgment, for it was after 1843 that the time would arrive for Daniel, as part of God's people, to stand in the pre-Advent judgment which was to begin in 1844.

c. The pre-Advent judgment and the atonement.

Since the beginning of 1850 the mission of Sabbatarian Adventists had resulted in the conversion of various non-Adventists through the contents of the proclamation of the three angels' messages. The possibility of their salvation was principally based on the argument of "ignorance" which implied that they had not rejected the Advent doctrine because it was not fully understood. They, therefore, had not grieved the Holy Spirit and closed their individual probation. Yet, at the same time, there was the important influence of Crosier's sanctuary theology which advocated a continued atonement but interpreted Christ's ministry before 1844 as an atoning ministry for the forgiveness of sins for mankind, and after 1844 as an atoning ministry for the blotting out of sins for the house of Israel. Two attempts were made to reconcile the sanctuary theology with the phenomenon of non-Adventists joining the Sabbatarian Adventists. The first attempt came through the "breastplate of judgment" concept which permitted those ignorant of the Advent doctrine in 1844 to enter the most holy place of the heavenly sanctuary to receive the benefits of Christ's intercessory ministry

---

38   [Smith], "The 1335 days," p. 100.
39   Smith, "Daniel," pp. 36, 37 (*Daniel*, pp. 367, 368). To anyone who questioned whether these events were the blessing of Dan. 12:12, he remarked, "Listen to the Saviour's words: 'Blessed are your eyes,' said he to his disciples, 'for they see; and your ears, for they hear.' Matt. 13;16. And again he told his followers that prophets and kings had desired to see the things which they saw, and had not seen them. But 'blessed,' said he to them, 'are the eyes which see the things ye see.' Luke 10:23, 24. If a new and glorious truth was a blessing in the days of Christ to those who received it, why not equally so in A.D. 1843?" (*ibid.*, p. 37; [*Daniel*, pp. 367, 368]). Cf. [Smith], "The 1335 Days," p. 100.

before the Father. The concept was based on the assumption that the names of these individuals had already been written on the breastplate of the High Priest before October 22, 1844. When the transition in Christ's ministry occurred, they were assured of His continual mercy because of their presence on His breastplate. This implied, according to Edson, that "all who were borne in on the breast plate of judgment, and have not sinned wilfully, may repent and find forgiveness."[40] The second attempt came through an analysis of the sacrifices offered on the Day of Atonement and their antitypical significance which revealed that on that specific day besides the blotting out of sins there was an opportunity for forgiveness of sins. Edson commented that "in the type, on the tenth day of the seventh month, the daily, the morning and evening sacrifice, and other offerings for the forgiveness of sins were kept up. See Num. xxix, 7-11."[41] This signified the possibility of forgiveness of sins during the antitypical Day of Atonement. Thus in 1850 there was, at least in the mind of Edson, a theological breakthrough of the limited soteriology of the sanctuary theology. One should add that it was especially the mission praxis which forced Sabbatarian Adventists to define more specifically the implications of a continued atonement for non-Adventists.

In 1853 Andrews provided the first extensive exposition on the possibility of forgiveness of sins in the context of the sanctuary theology. Analyzing the function of the blood shed on the typical Day of Atonement, he stated that it was offered for two purposes: "1. 'To make an atonement for the children of Israel, for all their sins.' 2. To cleanse, or 'make an atonement for the holy sanctuary.'"[42] From Lev. 16 he concluded that

> in the most holy place, blood was offered for the sins of the people to make an atonement for them. Verses 5, 9, 15, 17, 30, 33, 34; Heb. ix, 7. . . . the two holy places of the sanctuary, and also the altar of incense were on this day cleansed from the sins of the people, which . . . had through the year been born[e] into the sanctuary and sprinkled upon it. Verses 16, 18-20, 33; Ex. xxx.10.[43]

The implications for the antitypical Day of Atonement, according to Andrews, were that "our High Priest stands by the MERCY-SEAT (the top of the ark,) and there he offers his blood, not merely for the cleansing of the sanctuary, but also for the pardon of iniquity and transgression."[44] This meant to him an "*open door* in the heavenly sanctuary [Rev. iii, 7, 8; Isa. xxii, 22-25]," to which he invited "those to come for pardon and salvation, who have not sinned away the day of grace."[45] This exposition signified the end

---

40 Edson, "Appeal," p. 3. See *supra*, p. 160.
41 *Ibid.*
42 Andrews, "Sanctuary," p. 146 (*Sanctuary*, p. 57).
43 *Ibid.*, p. 146 (*Sanctuary*, p. 58).
44 *Ibid.*, p. 148 (*Sanctuary*, p. 71). Cf. Smith, "The Sanctuary," *RH*, April 4, 1854, p. 84 (*Sanctuary*, p. 23).
45 Andrews, "Sanctuary," p. 148 (*Sanctuary*, p. 71). (Brackets his.) Cf. Smith, "Sanctuary," p. 84 (*Sanctuary*, p. 23). He said also that Christ "is now performing his last ministration for a fallen world" (*ibid.*).

of the limited soteriology, which confined Christ's post-1844 ministry to blotting out of sins, and was immediately published in pamphlet form and recommended as "the best work that has been published on present truth."[46]

Two years later (1855), Smith and Andrews provided additional support for the possibility of pardon or forgiveness of sins on the antitypical Day of Atonement. The blood of Christ, Smith said, was ministered in both apartments of the heavenly sanctuary, and as long as this was the case "mankind" had the "privilege to avail themselves of the merits of his blood by faith in him [Christ]."[47] He added that "while Christ exercises the office of Priest he is a mediator between God and man, and those who will come unto him may avail themselves of his mediation. He is Priest in the second apartment as well as the first. If we confess our sins, he is yet 'faithful and just to forgive us our sins.'"[48] Andrews indicated that the two-fold nature of Christ's work in the most holy place — the cleansing of the sanctuary and the forgiveness of the sins of God's people — is taking place simultaneously, stating that "the sins of the whole church for 6000 years may be disposed of as individual cases, and all the while that the great work is being accomplished, the blood of Jesus still may avail for us in the presence of God."[49] He argued on the basis of the James Macknight translation[50] of Heb. 10:19, "Well then, brethren, having boldness in the entrance of the holy places, by the blood of Jesus," that "the blood of Jesus avails for us in both the holy places of the heavenly tabernacle," indicating a "complete refutation of the doctrine that probation closes with our Lord's entrance within the second vail."[51]

The theme of forgiveness was further worked out by another SDA leader, J. H. Loughborough,[52] in 1865. He saw evidences of continual

---

46   [J. White], "Bro. Andrews' Work on the Sanctuary," *RH*, March 31, 1853, p. 184.

47   Smith, "Cleansing of the Sanctuary," p. 54.

48   *Ibid.*

49   Andrews, "The Sanctuary and Its Cleansing," *RH*, Oct. 30, 1855, p. 69.

50   Macknight, *Apostolic Epistles*, pp. 555, 556. James Macknight (1721-1800) was a Presbyterian divine and Bible critic. He studied at the Universities of Glasgow and Leiden. The complete translation of the "Apostolic Epistles" was published in 1795. His text was reprinted several times in Britain and the U.S.A.

51   Andrews, "Sanctuary and Its Cleansing," p. 69. The question "if the offering of the high priest in the holiest could avail for a sin committed while he was there before God" was answered by Andrews who said that the Bible was silent on this point. However, he pointed out that "as far as we know in the whole work of the year the transgression preceded the offering. That is, this was at least as much the case in one apartment as the other. How then is it with our Lord? He shed his blood before entering the tabernacle in heaven at all. And that blood once shed avails for sin committed before or after his death. So that a moment's reflection will show that this objection bears equally against forgiveness' being found in either apartment" (*ibid.*). Furthermore, he felt that there was "just as much mercy implied in the sin offering in the holiest as in the other offerings on that day" (*ibid.*). Later on, this article was referred to as providing the evidence for the availability of mercy during the cleansing of the sanctuary. See e.g., [J. White], "Is There Probation During the Cleansing of the Sanctuary?" *RH*, June 2, 1863, p. 2.

52   John N. Loughborough (1832-1924) was a preacher among Adventists for three years before he accepted the third angel's message in 1852. He served as a pioneer missionary,

intercession and mercy on the typical Day of Atonement with post-1844 implications in the fact that on that day other offerings were offered (e.g. the continual burnt offering) besides the offering of blood to cleanse the sanctuary which required the service of the priests and high priest.[53] He remarked that these other sacrifices made on the Day of Atonement "meet their antitype in that consecration to God, and devotion to his cause, which must now be manifest on the part of those seeking an interest in the atonement of Christ our High Priest."[54] As additional evidence for forgiveness of sins on that special day he pointed to Lev. 23:29; 16:33, suggesting that an atonement "was made for the entire congregation which availed in the case of every individual who afflicted his soul," and to Lev. 16:18-20, indicating that the cleansing of the altar represented the removal of sins placed upon it during the Day of Atonement.[55]

It was not until 1858 that E. G. White made any statement in reference to an atonement in connection with Christ's ministry after 1844. She employed the terms "special atonement" and "final atonement." The term "special atonement" seems to refer to an atonement specifically related to the pre-Advent judgment. She pointed to the necessity of Jesus' entering into "the Most Holy place of the heavenly Sanctuary to cleanse it; to make a special atonement for Israel, and to receive the kingdom of his Father, and then return to earth and take them to dwell with him forever."[56] It was in 1844, she said, that Jesus "had gone to cleanse the Sanctuary, and to make a special atonement for Israel."[57] The term "final atonement" seems to include the whole atoning ministry of Christ after 1844. She remarked that Jesus entered "the Most Holy of the heavenly, at the end of the 2300 days of Dan. viii, in 1844, to make a final atonement for all who could be benefited by his mediation, and to cleanse the Sanctuary."[58] She indicated that now He made "his final intercession for all those for whom mercy still lingers, and for those who have ignorantly broken the law of God. This atonement is for the righteous dead as well as for the righteous living."[59] Here she added the new perspective that "Jesus makes an atonement for those who died, not receiving the light upon God's commandments, who

---

administrator, and writer. He was the author of *Rise and Progress of the Seventh-day Adventists . . .*, 1892, the first general SDA history.

53 Loughborough, "Thoughts on the Day of Atonement," *RH*, Aug. 15, 1865, p. 82. He also remarked that "we would not understand from the fact that an offering was made after the work of blotting out sins in the type [Lev. 26:23, 24], that there is to be mercy after Christ has completed the work of blotting out sins, but this shows in the clearest manner that the entire day of atonement in the type was a day in which pardon for sins might be found" (*ibid.*). Textual evidence for the continual burnt offering was Num. 29:7-11; Lev. 6:12, 13; 16:3, 5; Ex. 29:38-42 (*ibid.*).
54 *Ibid.*
55 *Ibid.*
56 E. G. White, *SG*, I, 149.
57 *Ibid.*, p. 158.
58 *Ibid.*, p. 162. Cf. Letter, Crosier to Pearson, p. [4].
59 E. G. White, *SG*, I, 163.

sinned ignorantly."[60] During His ministry, she said, when there was "the atoning blood to cleanse from sin and pollution,"[61] the judgment of the righteous dead was going on, and was to be followed by that of the righteous living.[62] At the end of the antitypical Day of Atonement "Jesus had blotted out the sins of his people. He had received his kingdom, and the atonement had been made for the subjects of his kingdom."[63] E. G. White's term "final atonement" could be equated with her term "final intercession," for this intercession was designated as an atonement. The final atonement, therefore, was an atonement dealing with the righteous living and the righteous dead. In view of the new formulations of the pre-Advent judgment and Christ's atoning ministry of forgiveness and blotting out of sins, the significance of the "final atonement" could be described as follows: (1) It provided an atonement for the forgiveness of sins "for all those for whom mercy still lingers," implying a continuation of Christ's pre-1844 ministry; (2) it provided a special atonement for the pre-Advent judgment which included three atoning phases: (a) pardon or forgiveness of sins "for those who died, not receiving the light upon God's commandments, who sinned ignorantly"; (b) blotting out of the sins of the righteous dead; (c) blotting out of the sins of the righteous living.[64] Thus, she confirmed both the ideas of a pre-Advent judgment and the continual availability of mercy for pardon through the intercession of Christ.

Not all her comments on the atonement seem to pertain to the post-1844 period. In 1858 she remarked that after the Crucifixion, when "the great Sacrifice had been offered," the Holy Spirit directed the attention of the disciples to the heavenly sanctuary "where Jesus had entered by his own blood, and shed upon his disciples the benefits of his atonement."[65] At that time various views on the atonement circulated among believers. It seems likely that those who applied the concept of the atonement exclusively to Christ's sanctuary ministry[66] would interpret her remark as a reference to

60 *Ibid.*
61 *Ibid.*, III, 1864, p. 134.
62 *Ibid.*, I, 198.
63 *Ibid.*
64 Many years later E. G. White expressed herself more specifically about the typological aspects of the sanctuary service and mentioned the necessity of an atonement for each of the two apartments. In the first apartment an atonement was made which transferred the sins from the sinner to the sanctuary. This action provided pardon and acceptance for the sinner but no cancellation of the sins because the claims of the law had not yet been satisfied. In the second apartment an atonement for the removal or blotting out of sins began which was to make satisfaction for the claims of the law. This remission or putting away of sins was called the cleansing of the sanctuary. But before this process could be accomplished there was the necessity of a pre-Advent judgment to determine who were entitled to the benefits of this atonement (*GC*, pp. 418-22). Yet, during this atoning ministry for the blotting out of sins, she said, the atonement for pardon or forgiveness of sins as performed in the first apartment before 1844 continued after this date in the second apartment (*ibid.*, pp. 429, 430).
65 E. G. White, *SG*, I, 170. Cf. *ibid.*, IV, a, 1864, p. 149.
66 See *supra*, p. 128. Because of the influence of Crosier's sanctuary doctrine it can be assumed that many would adhere to this view. There developed a trend which seems to limit the atonement to the cleansing of the sanctuary; see e.g., *The Bible Student's Assistant: or A*

His atonement in the heavenly sanctuary. Other believers who included Christ's death on the cross as a significant aspect of the atonement[67] might have interpreted her remark as a reference to Christ's atonement on the cross.[68] One of the first instances in which E. G. White clearly referred to the atonement as Christ's death was in 1864, when the term "atonement" was used to describe Jesus' offer "as a sacrifice for man, to take their guilt and punishment upon himself, and redeem them from death by dying in their place, and thus pay the ransom."[69] She also indicated that the deliverance of Israel from Egypt "was typical of the great atonement which Christ made by the sacrifice of his own life for the final deliverance of his people,"[70] and stated that "the sacrifices which they [Jews] performed under the law were typical of the Lamb of God, and illustrated his great atonement."[71] In 1869 she seems to refer to Christ's afflictions and death on the cross as "the great work of the atonement"[72] and "the atonement,"[73] though the context of these terms suggests that the atonement could include every aspect of Christ's sufferings throughout salvation history.

From these sources one discovers that E. G. White supported the developments of the pre-Advent judgment in the sanctuary theology. Her remarks on Christ's post-1844 ministry were qualified by terms like "special" and "final" atonement, and by 1864 it was clear that she did not support Crosier's idea that the atonement began after Christ's ascension

---

Compend of Scripture References, 1858, p. 11; Waggoner, "The Atonement — Part II," *RH*, Nov. 17 and 24, 1863, pp. 197, 206 (*The Atonement . . .*, 1868, pp. 103-12; 2nd ed., 1872, pp. 109-18); *A Declaration of the Fundamental Principles . . .*, 1872 (Appendix II, Principle II). Cf. Smith, *The Sanctuary and the Twenty-Three Hundred Days of Daniel VIII, 14*, 1877, pp. 179-85; *A Brief Sketch of . . . the Seventh-day Adventists*, 1888, p. 41.

67 This aspect of the atonement was advocated in Andrews, "The Perpetuity of the Law of God," *RH*, Jan. and Feb. 1851, pp. 34, 35, 41 (*Thoughts on the Sabbath . . .*, 1851, pp. 10, 16, 25); J. M. Stephenson, "The Atonement," *RH*, Aug. 22, Oct. 31, Nov. 21, Dec. 5, 1854, pp. 9, 90-91, 114, 123 (*The Atonement*, 1854, pp. 3-5, 93-97, 150-56, 181-86); Snook, *Review of W. G. Springer . . .*, 1860, pp. 87, 88; Moses Hull, "The Two Laws, and Two Covenants," *RH*, May 13, 1862, p. 189 (*The Two Laws . . .*, 1862, p. 27). Stephenson's book was highly recommended for a number of years. See [J. White], "New Works," *RH*, Dec. 19, 1854, p. 144; *RH*, 1855-57.

68 Against the background of a charge that SDA were "minimizing the atoning sacrifice completed on the cross, reducing it to an incomplete or partial atonement that must be supplemented by Christ's priestly ministry," several commentators interpreted her term "his atonement" in the light of her later comments as being Christ's sacrificial atonement on the cross which was followed by His heavenly ministry during which "the benefits" of this sacrificial atonement were applied. Thus it was felt that her remark supported the view that "Christ is now making application of the benefits of the sacrificial atonement He made on the cross" (*Seventh-day Adventists Answer Questions on Doctrine . . .*, 1957, pp. 349, 355, 661-64). For early references to the term "atoning sacrifice," see e.g., Stephenson, "Atonement," *RH*, Nov. 21, 1854, p. 114 (*Atonement*, pp. 150-56); [Andrews], "Christ As an Atoning Sacrifice," *RH*, Oct. 5, 1860, p. 120; Andrews, *Sermons on the Sabbath and Law . . .*, 1869, p. 94. This term was frequently used by E. G. White after 1876.

69 E. G. White, *SG*, III, 46, 47. Cf. E. G. White, *TC*, No. 17, 1869, pp. 17, 19 (*T*, II, 1948, pp. 213, 215).

70 E. G. White, *SG*, III, 228.

71 *Ibid.*, IV, a, 118.

72 E. G. White, *TC*, No. 17, p. 1 (*T*, II, 200).

73 *Ibid.*, pp. 17, 19 (*T*, II, 213, 215).

when He commenced His high-priestly ministry. By introducing terms like "the atonement," "the great atonement," and "the great work of the atonement" to include Christ's death she stimulated a development toward a broader view of the atonement. It took, however, decades before her view was accepted by the main body of believers. E. G. White's concept of atonement, depending on the context, could refer to Christ's death on the cross, His sanctuary ministry, or both. The "special" and "final" atonement could be interpreted as a "special" and "final" benefit of the atonement for mankind through Christ's death on the cross and high-priestly ministry in the sanctuary. The "special atonement" referred to Christ's atonement during the pre-Advent judgment, the "final atonement" to both the "special atonement" and His atonement for pardon or forgiveness of sins. In this context the function of the pre-Advent judgment seems to be an agency in determining who is eligible for receiving the "special atonement."

d. The relational significance of Dan. 8 and 9.

The calculation of the 2300 days as expounded by the Seventh Month movement[74] remained the standard interpretation among the Sabbatarian Adventists. In 1850 J. White emphatically stated "THE 2300 DAYS — this prophetic period has been, and still is, the main pillar of the Advent faith,"[75] which signified, as it did to the Millerites, that this "pillar" was based on the presupposition that Dan. 9:24-27 was the key to an understanding of Dan. 8:14, implying that both the 70 weeks and the 2300 days had a common starting point: 457 B.C. as the seventh year of Artaxerxes.[76] Commenting on the accuracy of the 457 B.C. date, J. White said, "it is by the Canon of PTOLEMY that the great prophetical period of seventy weeks is fixed. This Canon places the seventh year of ARTAXERXES in the year B.C. 457; and the accuracy of the Canon is demonstrated by the concurrent agreement of more than twenty eclipses."[77] Among SDA the year of Christ's death never had the importance in calculating the termination of the 2300 days that it had among the Millerites.[78]

Referring to the significance of Dan. 9:20-27 for Dan. 8:14, Andrews pointed out that the 70 weeks indicated how much of the 2300 days pertained to the earthly sanctuary ministry.[79] The reference to the anointing of "the most holy" (Dan. 9:24), he said, signified "the heavenly sanctuary receiving its consecration preparatory to the priesthood of Christ therein," and indicated that "at the very point where the earthly sanctuary ceases to

74   See *supra*, pp. 93-95.
75   J. White, "Our Present Position," *RH*, Dec. 1850, p. 13. Cf. J. White, "Parable," p. 100 (*Parable*, p. 12); E. G. White, *SP*, IV, 258.
76   See *supra*, pp. 36, 94. Cf. Storrs, "Exposition of Daniel, 8th Chapter . . . ," *MC*, Jan. 27, 1843, p. [11] (*Examiner*, pp. 47-50), repr. in "The 70 Weeks a Part of the 2300 Days," *RH*, Feb. 17, 1853, p. 154.
77   J. White, "Present Position," p. 14; "Lecture on Chronology," *AH*, March 2, 1850, p. 36. See *supra*, p. 94, n. 96.
78   See *supra*, pp. 36, 86, 87, 94, 95.
79   Andrews, "Temple in Heaven," p. 115.

be the subject of prophecy, the heavenly sanctuary is introduced, and with it the prophecy is filled out."[80] The contribution of Dan. 8 and 9 to the understanding of the different phases of Christ's high-priestly ministry was expressed by J. White in the following words: "As the ministration in the holy place of the temple in Heaven began immediately after the end of the typical system, at the close of the sixty-nine and a half weeks, Dan. 9:27, so the ministration in the holiest of all, in the heavenly sanctuary, begins with the termination of the 2300 days."[81]

2. The identification of the first angel with the angel of Rev. 10.

In the preceding years many Adventists had realized the special relationship of the angel of Rev. 10 to the angel of Rev. 14:6, 7.[82] The chapters of Rev. 9 and 10 were seen as a chronological sequence of salvation-historical events, for it was thought that only after the termination of "the second woe," which terminated with the end of the political domination of the Ottoman empire on August 11, 1840, the angel of Rev. 10 descended from heaven to proclaim the message of Rev. 14:6, 7.[83] Andrews remarked that "the angel of Chap. x, preaches from this little book [Rev. 10:2], and it is this prophecy of Daniel [Dan. 8:14] that contains the prophetic time on which the angel of Chap. xiv, 6, bases his proclamation."[84] Smith suggested the following arguments that the two angels were identical: (1) They both proclaimed a special message; (2) they did it with a loud voice; (3) they used similar language in referring to the Creator; (4) they proclaimed time: the one, that time shall be no more, and the other that the hour of God's judgment has come.[85]

This identification provided believers with another argument of seeing the Advent movement in the light of a successive series of events in salvation history. No wonder this awareness was an additional stimulus to their self-image and especially important in view of the fact that witnessing about their past experience was an integral part of their present mission.

3. The first angel and mission.

During the 1850s many Sabbatarian Adventists still adhered to the Millerite view that the proclamation of the "everlasting gospel" of the first angel's message (1840-44) had been fulfilled in the proclaiming of "the gospel of the kingdom" (Mt. 24:14).[86] Although arguments for this position

80 *Ibid*. See *supra*, p. 87, n. 57.
81 J. White, "Faith and Hope," *RH*, March 22, 1870, p. 105 (*Sermons*, p. 164).
82 Edson, "The Commandments of God . . . ," *RH*, Sept. 2, 1852, p. 65.
83 Cf. e.g., Andrews, "TAR," p. 169 (*TAR*, p. 20).
84 *Ibid*.
85 Smith, "Thoughts on the Revelation," *RH*, Oct. 21, 1862, p. 164 (*Thoughts . . . on the Book of Revelation*, 1865, pp. 179, 180).
86 E.g., J. White, "Signs of the Times," *RH*, Sept. 8, 1853, p. 70 (*The Signs of the Times . . . ,* 1853, p. 90); Andrews, "TAR," p. 169 (*TAR*, p. 21); [J. White], "Signs of the Times," *RH*, Oct. 1, 1857, p. 169.

were taken from Millerite literature and did not contribute new insights, the interpretation of Mt. 24:14 as a fulfilled sign of the times continued to focus attention on the imminent return of Christ.

In harmony with this view of the first angel and the current idea that the three angels represented successive periods in salvation history, J. White interpreted the first angel in 1850 as the "last mission of mercy to the world" given by the Millerites,[87] and stated that "it closed up for the world more than six years since,"[88] indicating that its relevance was in the past. He felt, however, that the "everlasting gospel" (Rev. 14:6) still had significance for the few non-Adventists who joined the Sabbatarian Adventists at that time, explaining that it "has not lost its power to affect the hearts of those who are still within the reach of mercy, and salvation; but that it has ceased to arouse any more men to repentance as in 1843, no sane man will deny."[89] In referring to Rev. 14:6, 7 as a major event in the past, Andrews remarked that "the world and church have been tested by this great truth. . . . It has tested the present generation as the great truths of the first advent tested the people of that time,"[90] indicating that the burden of the message of the first angel was in the past.[91]

It was E. G. White who called attention to the continued relevance of the first angel's message for missionary outreach because she felt it was essential for an explanation of their present position.[92] Said she, "the burden of the message should be the first, second, and third angels' messages, and those who had any hope in God would yield to the force of that truth."[93] Even in the missionary approach to Seventh Day Baptists the need was seen to provide background information of the first and second angels' messages.[94] A few years later E. G. White stated that the three angels' messages formed a "perfect chain of truth" and that non-Adventists would embrace them in their order, and follow "Jesus by faith into the heavenly Sanctuary. These messages were represented to me as an anchor to hold the body."[95]

The developments in the understanding of the first angel's message in the light of Christ's high-priestly ministry and increasing mission work among non-Adventists added to the importance of the message and made it an

---

87   J. White, "TAM," p. 65 (*TAM*, p. 3).

88   J. White, "Present Position," p. 14.

89   *Ibid.*

90   Andrews, "Thoughts on Revelation XIII and XIV," *RH*, May 19, 1851, p. 81.

91   *Ibid.*; [J. White], "The Angels of Rev. XIV — No. 2," *RH*, Sept. 2, 1851, p. 20 (*AR*, 1851, p. 6). Cf. J. White, "Present Position," p. 14. J. White's exposition on Rev. 14 was published in four articles in the *RH* of Aug. 19, Sept. 2, Dec. 9 and 23, 1851. These articles will be abbreviated as "Angels No. 1," etc.

92   She said that "such subjects as the Sanctuary, in connection with the 2300 days, the commandments of God, and the faith of Jesus, are perfectly calculated to explain the past Advent movement, show what is our present position, and establish the faith of the doubting, and give certainty to the glorious future. These, I have frequently seen, were the principal subjects on which the messengers should dwell" (*CEV*, p. 51 [*EW*, p. 63]).

93   E. G. White, MS 11, 1850

94   Cottrell, "To Sabbath-Keepers Who Have Not Heard the Third Angel's Message," *RH*, June 10, 1852, p. 22.

95   E. G. White, *SG*, I, 165, 166.

indispensable prerequisite for a comprehension of the significance of the third angel's message and the SDA theology of mission.

B. The Second Angel's Message.

The interpretation of Rev. 14:8 was basically the same as in 1844; though during the years, there was further specification of the characteristics of Babylon. The concept of "Babylon" determined Sabbatarian Adventist evaluations of contemporary religious revivals among non-Adventists, their view of church unity, and the question of a possible cooperation with other Christians. It also contributed significantly to the understanding of the raison d'être of this religious body and its mission.

1. The moral fall of Babylon.

In 1850 the question of what constituted Babylon was not yet settled. According to J. White, the first angel's message had been preached to the Protestant churches but was rejected, resulting in the proclamation of the second angel's message to God's people in these churches. This, he said, signified that the term "Babylon" in this message was not concerned with the Roman Catholic Church, for "God's people were not in that church,"[96] so indicating that people did not come out of that church but "out of the Protestant Sects."[97] Andrews, however, was of the opinion that "Babylon includes Protestant as well as Catholic churches."[98] Although in 1859 J. White seemed to have broadened his concept when he applied the Babylon of the Apocalypse to "all corrupt Christianity," he probably still meant by this Protestantism.[99] Later, the view that Babylon included the Protestant and Catholic churches became the accepted one.

96 J. White, "TAM," p. 66 (TAM, p. 5). Even in 1859 he did not think that God's people were in the Roman Catholic Church (J. White, "Babylon," RH, March 10, 1859, p. 122). The heading "Conversion of a Roman Catholic," RH, July 17, 1866, p. 56, indicates the uniqueness of this event. At the 1873 General Conference J. White mentioned the presence of "quite a representation from the Roman Catholic church" ("Conference Address . . . ," RH, May 20, 1873, p. 180).

97 [J. White], "Angels No. 3," p. 64 (AR, p. 11).

98 Andrews, "TAR," RH, March 6, 1855, p. 186 (TAR, p. 57). He added that it was certain "that the people of God at the time of the preaching of the hour of his judgment were in all the popular churches. And this fact is a most striking testimony as to what constitutes the great city of confusion" (ibid.).

99 J. White, "Babylon," RH, March 10, 1859, p. 122. In this early period there was frequently a difference between the interpretation of Babylon of Rev. 14:8 and Rev. 17. Rev. 14:8 was interpreted in the context of the 1844 experience as referring to the Protestant churches, while Babylon of Rev. 17 was applied to the Roman Catholic Church as the mother harlot and Protestant churches as her harlot daughters. The importance of Rev. 14:8 seems to have determined J. White's view of Rev. 17 (ibid.). A distinction between Rev. 14:8 and Rev. 17 was also seen by E. G. White. In 1884 she applied Babylon, symbolized by the harlot of Rev. 17, to the Roman Catholic Church and interpreted Rev. 14:8 as a description of the fall of the Protestant harlot daughters (SP, IV, 232, 233). Later she enlarged her view of Rev. 14:8, stating that "it cannot refer to the Roman Catholic Church alone" (GC, 1911, p. 383). This implied an inclusion of both Protestant and Roman Catholic churches.

Babylon was characterized by Andrews as "the professed church united with the kingdoms of the world. In other words, 'Babylon is the apostate churches.' "[100] Nichols designated Babylon, the great city, as a symbol of "the church incorporated, and united to the state."[101] Andrews further indicated that there existed a typological relationship between ancient Israel and contemporary Christianity. In the context of Rev. 17 he pointed out that "she [church] became a harlot by seeking the friendship of the world. James iv, 4. It was this unlawful connection with the kings of the earth that established her the great harlot of the Apocalypse."[102] He said "the Jewish church which was represented as espoused to the Lord, [Jer. ii; iii; xxxi, 32,] became an harlot in the same manner, Eze. xvi,"[103] and "the fact that Babylon is distinct from, though unlawfully united with, the kings of the earth, is positive proof that Babylon is not the civil power" but a "professedly religious body," for God's people were to be in Babylon before her destruction, which could only mean that "the woman, Babylon of Rev. xvii, symbolizes the professed church unlawfully united to the world."[104]

The "unlawful union" of the church with the world was closely related to the fact that "she made all nations drink of the wine of the wrath of her fornication" (Rev. 14:8). According to Andrews, "this harlot, in consequence of her unlawful union with the powers of earth, has corrupted the pure truths of the Bible, and with the wine of her false doctrine, has intoxicated the nations."[105] Loughborough suggested that Babylon "causes the nations to drink by enforcing these doctrines upon their minds, and calling them to enforce them by law upon the people."[106] In Cottrell's opinion "all nations" had tasted the wine of Babylon "whether Catholic, Greek, or Protestant, and 'the inhabitants of the earth have been made drunk with the wine of her fornication.' "[107] The wine, he said, was "especially the lust of

100   Andrews, "Revelation," p. 81.
101   Nichols, "Babylon," *RH*, Jan. 13, 1852, p. 75.
102   Andrews, "TAR," *RH*, Feb. 20, 1855, p. 178 (*TAR*, p. 51).
103   *Ibid.* (Brackets his.) Cf. Cottrell, "The Closing Messages. —" No. 10, *RH*, Oct. 19, 1869, p. 133.
104   Andrews, "TAR," p. 178 (*TAR*, p. 51).
105   Andrews, "TAR," p. 185 (*TAR*, p. 54). Cf. E. G. White, *SP*, IV, 234, 235. As false doctrines Andrews mentioned the doctrine of natural immortality, infant baptism, the change of the fourth commandment of the Decalogue, postmillennialism and the concept of a spiritual parousia ("TAR," pp. 185, 186 [*TAR*, pp. 54, 55]). Cf. E. G. White, *SP*, IV, 235.
106   Loughborough, "Questions for Bro. Loughborough," *RH*, Nov. 12, 1861, p. 192.
107   Cottrell, "Closing Messages," No. 10, p. 133. Later E. G. White qualified this statement by saying that Rev. 14:8 "did not reach its complete fulfillment in 1844. The churches then experienced a moral fall, in consequence of their refusal of the light of the Advent message; but that fall was not complete. As they have continued to reject the special truths for this time, they have fallen lower and lower. Not yet, however, can it be said that 'Babylon is fallen, . . . because she made *all nations* drink of the wine of the wrath of her fornication.' She has not yet not made all nations do this. The spirit of world-conforming and indifference to the testing truths for our time exists and has been gaining ground in the churches of the Protestant faith in all the countries of Christendom; and these churches are included in the solemn and terrible denunciation of the second angel. But the work of apostasy has not yet reached its culmination" (*GC*, p. 389). She added that not until the condition described in 2 Thes. 2:9-11 is reached and "the union of the church with the world shall be fully accomplished, throughout Christendom, will the fall of Babylon be complete. The change is a

civil power, which, when attained by an apostate church . . . never fails to lead to oppression and persecution."[108] Although Babylon was a dangerous force, E. G. White saw the greatest threat from the side of apostate Sabbatarian Adventists[109] and "Adventists who oppose the law of God."[110]

It was the general opinion that the fall of Babylon in 1844 could have been avoided. The first angel's message was seen to be a reformative instrument and a medicine which could cure Babylon,[111] but when it was rejected her fall became inevitable. In 1851 Andrews called Babylon's fall a "moral fall" which preceded her final destruction, "for the people of God are called out of her after her fall, and while her destruction is yet pending. Rev. xviii."[112] His rationale for calling it a "moral fall" was the rejection of "truth" by the "professed church."[113] In harmony with the criticism on Babylon E. G. White stated in 1853 that "coldness and death reigned" in the "nominal churches," and, by pleasing men, "God's spirit left them."[114] A few years later she also mentioned that "they have shut out the gifts God has placed in the church,"[115] and depicted the rejection of the first angel's message in the context of salvation history, stating that "as they rejected the light from heaven they fell from the favor of God"[116] and Jesus "turned his face from the churches."[117] Assuming a typological relationship between Jews of Christ's time and contemporary Christianity, she remarked:

> The nominal churches, as the Jews crucified Jesus, had crucified these [angels'] messages, and therefore they have no knowledge of the move made

---

progressive one, and the perfect fulfillment of Rev. 14:8 is yet future" (*ibid.*, pp. 389, 390).

108   Cottrell, "Closing Messages," No. 10, p. 133. As examples of religious persecution in the U.S.A. he mentioned Baptists and Quakers (*ibid.*).

109   E. G. White, "Testimony to the Church," *RH*, Nov. 26, 1861, p. 205. She added, "unfaithful Sabbath-keepers are the worst enemies the truth can have." Here she seems to refer to opposition of former believers like Ransom Hicks, R. R. Chapin, H. S. Case, C. P. Russel, J. M. Stephenson and D. P. Hall. Cf. the opposition of Snook, Brinkerhoff, Carver, Gilbert Cranmer, A. C. Long, W. C. Long, Preble, and Canright.

110   E. G. White, *TC*, No. 25, 1875, pp. 173, 175, 178 (*T*, III, 1948, pp. 571, 572, 574). For the context of this remark, see e.g., criticism on SDA in the *Voice of the West*, 1865-69, and the *World's Crisis*, 1865-75. Cf. the opposition of Grant, Wellcome, and Sheldon.

111   Andrews, "Revelation," p. 82. In 1855 he stated that "the preaching of the hour of God's judgment and the immediate coming of the Lord, was at once the test of the church, and the means by which she might have been healed" ("TAR," p. 186 [*TAR*, p. 57]). Cottrell said that Babylon "rejected the only medicine that could effect a cure. God, in his providence and in fulfillment of his prophetic word, provided a remedy. It was the gospel of the kingdom. . . . Matt. xxiv, 14; Rev. xiv, 6, 7" ("Babylon Might Have Been Healed," *RH*, Aug. 4, 1853, p. 46). Cf. E. G. White, *SP*, IV, 236.

112   Andrews, "Revelation," p. 82.

113   *Ibid.* Cf. E. G. White, *SP*, IV, 232.

114   Letter, E. G. White to Kellogg, No. 9, 1853. Cf. J. White, "TAM," p. 66 (*TAM*, p. 5). Here he reasoned that due to the rejection of the first angel's message by the Protestant churches, "Jesus, and the Spirit of truth left them forever, and the churches or Babylon fell." Later, E. G. White stated more specifically that "the churches have grieved the Spirit of the Lord, and it has been in a great measure withdrawn" (*SP*, IV, 237).

115   Letter, E. G. White to Friends in Mansville, No. 7, c. 1856.

116   E. G. White, *SG*, I, 140.

117   *Ibid.*, p. 136.

in heaven, or of the way into the Most Holy, and they cannot be benefited by the intercession of Jesus there. Like the Jews, who offered their useless sacrifices, they offer up their useless prayers to the apartment which Jesus has left, and Satan, pleased with the deception of the professed followers of Christ, fastens them in his snare, and assumes a religious character, and leads the minds of these professed Christians to himself, and works with his power, his signs and lying wonders.[118]

Later she applied typological reasoning to postmillennial views in Christ's time to illustrate the condition of the Christian world.[119]

In looking backward she noticed in 1858 that the spiritual condition of the churches after their fall had further declined, and that "they have been growing more and more corrupt; yet they bear the name of being Christ's followers. It is impossible to distinguish them from the world. . . . Satan has taken full possession of the churches as a body."[120] In 1859 J. White found support for the designation "moral fall" in the fact that a progressive decline indicated a "moral change."[121] First, he said, Babylon "falls"; then "she *becomes* the habitation of devils, and 'the hold of every foul spirit,' &c."; next "God's people are called out of her"; and finally "her plagues are poured out upon her, and she is thrown down with violence, 'like a great millstone cast into the sea,' and 'found no more at all.' "[122] Cottrell saw an illustration of the moral fall in a typological relationship between the "Jewish church" of Christ's time and the contemporary Christian church. He stated that

> a moral fall or apostasy of a religious body is always a gradual work; but it cannot be announced till it reaches a certain point. That point was reached by the Jewish church when they rejected Jesus Christ. Then their house was left unto them desolate [Mt. 23:38]. So the professed Christian church of the last days, will reach, if they have not already, a similar point; and then their fall will be announced, in fulfillment of the second message.[123]

He also said that the moral fall was "a point in her apostasy where God

118 *Ibid.,* pp. 171, 172.
119 E. G. White stated that "the churches of our time are seeking worldly aggrandizement, and are as unwilling to see the light of the prophecies, and receive the evidences of their fulfillment which show that Christ is soon to come, as were the Jews in reference to his first appearing. They were looking for the temporal and triumphant reign of Messiah in Jerusalem. Professed Christians of our time are expecting the temporal prosperity of the church, in the conversion of the world, and the enjoyment of the temporal millennium" ("The First Advent of Christ," *RH,* Dec. 24, 1872, p. 10).
120 E. G. White, *SG,* I, 189. She added, "Jesus had left the Holy place of the heavenly Sanctuary, and had entered within the second vail, the churches were left as were the Jews; and they have been filling up with every unclean and hateful bird" (*ibid.,* p. 190). For the decline of the churches, see M. E. Cornell, *Facts for the Times . . . ,* 1858, pp. 37-51; [Nathaniel Hawthorne], *The Celestial Railroad* [rev. ed., 1866]; Cornell, *The State of the Churches,* [1868]. Cf. Robert Atkins, *A True Picture: or A Thrilling Description of the State of the Churches Throughout Christendom . . .* (Boston: J. V. Himes, 1843), which was repr. by Sabbatarian Adventists in 1853.
121 J. White, "Babylon," *RH,* March 10, 1859, p. 122.
122 *Ibid.*
123 Cottrell, "Unity," p. 125. Cf. Cottrell, "Closing Messages," No. 9, *RH,* Oct. 12, 1869, p. 126.

abandons her, the spirits of devils rush in to fill the place of the Spirit of God, and worldly, unconverted persons flock in and make her a cage of every unclean and hateful bird."[124]

The believers saw in the rise of Spiritualism and its penetration of religious bodies after 1844 strong evidence for their interpretation that Rev. 14:8 signified the moral fall of Babylon. In 1853 Cottrell indicated that "'the rapping spirits' have commenced their work since 1844, and are filling the professed churches with their delusions."[125] J. White expressed that it was "a startling fact, that since 1844 has been the period for the rise of foul spirits."[126] Andrews remarked that "as a demonstration that we are correct in regard to the application of Rev. xiv, let the present movement respecting the spirits of the dead answer. An innumerable host of demons are spreading themselves over the whole country, flooding the churches and religious bodies of the land to a very great extent."[127] Later, Cottrell described as evidence of the moral fall "the advent of what is called spirit manifestations; which we might denominate, (considering the great number possessed of foul spirits in the days of the first advent of Christ,) the second advent of the devil and his angels."[128] The newly accepted view on the conditional immortality of man was considered an antidote for Spiritualism.[129]

As a result of this understanding of Spiritualism a distinction was made between the fall of Babylon in Rev. 14:8 and the one in Rev. 18:2. While Rev. 14:8 was seen as the moral fall in 1844, Rev. 18:2, "Babylon the great is fallen, is fallen, and she is become the habitation of devils, and the hold of every foul spirit, and a cage of every unclean and hateful bird" was interpreted as a future mission proclamation repeating Rev. 14:8 and adding a denouncement of the corruption and sins of contemporary Christianity caused by Spiritualism after the moral fall.[130] According to J. White, Rev.

124 Ibid., No. 13, RH, Nov. 9, 1869, p. 157.
125 Cottrell, "Babylon," p. 46.
126 J. White, "Signs," p. 71 (Signs, p. 95). Cf. R. Lawrence Moore, "Spiritualism," in Gaustad, Adventism, pp. 79-103; Clark, 1844, I, 327-82.
127 Andrews, "TAR," p. 187 (TAR, p. 66). He added that "the immortality of the soul . . . is the basis and foundation of all their work" (ibid.).
128 Cottrell, "Closing Messages," No. 16, RH, Nov. 30, 1869, p. 182. Concerning the recent rise of Spiritualism he remarked that "its progress has been unprecedented and unparalleled by any movement affecting the faith or the infidelity of the people, since the world began. In the short space of a score of years its converts are numbered by millions; and all these are infidels, rejecting the great truths revealed in the Bible. Such a tremendous evil could not suddenly burst upon our world, but by God's permissive providence; and his providence would not permit it without a cause. That cause must be departure from God and rejection of his truth" (ibid.). In 1872 an article was published stating that Spiritualism had now nearly embraced the whole world (Editorial, "Spiritualism in Asia," RH, Dec. 3, 1872, p. 200).
129 J. White interpreted as providential that conditionalism was introduced among Millerites by Storrs before the rise of Spiritualism (Life, p. 154).
130 Cf. Cottrell, "Babylon," p. 46. J. White stated, "Mesmerism, Satan's mildest bait, was but little known in this country prior to 1844; since then the church has been bewitched with its damning influences. Psychology was not mentioned; and no one so much as dreamed of all this clattering of ten thousand demons from the infernal regions, rapping, moving chairs, stands, tables, &c. That Babylon's cup is full, that she is now a 'hold of every foul spirit,' we do not believe. But the present movements of Spiritualism show the text fast fulfilling" ("Signs," p. 70 [Signs, pp. 91, 92]).

18:2 could not be applied to the churches before 1844, but in 1856 it was "fast becoming their real condition."[131]

Besides manifestations of Spiritualism Cottrell found support for the moral fall in a "great spiritual dearth" in the churches[132] and in a rapid decline in morality evinced by organized gambling, religious balls, and parties for "the purpose of building churches, or the support of the ministry."[133]

2. The evaluation of religious revivalism.

The negative attitude of Sabbatarian Adventists toward religious revivals within contemporary Christianity was the result of their interpretation of the fall of Babylon. The religious revivals going on in 1849 were described by E. G. White as "false reformations."[134] Her evaluation was determined on the basis that individuals associated with these revivals had rejected the truth,[135] which seemed to explain the fact that there was no more "the travel [travail] of soul for sinners as used to be."[136] Therefore, she could state that these revivals "were not reformations from error to truth; but from bad to worse."[137] In the sanctuary context she commented that

> the excitements and false reformations of this day do not move us, for we know that the Master of the house rose up in 1844, and shut the door of the first apartment of the heavenly tabernacle; and now we certainly expect that they will "go with their flocks," "to seek the Lord; but they shall not find him; he hath withdrawn himself [Hos. 5:6] (within the second vail) from them."[138]

Thus the powerful manifestations taking place during these revivals, she said, were "a mere human influence, and not the power of God."[139]

Not every Sabbatarian Adventist took such a determined stand against revivals. In 1854 a correspondent of the *Review and Herald* describing the various attitudes said, "Some are reasoning and doubting about this so-called work of God, feeling unprepared to deny that it is such; others believe there are true converts among them; some think they have nothing to do there; others have a mind to go and see; and a few take a firm stand

---

131 J. White, "The Third Angel's Message," *RH,* Aug. 14, 1856, p. 116.
132 Cottrell, "Closing Messages," No. 15, *RH,* Nov. 23, 1869, p. 173.
133 *Ibid.,* No. 17, *RH,* Dec. 17, 1869, p. 189.
134 E. G. White, "DBS," p. 22 (*EW,* pp. 43, 44). She also predicted that false revivals would increase (*ibid.,* p. 22 [*EW,* p. 45]). Smith considered this a prophecy being fulfilled in the 1858 revivals ("Visions," p. 63).
135 E. G. White, *SCEV,* p. 4 (*EW,* p. 45). See *supra,* p. 154.
136 E. G. White, "DBS," p. 22 (*EW,* p. 45). Cf. Smith, "Visions," p. 63; E. G. White, *SCEV,* p. 4 (*EW,* p. 45). See *supra,* p. 154.
137 E. G. White, "DBS," p. 22. She added that "those who professed a change of heart, had only wrapt about them a religious garb, which covered up the iniquity of a wicked heart. Some appeared to have been really converted, so as to deceive God's people; but if their hearts could be seen, they would appear as black as ever" (*ibid.*).
138 *Ibid.,* p. 64. Cf. J. White, "Parable," p. 102 (*Parable,* pp. 19, 20).
139 E. G. White, "DBS," p. 64.

184

against it as the work of Satan."[140]

In referring to revivals of the churches which had rejected the 1844 Advent doctrine (including those during the late 1850s), E. G. White remarked that "the churches were elated, and considered that God was marvelously working for them, when it was another spirit."[141] She stated that Satan "hopes to deceive the honest, and lead them to think that God is still working for the churches" and predicted that the revivals "will die away and leave the world and the church in a worse condition than before."[142] This statement seemed to be confirmed in a pessimistic evaluation of the revivals by two religious periodicals.[143] J. White commented that this evaluation "coming from two very high sources, in the religious world, makes the real condition of fallen Babylon appear worse than before her spurious revivals,"[144] and felt that apostasy of the majority of new converts and increasing worldliness within the churches was evidence that the revivals were not genuine.[145]

Cottrell saw revivalism as a necessary element in SDA eschatological expectations. He remarked that "the word of God points us to a Protestant persecution just before us," which implied that "there must be an increase of religion among the sects, in order to bring it about."[146] In the light of the SDA movement he felt that there was only one genuine revival, "the great revival," which was described as "the revival of genuine Christianity, a coming up to the standard of truth and holiness" and "the revival of long-neglected and down-trodden truth — 'the commandments of God and the faith of Jesus' — without which no real, permanent good can be accomplished for this generation."[147] He justified his use of the term "great revival" because it was "the revival of primitive faith and practice, and because it will sanctify God's peculiar people, and prepare them to be translated to Heaven without seeing death."[148] He had no expectations,

---

140 Letter, Albert Belden to J. White, RH, Feb. 28, 1854, p. 47. Another correspondent remarked, "many no doubt, are honestly deceived by these false guides, and may perhaps be eventually saved under the loud cry of the third angel" (E. R. Seaman, "Can Ye Not Discern the Signs of the Times?" RH, Feb. 21, 1854, p. 37).

141 E. G. White, SG, I, 172.

142 Ibid.

143 Congregationalist (Boston), Nov. 19, 1858, and the Watchman and Reflector (Boston), n.d., were quoted in J. White, "Babylon," RH, March 10, 1859, p. 122. For a positive interpretation of these revivals, see T. L. Smith, Revivalism and Social Reform . . . , 1957.

144 J. White, "Babylon," RH, March 10, 1859, p. 122. Cf. Smith, "Religious Declension of These Days," RH, Feb. 24, 1874, p. 85.

145 J. White, "New Fields," RH, Oct. 6, 1859, p. 156. He said: "Church festivals, fairs, pic-nics, donation-parties, exhibitions and theatrical performances to raise money for church purposes, have greatly increased since the revivals of 1858. These things exist in the greatest contrast with the religion taught by Christ and the apostles, which is preparing thousands to renounce the popular religion of the day, and embrace Bible truth and Bible religion" (ibid.). Cf. J. H. Cook, "The Two Proclamations," RH, July 16, 1872, p. 33.

146 Cottrell, "The Present 'Revivals' in Babylon," RH, May 13, 1858, p. 206.

147 Cottrell, "The Great Revival Here," RH, Aug. 29, 1865, p. 100.

148 Ibid., p. 101.

however, that it would "convert the world, but one that was destined to gather out a few — the little flock."[149]

3. Christian unity and cooperation.

The Sabbatarian Adventist view of Christian unity and attitude toward ecumenical trends in contemporary Christianity was fully determined by the second angel's message. Already in 1851 Cottrell stated that "the union of Christians is an object for which we all pray,"[150] being achieved only "if we would attend to the 'essentials' of religion, and leave off contending for the 'non-essentials.' " Essentials, he said, were recorded in the Bible, non-essentials "those which are wisely left out."[151] J. White felt that "the church should be *one*; that the world might believe that God had sent his Son to save lost men."[152] The responsibility that this had not been accomplished rested on Babylon, for "the confusion of this great Babylon has filled the world with infidelity."[153] He criticized attempts to achieve church unity among non-Adventists, pointing out that frequently various denominations had organized united efforts for "the conversion of sinners" but when the time came "to bend the converts to the different man-made creeds; then what confusion has followed, and what wounds have been inflicted upon the cause of Christ."[154] Therefore, he said that it was "no wonder that men have doubted the reality of the Christian religion."[155]

In 1870 Cottrell distinguished three ecumenical movements. The first movement, Roman Catholicism, had called "its Ecumenical Council, and declared the infallibility of the pope as the bond of union."[156] The second movement, Protestant ecumenism, was represented in the proposed scheme of church union of a "Protestant Ecumenical Council" which was to convene shortly.[157] This scheme, Cottrell said, advocated "an open communion, and the recognition of one evangelical ministry, by the interchange of pulpits, thus to make *visible* the *unity* of the church,"[158] and indicated that "denominational distinctions are not inconsistent with true Christian unity" because one "may be of Paul, another of Apollos, another of Cephas,

149 *Ibid.*, p. 100.
150 Cottrell, "From 'A Letter to the Disciples of the Lord,' " *RH,* April 7, 1851, p. 61.
151 *Ibid.* Examples of non-essentials were Sunday observance and infant baptism (*ibid.*).
152 [J. White], "Babylon," *RH,* June 10, 1852, p. 20.
153 *Ibid.*
154 *Ibid.*
155 *Ibid.*
156 Cottrell, "Unity of the Church," *RH,* Oct. 18, 1870, p. 141. This was a reference to the Vatican Council (1869-70).
157 *Ibid.*
158 *Ibid.* At that time the SDA opposed the idea of an open communion (see e.g., Butler, "Open and Closed Communion," *RH,* May 27, 1873, p. 186). On the question of participation at the Lord's supper Butler said: "Those who have been truly baptized by gospel baptism, and who take God's holy law as their rule of morality, and take upon themselves the obligations of the church covenant when practicable, and live consistent Christian lives, are the proper ones to partake of the emblems of Christ's broken body" (*ibid.*).

186

and yet all of Christ. 1 Cor. 1:13, 3:3, 4."[159] He concluded, therefore, that "they can all agree upon certain unscriptural dogmas of the Bible," and when they disagree on Biblical doctrines "they can compromise these as things non-essential, agree to disagree, and so form a sort of union which perhaps I cannot characterize better than by the expression, harmonious jargon, or disjunctive conjunction."[160] The third movement for Christian unity he saw in the SDA movement with its platform of "the commandments of God and the faith of Jesus."[161]

Improved relationships between Protestants and Roman Catholics were looked upon critically and with apprehension. When, in 1871, Protestants of various denominations made donations for the construction of a Catholic church and attended its consecration ceremony, the headlines of the article reporting these activities read: "Protestantism and Catholicism Joining Hands."[162]

Some years later skeptical notes were heard about the Evangelical Alliance.[163] Cottrell called it "a mere confederacy of distinct and differing sects, each still holding their distinguishing doctrines," not aimed at "correcting their errors" but at compromising their differences "to unite their power."[164] He contrasted it with the "perfect union in the truth" as expressed in Jn. 17:21, 23; 1 Cor. 1:10 and "based on the promise of God in prophecy (Rev. 14:9-12)" which was "to test out the true children of God, perfectly uniting them in the commandments of God and the faith of the gospel."[165]

It was obvious that Sabbatarian Adventist concepts of unity and Babylon prevented any form of cooperation with other church organizations.[166] In 1859 E. G. White expressed herself against the practice of being a "surety for unbelievers"; that is, being financially responsible for, or in "partnership with unbelievers. God's people trust too much to the words of strangers, and ask their advice and counsel when they should not," because "the enemy makes them his agents, and works through them to perplex and take from God's people."[167] Joseph Clarke, a correspondent of the *Review and*

159 Cottrell, "Unity of the Church," p. 141.

160 *Ibid.* He added that this signified that "I can fellowship whatever of Bible truth you hold, provided you will acknowledge my errors upon these subjects to be equally as good as the truth. By such mutual concessions and compromises the 'visible unity' of the church is to be effected" (*ibid.*).

161 *Ibid.*

162 F.A.B., "Protestantism and Catholicism Joining Hands," *RH*, May 16, 1871, p. 171. Cf. E. G. White, *SP*, IV, 405.

163 C. H. Bliss, "The Evangelical Alliance," *RH*, Dec. 16, 1873, p. 7. The Evangelical Alliance was formed in London in 1866; the article referred to its 6th General Conference.

164 Cottrell, "The 'Evangelical Alliance' vs. True Christian Union," *RH*, Feb. 24, 1874, p. 85.

165 *Ibid.*

166 Cf. Stephenson, "The Number of the Beast," *RH*, Nov. 29, 1853, p. 166. There was also a warning given to prevent children from "associating with wicked children" ([J. White], "An Address . . . ," *YI*, Aug. 1852, p. 2).

167 E. G. White, *TC*, No. 5, 1859, p. 21 (*T*, I, 1948, p. 200). The term "unbelievers" generally signified those who were not Sabbatarian Adventists.

Herald, saw biblical support for this prohibition in the experience of Asa and Jehoshaphat, kings of Judah (2 Chron. 16:7, 8; 18-19:2; 20:35-37).[168]

All non-SDA, however, were not viewed in the same way. In 1868 E. G. White alluded to the existence of a unity based on spiritual qualities like not being self-confident, a meek and quiet spirit, unselfishness, obedience, justice, purity, and true holiness which characterized "the oneness of Christ's followers the world over."[169] A similar view of unity, composed of individuals rather than of organized churches, she recognized when stating that "the children of God, the world over, are one great brotherhood."[170]

The Seventh Day Baptists were viewed from a different perspective than other church organizations. In 1869 they were compared with the 7,000 who had not bowed their knee before Baal in the days of Elijah (1 Ki. 19:18).[171] At the 1869 General Conference of SDA the suggestion was made "that we ought to cultivate fraternal feelings with all those who keep the commandments of God and teach men so."[172] To improve relationships it was felt necessary to confess wrong attitudes of the past, and it was openly acknowledged that "some of our brethren have not pursued the most judicious course in regard to them."[173] A communication was sent to the Seventh Day Baptists resulting in the appointment of Professor Jonathan Allen as a delegate to the 1870 General Conference of SDA.[174] The resolutions of this conference expressed an earnest desire "to maintain with them relations of Christian friendship, and, as far as the circumstances of our respective bodies permit, to co-operate with them in leading our fellow-men, to the sacred observance of the fourth commandment."[175] In the same year the Seventh Day Baptist General Conference, attended by Cottrell,[176] approved a resolution pertaining to cooperation with Seventh-day Adventists "without compromising any distinctive principles."[177] Following the 1871 General Conference of Seventh Day Baptists, Andrews, a delegate, gave a

---

168   Jos. Clarke, "Partnership, Suretiship," *RH,* May 20, 1862, p. 198.

169   E. G. White, *TC,* No. 16, 1868, pp. 18, 19 (*T, II,* 127).

170   *Ibid.,* No. 21, 1872, p. 74 (*T, III,* 52).

171   Editorial, "More Sabbath-Keepers," *RH,* May 11, 1860, p. 160.

172   General Conference Report, *RH,* May 25, 1869, p. 173.

173   *Ibid.* J. White confessed that "the REVIEW has not always spoken of those who differ from us with all that patience, kindness, and respect that it should" ("Eastern Tour," *RH,* Sept. 14, 1869, p. 93).

174   Seventh Day Baptists, *Minutes of the General Conference,* 1869, p. 10. The response to this communication indicated that the imminent Second Advent and its motive for Sabbath observance was a major difference between the two organizations (*ibid.*).

175   General Conference Report, *RH,* March 22, 1870, p. 109. At the 1870 General Conference of Seventh Day Baptists Allen reported that J. White had made the following proposal which received a "hearty response" from the SDA General Conference: "From this good hour onward, let us not obtrude upon Seventh Day Baptists those doctrines wherein we differ from them; defend these points when attacked; let your light shine; but let us no longer be aggressors upon them; henceforth let there be peace between us" (J. Allen, "The Seventh Day Adventist Anniversaries," *Sabbath Recorder,* April 21, 1870, p. 66).

176   J. White had been appointed as a delegate but he was unable to attend the conference (Letter, Cottrell to Editor, *Sabbath Recorder,* Sept. 29, 1870, p. 150).

177   Seventh Day Baptists, *Minutes of the General Conference,* 1870, p. 8.

favorable report but pointed out some of the difficulties of direct cooperation between the two religious bodies. He stated that "in some important
points our views of divine truth are different," adding that "we cannot, for
the sake of united action surrender any portion of God's precious truth, nor
can we ask of the S. D. Baptists that they should on their part do anything of
the kind."[178] Nevertheless, he expressed the hope that even "if we cannot
act as one people, we can so conduct ourselves, as distinct bodies, that there
may be true Christian friendship existing between us."[179] Smith was the
SDA delegate in 1872, Andrews again in 1873.[180] The 1873 General Conference of SDA once more discussed the subject of cooperation and resolved to recognize Seventh Day Baptists as "a people whom God has
highly honored in making them in past ages the depositories of his law and
Sabbath" and "so far as practicable, to co-operate with them in leading men
to the conscientious observance of the commandments of God."[181] Later
such friendly relations were discontinued.

4. The second angel and mission.

The message of Rev. 14:8 as part of the SDA theology of mission had a
considerable influence on the SDA self-image, and the attitude to contemporary Christianity and ecumenism. The message explained the very raison
d'être of Adventists as a separate religious body. J. White stated that "had it
not been for this Message, the Advent people generally would have remained with the several churches," and felt that "those who rejoice that
they are Adventists, should prize highly the means that separated them
from the churches, and made them what they are."[182] In fact both the first
and second angels' messages played a vital role in the formation of the
Adventists as a separate religious entity. J. White said that "if we had never
heard the judgment hour cry, which was based on definite time, we never
should have been led to bear a testimony which, being rejected by our own
brethren, made it necessary for us to separate from the churches."[183] He
affirmed that "the Advent cause owes its very existence to the first and the
second angels' messages of Rev. xiv,"[184] and thought it extremely inconsistent when individuals called themselves Adventists while rejecting the validity of these messages.[185] Speaking in the context of salvation history,
E. G. White pointed out that "prophecy was fulfilled in the first and second
angels' messages. They were given at the right time, and accomplished the

178   Andrews, "Visit to the S. D. Baptist General Conference," *RH,* Sept. 19, 1871,
p. 108.
179   *Ibid.*
180   Seventh Day Baptists, *Minutes of the General Conference,* 1872, p. 1; *ibid.,* 1873, p. 2.
181   General Conference Report, *RH,* Nov. 25, 1873, p. 190.
182   J. White, "Third Angel's Message," p. 116.
183   [J. White], "Call to Remembrance the Former Days," *RH,* Jan. 13, 1852, p. 76.
184   *Ibid.*
185   J. White, "Third Angel's Message," p. 116; [J. White], "Call to Remembrance," *RH,*
Jan. 13, 1852, p. 76.

work God designed they should,"[186] and Andrews indicated that the angel of Rev. 14:8 "in connection with the Midnight Cry, moved forward with the power of the God of heaven, and accomplished his purpose."[187]

The characterization of Babylon as a union of Church and State was used by some believers as an argument to prevent the organization of Sabbatarian Adventists into an effective missionary church. Any organization required legal incorporation as a religious body under the laws of the State which necessarily would involve the adoption of a name for the new church. The initial step of the adoption of an official name, to "make us a name" (Gen. 11:4), Cottrell felt, formed the basis of Babylon.[188] J. White objected to the argument because it was "the confusion of languages among the Babel-builders" which lay at the foundation of Babylon.[189] The refutation of this and other arguments[190] freed the way for the organization of Sabbatarian Adventists into the SDA Church in 1863.

The emergence of the Sabbath doctrine was described as a result of the proclamation of Rev. 14:8. J. White indicated, "the second angel's message called us out from the fallen churches where we are now free to think, and act for ourselves in the fear of God," and immediately afterward "the Sabbath truth came up in just the right time to fulfill prophecy."[191]

One of the functions of Rev. 14:8 in the emerging theology of mission was to inform people about the fallen condition of contemporary Christianity so as to weaken their confidence in any church except that of the Sabbatarian Adventists. Cottrell stated that "the object of this message is to cut every honest soul loose from their allegiance to the religious bodies with which they may be connected, so that they may be prepared to act upon their own individual responsibility, in reference to the third message."[192] A knowledge of the second angel's message, therefore, was a prerequisite to an understanding of the third angel and functioned as part of the "burden" of the missionary proclamation.[193]

Owing to the rise of Spiritualism, a distinction was made between the proclamation of Rev. 14:8 and that of Rev. 18:2: The former was seen as an announcement of the moral fall of Babylon, the latter as its final fall.[194] In J. White's opinion the message of Rev. 18:2 "in connection with the great truths of the third angel of Rev. xiv, will manifest the 144,000, who are to be 'redeemed from among men,' and changed to immortality at the coming of Christ."[195] Regarding the success of its future mission, he predicted already in 1852 that it was "to affect the world, arrest the public mind, and

---

186 E. G. White, SG, I, 150.
187 Andrews, "Revelation," p. 82.
188 Cottrell, "Making Us a Name," RH, March 22, 1860, p. 140.
189 J. White, " 'Making Us a Name,' " RH, April 26, 1860, p. 180.
190 See infra, pp. 206, 207.
191 J. White, "TAM," p. 68 (TAM, p. 12).
192 Cottrell, "Unity," p. 125 (Unity, p. 15).
193 Cf. E. G. White, MS 11, 1850; Cottrell, "Sabbath-Keepers," pp. 20, 22.
194 [J. White], "Babylon," RH, June 24, 1852, pp. 28, 29.
195 Ibid., p. 29.

call out from this great Babylon the scattered members of the body of Christ."[196] E. G. White shared similar convictions and saw in the Advent experience a type of the final call for separation from Babylon (Rev. 18:4), stating that "this message seemed to be an addition to the third message, and joined it, as the midnight cry joined the second angel's message in 1844."[197] Even at the present time J. White felt it his duty to say "to God's people, wherever they may be in this great Babylon, whether with the Baptist, Methodist, Adventist, or any other sect, 'Come out of her,' flee from her foul spirits lest ye receive Babylon's plagues."[198]

The object of the mission efforts was "to recover the remnant" of God's people.[199] In 1853 J. White stated that even non-Adventist ministers were "striving for heaven amid the moral darkness" surrounding Babylon and must be reached with the final proclamation of Babylon's fall.[200] It was during that year that J. B. Frisbie,[201] a Methodist minister who strongly opposed Sabbatarian Adventists, reversed his position and began to proclaim the Sabbath. With his recent understanding of the spiritual condition of other churches he observed in 1854 that "many of God's dear children are in Babylon."[202] During the revivals of the late 1850s Cottrell urged missionary work "to enlighten" the "many honest souls united and uniting with the fallen, corrupt and corrupting churches of the present day."[203] He was confident that these individuals, "when they have the light, will obey the voice from heaven, Come out of her my people."[204]

There was also a positive view of other church organizations. Their progressive mission work E. G. White used as an incentive for SDA. In 1874 she pointed out that "in missionary efforts we have done comparatively nothing, and yet we profess to be bearing a message of infinite importance which is to test the world. We are far behind other denominations in missionary work, who do not claim that Christ is soon to come, and that the destiny of all must soon be decided."[205] At the same time George I. Butler[206] contrasted the fact that "many of the leading bodies of Christians

196 *Ibid.* Since the beginning of 1850 the hymnal of believers included a hymn on the fall of Babylon with the phrase "Come 'my people' and forsake her" ([J. White], *Hymns*, p. 42).

197 E. G. White, *SG*, I, 194, 195. Observing the growing influence of Spiritualism and people's preference for the doctrines of the Roman Catholic Church above those of the third angel's message, Cottrell concluded that "it is easy to see how the second announcement of the fall of Babylon will unite with the third message, as its first announcement joined with the first in 1844" ("The Repeated Announcement," *RH*, April 27, 1869, p. 140).

198 [J. White], "Babylon," *RH*, June 24, 1852, p. 29.

199 E. G. White, *CEV*, p. 47 (*EW*, p. 70).

200 [J. White], "Signs," p. 72 (*Signs*, p. 95).

201 Joseph B. Frisbie (1816-82) preached for the Methodists since 1843 and was ordained in 1846. In 1853 he became a Sabbatarian Adventist. His early articles in the *RH* advocated church organization.

202 J. B. Frisbie, "Church Order," *RH*, Dec. 26, 1854, p. 147. Cf. E. G. White, *GC*, pp. 383, 390. She stated that "the great body of Christ's true followers" were still outside of SDA (*ibid.*, p. 390). The majority of these people were in the Protestant churches (*ibid.*, p. 383).

203 Cottrell, " 'Revivals' in Babylon," p. 206.

204 *Ibid.*

205 E. G. White, "The Spirit of Sacrifice . . . ," *TrM*, Jan. 1874, p. 1.

206 George I. Butler (1834-1918) was an influential SDA who served as a minister and

consider it a duty to send the light of Christianity to others in heathen darkness" with the absence of such convictions among SDA.[207] He openly admitted that "we sometimes speak of these as the 'nominal churches,' i.e., those in name merely. But where have we shown the genuine spirit of Christian sacrifice, such as the Judsons, the Boardmans, and hundreds of others, have manifested?"[208] The purpose of this confession was obviously to inspire believers with a greater vision of their mission. These concluding remarks ought also to be viewed in the context of the development of the SDA mission outreach which will be discussed in Chapter VI.

C. The Mission of the Third Angel's Message.

During the period 1845-49 the third angel's message gradually emerged and became the central theme of the new Sabbatarian Adventist theology of mission. Much time was spent in theological reflection and discussion, and basic differences were ironed out at a series of conferences in 1848.

In 1849 the emphasis of the third angel's message was on "the commandments of God and the faith of Jesus" (Rev. 14:12). It was designated as "present truth" and considered the sealing message which was to protect its adherents from God's final judgments. Those who rejected this message would eventually receive the mark of the beast.

Developments after 1849 dealt with a further quest into the significance of Rev. 14:12 and its relation to the spiritual, mental and physical dimensions of man, the interpretation of "the beast and his image" (Rev. 14:9, 11); the implications of God's wrath (Rev. 14:10, 11); the future missionary role of the third angel, and its relationship to the other angels' messages. During the years the third angel's message was developed into a more elaborate theological system which became the basic structure of the SDA theology of mission.

1. The central theme of the third angel.

The central theme of the third angel's message was described in Rev.

---

administrator. For a number of years he was president of the General Conference of SDA.

207 Butler, "What Have We Been Doing for Other Nations?" *TrM*, March 1874, p. 21.

208 *Ibid.* He added that "here were men and women, refined and highly educated, fitted to shine in almost any sphere, who voluntarily relinquished many of the comforts of life and the society of friends, to place themselves among heathen, to endure every evil almost that could be conceived, and in many cases to die a lingering death, that they might elevate poor heathen in the scale of being, and bring them to Christ their Lord.

"The obstacles they had to contend against before they could reasonably hope for success were tenfold more than we should have to meet in sending missionaries to civilized Europe" (*ibid.*). Yet the tragic thing, he said, was that after the specific SDA message had been preached for more than 25 years there was not "one single instance of a native American, S. D. Adventist who has yet voluntarily consecrated himself to the work of becoming a missionary to the enlightened nations of modern Europe" (*ibid.*). For a major reason for this lack of enthusiasm, see *infra*, p. 291, n. 164.

14:12: "Here is the patience of the saints: here are they that keep the commandments of God, and the faith of Jesus." In 1849 the phrase "the commandments of God" was identified with the continued validity of the Decalogue with special emphasis on the Sabbath, the expression "the faith of Jesus" equated with the past Advent experience,[209] and the central theme incorporated into the earliest Sabbatarian Adventist hymnbook entitled *Hymns for God's Peculiar People That Keep the Commandments of God and the Faith of Jesus.*[210]

In 1850 J. White stated that the open door of the Philadelphian church (Rev. 3:8) pointed to the new insights in the significance of the Decalogue after 1844 which gave relevance and power to Rev. 14:12.[211] When in November 1850 the periodicals the *Present Truth* emphasizing the Sabbath doctrine and the *Advent Review* stressing the 1844 Advent experience were united into the *Second Advent Review and Sabbath Herald,* Rev. 14:12 was chosen as its motto.[212] In this way both aspects of the central missionary message — the Sabbath and the Advent experience — had been united in the name and motto of the periodical which was the representative voice of the theological views of the Sabbatarian Adventists.[213] In 1850 Nichols published a *Pictorial Illustration of the Visions of Daniel & John* designed by Samuel W. Rhodes.[214] On this chart the third angel was indicated by the motto "The Commandments of God and the Faith of Jesus."[215] When in 1863 J. White designed a prophetic chart (Appendix V), no change was made in regard to the central message of the third angel.[216] In 1851 E. G.

209   [J. White], "Repairing the Breach," p. 28; Edson, "Beloved Brethren," p. 34. At this time the terms "faith of Jesus" and "testimony of Jesus" were used interchangeably ([J. White], "Repairing the Breach," p. 28). Cf. [J. White], "Angels No. 4," p. 71 (*AR,* p. 25). He paraphrased Rev. 14:12; 12:17 as "the commandments of the Father" and "the faith or testimony of the Son" (*ibid.*).

210   [J. White], *Hymns.* Cf. titles of hymnbooks published in 1852, 1855 and 1869.

211   J. White, "TAM," pp. 68, 69 (*TAM,* p. 14).

212   See, *RH,* Nov. 1850, p. 1. For nearly a century Rev. 14:12 appeared under the title or name of this periodical. After Dec. 29, 1938, it was discontinued, probably because of a diminishing historical consciousness of the SDA self-image. The abbreviation of the name of the periodical to *Review* since Sept. 7, 1967 might also be attributed to similar reasons. In March 18, 1971 the original title was reintroduced but at the same time the popular title *Review* was retained. In 1853 E. G. White said that the *RH* was "the only paper in the land owned and approved of God" (Letter, E. G. White to the Dodges, No. 5, 1853). To J. White it had to be "the best religious paper in the world" ("The Review and Herald," *RH,* Dec. 6, 1870, p. 200).

213   As its objectives it was stated that "the REVIEW and HERALD is designed to be strictly confined to those important truths that belong to the present time" which implied "a simple and clear exposition of those great and sanctifying truths embraced in the message of the third angel, viz: the 'commandments of God and the faith of Jesus' " ([J. White], "To Our Readers," *RH,* Nov. 1850, p. 7). During the early decades of the movement, the *RH* was used not only as a church paper but also as a missionary publication. Various articles and series of articles were later published in the form of pamphlets or books.

214   The necessity for this visual aid was stressed in a vision (Letter, E. G. White to the Lovelands, No. 26, 1850; Letter, E. G. White to the Church in Hastings' House, No. 28, 1850). Samuel W. Rhodes (1813-83) had been a Millerite preacher. In 1850, through the influence of Edson, he became a Sabbatarian Adventist and participated in missionary work.

215   [Rhodes], *1850 Chart.*

216   [J. White], *A Pictorial Illustration of the Visions of Daniel & John,* 1863. Further references will be indicated as *1863 Chart.*

White stated that Rev. 14:12 in connection with the sanctuary doctrine could very well "explain the past Advent movement, show what is our present position, and establish the faith of the doubting, and give certainty to the glorious future."[217] She added that these "were the principal subjects on which the messengers should dwell."[218] Cottrell indicated the importance of Rev. 14:12 by calling it "the primitive, apostolic platform" upon which "the remnant of God's people" would be brought together.[219]

During the 1850s various attempts were made to define the "faith of Jesus." In 1851 E. G. White wrote that "the faith of Jesus takes in the whole life and divine character of Christ."[220] In the same year J. White said that the faith of Jesus "embraces all the doctrines and precepts taught by Christ and his apostles, peculiar to the new covenant."[221] In 1852 he defined it as embracing (1) "all the requirements and doctrines of the New Testament, peculiar to this dispensation" which included "every requirement peculiar to the gospel," (2) "the suffering, death, resurrection and ascension of Christ, also his priesthood in the True Tabernacle above, including his work of cleansing the Sanctuary since the termination of the 2,300 days, and his coming the second time in glory to reign in judgment," (3) the good works mentioned in Mt. 5:2-16, particularly the missionary obligation to be the "salt of the earth" and the "light of the world."[222] In 1854 he expressed the phrase "faith of Jesus" more concisely as "the gospel system, embracing all the doctrines and requirements spoken by Jesus in person, and those written by his inspired apostles."[223] Not everyone had accepted such interpretation because in 1857 some believers confined the expression as a reference to the healing of the sick. In an attempt to change this view E. G. White pointed out that "it is not healing the sick, merely, but it is *all* the teachings of Jesus in the New Testament. 'The Commandments of God and the faith of Jesus.' I saw that it was the whole New Testament which relates to Jesus."[224]

For several years the term "the testimony of Jesus" (Rev. 12:17) was used synonymously with "the faith of Jesus."[225] In 1855, as a result of a renewed emphasis on the function and value of spiritual gifts among Sabbatarian Adventists, a new interpretation of the testimony of Jesus began to emerge. According to J. White, the only biblical answer as to the meaning of this

217 E. G. White, *CEV*, p. 51 (*EW*, p. 63).
218 *Ibid.*
219 Cottrell, "Unity," p. 125 (*Unity*, p. 16).
220 Letter, E. G. White to [Stephen] Pierce, No. 2, 1851.
221 [J. White], "Angels No. 4," p. 71 (*AR*, p. 26).
222 [J. White], "The Faith of Jesus," *RH*, Aug. 5, 1852, pp. 52, 53.
223 [J. White], "The Faith of Jesus," *RH*, March 7, 1854, p. 53.
224 Letter, E. G. White to Pierce, Nov. 4, 1857.
225 See *supra*, pp. 141; 193, n. 209. In describing the differences between the various Sabbath-observing religious groups on the basis of Rev. 12:17, Bates said that the Jews did not believe the testimony of Jesus, the Seventh Day Baptists accepted only part of it, but those belonging to the Philadelphian church acknowledged the whole testimony as expounded by the sanctuary theology and the angels' messages ("The Holy Sabbath," *RH*, April 7, 1851, p. 58).

term was found in Rev. 19:10, "the testimony of Jesus is the spirit of prophecy."[226] Interpreting Rev. 12:17 in this light he suggested that it was especially the "spirit of prophecy" within the remnant of God's people which would provoke the anger of the dragon.[227] The term "spirit of prophecy" came to be associated with the testimony of E. G. White.[228] This interpretation was generally accepted and integrated into the missionary proclamation of the SDA Church, but it did not become as prominent as the central message of Rev. 14:12.

2. The "beast and his image."

The next step in the quest for the significance of the third angel was the interpretation of "the beast and his image" which formed the key to the understanding of Rev. 14:9-11. In 1851 one of the most influential attempts in this direction was made by Andrews, who determined the meaning of this expression in the context of the symbolism of Rev. 13 in which it was used several times.[229]

a. The beast.

Andrews identified the beast of Rev. 14:9-11 as the beast of Rev. 13:1-10, the latter of which was identified with the fourth beast of Dan. 7. The identification of the first beast of Rev. 13 with the fourth of Dan. 7 he based on the fact that (1) in John's time three of the beasts (empires)[230] had passed away, making it logical that only Daniel's fourth beast was shown to John; (2) both beasts ascended out of the sea.[231] He concluded that the beast of Rev. 13 "is evidently the Papal form of the fourth beast, for it receives its seat and dominion from the dragon [Rev. 13:2], Rome Pagan. The seat is Rome, which was given to him at the same time that his power was given."[232] The period of persecution under this beast during forty-two

226 J. White, "The Testimony of Jesus," *RH,* Dec. 18, 1855, p. 92. Cf. Editorial, " 'False Prophets,' " p. 124.

227 J. White, "Testimony of Jesus," pp. 92, 93. Cf. Letter, James Newman, *True Day Star,* Dec. 29, 1845, p. 4.

228 In order to make the view of E. G. White as being a manifestation of spiritual gifts within the church more acceptable, a publication appeared which provided evidence for the doctrine of the perpetuity of the New Testament gifts of the Spirit throughout the history of the Christian church. See Cornell, *Miraculous Powers . . . ,* 1862. J. White wrote the introductory essay, "Perpetuity of Spiritual Gifts" (*Perpetuity of Spiritual Gifts,* [1870]).

229 Andrews, "Revelation," pp. 82-86. See e.g., his influence in Bates, "The Beast with Seven Heads," *RH,* Aug. 5, 1851, p. 4; [J. White], "Angels No. 4," pp. 69, 70 (*AR,* pp. 14-20); Loughborough, "THB," *RH,* March 21 and 28, 1854, pp. 65-67, 73-75, 79 (*THB,* 1854).

230 See *supra,* p. 23.

231 Andrews, "Revelation," p. 82.

232 *Ibid.* Later he added that "the seat of the empire was by the emperor Constantine removed from Rome to Constantinople. And that Rome itself, at a later period, was given to the Popes by the emperor Justinian" ("TAR," *RH,* March 20, 1855, p. 194 [*TAR,* p. 74]). Cf. E. G. White, *SP,* IV, 276. She said that "through the great powers controlled by paganism and the papacy, symbolized by the dragon and the leopard-like beast, Satan for many centuries destroyed God's faithful witnesses." Later she defined more precisely that "while the dragon, primarily, represents Satan, it is, in a secondary sense, a symbol of pagan Rome" (*GC,* p. 438).

months (Rev. 13:5), or 1260 years, terminating in 1798 with a "deadly wound [Rev. 13:3] which has been healed," was also seen to support his views of Rev. 13:1-10.[233] Andrews' interpretation closely followed that of Litch.[234]

b. The two-horned beast.

In order to define the "image of the beast" it was first necessary to determine the significance of the "two-horned beast" (Rev. 13:11-18). Andrews felt that the two-horned beast was "another and distinct power," not another form of the fourth beast of Dan. 7 or the first beast of Rev. 13 healed of its deadly wound, or the Roman Catholic Church as some Millerites had believed.[235] Some interpreters who seemed to have made similar observations associated this beast with Protestantism.[236] In determining the time of its appearance in history, Andrews said that from its rise it would be "a power *cotemporary* [sic] with the beast whose deadly wound was healed

233 Andrews, "Revelation," p. 82. The history of the first beast as described in Rev. 13:1-3 he saw repeated in Rev. 13:4-10 ("TAR," p. 194 [*TAR*, pp. 74, 75]).

234 See Litch, *PE*, I, 95-105; Litch, *The Restitution* . . . , 1848, pp. 119, 120. Litch's arguments for the identity of the little horn of Dan. 7 with Rev. 13:1-10 were adopted by Sabbatarian Adventists. These arguments were: "1. The little horn was to be a *blasphemous power.* 'He shall speak great words against the Most High.' Dan. vii, 25. So, also was the beast of Rev. xiii, 6, to do the same. 'He opened his mouth in blasphemy against God.' 2. The little horn 'made war with the saints and prevailed against them.' Dan. vii, 21. Thus the beast of Rev. xiii, 7, 'was to make war with the saints, and to overcome them.' 3. The little horn had 'a mouth that spake very great things.' Dan. vii, 8, 20. So, likewise, there was given the beast of Rev. xiii, 5, 'a mouth speaking great things and blasphemies.' 4. Power was given the little horn of Dan. vii, 25, 'until a time, times, and the dividing of time.' To the beast, also, power was given 'to continue forty and two months.' Rev. xiii, 5. 5. The dominion of the little horn was to be taken away at the termination of that specified period. The beast of Rev. xiii, 10, who led into captivity and put to death with the sword so many of the saints, was himself to be led into captivity and killed with the sword, at the end of the forty and two months" (Andrews, "TAR," pp. 193, 194 [*TAR*, p. 73]; Litch, *Restitution*, pp. 119, 120). Cf. Litch, *PE*, I, 96, 97. See also *supra*, p. 25. One year before Andrews published his views, Geo. W. Holt mentioned the Roman Catholic Church as "the beast" of Rev. 13:1 (Letter, Geo. W. Holt to Dear Brethren, *PT*, March 1850, p. 74). [Rhodes], *1850 Chart*, defined Rev. 13:1-7 as "papal Rome." So did Bates, "Beast with Seven Heads," p. 3.

235 Andrews, "Revelation," p. 82. Cf. Miller, *ESH*, 1836, p. 56. Litch had taken the position that Napoleon Bonaparte was the two-horned beast (*PE*, I, 106, 107), but in 1848 he had given up this view and expected that power to develop in the future (*Restitution*, pp. 132, 133).

236 See e.g., John Bacon, *Conjectures on the Prophecies; Written in the Fore Part of the Year 1799*, 1805, p. 26; Samuel M. M'Corkle, *Thoughts on the Millennium, with a Comment on the Revelations* . . . , 1830, pp. 54-58. Some called the two-horned beast the "Image Beast," e.g., J. White, *WLF*, pp. 8-10; Letter, Holt to Dear Brethren, p. 64. [Rhodes], *1850 Chart*, designated it as "Image of Papacy." [J. White], *1863 Chart* (Appendix V), indicated it as "Protestantism." To Edson it was "Protestant Rome" ("Appeal," p. 9). Prior to Andrews the most extensive treatment of the two-horned beast was by Edson (*ibid.*, pp. 9, 10, 12, 13). For a discussion on the various interpretations, see Loughborough, "THB," p. 65 (*THB*, pp. 1-7); Andrews, "TAR," pp. 194, 195 (*TAR*, pp. 77-86). Similarities in action between the two-horned beast and the false prophet (Rev. 19:20) suggested to Andrews that they were identical. Their contextual situations seemed to him of a complementary nature, for "the Bible gives us the origin of the two-horned beast, but does not, under that name, give us its final destiny. The origin of the false prophet is not given under that name but his destiny is clearly revealed" ("Revelation," p. 84). Cf. Editorial, "Human Sympathy," *JS*, Aug. 7, 1845, p. 165.

[Rev. 13:12]," because the two-horned beast "exerciseth all the power of the first beast before him" (13:12).[237] He concluded that it would "come on the stage of action about the close of the first beast's dominion, at the end of the 1260 years"[238] and was to "cause the world to worship the first beast whose deadly wound was healed, which shows that its period of action is this side of 1798."[239]

The identification of the two-horned beast Andrews based on a number of arguments: (1) "The *location* of the two-horned beast is not in the ten kingdoms of the fourth beast" because the first beast of Rev. 13 did not give its seat to another power.[240] (2) His allusion to a theory that the course of the world empires was westward indicated that "the seat of the Babylonian and Persian empires was in Asia. The seat of the Grecian and Roman empires was in Europe. The Roman empire, in its divided state as represented by the ten horns, occupies all the remaining territory west to the Atlantic Ocean. Hence we still look westward for the rise of the power described in this prophecy."[241] (3) The third angel's message "pertains almost entirely to the action of the two-horned beast," making it "the last one with which the people of God are connected" (cf. Rev. 14:9-11 with 13:11-18).[242] (4) The westward course of Christianity implied that the territory of the two-horned beast "is to be the field of the angels' messages, the land where the crowning truths of the gospel, ere it finishes its course, are to be brought out."[243] (5) The rise of the two-horned beast was different from that of the beasts of Dan. 7 and the first beast of Rev. 13. These latter beasts arose out of the sea as a result of the striving of the winds (Dan. 7:2, 3; Rev. 13:1)[244] and symbolized the overturning of "the powers that preceded them, by means of general war."[245] This was a direct contrast to the rise of the second beast of Rev. 13 which "seems to arise in a peaceful, or lamb-like manner from the earth."[246] On the basis of these arguments Andrews was led to conclude that the two-horned beast pointed to nothing less than the U.S.A.[247] He

237 Andrews, "Revelation," p. 82. The healing of the wound (Rev. 13:3) of the Roman Catholic Church Bates dated from 1815 onward ("Beast with Seven Heads," p. 4). Cf. [J. White], "Angels No. 4," p. 69 (AR, p. 14).

238 Andrews, "Revelation," p. 82. Cf. E. G. White, SP, IV, 276.

239 Andrews, "Revelation," p. 82. In this context he quoted Litch who had said that "the two-horned beast is represented as a power existing and performing his part, after the death and revival of the first beast. . . . I think it is a power yet to be developed or made manifest as an accomplice of the Papacy in subjecting the world" (*ibid.*; Litch, *Restitution*, pp. 131, 133).

240 Andrews, "Revelation," p. 82.

241 *Ibid.*, pp. 82, 83.

242 *Ibid.*, p. 83. Cf. Andrews, "TAR," pp. 195, 196 (TAR, p. 88). Here a poem on America by Bishop Berkeley was cited which mentioned the westward course of civilization.

243 Andrews, "Revelation," p. 83.

244 On the basis of Rev. 7:1-3; 17:15 the winds were interpreted as wars or strife, the waters as people and nations (*ibid.*, p. 82).

245 *Ibid.* Cf. E. G. White, SP, IV, 277.

246 Andrews, "Revelation," p. 82.

247 For earlier attempts by Adventists to relate the U.S.A. to prophecy, see e.g., E. R. Pinney and O. R. Fassett, "The Vision of the Eagle," VT, Jan. 1, 1845, pp. 193, 194 (WMC, Jan. 14, 1845, pp. 38-40); Woodcock, "True Millennium," p. 31.

added that since its discovery, this country had been a refuge for many Christians who desired to obtain religious freedom during the Reformation and post-Reformation times. The fact that these people "did not establish their power by overturning another power, but . . . planted themselves in an uncultivated waste and laid the foundation of a new government" was typical of the emerging two-horned beast "out of the earth" (Rev. 13:11) in a "peaceful manner."[248] In summary he stated that

> the progress of our own country since its first settlement, has indeed been wonderful. We trace its rise from the time of its settlement by those who fled from the oppression of the fourth empire, onward till it assumes its station among the great powers of earth, a little previous to the end of the 1260 years. Its territory has trebled since that period, by addition of the vast territories of Louisiana, Florida, Texas, New Mexico and California, and the extension of an undisputed title to Oregon. Thus extending its dominion to the vast Pacific. This power was seen *arising* from the earth, as though it had not time to develop itself in full, before the end. Mark its onward progress and tell, if it be possible, what would be its destiny, if the coming of the Just One should not check its astonishing career?[249]

Additional evidence for its location was provided by Loughborough in 1854. The characteristic of the two-horned beast, exercising "all the power of the first beast before him" (Rev. 13:12), he interpreted on the basis of the translation by Nathan N. Whiting[250] which used the expression "in his sight" instead of "before him." Thus Loughborough could remark that "the Papal beast exists on the eastern continent; his seat is definitely at Rome; and while the two-horned beast is located in the west, and is performing his wonders, they of the eastern world behold, wondering."[251] The existence of slavery in the United States at that time he saw as another confirmation of the locality of the two-horned beast and stated that Rev. 13:16, "And he causeth all, both small and great, rich and poor, *free* and *bond*, to receive a mark in their right hand, or in their foreheads," indicated that the two-horned beast was to operate "where there are 'bondmen.' "[252] Reviewing the slavery situation in the world he concluded that the fact that "all other nations have abolished slavery, or declared it to be piracy, and the traffic is

248 Andrews, "Revelation," p. 83. He supported this view with a description of the progress and power of the U.S.A. by *The Dublin Nation*, n.d. Cf. E. G. White, *SP*, IV, 277.

249 Andrews, "Revelation," p. 83.

250 Whiting, *The Good News of Our Lord, the Anointed; from the Critical Greek Text of Tittman*, 1849. This was a translation of the N.T. based on the Greek text of J. A. H. Tittman as revised by Aug. Hahn and edited by Prof. Edward Robinson, 1842.

251 Loughborough, "THB," p. 73 (*THB*, p. 25). Cf. Smith's analysis of the major powers of the Eastern and Western Hemisphere in relation to prophetic symbolism ("The United States in the Light of Prophecies," *RH*, Oct. 17, 1871, p. 141 [*The United States . . .* , 1872, pp. 16-19]). His conclusion was that "of all the symbols mentioned, one, the two-horned beast of Rev. 13, is left; and of all the countries of the earth respecting which any reason exists why they should be mentioned in prophecy, the United States alone is left. Do the two-horned beast and the United States belong together? If they do, then all the symbols find an application, and all the ground is covered" (*ibid.*, p. 141 [*United States*, p. 19]).

252 Loughborough, "THB," p. 75 (*THB*, p. 39).

dying away" while it still existed in the U.S.A. was firm evidence as to the territory of the two-horned beast.[253]

The symbolic significance of the lamb-like horns of the two-horned beast Andrews determined through illustrations from Dan. 7 and 8. He referred to the commonly accepted idea that the horns of the ram of Dan. 8 symbolized the kings of Media and Persia, the great horn of the goat (Greece) indicated its first king, the ten horns of the fourth beast of Dan. 7 signified the ten kingdoms of the divided Roman empire, and "the little horn which came up after them denoted the Papal church *which was afterward clothed with civil power.*"[254] Thus, he inferred, "it is evident that the horns of these beasts, symbolize the entire power of the beasts. From these facts we learn that the horns of the preceding beast [Rev. 13:1-10; Dan. 7:7, 8, 19-22], denoted civil and religious powers. Hence we regard the horns of this latter beast [Rev. 13:11] as symbols of civil and religious power."[255] Being more specific, he said that the horns of the two-horned beast represented "the civil and religious power of this nation — its Republican civil power, and its Protestant ecclesiastical power."[256] In summarizing his interpretation he said that

> no civil power could ever compare with Republicanism in its lamb-like character. The grand principle recognized by this form of power is thus expressed: "All men are born free and equal, and endowed with certain inalienable rights,

253 *Ibid.*, p. 75 (*THB*, p. 40). On the slavery situation in the world he quoted from an article on the Nebraska Bill, *New York Tribune*, Feb. 18, 1854 (*ibid.*).

254 Andrews, "Revelation," p. 83.

255 *Ibid.*

256 *Ibid.* Earlier Bacon referred to the "mild and benevolent principles of *civil and religious liberty,* which constitute the *equal rights of men*" (*Conjectures on the Prophecies*, p. 27). Cf. E. G. White, *SP*, IV, 277. To the objection that the republican civil power was a form of government and that it, therefore, ought to represent the beast rather than a horn, Andrews replied that "the civil power of the Macedonian kingdom, was represented by the great horn of the goat. And that when that civil power was broken the beast still remained, and in the place of that one civil government, four arose in its stead. And we may add further that when the dominion of the different beasts of Dan. vii, was taken away, their lives were prolonged for a season and time [Dan. 7:12]. That is the nation still lived, though the dominion of the nation was destroyed. Hence we understand that the beasts denote the nations which constitute the different kingdoms, and the horns of the beasts denote the civil government or governments of these nations" ("Revelation," p. 83). The objection that Protestantism cannot be applied to a horn he answered by stating that "Papacy was reckoned as a horn, before it had plucked up three of the first horns [Dan. 7:8], — before it had civil power conferred on it" (*ibid.*). One year earlier Holt referred to the Protestant and Republican character of the "image beast" when he identified the two-horned beast with the image (Letter, Holt to Dear Brethren, p. 64). To Edson the two horns signified the "civil and ecclesiastical power" ("Appeal," p. 9). H. S. Case, who was a Sabbatarian Adventist minister for a few years, determined the character of the two-horned beast by comparing it with the first beast of Rev. 13. He stated that "the two horned beast is the power of Church and State. It is an 'image' of the Papal Beast to whom the dragon gave 'his power, and his seat, and great authority.' The Papal Beast was church and state united. An image must be like the thing imitated; therefore, the image-beast is composed of church and state united — Protestant churches and Republicanism" (Letter, Hiram S. Case to J. White, *PT*, Nov. 1850, p. 85). The references to Republicanism and Protestantism on the *1850 Chart* are not absolute evidence of an 1850 position, for their presence was the result of later changes ([Rhodes], *1850 Chart*).

as life, liberty, and the pursuit of happiness." Hence, all have a right to participate in making the laws, and in designating who shall execute them. Was there ever a development of civil power so lamb-like before? And what, in religious matters, can be compared with Protestantism? Its leading sentiment is the distinct recognition of the right of private judgment in matters of conscience. "The Bible is the only religion of Protestants." Was there ever in the religious world any thing to equal this in its lamb-like professions? Such we consider the meaning of the "two horns like a lamb."[257]

The command of the two-horned beast "to them that dwell on the earth, that they should make an image to the beast" (Rev. 13:14) was interpreted by Loughborough as clear evidence of an action by the republican form of the United States government, indicating that "the dwellers on earth, or the territory of this beast . . . have a part to act in this work."[258] It portrayed, he said, especially "the manner in which laws are made here: by the representatives of the people."[259] Smith saw in this text "that the supreme power is vested in the people, and that the government is consequently republican."[260]

The absence of crowns on the horns of the two-horned beast (in contrast with those of the first beast of Rev. 13) Andrews interpreted as another allusion to the U.S.A. because the "two-horned beast is emphatically a government of the people; and whatever is done by the people may be said to be done by the beast."[261] To Smith its significance was that "this power is not monarchical or kingly."[262] The relevance of this argument has to be seen against the background that the monarchy was the generally accepted form of government at that time.

The technological advancement in the U.S.A. Andrews saw as one possible fulfillment of Rev. 13:13, "And he doeth great wonders, so that he maketh fire come down from heaven on the earth in the sight of men." He observed that " 'the increase of knowledge' [Dan. 12:4] in every department of the arts and sciences, has indeed been without precedent in the world's past history."[263] The complete fulfillment of Rev. 13:13, however, he as-

257 Andrews, "Revelation," p. 83. Cf. E. G. White, *GC*, p. 441. M. E. Cornell, an influential Sabbatarian Adventist, defined the profession of the two horns by stating that "the Republican's creed is the Declaration of Independence. The Protestant's creed is the Bible" ("The Two Horns," *RH*, Feb. 4, 1862, p. 78).
258 Loughborough, "THB," p. 74 (*THB*, p. 37). Cf. E. G. White, *GC*, p. 443.
259 Loughborough, "THB," p. 74 (*THB*, p. 37). He added that "as all men by the declaration, are declared to be 'equal', it became necessary that some course should be taken by which all could have equal privileges in the construction of the laws. If the whole mass were called together, there would be an endless discussion and no laws made. Therefore, the people were to elect such representatives as would carry out their principles; and they were to meet and make laws, which, when passed, should be considered the laws of the people. The image is to be formed by the people or their representatives" (*ibid.*, pp. 74, 75 [*THB*, pp. 37, 38]).
260 Smith, "Thoughts on Revelation," *RH*, Nov. 11, 1862, p. 188. Cf. Smith, *Revelation*, p. 221.
261 Andrews, "TAR," *RH*, April 3, 1855, p. 201 (*TAR*, p. 95)
262 Smith, "Revelation," p. 188. Cf. Smith, *Revelation*, pp. 220, 221.
263 Andrews, "Revelation," p. 84. He commented: "We see the chariots with the speed of lightning coursing their way through the land, and with similar speed are men enabled to

cribed to wonders of a different class: It was Spiritualism or "necromancy" that would deceive the world.[264] He also indicated that the principles of Republicanism and Protestantism could be considered as wonders necessary to liberate the oppressed of the world,[265] for they would raise the expectation of many that the moment had arrived for "the ushering in of the period when the nation shall learn war no more, and a universal spiritual kingdom shall be set up and fill the whole earth. Micah iv, 1-5."[266] The reality, according to Andrews, was quite different because the rejection of the Advent truth had left "the great mass . . . to the deception which is already beginning to come on the nations of earth. . . . Peace and safety is the delusive dream in which men indulge whilst the wrath of God hangs over them."[267]

On the deceptive character of the two-horned beast with its pretensions of being a lamb but in reality manifesting dragon-like qualities, Andrews remarked that in appearance it was "the mildest form of power which ever existed, but it is after having deceived the world with its wonders, to exhibit all the tyranny of the first beast."[268] In the current political situation in the U.S.A. he saw evidences for this paradoxical character in the contrast between the statement of the Declaration of Independence that "all men are born free and equal" and the fact that there were "three millions of slaves in bondage. . . . reduced to the rank of chattels personal, and bought and sold like brute beasts."[269] The religious side of this paradox he found in the expulsion of the Adventists from the churches during their 1843-44 experi-

---

traverse the mighty deep. Nahum ii. 'The fire of God' (the lightning, Job i, 16; Exodus ix, 16) is literally brought down from heaven. Such is the wonderful power man has obtained over the elements. And the lightning thus brought down from heaven is sent as a messenger from one end of the land to the other. They 'send the lightnings, and they go and say here we are!' Job xxxviii, 35. And all those wonders bid fair to be eclipsed by others still astonishing" (ibid.). Cf. Edson, "Appeal," p. 12; Loughborough, "THB," p. 74 (THB, pp. 31-33). Regarding Dan. 12:4 Miller said: "View this in any point you please, whether theological or scientifical, it is literally true in this day of invention and improvement, knowledge increases" (ESH, 1836, p. 214). Cf. supra, p. 51. In 1869 Andrews interpreted the bringing down of fire from heaven as an imminent future event ("The Proclamation of Rev. XIV, 9-12," RH, June 22, 1869, p. 204).

264 Andrews, "Revelation," p. 84. He said: "We notice those astonishing developments from the land of spirits, which are causing the world to wonder. It would seem that communications with the spirits of the departed dead are now freely held, and men are brought into immediate connection with the spirit world. Such communications, though rare in past ages, have become of every day occurrence. . . . And Protestants are the chief actors in all this" (ibid.). Cf. Edson, "Appeal," p. 13; Loughborough, "THB," p. 74 (THB, pp. 34, 35); Andrews, "TAR," p. 202 (TAR, pp. 99-103).

265 Andrews, "Revelation," p. 84. He remarked: "What is needed throughout the world to relieve its inhabitants of their oppressions, but that Republicanism should remodel all their civil governments? The leaven of its principles has deeply diffused itself throughout the nations of earth. In proof of this, witness the revolution of 1848, which shook nearly all the thrones of Europe. And what is so well calculated to develop, and to maintain religious freedom, as Protestantism. With the diffusion of these free principles may we not expect a scene of prosperity and triumph to the church; a period of emancipation to the poor enslaved nations of earth?" (ibid.).

266 Ibid.

267 Ibid. Cf. Edson, "Appeal," p. 12.

268 Andrews, "Revelation," p. 84.

269 Ibid. Loughborough expressed that the "very national executive body, who have be-

ence, which indicated a violation of "the right of private judgment," for greater value was placed on the creeds of the religious bodies than on the word of God.[270] His future outlook on the U.S.A. was that it would enforce at the penalty of death the claims of the first beast so that the world would receive the special mark of the Roman Catholic Church, the institution of the Sunday.[271]

Already in 1854 Loughborough saw trends toward a religious persecution.[272] The articles of the Constitution which he and other Sabbatarian Adventists highly valued were those safeguarding the principles of religious freedom based on a separation of Church and State:

> *Constitution of the United States. Art. 6. Sec. 2.*
> "This constitution, and the laws of the United States which shall be made in pursuance thereof, . . . shall be the supreme law of the land; and the judges in every state shall be bound thereby, anything in the constitution or laws of any state to the contrary notwithstanding."
> Sec. 3. "The members of the several state Legislatures, and all executive and judicial officers, both of the United States, and of the several states, shall be bound by oath or affirmation to support the constitution; but no religious test shall ever be required as a qualification to office or public trust under the United States."
>
> *Amendments to the Constitution. Art. 1st.*
> "Congress shall make no law respecting an establishment of religion, or prohibiting the free exercise thereof."[273]

In Loughborough's opinion these articles had been violated by the two-horned beast in regard to Sunday legislation. He stated that the Constitution

> is already transgressed in a large number of the States of this Union; in the

---

fore them this declaration of Independence, and profess to be carrying out its principles, can pass laws by which 3,500,000 slaves can be held in bondage. Slaves, what are they! men like ourselves, except perhaps in their complexion. The Declaration of Independence should have a clause supplied, and should read, All men are created *free* and *equal* except 3,500,000" ("THB," p. 66 [*THB*, p. 14]). He also attacked vigorously the Fugitive Slave Law, the efforts in Virginia to keep the blacks illiterate, and the condemnation of a slave to be burned at the stake (*ibid.,* pp. 66, 67 [*THB*, pp. 14-18]). The interpretation of Rev. 13:16 in the context of slavery was one of the reasons why for many years the SDA were not successful in penetrating the southern part of the U.S.A. (Roger G. Davis, "Conscientious Cooperators: The Seventh-day Adventists and Military Service, 1860-1945," Ph.D. dissertation, 1970, pp. 47, 48). After the Civil War, the slavery interpretation was disregarded. Cf. Andrews, *TAR,* pp. 105, 109 with Andrews, *The Three Messages . . . ,* 3rd ed., rev., 1872, pp. 87, 91.

270   Andrews, "Revelation," p. 84. The formulation of a creed was considered by Loughborough as the first step in apostasy and the basis for the formation of both the beast and his image ("The Image of the Beast," *RH,* Jan. 15, 1861, p. 69; "Battle Creek Conference Report," *RH,* April 30, 1861, p. 189).

271   Andrews, "Revelation," p. 85.

272   Loughborough, "THB," p. 67 (*THB*, pp. 18-23). Cf. Letter, Mary L. Priest to Editor, *RH,* Oct. 18, 1853, p. 120.

273   Loughborough, "THB," p. 67 (*THB*, pp. 18, 19). In this article he supported his interpretation with a letter of George Washington to a Baptist society in Virginia, Aug. 4, 1789, regarding the Constitution and religious liberty.

northern portion there are laws respecting the resting from labor on the *first day of the week*. And in four states of the Union at least, the laws are such, that the rights of those are infringed upon who keep the *seventh day*, because they do not also keep the *first*.[274]

As specific examples he mentioned a report concerning a decision by the Supreme Court of Pennsylvania declaring Sunday traveling illegal, and the condemnation of eight Seventh Day Baptists for working on Sunday in that State. This, he said, could only be interpreted as "a fulfillment of the text, 'And he spake as a dragon.' "[275] In 1855 Andrews remarked that the current movements toward Sunday legislation signified that a Roman Catholic institution was "enforced by a Protestant government," which was a violation of the Constitution and "a most striking instance of the union of church and state in this country."[276] He warned that when "most of the State governments, which have no right to infringe upon the constitution, have already decided that the Sabbath of the Bible shall be kept on Sunday, and the judges have decided such laws to be constitutional," then "there is an end to the principle of religious liberty."[277] The constitutional separation of Church and State was seen to be a necessity for maintaining the principle of religious liberty. The Sabbatarian Adventists realized that as long as this separation was preserved, their freedom of worship on the Sabbath was guaranteed. However, their interpretation of Rev. 13:11-18 pointed to a period of religious persecution in the near future due to the increased violation of the principle of religious liberty.

c. The image of the beast.

Finally, after having defined "the beast" and "the two horned beast," Andrews interpreted "the image of the beast" (Rev. 13:14, 15). On the basis of his previous interpretation that "the beast was, in truth, a church clothed with civil power and authority by which it put to death the saints of God. Rev. xiii, 5-8; Dan. vii, 23-26," he drew the conclusion that "an image to the beast then must be another church clothed with civil power and authority to put the saints of God to death."[278] This, Andrews said, could be "nothing else but the corrupt and fallen Protestant church."[279] In the con-

274 *Ibid.*, p. 67 (*THB*, pp. 21, 22).
275 Loughborough, "THB," p. 67 (*THB*, pp. 22, 23).
276 Andrews, "TAR," p. 204 (*TAR*, p. 117). See W. H. Littlejohn, *The Constitutional Amendment: or The Sunday, the Sabbath, the Change, and Restitution*, 1873, pp. iii, 72-74 for a discussion of the National Reform Association which was founded in 1863 and had as one of its aims the legislation of the observance of Sunday as a day of worship. For later developments of Sunday legislation in the U.S.A. and the SDA response, see Warren L. Johns, *Dateline Sunday, U.S.A.: The Story of Three and a Half Centuries of Sunday-law Battles in America*, 1967; Eric D. Syme, "Seventh-day Adventist Concepts on Church and State," Ph.D. dissertation (American University), 1969, pp. 80-150, 234-53.
277 Andrews, "TAR," p. 204 (*TAR*, p. 117).
278 Andrews, "Revelation," p. 84. Cf. Andrews, "TAR," p. 203 (*TAR*, p. 108); E. G. White, *SP*, IV, 278.
279 Andrews, "Revelation," p. 84. Cf. Andrews, "TAR," p. 203 (*TAR*, p. 108); E. G. White, *GC*, p. 445. Already in 1847 J. White stated that Christendom, "the last power that treads down the saints is brought to view in Rev. 13:11-18" (*WLF*, pp. 8, 9). Cf. Letter, E. G.

text of the Sabbatarian Adventist view of the Babylon of the second angel's message, this interpretation was not surprising.

Loughborough further elaborated the concept of the image of the beast. Focusing on the Church-State relationship, he stated that "all that is wanting to complete an image to Papacy, is simply a union of action in Church and State, and for the churches to have control of the laws so as to inflict penalties on heretics, or those who do not obey *their* sentiments."[280] The fact that several States had provided a legal basis for Sunday observance he saw as evidence that the image was in the process of being formed,[281] and its completion was to take place in the U.S.A. in the near future after the abolishment of the separation of Church and State. He predicted that "were the United States as a body to pass a law that *Sunday* should be kept holy, or not profaned by labor, *there* would be, I conceive, an image to Papacy; for law would then be in the hand of the church, and she could inflict penalties on those who did not obey the Sunday institution."[282] It was only "when moral restraint is taken from men, and the honest in heart have been called from Babylon,"[283] he explained, that a "decree will be passed that all who will not 'worship (keep the laws of) the image shall be killed' [Rev. 13:15]; then you will witness a *living* image, breathing out the venom of a Romish Inquisition."[284] Andrews saw a typological relationship between the condition of Daniel's three friends when a decree was issued to worship the image of Nebuchadnezzar (Dan. 3) and "the situation of the church when the decree goes forth that all shall worship the image of the beast on pain of death."[285] In the context of a similar eschatological conflict Cottrell pointed to an analogy between the power and authority of the beast and its image:

White to Bates, *WLF*, p. 19. Here she described the "Image Beast" as following a religious practice of the beast.

280 Loughborough, "THB," p. 74 (*THB*, p. 37).

281 *Ibid.*

282 *Ibid.*, p. 75 (*THB*, p. 39). He stated further that the U.S.A. "already has it in its 'power to give life to the image of the beast,' [Rev. 13:15] or cause the decree to be made and executed. Is it not in the power of the United States to pass such laws? . . . We see the mass hold the first day of the week as a holy day. If a memorial should be sent into congress with 1,000,000 names signed to it, declaring that their rights were infringed upon, and praying them to pass a solemn enactment that the first day should not be profaned by labor, how soon the result would be a law upon this point." In the context of an article on the "Political Effect of Religious Union" in the *Examiner and Chronicle* (New York), n.d., Cottrell said that "we see it [the current of public sentiment] drifting more and more in favor of a union of religion and politics, of Church and State" ("'Make an Image,'" *RH*, July 20, 1869, p. 26). Cf. E. G. White, *SP*, IV, 278. Here she said: "When the churches of our land, uniting upon such points of faith as are held by them in common, shall influence the State to enforce their decrees and sustain their institutions, then will Protestant America have formed an image of the Roman hierarchy. Then the true church will be assailed by persecution, as were God's ancient people."

283 Loughborough, "THB," p. 75 (*THB*, p. 39). Cf. J. White, "Our Faith and Hope . . . ," *RH*, May 10, 1870, pp. 161, 162.

284 Loughborough, "THB," p. 75 (*THB*, p. 39). In the context of God's wrath in the seven last plagues E. G. White had already mentioned the issuance of a decree to kill the righteous ("DBS," p. 22 [*EW*, pp. 36, 37]).

285 Andrews, "TAR," *RH*, May 1, 1855, p. 217 (*TAR*, p. 143). Cf. Edson, "Appeal," p. 13.

The first beast received the power to kill of the dragon: the image will receive the same power and authority from the two-horned beast. The dragon power of the ten-horned monster gave his seat and authority to the Catholic church: the dragon power of "another beast" will give his authority to another church. Give civil power into the hands of Protestants, and the result will be a "holy war" against heretics.[286]

d. The number 666.

During the early years of the movement there existed several interpretations of the number 666 (Rev. 13:18). After the Disappointment a correspondent of the *Western Midnight Cry* referred to it as signifying the number of denominations, presumably in the U.S.A.[287] In 1847 J. White stated that the "last power [Christendom] that treads down the saints is brought to view in Rev. 13:11-18. His number is 666."[288] At the same time he referred to this passage as a description of "the closing strife with the Image Beast."[289] This seems to imply that the term "image beast" was used as a descriptive term for the two-horned beast which had been interpreted as an image of the first beast of Rev. 13.[290] Thus, to J. White the image beast, or two-horned beast, represented Christendom while its number was 666.[291] In 1850 George W. Holt[292] also defined the image beast as the two-horned beast with its number 666.[293] The *1850 Chart* designated the two-horned beast as the "image of the Papacy" having 666 as its number.[294] In 1851 Andrews suggested that "the Protestant Church [image to the beast] may, if taken as a whole, be considered as a unit; but how near its different sects number six hundred three score and six, may be a matter of interest to determine."[295] Later, Loughborough quoted J. M. Stephenson —

286 Cottrell, "Speaking of the Image," *RH,* Dec. 12, 1854, p. 134. In the context of a fast-growing Roman Catholic Church in the U.S.A. the formation of a united front of Protestants seemed to him the solution to prevent annexation by the Catholics. He thought it inevitable that "Protestants must unite to oppose this law-making church by the exercise of the same kind of power: by constituting themselves another law-making church. The moment this is done, the Image of the beast will be complete. The beast was church and state united; the Image will be the same" ("What Will Cause the Image?" *RH,* Nov. 14, 1854, p. 110).

287 Letter, J. H. Thomas to Jacobs, *WMC,* Dec. 21, 1844, p. 28. At that time there seemed to be over 640 denominations in the U.S.A. (*ibid.*).

288 J. White, *WLF,* pp. 8, 9.

289 *Ibid.,* pp. 9, 10. Cf. use of the term "image beast" for the two-horned beast; J. White, "TAM," p. 66 (*TAM,* p. 6).

290 Cf. Letter, H. S. Case to J. White, p. 85; Letter, Holt to Dear Brethren, p. 64; *supra,* p. 25, n. 124.

291 Cf. Letter, E. G. White to Bates, *WLF,* p. 19.

292 George W. Holt (1812-77) was an early Sabbatarian Adventist who had also been a Millerite preacher.

293 Letter, Holt to Dear Brethren, p. 64.

294 [Rhodes], *1850 Chart.*

295 Andrews, "Revelation," p. 85. Cf. J. White, *WLF,* pp. 8, 9; Letter, E. G. White to Bates, *WLF,* p. 19. In 1855 Andrews stated that "the image of the beast . . . is made up of apostate religious bodies. The name of the beast, as given in verse 1 [Rev. 13], is blasphemy. The image it appears is made up by legalizing the various classes that will acknowledge the blasphemous claims of the beast, by taking his mark. Every class that will therefore acknowledge the authority of the beast may be legalized and form a part of this image; but when this is

a Sabbatarian Adventist minister for a few years — who had stated that 666 was the number of a man, the man of sin, representing the Roman Catholic Church. This church according to Stephenson continued to be a unit until the Reformation, when it started to break up, and "these divisions have continued dividing and subdividing until, according to the Encyclopedia of Religious Knowledge, they now number about six hundred three score and six,"[296] indicating an intimate relationship between contemporary Protestantism and historic Roman Catholicism. Thus, he could also state about the Protestant churches that "their number is the number of a man, (the man of sin,) and his number is six hundred three score and six. Those churches collectively or individually, have that number."[297]

In 1860 steps were taken to organize the Sabbatarian Adventists officially into an effective organizational structure for missionary outreach which implied legal incorporation of church property under the laws of the State. Plans for organizational unity were resisted by those believers who maintained that the number 666 referred to the two-horned beast and signified the total number of legally organized churches in the U.S.A. According to J. White, these opponents felt that "in order to get the victory over the number of his name, it is supposed to be necessary to reject all sectarian names."[298] One opponent to organization, Cottrell, advocated the principle of a *total* separation of Church and State and warned that the consequence of getting "incorporated as a religious body according to law" would imply a "name with the two-horned beast" and "spiritual fornication" with the kings of the earth, for it would mean that one would "look to the civil arm for aid and protection."[299] To this J. White replied that the number 666 referred to "the papal beast," not to the two-horned beast,[300] and added that already in

---

accomplished, woe to all dissenters! It is thus that we understand the number of the beast as six hundred three-score and six" ("TAR," p. 204 [*TAR*, p. 114]). This statement appeared also in Andrews, *Three Messages*, 1860; [2nd ed.], 1864. However, it was left out in *ibid.*, 3rd ed., rev. Smith's interpretation of 666 was included in *ibid.*, 4th ed. rev. Cf. *ibid.*, 1872, p. 95 with *ibid.*, 1876, p. 61.

296 Loughborough, "THB," p. 79 (*THB*, pp. 47, 48); Stephenson, "Number of the Beast," p. 166.

297 *Ibid.*; Loughborough, "THB," p. 79 (*THB*, p. 48). Cf. Loughborough, *The Two-Horned Beast . . .* , 1857, p. 64.

298 [J. White], "Organization," *RH*, July 16, 1861, p. 52.

299 Cottrell, "Making Us a Name," p. 140. Cf. Cottrell, "Speaking of the Image," p. 134. Cottrell supported his position with Andrews' 1855 view which related the incorporation by law of an organization to the concept of Babylon. Andrews had stated that "the United States disclaim a national religion, and yet nearly all her religious bodies are incorporated by the State. Babylon has made all the nations drunken with her wine; it can therefore symbolize nothing less than the universal worldly church" (Letter, Cottrell to Smith, in J. White, "Making Us a Name," *RH*, June 5, 1860, p. 20). In the next edition of Andrews' *TAR* this statement had been left out. Cf. Andrews, "TAR," p. 178 (*TAR*, pp. 46, 47) with Andrews, *Three Messages*, 1860, p. 44. J. White accused Cottrell of not having his premises correct, for it was "the confusion of languages among the Babel-builders" which lay "at the foundation of Babylon" ("'Making Us a Name,'" p. 180).

300 *Ibid.*, pp. 181, 182. Smith also applied it to the Roman Catholic Church ("Revelation," p. 188). Cf. Smith, *Revelation*, p. 224; J. White's earliest position, *WLF*, p. 9.

1845 "some declared the number 666 to be full — that there was that number of legally organized bodies. Since that time there have been almost numberless divisions, and new associations, and still the number is just 666!"[301] Also rejected by J. White was the idea that "to hold a legal property of any kind" would be "spiritual fornication," because obedience to the laws of the country, as long as they did not interfere with God's laws, was not violation of the principle of Church-State separation.[302] Thus a change of attitude was brought about toward the government of the U.S.A. which paved the way for the official organization of the religious body in 1863.

Although now the number 666 was thought to refer to the first beast of Rev. 13, there was still uncertainty about its significance.[303] However, in 1865 Smith gave an explanation which was generally accepted by the SDA. In referring to an anonymous work entitled *The Reformation*, 1832, he stated that "the most plausible name we have ever seen suggested as containing the number of the beast, is the blasphemous title which the pope applies to himself, and wears in jeweled letters upon his miter or pontifical crown."[304] He explained that the Latin letters of the pope's title "Vicarious [sic] filii Dei: 'Viceregent of the Son of God' "[305] had the numerical value of 666: "We have V, 5; I, 1; C, 100; (a and r not used as numerals;) I, 1; U (formerly the same as V), 5; (s and f not used as numerals;) I, 1; L, 50; I, 1; I, 1; D, 500; (e not used as numeral;) I, 1. Adding these numbers together, we have just 666."[306] Smith saw this number as "the number of a man, even the 'man of sin,' " and considered the selection of the pope's title somewhat providential, showing "the blasphemous character of the beast, and then cause it to be inscribed upon his miter, as if to brand himself with the number 666."[307]

3. *The final conflict.*

301   J. White, " 'Making Us a Name,' " p. 182. Cf. Letter, Thomas to Jacobs, p. 28.
302   J. White, " 'Making Us a Name,' " p. 181. He said that "while we are stewards of our Lord's goods here in the land of the enemy, it is our duty to conform to the laws of the land necessary to the faithful performance of our stewardship, as long as human laws do not oppose the divine law" (*ibid.*). Loughborough had earlier pointed out that "there is quite a difference between our being in a position that we can protect our property by law, and using the law to protect and enforce our religious views" ("Legal Organization," *RH,* March 8, 1860, p. 125).
303   Cf. Smith, "Revelation," p. 188.
304   Smith, *Revelation*, p. 225.
305   *Ibid.* Later he used the spelling "Vicarius Filii Dei" ("The United States in the Light of Prophecy," *RH,* Feb. 13, 1872, p. 68 [*United States*, p. 158]).
306   Smith, *Revelation*, p. 225. Cf. *SDABC,* VII, pp. 823, 824. One of the earliest expositors of this interpretation seemed to be Andreas Helwig (c. 1572-1643) (Froom, *PFF,* II, 605-608). For other similar pre-Sabbatarian Adventist expositions, see *ibid.*, II, 649; III, 228, 242, 412; IV, 112, 197, 372. Cf. Robert Fleming, *Apocalyptical Key,* 1793, p. 138; Fleming, *Apocalyptical Key,* 1809, pp. 107-110; Shimeal, *Age of the World,* pp. 246-48; John Leland, *American Sentinel,* 1797, quoted in "The Number 666 in Roman Letters," *MC,* Feb. 24, 1843, p. 13; Editorial, "The Number of the Name of the Beast," *JS,* April 3, 1845, p. 27.
307   Smith, *Revelation,* p. 226. Later, he said that "it is the number of the beast, the papacy; it is the number of his name; for he adopts it as his distinctive title; it is the number of a man; for he who bears it is the 'Man of sin' " ("United States," p. 68 [*United States*, p. 158]).

The third angel's message was interpreted by Sabbatarian Adventists as a message of warning for the coming confrontation between the powers of light and darkness. The scene of this conflict was described in Rev. 13:11-18 with the "two-horned beast" and the "beast and his image" as the enemies of God's people. Concerning this conflict Andrews pointed out that "its fearful character may be learned from the thrilling and dreadful import of the angel's message. The Bible nowhere else depicts such dreadful wrath."[308] In comparing Rev. 13:11-18 with Rev. 14:9-12 he saw the final issue as follows: "On one side stands the decree of the beast who is to exercise all the power of the first beast before him, that all who will not worship the image and receive his mark shall be put to death [Rev. 13:12, 15]; on the other hand stands the solemn warning of the third angel."[309] Thus, the issue was two-fold: "We can worship the beast and his image, and as the penalty, drink the wine of the wrath of God, or we can refuse, and peril our lives that we may obey God."[310] It was obvious to Andrews that the third angel's message would "draw a line between the worshippers of God and the worshippers of the beast and his image, for on either hand it reveals a dreadful penalty and leaves no chance for half way work."[311] The visible characteristics of both classes, he stated, were that "one class is designated by the mark of the beast, the other class is seen in the patience of the saints keeping the commandments of God,"[312] which implied that the law of God was "a great testing truth to draw a line between the subjects of the fourth and fifth kingdoms [Dan. 2; 7]."[313] As to the preparation for the conflict he remarked that the "third angel's proclamation will prepare the people of God for the coming crisis: and the formation of the image and the reception of the mark will prepare all the various classes of adherents to the beast, to receive the vials of the wrath of God, the seven last plagues."[314] Smith predicted that "society will eventually resolve itself into two classes: Sabbath-keepers and Sunday-keepers."[315] From this it seems that the apocalyptic eschatology of Sabbatarian Adventists indicated that the central issue in the final conflict was the choice between the mark of the beast and the seal of God.

a. The mark of the beast.

308   Andrews, "Revelation," p. 85. E. G. White said that the third angel proclaimed "the most terrible threatening ever borne to man" (SG, I, 162).
309   Andrews, "Revelation," p. 85.
310   Ibid.
311   Ibid.
312   Ibid. Cf. Edson, Time of the End, p. 21; J. White, "TAM," p. 69 (TAM, p. 15).
313   Andrews, "Revelation," p. 85.
314   Andrews, "TAR," pp. 203, 204 (TAR, p. 114). Cf. J. White, "TAM," p. 69 (TAM, p. 15). Here he stated that "one class keep the commandments, and are marked or sealed with the seal of the living God, and are to be protected in the day of slaughter. The other class have an opposite mark, which is of the beast, and they are to drink the wrath of God."
315   [Smith], "The Seal of the Living God," RH, May 1, 1856, p. 20. This subject was published in two articles in the April 24 and May 1, 1856 issues of the RH. These articles will be abbreviated as "Seal," I and "Seal," II.

As early as 1847 Bates had designated Sunday observance as "a mark of the beast."[316] Later this mark came to be more precisely defined. In 1850 J. White stated that the mark of the beast was "very conspicuous" and did not refer to a literal mark but to "a prominent point of religious faith introduced by the Papal power, which is the observance of the first day of the week as a holy day of rest instead of the seventh."[317] In 1852 he rejected the idea that those who presently did not observe the Sabbath were already in possession of the mark because it was to be received in the future "when the line shall be drawn between the worshipers of the beast and image, and the worshipers, or servants of God."[318] The third angel's message, he saw, was a warning "not to receive the mark," which implied that "it is yet to be received by the worshipers of the beast."[319] Therefore, White said, "Christians who have conscientiously observed the first day of the week, in time past, whose minds were never called to investigate the Sabbath question, certainly did not *receive* the mark of the beast."[320] The time for the reception of the mark he described as follows: "After the true light on this subject shall be given, and that period of anguish when the mark of the beast shall be enforced shall have come, and the division made between the worshipers of God and the worshipers of the beast, *then* will be the danger of receiving the mark of the beast."[321] In 1856 he commented on this event saying, "when the claims of the Sabbath of the fourth Commandment are urged upon the mind in opposition to the practice of Sundaykeeping, it is then that men choose, and receive either the Mark of the Beast, or the Seal of the living God."[322]

b. The seal of the living God.

For the people of God the third angel's message seems to have a positive sound. In 1849 J. White had already interpreted it as the "sealing message" which carried "the sealing mark, the Sabbath, to the saints."[323] The following year he referred in the context of the sealing to a typological relationship between Ezek. 9 and the third angel's message.[324] E. G. White remarked that "the third angel is binding them (sealing them) [God's people] in bundles for the heavenly garner."[325] In 1852 Cottrell suggested that the

316 See *supra*, p. 141.
317 J. White, "TAM," p. 67 (*TAM*, p. 8).
318 [J. White], "Remarks in Kindness," *RH*, March 2, 1852, p. 100.
319 *Ibid.*
320 *Ibid.* Cf. E. G. White, *SP*, IV, 281, 282. See *supra*, p. 140, n. 213.
321 [J. White], "Remarks," p. 100. Cf. E. G. White, *SP*, IV, 282. Here she said that "the test upon this question does not come until Sunday observance is enforced by law, and the world is enlightened concerning the obligation of the true Sabbath. Not until the issue is thus plainly set before the people, and they are brought to choose between the commandments of God and the commandments of men, will those who continue in transgression receive the mark of the beast."
322 J. White, "The Third Angel's Message," *RH*, Aug. 7, 1856, p. 108.
323 Letter, J. White to Bowles, Nov. 8, 1849; see *supra*, p. 145; cf. E. G. White, "DBS," p. 21 (*EW*, pp. 42, 43); J. White, "TAM," p. 69 (*TAM*, p. 15); Letter, Cottrell to J. White, *RH*, Feb. 3, 1852, p. 87.
324 J. White "TAM," p. 69 (*TAM*, p. 15).
325 E. G. White, *SCEV*, p. 7 (*EW*, p. 89).

seal "imprints the Father's name in the forehead [Rev. 14:1] of those who have not the mark of the beast in that place."[326] He associated the seal with the third angel's message, because the commandments of God (Rev. 14:12), in particular the fourth commandment of the Decalogue, contained the Father's name, being "the only one of the ten that distinguishes the Lord from every other God, as being the Maker of all things."[327] Edson pointed out that "the fourth commandment is the only precept in the great constitution that points out the true God" and it had to be interpreted that this commandment "contained his [God's] signature and seal."[328] He saw the mission of the third angel as a means of restoring the seal of the living God, the Sabbath, to the Decalogue.[329] Several years later, Smith commented on the significance of the fourth commandment as a seal on the basis of an analogy between the seal of a secular ruler and the seal of the Decalogue. He argued that for "any document from any earthly monarch to be valid [it] must possess his name and title of royalty, by which his subjects will know who it is that demands obedience, and by what right he demands it."[330] From analogy he reasoned that if God had given mankind a law then "in order for it to be valid it must declare who he is, contain his title of royalty, the extent of his dominion, and his right to reign; and whatever portion of the law does this, by just and appropriate figure may be called 'his seal,' 'the seal of the law.' "[331] In applying these criteria to the Decalogue, he said that only in the fourth commandment "we are reading the requirements of Him who made heaven and earth, and all things therein. We realize at once that the Maker of heaven and earth, is the Supreme Ruler over all his works; that the extent of his dominion is the extent of his creation; and that he has a right to demand obedience from all his creatures."[332] Thus, he concluded that "this commandment brings to view his title of royalty, the extent of his dominion, and his right to reign."[333]

As Bates had done previously,[334] Smith equated the Sabbath as a sign (Ex. 31:13, 17) with a seal, stating that "the Lord told his ancient people Israel, that it [Sabbath] should be a *sign* between him and them *forever.* This must include, not the literal descendants only, but spiritual Israel also."[335] He suggested that the command to hurt "only those men which have not the seal of God in their foreheads" (Rev. 9:4) indicated that there were

326 Letter, Cottrell to J. White, p. 87. Already in 1844 the seal of the living God, although undefined, was related to the 144,000 (E. G. White [E. G. Harmon], "RSA," p. 17). Cf. *ibid.,* p. 14.

327 Letter, Cottrell to J. White, p. 87.

328 Edson, "Commandments of God," p. 65.

329 *Ibid.* Earlier E. G. White wrote that "the Sabbath was set apart to be kept in honor of God's holy name" (Letter, E. G. White to Bates, *WLF,* p. 18).

330 [Smith], "Seal," I, p. 12. Cf. Cottrell, "Mark of the Beast, and Seal of the Living God," *RH,* July 28, 1859, p. 78 (*Mark of the Beast . . . ,* 1859, p. 5).

331 [Smith], "Seal," I, p. 12.

332 *Ibid.* Cf. Cottrell, "Mark of the Beast," p. 78 (*Mark of the Beast,* pp. 6, 7).

333 [Smith], "Seal," I, p. 12.

334 See *supra,* pp. 143, 144.

335 *Ibid.,* II, p. 20. Cf. *ibid.,* I, p. 12.

individuals living during the sounding of the fifth angel (A.D. 1299 — A.D. 1449)[336] who had "the seal of God in their foreheads."[337] However, the work of the third angel's message and the sealing angel of Rev. 7:2 pointed to "a particular reform, a special work, at a special time."[338]

Although the third angel's message was identified as the sealing message, J. White rejected in 1852 the idea that "all Sabbath-keepers have the seal of the living God" or that "the 'Review and Herald' teaches that those who embrace the Sabbath are now sealed and sure of heaven."[339] The difference, however, between the present and future reality of the sealing had not yet been solved, because it was not understood that though the sealing message had been proclaimed for years, no one seemed to be sealed in the absolute sense. In 1856 Smith analyzed the sealing process by introducing a distinction between "the possession of the seal" and "the state of being sealed."[340] He acknowledged the possibility "that people in times past have been in possession of the seal" but stated that no one who had ever lived had experienced the sealing as described in Rev. 7.[341] In order to possess the seal, he argued, one had to observe the Sabbath, because "if the Sabbath is the seal, a correct theory on this question, and an observance of the fourth commandment according to the letter, would of course put one in possession of the seal."[342] But, he said, to be in a state of being sealed required much more, for these Sabbath-observing individuals could still "be destitute of saving faith or the Spirit of God," and added that "a mere theory of the truth will not save us."[343] Smith stressed that in the work of personal salvation the Holy Spirit had an essential part to play, remarking that *"while we believe the Sabbath to be a seal, we believe the Holy Spirit to be the sealer."*[344] He, therefore, concluded that the condition of "our being sealed, is not only to be in possession of the seal, but also to fulfill every other requirement of the Holy Spirit; as saith the Apostle, 'Grieve not the Holy Spirit of God, *whereby* (by whom — Whiting) ye are sealed unto the day of redemption. Eph. iv, 30.'"[345] Smith's concept of the mission of the sealing angel contributed to the harmonization of the present and future sealing because

336 See *supra*, p. 27.
337 *Ibid.*, II, p. 20.
338 *Ibid.*
339 [J. White], "Remarks," p. 100. Nichols had stated that those who had been sealed could fall away by yielding to temptation ("Extracts of Letters," *AdR,* Sept. 1850, p. 48).
340 [Smith], "Seal," II, p. 20.
341 *Ibid.*
342 *Ibid.*
343 *Ibid.* In 1852 J. White already made this remark that when individuals "keep *all* the commandments, and repent before God of past transgression of his holy law, their only hope of salvation is through faith in the atoning blood of Jesus," and he added that "a man may outwardly observe all ten of the commandments of God, yet if he is not benefited by the atonement of Jesus it will profit him nothing" ("Remarks," p. 100).
344 [Smith], "Seal," II, p. 20. Commenting on Eph. 2:13, Nichols said earlier that "the *gospel* testimony was the *seal* and the *Holy Spirit* the *sealer.* The testimony must first be *preached,* and then *believed,* before the Holy Spirit can seal us with the truth" ("Extracts," p. 48).
345 [Smith], "Seal," II, p. 20.

the truth by those who would be sealed" and the guidance "in all things by the Spirit of truth that we may keep the Commandments of God *and* the Faith of Jesus."[346] Thus, owing to its broad reformatory work the sealing message had not yet sealed individuals in the absolute sense, though it had been proclaimed for several years and they had been in the possession of the seal by observing the Sabbath. In 1866 Smith viewed the sealing time as "a period during which a progressive work is carried on upon the earth," the nature of which was "the development of a holy character, by obedience to the truth. . . . to a position where they [people] can be sealed absolutely, in the sense of having their cases forever decided for Heaven."[347] He felt that Christ's post-1844 ministry could also be designated as a sealing work because it involved a judgment on the character of human beings. Therefore, parallel with the proclamation of the sealing message on earth a sealing work was going on in heaven where, during the pre-Advent judgment, decisions were made which sealed the eternal destiny of individuals.[348]

In 1852 Edson explored Bates' allusion[349] to the existence of a relation between Rev. 14 and Rev. 7 in a different way, suggesting that the work of the third angel and that of the sealing angel of Rev. 7:2 were identical. He found support for this view in the fact that the events and consequences which followed both angels were similar. The seven plagues (Rev. 15; 16) following the third angel, and the loosing of the four winds (Rev. 7:1-3) after the sealing were seen to be related events, because in both instances it affected the earth, the sea, and the trees.[350] In 1856 Smith held similar views on the two angels and added that they also prepared the people of God for the final events.[351] In 1866, however, he seemed to imply that the sealing message of the third angel performed a preparatory work for the reception of the final sealing performed by the sealing angel of Rev. 7 who would begin his sealing work when the pre-Advent judgment would take up the cases of the living. Those who would be found righteous in that judgment would then be sealed with the "seal of the living God" and be in the "state of being sealed."[352]

346 *Ibid.*
347 Smith, "The Visions — Objections Answered," *RH,* July 10, 1866, p. 42 (*The Visions of Mrs. E. G. White . . . ,* 1868, p. 87).
348 *Ibid.*
349 See *supra,* p. 144.
350 Edson, "Commandments of God," p. 65. He said that "the first vial will be poured out upon the *earth.* — The second will be poured out upon the *sea.* The fourth will be poured out upon the sun, and power will be given unto him to scorch men with fire and great heat. Under this plague the trees will be hurt as predicted in Joel i, 10-12, 18-20. Thus it is seen that the *earth* and *sea* and *trees* are to be hurt by the pouring out of the plagues, the same as by the loosing of the four winds" (*ibid.*). Cf. [Smith], "Seal," I, p. 12.
351 *Ibid.*
352 Smith, "Visions — Objections," p. 42 (*Visions,* p. 87). Rev. 7 pictured to Cottrell two distinct classes of individuals: the 144,000 (Rev. 7:1-8) and a great multitude (Rev. 7:9-17) ("Mark of the Beast," p. 77 [*Mark of the Beast,* p. 3]). The 144,000 seemed to be the living righteous who, after having gone through the final conflict and trouble, would be translated into immortality without experiencing death; see e.g., E. G. White [E. G. Harmon], "RSA," pp. 14, 15 (*EW,* pp. 15, 16); E. G. White, "DBS," p. 22 (*EW,* p. 37); J. White "The One Hundred and Forty Four Thousand," *AdR,* Sept. 1850, pp. 56, 57.

c. The location of the mark and seal.

Additional aspects of the nature of the seal of God and the mark of the beast were discovered when a comparison was made regarding their location. The seal was to be placed in the forehead of the individual,[353] the mark of the beast on the hand or forehead (Rev. 13:16; 14:9). Smith located the seal in the forehead, for he identified those who had the seal with those who had the Father's name written in their foreheads (Rev. 14:1).[354] In this context Cottrell described the difference between the possessors of the seal and mark:

> Those who receive the seal of God, have the Lamb's "Father's *name* written in their foreheads." Rev. xiv, 1. Those who receive the mark of the beast receive "the mark of his *name.*" Verse 11. Name is used in a figurative sense to denote authority. . . . In the name of Jesus Christ, means by the authority of Jesus Christ. Hence, the mark of the beast is a sign or token of his authority, standing in opposition to the sign of the authority of the Father.[355]

The seal and mark were not considered as visible signs in a literal sense.[356] The location in the forehead indicated to Smith that the difference in issue was of a doctrinal nature. The forehead, he remarked, was "the seat of the mind by which we receive or reject all theories presented to us, the seal and the mark there located, must evidently signify some prominent doctrines which distinguish the worshipers of the beast and the worshipers of God."[357] According to Cottrell, the forehead was "a symbol of mind and affections, since the forehead is the seat of the intellectual faculties."[358] Therefore, the "seal of God can be received nowhere else. He accepts of no obedience but that which is from the heart."[359] This was different from the beast which was "more accommodating," for sincerity was not a prerequisite, so that "if you do not choose his mark in your forehead, you may receive it in your right hand. If you do not believe and love his institutions, you may obey them outwardly — carry out his requirements with your right hand, which is a symbol of outward actions."[360] In this light he called attention to the significance of the mission of the third angel as a message of warning "against submitting to the authority of the beast and receiving the mark of his authority, and presents us the 'commandments of God (the Father) and the faith of Jesus,' (the Son)."[361]

---

353   See e.g., Bates, *SLG,* p. 37 (he referred to Rev. 9:4 as one of the arguments to place the seal in the forehead [*ibid.*]); E. G. White, "DBS," p. 23 (*EW,* p. 38); Nichols, "Extracts," p. 48.
354   [Smith], "Seal," II, p. 20.
355   Cottrell, "Mark of the Beast," p. 78 (*Mark of the Beast,* p. 5).
356   *Ibid.,* p. 77; [Smith], "Seal," II, p. 20.
357   *Ibid.* Cf. Nichols, "Extracts," p. 48.
358   Cottrell, "Mark of the Beast," p. 77 (*Mark of the Beast,* p. 4).
359   *Ibid.*
360   *Ibid.,* p. 78 (*Mark of the Beast,* p. 4).
361   *Ibid.* (*Mark of the Beast,* p. 5).

4. The wrath of God.

During the latter part of the 18th century and the early part of the 19th century the "seven last plagues" filled with the wrath of God (Rev. 15:1) were frequently interpreted as being in the past or in process, while some placed them in the future.[362] In the beginning of 1846 J. White adopted the position that "the seven last plagues were all in the future, and that they were all to be poured out before the first resurrection."[363] From the reference in Rev. 15:1 to the "seven angels having the seven last plagues; for in them is filled up the wrath of God" he inferred that "as the 'wrath of God' on the living wicked is *filled up* in the plagues, and as the day of wrath is future, it follows that the plagues are all future."[364] For further evidence he used typological argumentation. The plagues on ancient Egypt, he said, were poured out "just before, and at the deliverance of Israel; so we may expect the last plagues on the wicked, just before and at the deliverance of the saints."[365] In the destruction of the unrighteous after the sealing time described in Ezek. 9 he saw a type of the future wrath of God.[366] He integrated the wrath of God into the sanctuary theology by associating the termination of Jesus' sanctuary ministry with the beginning of the seven last plagues on the living unrighteous.[367]

When the third angel's message began to occupy a central place in the Sabbatarian Adventist theology of mission the concept of the wrath of God in Rev. 14:10, 11 came to prominence. From 1850 onward the seven last plagues formed an integral part of the third angel's message. In that year Holt identified the wrath of God in Rev. 15:1 with the one in 14:10, and stated that it "will be fulfilled in the pouring out of the seven last vials" on the worshippers of the "beast and his image."[368]

The extent of the wrath of God as pictured in the third angel's message was, according to J. White, not to be confined to "a warning of the terrors of

362   See, Froom, *PFF,* IV, 80, 86, 92, 95, 96, 132, 136, 159, 162, 187-90, 199, 225, 241, 261, 267, 311, 319, 341, 342, 394, 401, 701.

363   J. White, *WLF,* p. 1. In the fall of 1845 he had become acquainted with E. G. Harmon's view that "the saints must pass through the 'time of Jacob's trouble,' which was future" (*ibid.,* p. 22). In 1843 Litch had placed the plagues in the future ("The Seven Last Plagues," *MC,* Aug. 17, 1843, p. 205).

364   J. White, *WLF,* p. 2. The execution of these judgments on the living unrighteous he did not consider as being "the final execution of the judgment. That will be at the second death" (*ibid.,* p. 24). Cf. E. G. White, "DBS," p. 86 (*EW,* p. 52).

365   J. White, *WLF,* p. 3. This typology showed him that the seven last plagues were of a literal nature ("Angels No. 4," p. 70 [*AR,* p. 22]). The deceptive power of Pharaoh's magicians "just before, and in connection with the plagues of Egypt" he saw as a type of the deception "by the 'wonders,' and 'miracles,' [Rev. 13:13, 14] performed by the two-horned beast" which would deceive the worshipers of the beast and his image "prior to, and in connection with, the last plagues" (*ibid.*). Cf. J. White, *WLF,* p. 9.

366   *Ibid.,* p. 3. Cf. J. White, "TAM," p. 69 (*TAM,* p. 15).

367   J. White, *WLF,* pp. 2, 3. Cf. E. G. White, "DBS," p. 22 (*EW,* p. 36); E. G. White, "DBS," p. 86 (*EW,* p. 52). She wrote that "the seven last plagues will be poured out, after Jesus leaves the Sanctuary, Said the angel — It is the wrath of God and the Lamb that causes the destruction or death of the wicked" (*ibid.*).

368   Letter, Holt to Dear Brethren, p. 64. Cf. [J. White], "Angels No. 4," p. 70 (*AR,* p. 22).

214

the first death of the worshippers of the beast and his image, by the seven last plagues" but included "the second death at the end of the 1000 years of Rev. xx," for it is then that "the wicked dead will be raised with bodies capable of standing in the presence of the Lamb and the holy angels [Rev. 14:10]. And as the host of 'Gog and Magog' gather up around the Beloved City the final execution of the judgment will take place. 'Fire from God out of heaven' will *'devour'* them [20:8, 9]."[369] Thus God's wrath ended with the annihilation of the wicked.

It was Andrews who interpreted the seven last plagues as an integral part of the judgments of God under the angels with the seven trumpets. His rationale for the relationship between the seven trumpets and the finality of God's wrath in the seven last plagues was the following:

> The seven trumpets represented terrible judgments of God upon wicked men. The judgments that made up this series are called plagues. When six of these trumpets had been blown, and their judgments had been felt by the wicked inhabitants of earth, we read that those who were left who had not been killed by THESE PLAGUES repented not of their wickedness. Rev. ix, 20, 21. So another series of plagues must come upon men, even the seven LAST plagues which fill up God's wrath.[370]

He identified the seven last plagues with the "third woe" under the sounding of the seventh angel (Rev. 11:14, 15). His argumentation was: (1) Under the sounding of the fifth and sixth trumpet there had been a full account of the first and second woes (Rev. 9); (2) the third woe under the seventh trumpet, though simply indicated by the statement "thy wrath is come" and the time to "destroy them which destroy the earth" (Rev. 11:18), was more fully described in the completion of God's wrath in the seven last plagues of Rev. 15 and 16.[371] J. White, who identified the third woe with the seventh angel, concluded that its duration "reaches to the second death at the close of the 1000 years of Rev. xx, covering all woe."[372]

The understanding of the third angel's message in the context of the sanctuary theology provided an explanation why God's wrath had been prevented from being poured out after 1844. Jesus' high-priestly ministry and the sealing mission of the third angel were a restraining influence on the seven last plagues. E. G. White stated that the "wrath of God could not come until Jesus had finished his work in the Most Holy Place — laid off his priestly attire and clothed himself with the garments of vengeance."[373] It was not until the sealing was completed that God's wrath in the seven last

369 *Ibid.* (AR, pp. 23, 24).

370 Andrews, "The Seven Last Plagues," *RH,* Dec. 29, 1868, p. 5.

371 *Ibid.* Cf. Andrews, "TAR,"*RH,* April 17, 1855, pp. 209, 211 (*TAR,* pp. 120, 137). He interpreted Rev. 15:5-8; 16 as an expanded version of Rev. 11:15-19, for both accounts referred to scenes taking place when the temple in heaven was opened, and ended in the same manner with events of the last plague (*ibid.,* p. 209 [*TAR,* p. 120]).

372 J. White, "The Mystery of God," *RH,* March 27, 1856, p. 205. Cf. J. White, "The Seventh Angel," *RH,* March 27, 1856, p. 204.

373 E. G. White, "DBS," p. 22 (*EW,* p. 36).

plagues would be poured out.[374] In 1851 J. White summarized the various restraining factors in this way:

> The wrath of God in the seven last plagues will constitute the "time of trouble such as never was," after Michael stands up. Dan. xii, 1. The mediation of Jesus in the Heavenly Sanctuary, prevents the wrath of God from coming on a guilty world. The four angels [Rev. vii, 1-3] hold the four winds until the servants of God are sealed by the last warning message. When that work is done, Christ will lay aside his priestly attire, put on the "garments of vengeance," [Isa. lix.17,] and take his position on the "white cloud," [Rev. xiv, 14] with a "sharp sickle" to reap the harvest of the earth. Then the four angels will cease to hold the four winds [Rev. vii, 1-3,] and the wrath of God, in the seven last plagues, will be poured out.[375]

The reason, according to Andrews, why the "third woe, or seven last plagues" did not take place in 1844 when the trumpet of the seventh angel began to sound was that "a period of days is occupied in finishing the mystery of God [Rev. 10:7]."[376] The mission of the third angel and Jesus' post-1844 ministry he identified as aspects of the finishing of the mystery of God, or the "work of salvation for sinful men."[377]

5. The last warning.

From 1850 onward the mission of the third angel's message came to be called "the last message of mercy" or "the last warning message."[378] In 1853 J. White explained that the expression "the last mesage of mercy to man" was based on the fact that there was "nothing but unmingled wrath beyond this message."[379] Later E. G. White referred to the relevance of the mission of the warning message as follows: (1) It was "designed to put the children of God upon their guard, and show them the hour of temptation and anguish that was before them" because of the final conflict with the "beast and his image";[380] (2) it was to bring individuals together and, through a process of purification through obedience to the truth, to prepare them for translation from mortality to immortality;[381] (3) due to the fact that the law of God had been lightly regarded by man "the Lord would not come to punish the transgressors of his law without first sending them a message of

---

374 *Ibid.* (*EW*, p. 44); *ibid.*, p. 32 (*EW*, p. 48).

375 [J. White], "Angels No. 4," p. 70 (*AR*, p. 22). (Brackets his.)

376 Andrews, "TAR," p. 211 (*TAR*, p. 137). On Rev. 10:7, see *supra*, pp. 43, 44, 131.

377 *Ibid.*

378 See e.g., Edson, *Time of the End*, p. 21; J. White, "TAM," p. 69 (*TAM*, p. 15); J. White, "Third Angel's Message," p. 108. He also used the phrase "the last merciful warning to dying men" ("Conference Address," *RH*, June 9, 1859, p. 21). E. G. White used expressions like "the last notes of warning to the world" (*SG*, II, 202), "the last message of mercy to the world" (*ibid.*, p. 213), "the last great message of mercy to the world" (*ibid.*, p. 231).

379 [J. White], "Remarks on Luke XIII, 23-25," *RH*, May 26, 1853, p. 4.

380 E. G. White, *SG*, I, 162.

381 Letter, E. G. White to Friends, No. 13, 1859. She added the necessity of being "baptized with the third angel's message, the soul purifying truth for this time" (*ibid.*). Cf. Letter, E. G. White to Buck, No. 18, 1861.

warning. The third angel proclaims the warning message."[382] In 1854 E. G. White associated the mission of the third angel with the closing work of salvation;[383] and in 1856 J. White described the mission of the "last warning Message" as the "closing work of salvation through Jesus Christ."[384] The response to its closing mission, he said, was to "ripen the harvest of the earth," for "on the manner in which this Message is treated, hangs the eternal destiny of this generation" and "all will be fitted for immortality or the seven last plagues."[385]

The "closing work of the gospel of Jesus Christ" through the "last message of mercy" J. White identified with the "finishing of the mystery of God"[386] and suggested the existence of a very close relationship between the gospel and "the mystery of Christ in the Heavenly Sanctuary":

> As the tenth day atonement for the cleansing of the sanctuary of the first covenant was the finishing up of the work of that year, so the ministration of Christ for the cleansing of the Heavenly Sanctuary after the termination of the 2300 days of Dan. viii, is the finishing up of Christ's entire work as Priest. And while his work as Priest is being finished in heaven, the mystery of God, which is the gospel to the world, is being finished on earth in the third message, which is the last that offers salvation.[387]

The warning mission of the third angel's message was also associated with the measuring of "the temple of God, and the altar, and them that worship therein" (Rev. 11:1). One of the most complete expositions on the measuring process was provided by Smith in 1862. This process, he felt, depicted the nature of the prophetic message of the previous verse (10:11).[388] The importance of the measuring was emphasized by the command not to measure the court outside the temple (11: 2), meaning that "the attention of the church is now directed to the inner temple, and the services there," for matters related to the court were presently of less relevance.[389] In defining the temple and its worshipers he argued that the temple of God could not be interpreted as the church, "for the church is brought to view in connection with this temple as 'them that worship therein.' The temple is therefore the literal temple in heaven, and the worshipers the true church on earth."[390] The worshipers, he remarked, "are to be measured as *worshipers;*

382   E. G. White, *TC*, No. 22, 1872, p. 49 (*T*, III, 161).
383   E. G. White, *SCEV*, pp. 3, 4 (*EW*, pp. 85, 86).
384   J. White, "Third Angel's Message," p. 108.
385   *Ibid.* He said: "Those who receive it, and live up to their profession of faith, who really keep the Commandments of God and the Faith of Jesus, will be ripened for immortality; while those who reject it, will be left of God to the delusions of Satan, and thus ripen for the vials of Jehovah's wrath" (*ibid.*). Later, he stated that the third angel's message "will be a test to all men" ("The Loud Voice of the Third Angel," *RH*, Oct. 20, 1859, p. 172).
386   J. White, "Mystery," p. 205. Cf. Andrews, "TAR," p. 211 (*TAR*, 137).
387   J. White, "Mystery," p. 205.
388   Smith, "Thoughts on Revelation," *RH*, Oct. 28, 1862, p. 172 (*Revelation*, p. 187).
389   *Ibid.* (*Revelation*, p. 189). Rev. 11:2 signified to Smith a transition to the 1260 years of persecution as a new series of events (*ibid.*).
390   *Ibid.* (*Revelation*, p. 187).

hence the measurement has to do with character; and character can be measured only by some standard of right, namely, a law or rule of action."[391] From this he concluded that the measuring rod which the angel placed into the hands of John embraced "the ten commandments, the standard which God has given by which to measure 'the whole duty of man,'" and had been put into the hands of the church in the form of the third angel's message as "the standard by which the worshipers of God are now to be tested."[392] The call to rise and measure the temple he saw as a "prophetic command to the church to give the subject of the temple or sanctuary a special examination."[393] In summary Smith stated that

> the measuring rod is the special message now given to the church, which embraces all the truths peculiar to this time, including the ten commandments. By this message our attention has been called to the temple above, and through it the light and truth on this subject has come out. Thus we measure the temple and the altar, or the ministration connected with that temple, the work and position of our great High Priest; and we measure the worshipers with that portion of the rod which relates to character, namely, the ten commandments.[394]

In 1872 he described the significance of Rev. 11:1 as "the last testing work to be brought to bear upon the church, to determine their fitness to be translated to Heaven, their preparation for the issues of eternity."[395] Concerning the accomplishment of the testing (measuring) work, he said that one measured "the temple by first accepting the truth of its existence above, studying into the purpose for which it exists, connecting therewith the work of Christ as our great High Priest, examining into the nature and duration of that work, and the present stage of its progress."[396] Although the worshipers were in a general sense to be tested by the Decalogue, he felt that because of the deceitfulness of the heart and the fact that God's law was exceedingly broad, a divine aid for this testing work had been provided in "two great instrumentalities for the perfection of character" which were brought to view in the third angel's message, namely, "the commandments of God *and the faith of Jesus*."[397] This, in fact, meant that the worshipers were to be measured by the Decalogue and the various new truths discovered since the Disappointment.[398]

From the early beginnings of their movement Sabbatarian Adventists had been conscious of the success of their missionary activity in proclaiming the

391 *Ibid.* (*Revelation*, p. 188).
392 *Ibid.* In 1854 Loughborough mentioned the third angel's message as the agent to perform this measuring process with the Decalogue as measuring rod ("The Hour of His Judgment Come," *RH*, Feb. 14, 1854, p. 30).
393 Smith, "Revelation," p. 172 (*Revelation*, p. 188).
394 *Ibid.* (*Revelation*, pp. 188, 189).
395 Smith, "Nature of the Closing Work," *RH*, Nov. 19, 1872, p. 178.
396 *Ibid.*
397 *Ibid.*
398 *Ibid.*, pp. 178, 179.

message of warning. Already in 1847, E. G. White had pointed to the beginning of "the time of trouble" when the believers, who were filled with the Holy Spirit, would be engaged in a missionary work resulting in a strong positive and negative response from other Christians and their organizations.[399] A few years later when the third angel's message had become the dominant factor in their theology, added support was given to the idea that their missionary work would succeed because the proclamation of the warning message was to take place with a "loud voice" (Rev. 14:9).[400] Since 1850 this final future proclamation of the last warning message came to be identified by the term "the loud cry" of the third angel or of the third angel's message.[401] Both in 1851 and 1856 it was thought that the time had come for the loud cry.[402] After 1856 the rationale for the delay of the loud cry was seen in the unprepared and unsanctified condition of the believers.[403]

In 1858 E. G. White described the loud cry in the context of an invisible angelic activity as a joint action of the proclamations of the angel of Rev. 18:1 and the third angel. The mission of the angel of Rev. 18:1, which provided "power and force" for the third angel's message, she saw described in Rev. 18:2.[404] This proclamation indicated that "the message of the fall of

399 Letter, E. G. White to Bates, *WLF*, p. 19. This "time of trouble," she remarked, "does not refer to the time when the plagues shall begin to be poured out; but to a short period just before they are poured out, while Christ is in the Sanctuary. At that time, while the work of salvation is closing, trouble will be coming on the earth, the nations will be angry, yet held in check, so as not to prevent the work of the third angel. At that time the 'latter rain,' or refreshing from the Lord, will come [Acts 3:19], to give power to the loud voice of the third angel, and prepare the saints to stand in the period when the seven last plagues shall be poured out" (*SCEV*, pp. 3, 4 [*EW*, pp. 85, 86]).

400 Cf. J. White, "TAM," p. 69 (*TAM*, pp. 14, 15).

401 See e.g., Letter, Bates to Editor, *PT*, Nov. 1850, p. 88; [J. White], "Present Work," p. 12; E. G. White, *SG*, I, 193-96; II, 224.

402 See [J. White], "Present Work," p. 12; J. White, "Where Are We?" *RH*, Dec. 11, 1856, p. 45. E. G. White commented on the 1856 situation that "nearly all believed that this message [Laodicean Message when it was first presented] would end in the loud cry of the third angel" (*TC*, No. 5, p. 4 [*T*, I, 186]). See *infra*, p. 247.

403 In 1857 J. White stated that "all that is necessary to introduce the loud cry of the Third Angel, is for the remnant to arouse and perfect their faith by corresponding works. Then Jesus (who is now without, knocking) will come in. The gifts will revive in the church, and the mighty truths of the Third Message will be set home to the honest in heart by the power of the Holy Ghost" ("Western Tour," *RH*, Jan. 1, 1857, p. 69). As another prerequisite for the loud cry he mentioned the existence of unity among believers. He said that when the believers "shall fully reach that standard [Bible standard of unity], then, and not until then, will he [God] trust them with the loud cry" because God would not allow others to be called out of Babylon in order "to be scattered, confused and destroyed by discordant sentiments and spirits" ("Loud Voice," p. 173). In 1859 E. G. White explained the delay in terms of a preparatory process of the church by the Laodicean message of 1856. This message which was designed to prepare people for the loud cry included both a work of repentance among God's people so that "they might be favored with the presence of Jesus" and a work of character development which required time to prove its genuineness (*TC*, No. 5, pp. 4, 5 [*T*, I, 186, 187]). In 1867 she strongly criticized the attitude of church members who waited for divine power to prepare them for the loud cry without their cooperation in the process of personal sanctification (*ibid.*, No. 11, 1867, pp. 41, 42 [*T*, I, 486]; *ibid.*, No. 13, 1867, pp. 67, 68 [*T*, I, 619]). Cf. E. G. White, *CEV*, pp. 58, 59 (*EW*, p. 71); E. G. White, *SCEV*, p. 4 (*EW*, p. 86).

404 E. G. White, *SG*, I, 194. J. White remarked that both the angel of Rev. 18:1 and the third angel "symbolize different parts of the same great work, preparatory to the plagues."

Babylon, as given by the second angel, is again given, with the addition of the corruptions which have been entering the churches since 1844."[405] Other angels would assist the angel of Rev. 18:1, producing the effect that everywhere the call was heard of Rev. 18:4, "Come out of her, my people, that ye be not partakers of her sins, and that ye receive not of her plagues."[406] She remarked that "this message seemed to be an addition to the third message, and joined it, as the midnight cry joined the second angel's message in 1844," implying that the Advent experience of the summer of 1844 was a type of the loud-cry experience.[407] E. G. White foresaw that the response to this "last solemn warning, proclaiming the fall of Babylon, and calling upon God's people to come out of her; that they might escape her fearful doom" had as a result that "those who had any light in the churches, who had not heard and rejected the three messages, answered to the call, and left the fallen churches."[408] Efforts to persuade people to sever their religious affiliation during the loud cry were seen as a type of the manner in which Lot was persuaded to leave Sodom before its destruction.[409] In an attempt to counteract the success of the last mission of warning, she stated that prior to the loud cry Satan would create "an excitement in these religious bodies, that those who have rejected the truth may think God is with them. He hopes to deceive the honest, and lead them to think that God is still working for the churches."[410] She predicted, however, that this false revival would not prevent the last warning message from accomplishing its work.[411] The concept of the loud cry had important missiological consequences, for it continually inspired believers to new hopes, provided a strong incentive to persevere in mission work — especially in times of discouragement and disappointment —, and was an ever-present factor in the development of missionary strategy.

The relationship between the angelic and human activity in mission was especially brought out by E. G. White.[412] Her views depicted angels sent from God as being responsible for influencing His people to engage in their God-appointed mission. From the viewpoint of human activity believers could identify their missionary proclamation with the cry of the angels' messages. However, the general understanding seems to be that the messages of Rev. 14 and 18 were proclaimed through the united efforts of both the visible and invisible realities.

Presently, it was the time of the third angel while the time of the angel of Rev. 18:1 was future and would "introduce the loud cry of the third message" ("Loud Voice," p. 173).

405 E. G. White, *SG*, I, 194.
406 *Ibid.* Cf. Frisbie, "Church Order," p. 147.
407 E. G. White, *SG*, I, 194, 195.
408 *Ibid.*, p. 195. She added that "the third message was to do its work; all were to be tested upon it, and the precious ones were to be called out from the religious bodies" (*ibid.*).
409 *Ibid.*, p. 196.
410 *Ibid.*, p. 172.
411 *Ibid.*, pp. 172, 173.
412 See *ibid.*, pp. 128-96.

6. Health reform.

During the first half of the 19th century, there was a general ignorance of principles of healthful living and treatment of disease.[413] However, movements advocating a healthier life style and improved rational methods of treating disease began to emerge both in Europe and in the U.S.A. and created increasing interest in temperance, therapeutic reform, diet reform, dress reform, etc.[414] In the U.S.A. the origin of such a movement, called the health reform movement, could be traced back to factors such as a long tradition of health literature, a general dissatisfaction with the medical profession, a widespread prevalence of dyspepsia,[415] and a growing agitation by Christians against intemperance.[416] Some of the special characteristics[417] of this movement, which already flourished before the SDA Church was organized, were its opposition to the use of tea, coffee, tobacco, and alcohol, its support for dietary reform and natural remedies, and its evangelical fervor which made health reform a holy cause.[418] Many participants could not accept the general notion that disease was a divine punishment for sin, but felt that disease was caused by man's failure to live under the laws of nature. Health reform was seen as a means to bring man's behavior in

413 D. E. Robinson, *The Story of Our Health Message* . . . , 1965, pp. 13-27.
414 *Ibid.*, pp. 28-49. Cf. Clark, *1844*, II, 199-275.
415 W. C. Gage, *Dyspepsia: Its Causes, Prevention, and Cure*, 1874, p. 1; John B. Blake, "Health Reform," in Gaustad, *Adventism*, p. 46.
416 Already in the 18th century the Methodists and Quakers had expressed their concern about the excessive use of alcohol. In 1743 John Wesley appealed to Christians to abstain from "drunkenness, buying or selling spirituous liquors, or drinking them, unless in cases of extreme necessity." He also opposed the use of snuff and tobacco unless prescribed by a physician, and objected to the drinking of tea. See L. Tyerman, *The Life and Times of the Rev. John Wesley, M.A., Founder of the Methodists*, I, 1870, pp. 464, 521-23; II, 1880, p. 390; III, 1872, pp. 44, 133; Henry Wheeler, *Methodism and the Temperance Reformation*, 1882, pp. 11-110. A publication entitled *An Inquiry into the Effects of Spirituous Liquors on the Human Body*, 1790, by Dr. Benjamin Rush, a well-known Quaker physician and one of the signers of the Declaration of Independence, and the *Six Sermons on Intemperance* . . . , 1827, by Lyman Beecher were very influential in generating public support for the American temperance cause. In 1826 the American Temperance Society was established, which advocated abstinence from intoxicating liquors. The leaders in the temperance movement were almost entirely Christians. In 1836 the American Temperance Union was founded. Its aim was total abstinence from all alcoholic beverages (teetotalling) and it received support of many Methodists, Quakers, Presbyterians, and Congregationalists. See e.g., Paul C. Conley and Andrew A. Sorensen, *The Staggering Steeple* . . . , 1971, pp. 30-40.
417 See e.g., Blake, "Health Reform," p. 47.
418 The cause of health reform was especially promoted in the U.S.A. by Sylvester Graham, a former Presbyterian minister. He turned health reform into a moral crusade. His most influential work was a two-volume *Lectures on the Science of Human Life*, 1839. One of his fundamental ideas was that the closer man lived to nature the more he lived in harmony with the divine laws of the human organism and the healthier would be his body and his moral and intellectual faculties. Through the influence of his lectures, the American Physiological Society was established in 1837 with its purpose to provide practical information on human physiology in order to promote health and longevity. One of the reports of the society stated that several ministers were beginning to recognize the importance of obedience to the laws of nature as a part of God's laws. In 1850 the American Vegetarian Society was founded. See Blake, "Health Reform," pp. 36-44.

harmony with the divine laws of the human organism in order to develop a healthy constitution.[419]

Various aspects and principles of the reforms advocated by this movement were adopted by few Sabbatarian Adventists before 1863 but, especially through the influence of E. G. White, there was a general acceptance of such reforms by SDA after 1863.[420] These reforms became designated among SDA under the general term of "health reform." The primary reason for their acceptance of the reforms was that they were incorporated into their religious experience. It was admitted that SDA did not "profess to be pioneers in the general principles of the health reform," but they did claim the uniqueness of integrating health reform into their theology.[421] The integration of health reform into the third angel's message made it a vital part of their theology of mission and accounts for the emphasis in SDA thought on the intimate relationship of the human body and mind to the religious experience of the individual. In this section, first attention will be focused on the early developments of the relationship between religion and health among Sabbatarian Adventists. Then, after the organization of the movement into the·SDA Church, a description will be given of the integration of health reform into the third angel's message and its missiological consequences. The reason for this division was due to the strong influence E. G. White had on the adoption and integration of health reform after 1863.

a. Relationship between religion and health (1848-63).

The initial indication that abstinence from harmful products for the human body would become a part of the Sabbatarian Adventist profession, was a vision of E. G. White in the autumn of 1848. Here attention was called to the "injurious effects of tobacco, tea, and coffee."[422] The following year Bates, who had been an active participant in the Temperance movement for many years,[423] drew the attention of believers to this vision and reminded them of a departure from their 1844 self-sacrificing practice

---

419 *Ibid.*, p. 47.

420 See *supra*, p. xv. For an understanding of healthful living among believers before and after 1863, see e.g., A. W. Spalding, *Origin and History of Seventh-day Adventists*, I, 1961, pp. 335-52.

421 Waggoner, "Present Truth," *RH*, Aug. 7, 1866, p. 77. Non-SDA health reform influences were to be seen in one of the earliest SDA health reform publications, *Health: or How to Live*, which was prepared by E. G. White in 1865. This publication was "made up chiefly from the most spirited and valuable articles and extracts from Trall, Jackson, Graham, Dio Lewis, Coles, Horace Mann, Gunn, and many others" (J. White, "Health Reform," No. 4, *HR*, Feb. 1871, p. 152). It should be noticed that the general objective in the publication *How to Live* was to set forth the E. G. White teachings on the major points of health reform, and then to put with these supportive materials from medical authorities, showing that what she was saying could be substantiated (cf. E. G. White, "Questions and Answers," *RH*, Oct. 8, 1867, p. 260). So, while from a quantity standpoint the six pamphets, *How to Live*, were made up chiefly of valuable articles from others, the prime article in each case was written by E. G. White.

422 J. White, "Western Tour," *RH*, Nov. 8, 1870, p. 165.

423 Bates, *Autobiography*, pp. 205-8, 211, 228-31, 262. For a view of Bates' personal maturing on the subject of temperance, see *ibid.*, pp. 97, 143, 150, 168, 173, 179, 234, 235.

of abstaining from tobacco and snuff.[424] He urged them to refrain from such unhealthful habits, including the use of alcohol.[425] The same year Edson reported that in western New York State the "brethren have seen the importance of leaving their useless habits; — therefore they have put away snuff and tobacco, as useless, filthy, and unclean."[426] From the early part of the 1850s onward, one could distinguish predominantly three categories of appeals stressing the necessity for healthful living: (1) Appeals for health resulting in improvement in spirituality; (2) appeals to the importance of health in the light of the imminent Second Advent; (3) appeals for abstinence to provide means for financial support of missionary activity. Although there is some overlapping, each category has been treated separately.

i. *Spirituality and health.* In 1851 E. G. White pointed to the necessity of discontinuing the use of tobacco because it was "an idol" and said that "unless it is given up the frown of God will be upon the one that uses it."[427] Later a correspondent of the *Review and Herald* supported the concept of idolatry with Eph. 5:5 and Col. 3:5, indicating that the condemnation of tobacco as idolatry was based on the idea that one using tobacco was a "covetous man" and that in turn "covetousness" was "idolatry."[428] In discussing the use of tobacco and alcohol, J. H. Waggoner[429] exhorted believers to "keep yourselves from idols [1 John 5:21]."[430] In 1861 E. G. White classified not only tobacco, but also tea and coffee, as idols.[431] According to D. T. Bourdeau[432] it was obvious that "self, tea, and tobacco, etc., are idols, to which many bow and sacrifice."[433] This indicates that when physical habits were seen to influence spirituality negatively, an appeal for renunciation of such habits was inevitable.

The relationship between religion and health was also described in a "selected" article published in the *Review and Herald* which pointed out that "religion, for its full development, demands all our mental powers."[434] Because tobacco impaired the mental powers, it was concluded that a person who "uses tobacco, cannot be as good a Christian as he could be without

424 Bates, *SLG*, p. 67. See *supra*, p. 98.
425 *Ibid.*, p. 68. See *infra*, p. 226.
426 Edson, "Beloved Brethren," p. 34.
427 Letter, E. G. White to Barnes, No. 5, 1851.
428 J. M. McLellan, "The Temple of God Is No Place for Idols," *RH*, Oct. 9, 1856, p. 182. Cf. Cornell, "The Tobacco Abomination," *RH*, May 20, 1858, p. 1.
429 Joseph H. Waggoner (1820-89), a former Baptist, became a Sabbatarian Adventist in 1852. From then onward he was actively engaged in missionary work. He wrote several doctrinal books and was corresponding editor of the *RH* for some time.
430 Waggoner, "Tobacco," *RH*, Nov. 19, 1857, p. 13.
431 E. G. White, *TC*, No. 6, pp. 20, 24 (*T*, I, 222, 224).
432 Daniel T. Bourdeau (1835-1905), a former Baptist, was ordained to the Sabbatarian Adventist ministry in 1858. He and his brother, A. C. Bourdeau, were pioneer missionaries among the French-speaking population of North America. They were among the first of French descent to accept the third angel's message.
433 D. T. Bourdeau, "Tobacco and Tea," *RH*, March 17, 1863, p. 125.
434 "Tobacco," *RH*, Dec. 13, 1853, p. 178.

it."[435] A recommended article written by a non-Sabbatarian Adventist brought out that violation of the physical laws of the human body, especially through the use of tobacco, was a moral issue involving a sin against the Creator. It stated that God was the author of "man's organic structure," which implied that "God's will is as manifest in this organism as in the ten commandments."[436] Then it was argued that "whoever injures this 'divine workmanship,' by the use of a deadly thing, plants his will in conflict with God's will," which signified "rebellion against God" and "sin."[437] Sin, therefore, was seen as "the transgression of law, written by the finger of God on the whole organism of a man, as well as in the Bible."[438] It was considered "merely a sin of ignorance" when the physical laws of the organism were violated unconsciously, but the moment when one "becomes conscious of this violation, the violation is no longer simply physical, but moral; the act becomes a sinning act, a sin, and the actor a sinner."[439] In 1863 D. T. Bourdeau approached the moral dimension of healthful living from a different perspective when he associated the use of tea and tobacco with transgression of the Decalogue, not with the transgression of the laws of the human organism. He reasoned that "if tea and tobacco are injurious to our health, as far as we use these herbs, we violate a principle of the sixth commandment, which says, 'Thou shalt not kill.' And let us remember that we profess to show a respect for all of God's commandments."[440]

The Sabbatarian Adventists placed great importance on the temporal significance of the human body in relation to their religious experience. The body was seen as a temple of God designed as the habitation of the Holy Spirit. According to J. White, it was not likely that the Holy Spirit would dwell in those who used tobacco, snuff, and tea.[441] The believers frequently referred to 1 Cor. 3:16, 17, "Know ye not that ye are the temple of God, and that the Spirit of God dwelleth in you? If any man defile the temple of God, him shall God destroy; for the temple of God is holy, which temple ye are," and 1 Cor. 6:19, "What? know ye not that your body is the temple of the Holy Ghost which is in you, which ye have of God, and ye are not your own?"[442] These texts were quoted synonymously, so that the "temple of God" in 1 Cor. 3:16, 17 was identified with the human body as "the temple

435   Ibid. Cf. [J. White], "The Faith of Jesus," RH, March 14, 1854, p. 60.
436   George Trask, "Popular Poisons," RH, Oct. 16, 1855, p. 62 (repr. from AH, Sept. 29, 1855, p. 305).
437   Ibid.
438   Ibid. See infra, pp. 230, 231.
439   Ibid., p. 63.
440   D. T. Bourdeau, "Tobacco and Tea," p. 125.
441   J. White, "The Office," RH, July 24, 1855, p. 13. Cf. Letter, Dexter Daniels to Smith, RH, Feb. 5, 1857, p. 110. Here the use of tobacco, snuff, and "intoxicating spirits" was criticized. Reflecting on his behavior when he was twenty years of age (1841), J. White said: "I had never descended to the common sin of profanity, and had not used tobacco, tea and coffee, nor had I ever raised a glass of spirituous liquor to my lips" (Life, p. 15).
442   Andrews, "The Use of Tobacco a Sin Against God," RH, April 10, 1856, p. 5; McLellan, "Temple of God," p. 182; J. F. Case, "Tobacco," RH, Sept. 24, 1857, p. 166; Cornell, "Tobacco Abomination," p. 1.

of the Holy Ghost" in 1 Cor. 6:19.[443] Interpreted in a similar way but used less frequently was 2 Cor. 6:16: "And what agreement hath the temple of God with idols? for ye are the temple of the living God; as God hath said, I will dwell in them, and walk in them; and I will be their God, and they shall be my people."[444] All these texts were seen to allude to individual responsibility to preserve the human organism in the best possible condition. A biblical passage often used as having specific reference to the cleanliness of the human body as a necessary aspect of Christian perfection in a non-eschatological as well as in an eschatological sense was 2 Cor. 7:1: "Having therefore these promises, dearly beloved, let us cleanse ourselves from all filthiness of the flesh and spirit, perfecting holiness in the fear of God."[445] The concept of *gloria Dei* was also regularly employed as referring to a healthful treatment of the physical organism. Both 1 Cor. 6:20, "For ye are bought with a price: therefore glorify God in your body, and in your spirit, which are God's," and 1 Cor. 10:31, "Whether therefore ye eat, or drink, or whatsoever ye do, do all to the glory of God," were quoted in this context.[446] Another text which was often mentioned to stress the significance of a healthy body was Rom. 12:1: "I beseech you therefore, brethren, by the mercies of God, that ye present your bodies a living sacrifice, holy, acceptable unto God, which is your reasonable service."[447] Although other texts were used,[448] the above mentioned passages were most frequently used as non-eschatological arguments to support the religious responsibility for the care of the human body.

ii. *Eschatology and health.* Healthful living came to be seen as an indis-

443   See e.g., McLellan, "Temple of God," p. 182; Cornell, "Tobacco Abomination," p. 1.

444   See e.g., J. F. Case, "Tobacco," p. 166; Cornell, "Tobacco Abomination," p. 1. McLellan used this text to show the incongruity of the temple of God with the tobacco idolatry ("Temple of God," p. 182).

445   [J. White], "Faith of Jesus," *RH,* March 14, 1854, p. 60; Stephen Pierce, "The Use of Tobacco," *RH,* Dec. 4, 1855, p. 79; Andrews, "Tobacco," p. 5; McLellan, "Temple of God," p. 182; Letter, Daniels to Smith, p. 110; Waggoner, "Tobacco," p. 12; Cornell, "Tobacco Abomination," p. 110; D. T. Bourdeau, "Tobacco and Tea," p. 125.

446   E. G. White, MS 1, 1854 (here, eating to the glory of God was interpreted in the context of the denial of unhealthy appetite); [J. White], "Faith of Jesus," *RH,* March 14, 1854, p. 60; Pierce, "Tobacco," p. 79; J. F. Case, "Tobacco," p. 166; Waggoner, "Tobacco," p. 12; D. T. Bourdeau, "Tobacco and Tea," p. 125; M. B. Smith, "Coffee — Its Effects," *RH,* Oct. 1, 1861, p. 142. He stated that "if the use of coffee as an article of daily consumption is contrary to organic laws (and organic laws are the laws of God), then we cannot use it 'to the glory of God' " (*ibid.*).

447   McLellan, "Temple of God," p. 182; J. Clarke, "Sacrificing," *RH,* Oct. 15, 1857, p. 192; Waggoner, "Tobacco," p. 12; Cornell, "Tobacco Abomination," p. 1.

448   Pierce referred also to James 1:21 ("Tobacco," p. 79). Cf. Waggoner, "Tobacco," p. 12. Andrews mentioned Gal. 5:24, Titus 2:11, 12, 13 ("Tobacco," p. 5). McLellan used 1 Tim. 6:9; 2 Tim. 2:21, 22; 2 Cor. 5:17; 1 Cor. 5:7 ("Temple of God," p. 182). J. F. Case alluded to 1 Pet. 2:11; 2 Cor. 5:17; Rom. 8:7, 13 ("Tobacco," p. 166). Cornell, who provided probably the most elaborate textual evidence among the Sabbatarian Adventists, pointed further to the sin of gratification of worldly, fleshly lusts as referred to in Rom. 13:13, 14; Gal. 5:16; 6:8; Eph. 2:2, 3; Titus 2:12; James 4:3; 1 Pet. 2:12; 4:1, 2 and called attention to Rom. 14:21 and 1 Cor. 8:12, 13 for the principle of avoiding being a stumbling block because *"tobacco is very offensive to the saints"* ("Tobacco Abomination," p. 1). J. White indicated the significance of temperance in 2 Pet. 1:5, 6 ("Conference Address," *RH,* June 9, 1859, p. 22).

pensable facet of an individual preparation for the parousia. In 1849, in the light of the sealing time, Bates appealed for abstinence from tobacco, snuff, and alchohol.[449] He especially stressed the necessity of the cleansing of body and spirit, and perfecting holiness (2 Cor. 7:1; Is. 52:11), because continuation of defiling practices would prevent the entrance into the New Jerusalem (Rev. 21:27).[450] Two years later E. G. White indicated the consequences of the use of tobacco for the sealing process when she said that the tobacco consumer "cannot be sealed with the seal of the living God."[451]

In associating Christian perfection with the Second Advent, E. G. White said: "I saw that Christ will have a church without *spot* or *wrinkle* or *any such thing* to present to his Father [Eph. 5:27]."[452] In 1854 E. G. White made an appeal for greater "cleanliness among Sabbath-keepers" as a part of the preparatory process for Christ's return because "God would have a clean and holy people, a people that He can delight [in]."[453] She continued to say that "God would not acknowledge an untidy and unclean person as a Christian. His frown was upon such. Our souls, bodies, and spirits are to be presented blameless by Jesus to His Father [1 Thes. 5:23], and unless we are clean in person and pure in heart, we cannot be presented blameless to God."[454] In 1856 Andrews made an appeal to the tobacco consumer to be perfect for the Second Coming:

> Do you indulge in this inexcusable worldly lust? If so let me beg you to consider that you cannot thus be presented without spot or wrinkle or fault before God. Eph. v, 27; Rev. xiv, 5. Deceive not yourself. If you would stand with the Lamb on mount Zion [Rev. 14:1], you must cleanse yourself from all filthiness of flesh and spirit, and perfect holiness in the fear of God [2 Cor. 7:1].[455]

In view of Christ's imminent return, one correspondent of the *Review and Herald* urged people to "crucify the lusts of the flesh [Gal. 5:24], and make no delay. We are living in the perilous times of the last days. We must be overcomers, or we cannot stand before the Lord at his coming."[456] In 1857 when the Laodicean message[457] was emphasized, another correspondent

---

449 Bates, *SLG,* pp. 67, 68. He added: "I know not how he [God] can approbate one of the 144,000 that uses or traffics in alcoholic drinks, from brandy to cider, and beer."

450 *Ibid.,* p. 68.

451 Letter, E. G. White to Barnes, No. 5, 1851.

452 *Ibid.* Here she also stated that "we must be *perfect Christians,* deny ourselves all the way along, tread the narrow thorny pathway that our Jesus trod, and then if we are final overcomers, Heaven sweet Heaven will be cheap enough."

453 E. G. White, MS 1, 1854.

454 *Ibid.* For the use of 1 Thes. 5:23, see J. F. Case, "Tobacco," p. 166; M. B. Smith, "Tea — Its Effects," *RH,* May 21, 1861, p. 6; M. B. Smith, "Coffee," p. 142. The call for blameless bodies implied the necessity of becoming acquainted with "the organic laws by which we are governed" so that practices contrary to these laws might be abolished for the sake of God's glory (*ibid.*)

455 Andrews, "Tobacco," p. 5.

456 McLellan, "Temple of God," p. 182.

457 See *infra,* pp. 244-48.

pointed out that a healthy body was an indispensable part of the preparation for the latter rain, the antitypical outpouring of "the Spirit of the day of Pentecost" just before the Second Advent. He remarked that to get ready for "a baptism of fire or the Holy Ghost" it was necessary that

> we must be pure in body and soul. We must cleanse ourselves from all filthiness of the flesh and of the spirit, perfecting holiness in the fear of God [2 Cor. 7:1]. We must not use tobacco, or snuff, or intoxicating spirits; for if we do we are filthy. The holy Spirit cannot dwell in such temples [1 Cor. 3:16]. We must cast away all such filthy things.[458]

In the pre-1863 period the above biblical references formed the general eschatological appeal while no connection had yet been established between healthful living and the third angel's message.

iii. *Mission financing and health*. When the missionary activity of Sabbatarian Adventists began to expand, there was an ever growing demand for financial support. In 1854 E. G. White called for a denial of unhealthful appetite so that money saved in this way could be "put into the treasury of the Lord."[459] In appealing for financial assistance she employed arguments of economy, healthful living, and divine favor:

> If all would study to be more economical in their articles of dress, and deprive themselves of some things which are not actually necessary, and lay aside such useless and injurious things as tea, &c., and give what they cost to the cause, they would receive more blessings here, and a reward in heaven.[460]

When some pleaded poverty as a reason for not sustaining the *Review and Herald*, J. White described them as being "too poor to help a brother send out the bread of heaven to the scattered flock, but have means enough to obtain tobacco, snuff and tea!"[461] In 1856 he estimated that if Sabbatarian Adventists would donate their yearly expenses they had or used to have for the purchase of tea and tobacco, the amount "would be sufficient to sustain thirty Missionaries in new fields of labor."[462] In 1861 E. G. White stated that "those who use tobacco, tea and coffee should lay these idols aside, and put their cost into the treasury of the Lord."[463] One correspondent condemned the consumption of coffee because it was unhealthy and used "the Lord's money for that which at most only gratifies the taste without nourishing the body."[464] Evaluating the results of these agitations by 1863, D. T. Bourdeau optimistically said that "as far as organization and church order are adopted and carried out among us, tobacco and tea are being laid aside."[465]

---

458   Letter, Daniels to Smith, p. 110.
459   E. G. White, MS 1, 1854.
460   E. G. White, *SCEV*, p. 42 (*EW*, pp. 121, 122).
461   J. White, "Office," p. 13. Cf. M. B. Smith, "Tea," p. 6.
462   J. White, "Tobacco and Tea," *RH*, May 1, 1856, p. 24.
463   E. G. White, *TC*, No. 6, p. 20 (*T*, I, 222). Cf. J. White, *An Appeal to the Working Men and Women in the Ranks of Seventh-day Adventists*, 1872, pp. 94-97.
464   M. B. Smith, "Coffee," p. 142.
465   D. T. Bourdeau, "Tobacco and Tea," p. 125.

b. Health reform and the third angel's message (1863-74).

From the year 1863 onward more emphasis was placed on the necessity of healthful living habits. Gradually the term "health reform" was adopted by SDA to designate a variety of reforms which would lead to restoration as well as preservation of health. In its broadest sense health reform signified an intelligent understanding of the laws of life and nature, seen as divine laws, resulting in a series of reformations so individuals could enjoy the greatest measure of physical, mental, and spiritual health. Health reform principles were considered to have a biblical basis and to be a gift from God to humanity. A major reason for the growing pre-occupation with the importance of a healthy human organism for the religious experience of the individual could be traced back to E. G. White's visions on this subject in 1863 and 1865.[466] The successful acceptance of health reform among SDA resulted, according to Waggoner, from its integration into the third angel's message. In 1866 he stated that the principles of health reform "as mere physiological and hygienic truths" could be studied or laid aside as of no importance, but

> when placed on a level with the great truths of the third angel's message by the sanction and authority of God's Spirit, and so declared to be the means whereby a weak people may be made strong to overcome, and our diseased bodies cleansed and fitted for translation, then it comes to us as an essential part of *present truth*, to be received with the blessing of God, or rejected at our peril.[467]

One year later, E. G. White indicated the significance of health reform for ministers by saying that "one important part of their work is to faithfully present to the people the Health Reform, as it stands connected with the third angel's message, as part and parcel of the same work."[468] She stated further that "the Health Reform is a part of the third angel's message, and is just as closely connected with this message, as the arm and hand with the human body."[469] However, a warning was issued against making it the prominent message when she said that "the Health Reform is closely connected with the work of the third [angel's] message, yet it is not the message. Our preachers should teach the Health Reform, yet they should not make this the leading theme in the place of the message."[470] She added that "its place is among those subjects which set forth the preparatory work to meet the events brought to view by the message, among which it is prominent."[471] At the 1869 General Conference a resolution was passed stating

466 See e.g., Robinson, *Health Message*, pp. 75-171.
467 Waggoner, "Present Truth," p. 77.
468 E. G. White, *TC*, No. 11, p. 19 (*T*, I, 469, 470).
469 *Ibid.*, p. 41 (*T*, I, 486). In 1872 she said that "health reform is as closely connected with the third angel's message as the hand is united to the body" (*ibid.*, No. 21, p. 90 [*T*, III, 62]). Cf. *ibid.*, No. 22, p. 49 (*T*, III, 161).
470 *Ibid.*, No. 12, 1867, p. 85 (*T*, I, 559).
471 *Ibid.* She said: "We should take hold of every reform with zeal, yet should avoid giving the impression that we are vacillating, and subject to fanaticism" (*ibid.*).

228

"that we consider the Health Reform as an important auxiliary to the cause of present truth, and recommend to all our ministers to urge it to a proper extent upon the churches, and to endeavor to be examples to all in this respect."[472] In 1870 on the presupposition that "every real reform, which is calculated to improve man's present condition, and which has a bearing on his future happiness, is under the direct providence of God," J. White concluded that "the great cause of health reform is from Heaven."[473]

i. *The integration of health reform.* A basic principle in health reform indicated that transgression of the laws of the human organism was a moral issue, and thus sinful, so that transgression of these laws could be considered as transgression of God's law, the Decalogue. It was at this point that the integration of health reform into the third angel's message took place, because its central theme summoned the observance of God's commandments (Rev. 14:12). Therefore, health reform by calling people to obedience to the laws of nature supported obedience to God's commandments, an object similar to the mission of the third angel's message.

Various approaches were made to explain violation of the laws of the human organism as a sin. One approach was by evaluating disobedience to these laws through using the Decalogue as a criterion. One of the first to discuss the relation of health reform to the third angel's message in this context was D. T. Bourdeau. In 1867 he pointed out that

> the Health Reform has come to us as a part of the message; being based on the laws of our being, which are very comprehensive; growing out of the commandments of God and the faith of Jesus [Rev. 14:12], especially the sixth commandment; making it obligatory upon us to use all proper and available means within our reach to ameliorate and preserve our health and prolong our lives; making it a sin for us to be sick, if we knowingly and carelessly bring sickness upon ourselves by a violation of the laws of health.[474]

472 General Conference Report, *RH,* May 1869, p. 173.
473 J. White, "Health Reform," No. 1, *HR,* Nov. 1870, p. 90. He added that "though Jews, Turks, skeptics, Christians, or modern Judases, who would sell their Lord for money, may act a part in it, the reform, nevertheless, is of God" (*ibid.*).
474 D. T. Bourdeau, "Advantages of God's People . . . ," *RH,* Feb. 26, 1867, p. 134. Earlier he had said that "the sixth commandment, in particular, regulates our course with regard to preserving life and health. It is one of the negative precepts, and not only prohibits the sin of destroying our lives and the lives of others, but it includes the injunction of the contrary duty, viz. to make use of all proper and available means to ameliorate and preserve health, and prolong our existence and the existence of others" (*Sanctification, or Living Holiness,* 1864, p. 120). See *supra,* p. 224. Another connection between health reform and the third angel he found in the "patience of the saints" (Rev. 14:12): "We cannot have the patience of the saints without it [Health Reform], while we are constantly lessening our vitality, and abusing our nervous system by intemperance" ("Advantages," p. 134). Commenting on the relation between sin and sickness E. G. White said: "It is a sin to be sick; for all sickness is the result of transgression. Many are suffering in consequence of the transgression of their parents. They cannot be censured for their parents' sin; but it is nevertheless their duty to ascertain wherein their parents violated the laws of their being, which has entailed upon their offspring so miserable an inheritance; and wherein their parents' habits were wrong, they should change their course, and place themselves by correct habits in a better relation to health" ("Duty To Know Ourselves," *HR,* Aug. 1866, p. 2). She also stated that God required people "to obey natural law, to preserve physical health" (*TC,* No. 21, p. 92 [*T,* III, 63]).

Waggoner argued that the preservation of health was a moral duty. The sixth commandment of the Decalogue, he said, "as truly forbids injury to our own lives as to the lives of others," which meant that it could be interpreted as " 'Thou shalt not kill' *thyself*, as justly as, 'Thou shalt not kill' *thy neighbor*."[475] This led him to conclude that "*it is morally wrong*, according to the sixth commandment, *to do anything tending to abridge the lives either of ourselves or others*."[476] This approach with its emphasis on *physical killing* resulting from the violation of the laws of the body indicated a transgression of the Decalogue and formed a point of contact between health reform and the third angel's message.

Another approach evaluated disobedience to the laws of the human organism in the context of God's creatorship. It considered these laws divine, which meant that transgressing them was a sinful act. E. G. White pointed out that "God has formed laws which govern our constitutions, and these laws which he has placed in our being, are divine, and for every transgression there is affixed a penalty, which must sooner or later be realized."[477] This suggested that the law of God included both the moral law and the laws of the human organism. J. White interpreted the phrase "sin is the transgression of the law" (1 Jn. 3:4) as referring "particularly to the moral code, yet the transgression of law, moral or physical, established by our beneficent Creator to govern our actions, is sin."[478] This approach of designating divine status to the laws of the human organism also provided a point of contact between health reform and the third angel's message.

A third approach viewed the violation of the laws of nature by its consequences on the body. On the basis of E. G. White's description, the consequences can be designated as "soma-psycho-pneumatic" because each violation of the laws of health affected the physical, mental, and spiritual constitution of man. In 1864 her first extensive treatment on principles of healthful living was published, describing the "soma-psycho-pneumatic" consequences. The effect of the use of fermented wine on the body, she said, was that it impaired the mind, which in turn negatively affected spirituality. As an example she referred to the death of Nadab and Abihu (Lev. 10:1, 2), stating that they, by drinking wine, "beclouded their reasoning faculties, and so lost their sense of sacred things, that they thought they could as well offer common fire as sacred [Lev. 10:9, 10]. God did not excuse them because the brain was confused. Fire from his presence destroyed them in their sin."[479] Concerning the effects of tobacco, she said: "It is a slow poison. It affects the brain and benumbs the sensibilities, so that

475 Waggoner, "Moral Duty of Preserving Health," *HR*, Feb. 1872, p. 51.

476 *Ibid.*

477 E. G. White, "Parents Their Own Physicians," *HR*, Oct. 1866, p. 36 (*Counsels on Diet and Foods*, 1946, p. 19).

478 [J. White], "Redemption," *HR*, Dec. 1872, p. 371. In this setting an allusion was made to Mt. 1:21 about the redemptive work of Jesus, whose mission was "to save man *from*, not in, the transgression of law" (*ibid.*).

479 E. G. White, *SG*, IV, a, 125. The prohibition against alcoholic drinks in Lev. 10:9, 10 was seen as a direct consequence of the events in 10:1, 2.

the mind cannot clearly discern spiritual things, especially those truths which would have a tendency to correct this filthy indulgence. Those who use tobacco in any form are not clear before God."[480] In her opinion, people who "indulge a perverted appetite, do it to the injury of health and intellect. They cannot appreciate the value of spiritual things. Their sensibilities are blunted, and sin does not appear very sinful, and truth is not regarded of greater value than earthly treasure."[481] In 1866 she summarized her views, saying that "every violation of principle in eating and drinking, blunts the perceptive faculties, making it impossible for them to appreciate or place the right value upon eternal things."[482] Describing this "soma-psycho-pneumatic" process, she stated that

> in order to render to God perfect service, you want clear conceptions of his requirements. You should indulge in the use of the most simple food, prepared in the most simple manner, that the fine nerves of the brain be not weakened, benumbed nor paralyzed, making it impossible for you to discern sacred things, and to value the atonement, and the cleansing blood of Christ as of priceless worth.[483]

It should be no surprise that the conclusion was that if violation of the laws of the human organism would lessen one's spiritual discernment, it would also negatively affect one's obedience toward the moral law of God. Thus, E. G. White remarked that "men and women cannot violate natural law in the indulgence of depraved appetite, and lustful passions, and not violate the law of God."[484] Through the analysis of the "soma-psycho-pneumatic"

480 *Ibid.*, p. 126.

481 *Ibid.*, p. 129. She also remarked that if individuals "gratify a gross appetite and by so doing blunt their sensibilities, and becloud their perceptive faculties so that they cannot appreciate the exalted character of God, or delight in the study of his Word, they may be assured that God will not accept their unworthy offering any sooner than that of Cain" (*ibid.*, p. 148). For the relationship between appetite and sanctification, see D. T. Bourdeau, *Sanctification*, pp. 43-47.

482 E. G. White, "Duty," p. 3.

483 E. G. White, *TC*, No. 15, 1868, p. 34. Later the verb "use" replaced "indulge in the use of" (E. G. White, *T*, II, 46). Cf. Waggoner, " 'The Gospel of Health,' " *HR*, Sept. 1871, p. 80. For the relation between health reform and atonement, see also E. G. White, *TC*, No. 11, p. 43 (*T*, I, 488); *ibid.*, No. 18, 1870, pp. 15, 16 (*T*, II, 364). Due to the "soma-psycho-pneumatic" consequences of the violation of the laws of the human body, she stressed the necessity that "the animal part of our nature should never be left to govern the moral and intellectual" (*ibid.*, p. 16 [*T*, II, 364]. Cf. E. G. White, "Life and Mission of John," *RH*, Jan. 7, 1873, p. 26; *TC*, No. 11, p. 42 [*T*, I, 487]). In this context health reform provided for God's people insights so that they would not endanger their spirituality but would have "strength and clearness to discern the sacred chain of truth, and turn from the bewitching errors and pleasing fables that are flooding the world" (E. G. White, "Life and Mission of John," p. 26).

484 E. G. White, *TC*, No. 22, p. 49 (*T*, III, 161). One of the points of the platform of the Western Health Reform Institute stated that "the moral and physical natures of man are so intimately related that it is impossible to live in violation of either of these laws without doing violence to the other. Physical law, therefore, in its sphere, is as sacred and binding upon man as moral law" (Editorial, "Our Health Institute," *HR*, Feb. 1872, p. 48). Cf. E. G. White, "Duty," p. 3. Here she stated that "every needless transgression of the laws which God has established in our being, is virtually a violation of the law of God, and is as great a sin in the sight of Heaven as to break the ten commandments."

consequences another point of contact was established with God's law, which formed a part of the third angel's message.

The fact that there was an intimate relationship between the violation of the laws of the body and those of God's moral law was, according to E. G. White, one of the major reasons that God "permitted the light of health reform to shine upon us, that we may see our sin in violating the laws God has established in our being."[485] She also stressed the spiritual consequences of rejecting health reform by stating that "those who will not, after the light has come to them, eat and drink from principle, instead of being controlled by appetite, will not be tenacious in regard to being governed by principle in other things."[486] Such a rejection would result in the hardening of the heart with the possibility of losing salvation. She said: "Whoever turns from the light in one instance hardens his heart to disregard the light in other matters. Whoever violates moral obligations in the matter of eating and dressing, prepares the way to violate the claims of God in regard to eternal interests."[487] The above arguments were used to appeal for a total acceptance of health reform because it was a part of the third angel's message.

ii. *Eschatological aspects of health reform.* Some of the eschatological arguments for accepting health reform were similar to those used before 1863, but the fact that they were integrated into the third angel's message made them much more forceful. Their thrust was made in the context of a preparation for the difficult times ahead and Christ's return. In 1867 D. T. Bourdeau stated that health reform would prepare the people of God for the time of refreshing (Acts 3:19) or latter rain, the seven last plagues, and the time of trouble.[488] Similar arguments[489] were used by Loughborough, D. M. Canright,[490] and Stephen Pierce.[491] Health reform was seen as indispensable in maintaining a state of watchfulness for the "day of the Lord" (Lk. 21:34).[492] In commenting on a negligent attitude toward health reform E. G. White stated that "ministers and people must act in concert. God's

---

485   E. G. White, *TC*, No. 22, p. 49 (*T*, III, 161). She added that God "in love and pity to the race, causes the light to shine upon health reform. He publishes his law, and the penalty that will follow the transgression of it, that all may learn, and be careful to live in harmony with natural law."

486   E. G. White, "Duty," p. 3.

487   E. G. White, *TC*, No. 21, pp. 90, 91 (*T*, III, 63).

488   D. T. Bourdeau, "Advantages," p. 134.

489   Loughborough, "Report . . . ," *RH*, Aug. 14, 1866, p. 84; D. M. Canright, "The Three Messages of Rev. XIV, 6-13," *RH*, Jan. 1, 1867, p. 39; Pierce, "Eating Not of Faith," *RH*, March 12, 1867, p. 158.

490   Dudley M. Canright (1840-1919) was a minister, polemic writer and administrator. He was ordained to the SDA ministry in 1865. Later he renounced his church affiliation and became one of the foremost critics of the SDA.

491   Stephen Pierce (c. 1804-1883) was one of the early Sabbatarian Adventists who participated in the 1848 conferences. He functioned in the capacity of a minister, administrator, and corresponding editor of the *RH*.

492   John Matteson, "Godly Sorrow," *RH*, June 19, 1866, p. 21; Waggoner, " 'Gospel of Health,' " *HR*, Sept. 1871, p. 80.

people are not prepared for the loud cry of the third angel."[493]

The majority of arguments were focused on the Second Advent and especially the preparation for the moment when the mortal body would be translated into immortality. Obedience to health reform principles had a purifying influence on the body, and, according to Waggoner, was a means "whereby a weak people may be made strong to overcome, and our diseased bodies cleansed and fitted for translation."[494] E. G. White remarked that

> in order for the people of God to be fitted for translation, they must know themselves. They must understand in regard to their own physical frames, that they can, with the psalmist, exclaim, "I will praise Thee, for I am fearfully and wonderfully made" [Ps. 139:6]. They should ever have the appetite in subjection to the moral and intellectual organs. The body should be a servant to the mind, and not the mind to the body.[495]

The implication of obedience to principles of healthful living for sanctification and translation she expressed by stating that "if man will cherish the light that God in mercy gives him upon health reform, he may be sanctified through the truth, and fitted for immortality. If he disregards light, and lives in violation of natural law, he must pay the penalty."[496] In a similar context D. T. Bourdeau interpreted the wilderness experience of ancient Israel before entering into Canaan as a type of the experience of SDA before entering into the heavenly Canaan, stating that

> they [Israelites] must repent thoroughly of their sins, and reform. They must cleanse themselves physically as well as spiritually. And is God less particular now than he was then? Can we meet the Lord when he comes in the glory of the Father, and with all the holy angels, without cleansing ourselves of all filthiness of the flesh and spirit? without overcoming those habits that are injurious to both body and mind? Will God change the wrong habits of those who shall never taste of death, but shall be translated alive to the heavenly Canaan, without their co-operation?[497]

As a result of E. G. White's June 6, 1863 vision believers were encouraged to adopt a vegetarian diet.[498] In providing biblical support for this diet

---

493 E. G. White, *TC*, No. 11, p. 41 (*T*, I, 486).
494 Waggoner, "Present Truth," p. 77. Cf. Loughborough, "Report," p. 84.
495 E. G. White, *TC*, No. 11, p. 42 (*T*, I, 486, 487).
496 *Ibid.*, No. 22, p. 52 (*T*, III, 162). Cf. *ibid.*, No. 18, p. 33 (*T*, II, 375, 376).
497 D. T. Bourdeau, "Report from California," *RH*, Feb. 23, 1869, p. 69.
498 E. G. White, *SG*, IV, a, 153; E. G. White, "Questions and Answers," p. 260. For additional biblical arguments used to support vegetarianism, see E. G. White, *SG*, IV, a, 120-22; D. T. Bourdeau, "Health," No. 2, 3, *HR*, Sept. and Oct. 1866, pp. 25-27, 33-35; [J. White], "Bible Hygiene," *HR*, July, Aug. and Sept. 1871, pp. 17, 18, 48, 82, 83; Sept. 1872, pp. 274-76; "The Food of John the Baptist," *HR*, Sept. 1871, p. 83; [J. White], "Flesh as Food . . . ," *HR*, Jan. 1872, pp. 16-18; E. G. White, *Diet and Foods*, pp. 373-405. Cottrell interpreted the Mosaic law on clean and unclean animals as a divine criterion to indicate the healthfulness of food for human consumption. However, he felt that due to the fact that even the clean animals were not the healthiest kind of foods and that disease among animals was on the increase, the safest course would be to return to the antediluvian diet ("The Health Reform As

J. White pointed out that God's promise, "Behold, I make all things new" (Rev. 21:5), would be fulfilled in the restoration and restitution of this earth to the condition of Eden "before the fall," which implied a return to the vegetarian Edenic diet described in Gen. 1:29.[499] He remarked that pain, death, the killing of God's creatures, and the habit of eating meat were the result of sin and did not form a part of the original divine plan for mankind. Therefore, he made an appeal for vegetarianism by stating that "flesh-eating being of so doubtful origin, its continued practice, especially by those who look upon sin with abhorrence, and seek for purity and true holiness, may with propriety be called in question."[500] He added that "those who 'seek for glory, honor, immortality, eternal life' [Rom. 2:7], will wisely and safely come as near as possible in conformity to God's original plan when all creation was robed in spotless purity."[501]

iii. *Non-eschatological aspects of health reform.* After 1863, the non-apocalyptic thrust for health reform was on temperance. In 1865 Andrews observed that "we begin to understand not only that temperance is a Christian virtue, but also that it is the real foundation of good health."[502] The following year he described the SDA position as very unique: "As a people, we have undertaken to do what no other religious denomination, to my knowledge, has ever attempted. We have taken in hand the idea of Christian temperance as set forth in the Bible and endeavored to make it a practical matter throughout our whole body."[503] The major expositor on temperance was E. G. White who pointed to the duty of taking a stand against "intemperance of every kind."[504] The fall of man she used as an illustration of the consequences of an intemperate appetite. The hope for mankind, she said, was Christ's example, for "as Adam fell, through appetite, and lost blissful Eden, the children of Adam may, through Christ, overcome appetite, and through temperance in all things [1 Cor. 9:25] regain Eden."[505] The relation between intemperance and salvation she described by referring to the "soma-psycho-pneumatic" effects, stating that

---

Connected with the Third Angel's Message," *RH,* May 16, 1871, p. 173). Cf. the contrasting attitude on meat eating before 1863: [J. White], "Swine's Flesh," *PT,* Nov. 1850, pp. 87, 88; [J. White], "Swine Flesh," *RH,* May 23, 1854, p. 140. Cf. E. G. White, *TC,* No. 5, p. 20 (*T,* I, 206, 207).

499 [J. White], "Flesh As Food . . . ," *HR,* Aug. 1872, p. 242.

500 *Ibid.*

501 *Ibid.* Pierce remarked that "we are trying to bring ourselves back to the course of living practiced in Eden; in preparation for the heavenly Eden, where there will be no beasts slain for the gratification of carnivorous appetites; where the wolf shall dwell with the lamb, the leopard shall lie down with the kid, the calf and the young lion and the fatling together. Isa. xi, 6" ("Eating," p. 158).

502 Andrews, "How To Live," *RH,* Sept. 12, 1865, p. 116.

503 Andrews, "The Health Institute at Battle Creek," *RH,* Sept. 11, 1866, p. 120. He added: "Considering the difficulties of the undertaking, we have met with great success" (*ibid.*).

504 E. G. White, MS 1, 1863.

505 E. G. White, *TC,* No. 22, p. 50 (*T,* III, 161, 162). Cf. E. G. White, *SG,* IV, a, 120.

intemperate appetite had resulted in disease, weakening of the moral faculties, and an inability to "appreciate the sacred truth, the value of the atonement, which is essential to salvation."[506] The phrase "temperance in all things" became central in this thrust.[507] It signified to E. G. White temperance in the exercise of the passions and total abstinence from all "stimulating, hurtful indulgences," including excessive labor, drinking of tea and coffee, and use of meat.[508] In 1872 she connected temperance with the third angel's message and remarked that "temperance in all things is to be connected with the message, to turn the people of God from their idolatry, their gluttony, their extravagance in dress and other things."[509] Temperance was an important tool in the successful introduction of health reform. A major reason was, according to J. White, that E. G. White "appealed to the people upon the subject of Christian temperance from a Bible standpoint."[510]

Closely related to temperance was the argument of self-denial. It was associated with Christ's redemptive acts of self-denial in His incarnation[511] and His temptation in the wilderness.[512] Describing the importance of self-denial and temperance E. G. White said: "Providence has been leading the people of God out from the extravagant habits of the world, away from the indulgence of appetite and passion, upon the platform of self-denial and temperance in all things."[513]

Another thrust of arguments which motivated people to accept health reform was related to the various aspects of sanctification, such as perfection, the concept of *gloria Dei,* the bodily temple, being a living sacrifice, etc. E. G. White pointed out that the object of a health institute to be established by SDA should not be "only health, but perfection and the spirit of holiness, which cannot be attained to with diseased bodies and minds."[514]

506   E. G. White, *TC,* No. 14, 1868, p. 80 (*T,* I, 693, 694).
507   See e.g., E. G. White, *SG,* IV, a, 146; E. G. White, "Duty," p. 3; Pierce, "Eating," p. 158; Editorial, "Our Health Institute," p. 48; E. G. White, *TC,* No. 21, p. 91 (*T,* III, 63).
508   See e.g., E. G. White, *An Appeal to Mothers . . . ,* 1864; Letter, E. G. White to Morrell, No. 20, 1867; E. G. White, "Appeal to Mothers," "The Marriage Relation," "Obedience to the Law of God," "Female Modesty" and "Sentimentalism" in J. White, ed., *A Solemn Appeal Relative to Solitary Vice, and the Abuses and Excesses of the Marriage Relation,* 1870, pp. 49-80, 102-81 (E. G. White, *Child Guidance,* 1954, pp. 114, 115, 351, 444-46, 449, 450, 457-60, 462-68; E. G. White, *SM,* II, 420-40; E. G. White, *TC,* No. 18, pp. 139-88 [*T,* II, 448-83]).
509   *Ibid.,* No. 21, p. 90 (*T,* III, 62).
510   J. White, "Health Reform," No. 4, p. 152. However, the audience to whom she presented the subject consisted of "men and women who held the Bible as the highest and safest authority" (*ibid.*).
511   E. G. White, *SG,* IV, a, 149.
512   [J. White], "Redemption," p. 371; Jesus' first temptation in the wilderness was interpreted as of special significance for the relation between self-denial and health reform: "Man fell under the power of appetite. The Redeemer took hold of redemption just where the ruin occurred. In order to be better qualified to redeem man, sold in transgression of moral and physical law, the Redeemer subjected himself to a total fast of nearly six weeks at the time of the temptation in the wilderness. In this, he set his people an example of self-denial. . . . But what of the professed followers of Jesus Christ, who are really drunkards and gluttons?" (*ibid.*).
513   E. G. White, *TC,* No. 21, p. 91 (*T,* III, 63).
514   *Ibid.,* No. 12, p. 78 (*T,* I, 554).

She said that it was God who through His love permitted "light to shine, that man may see that, in order to live a perfect life, he must live in harmony with those natural laws which govern his being."[515] Thus it was of great importance that man should know "how to live, that his powers of body and mind may be exercised to the glory of God."[516] The concept of God's glory was explained both in the context of the body as a temple of God (1 Cor. 6:19, 20) and the one of 1 Cor. 10:31.[517] The argument of creation was used by E. G. White in appealing for bodily perfection. The fact that man was formed in God's image (Gen. 1:26, 27), she said, signified the "sacred duty . . . to keep that image in as perfect a state as possible."[518] From God's creatorship she inferred that He is the owner of the body, so that "we are in duty bound to become intelligent in regard to the best means of preserving the habitation he has given us from decay."[519] The preservation of the body as a sacrifice (Rom. 12:1) was also used to stress the necessity of bodily perfection.[520] According to E. G. White, this text had implications for salvation, for it indicated that man "can make the body unholy by sinful indulgences. If unholy, they are unfitted to be spiritual worshipers, and are not worthy of Heaven."[521] From the intimate relationship between religion and health, and the biblical appreciation for body, mind, and spirit, J. White concluded that "the sanctification of the Bible is nothing short of the sanctification of the entire man" while referring to 1 Thes. 5:23.[522] Although other biblical arguments were used, the above mentioned provided the major emphasis.[523]

In addition to these arguments the prospect of enjoying better health also motivated people to accept the principles of health reform.[524]

iv. *Mission and health reform.* The thrust of health reform was at first directed toward SDA themselves, of whom many suffered from ill health caused by the tensions and problems experienced during the Civil War period of 1861-65.[525] In 1866 an editorial in the *Review and Herald* stated

515 *Ibid.*, No. 22, p. 52 (*T*, III, 163).
516 *Ibid.*
517 For 1 Cor. 6:19, 20, see E. G. White, *SG*, IV, a, 126, 148. For 1 Cor. 10:31, see Waggoner, " 'Gospel of Health,' " *HR*, Sept. 1871, p. 80. On the body temple, see E. G. White, *SG*, IV, a, 148; E. G. White, *TC*, No. 21, p. 91 (*T*, III, 63).
518 E. G. White, *SG*, IV, a, 148.
519 E. G. White, *TC*, No. 21, p. 91 (*T*, III, 63).
520 E. G. White, *SG*, IV, a, 149; E. G. White, *TC*, No. 21, p. 91 (*T*, III, 63); *ibid.*, No. 22, p. 52 (*T*, III, 163).
521 *Ibid.*, pp. 51, 52 (*T*, III, 162).
522 J. White, "Health and Religion," *HR*, Feb. 1874, p. 34.
523 See e.g., 2 Cor. 7:1, E. G. White, *SG*, IV, a, 148; 1 Pet. 2:11, *ibid.*, p. 149; 1 Thes. 5:23, James 1:21, Pierce, "Eating," p. 158; 1 Cor. 9:24-27, E. G. White, *TC*, No. 15, p. 34 (*T*, II, 46); 1 Tim. 4:8, Waggoner, " 'Gospel of Health,' " *HR*, July 1871, p. 11, J. White, "Health and Religion," p. 34; 2 Cor. 6:16-18; 7:1, *ibid.*, J. White, "Health Reform," No. 1, p. 91; Heb. 10:22, J. White, "Health and Religion," p. 34; Rev. 7:14, [J. White], "Redemption," p. 372; Rev. 3:21, *ibid.*
524 See e.g., E. G. White, *TC*, No. 12, p. 77 (*T*, I, 554); [J. White], "Progress of the Cause," *HR*, Aug. 1873, p. 242.
525 Some of the major problems were the organization of the SDA Church, the costly

that because of the insights provided by "the great subject of health reform
. . . all will be enabled to adjust their labors to their physical capabilities,
and thus have the surest gurarantee against breaking down, and becoming
inefficient in the future."[526] E. G. White remarked that one important part
of the work of the ministry was to urge health reform connected with the
third angel's message "upon all who profess to believe the truth."[527] A
resolution of a similar nature was passed at the 1869 General Conference.[528] The introduction of health reform did not take place without opposition;[529] however, when J. White observed the behavior of SDA at
camp meetings from Maine to Kansas during the summer of 1870, he reported that "with hardly an exception they discarded flesh-meats, and partake of food but twice each day."[530]

E. G. White indicated that the mission of health reform was much
broader than to be confined only to SDA. In referring to intemperance she
stated that it was of "the greatest importance that mankind should not be
ignorant in regard to the consequences of excess."[531] Commenting on
health reform, J. White said that "the burden of our mission is to teach the
people how to live so that those who enjoy health may remain well, and that
those who are running down in health may return from wrong habits to
correct ones, and live."[532] He also called for "intelligent, big-hearted, devoted hygienic missionaries, who will assist us in our mission of sending rays
of light and truth everywhere, upon the great subject of how to live."[533]

Health reform was seen as a means which would prepare the ground for
the third angel's message. J. White remarked that it was "a sort of John [the]
Baptist to prepare the way for the greater light of the last message of
mercy."[534] E. G. White stated that "the great subject of health reform shall
be agitated, and the public mind deeply stirred to investigate, for it is
impossible for men and women, with all their sinful, health-destroying,
brain-enervating habits, to discern sacred truth."[535] The work of educating
people on the importance of "natural law, and urge the obedience of it" was
to be associated with the third angel's message.[536]

---

attempts to exempt believers from military service, the formulation of a position on war and
military service, and the function and credibility of E. G. White.

526 Editorial, "The New Volume," *RH*, June 5, 1866, p. 4.
527 E. G. White, *TC*, No. 11, p. 19 (*T*, I, 469, 470).
528 General Conference Report, *RH*, May 25, 1869, p. 173.
529 E. G. White, *TC*, No. 11, p. 43 (*T*, I, 487).
530 J. White, "Health Reform," No. 3, *HR*, Jan. 1871, p. 130. He denied the idea that
adoption of these dietary habits had anything to do with "a denominational law" and said that
"their church organization and discipline have nothing to do with regulating such domestic
matters as the kind of food to be eaten, and how often" (*ibid.*).
531 E. G. White, "Duty," p. 3. Cf. E. G. White, MS 1, 1863.
532 [J. White], "Progress of the Cause," *HR*, Aug. 1873, p. 242.
533 *Ibid.*, p. 243.
534 J. White, "Hygienic Book Fund," *RH*, Aug. 20, 1872, p. 77.
535 E. G. White, *TC*, No. 22, p. 51 (*T*, III, 162).
536 *Ibid.*, p. 50 (*T*, III, 161).

In 1866, as a direct result of E. G. White's December 25, 1865 vision,[537] the Western Health Reform Institute was established in Battle Creek, Michigan. Its functions were the treatment of disease and the teaching of health reform principles. An editorial in the *Review and Herald* stated that this institution was "a present necessity with our people, not only as a place where the sick can be treated, but where people may come and see the practical workings of the Reform, and learn more of its principles, and how to carry them out at their homes."[538] The institution was established especially for the benefit of SDA because it was felt that their faith and religious principles should not be endangered by the worldly atmosphere of secular institutions.[539] The health-reform educational program of the institution was seen to be of vital importance in the preparation of SDA for the final conflict which would culminate in the translation of God's people at the Second Advent.[540] E. G. White brought out that "this Institution is designed of God to be one of the greatest aids in preparing a people to be perfect before God."[541] The institution was also considered as an important aspect of the missionary thrust. When non-SDA would attend it, Loughborough remarked, they might also "become acquainted with the character and ways of our people, see a beauty in the religion of the Bible, and be led into the Lord's service."[542] He felt that even if people would never accept the truth, their favorable impression of the institute would make them defenders of the SDA cause.[543] E. G. White stated that if the institution were rightly conducted it "would be a means of bringing our views before many whom it would be impossible for us to reach by the common course of advocating the truth."[544] She further stated that

> as unbelievers shall resort to an institution devoted to the successful treatment of disease, and conducted by Sabbath-keeping physicians, they are brought directly under the influence of the truth. By becoming acquainted with Sabbath-keepers and our real faith, their prejudice is overcome, and they are favorably impressed. By thus being placed under the influence of truth, some will not only obtain relief from bodily infirmities, but their sin-sick souls will find a healing balm.[545]

E. G. White referred to this healing of "sin-sick souls" as "one of the great

537 *Ibid.*, No. 12, p. 76 (*T*, I, 553).
538 Editorial, "The Health-Reform Institute," *RH*, July 10, 1866, p. 48. Cf. E. G. White, *TC*, No. 12, p. 76 (*T*, I, 553). The editorial further stressed that "the Health Reform must be put in practice by us all" ("Health-Reform Institute," p. 48).
539 E. G. White, *TC*, No. 11, p. 47 (*T*, I, 490). Cf. *ibid.*, No. 14, p. 4 (*T*, I, 633).
540 Loughborough, "Report," p. 84. Cf. General Conference Committee, "Health Institute," *RH*, May 3, 1870, p. 160. This fact, according to Loughborough, was evidence that the establishment of such an institution was not a denial of faith in the imminence of the parousia, but rather a confirmation of the genuineness of their faith (Loughborough, "Report," p. 85).
541 E. G. White, *TC*, No. 22, p. 57 (*T*, III, 166).
542 Loughborough, "Report," p. 84.
543 *Ibid.*, p. 85. Cf. E. G. White, *TC*, No. 11, p. 51 (*T*, I, 493).
544 *Ibid.*, p. 50 (*T*, I, 492, 493).
545 *Ibid.* (*T*, I, 493).

objects of our Health Institute," and indicated that it was the function of health-reform education "to direct the sin-sick soul to the great Physician, the true healing fountain and arouse their attention to the necessity of reform from a religious standpoint, that they no longer violate the law of God by sinful indulgences."[546] In comparing this institution with secular institutions, she said that SDA managers

> do not labor selfishly for means alone; but for humanity's sake, and for Christ's sake. The managers of our Health Institute are seeking to benefit suffering humanity, to heal the diseased mind, as well as the suffering body, by directing invalids to Christ, the sinner's friend. They do not leave religion out of the question, but make God their trust and dependence. The sick are directed to Jesus.[547]

Therefore, as far as she was concerned, the missionary nature of the institution was clear: "The great object of receiving unbelievers into the institution is to lead them to embrace the truth."[548]

The qualifications for physicians engaged in the restoration of "sin-sick souls" were, according to E. G. White, that they should be able not only "to treat the body merely to cure disease, thus working from the popular physician's standpoint, but be spiritual fathers, to administer to minds diseased, and point the sin-sick soul to the never-failing remedy, the Saviour who died for them."[549] The spiritual and physical restoration of the paralytic by Jesus (Mt. 9:2-8; Mk. 2:3-14; Lk. 5:18-26) she used as biblical rationale to indicate that "physicians who would be successful in the treatment of disease, should know how to administer to a mind diseased."[550] Regarding the role of the physician, the 1872 platform of the Institute stated: "We recognize in nature the power to restore to health without the aid of medicines. The true Physician supplies conditions: Nature Cures." It added: "Our

546 *Ibid.*, No. 22, p. 64 (*T*, III, 170). In describing the process toward a total commitment to the principles of health reform Matteson said that the essential steps were, first, "to acknowledge your sin. Then to feel godly sorrow for sin, repent of sin, and turn away from it to Jesus. There, and there only, you can find help to truly reform. But when you get Jesus to help you, how easy everything goes. Then you will have the health reform connected and interwoven with your religion, and you will praise the Lord for his loving kindness also in this respect" ("Godly Sorrow," p. 21).

547 E. G. White, *TC*, No. 22, p. 87 (*T*, III, 184). From the viewpoint of the psychology of mission strategy she warned against the presentation of specific SDA doctrines to the patients. She said: "Our peculiar faith should not be discussed with patients. Their minds should not be unnecessarily excited upon subjects wherein we differ, unless they themselves desire it, and then great caution should be observed, not to agitate the mind by urging upon them our peculiar faith. The Health Institute is not the place to be forward to enter into discussion upon points of our faith wherein we differ with the religious world generally" (*ibid.*, p. 58 [*T*, III, 166]). She suggested that prayer meetings at the institution, where topics on general Bible themes should be discussed, would be a means to create mutual confidence and remove prejudice. This would result in a desire by the patients to attend also the church service. It was during the church service that the patients should have the opportunity to be exposed to the specific SDA doctrines (*ibid.*, pp. 59, 60 [*T*, III, 167]).

548 *Ibid.*, No. 12, p. 86 (*T*, I, 560).

549 *Ibid.*, No. 22, pp. 60, 61 (*T*, III, 168).

550 *Ibid.*, p. 62 (*T*, III, 169).

materia medica: Good food, pure air, pure, soft water, light, heat, exercise, proper clothing, rest, sleep, moral and social influence."[551]

As a criterion to evaluate the missionary effectiveness of the Institute, E. G. White employed the narrative of the ten lepers who were restored to health by Jesus while only one returned and glorified God (Lk. 17:11-19). In similar manner, she said, the efforts of the physicians of the institution would be treated by their patients. Nevertheless she stated that if

> one out of twenty makes a right use of the benefits received and appreciates the efforts in his behalf, the physicians should feel satisfied and grateful. If one life is saved in ten, and one soul is saved in the kingdom of God in one hundred, all connected with the Institute will be amply repaid for all their efforts.[552]

She added that if the work of the "King of glory, the Majesty of Heaven" for suffering humanity was appreciated by so few, "the physicians and helpers at the Institute should blush to complain if their feeble efforts are not appreciated by all and seem to be thrown away on some."[553]

The establishment of the Western Health Reform Institute, which took only several months,[554] was not considered as a denial of their faith in the soon return of Christ. Because much of the leadership suffered from ill health and spirituality of many believers needed much improvement, indicating that the imminence of the Second Advent had lost some of its momentum, the founding of the institution was seen as a means which would effectively aid the mission of the church and hasten the Second Advent. Thus D. T. Bourdeau pointed out that the Institute was "one of the strongest proofs that the Lord is near" because it functioned as a mighty agency in bringing about "a state of preparation" for Christ's return.[555] According to Loughborough, the Institute would provide SDA with an opportunity to learn in the "shortest possible time" how to apply the principles which would prepare them for a state of excellent health and for the Second Advent.[556]

Besides a health reform institution, SDA began publishing in 1866 a periodical named the *Health Reformer*. Its object was to educate people in the principles of health reform, especially those who did not have sufficient funds to attend the institution.[557] Later, the objectives were seen in a

551 "Our Health Institute," *HR*, Feb. 1872, p. 48. In reprints of this platform the term "physician" was used instead of "Physician." See e.g., R. T. Trall, *The Hygienic System*, 1872, p. 84.
552 E. G. White, *TC*, No. 22, p. 80 (*T*, III, 180). Cf. *ibid.*, No. 11, pp. 50, 51 (*T*, I, 493).
553 *Ibid.*, No. 22, p. 80 (*T*, III, 180).
554 In July 1866 a property was bought on which there was already a large building. Before this could be used it needed to be remodelled and furnished with equipment. It was estimated that the first patients could be accommodated in Aug. or Sept. of 1866. Cf. Loughborough, "Report," p. 85; E. G. White, *T*, VII, 1902, p. 97.
555 D. T. Bourdeau, "The Health Reform," *RH*, June 12, 1866, p. 12.
556 Loughborough, "Report," p. 85.
557 Cf. [H. S. Lay], "Items for the Month," *HR*, May 1867, p. 160; E. G. White, *TC*, No. 12, p. 76 (*T*, I, 553).

broader perspective when J. White stated that "its mission is to contribute to the improvement of mankind physically, mentally, and morally."[558]

The above philosophy on health reform formed the basis of a future world-wide system of sanitariums and hospitals which was to be considered as a powerful missionary tool to spread the third angel's message to mankind. The elaborate outlay of means in the establishment of many of these medical institutions, however, is at the same time evidence that the expectation of the soon coming Savior had lost some of its urgency.

7. Unity between the third angel's message and the Sabbath.

The SDA missionary thrust indicated that an inseparable connection between the third angel's message and the Sabbath was of vital importance. The central position of the Sabbath in the third angel's message has already been mentioned earlier.[559]

When in 1862 some had accepted the Sabbath and considered themselves SDA but rejected the current views on the third angel's message, E. G. White described them as being in a "dark position."[560] She strongly opposed the fact that any influence was given to these individuals, stating that they had "an independent faith of their own. Such are allowed to have influence when no place should be given to them, notwithstanding their pretensions to honesty."[561] Commenting that a connection between the third angel's message and the Sabbath lay at the foundation of the success of the SDA mission, E. G. White said: "Separate the Sabbath from the messages and it loses its power; but the Sabbath connected with the message of the third angel, has a power attending it which convicts unbelievers and infidels, and brings them out with strength to stand, to live, grow, and flourish in the Lord."[562] It was in this respect, she remarked, that the position of SDA on the Sabbath differed from that of Seventh Day Baptists.[563] In the light of the SDA theology of mission, therefore, the acceptance of the Sabbath also implied the acceptance of the eschatology of Rev. 14:9-12 as a necessary aspect for a successful missionary proclamation.

8. Relationship between the three angels' messages.

From the beginning Sabbatarian Adventists saw a close interrelationship between the three angels' messages. In 1850 E. G. White stressed the validity of the three angels' messages as a central part of their missionary

558 [J. White], "The Health Reformer," HR, Dec. 1873, p. 372. He remarked that the most important subjects of health reform education in the periodical were "how to recover health, and how to retain it" (ibid.).
559 See supra, pp. 140-42.
560 E. G. White, TC, No. 8, 1862, p. 29 (T, I, 326).
561 Ibid. Cf. [Smith], "A Good Move in Iowa," RH, Feb. 20, 1866, p. 94.
562 E. G. White, TC, No. 8, p. 43 (T, I, 337).
563 Ibid.

proclamation, indicating that "the burden of the message should be the first, second, and third angels' messages."[564] In 1852 J. White stated that a knowledge of the first and second angels' messages was a prerequisite for an understanding of the third angel's message and pointed out that "those who might embrace the third message without inquiring for the first and second, would not be likely to stand a very fierce storm of opposition against the truth."[565] During that same year, Andrews united the three angels' messages with the gospel by stating that they formed "a part of the gospel of Jesus Christ," and more specifically "the *closing* part of that 'great salvation.' "[566] In 1858 E. G. White described the three angels' messages in the context of salvation history.[567] She pointed out that it was the third angel's message that had made the 1844 experience relevant to Sabbatarian Adventists, and said that "the third angel has lighted up the past, present and future, and they know that God has indeed led them by his mysterious providence."[568] This message provided a major contribution to the explanation of the Disappointment. The three angels' messages were to her a "perfect chain of truth," "an anchor to hold the body," and "as individuals receive and understand them, they are shielded against the many delusions of Satan."[569] The messages she designated as a "firm platform," or a "solid, immovable platform,"[570] and remarked that those who were criticizing its foundation were fighting against God.[571] In this context she stressed that "the true understanding of these messages is of vital importance. The destiny of souls hangs upon the manner in which they are received."[572] The 1844 experience, E. G. White pointed out, had taught the necessity of the acceptance of the first two messages before the third could be comprehended, because

> those who rejected the first message could not be benefited by the second, and were not benefited by the midnight cry, which was to prepare them to enter with Jesus by faith into the Most Holy place of the heavenly Sanctuary. And by rejecting the two former messages, they can see no light in the third angel's message, which shows the way into the Most Holy place.[573]

Thus, it was obvious that the third angel's message could be fully comprehended only in the historical context of the proclamation of the first and second angels' messages in the 1844 Advent experience.

564 E. G. White, MS 11, 1850.
565 [J. White], "Babylon," *RH,* June 10, 1852, p. 20. Cf. J. White, "Third Angel's Message," p. 116.
566 Andrews, "Reply to Mary A. Seymour," *RH,* March 2, 1852, p. 101.
567 E. G. White, *SG,* I, 133-73.
568 *Ibid.,* p. 164.
569 *Ibid.,* pp. 165, 166.
570 *Ibid.,* p. 169. Cf. E. G. White, "Notes of Travel," *RH,* Nov. 27, 1883 (*Ev,* 1946, p. 223).
571 E. G. White, *SG,* I, 168-72.
572 *Ibid.,* p. 168.
573 *Ibid.,* p. 171.

D. The Ecclesiological Self-understanding.

During 1850-74, a number of ecclesiological motifs developed which became a part of the SDA theology of mission. These motifs were of paramount importance for the improvement of the spiritual climate for mission work and for the understanding of the self-image of the religious body, which called attention to its unique role in the history of the Christian church. As a result there was an increased dedication and self-consciousness of its missionary task toward other churches and the world. The two major categories of ecclesiological motifs that could be distinguished were eschatological motifs and typological motifs.

1. The eschatological motifs.

There were two categories of eschatological motifs: (1) The Remnant motif, which indicated the uniqueness of Sabbatarian Adventists as the remnant of God's people who continued to adhere to the major positions of the Advent movement; (2) the Laodicean motif, which succeeded the Philadelphian motif, and reflected the spirituality of the believers, contributed to an anti-triumphalistic dimension in ecclesiology, and created a spirit of self-investigation resulting in greater dedication toward missionary endeavor.

a. The Remnant motif.

The Sabbatarian Adventists designated themselves as "the remnant,"[574] "the remnant people of God,"[575] and "the remnant church."[576] It seems probable that they took the term "remnant" initially from Rev. 12:17,[577] though in many cases this text was not mentioned in the context.[578] Explaining the significance of "the remnant," J. White stated that they "must be the last end of the church; those who live in the last generation before Christ comes. Sabbath-keepers will understand it, when they are reviled, and called Jews, fools, fanatics, &c. The dragon is to make war on the remnant [Rev. 12:17]."[579] On the basis of this text he pointed out that the remnant were especially noted for the fact that "they teach the observance of the ten commandments, and the revival of the gifts, and acknowledge the gift of prophecy among them."[580] In a few instances the remnant concept was used

---

574 See *supra*, p. 147.
575 E.g., E. G. White, *SG*, II, 169. Cf. E. G. White, *TC*, No. 10, 1864, p. 47 (*T*, I, 439).
576 E.g., [J. White], "The Cause," *RH*, Oct. 24, 1854, p. 84; E. G. White, *TC*, No. 32, 1885, pp. 228, 229 (*T*, V, 1948, pp. 472, 473).
577 Cf. J. White, "TAM," p. 66 (*TAM*, p. 7); J. White, "Signs," p. 75 (*Signs*, pp. 114, 115); E. G. White, *CEV*, p. 54 (*EW*, p. 66).
578 E.g., E. G. White, *SCEV*, pp. 34, 35, 39, 40 (*EW*, pp. 114, 119); E. G. White, *SG*, I, 164, 173.
579 J. White, "Signs," p. 75 (*Signs*, p. 115).
580 J. White, *Life*, p. 326. See *supra*, pp. 194, 195.

with a different significance. When in 1850 E. G. White wrote that the "hand of the Lord is set to recover the remnant of his people [Is. 11:11],"[581] she apparently referred to saving the remnant of God's people outside the Sabbatarian Adventists. In regard to the success of this mission in terms of quantity she was not too optimistic, later (1870) pointing out that "a few, yes, only a few, of the vast number who people the earth, will be saved unto life eternal" while "the masses" would perish because of disobedience.[582]

The Remnant motif does not appear to have directly contributed to the growth of SDA missionary consciousness, but it surely did indirectly by providing a positive argument for their uniqueness in the history of salvation as God's faithful remnant participating indispensably in His final rescue mission.

b. The Laodicean motif.

After the 1844 experience, Sabbatarian Adventists identified themselves with the much desired character of the Philadelphian church,[583] other Adventists with the Laodicean church,[584] and non-Adventists with the Sardis church.[585] As time passed, however, it became increasingly apparent that the spiritual condition of Sabbatarian Adventists did not adequately resemble Philadelphian characteristics. In 1851 E. G. White brought out that "the remnant were not prepared for what is coming upon the earth. Stupidity, like lethargy, seemed to hang upon the minds of most of those who profess to believe that we are having the last message."[586] She also portrayed critically the lack of sacrifice for mission activities among those believers "who were not willing to dispose of this world's good to save perishing souls by sending them the truth, while Jesus stands before the Father, pleading his blood, his sufferings, and his death for them."[587] A self-critical attitude developed. In 1854 J. White ventured to say that "the reason why the work does not progress more rapidly is because so many who profess the truth are not real Bible Christians."[588] In another article he pointed to the failure to achieve "gospel order" as the reason for the lack of missionary progress, stating that

581   E. G. White, *CEV*, pp. 57, 61 (*EW*, pp. 70, 74).
582   E. G. White, *TC*, No. 18, p. 71 (*T*, II, 401, 402). Cf. *ibid.*, No. 17, p. 169 (*T*, II, 334); Smith, "Visions — Objections Answered," *RH*, June 19, 1866, p. 18 (*Visions*, p. 30). E. G. White later indicated that in the future these "few" may signify as many "in a day as there were on the day of Pentecost, after the disciples had received the Holy Spirit" ("The Need of Home Religion," *RH*, June 29, 1905, p. 8 [*Ev*, p. 692]). This reference was made in regard to mission among modern Jews. Cf. D. T. Bourdeau, "The Council at Bale, Suisse," *RH*, Nov. 10, 1885, p. 100 (E. G. White, *Ev*, p. 693).
583   See *supra*, p. 148. See e.g., J. White, "TAM," p. 68 (*TAM*, p. 14); [J. White], "The Seventh Month Movement," *AdR*, Sept. 1850, p. 64; Bates, *TAS*, pp. 13, 14.
584   See *supra*, p. 148. See e.g., E. G. White, MS 11, 1850; Bates, *TAS*, pp. 13, 14; Arnold, "Miller's Dream," p. 11.
585   See *supra*, p. 148. Bates, *TAS*, pp. 13, 14.
586   E. G. White, *SCEV*, pp. 39, 40 (*EW*, p. 119).
587   E. G. White, *CEV*, pp. 30, 31 (*EW*, p. 49).
588   [J. White], "The Angry Nations," *RH*, March 7, 1854, p. 53.

God will not suffer this holy cause to move faster than it moves right. . . . And he is waiting for his people to get right, and in gospel order, and hold the standard of piety high, before he adds many more to our numbers. . . . God will not intrust many souls to our watch-care, brethren, until we get into a position to lead them on in the path to eternal life.[589]

Smith agreed with the assertion that the believers themselves were responsible for the failure in mission work and said that only "when the people of God are prepared so that he [God] can, consistently, and without danger to themselves, manifest his power through them, there will be delay no longer."[590] The necessary preparation he saw in personal sanctification and holy living so that individuals could become instruments of the Holy Spirit.[591] In 1855 the attitude of Sabbatarian Adventists toward mission was of such a nature that it was compared with the experience of the people of Meroz who were cursed because of their sin of doing nothing (Judg. 5:23).[592]

In the face of declining spirituality and lethargic missionary endeavor, it seemed incongruous to continue styling the Sabbatarian Adventists the Philadelphian church. When in 1856 J. White brought out (possibly through the influence of his wife)[593] that the present condition of the believers was that of the Laodicean church of Rev. 3, it came as a surprise to many, but was readily conceded, only confirming as it did the current spiritual lethargy. However, this shift in ecclesiological self-understanding from a triumphalistic to an anti-triumphalistic attitude was immediately accepted and provided a powerful incentive to awaken believers to participate in missionary activity. J. White explained the hermeneutic for such interpretation by stating that

> it has been supposed that the Philadelphia church reached to the end. This we must regard as a mistake, as the seven churches in Asia represent seven distinct periods of the *true church,* and the Philadelphia is the sixth, and not the last state. The true church cannot be in two conditions at the same time, hence we are shut up to the faith that the Laodicean church represents the church of God at the present time.[594]

589   [J. White], "Gospel Order," *RH,* March 18, 1854, p. 76. Cf. E. G. White, *T,* VI, 1900, p. 371.

590   Smith, "Prepare Ye the Way of the Lord," *RH,* May 30, 1854, p. 148.

591   *Ibid.*

592   "The Sin of Doing Nothing," *RH,* Aug. 21, 1855, p. 32, quoted from "an old religious magazine."

593   It is not quite clear whether he was influenced through one of his wife's visions or that she confirmed his views. Cf. E. G. White, *TC,* No. 3, 1857, p. 1 (*T,* I, 141); *TC,* No. 5, p. 4 (*T,* I, 186). Already in 1853 there was a suggestion that Rev. 3:18 had relevance for believers (N. W. Rockwell to J. White, *RH,* Sept. 8, 1853, p. 71). In 1855 E. G. White pointed to the significance of Rev. 3:15, 16 (*TC,* [No. 1], 1855, p. 16 [*T,* I, 126]).

594   J. White, "The Seven Churches," *RH,* Oct. 16, 1856, p. 189. Cf. J. White, "Watchman, What of the Night?" *RH,* Oct. 9, 1856, p. 184. Regarding the "conditional promises to the Philadelphia church," he said that they were "yet to be fulfilled to that portion of that church who comply with the conditions, pass down through the Laodicean state, and overcome" ("Seven Churches," p. 189).

J. White further remarked that if the "nominal churches" and the organized "nominal Adventists" were characterized as cold, the only ones who would qualify to represent the lukewarm Laodicean church must be those who professed the third angel's message.[595] The name "Laodicea" was seen as timely and signified to him " 'the judging of the people,' or according to Cruden, 'a just people,' and fitly represents the present state of the church, in the great day of atonement, or judgment of the 'house of God' while the just and holy law of God is taken as a rule of life."[596]

From this time onward the tenor of the ecclesiological self-understanding was more anti-triumphalistic. Referring to the Laodicean spirit among the Sabbatarian Adventists J. White stated that

> our positions are fully sustained by an overwhelming amount of direct scriptural testimony. . . . but we, as a people, have evidently rested down upon a theory of truth, and have neglected to seek Bible humility, Bible patience, Bible self-denial, and Bible watchfulness, and sacrifice, Bible holiness, and the power and gifts of the Holy Ghost. . . . Hence it is said, "And knowest not that thou art wretched, and miserable, and poor, and blind, and naked [Rev. 3:17]." What a condition![597]

He also pointed out that the church had to be "stripped from self-righteous views and feelings" and had to experience a thorough repentance.[598] The current attitude he denounced as "hypocritical," for in living with the expectancy of the imminent Second Advent and God's judgments on those who disobeyed the third angel's message, "professed believers rush on in their worldly pursuits, taxing their entire energies in pursuit of this world as if there was no coming Jesus, no wrath of God to fall upon the shelterless, and no flaming Judgment-bar, where all deeds will receive a recompense."[599]

At this time a parallel was discovered between the third angel's message and the Laodicean message: The third angel's message was seen as the final message of mercy to "a rebellious world," and the Laodicean, as the final message to "a lukewarm church."[600] Waggoner stated that "the last warning to the world is the Third Angel's Message, and the last admonition to the church is the letter to the Laodiceans."[601]

595 J. White, "Watchman," p. 184.

596 J. White, "Seven Churches," p. 189. Cf. letter, E. Everts to the Brethren, *RH,* Jan. 1, 1857, p. 72; Snow, "Laodicean Church," p. 117.

597 J. White, "Seven Churches," p. 189.

598 J. White, "The Laodicean Church," *RH,* Nov. 13, 1856, p. 13.

599 *Ibid.* According to Stephen H. Haskell, there had probably never been a time that a theory of the third angel's message was better understood; yet, it was a well-known fact that there was a "very great, lukewarmness throughout the entire church. Pride, popularity, a worldly-mindedness, &c., &c., are in the ranks of the remnant" ("A Few Thoughts on the Philadelphia and Laodicean Churches," *RH,* Nov. 6, 1856, p. 6). Cf. E. G. White, *TC,* No. 3, p. 1 (*T,* I, 141). Here she said: "Worldly-mindedness, selfishness and covetousness, have been eating out the spirituality and life of God's people."

600 [Smith], "The Last Way-Marks," *RH,* Dec. 11, 1856, p. 44.

601 Letter, Waggoner to Smith, *RH,* Dec. 25, 1856, p. 61. See *supra,* p. 168.

Three years after its first presentation E. G. White observed that the Laodicean message had initially stirred the Sabbatarian Adventists everywhere and "nearly all believed that this message would end in the loud cry of the third angel" — a lofty hope which was not realized because, as the believers "failed to see the powerful work accomplished in a short time, many lost the effect of the message."[602] She pointed out that the message was "designed to arouse the people of God, to discover to them their backslidings, and lead to zealous repentance, that they might be favored with the presence of Jesus, and be fitted for the loud cry of the third angel," a process requiring individual character development over a certain period of time.[603] Nevertheless, even with the drawback from full acceptance of the Laodicean message some progress had been achieved in missionary activity. Were it not for "the hardness of their hearts," E. G. White said, the results could have been greater. Yet, she added, "the efforts made since the message has been given have been blessed of God, and many souls have been brought from error and darkness to rejoice in the truth."[604]

The Laodicean message, functioning as a criterion for self-evaluation, became an integral part of the SDA theology of mission and helped create a better climate for mission work after it was used quite indirectly as a basis for self-criticism. In 1867 E. G. White revealed "the startling fact that but a small portion of those who now profess the truth will be sanctified by it, and be saved."[605] This implied that only a remnant of the remnant church would gain the victory. One year later she remarked that "not one in twenty of those who have a good standing with Seventh-day Adventists . . . is living out the self-sacrificing principles of the word of God."[606] She called on all SDA to engage in the work for "the salvation of souls who are perishing."[607] According to her, it was the responsibility of "each member of the church" to come "to the help of the Lord [Judg. 5:23]"; and unless he would obey he would be subject to the curse on Meroz.[608] In 1871 she sharply criticized the lack of missionary progress by stating that "the efforts made in getting the truth before the people are not half as thorough and extensive as they should be. Not a fiftieth part is now being done that might be, in extending the truth by scattering publications on present truth, and in bringing

602 E. G. White, *TC*, No. 5, p. 4 (*T*, I, 186).

603 *Ibid.*, pp. 4, 5 (*T*, I, 186, 187).

604 *Ibid.* (*T*, I, 186). In 1857 J. White thought there were "several thousand" believers. The weekly *RH* had a circulation of "near two thousand" ("Cause," *RH*, July 23, 1857, p. 93).

605 E. G. White, *TC*, No. 13, p. 54 (*T*, I, 608). Cf. H. F. Davis, "Few That Be Saved," *RH*, Nov. 10, 1868, p. 235. In this context E. G. White referred to ancient Israel's wilderness experience during which nearly all of the adults perished (*TC*, No. 13, p. 54 [*T*, I, 609]). See *infra*, p. 250.

606 *Ibid.*, No. 14, p. 4 (*T*, I, 632). In 1874 she stated that "we were not doing one-twentieth part of the work that we should for the salvation of souls" ("Sacrifice," p. 1). Cf. Butler, "Nations," pp. 20, 21; Mary Martin, "Not Doing One-Twentieth of What We Might," *TrM*, March 1874, p. 24; E. G. White, "Tithes and Offerings," *RH*, Dec. 15, 1874, p. 195 (*T*, III, 407).

607 E. G. White, *TC*, No. 16, p. 64 (*T*, II, 165).

608 *Ibid.* (*T*, I, 166). See also *ibid.*, No. 17, p. 65 (*T*, II, 247); *infra*, p. 263.

friends, and all that can be induced, within the sound of the truth."[609] The continual self-criticism, which seems to grow in severity as the years passed, obviously indicated that the Laodicean spirit of lukewarmness continued to characterize the majority of SDA. In 1873 J. White concluded that "God has had those to lead out in this work who could forsee the wants of the cause, and suggest new and more extensive enterprises and missions. But the body of our people have ever been too slow to move out, which has increased their labors."[610] In the same year E. G. White declared that among the SDA "faith in the soon coming of Christ is waning. 'My Lord delayeth his coming [Mt. 24:48; Lk. 12:45]' is said not only in the heart, but expressed in words, and most decidedly in works. Stupidity in this watching time is sealing the senses of God's people as to the signs of the times."[611]

This anti-triumphalism in the Laodicean context has continued to be an important factor in the SDA theology of mission up till the present. It has not only improved the spiritual climate for mission work but has also provided a rationale for the delay of the parousia.

2. Typological motifs.

Several ecclesiological motifs in the category of "types" were employed to elucidate the past, present, and future experience of Sabbatarian Adventists. For example, the "Israel" motif, referring to the period between the Exodus experience and the entry into the promised land, was seen to typify the period between the Advent experience and Christ's return. The "Elijah" motif focused on the restoration of true worship in the context of a general apostasy, while specific motifs in the lives of John the Baptist, Noah, and Enoch were also seen as typifying the mission of Sabbatarian Adventists. All these motifs contributed to the missionary ecclesiology and helped substantiate the already unique self-image of this religious body.

a. The Israel motif.

Immediately after the Disappointment various Adventists saw in Israel's exodus from the bondage of Egypt a type of the final deliverance of the faithful Adventists.[612] In 1847 E. G. White designated those who observed the Sabbath as "the true Israel of God."[613] Three years later J. White indicated that after the deliverance from Egypt, God led Israel into the desert to test them for forty years (Deut. 8:2); "in like manner," White continued, "he called us from the bondage of the churches in 1844, and

---

609 *Ibid.*, No. 20, 1871, p. 117 (*T*, II, 655).
610 J. White, "Permanency of the Cause," *RH*, July 8, 1873, p. 28.
611 E. G. White, "The Laodicean Church," *RH*, Sept. 16, 1873, p. 109. Cf. E. G. White, "Sacrifice," p. 1.
612 Cf. Editorial, "The Midnight Cry," *WMC*, Dec. 11, 1844, p. 22; "J. B. Cook," *WMC*, Jan. 9 and 23, 1845, pp. 36, 41; Letter, Mary Fall to Jacobs, *DS*, April 1, 1845, p. 27; Letter, Minor to Jacobs, *DS*, May 20, 1845, p. 6.
613 Letter, E. G. White to Bates, *WLF*, p. 19. See *supra*, p. 148.

there humbled us, and has been proving us, and has been developing the hearts of his people, and seeing whether they would keep his commandments."[614] Others interpreted the Advent experience as an Exodus from the bondage of "spiritual Egypt"[615] or "antitypical Egypt."[616] In 1850 Edson explained that "by the proclamation of the hour of his judgment, the fall of Babylon and the midnight cry, he [God] brought them out of spiritual Egypt, into the wilderness of the people, and when we passed the midnight cry, our pillar of light was behind us [Ex. 13:21; 14:19]."[617] He added that just as the typical pillar of fire was darkness to the Egyptians but light to the Israelites, so the antitypical pillar of fire manifest in the events of 1844 was a "brilliant light" to Sabbatarian Adventists but darkness to their enemies.[618] Several years later, A. C. Bourdeau[619] interpreted the pillar of fire in the context of the progress of the SDA Church as God guiding "his people by his Spirit; and causes light to shine on their path just as they can bear it, and leads them in the truth, step by step, as fast as they are prepared to practice it."[620]

Mount Sinai suggested yet another typological relationship. Right after the Exodus Israel was confronted with the Sabbath commandment (Ex. 16:14, 28). Even so, Edson stated, "the first important truth brought to our minds after we came into the wilderness of the people, this side of '44, was the Sabbath truth."[621]

In 1867 A. C. Bourdeau alluded to a hygienic parallel. The Israelites in the wilderness were given "manna" to eat and the promise that, if they obeyed Him, God would keep them from the diseases that the Egyptians suffered (Ex. 15:26). SDA in their turn received the "health reform" message.[622] Bourdeau remarked that in both Exodus and Advent experiences God had not revealed the disappointing future. According to him, Israel would never have left Egypt in a rush if they had known about their forty years of wilderness wanderings. Similarly, he said that if the Adventists had known about the delay of Christ's return, "they would not have proclaimed the doctrines of the second advent with the spirit and power that they did."[623] Furthermore, he paralleled those who perished in the Exodus with

614 J. White, "TAM," p. 68 (*TAM*, p. 12). A. C. Bourdeau stated that as it was impossible for Israel to receive the necessary preparation for the entry into the promised land of Canaan by remaining in Egypt, so "God's honest people cannot get a preparation to enter the antitypical land of Canaan while they are bound by popular orthodoxy, or connected with fallen professors of Christianity" ("Our Present Position . . . ," *RH*, May 28, 1867, p. 278).
615 Edson, "Appeal," p. 4.
616 Letter, Lewis Bean to Smith, *RH*, May 29, 1856, p. 46.
617 Edson, "Appeal," p. 4.
618 *Ibid.*
619 Augustin C. Bourdeau (1834-1916), a former Baptist preacher, joined the Sabbatarian Adventists in 1847. For a number of years, he and his brother D. T. Bourdeau were pioneer missionaries among the French-speaking population of North America.
620 A. C. Bourdeau, "Present Position," p. 278.
621 Edson, "Appeal," p. 4. Cf. A. C. Bourdeau, "Present Position," p. 278.
622 *Ibid.*
623 *Ibid.*

"the mass of professors of Christianity" who rejected the Advent message in 1844, and likened those who died in the wilderness to the Adventists who refused the SDA explanation of the Disappointment.[624]

In the same year E. G. White illustrated the "startling fact" that only a few of the then living SDA would be saved, and warned that "but two of the adults of that vast army that left Egypt entered the land of Canaan. Their dead bodies were strewn in the wilderness because of their transgressions. Modern Israel are in greater danger of forgetting God and being led into idolatry than was God's ancient people."[625] In 1872 she again used typology to alert SDA to their danger. The Israelites, she said, "had great light and exalted privileges, yet they did not live up to the light or appreciate their privileges and their light became darkness, and they walked in the light of their own eyes instead of the counsel of God. The people of God in these last days are following the example of ancient Israel."[626] Identification of SDA as antitypical Israel could have led to a triumphalistic attitude, but increasing emphasis on ancient Israel's failures seemed to be a deterrent at the time. The self-critical dimension in this typology was used to improve the commitment of believers to greater missionary endeavor.

b. The Elijah motif.

Elijah's mission of restoration in a day of general apostasy was also seen to parallel the mission of Sabbatarian Adventists. As early as 1846 a reference was made to the restorative work of Elijah in the context of the Sabbath,[627] a theme Edson treated more fully in 1850 in a polemic against other Adventists. Referring to Mal. 4:5, "Behold I send you Elijah the prophet before the coming of the great and dreadful day of the Lord" and Jesus' statement in Mk. 4:5, "Elias truly shall first come and restore all things," Edson asserted that "the work of Elijah, in the last days, is to restore, to 'raise up the foundations of many generations' [Is. 58:12], repair the breach in the law of God, and to restore the true worship of the true God."[628] He continued: "Those who are engaged in this restoration, are the Elijah that was to immediately precede the second advent, the same as was John the Baptist

624 *Ibid.* The impatience of Israel which led to the creation of a golden calf while enduring the delay in Moses' descent from the mount (Ex. 32) was to Edson a type of the impatience of the majority of Adventists after the Disappointment: "They expected Jesus [the antitypical Moses] would then descend from heaven, but being disappointed, and impatient, many of them organized at the Albany conference, in 1845, and made to themselves leaders to go before them" ("Appeal," pp. 4, 5). (Brackets his.)

625 E. G. White, *TC*, No. 13, p. 54 (*T*, I, 609).

626 Letter, E. G. White to Lay, No. 1a, 1872.

627 See *supra*, p. 139. Immediately after the Disappointment reference was made to Elijah as being a type of the Advent movement (Letter, Clayton to Miller, Oct. 26, 1844; Editorial, "Elijah," *WMC*, Dec. 21, 1844, p. 27; "The Watching Time," *MW*, Jan. 30, 1845, p. 37). Cf. Letter, Minor to Pearson, *HI*, repr. in *DS*, April 15, 1845, p. 35. In 1843 a Second Advent periodical, *The Voice of Elijah!*, was published in Sherbrooke, Canada East.

628 Edson, "Appeal," p. 5. Cottrell remarked that Mal. 4:5 had "a primary, or incipient, fulfillment in the mission of John the Baptist" but added that contextual evidence showed that the text "must have a more striking and complete fulfillment just before" Christ's return ("Elijah the Prophet," *RH*, July 9, 1867, p. 49).

who went before Jesus, in the spirit and power of Elijah, at the first advent."[629] The three-and-a-half-year period of drought (Lk. 4:25) he interpreted as a type of the period after the Disappointment until 1848 when there was a spiritual famine among Adventists in general.[630] Commenting on the fact that after this drought Elijah emerged from his seclusion (1 Ki. 18:1), he said that "the word of the Lord contained in the sealing message of the third angel came to the true people of God, more clearly in 1848, after they had been hid in the wilderness of the people three and a half years."[631] In Ahab's reaction to Elijah's appearance, "Art thou he that troubleth Israel?" (1 Ki. 18:17), Edson saw a parallel with the reaction of other Adventists to the Sabbatarian Adventists' missionary activity among them and stated that "when we urge the keeping of all the commandments of God, we are charged with troubling Israel, and sowing discord, and of causing divisions, &c."[632] The climax of the battle for the restoration of true worship, when Elijah confronted the people with the crucial question "How long halt ye between two opinions? if the Lord be God, follow him, but if Baal, then follow him" (1 Ki. 18:21), Edson interpreted as the current (1850) confrontation between Sabbatarian and non-Sabbatarian Adventists over the crucial question of Sabbath versus Sunday as the true day of worship.[633] The rain which came down in answer to Elijah's prayer (1 Ki. 18:42-45) he regarded as "an example of the latter rain, the time of refreshing from the presence of the Lord, which will come upon the remnant, just at their entering the great day of the Lord, to prepare them to endure the time of trouble."[634] The final phase of the restoration theme occurred at Jezreel when confronted with Jezebel's death decree.[635] Elijah had to flee for his life to Horeb, the mount of God (1 Ki. 18:46; 19:1-8). Jezreel, Edson said, was a type of the Day of the Lord, and Jezebel's decree, a type of the death decree in Rev. 13:15. From these he concluded the antitype of the final conflict will be realized "in the great day of JEZREEL, or day of the Lord [Hos. 1:11]. As Elijah had to flee for his life, so also, all that will not worship the image [Rev. 13:15], . . ."[636]

629 Edson, "Appeal," p. 5. Cf. Cottrell, "I Can Do More Good," RH, May 29, 1856, p. 44.

630 Edson, "Appeal," p. 6. He remarked that "while Elijah was hid by Jordan, the people supposed he was dead. So also after '44, the funeral sermon of Millerism was preached, and many supposed that Millerism was dead" (ibid.).

631 Ibid.

632 Ibid. Cf. Cottrell, "Extract from 'Elijah the Tishbite,'" RH, Oct. 1, 1861, p. 141.

633 Edson, "Appeal," pp. 6, 7; Cf. Cottrell, "I Can Do More Good," p. 44.

634 Edson, "Appeal," p. 7.

635 In Jezebel he saw a symbol of the Roman Catholic Church which had killed "millions of Christians" (ibid., p. 6). Cf. Cottrell, "I Can Do More Good," p. 44; Cottrell, "Elijah the Prophet," p. 50. Jezebel was also associated with "the image of the beast" (Edson, "Appeal," p. 7).

636 Ibid. Cf. Cottrell, "Elijah the Prophet," p. 50. Elaborating on Elijah's flight, Cottrell said that "as it was with Elijah, so it will be with the remnant of God's people on the earth, those who are alive and remain to the coming of the Lord. After bearing a bold testimony for the truth — 'the commandments of God and the faith of Jesus' — their lives will be threatened by family and followers of 'that woman Jezebel.' In their extremity they may desire death rather than life; but as God had ordained that Elijah should not die, so he has decreed in respect to the remnant of his people. Jezebel's threat failed of execution; and the dogs ate her

They will find their only refuge on Mount Zion.[637]

In 1856 Cottrell used a somewhat similar argument to bring out the theme of restoration in the mission of Sabbatarian Adventists. His remarks were, however, placed in a broader and more general setting than Edson's. Stating with Edson that "the office of Elijah is to counteract the effects of apostasy, and restore the commandments of God," he added that the "antitypical Baal is the beast of Revelation, Paul's man of sin, and Daniel's little horn."[638] To Cottrell, the choice which Elijah offered the people was the same choice presented by the third angel's message under which people "are called upon to decide whether they will keep the Commandments of God, or those of the beast."[639] Several years later, Cottrell summarized his position. Drawing an analogy between the general apostasy of Elijah's day and the contemporary religious situation, he pointed out that "Elijah had a message for the people of his time, very similar to the third angel's message, which is addressed to the last generation of earth."[640] Alluding to the theme of restoration, he said that "those that heeded Elijah turned back from Baal to the commandments of God. So will those that heed the third message. Elijah restored the commandments to the true Israel; so will this message."[641] Furthermore, "Elijah was accused of troubling Israel; so are those accused that preach this last message."[642] And finally, influenced by the book *Elijah the Tishbite,*[643] he referred to an "analogy between Elijah in the time of drought and famine which had come according to his word, and the saints remaining on earth in the time of trouble, and while the seven last plagues are being poured out."[644]

In 1864 Canright suggested that the prediction in Mal. 4:5 regarding the coming of Elijah as "prophet" found its antitypical fulfillment in the remnant church which had the "gift of prophecy among them."[645] Referring to Elijah's ascension to heaven, he stated that "after warning a fallen church and a godless world of the wrath to come, the 'remnant' will be translated without tasting death. 1 Thess. iv, 15-17. So was Elijah."[646] In 1867 there

---

flesh by the wall of Jezreel. Thus will the unburied carcasses of the enemies of the Lord be devoured by beasts and birds in the day of the Lord. Jer. xvi, 4; Rev. xix, 17, 18; Eze. xxxix, 17" *(ibid.).*

637   Edson, "Appeal," p. 8. Cf. Cottrell, "Elijah the Prophet," p. 51.
638   Cottrell, "I Can Do More Good," p. 44.
639   *Ibid.*
640   Cottrell, " 'Elijah the Tishbite,' " p. 141.
641   *Ibid.* He added that "Elias must first come and *restore* all things" (Mt. 17:11).
642   *Ibid.*
643   See F. W. Krummacher, *Elijah the Tishbite,* English translation (London), 1836, American Tract Society ed., n.d.
644   Cottrell, " 'Elijah the Tishbite,' " p. 141.
645   Canright, "Elijah the Prophet," *RH,* Dec. 6, 1864, p. 9.
646   *Ibid.* Elijah's escape and subsequent translation were interpreted by Cottrell as "a feature which will be filled up in the history of that people who shall preach the last message of reform, that of the 'third angel,' before the coming of the great and dreadful day of the Lord, and who will be alive and remain unto the coming of the Lord. These will be translated as Elijah of old, and then the characteristics and history of Elijah will have met their antitype" ("Elijah the Prophet," p. 50). Cf. Editorial, "Elijah," p. 27; "Watching Time," p. 37.

appeared an extensive treatment of the subject by Cottrell, who combined the already existing arguments.[647]

E. G. White's first known use of the Elijah typology occurred in the context of the Advent proclamation by Miller. In 1858 she commented that "thousands were led to embrace the truth preached by Wm. Miller, and servants of God were raised up in the spirit and power of Elijah [Lk. 1:17] to proclaim the message."[648] The current interpetation of Mal. 4:5, 6 in relation to SDA she endorsed in 1872 when, discussing the importance of health reform, she remarked that "those who are to prepare the way for the second coming of Christ are represented by faithful Elijah, as John came in the spirit of Elijah to prepare the way for his first advent. The great subject of reform is to be agitated, and the public mind is to be stirred."[649]

More than any other ecclesiological motif, the Elijah theme brought out the mission of restoration — the specific burden of the third angel's message. As a result the Elijah motif became an integral part of the SDA theology of mission.

c. Other typological motifs.

Closely related to the Elijah motif is the "John the Baptist" theme. Christ had associated the work of the two men, and the fact that Sabbatarian Adventists considered themselves as preparing the world for the Second Advent inevitably led to an identification not only with Elijah, as we have seen, but also with John the Baptist, who was engaged in preparing the Jewish nation for the First Advent. In 1850 in the context of the Elijah motif Edson referred to a similarity between John's mission and that of Sabbatarian Adventists.[650] Later, in 1858, E. G. White drew a parallel between the mission of the Millerites and that of John, stating that "as John the Baptist heralded the first advent of Jesus, and prepared the way for his coming, so also, Wm. Miller and those who joined with him, proclaimed the second advent of the Son of God."[651] Several years later, she called attention to similarities between the mission of John the Baptist as a "reformer" preparing the way of the Lord and the mission of the SDA with the health-reform message preparing for Christ's return.[652] John, she said, "was a representative of those living in these last days to whom God has entrusted sacred truths to present before the people, to prepare the way for the second appearing of Christ."[653]

The SDA mission included more than preparation and reformation. It also announced the imminence of judgment, a theme which was brought

---

647   Cottrell, "Elijah the Prophet," pp. 49-51.
648   E. G. White, SG, I, 134.
649   E. G. White, TC, No. 21, pp. 89, 90 (T, III, 62).
650   Edson, "Appeal," p. 5. Cf. E. G. White, TC, No. 21, pp. 89, 90 (T, III, 62).
651   E. G. White, SG, I, 129, 130.
652   E. G. White, TC, No. 21, pp. 88, 89 (T, III, 61, 62). The instruction of the angel to Zacharias to give his son neither "wine nor strong drink" (Lk. 1:15) was interpreted as "a discourse upon health reform"; John's ascetic life style was also recommended (ibid.).
653   Ibid., p. 89 (T, III, 62).

out by means of the "Noah" motif. In 1872 E. G. White wrote that "as the preaching of Noah warned, tested, and proved the inhabitants of the world before the flood of waters destroyed them from off the face of the earth, so is the truth of God for these last days doing a similar work of warning, testing, and proving the world."[654]

Finally, there was the "Enoch" motif, based primarily on Gen. 5:24, "And Enoch walked with God: and he was not; for God took him." Commenting on this, a correspondent of the *Review and Herald* wrote that "the remnant in these last days must walk closely with God, if they ever expect to be translated as Enoch was."[655]

These motifs represent the early development of SDA missionary ecclesiology. They have been further developed and frequently employed in the framework of SDA mission until the present time.

3. The SDA Church as a missionary organization.

It has not been the purpose to write a detailed account of the organization of Sabbatarian Adventists into the SDA Church. This section will deal with only two aspects of the SDA self-image which are of direct relevance to the understanding of its missionary nature: Their name and the authority of the religious body.

a. The name "Seventh-day Adventists."

The first to use the name "Seventh-day Adventists" appear to have been their opponents. One of the earliest references to the name Seventh-day Adventists occurred in the *Advent Herald,* the main publication of the non-Sabbatarian Adventists, in 1847.[656] In 1853 the Seventh Day Baptist Central Association designated the Sabbatarian Adventists as the "Seventh-day Advent people."[657] Although during the 1850s the need for organization grew, there were theological obstacles regarding the adoption of a name and the formation of a legal organization which were only slowly overcome.[658]

There were some Sabbatarian Adventists who preferred to be called simply "Christians" or "disciples" because these names had apostolic connotations,[659] while others advocated the name "the Remnant" due to its biblical basis.[660] In 1860 J. White suggested "that we unanimously adopt the name *Church of God,* as a scriptural and appropriate name by which to be

---

654   *Ibid.,* No. 22, p. 124 (*T,* III, 207).

655   Letter, Hannah Clough to Dear Brother, *RH,* May 29, 1856, p. 47. Cf. [Smith], "Enoch's Testimony," *RH,* Jan. 8, 1857, p. 76. E. G. White, *SG,* III, 57, 59. For the antitypical significance of Enoch's holiness of life, his warning of the world, and his translation, see *ibid.,* pp. 54-59.

656   Editorial, "Advent Question," p. 133. See *supra,* p. 114, n. 78.

657   Letter, J. C. Rogers to J. White, in J. White, "Resolution of the Seventh-day Baptist Central Association," *RH,* Aug. 11, 1853, p. 52.

658   See *supra,* pp. 190, 206, 207.

659   Cottrell, "Making Us a Name," *RH,* May 29, 1860, p. 9.

660   Cf. J. White, " 'I Want the Review Discontinued,' " *RH,* Sept. 25, 1860, p. 148.

known."[661] At this time some believers in Michigan had named tnemselves the Church of God.[662] There was, however, no uniformity in the names chosen by the various independent communities of believers.[663] At the 1860 Battle Creek Conference of Sabbatarian Adventists the decision was made to adopt an official name. When the name "Church of God" was proposed, the objection was made that "that name was already in use by some denominations, and on this account, was indefinite, besides having to the world an appearance of presumption."[664] J. White made the suggestion that the name chosen "should be one which would be the least objectionable to the world at large."[665] Then the name "Seventh-day Adventists" was proposed as "a simple name and one expressive of our faith and position."[666] After discussion it was adopted by those present at the conference and recommended to the believers at large. In general it was well received, though a few communities opposed it.[667] E. G. White viewed it favorably as "a standing rebuke to the Protestant world,"[668] and commenting on its missionary significance she said that "the name Seventh-day Adventists carries the true features of our faith in front and will convict the inquiring mind. Like an arrow from the Lord's quiver it will wound the transgressor of God's law, and will lead to repentance toward God, and faith in our Lord Jesus Christ."[669]

b. The organization and its authority.

As had been realized in previous years, church order and unity were a necessity for effective operation and success in mission endeavors. The larger the religious body became, the more urgent the need was felt for unity and organization to prevent general confusion, and especially so during the Civil War.[670] Finally in 1863, having overcome the theological obstacles to organization, the SDA organized legally with the specific purpose of "securing unity and efficiency in labor and promoting the general

661 J. White, "Organization," *RH*, June 19, 1860, p. 36. As textual evidence he referred to Acts 20:28 ("Review Discontinued," p. 148). Cf. Letter, S. B. Craig, Jona. Lamson, J. B. Lamson to J. White, *RH*, Jan. 10, 1854, p. 207; Frisbie, "Church Order," p. 147; Frisbie, *Order of the Church of God*, 1859, p. 1.
662 Editorial, "A New Sect," *RH*, July 17, 1860, p. 72. See *supra*, p. 115, n. 81.
663 Battle Creek Conference Report, *RH*, Oct. 23, 1860, p. 179.
664 *Ibid.*
665 *Ibid.*
666 *Ibid.*
667 J. White, "Secession," *RH*, April 9, 1861, p. 164; Waggoner, "Meetings in Southern Iowa," *RH*, Aug. 6, 1861, p. 76; Cornell, "Meetings In Ohio," *RH*, Nov. 12, 1861, p. 190.
668 E. G. White, *TC*, No. 6, p. 23 (*T*, I, 223).
669 *Ibid.* (*T*, I, 224).
670 See e.g., E. G. White, "Communication from Sister White," *RH*, Aug. 27, 1861, pp. 101, 102; E. G. White, "The Cause in Northern Wisconsin," *RH*, May 6, 1862, p. 178; J. Clarke, "Stone of Stumbling," *RH*, Nov. 18, 1862, pp. 197, 198; E. G. White, *TC*, No. 7, 1862, p. 25 (*T*, I, 270). For some forces of disunity, see *ibid.*, No. 8, pp. 29, 30, 43 (*T*, I, 326, 327, 337); R. G. Davis, "Conscientious Cooperators," p. 67. Cf. Editorial, "To Correspondents," *RH*, Sept. 9, 1862, p. 118.

interest of the cause of present truth."[671] That same year for the first time the idea was brought forward among SDA that the church was "a missionary society" established by Christ and still under obligation to obey the Great Commision,[672] a motive widely advocated by other Christians at that time.[673]

A conference address[674] on organization was published as part of the 1863 General Conference Report. This address indicated two categories of church officers in the New Testament: "Those who hold their office by virtue of an especial call from God, and those selected by the church: the former embracing apostles and evangelists; and the latter elders, bishops, pastors, and deacons."[675] It was brought out that the office of apostle was not confined to the 12 apostles of Christ[676] and could not be restricted to New Testament times.[677] An apostle was seen as "one sent forth, a messenger," so that "anyone especially sent out of God in any age" leading out in "any new truth or reform" could be called an apostle.[678] An evangelist was described as "a preacher of the gospel, not fixed in any place, but traveling as a missionary to preach the gospel, and establish churches."[679] At this time any one in the first category was also called a minister.[680] Regarding the second category, it was pointed out that the names elder, bishop, and pastor are synonymous and denote an identical office.[681] This reduced the number of officers to be appointed by the individual churches to two: elders and deacons. As far as the respective responsibilities were concerned, the work of a deacon was to be confined "exclusively to the tem-

671   General Conference Report, *RH*, May 26, 1863, pp. 204, 205.

672   Snook, "The Great Missionary Society," *RH*, July 7, 1863, p. 46. Cf. Cottrell, "Proselytism," *RH*, July 3, 1866, p. 36; Cottrell, "The Gospel Is Free," *RH*, Jan. 20, 1874, p. 45.

673   Cf. R. Pierce Beaver, "Missionary Motivation through Three Centuries," in Brauer, *Reinterpretation in American Church History*, 1968, pp. 141, 142.

674   This address was first presented in behalf of the ministers of the Michigan Conference of SDA by Loughborough, Hull, and Cornell on the 1861 Battle Creek Conference. They were assisted by Smith ([J. White], "The Conference Address," *RH*, Oct. 15, 1861, p. 156).

675   Loughborough, Hull, and Cornell, "Conference Address," *RH*, Oct. 15, 1861, p. 156 (SDA, *Report of the General Conference of Seventh-day Adventists*, 1863, p. 10).

676   *Ibid.* (SDA, *Report*, p. 11). The argument was that Christ, Paul, and Barnabas were called apostles (Heb. 3:1; Acts 14:4, 14) and the Greek text designated also Epaphroditus, Titus, and others as apostles (Phil. 2:25; 2 Cor. 8:22, 23).

677   *Ibid.* One evidence was seen in Eph. 4:11-13 which suggested that "the office of apostles runs co-extensive with that of pastors and teachers, and other spiritual gifts, and is to last till the church, the body of Christ, all come into the unity of the faith" (*ibid.*).

678   *Ibid.* As examples were given the names of Luther, Melanchthon, and Miller.

679   *Ibid.* (SDA, *Report*, p. 12). Reference was made to Acts 21:8; Eph. 4:11; and 2 Tim. 4:5. The apostles and evangelists were the only officers qualified to organize churches (*ibid.*, p. 157 [SDA, *Report*, p. 14]).

680   Those who felt a call from God to become ministerial workers were advised to express their convictions before a Conference Committee. If they were considered qualified they would receive a license (General Conference Report, *RH*, May 26, 1863, p. 205 [SDA, *Report*, p. 8]). The Executive Committee of the General Conference had the "general supervision of all ministerial labor," functioned as a "missionary board," and had "the special supervision of all missionary labor" and "the power to decide where such labor is needed, and who shall go as missionaries" (*ibid.* [SDA, *Report*, p. 3]).

681   Loughborough, *et al.*, "Conference Address," p. 156 (SDA, *Report*, pp. 12, 13). Reference was made to Tit. 1:5, 7 and Acts 20:17, 18.

poral matters of the church; such, for instance, as taking charge of its finances, making preparation for the celebration of the ordinances, &c" while the work of the elder was "to take the lead and oversight of the church in spiritual things" and function as "chairman in all its business meetings."[682] Both the elder and the deacon were to be ordained by a minister.[683] The mutual relationship between the various offices was expressed by the following rule: "That no person by virtue of a lower office can fill a higher one; but any one filling a higher office, can by virtue of that office, act in any of the lower."[684]

In the newly organized church a distinction was made between the leadership and the laity in regard to the question of authority. Referring to church organizations, E. G. White pointed out (in association with Heb. 13:17, 1 Thes. 5:12, 13, and Mt. 18:15-18) that "there is no higher tribunal upon earth than the church of God. And if the members of the church will not submit to the decision of the church, and will not be counseled and advised by them [local and traveling elders], they cannot be helped."[685] A warning was given that "God has bestowed power on the church and the ministers of the church, and it is not a light matter to resist the authority and despise the judgment of God's ministers."[686] However, as far as the mission of the movement was concerned she stated that "the work does not depend alone upon the ministers. The church — the lay members — must feel their individual responsibility and be working members."[687] Regarding the subject of "new light" or "new truth," she suggested that, in order to prevent confusion and disunity, "no new views should be advocated by preachers or people upon their own responsibility. All new ideas should be thoroughly investigated and decided upon. If there is any weight in them they should be adopted by the body; if not, rejected."[688]

During the 1870s a discussion arose on the question of leadership. In 1873 J. White declared that "our General Conference is the highest author-

682 Ibid., p. 157 (SDA, Report, pp. 14-16). Cf. Frisbie, Church of God, p. 14. Although the offices of deacon and elder were different, he felt they were of equal importance (ibid.).
683 Loughborough, et al., "Conference Address," p. 157 (SDA, Report, p. 15). Textual evidence: Acts 6:6; Tit. 1:5 (ibid.).
684 Ibid. (SDA, Report, p. 14). It was added that "a deacon cannot by virtue of his deaconship, act as an elder, nor an elder as evangelist, nor an evangelist as an apostle; but an apostle can act as an evangelist, elder or deacon; an evangelist as an elder or deacon; and an elder as a deacon."
685 Letter, E. G. White to the Scotts, No. 5, 1863.
686 Ibid. In case the church should make a judgmental error, she said, "God could take hold of this matter in His own time and vindicate the right" (ibid.).
687 Letter, E. G. White to Edson and Emma White, No. 19b, 1874. For her concept of the laity, see also Letter, E. G. White to the Smiths, No. 25, 1874; E. G. White, MS 6, 1902; E. G. White, T, VIII, 1904, pp. 37, 99, 245, 246, 253; T, IX, 1909, pp. 86, 87. During the 19th century the lay character of American Protestantism was particularly marked (Latourette, Christianity, III, p. 13).
688 Letter, E. G. White to Sawyer, No. 8, 1863. She also said: "It is not in the order of God for one to feel at liberty to express his views independent of the body, another express his, and so on. If such a course should be taken we should not all speak the same things and with one mind glorify God" (ibid.).

ity with our people, and is designed to take charge of the entire work in this and all other countries."[689] In the same year Butler wrote an essay in which he developed the idea that the highest authority of the church should be invested in one individual, namely, J. White.[690] The reason for Butler's position was his desire, as president of the General Conference, to eliminate some problems in regard to responsibility which had arisen among SDA leaders and to improve the unity among them.[691] His view was fully endorsed by the General Conference of November, 1873. After a few weeks of reflection, however, J. White took a position against this concept of leadership. In the context of Christ's being the head of the church, he stressed the servant aspect of leadership and advocated the "true doctrine of the leadership of Christ and the equality of the ministerial brotherhood."[692] He reiterated his previous view that the General Conference is the highest authority of God on earth, and conceding that it could make mistakes, he urged that "in view of the authority Christ has invested in the church, and the tender care he has had for our cause, the only safe course for our ministers, and for our people, is to respect the decisions of our General Conference."[693] In the discussion J. White was supported by his wife. She wrote to Butler that "no man's judgment should be surrendered to the judgment of any one man. But when the judgment of the General Conference, which is the highest authority that God has upon the earth, is exercised, private independence and private judgment must not be maintained, but be surrendered."[694] Faced with such opposition to Butler's views, the General Conference reversed itself.[695]

Additional insight into SDA missionary ecclesiology was provided by E. G. White when she expounded the function of the SDA Church in the context of Christ's mission for the salvation of man. Stressing the importance of the organized church, she said that "the Son of God identified Himself with the office and authority of His organized church. His blessings were to come through the agencies he has ordained," and she

689 J. White, "Organization," RH, Aug. 5, 1873, p. 60.
690 Butler, Leadership, 1873. Cf. Butler, "Leadership," RH, Nov. 18, 1873, pp. 180, 181. He based his views on an analysis of Scripture and statements by E. G. White.
691 Letter, Butler to C. C. Crisler, Sept. 25, 1914.
692 J. White, "Leadership," RH, Dec. 1, 1874, p. 180 ("Leadership," in E. G. White, TC, No. 25, p. 187). Cf. J. White, "Leadership," ST, June 4-July 9, 1874, pp. 4, 5, 12, 20, 28.
693 J. White, "Leadership," in E. G. White, TC, No. 25, p. 192.
694 Ibid., p. 43 (T, III, 492). This she seems to interpret in the context of the General Conference in session when "the judgment of the brethren assembled from all parts of the field is exercised" (T, IX, 260).
695 The 1875 General Conference passed a resolution to revise Butler's essay (General Conference Report, RH, Aug. 26, 1875, p. 59). At the 1877 General Conference it was decided to rescind all portions of the essay which taught that the leadership of the church was to be confined to any one man. This was followed by a resolution which stated that "the highest authority under God among Seventh-day Adventists is found in the will of the body of that people, as expressed in the decisions of the General Conference when acting within its proper jurisdiction; and that such decisions should be submitted to by all without exception, unless they can be shown to conflict with the word of God and the rights of individual conscience" (General Conference Report, RH, Oct. 4, 1877, p. 106).

added, "the Redeemer of the world does not sanction the experience and exercises in religious matters independent of his organized and acknowledged church, where he has a church."[696] The biblical principles for this view she found in the conversion experience of Saul in Acts 9. The fact that after his encounter with Jesus on the road to Damascus Saul was brought in contact with the Christian church in that city she interpreted as follows:

> He [Jesus] directs Saul to the church thus, acknowledging the power he has placed upon the church as a channel of light to the world. It is Christ's organized body upon the earth and respect was required to be paid to his ordinances. Ananias represents Christ in the case of Saul. He also represents Christ's ministers upon the earth who are appointed to act in Christ's stead.[697]

With this ecclesiological self-image the SDA Church saw itself in a highly responsible position in the history of salvation. It was cautioned by E. G. White, however, that the spiritual heritage the SDA had received from the Christian church of history should be highly appreciated. She remarked, "God's workers to-day constitute the connecting link between the former workers, the church of history, and the church that is to be called out from the world and prepared to meet their Lord," adding that "all the excellencies that have come through the belief of the truth, from past ages to the present time, are to be treated with the utmost respect."[698]

E. The Mission of God.

The concept that mission is the very work of God, not of man, — the *missio Dei* —, had strong roots in the New England Puritan tradition.[699] Among Sabbatarian Adventists it functioned especially in an eschatological setting. In 1850, commenting on the successful progress of their message since 1848,[700] J. White explained it to be a realization of God's activity as pictured in Ezek. 34: "God has promised to gather his flock that have been scattered in this dark and cloudy day [Ezek. 34:12], since 1844." It was his conviction that "before Jesus comes, the 'little flock' will be gathered into 'the unity of the faith.' Jesus is now purifying 'unto himself a peculiar

---

696 Letter, E. G. White to Charles Lee, No. 54, 1874 (*T*, III, 432, 433). She added that Christ "has all power both in heaven and upon earth, but he respects the means he has ordained for the enlightenment and salvation of men" (*ibid.* [*T*, III, 433]).

697 *Ibid.* Furthermore, she stated that "Saul was a learned teacher in Israel but while under the influence of blind error and prejudice, Christ reveals Himself to him and then places Saul in communication with His church, who are the light of the world. They were to instruct this educated popular orator in the Christian religion. In Christ's stead, Ananias touches his eyes that they may receive sight. In Christ's stead he lays his hands upon him praying in Christ's name, Saul receives the Holy Ghost. All is done in the name and authority of Christ. Christ is the fountain; the church is the channel of communication" (*ibid.*).

698 E. G. White, MS 1, 1874 (*SpT*, [Series A], No. 7, 1897, p. 11).

699 Cf. Beaver, "American Missionary Motivation before the Revolution," *Church History*, XXXI (June 1962), 218.

700 See *supra*, p. 143.

people, zealous of good works' [Titus 2:14]."[701] Regarding God's current mission E. G. White remarked that the Lord "had stretched out his hand the second time to recover the remnant of his people [Is. 11:11],"[702] — a "quick work" which "would soon be cut short in righteousness."[703]

The *missio Dei* was frequently equated with the providence of God. J. White was convinced that Providence was opening a way to present "the truth" to people, and urged that "the church should keep pace with the opening providence of God."[704] E. G. White, however, warned not to move faster than "the unmistakable providence of God opens the way."[705] She also indicated the great need for individuals with "energy equal to the opening providence of God"[706] and said that "if we would follow the opening providence of God, we should be quick to discern every opening, and make the most of every advantage within our reach, to let the light extend and spread to other nations."[707]

The manner in which God influenced non-Adventists was described in various ways. J. White attributed their growing interest in his message to the fact that "the Spirit of God is moving upon many to investigate."[708] Bates used the phrase, "the Lord wrought for Israel."[709] In 1857 E. G. White pointed out that God's providence had a definite direction depending on time and circumstances. The fact that certain geographical areas in the U.S.A. were more responsive to "the present truth" than others, she felt, was the result of the activity of "the angels of God," who were preparing individuals to be receptive.[710] Thus, from the viewpoint of church growth, it was important that "special efforts should be made at the present time where most good can be accomplished."[711] Later the work of angels in the *missio Dei* was described more specifically in an eschatological context. She stated that angels were "moving on the hearts and consciences" of people in various places with the result that "honest souls are troubled as they witness the signs of the times in the unsettled state of the nations. The inquiry arises in their hearts, What will be the end of all these things?"[712] At

---

701   J. White, "Miller's Dream," p. 75 (*Miller's Dream*, pp. 9, 10). Cf. Andrews, "Brethren and Sisters," p. 39.

702   E. G. White, *CEV*, p. 61 (*EW*, p. 74). Cf. E. G. White, *SCEV*, p. 4 (*EW*, p. 86). To Edson the Exodus experience of ancient Israel was a type of the Exodus referred to in Is. 11:11. The Lord was the leader in the antitypical Exodus "out of spiritual Egypt" ("Appeal," p. 4).

703   E. G. White, *CEV*, p. 31 (*EW*, p. 50).

704   [J. White], "The Cause," *RH*, Oct. 24, 1854, p. 84. Cf. E. G. White, *TC*, No. 10, p. 29 (*T*, I, 420); *ibid.*, No. 21, p. 11 (*T*, III, 14).

705   *Ibid.*, No. 12, p. 86 (*T*, I, 560).

706   E. G. White, *TC*, No. 21, p. 25 (*T*, III, 23).

707   E. G. White, "Sacrifice," pp. 1, 2 (*Ev*, p. 62).

708   [J. White], "Laborers," *RH*, Feb. 3, 1853, p. 149.

709   Letter, Bates to J. White, *RH*, March 14, 1854, p. 63.

710   E. G. White, *TC*, No. 3, p. 10 (*T*, I, 148, 149). Cf. J. White, "Third Angel's Message," p. 141.

711   E. G. White, *TC*, No. 3, p. 8 (*T*, I, 147). Cf. J. White, "Third Angel's Message," p. 141.

712   E. G. White, *TC*, No. 22, p. 115 (*T*, III, 202). Cf. E. G. White, *Ed*, pp. 179, 180.

this point these people seemed to be ready for the proclamation of "the present truth," though it was stressed that only the grace of God could convict the heart.[713] When some wealthy persons joined the Sabbatarian Adventists E. G. White interpreted it as the result of God's mission so that their financial resources would assist the advancing mission of the church.[714] The centripetal dynamic of the mission of God was also perceived when individuals of other nations came under the "influence of the truth."[715]

Often the result of divine activity was a Macedonian call, "Come over . . . and help us" (Acts 16:9),[716] a response long appreciated in the New England Puritan tradition.[717] Frequent calls from individuals interested in "present truth" led to the conclusion that the harvest was great (Lk. 10:2; Mt. 9:37),[718] the fields "already white to harvest" (Jn. 4:35),[719] but the "laborers were few" (Lk. 10:2; Mt. 9:37, 38).[720] The Adventist leadership found a basis here for persuading believers to enter into mission service. The idea of a great harvest did not contradict the concept that only a remnant would be saved, for it was generally understood that the majority of God's people were still outside the remnant church.[721]

The *missio Dei* concept included as participants both angels and men, whose mutual relation E. G. White expressed as follows: "Angels of God have charge of the work, and they counsel and direct God's people through chosen agents, and thus the work moves forward."[722] It was added that "simple instruments" would be chosen "to carry forward this great work, but they only carry out the mind and will of the great Master at the head of the work."[723] Besides being God's instruments she stated that "those who are engaged in the work of saving souls, are co-workers with Christ."[724]

713 E. G. White, *TC*, No. 22, p. 128 (*T*, III, 210). Cf. E. G. White, "Sacrifice," p. 2.
714 E. G. White, *TC*, No. 4, 1857, pp. 25, 29 (*T*, I, 174, 177).
715 *Ibid.*, No. 22, p. 121 (*T*, III, 205).
716 See e.g., [J. White], "The Review and Herald," *RH*, March 2, 1852, p. 104; [J. White], "The Faith of Jesus," *RH*, Aug. 19, 1852, p. 61; Holt, "Pultney Conference," *RH*, Sept. 16, 1852, p. 80; Letter, M. G. Kellogg, *RH*, March 3, 1853, p. 168; Letter, Loughborough to Editor, *RH*, Jan. 31, 1854, p. 16; Letter, Bates to J. White, *RH*, March 14, 1854, p. 63; E. G. White, "Offerings," p. 195 (*T*, III, 404).
717 Cf. Beaver, "American Missionary Motivation," p. 219.
718 See e.g., [J. White], "Cause," *RH*, Oct. 24, 1854, p. 84; [Smith], "Calls for Help," *RH*, March 6, 1856, p. 180; E. G. White, *TC*, No. 9, 1863, p. 13 (*T*, I, 368). E. G. White said: "The harvest of the earth is nearly ripe" (*ibid.*, No. 7, p. 13 [*T*, I, 261]).
719 See e.g., [J. White], "Dangers to Which the Remnant Are Exposed," *RH*, March 3, 1853, p. 164; J. White, "New Fields," *RH*, Oct. 6, 1859, p. 156; E. G. White, "Offerings," p. 195 (*T*, III, 408); E. G. White, *T*, VII, p. 98.
720 See e.g., [J. White], "Cause," *RH*, Oct. 24, 1854, p. 84; [Smith], "Calls for Help," p. 180; E. G. White, *TC*, No. 9, p. 13 (*T*, I, 368).
721 Up until 1874 there were relatively few SDA in comparison with the 144,000 which were expected to make up the number of the remnant church at the time of the Second Advent. For membership statistics, see *infra*, p. 285, n. 107.
722 E. G. White, *SG*, II, 282.
723 E. G. White, MS 4, 1866. Cf. E. G. White, *SG*, II, 283; Haskell, "By My Spirit, Saith the Lord," *RH*, Dec. 23, 1873, pp. 12, 13.
724 E. G. White, *TC*, No. 10, p. 40 (*T*, I, 431). Cf. *ibid.*, No. 22, p. 129 (*T*, III, 210); E. G. White, MS 19, 1910 (*Ev*, p. 67).

Already during the Great Awakening the concept of cooperation had been advocated by Jonathan Edwards.[725] According to E. G. White, the goal of divine-human cooperation was primarily that of satisfying man's basic need for happiness, character development, and God-like-ness.[726] Among the ways in which man may cooperate in God's mission were these: (1) Follow the providence of God and respond to the "Macedonian cry";[727] (2) carry out God's will and work in "unison with Christ" for the salvation of others;[728] (3) avoid interfering with the advancement of God's mission by inactivity or lack of faith;[729] (4) engage in acts of benevolence and self-denial, and contribute tithes and offerings to assist in the work of salvation.[730]

Regarding the success of this cooperation J. White promised that "the Lord of the harvest will take care of the results, if his servants do their duty."[731] He pointed out that it was the Lord who converted individuals,[732] added them to the church (Acts 2:47),[733] and established churches.[734] E. G. White stated: "The seed of truth we must sow, and trust in God to quicken it to life."[735]

The concept of divine-human cooperation seemed to imply the self-limitation of the Omnipotent in the salvation of man. E. G. White indicated that God "could send means from heaven to carry on his work; but this is out of his order. He has ordained that men should be his instruments."[736] This placed a tremendous responsibility on SDA, one which at first they did

---

725   Cf. Beaver, "American Missionary Motivation," p. 220; Beaver, "Missionary Motivation," pp. 121, 124.

726   E. G. White, "Tithes and Offerings," *RH*, Aug. 25, 1874, pp. 73, 74 (*T*, III, 382, 383, 390, 391). To her the philosophy of cooperation was based on "the law of action and reaction." This law she explained as follows: "God could have reached his object in saving sinners without the aid of man; but he knew that he could not be happy without acting a part in the great work in which he should be cultivating self-denial and benevolence. That man might not lose the blessed results of benevolence, our Redeemer formed the plan of enlisting him as his co-worker. By a chain of circumstances which would call forth his charities, he brings man under the best means of cultivating benevolence, and keeps him habitually giving to help the poor, and to advance his cause. He sends his poor as the representatives of himself. A ruined world is drawing forth from us by their necessities talents of means and of influence to present to them the truth, of which they are in perishing need. And as we heed these calls, by labor and acts of benevolence, we are assimilated into the image of him who for our sakes became poor. In bestowing, we bless others, and thus accumulate the true riches" (*ibid.*, p. 73 [*T*, III, 282, 283]).

727   [J. White], "Cause," *RH*, Oct. 24, 1854, p. 84. See *supra*, p. 261.

728   E. G. White, *SG*, II, 283; E. G. White, "The Work for This Time," *TrM*, Feb. 1874, p. 9.

729   E. G. White, "Offerings," p. 74 (*T*, III, 389); E. G. White, *TC*, No. 22, p. 127 (*T*, III, 209).

730   E. G. White, "Offerings," pp. 73, 74 (*T*, III, 382, 383, 390-92, 396).

731   J. White, "New Fields," p. 156. Their mission was in the context of Joel 2:1, Is. 58:1. E. G. White said: "We are to do our work, leaving the result with God" (*TC*, No. 22, p. 188 [*T*, III, 248]).

732   [J. White], "Who May Hear the Truth?" *RH*, Feb. 17, 1852, p. 94.

733   [J. White], "Our Tour West," *RH*, Feb. 17, 1852, p. 94. Cf. Frisbie, "Church Order," p. 147; E. G. White, *T*, IX, 110.

734   [J. White], "Truth," p. 94.

735   E. G. White, *TC*, No. 22, p. 188 (*T*, III, 210).

736   *Ibid.*, No. 4, pp. 25, 26 (*T*, I, 174).

not seem to grasp: "Sinners, who are perishing for lack of knowledge, must be left in ignorance and darkness, unless men shall carry to them the light of truth. God will not send angels from Heaven to do the work which he has left for man."[737]

Non-participation in the *missio Dei* was looked upon as a grievous neglect comparable with the sin of Meroz (Judg. 5:23).[738] "A bitter curse," said E. G. White, "is pronounced on those [church members] who come not up to the help of the Lord."[739] She explained the reason: "What had Meroz done? Nothing. And this was their sin. They came not up to the help of the Lord against the mighty."[740] Their responsibility as co-workers with God in the salvation of man and the threat of the curse of Meroz were factors in motivating SDA to engage in mission.

F. Non-Apocalyptic Dimensions.

During the period 1850-74 there was a gradual emergence of non-apocalyptic dimensions in the SDA theology of mission, most of which had roots in Protestant mission traditions in the U.S.A.[741] Among SDA the greatest contribution to these motives for mission came from E. G. White. The classification of the following motives was determined by the thrust of the primary source material. In certain instances it was impossible to avoid some overlapping because of the close relationships among the various categories.

1. The Imitatio Christi.

The concept of Christlikeness was especially used by E. G. White as a motive for mission. She frequently appealed "to all who profess to believe the truth, to consider the character and life of the Son of God. He is our example. His life was marked with disinterested benevolence. He was ever touched with human woe. He went about doing good. There was not one selfish act in all his life."[742] It was her deepest desire that SDA should study

737 E. G. White, "Offerings," p. 74 (*T*, III, 391). Here she added that God "has given all a work to do, for the very reason that he might prove them, and that they might reveal their true character." Already in 1854 J. White had appealed to the responsibility of the "remnant church" by stating that "the destiny of souls hangs upon her faithfulness" ("Cause," *RH*, Oct. 24, 1854, p. 84).
738 Cf. "Sin of Doing Nothing," p. 32; J. Clarke, "Rising with the Message," *RH*, May 10, 1860, p. 197.
739 E. G. White, *TC*, No. 16, p. 64 (*T*, II, 165, 166).
740 *Ibid.*, No. 17, p. 65 (*T*, II, 247). See *supra*, p. 247.
741 Cf. Beaver, "American Missionary Motivation," pp. 217, 222-26; Beaver, "Missionary Motivation," pp. 120-23, 139-42.
742 E. G. White, *TC*, No. 11, p. 36 (*T*, I, 482). Cf. *ibid.*, No. 12, p. 45 (*T*, I, 519); *ibid.*, No. 22, p. 115 (*T*, III, 202); J. White, "The True Missionary," *TrM*, Jan. 1874, p. 4. In a particular instance she said: "Become like your self-denying Redeemer, pure and unselfish, your life characterized with disinterested benevolence" (*TC*, No. 19, 1870, p. 59 [*T*, II, 545]).

and imitate the life style of Christ and she often referred to the life and character of Christ when appealing for missionary activity.

"Disinterested benevolence" played an important role during the Second Great Awakening, being especially emphasized by Samuel Hopkins and other New England theologians as a vital element in the social responsibility of the Christian.[743] E. G. White explained the term in the context of Christ's complete unselfishness.[744]

Christ's sacrifice for man was also employed frequently by E. G. White to motivate individuals to participate in mission work. The believers were encouraged to follow Christ's redemptive activities because "as a great sacrifice was made to redeem them, they should act a part in this work of salvation, by making a sacrifice for each other."[745] Commenting on the close relation between mission and an accurate understanding of the atonement, she remarked, "when the atonement is viewed correctly, the salvation of souls will be felt to be of infinite value. In comparison with the enterprise of everlasting life, every other sinks into insignificance."[746] Citing 1 Pet. 2:9 she said that Christ had called His followers "to imitate his life of self-sacrifice and self-denial, to be interested in the great work of the redemption of the fallen race."[747] Christ, after having sacrificed everything for man, asked: "I have done all this for you, what are you willing to do for me? I have given you an example."[748] Those who excused themselves from being actively engaged in the salvation of others, E. G. White said, proved themselves "unworthy of the life to come, unworthy of the heavenly treasure which cost so great a sacrifice."[749]

2. The light of the world — the salt of the earth.

The various aspects of Mt. 5:13-16 from the Sermon on the Mount were often quoted to motivate the believers to engage in mission work. The most frequently used appeals were made to the phrases, "Ye are the light of the

743 Hopkins associated sin with self-love and holiness with disinterested benevolence. This benevolence was very much concerned with the unselfishness of Christ and the public interest, the highest good for the largest number. Thus a dedicated Christian would sacrifice his personal interests for the greatest happiness of the whole. Hopkins' view had strong missionary implications which were manifested in his own life when he supported some reform movements (Hopkins, *The System of Doctrines . . . ,* I, 2nd ed., 1811, pp. 461-91; Hudson, *Religion in America,* p. 152; Olmstead, *United States,* p. 189).

744 E. G. White, *SG,* I, 183; E. G. White, "Sacrifice," p. 1; E. G. White, *TC,* No. 9, p. 13 (*T,* I, 369); *ibid.,* No. 10, p. 40 (*T,* I, 431).

745 *Ibid.,* No. 4, p. 26 (*T,* I, 174). Cf. *ibid.,* No. 10, p. 40 (*T,* I, 431). She said: "In view of what Christ has done for us, and has suffered for sinners, we should, out of pure, disinterested love for souls, imitate his example in sacrificing our own pleasure and convenience for their good" (*ibid.,* No. 16, p. 5 [*T,* II, 115]).

746 *Ibid.,* No. 17, p. 19 (*T,* II, 215).

747 *Ibid.,* No. 16, p. 68 (*T,* II, 169).

748 E. G. White, "Sacrifice," p. 1. Cf. [J. White], "Present Work," p. 13. According to Cottrell "the mercy of God to us has brought upon us a debt of gratitude and love which it is impossible for us to overpay" ("The Gospel Is Free," *RH,* Jan. 20, 1874, p. 45).

749 E. G. White, *TC,* No. 12, p. 67 (*T,* I, 546).

world" (5:14)[750] and "Ye are the salt of the earth" (5:13).[751] These were used even before a concept of world-wide mission had been developed. E. G. White expressed the relationship between Christ and His people as follows: "Jesus is light, and in him is no darkness at all [1 Jn. 1:15]. His children are the children of light [1 Thes. 5:5]. They are renewed in his image, and called out of darkness into his marvelous light [1 Pet. 2:9]. He is the light of the world [Jn. 8:12], and they that follow him are the light of the world [Mt. 5:14]."[752] To be the light of the world also implied a responsibility for the laity. She indicated that "God requires his people to shine as lights in the world [Mt. 5:16]. It is not merely the ministers who are required to do this, but every disciple of Christ."[753] Both the ministers and the laity were responsible for the mission of the church.[754] All, she said, who were "consecrated to God . . . are channels of light. God makes them instruments of righteousness to communicate the light of truth, the riches of his grace [Eph. 1:7], to others."[755]

The concept of being the light of the world and the salt of the earth was employed against the current practice of the formation of colonies of Sabbatarian Adventists. Already in 1856 J. White rebuked the tendency "to huddle together for the sake of the society of those of like faith," for it signified hiding a light under a bushel (Mt. 5:15) and prevented the outpouring of the Holy Spirit.[756] Several years later he said that it was a mistake to think that the message would have any impact on the world when the believers were "shut up in a corner, so excluded from the world, or so singular in their general deportment, as to have no influence in the world."[757] E. G. White criticized the movements among SDA to concentrate in Battle Creek, Michigan, and Bordoville, Vermont.[758] In regard to

750 See e.g., Letter, J. White to Bowles, Oct. 17, 1849; [J. White], "Faith of Jesus," RH, March 7, 1854, p. 53; Letter, F. Wheeler to J. White, RH, Nov. 25, 1852, p. 109; Loughborough, " 'Ye Are the Light of the World,' " RH, May 23, 1854, pp. 140, 141; E. G. White, TC, No. 8, pp. 1, 53 (T, I, 303, 345).

751 [J. White], "Faith of Jesus," RH, March 7, 1854, p. 53; E. G. White, TC, No. 8, pp. 1, 53 (T, I, 303, 345); ibid., No. 7, p. 14 (T, I, 262).

752 Ibid., No. 10, pp. 15, 16 (T, I, 405, 406). She said: "We must study the life of Christ, and learn what it is to confess him before the world" (ibid., No. 8, p. 1 [T, I, 303]).

753 Ibid., No. 16, p. 13 (T, II, 122). She added that "their conversation should be heavenly. And while they enjoy communion with God, they will wish to have intercourse with their fellowmen, in order to express by their words and acts the love of God which animates their hearts. In this way they will be lights in the world" (ibid., pp. 13, 14 [T, II, 122, 123]).

754 See supra, p. 257.

755 Ibid., No. 20, pp. 83, 84 (T, II, 632). Here she stated that "every follower of Jesus has his or her work to do as missionaries for Christ, in their families, in their neighborhoods, and in the towns and cities where they live." Mt. 5:13, 14 was not only associated with the communication of spiritual realities but she applied it also to the personal appearance of the SDA as far as their dress was concerned (ibid., No. 10, p. 33 [T, I, 425]; ibid., No. 11, p. 7 [T, I, 460]).

756 J. White, "Third Angel's Message," p. 141. Cf. [J. White], "The Scattered Flock," RH, April 14, 1863, p. 156.

757 [J. White], "The Light of the World," RH, April 21, 1863, p. 165.

758 E. G. White, TC, No. 16, pp. 2-6 (T, II, 113-16); ibid., No. 20, pp. 82-89, 137, 138 (T, II, 631-36, 669).

the believers in Bordoville, she stated that "the plan of gathering together in large numbers, to compose a large church, has contracted their influence, and narrowed down their sphere of usefulness, and is literally putting their light under a bushel."[759] She further remarked that the SDA message should be given to the world and that God's people who were the light of the world "should be interspersed among the moral darkness of the world, as witnesses; their lives, their testimonies, and example, to be a savor of life unto life, or of death unto death [2 Cor. 2:16]."[760]

3. Love.

Love was regarded as fundamentally important as a motivating principle in missions. Although references to the subject of love could be found in the current SDA literature, yet during this period it was not so frequently employed in relation to mission activity as some of the other motivating factors. Love to God was seen as a prerequisite for love to others. E. G. White stated that "love, true love for our fellowmen, evinces love to God."[761] She further said that if the love of God would animate the heart it would manifest itself in word and deed toward our neighbors.[762] Another SDA pointed out that "if we would lead others to love Jesus, we must show that we love him."[763] Love, according to Stephen N. Haskell,[764] was "the motive from which the action springs. Love is an active principle, and cannot live without works. Its life consists in performing acts of disinterested benevolence. . . . It never becomes weary in doing good to others."[765] He also remarked that "Christ was the great example of this principle. And, as we are possessed of his Spirit, just in that proportion the work will be for the upbuilding of the cause for which he shed his blood."[766]

759 *Ibid.*, p. 85 (*T*, II, 633). She added that "the plan of colonizing, or moving from different localities where there is but little strength of influence, and concentrating the influence of many in one locality, is removing the light from places where God would have it shine." Cf. *ibid.*, p. 138 (*T*, II, 669).

760 *Ibid.* Another reason against centralizing was that "God cannot display the knowledge of his will, and the wonders of his grace, among the unbelieving world, unless he has witnesses scattered all over the earth" who would function as "bodies of light throughout the world" (*ibid.*, p. 82 [*T*, II, 631, 632]).

761 *Ibid.*, No. 16, p. 5 (*T*, II, 116). Cf. *ibid.*, No. 19, p. 64 (*T*, II, 549). She said that "divine love" was to be found "in the renewed heart, and where this exists, love will naturally flow out to your fellow men" (*ibid.*, No. 16, p. 68 [*T*, II, 169]).

762 *Ibid.*, pp. 13, 14 (*T*, II, 123); *supra*, p. 265, n. 753. She said: "With the love of Christ in the heart, Christians will work" ("Work for This Time," p. 10). Cf. Haskell, "Counterfeit," *RH*, Jan. 6, 1874, p. 29.

763 [G. H. Bell], "Who Will Be a Missionary?," *YI*, April 1, 1870, p. 52.

764 Stephen N. Haskell (1833-1922) began his preaching ministry as an Adventist in 1853. Later in that year he accepted the third angel's message. He occupied both important ministerial and administrative positions.

765 Haskell, "Missionary Spirit," *TrM*, April 1874, p. 28. In 1851 J. White stated that "those who really love the truth, will do all they consistently can for its advancement. 'Faith without works is dead'" ("Present Work," p. 13).

766 Haskell, "Missionary Spirit," p. 28.

4. Salvation of others.

Although the subject of the salvation of others was related to all non-apocalyptic motives, it had particular relevance for the believer's personal salvation. The priorities in life, according to E. G. White, were "to secure our soul's salvation and to save others. All importance should be attached to this, and everything beside should come in secondary."[767] Being actively involved in the salvation of others seemed to be a condition for personal salvation. She pointed out that "light, precious light, shines upon them [God's people]; but it will not save them, unless they consent to be saved by it, fully live up to the light, and transmit their light to others in darkness."[768] Financial support could not take the place of "personal efforts." No one was to be excused from personal involvement in the salvation of fellow men: "All will not be called to go to foreign missions, but you may be missionaries at home in your own families and in your neighborhoods."[769] She brought out that believers were "their brother's keeper," making them "in a great degree responsible for souls around them."[770] "We are one great brotherhood," she observed on another occasion, "and the welfare of our fellow-men should be our great interest."[771]

5. The parable of the talents.

The talents of God's people were considered of vital importance in the proclamation of the present truth. E. G. White emphasized the obligation of believers to dedicate their talents to the service of others and referred from time to time to the obligations implicit in God's ownership as Creator, Christ's redemptive sacrifices, and the fitness of a man's talents as tools in God's hand for reaching suffering humanity.[772] The parable of the talents (Mt. 25:14-20), she said, was especially given for "the benefit of Christians living

767   Ibid., [No. 1], p. 12 (T, I, 723). Cf. ibid., No. 16, pp. 11, 12 (T, II, 121). She also said that "the followers of Christ have one leading object in view. The one great work, the salvation of their fellow men. Every other interest should be inferior to this, and this great enterprise should engage the earnest effort and deepest interest" (ibid., p. 67 [T, II, 168]). Cf. Haskell, "Object of Missionary Work," TrM, April 1874, p. 28. To Andrews the only reasons on which the actions of ministers should be based were "the honor of God and the salvation of men" ("Preparation for the Work," TrM, Feb. 1874, p. 13).
768   E. G. White, TC, No. 16, p. 14 (T, II, 123).
769   E. G. White, "Work for This Time," p. 10. A similar sentiment was expressed by Haskell who defined a missionary as "one sent upon a mission to save souls" and concluded that it was not "necessary to go into a far country to be a true missionary; but wherever there are souls to save, there men and women should manifest the true missionary spirit. It should commence in our own hearts, and the fruits of it will be seen in our lives; and its influence will be felt in our own families and neighborhoods" ("Missionary Spirit," p. 28).
770   E. G. White, TC, No. 9, p. 13 (T, I, 368). She said that "the more closely our connections with our fellow-men, the greater is our responsibility" (ibid., No. 22, p. 126 [T, III, 209]).
771   Ibid.
772   Ibid.; ibid., No. 17, pp. 110, 111 (T, II, 284, 285); ibid., No. 20, pp. 122, 123 (T, II, 659); ibid., No. 22, p. 48 (T, III, 160).

in the last days."[773] Though she interpreted the talents in a variety of ways, they seemed to her to signify especially the "means," or money, which God has entrusted to individuals and which those in whose heart "the truth lives" will cheerfully expend "in sending the truth to others."[774] In fact she stated that "every soul saved, is a talent gained."[775] The employment of talents would result in the believers shining as lights in the world[776] and receiving a reward "proportionate to the talents improved."[777] Those who did not invest their talents in the advancement of God's work would be punished "according as the talents have been abused"[778] and were compared with the unfaithful servant in the parable who hid the Lord's talent in the earth. In this context E. G. White made the appeal that "God calls upon you to put all your strength with the work. You will have to render an account for the good you might have done had you been standing in a right position, but which you have failed to do."[779]

G. Summary.

During the period of 1850-74 the basic structure of the SDA theology of mission further developed the apocalyptic-eschatological dimensions of the three angels' messages. Those developments were possible through the consistent use of their historicist hermeneutic, making it possible for believers to interpret the current events, especially those in the U.S.A., as signs of the times indicating the nearness of the Second Advent. Although the third angel received the greatest attention, there was an intimate relationship among all these angels. A knowledge of the first two angels' messages was considered a prerequisite for the understanding of the third angel. The proclamation of the three angels' messages was seen as a part of the gospel of Jesus Christ.

The first angel's message came to be especially associated with the pre-Advent judgment aspect of Christ's post-1844 ministry. The successful mission praxis among non-Adventists was responsible for new soteriological developments in the sanctuary theology. There was a gradual maturing of the concept of the atonement which involved the sacrifice of Christ on the cross. The significance of this message for mission was its special rele-

---

773 *Ibid.*, No. 5, p. 18 (*T*, I, 197).

774 *Ibid.* (*T*, I, 197, 198).

775 *Ibid.*, No. 20, p. 124 (*T*, II, 660). Here she explained that "the one brought to a knowledge of the truth, if truly converted, will, in his turn, use the talents of influence and of means which God has given him, and will work for the salvation of his fellow-men."

776 Cf. *ibid.*, No. 21, p. 94 (*T*, III, 65).

777 *Ibid.*, No. 20, p. 136 (*T*, II, 668).

778 *Ibid.* Regarding those individuals she said that "they keep their possessions and means from doing good to God's cause. They claim that it is their own, and that they have a right to do what they please with their own; and souls are not saved by any judicious effort they make with their Lord's money." It was concluded that these unfaithful servants would perish in the time of slaughter (*ibid.*, No. 5, p. 18 [*T*, I, 198]).

779 E. G. White, MS 1, 1869.

vance for non-Adventists. Its proclamation prepared them to accept the other angels' messages and the awareness of a present pre-Advent judgment provided a warning of the nearness of Christ's return.

As a result of further developments of the second angel's message, a distinction was made between a moral fall of Babylon and a final fall. The concept of the fall of Babylon determined the evaluation of revivals among non-Adventists, prevented ecumenical cooperation, and stressed the unique unity, function, and raison d'être of SDA. The Seventh Day Baptists were the only religious body toward which they had a somewhat positive attitude. An important mission of this message was that it informed people about the spiritual condition of Christianity in contrast to that of the SDA.

The third angel's message was considered a message of restoration. Its central theme was the proclamation of the commandments of God and the faith of Jesus which explained the 1844 Advent experience and the present theological position. This message pointed out that the final conflict in the world was to be on the issue of worship: The worship of God versus the worship of the beast and his image. In this issue in which the Decalogue in general, and especially the Sabbath, played a central role, each individual would receive either the seal of God or the mark of the beast. The third angel's message was interpreted as a preparatory message restoring true worship and purifying God's people for the coming crisis and Second Advent and was considered as a vital part of the closing work of salvation through Jesus Christ because man's response to it was to ripen the harvest of the earth.

The strong emphasis on the Sabbath and the Decalogue may cause some to characterize this period as legalistic. A careful reading of contemporary literature, however, cannot support such a view.[780] The primary sources advocated a concept of salvation which revealed a close relationship between works of obedience to God and faith in Jesus Christ, a relationship also expressed in the central theme of the third angel's message.

Viewed as an important aid in the preparation for Christ's return, health reform became an integral part of the third angel's message. This reform advocated a series of changes in behavior based on the concept that the laws of nature are as divine as the Ten Commandments. Resultant, purifying influences on spiritual, mental, and physical faculties were expected to leave believers in a better condition to engage in mission work. Health institutions were to be established to facilitate not only the improvement of health among believers but also to restore others while reaching them with the gospel.

Further ecclesiological developments reflecting the character of the church created a better climate for mission work and contributed to the

---

780 See e.g., Andrews, "Perpetuity of the Law of God," pp. 33-37, 41-43 (*Thoughts on the Sabbath*, pp. 6-30); Cottrell, *The Bible Class . . .* , 1855, pp. 19-23, 60-69; Appendix II, Principle XV. Cf. D. T. Bourdeau, *Sanctification*, pp. 9, 10, 17, 18, 74-88; J. White, *Life*, pp. 343-59.

already unique position of SDA in the history of the Christian church. It was especially the Laodicean motif which brought out the anti-triumphalistic dimension in the missionary ecclesiology, while more than any other motif, the Elijah motif revealed the mission of restoration — the specific mission of the third angel's message.

The missionary nature of the church was evident in the general understanding that all believers were called to engage in missionary activity — though a distinction in authority was maintained between the leadership and the laity. The mission endeavors of the believers were placed in the framework of God's mission. It was felt that both angels and man played an active role in this divine mission. The relationship between God and man was seen as a cooperative one in the salvation of man.

During the period under discussion, apocalyptic-eschatological motives for mission dominated the movement. The development of non-apocalyptic motives could be attributed to E. G. White more than others, with her prevailing theme being the *imitatio Christi*.

This chapter dealt with the basic structure of the theology of mission, which slowly emerged into a harmonious system in which each component played an indispensable role. Even though different individuals emphasized different aspects, the published primary sources reveal a remarkable uniformity in regard to the eschatological thrust of the mission theology. Although the believers continued to stress the soon return of Christ, they realized that His coming could not take place at any moment; the process of preparation would take some time during which certain events in the history of salvation would occur. Thus the urgency of the imminent parousia changed into a view which expected the Second Advent in the near future, creating in turn a climate in which missionary consciousness could gradually develop to a concept of a world-wide mission responsibility. The next chapter discusses the development of the missionary consciousness during the same period in which the basic structure of the theology of mission emerged. The context of that discussion is the interaction of theology and missionary praxis.

In this chapter there is a further description of the development of the gradual expansion of the missionary outreach which can be considered as a continuation of the concept of mission in Chapter IV. As a result of the progress in mission additional modifications occurred in the shut-door concept. New insights in the interpretation of the parable of the ten virgins indicated not only its past but also its present relevance. The mission of the third angel emerged from being primarily a mission in North America to a mission on a world-wide scope. In bringing out the background of textual interpretations regarding the development of a concept of world-wide mission, close attention is given to the mission praxis.

A. Developments during 1850-59.

After 1849 various Sabbatarian Adventists realized that the scattering time had passed and the gathering time had commenced.[1] During the gathering time the shut-door concept continued to be modified through the influence of missionary progress and developments in the understanding of Christ's sanctuary ministry. David Arnold's shut-door concept of Mt. 25:10 reflected the influence of the March 24, 1849 vision of E. G. White[2] and the idea of an absence of mercy for the world in general. He stated that the door of the parable represented "not only a change in the position of the bridegroom, (Christ), but also shows a change in his relation to the world, from that which he previously had."[3] Except for children who were not accountable for their actions in 1844, "misguided souls" seemed to be beyond the possibility of salvation.[4] From this time onward there was a growing concern to work for the conversion of the children of Adventists.[5]

---

1 [J. White], "Repairing the Breach," p. 28; Edson, "Beloved Brethren," p. 34; Andrews, "Brethren and Sisters," p. 39; E. G. White, "DBS," p. 86 (*EW*, p. 74).
2 See *supra*, pp. 153, 154.
3 Arnold, "Shut Door," p. 43. Cf. *ibid.*, pp. 44, 45; Arnold, "Daniel's Visions," pp. 60, 63.
4 Arnold, "Shut Door," p. 45.
5 See e.g., Letter, Rebekah G. Whitcomb to J. White, with comments, *PT*, April 1850, p. 72; [J. White], "Conferences," *AdR*, Nov. 1850, p. 72; Bates, "Duty to Our Children," *RH*, Jan. 1851, pp. 39, 40; [J. White], "Our Tour East," *RH*, Nov. 25, 1851, p. 52. Already in 1848 E. G. White felt a burden for children (Letter, E. G. White to the Hastingses, No. 1, 1848).

In the beginning of 1850 E. G. White stressed the necessity for mission among other Adventists but not their leaders, stating that "our work was not to the shepherds who have rejected the former messages, but to the honest deceived who are led astray."[6] It seems that meetings were held among these Adventists which were also attended by some interested non-Adventists. The result was that even a few non-Adventists joined the Sabbatarian Adventists to that in February 1850 E. G. White could report that in Oswego, New York, "souls are coming out upon the truth all around here. They are those who have not heard the Advent doctrine and some of them are those who went forth to meet the Bridegroom in 1844."[7] In other areas, however, such as Vermont, New Hampshire, Maine, and Canada it was "next to impossible to obtain access to unbelievers" in 1850 because the Disappointment "had confused the minds of many, and they would not listen to any explanation of the matter."[8] Two months later J. White described the first angel's message as "the last mission of mercy to the world" which had been fulfilled in 1844, and the third angel's message as the "last message of mercy to the scattered flock."[9] He interpreted the open door of the Philadelphian church (Rev. 3:8) in the context of the sanctuary doctrine as a reference to the "tabernacle of the testimony which was then [1844] opened, that the light of the holy law of God might shine out upon the waiting saints."[10] The shut door of Mt. 25:10 he also explained in the setting of the sanctuary, stating that at the end of the 2300 days "the time had come for Jesus to shut the door of the Holy, and pass into the Most Holy, to receive the kingdom, and cleanse the Sanctuary. This change, so wonderfully described in Dan. vii. 13, 14, answers to the coming of the bridegroom and the shut door, in the parable."[11] Although he remarked that "the work for the world was closed up"[12] he denied that the door of mercy was shut in 1844 because "God's 'mercy endureth for ever.' See Ps. cxxxvi; cvi, 1; cxviii, 1."[13] The shut-door concept he applied to "the sinner, to whom Jesus had stretched out his arms all the day long, and who had rejected the offers of salvation."[14] On July 29, 1850, E. G. White had a

6 Letter, E. G. White to the Hastingses, No. 1, 1850. Cf. E. G. White, "DBS," p. 64.

7 Letter, E. G. White to the Collinses, No. 4, 1850.

8 E. G. White, "Travel," p. 721.

9 J. White, "TAM," pp. 65, 69 (TAM, pp. 3, 15). Cf. Edson, "Appeal," pp. 8, 10; the first angel seemed to have relevance for those few "who are still within the reach of mercy, and salvation" (J. White, "Present Position," p. 14). Cf. [J. White], "Angels No. 2," p. 20 (AR, pp. 5, 6). In Dec. 1850 E. G. White stated that "the burden of the message should be [the] first, second, and third angels' messages, and those who had any hope in God would yield to the force of that truth" (MS 11, 1850).

10 J. White, "TAM," p. 68 (TAM, p. 14). Cf. Edson, "Appeal," pp. 2, 3.

11 J. White, "Sanctuary," p. 79 (Sanctuary, p. 13). Cf. ibid., pp. 76, 77 (Sanctuary, p. 5).

12 Ibid., p. 78 (Sanctuary, p. 10). Cf. J. White, "Our Tour East," AdR, No. 1, Aug. 1850, p. 14; J. White, "Present Position," p. 14.

13 [J. White], "Sanctuary," p. 79 (Sanctuary, p. 14). Cf. [J. White], " 'Call to Remembrance the Former Days,' " RH, Sept. 16, 1851, p. 25. He also said: "He [God] is still merciful to his saints, and ever will be; and Jesus is still their advocate and priest" ("Sanctuary," p. 79 [Sanctuary, p. 14]).

14 Ibid. Here special reference was made to "the professed church." Hos. 5:6, 7 was used to describe its condition and new converts.

vision which indicated that disobedient Adventists would be purged out, but assurance was given that "others who had not heard the Advent doctrine and rejected it would embrace the truth and take their places."[15]

In August 1850, the *Advent Review* was published which reprinted many testimonies of leaders of the Advent movement from the period immediately following the Disappointment, affirming the validity of the Seventh Month movement and the extreme shut-door view. The purpose of this publication was to make "ashamed" the Adventist leadership who had later on rejected this movement.[16] From these reprints the conclusion should not be drawn that at this time Sabbatarian Adventists in general advocated a shut-door view such as was described in these testimonies.[17] That was made clear when J. White, commenting on this shut-door concept, stated that during the mission of the third angel's message some of "the scattered children of the Lord . . . who were not brought directly under the influence of the 'everlasting gospel' [Rev. 14: 6], are now coming into the clear light of the third angel's message."[18] These non-Adventists were considered to be saved "at the eleventh hour."[19]

In September 1850, Edson described the open and shut door of the Philadelphian church (Rev. 3:7, 8) in the context of the sanctuary theology.[20] Viewing the current missionary situation, he felt that they were in the "gleaning time," when, on the basis of the breastplate-of-judgment argument, non-Adventists who in 1844 belonged to one of the following categories could still be saved: (1) Those who had not had "the light on the second advent doctrine, and had not rejected it, but were living according to the best light they had"; (2) those who had "a sacred reverence for God and his word, and had his fear before their eyes, yet they made no profession of religion, or of conversion"; (3) "children who had not arrived to years of accountability."[21]

In the same year Bates interpreted the open and shut door of the Philadelphian church in the context of Rev. 11:19 and Lk. 13:25. He remarked that the Master of the house, who was identified with Christ the High

15 E. G. White, MS 5, 1850. Cf. Edson, "Appeal," p. 3. During the summer of 1850, as a result of a vision, E. G. White seems to have admonished Washington Morse, a disappointed Adventist. In an autobiographical statement she said that "he did not think of the mercy of God in granting the world a longer time in which to prepare for his coming, that the warning of the judgment might be heard more widely, and the people tested with greater light. . . . He should have rejoiced that the world was granted a reprieve; and he should have been ready to aid in carrying forward the great work yet to be done upon the earth, in bringing sinners to repentance and salvation " ("Mrs. Ellen G. White," p. 165 [*LS*, p. 78]). See *supra*, p. 151, n. 280.

16 Letter, E. G. White to Arbella Hastings, No. 8, 1850. Cf. Letter, J. White to Brother, July 21, 1850.

17 This remark also applies to later reprints. See e.g., J. White, "The Seven Last Plagues," *RH*, Aug. 5, 1851, p. 1; [Hale], "Brother Hale's Article," *RH*, Sept. 16, 1851, pp. 27, 28.

18 J. White, "Voice of the Fourth Angel," p. 6.

19 J. White, "Tour East," *AdR*, No. 1, Aug. 1850, p. 15. Cf. [J. White], "The Work of the Lord," *RH*, May 6, 1852, p. 5.

20 Edson, "Appeal," pp. 2, 3.

21 *Ibid.*, p. 3. His shut-door concept included the possibility of repentance and forgiveness of sin for "all who were borne in on the breast plate of judgment, and have not sinned wilfully" (*ibid.*).

Priest, rose up (Lk. 13:25) and *"shut the outer door* of his daily ministration with the world, and no man can *open* it, and *opened the door into the holiest of all;* where the ten commandments are seen, [Rev. xi, 19], and *'no man can shut it.'* "[22] This change was for him evidence that "the door was shut; and that the last, and only safe one was then opened for the overcomers in the Philadelphian church."[23] His shut-door concept was modified by the breastplate-of-judgment argument which led him to conclude that there was mercy for "all honest believers, that had submitted to his [Lord Jesus'] will, and children that had not arrived to the years of accountability."[24] The idea that in 1844 the times of the gentiles had been fulfilled (Lk. 21:24) signified to him that now the gospel and "mercy" had been "extended to a remnant of literal Israel before the second advent. Rom. xi."[25]

In 1851, J. White conceded that the shut-door concept did not "exclude ALL conversions" because "conversion, in the strictest sense, signified a change from sin to holiness."[26] He applied the shut door to "those who heard the 'everlasting gospel' message and rejected it, or refused to hear it" and he distinguished three categories of individuals who could be converted: (1) The "erring brethren" of the Laodicean church — James 5:19, 20; (2) children who were not old enough to make an intelligent decision about the truth in 1844 because God "will give every intelligent being a chance to be saved"; (3) "a multitude of precious souls, some even in the churches" who were compared with the 7000 men who had not bowed before Baal (Rom. 11:14) and designated as "hidden souls" who "were living up to what light they had when Jesus closed his mediation for the world." J. White pointed out that God would manifest these people "IN HIS OWN TIME," but there was "no message to such now, still 'he that hath an ear to hear let him hear' [Rev. 3:13]. Our message is to the Laodiceans, yet some of these hidden souls are being manifested."[27]

J. White provided an extensive treatment of the parable of Mt. 25:1-12. He no longer considered the Advent experience as a literal fulfillment of the parable but as "likened, or compared, unto an eastern marriage," remarking that "the Second Advent people were to experience a series of events which were to have a natural application to the events of the eastern

22   Bates, "Laodicean Church," p. 8. (Brackets his.) Cf. Bates, *SLG,* pp. 19, 20; Bates, *TAS,* pp. 9, 10, 14, 15; Bates, "Our Labor in the Philadelphia and Laodicean Churches," *RH,* Aug. 1851, p. 13. In 1844 Christ's mediatorial work ceased "for the *whole* world forever" (Bates, *TAS,* p. 9). Cf. Bates, "Labor," p. 13. The two veils of the sanctuary he designated as two doors (*TAS,* pp. 11, 14).
23   Bates, "Laodicean Church," p. 8.
24   Bates, "Children," p. 39. Cf. Bates, "Labor," p. 13. He also said that "those that were believers before 1844" but who "are ignorant of this message [third angel] may, and undoubtedly will be saved if they die before Jesus leaves the Holiest" but "sinners and backsliders" were beyond hope ("Children," p. 39).
25   Bates, *TAS,* p. 12. Cf. Edson, *An Exposition . . . Showing the Final Return of the Jews in 1850,* 1849; Arnold, "Daniel's Visions," p. 63.
26   Reply, J. White to Marshall M. Truesdell, *RH,* April 7, 1851, p. 64. Cf. Letter, Adventist to Son, *RH,* Feb. 1851, p. 47.
27   Reply, J. White to Truesdell, p. 64.

marriage rehearsed by Christ."[28] The going of the wise virgins to the marriage was compared with the going into the most holy place of "all that had not rejected light and truth sufficient to be cut off from Israel" because they were carried on the breastplate of Christ the High Priest.[29] In the literal shutting of the door in the parable he saw an illustration of the change in Christ's ministry. Employing the sanctuary interpretation of Rev. 3:7, 8, J. White stated that Christ "closed the work or 'door' of the daily ministration in the Holy, and opened the door of the Most Holy. 'The tabernacle of the testimony' [Rev. 11:19] was then opened; but before this could be done, the 'door,' or work of Christ's continual mediation in the Holy had to be closed. This may well be 'likened' to the shut door in the parable."[30]

During 1850 E. G White stressed that the "message of the third angel must go, and be proclaimed to the scattered children of the Lord."[31] In August 1851, J. White reported on the opportunities for mission that "now the door is open almost everywhere to present the truth, and many are prepared to read the publications who have formerly had no interest to investigate."[32] He observed that many Sabbatarian Adventists believed that "the time has come to swell the loud cry of the third angel . . . and to sound the last note of warning to the scattered people of God."[33] The next month meetings were held with Seventh Day Baptists and because of their continued interest Edson expressed the conviction that among them there were some hidden souls.[34] Articles were published suggesting that the Gospel dispensation had not terminated in 1844. The *Review and Herald* reprinted Crosier's 1846 idea regarding a transition period from the Gospel dispensation to the following dispensation during which a proclamation of a prophetic message (Rev. 10:11) was to take place.[35] Nichols indicated that "the work under the third angel of Rev. xiv, and the tenth day atonement and ministration of Christ in the Most Holy are cotemporary [*sic*], and will finish the gospel dispensation."[36]

In the summer of this year it was decided not to publish any more visions of E. G. White in the *Review and Herald* because many readers of this missionary periodical were prejudiced against the manifestations of visions.[37] Prejudicial attitudes were also present among various Sabbatarian Adventists.[38] It was therefore decided to publish these visions separately for

---

28 J. White, "Parable," p. 97 (*Parable*, pp. 2, 3).
29 *Ibid.*, p. 102 (*Parable*, p. 17). Cf. *ibid.*, p. 101 (*Parable*, p. 15).
30 *Ibid.*, p. 102 (*Parable*, p. 18).
31 Letter, E. G. White to Brethren, *RH*, Extra, July 21, 1851, p. [4] (*EW*, p. 75).
32 [J. White], "Present Work," p. 13.
33 *Ibid.*, p. 12. There was a similar expectation in 1856. See *supra*, p. 247.
34 Letter, Edson to J. White, *RH*, Sept. 2, 1851, p. 24. Through the influence of Rhodes, a Seventh Day Baptist joined the Sabbatarian Adventists (Letter, Cottrell to J. White, *RH*, Nov. 25, 1851, p. 54).
35 [Crosier], "The Transition," *RH*, Sept. 2, 1851, p. 22. Cf. *supra*, p. 131.
36 Letter, Nichols to J. White, *RH*, Sept. 2, 1851, p. 22.
37 [J. White], Comments, *RH*, Extra, July 21, 1851, p. [4]. See *supra*, p. 121.
38 See e.g., Letter, E. G. White to the Howlands, No. 8, 1851; E. G. White, MS 5, 1851; J. White quoted in Spicer, *Pioneer Days of the Advent Message . . .* , 1941, p. 100.

the benefit of those who were convinced that God still communicated with His church through visions "*in the last days.*"[39] This resulted in the publication of *A Sketch of the Christian Experience and Views of Ellen G. White* in August 1851 which included several previously published visions. Some passages of these reprinted visions had been omitted, among which were two references to the shut door.[40] Frequently these deletions have been used by later critics as evidence that there was a deliberate attempt to suppress erroneous theological concepts.[41] The fact, however, that these

39   [J. White], Comments, p. [4].

40   Cf. E. G. White, "RSA," p. 14 with E. G. White, *CEV,* p. 10 (*EW,* p. 15); cf. E. G. White, "DBS," p. 22 with E. G. White, *CEV,* p. 27 (*EW,* p. 45). To E. G. White a major reason for deletions in the first vision was to "prevent repetition" (E. G. White, "Experience and Views," p. [2]). For other possible reasons pertaining to the size of publication and economy, see A. L. White, "Shut Door," pp. 34, 35.

41   For the tradition of this criticism, see Snook and Brinkerhoff, *E. G. White,* pp. 5, 7; Carver, *E. G. White,* pp. 51, 52, 60; Grant, *True Sabbath,* p. 93; Wellcome, *Second Advent Message,* p. 406; A. C. Long, *Comparison of the Early Writings of Mrs. White with Later Publications,* 1883; Canright, *Seventh-day Adventism,* pp. 139-46; Conradi, *E. G. White,* p. 31; Lindén, *Biblicism,* pp. 80-84; Ronald L. Numbers, *Prophetess of Health: A Study of Ellen G. White* (New York: Harper and Row, 1976), p. 27. This criticism can be traced back to Snook and Brinkerhoff, two ministers who left the SDA Church in 1865 (Butler, " 'Early Writings' and 'Suppression,' " *RH,* Supplement, Aug. 14, 1883, pp. 3-5; Butler, "A Brief History of the 'Marion' Movement," *ibid.,* pp. 7, 8). E. G. White described Snook and Brinkerhoff as "false ministers" who had gathered "testimonies of falsehood" from former believers like Moses Hull, Ransom Hicks, and participants in the Messenger party — the first secession from the Sabbatarian Adventists ("Our Late Experience," *RH,* Feb. 20, 1866, p. 89). This could be an indication that the charge of suppression goes back to an earlier date. Lindén came to the following conclusions: (1) The statement in the E. G. White letter to the Dodges, No. 4, July 21, 1851 that the "visions trouble many. They [know] not what to make of them" provided evidence that her fellow believers had already discussed the changes in the wording of the visions before they had been published. He concluded that in this context she, having seen her early printed visions while in the home of a fellow believer and being conscious of the changes, assured her friends that if all the details should not be printed she would like to write them out at their request; (2) J. White deleted the "heretical" shut-door concept in order to secure a smooth transition to the open-door view or unlimited evangelistic work; (3) the publication of *CEV* was followed by a reaction which resulted in the fact that E. G. White could not fully assert her authority until 1855. As evidence he pointed to her few articles in the *RH* during 1851-55 (Lindén, *Biblicism,* pp. 81, 82, 84 [Letter, Lindén to A. L. White, pp. 9, 11]). Cf. Letter, Lindén to the E. G. White Trustees, Sept. 2, 1971, pp. 4, 5. Regarding Lindén's first conclusion, contemporary sources indicate that the reason why the visions troubled many was that there existed a strong prejudice against visions even among Sabbatarian Adventists (*supra,* p. 275, n. 38). Lindén's translation and interpretation of his final quotation from this E. G. White letter, which he used as support for his argument, indicate that he misunderstood its grammatical construction (cf. Lindén, *Biblicism,* p. 81 with Letter, E. G. White to the Dodges, No. 4, 1851). Cf. Letter, A. L. White to Lindén, Oct. 21, 1971, p. 7. The immediate context of the original quotation indicates that it was not her early printed visions which she saw at the home of a believer but a vision. In her letter to her friends she said that if all the particulars of the vision she saw were not published in the forthcoming pamphlet she could write them out. This interpretation accounts for the grammatical structure of the original quotation in its contextual setting and the fact that a few days later she was occupied with the writing out of her latest visions in order to incorporate them in the pamphlet (Letter, E. G. White to Hastings and Harriet, No. 7, July 27, 1851). Compare the similarities between her comments in both letters on the publication of the pamphlet. These facts invalidate his first conclusion. Both his second and third conclusions are based on assumptions and not on contemporary sources. Regarding the third conclusion it should be noted that in July 1851, prior to the publication of *CEV,* J. White had announced that no more visions would be published in the *RH* as a concession to the prejudice of many individuals (Comments, p. [4]). This seems to be the major reason for

shut-door concepts could be interpreted in harmony with later shut-door statements may suggest a different reason for these deletions. A more plausible explanation seems to be that in 1850-51, when various non-Adventists became interested in the proclamation of the Sabbatarian Adventists, everything was done to avoid a perpetuation of a shut-door view that interfered with an expanding missionary outreach. Owing to the fact that the omitted shut-door statements could be interpreted in a way which was contrary to E. G. White's own interpretation, the decision might have been made not to include them in the current publication.[42]

During 1852 the mission of Sabbatarian Adventists among non-Adventists continued to be so successful that J. White could state that the "work is not confined to those only who have had an experience in the past advent movement. A large portion of those who are sharing the blessings attending the present truth were not connected with the advent cause in 1844."[43] This cannot but be the result of an active mission among non-Adventists in certain areas during the previous year. These new converts, according to J. White, consisted of individuals who came out of "the churches and the world at the 'eleventh hour'" and youth from Adventist parents.[44] As biblical evidence that people could still be saved from the fallen nominal Sardis church, he indicated that there were "'a few names even in Sardis,' (from which the Philadelphian church came out,) 'which have not defiled their garments.' Rev. iii, 4. . . . They are coming out of Babylon."[45] He expected their mission to affect "the world, arrest the public mind, and call out from this great Babylon the scattered members of the body of Christ."[46] In an attempt to reach members of his former Seventh Day Baptist Church, Cottrell published the article, "To Sabbath-Keepers who Have Not Heard the Third Angel's Message."[47] Various believers expressed the hope that the 144,000 would be sealed soon.[48]

In discussing the shut door of Mt. 25:10 J. White stated in 1852, "that

the absence of her visions in the *RH*. Cf. A. L. White, *Ellen G. White*, pp. 51-53. For an evaluation of Number's selective use of sources, see Ellen G. White Estate, *A Critique of Prophetess of Health*, 1976.

42   See *supra*, pp. 150, n. 271; 154, n. 298; cf. A. L. White, "Shut Door," p. 37.

43   [J. White], "Work of the Lord," pp. 4, 5. In another article he said: "Many of our brethren in this state [New York], who are fully with us in our views of the message of the third angel, had no part in the messages of the first and second angels" ("Truth," p. 94). On the success in Lorain, New York, he remarked that "the Lord has raised up quite a large company of Sabbath-keepers within a few months, many of whom had but little or no experience in the advent movement" ("Tour West," p. 94).

44   [J. White], "Work of the Lord," p. 5. For the success among children, see *ibid.*; [J. White], "The Work of Grace," *RH*, Feb. 17, 1852, p. 94. The concern to educate children of believers in the "present truth" resulted in the publication of the *Youth's Instructor* ([J. White], "A Paper for Children," *RH*, July 8, 1852, p. 37).

45   [J. White], "Babylon," *RH*, June 24, 1852, p. 29.

46   *Ibid.*

47   Editorial Remarks, *RH*, June 10, 1852, p. 21; Cottrell, "Sabbath-Keepers," p. 22. See *supra*, p. 275, n. 34. The following year Sabbatarian Adventists were approached by Seventh Day Baptists (J. White, "Resolution," pp. 52, 53).

48   See e.g., Letter, Bates to J. White, *RH*, Jan. 13, 1852, p. 80; Letter, Seaman to J. White,

event shuts out none of the honest children of God, neither those who have not wickedly rejected the light of truth, and the influence of the Holy Spirit."[49] The mission of the Philadelphian church among these non-Adventists became associated with the invitation "he that hath an ear, let him hear" (Rev. 3:13).[50] In referring to the open door of Is. 22:22 and Rev. 3:7, 8, J. White said:

> This OPEN DOOR we teach, and invite those who have an ear to hear, to come to it and find salvation through Jesus Christ. There is an exceeding glory in the view that Jesus has OPENED THE DOOR into the holiest of all, or has passed within the second vail, and now stands before the Ark containing the ten commandments. [Rev. 11:19 quoted here]. If it be said that we are of the OPEN DOOR and seventh day Sabbath theory we shall not object; for this is our faith.[51]

He also added that they had "never felt greater liberty in pointing out the way of life to sinners in past years, than to such now."[52] Although this emphasis on an "open door" concept reflected the current success of mission among non-Adventists, the shut-door concept based on the rejection of truth was retained. Thus the "large mass of mankind" or "the mass of the present generation" he considered as being lost because of the assumption that they had "rejected the doctrine of the Second Advent."[53] "Some" of the believers, however, still adhered to the extreme shut-door view.[54] From the above evidence it is clear that the Sabbatarian Adventist leaders did not advocate the extreme position at this time.[55] In fact, they, including E. G. White, tried to counteract this view.[56]

RH, Feb. 17, 1852, p. 96. For many years the idea continued to prevail that the mission would progress till there would be 144,000 living sealed believers. See e.g., Haskell, "The Cause Is Onward," *RH,* Oct. 13, 1874, p. 125; D. T. Bourdeau, "Future Enlargement of the Review," *RH,* April 2, 1867, p. 199. He expected hundreds of thousands to accept the message but because of apostasy only 144,000 would be sealed (*ibid.*). However, E. G. White said: "Our work is not done in this world for the good of others until Christ shall say in Heaven: 'It is done' [Rev. 22:11 quoted]" (*TC,* No. 11, p. 39 [*T,* I, 484]).

49   [J. White], "Call at the Harbinger Office," *RH,* Feb. 17, 1852, p. 94.

50   [J. White], "Truth," p. 94; Letter, Arnold to J. White, *RH,* March 23, 1852, p. 110; Andrews, "TAR," p. 211 (*TAR,* p. 137). Cf. *supra,* p. 274.

51   [J. White], "Harbinger Office," p. 95. Cf. [J. White], "The Shut Door," *RH,* April 14, 1853, p. 189. Wm. S. Ingraham, "The Parable — Matt. XXV," *RH,* June 9, 1853, p. 10.

52   [J. White], "Truth," p. 94.

53   *Ibid.*

54   Waggoner, *et al.,* "Conference Address," *RH,* June 11, 1861, p. 21 (E. G. White, MS 4, 1883 [*SM,* I, 64]).

55   Cf. Waggoner, " 'Suppression' and 'The Shut Door,' " *RH,* Supplement, Aug. 14, 1883, p. 1.

56   At a meeting in 1852 (*ibid.*; Letter, Waggoner to Smith, in *Vindication of the Business Career of Elder James White,* 1863, p. 11) a non-Adventist was "nearly refused the message" due to the fact that the "individual presenting it [had] doubts of the possibility of his salvation because he was not in the '44 move' " (Waggoner, *et al.,* "Conference Address," p. 21. [E. G. White, MS 4, 1883 (*SM,* I, 64)]). The situation was overruled by a vision of E. G. White which encouraged this individual "to hope in God and to give his heart fully to Jesus, which he did then and there" (*ibid.*). Waggoner identified himself as being this non-Adventist and added that none of the leaders had any doubts about his chances of salvation: "On the contrary, they

In 1853 the argument that the breastplate of judgment provided the possibility of salvation after 1844 was replaced by Andrews' argument that on the antitypical Day of Atonement the blood of Christ was employed not only to cleanse the sanctuary but also to pardon or forgive sins.[57] This interpretation harmonized the sanctuary theology with mission praxis.

In the same year J. White stressed that the parable of Mt. 25 only concerned individuals participating in the Advent movement, so that "those who were not in the movement, and did not reject its light, stand on the same ground for salvation, as though such a movement had never taken place."[58] The shut door, he said, pertained to "those moved by the proclamation of the Advent, who had none of the grace of God, no real faith" and "those who were foolish and wicked enough to reject, and fight against the glorious news of a coming Saviour."[59] He stated, however, that "we rejoice to publish to those that have an ear to hear, that there is an *Open Door* [context of Rev. 3:8; 11:19]."[60] As one of the first Sabbatarian Adventists J. White applied the shutting of the door by the Master of the house (Lk. 13:25) "to the close of Christ's mediation in the holiest of the heavenly Sanctuary."[61] Then, from his understanding of Christ's ministry and Rev. 3:7, he concluded that there were in fact two shut doors: "First, when his [Christ's] work closed in the holy place, at the termination of the 2300 days, and, second, when the atonement shall be finished, and Christ leaves the Sanctuary."[62] He added that "the last message of mercy is going forth, and soon the Master of the house will rise up, and shut to the door."[63] A few years later, Smith described the shut door of Mt. 25:10 in a contemporary setting by stating that "those who . . . with the present light on this subject [of Christ's high-priestly ministry], shall attempt to find in Christ a Saviour, while living in violation of that holy law, or shall seek him as minister in the first apartment of the Sanctuary, will find that he has withdrawn himself from them [Hos. 5:6], and knows them not."[64] Belonging to the foolish virgins, however, did not preclude a change for the better. The wise and foolish virgins he considered to represent a "class" and not individuals, meaning that "an individual may, without difficulty, though belonging at

---

hailed my conversion to the message with joy, and received me cordially" (Waggoner, " 'Shut Door,' " p. 1).

57   See *supra*, pp. 171, 172. Cf. [J. White], "The Sanctuary," *RH*, March 17, 1853, p. 176. Edson was one of the first who alluded to this argument (*supra*, p. 171).

58   [J. White], "Shut Door," p. 189. He added: "Those . . . who are now looking for the Lord, and are obeying the present truth, may now rejoice in the true application of the parable of the ten virgins, as well as those who shared in the past great and glorious movement."

59   *Ibid.*

60   *Ibid.* Here Mt. 25:11 was expected to have a future fulfillment.

61   [J. White], "Luke XIII, 23-25," p. 4.

62   *Ibid.*

63   *Ibid.* Cf. [J. White], "The Days of Noah," *RH*, Feb. 3, 1853, p. 149.

64   Smith, "Cleansing of the Sanctuary," p. 54; [Smith], "Synopsis of the Present Truth," No. 24, *RH*, April 29, 1858, p. 188.

one time to one class, at another, help compose the other."[65] Thus more and more the shut door of the parable was explained in the context of the sanctuary theology.[66]

In 1853 E. G. White was one of the first to say that the Sabbatarian Adventist mission had relevance for the world when she referred to it as "the last message of mercy that is ever to be given to a guilty world."[67] From this time onward others began using similar language to describe the mission of the third angel's message.[68] In general, during the 1850s the concept of their mission to the world was confined to the North American continent.[69] However, in commenting on the apocalyptic-eschatological scene of Rev. 18, E. G. White seemed to suggest that their mission would be much more extensive. She indicated that the loud cry of the third angel's message would enlighten "the earth," penetrate "every where" and close "with a power and strength far exceeding the midnight cry."[70] The interpretation of Mt. 24:14 was similar to that of the Millerites,[71] who saw its fulfillment in the proclamation of the gospel by the Christian church as well as in the preaching of the Second Advent, 1840-44.[72]

For several years SDA missionary strategy was influenced by a current idea that the three invitations to the marriage supper of Lk. 14:16-24 signified the special warnings of the three angels' messages.[73] From this J. White concluded that the mission of the third angel's message, which was identified with the last invitation, was not directed to the "self-righteous professors" or to the churches and the cities where the first two angels'

65 *Ibid.,* p. 189. Adventists who participated in a time-setting movement in 1854 were regarded by J. White as the foolish virgins ("Signs of the Times," *RH*, Nov. 12, 1857, p. 3).

66 Cf. *infra,* p. 283, n. 95. Haskell's interpretation was not normative for that time ("Philadelphia and Laodicean Churches," p. 6).

67 E. G. White, "To the Saints Scattered Abroad," *RH*, Feb. 17, 1853, p. 155. Cf. [J. White], "Babylon," *RH*, June 24, 1852, p. 29.

68 See e.g., Andrews, "TAR," p. 211 (*TAR*, p. 136); J. White, "The Third Angel's Message," *RH*, Aug. 28, 1856, p. 132.

69 When E. G. White wrote to an individual in Wisconsin "to give the last message of mercy to the world" and to show "to those around you that this world is not your home," it was obvious that the implications for this person were not in the context of a world-wide mission (*TC,* [No. 1], p. 6 [*T,* I, 118]). Cf. Letter, E. G. White to Brethren and Sisters, *RH*, Jan. 10, 1856, p. 118; E. G. White, *TC*, No. 10, p. 31 (*T,* I, 422). When J. White described Bates' successful missionary work in "all the world" he referred to Bates' mission in "the different States, and in the Canadas" ("A Sketch of the Rise and Progress of the Present Truth," *RH*, Jan. 14, 1858, p. 77). Cf. A. S. Hutchins, "The Field Is the World," *RH*, March 26, 1857, p. 168.

70 E. G. White, *SG*, I, 194, 196. Cf. *ibid.,* p. 197; J. White, "Babylon," *RH*, June 24, 1852, p. 29; J. White, "Loud Voice," pp. 172, 173. He stated that the third angel's message would be "a test to all men" (*ibid.,* p. 172).

71 Cf. *supra,* pp. 50-52.

72 J. White, "Signs of the Times," *RH*, Aug. 28 and Sept. 8, 1853, pp. 57, 58, 70 (*Signs,* pp. 27-36, 90); Andrews, "TAR," pp. 169-71 (*TAR*, pp. 21-35). For reprints of Millerite articles on this subject, see *RH*, July 21, 1853, p. 38 and March 21, 1854, p. 70.

73 See e.g., [J. White], "Cause," *RH*, Oct. 24, 1854, p. 84; Andrews, "TAR," *RH*, Jan. 23, 1855, p. 162 (*TAR*, pp. 15-17); cf. H. Heath, "The 'Great Supper,' " *AH*, Jan. 29, 1845, pp. 194, 195 (*RH*, Sept. 2, 1851, pp. 21, 22). Later this interpretation was modified (E. G. White, *TC*, No. 17, pp. 33, 34, 123 [*T,* II, 225, 226, 295]; E. G. White, *T,* VI, 412; VIII, pp. 71, 72; E. G. White, *COL*, pp. 219-37; 307-9).

messages had been given but to the "mixed multitude, in the high ways and hedges [Lk. 14:23], rich and poor, professors and non-professors."[74] In 1855 Bates suggested that a few publications on the third angel's message be sent "to some of the foreign missionary stations, especially to the Sandwich islands."[75] The following year J. White stated that there was a need for "a missionary spirit" — not, of course, to send "the gospel to the heathen; but to extend the solemn warning throughout the realms of corrupt Christianity [Joel 2:1; Is. 58:1 quoted],"[76] calling upon believers to "send the Message abroad throughout christendom."[77]

During the 1850s new interpretations of Rev. 10 reflected the contemporary mission expansion among the various groups of European immigrants in the U.S.A. The phrase, "There should be time no longer" (10:6), was no longer referred to as probationary time but as the end of "prophetic time," which was seen to have ended in 1844.[78] Since that date the "mystery of God" (10:7) was being "finished," a process defined by J. White as "the closing work of the gospel of Jesus Christ, embracing the last message of mercy to the world."[79] The mission of the third angel's message came to be identified with the prophetic call, "Thou must prophesy again before many peoples, and nations, and tongues, and kings" (10:11).[80] At first this text was not interpreted as having world-wide implications, and when, in the 1850s, European immigrants began to accept the message, it seemed to some that it would find fulfillment within North America.[81]

To reach these immigrants, publications were prepared between 1856 and 1858 in German, French, and Dutch.[82] In 1858 J. White reported that there were Sabbatarian Adventists in the U.S.A. whose mother tongues

74 J. White, "Cause," *RH,* Oct. 24, 1854, p. 84. Cf. J. White, "Third Angel's Message," p. 141. It further implied that the believers should "go forth from town to town, from country to country, and from state to state . . . and give the third and last call which has compelling power in it" (*ibid.*).
75 Letter, Bates to J. White, *RH,* May 29, 1855, p. 240. He expected a few results.
76 J. White, "Third Angel's Message," p. 141.
77 *Ibid.*
78 [Smith], "Synopsis of the Present Truth," No. 13, *RH,* Feb. 4, 1858, p. 100.
79 J. White, "Mystery," p. 205.
80 See e.g., Cottrell, "Definite Time," *RH,* June 26, 1855, p. 253.
81 See e.g., Hutchins, "World," p. 168; [Smith], "The Conference," *RH,* May 27, 1858, p. 13. To Smith Rev. 10:11 could have its fulfillment in the U.S.A. He stated that by reason of analogy it would seem that the mission of the third angel's message would be "co-extensive with the first: though this might not *perhaps* [italics mine] be necessary to fulfill Rev. x, 11, since our own land is composed of people from almost every nation" (Reply to A. H. Lewis, *RH,* Feb. 3, 1859, p. 87).
82 J. White, Note on the German Tract, *RH,* Jan. 28, 1858, p. 96; [Smith], "Business Items," *RH,* March 25, 1858, p. 152; J. White, "Publications in Other Languages," *RH,* May 6, 1858, p. 200; J. White, "From the Field," *RH,* July 8, 1858, p. 64. The first publication in Dutch was published in 1858. It contained translations of Waggoner, *Sabbath of the Fourth Commandment,* an extract from a Sabbath Manual, and several pages of the *Bible Student's Assistant* (J. White, "Field," *RH,* July 8, 1858, p. 64). It was entitled *De Natuur en Verbinding van den Sabbath Volgens het Vierde Gebodt; met Aanmerkingen op den Groten Afval en Zwaren Tyden in de Laatste Dagen,* trans. John Fisher. Already in 1855 there were preparations to publish a pamphlet in Swedish (Letter, Gustaf Mellberg to J. White, *RH,* Feb. 20, 1855, p. 183).

were "German, French, Norwegian, Swedish, Dutch, &c." and whose desire it was "to see publications on the present truth printed in their native languages, to circulate in America and in Europe."[83] Thus relatives and friends in Europe began to be exposed to the third angel's message through the sending of literature.[84] The result was that in 1859, in Ireland, S. E. Armstrong accepted this message as one of the first in Europe.[85] Perhaps the first attempt to reach American Indians was made in 1857.[86] In that same year a report was published on the authority of a French Baptist minister in Canada who claimed to have encountered individuals in France who also proclaimed the third angel's message.[87] In 1859 a Norwegian immigrant, who had become a Sabbatarian Adventist in the U.S.A., reported that he thought he had heard the third angel's message proclaimed by a Swede in Norway in 1848.[88] Neither report was confirmed in later publications.

B. Developments during 1860-74.

In the period 1860-74 the shut-door concept continued to be interpreted in terms of the sanctuary theology and the rejection of truth. Smith stated that the shut door (Mt. 25:10) signified the closing of the door of the holy place, implying a change in "the relation between God and the world," a termination of His "general ministry for the whole world."[89] Those who rejected the new insights and deliberately approached Him as if He were still in the holy place would not find Him there (Hos. 5:6), for "that door is

83 J. White, "Publications in Other Languages," *RH,* May 6, 1858, p. 200, Cf. Letter, M. B. Czechowski to E. G. White, *RH*, Sept. 23, 1858, p. 144; J. White, "Third Angel's Message," p. 141.

84 Letter, J. Andrews to Smith, in "Extract from a Letter from Ireland," *RH,* Aug. 14, 1860, p. 103; Letter, Jane Martin to J. White, in "The Sabbath in Ireland," *RH,* Nov. 19, 1861, p. 199; Letter, Jno. Sisley to J. White, *RH,* July 2, 1861, p. 47.

85 Letter, S. E. Armstrong to J. White, *RH,* Dec. 15, 1863, p. 23; Letter, Margaret Armstrong to J. White, in "Extract from a Letter from Ireland," *RH,* Aug. 14, 1860, p. 103. Since 1857 Margaret Armstrong's brother, J. Andrews, was the one who provided his relatives with literature. It is possible that both Margaret and her daughter Sarah accepted the third angel's message at the same time (*ibid.*).

86 A Seneca Indian settlement was visited by Cottrell and Ingraham ("The Cause in Western New York," *RH,* Feb. 12, 1857, p. 117). For the sermons given, see Cottrell, "Sermon Preached to the Seneca Indians," *RH,* May 14, 1857, pp. 12, 13; Cottrell, "A Discourse Written for the Seneca Indians, To Be Delivered Through an Interpreter. No. 2," *RH,* June 10, 1858, pp. 28, 29.

87 A. C. Bourdeau, "The French Baptists," *RH,* Feb. 5, 1857, p. 108. Cf. A. C. Bourdeau, "The Third Angel's Message in France," *RH,* March 26, 1857, p. 166.

88 Letter, Francis C. Johnson to Smith, *RH,* March 17, 1850, p. 134. Here Johnson stated that in 1848 he accepted the proclamation of "the Commandments of God and the Faith of Jesus . . . as truth, but did not keep the Sabbath; for we thought that we could wait till we got across the Atlantic to America where there would be no persecution." Cf. Matteson, "The Scandinavian Mission," in *Historical Sketches of the Foreign Missions of the Seventh-day Adventists,* 1886, p. 57.

89 Smith, "Visions — Objections," *RH,* June 19, 1866, pp. 17, 18 (*Visions,* pp. 23, 30).

shut."[90] He indicated, however, that salvation was still possible for "honest persons, who have not, on account of their rejection of truth, been given over to blindness of mind, and hardness of heart, should such die before hearing the truth, living up to the best light they have."[91] In Smith's opinion the mass of mankind were "hopeless rejecters of the truth, [with] but yet a few honest hearts remaining, for whose benefit the proclamation of the truth goes forth."[92] E. G. White stated that the example of believers who lived in accordance with the truth they professed was "saving a few, and condemning the many, leaving them with no excuse in the day when the cases of all will be decided."[93] She indicated, however, that mission efforts should include those who have "apostatized from the truth."[94] In the years following 1874 she interpreted the various aspects of the parable of the virgins in the context of the past Advent experience, the present situation of the church, and the future Second Advent.[95]

90 *Ibid.*, p. 18 (*Visions*, p. 26). Comparing the rejection of Christ by the Jews with the attitude of contemporary Christians, he said, "The second house of Israel, the professed people of God of the present day, have stumbled at the second advent of Christ, as the first house, the Jews, did at the first advent, and have thus brought themselves into similar condemnation" (*ibid.* [*Visions*, p. 31]).

91 Smith, "Visions — Objections," p. 18.

92 *Ibid.* (*Visions*, p. 31). Here he said: "A final message of mercy, the third angel, is sent forth to give mankind a last warning, and gather out the few who may not be given over to hardness of heart, and may be willing to comply with the terms of the truth" (*ibid.* [*Visions*, p. 30]).

93 E. G. White, *TC*, No. 17, pp. 169, 170 (*T*, II, 334). Cf. *ibid.*, No. 18, p. 74 (*T*, II, 402).

94 *Ibid.*, No. 15, p. 11 (*T*, II, 20). Only a few SDA felt this burden (*ibid.*). As biblical motivation Lk. 15:1-7 was referred to (*ibid.*, pp. 11-13 [*T*, II, 21, 22]).

95 E. G. White stated that "in the parable of the ten virgins . . . the experience of Adventists is illustrated by the incidents of an Eastern marriage" (*SP*, IV, 242, 243). See *ibid.*, pp. 243, 248, 249. Referring to Mt. 25:10 she said that in 1844 the Adventists "were not to be present in person at the marriage; for it takes place in Heaven, while they are upon the earth. . . . But they are to understand his [Christ's] work, and to follow him by faith as he goes in before God. It is in this sense that they are said to go in to the marriage.

"In the parable it was those that had oil in their vessels with their lamps that went in to the marriage. Those who, with a knowledge of the truth from the Scriptures, had also the Spirit and grace of God, and who, in the night of their bitter trial [Disappointment and the period immediately following it], had patiently waited, searching the Bible for clearer light, — these saw the truth concerning the sanctuary in Heaven and the Saviour's change of ministration, and by faith they followed him in his work in the sanctuary above" (*GC*, pp. 427, 428). Showing the present reality of this event, she added that "all who through the testimony of the Scriptures accept the same truths, following Christ by faith as he enters in before God to perform the last work of mediation, and at its close to receive his kingdom, — all these are represented as going in to the marriage" (*ibid.*, p. 428). The shut door of the parable was placed in the near future. She indicated that when this final work of Christ, which was described as "the investigative judgment" and illustrated by Mt. 22:11-13, would be completed, then "probation will close, and the door of mercy will be shut. Thus in the one short sentence, 'They that were ready went in with him to the marriage, and the door was shut,' [Mt. 25:10] we are carried down through the Saviour's final ministration, to the time when the great work for man's salvation shall be completed" (*ibid.*). She affirmed that there was also a shut door in 1844, but this door was associated with Rev. 3:7, 8 (MS 4, 1883 [*SM*, I, 63]; *SP*, IV, 269, 270) and referred to both the closed door in the heavenly sanctuary and "the condition of the careless and unbelieving among professed Christians, who are willingly ignorant of the work of our merciful High Priest" (*ibid.*). For her application of various aspects of the parable to the present and imminent future, see e.g., *TC*, No. 33, 1889, p. 13 (*T*, V, 485); "The Perils and

In the interpretation of Mt. 24:14, the period 1860-74 shows little change from the previous period, except that the text was not any more considered to be fulfilled, but *almost* fulfilled.[96] Millerite arguments were frequently employed to indicate the nearness of Christ's return. For example, the idea was repeated that the text did not require every individual to hear the Gospel but only that it be proclaimed as a "witness" to all nations.[97] Further, the "general" proclamation of the Gospel was regarded as having been almost accomplished by Christian missions, as evidenced by the history of Christian missions[98] and contemporary missionary activity.[99] The fulfillment of this text in the context of the "specific" proclamation of the Second Advent also continued to be supported by Millerite statements on the widespread nature of the first angel's message during the 1840s.[100] Regarding the end of the world, J. White stated in the setting of the three angel's messages that "when the purpose of God in the proclamation of the coming reign of Christ shall be accomplished, *then* will the end come."[101]

The text, "Thou must prophesy again before many people, and nations, and tongues, and kings" (Rev. 10:11), was frequently used to describe the present extent of SDA mission. The believers saw in Rev. 10 a prophetic account of the proclamation of the first angel's message, the Disappointment, and the mission of the third angel's message (10:11).[102] During the 1860s the feeling continued to exist that 10:11 could be fulfilled in the U.S.A. Smith pointed out that this country occupied "a providential place in

---

Privileges of the Last Days," *RH,* Nov. 22, 1892, p. 722 (*SDABC,* VII, 984); "Words to the Young," *YI,* Sept. 20, 1894, p. 297; Letter, E. G. White to the Olsons, 64a, 1895 (*TM,* p. 233); *COL,* pp. 406-16; *T,* VI, 129; *ibid.,* VIII, 212; *ibid.,* IX, 155; "The Ten Virgins," *Signs of the Times,* June 21, 1910, pp. 371, 372 (*SDABC,* V, 1956, p. 1099); "Go, Preach the Gospel," *RH,* Nov. 17, 1910, p. 7 (*Medical Ministry . . . ,* 1932, p. 331); *The Acts of the Apostles . . . ,* 1911, p. 55.

96   See e.g., Loughborough, "Questions for Bro. Loughborough," *RH,* Nov. 19, 1861, p. 200; J. White, "Faith and Hope," *RH,* Jan. 18, 1870, p. 25; Canright, "The Gospel Preached in All the World," *RH,* Dec. 1874, p. 197.

97   See e.g., Loughborough, "Questions," p. 200; [J. White], "Questions and Answers," *RH,* Dec. 23, 1862, p. 29; J. White, "Our Faith and Hope," *RH,* Dec. 27, 1870, p. 10 (*The Second Coming of Christ . . . ,* 1871, p. 21); [Smith], "The Gospel Preached in All the World," *RH,* July 16, 1872, p. 36. See *supra,* pp. 51, 52. Mk. 13:10 was identified with Mk. 24:14 (Loughborough, "Questions," p. 200).

98   See e.g., [J. White], "Questions," p. 29; "Signs of the Advent," *Voice of the Prophets,* repr. in *RH,* June 23, 1863, p. 25; J. White, "Faith and Hope," *RH,* Jan. 18, 1870, p. 25; J. White, "Faith and Hope," *RH,* Dec. 27, 1870, p. 10 (*Second Coming,* pp. 21, 22); Canright, "Present Condition of the World," *RH,* April 16, 1872, p. 138. See *supra,* p. 50.

99   See e.g., G. W. Amadon, "Fourteen Reasons Why I Believe the Lord Is Soon Coming," *RH,* Dec. 3, 1861, p. 7; Canright, "The Spread of the Gospel a Sign of the End," *RH,* Dec. 6, 1870, p. 196; Canright, "Condition of the World," p. 138; Canright, "Gospel," p. 197. See *supra,* p. 51.

100   J. White, "Faith and Hope," *RH,* Jan. 18, 1870, pp. 25, 26; J. White, "Faith and Hope," *RH,* Dec. 27, 1870, p. 10 (*Second Coming,* pp. 22-27). See *supra,* pp. 52, 54, 55. In 1861, in referring to Rev. 14:6-12, Amadon said: "For the last twenty years the globe has rung with the doctrine of the coming of the Son of man" ("Fourteen Reasons," p. 7).

101   J. White, "Faith and Hope," *RH,* Jan. 18, 1870, p. 26.

102   See e.g., J. White, "Conference Address," p. 180. Cf. Smith, "Revelation," pp. 164, 165 (*Revelation,* pp. 177-187).

history" because "in what other land could the proclamation of the truth reach at once so many 'peoples, nations and tongues?' Rev. x, 11. People from every civilized part of the globe are here to be found, as a settled and abiding portion of our population."[103] This text was also used as an incentive for the distribution of publications in other languages.[104] When individuals from the highest political level showed an interest in SDA literature, Haskell saw this as a fulfillment of the text, for "the truth" was also to go to "kings."[105] In the 1870s, however, the extent of Rev. 10:11 began to be designated as "world-wide."[106]

To comprehend the significance of statements made up till 1874 regarding the "world-wide" extent of the SDA mission, it is necessary to look at the numerical size of the new church and its mission outreach. In 1863 when the SDA Church was officially organized it had a membership of about 3500, not many of whom had much in the way of financial resources. By 1875, 8000 members (the official number)[107] attempted to manage two publishing houses, a medical institution, and a college, to supply a growing demand for workers, and to fund a rapidly expanding work in North America. Since 1861 the believers had been aware that several individuals had accepted the third angel's message in Ireland through reading literature sent by relatives in the U.S.A.[108] Publications had also been sent to England, and the "present truth" was accepted there.[109] By that time mission work was carried on among the French, Polish, Italian, Swedish, Danish, Norwegian and German immigrants in the U.S.A.[110] For years these immigrant converts had already been calling for publications in their native languages and pamphlets had been published in French, German, and

103 [Smith], Editorial Remarks, *RH*, Jan. 1, 1867, p. 48. Matteson stated that Rev. 10:11 was a promise of the kindness and mercy of Jesus to foreigners in the U.S.A. ("Report," *RH*, March 24, 1868, p. 237). Another believer felt that at the time of the loud cry immigrants would return to "their respective nations, and there proclaim the solemn warning of the third angel" (J. S. Miller, "The California Mission," *RH*, Aug. 25, 1868, p. 154).

104 Haskell, "Svensk Advent Harold," *TrM*, March 1874, p. 24.

105 Haskell, "The Cause Is Onward," *TrM*, Sept. 1874, p. 68.

106 See e.g., J. White, "Conference Address," p. 180; *infra*, p. 289.

107 The General Conference Report statistics on membership in the *RH* during 1867-75 provided the following data: 4320 members in 1867; 4475 in 1868; 4900 in 1869; 5440 in 1870; 4550 in 1871; 4801 in 1872; 5875 in 1873; 8022 in 1875. According to Smith there were in 1874 "291 churches with an enrollment of about 7500 members." However, due to the scattered conditions of the various individual believers "a large proportion" was unable to belong to any of the official churches. The total number of SDA was estimated to be between 12,000 and 15,000 ("Seventh-day Adventists," *RH*, Nov. 10, 1874, p. 156). Pre-1863 data: About 100 believers in 1849 (*supra*, p. 161); 1000 paying *RH* subscribers in 1854-55 and 2000 paying subscribers in 1858 (J. White, "Present Truth," p. 78). Andrews estimated the number of believers in 1859 at 10,000, and in 1862 at 12,000 (*History of the Sabbath . . .*, 1859, p. 90; *ibid.*, 1862, p. 340). Cf. Smith, *Both Sides on the Sabbath and Law*, 1864, p. 3.

108 M. Armstrong and Martin in "Sabbath in Ireland," pp. 198, 199; Letter, Martin to E. G. White, *RH*, Dec. 16, 1862, pp. 21, 22; *supra*, p. 282.

109 Letter, Sisley to J. White, p. 47. The acceptance took place in 1860 (*ibid.*).

110 See e.g., Czechowski, "The N.Y. Mission," *RH*, Sept. 4, 1860, p. 125; *supra*, p. 282. Czechowski called his mission among immigrants a work "in foreign nations" (*ibid.*).

Dutch.[111] In 1863 literature was sent to Australia[112] and J. White became one of the first to employ the expression "world-wide" in reference to SDA mission.[113] At the same time B. F. Snook, who was an SDA minister for a few years, made the remark that the Great Commission was still valid. He stated that "the same great commission that authorized them [disciples] to go out into all the world is yet in force, and Christ yet says to his people, 'Go ye into all the world, and preach the gospel to every creature' [Mk. 16:15]";[114] while John G. Matteson[115] expressed his hope that "the solemn sound of the third angel's message may be carried to the ends of the earth."[116] In that year there was the possibility that the SDA General Conference Executive Committee might send Snook as "a missionary to Europe before the close of 1863."[117] One of the workers, M. B. Czechowski,[118] volunteered to go as a missionary to Europe. When for certain reasons, which were generally of a personal nature,[119] this offer was not accepted, Czechowski discontinued his work for the SDA Church and left for Europe in May, 1864, as a missionary at large for the non-Sabbatarian Adventists who, incidentally, had become the strongest opponents of SDA.[120] By 1864

111   See *supra*, p. 281. Cf. J. White, "Publications in Other Languages," *RH,* Nov. 12, 1872, p. 173.
112   "Books Sent by Mail," *RH,* Sept. 1, 1863, p. 112.
113   [J. White], "Light of the World," p. 165.
114   Snook, "Missionary Society," p. 46.
115   John G. Matteson (1835-96) was born in Denmark. In 1854 he emigrated to the U.S.A. There he studied at the Baptist Theological Seminary in Chicago and was ordained in 1862. The following year he became a SDA and served as a successful minister and editor with a special concern for Scandinavians both in Europe and in the U.S.A.
116   Letter, Matteson to J. White, *RH,* Nov. 10, 1863, p. 191.
117   [J. White], "God's Free-Men," *RH,* June 2, 1863, p. 8. This may have been a response to a call from Ireland for a missionary ([J. White], "The Cause," *RH,* Feb. 16, 1864, p. 92). Already in 1862 there were plans to send a missionary to Ireland (Letter, Martin to E. G. White, p. 22).
118   Michael Belina Czechowski (1818-76) was born and educated for the priesthood in Poland. Later he became disillusioned with the Roman Catholic Church and immigrated to America. He attended a French Baptist school near Montreal, Canada and was sent to do mission work among the French-speaking people in the eastern part of the U.S.A. There he came in contact with Sabbatarian Adventists and joined them in 1857. When he returned to Europe he proclaimed the Sabbath in Italy, Switzerland, France, Germany, Hungary and Rumania.
119   See e.g., [Andrews], "The Seventh-day Adventists of Europe," *RH,* Nov. 30, 1869, p. 181; [J. White], "Cause in Switzerland," *RH,* Jan. 11, 1870, p. 22; Andrews, "The Case of Eld. M. B. Czechowski," *RH,* July 8, 1873, p. 29; Andrews, "Adresse au public," *Les signes des temps,* Jan. 1880, p. 340; Letter, Czechowski to [Albert] Vuilleumier, July 5, 1868 (Jacques Frei, "Recueil de documents concernant Michael Belina Czechowski," 1971, p. 19). Cf. Letter, E. G. White to Czechowski, No. 3, c. 1864. For Czechowski's later attitude toward the SDA Church, see e.g., Letter, Czechowski to Vuilleumier, July 5, 1868 (Frei, "Documents," pp. 18-20); Andrews, "Czechowski," p. 29. Cf. Czechowski, "Mission Letters from Hungary," *WC,* July 28, 1869, p. 80.
120   [Andrews], "Europe," p. 181; Letter, Czechowski to Grant, *WC,* May 31, 1864, p. 43. According to D. T. Taylor, Vice-President of the American Advent Missionary Society, Czechowski did not belong to a missionary society but was "a missionary at large for all the Adventists, — the [*Advent*] *Herald,* the [*World's*] *Crisis,* and *Voice* [*of the West*]" ("Our European Mission," *WC,* Nov. 22, 1865, p. 38). Cf. L. T. Cunningham, "Eld. M. B. Czechowski," *WC,* Dec. 22, 1869, p. 54. By 1869 Czechowski was calling his mission the "great European and

two missionaries in Africa had become "whole hearted Seventh-day Adventists" mainly through reading SDA literature.[121] A request was made for further literature and a missionary.[122] Another call for a missionary came from Ireland.[123] However, no missionary was sent. This seemed due less to financial than to manpower inadequacy. Because of a lack of workers for the great need in America, no man "could be spared."[124] Literature requests also came from Italy[125] and Switzerland.[126] The general impression of the leadership, however, was that the "principal theater of the third angel's message, the final message of mercy . . . seems to be in our own country."[127]

In the early part of 1868 news was received that since his return to Europe Czechowski had established, without the knowledge of his Adventist sponsors, groups of Sabbath-observing Adventists in Central Europe. One of these groups in Switzerland discovered that there were SDA in the U.S.A. Correspondence developed which revealed that there were about 50 Sabbatarian Adventists in Switzerland and Italy.[128] The following year

only evangelical Advent mission" established by the "American Advent Christian Union, resident in . . . Boston" ("Mission Letters," p. 80). Cf. Czechowski, "Letter from Hungary," *WC*, March 31, 1869, p. 12. At the end of 1866 he began publishing a weekly *L'Evangile Eternel*, which was sent to Italy, France, England, Holland, Germany, Poland, Hungary, and different parts of Switzerland ("Mission Letters from Switzerland," *WC*, Jan. 9, 1867, p. 66).

121 Hannah More, "The Sabbath in Africa," *RH*, March 29, 1864, p. 142. One of these was Hannah More, an American missionary. About 1862 she briefly met Haskell who presented her Andrews' *History of the Sabbath* and a few tracts. When in 1863 she left for Africa (Cape Palmas, Liberia), the *RH* and other publications were sent to her. Through her influence literature was sent to "every missionary station on [the] African shore" and to Wm. Muller, the manager of the Orphan Asylum in Bristol, England. The other missionary was Alexander Dickson, an Australian missionary, who had accepted the Sabbath through More. He returned to Australia with SDA publications (Haskell, "Tract and Missionary Work," *RH*, Dec. 17, 1872, p. 8; "Books Sent By Mail," *RH*, July 5, 1864, p. 48). Her death in 1868 was indirectly the result of a lack of concern and hospitality among SDA in Battle Creek (E. G. White, *TC*, No. 14, pp. 45-62 [*T*, I, 666-80]; *ibid.*, No. 16, pp. 34-40 [*T*, II, 140-45]). This also indicated an absence of interest for mission among people of other nations or religions.

122 "Books Sent By Mail," *RH*, Aug. 22 and Sept. 26, 1865, pp. 96, 136; More, "Letter from Africa," *RH*, Oct. 11, 1864, p. 155.

123 [J. White], "Cause," *RH*, Feb. 16, 1864, p. 92.

124 *Ibid.* In 1863 the SDA membership was 3500 with 30 evangelistic workers and 125 churches ("SDA Church," *SDAE*, p. 1181). A similar reason was given in 1869 when there was a call from Switzerland for a missionary (Letter, Andrews to Brethren [in Switzerland], April 2, 1869).

125 "Books Sent By Mail," *RH*, July 18, and Nov. 28, 1865, pp. 56, 207. These requests came from Joseph Jones and Mons le Comte Pierro Guicciardini who seemed to be converts of Czechowski in Italy (Czechowski, "The Italian Mission," *WC*, July 25, 1865, p. 74; Czechowski, "Mission Letters from Switzerland," *WC*, June 27, 1866, p. 58). Already in 1864 the *RH* was sent to Guicciardini ("Receipts for Review and Herald," *RH*, Sept. 13, 1864, p. 128).

126 "Books Sent By Mail," *RH*, Nov. 28, 1865, p. 207. This was requested by Czechowski.

127 General Conference Committee, "The Time Has Come!" *RH*, Feb. 21, 1865, p. 100.

128 See e.g., [Andrews], "Europe," p. 181. Among the first converts of Czechowski in Europe (Italy) were Catherine Revel and Jean David Geymet (Albert Vuilleumier in "Switzerland," *RH*, Aug. 26, 1873, p. 86; J. Vuilleumier, *Premiers jours de l'oeuvre en Europe*, p. 4 [*La revue adventiste*, May 1, 15 and June 1, 15, 1939; Frei, "Documents," p. 75]).

J. H. Ertzenberger (sometimes spelled Erzenberger or Erzberger)[129] was sent to the U.S.A. as a representative of the Swiss believers to gain a more complete understanding of SDA doctrines.[130] At that time the SDA Church received "almost daily applications to send publications to other lands."[131] Against this background, the General Conference of that year hailed "with joy every indication of the present truth going to the nations and tongues of the earth"[132] and decided to establish "the Missionary Society of the Seventh-day Adventists." Its object was "to send the truths of the Third Angel's Message to foreign lands, and to distant parts of our own country, by means of missionaries, papers, books, tracts, &c."[133] In 1870, in the context of the recent developments in Switzerland, J. White indicated that the SDA mission included "all Christian lands."[134] At the General Conference a resolution was passed concerning Czechowski's mission in Europe acknowledging "the hand of God in the establishment of a body of S. D. Adventists in Central Europe," and Christian fellowship was extended to these believers.[135] In the autumn of 1870 Ertzenberger returned to Switzerland to become the first ordained minister recognized by the SDA Church to extend their mission outside North America. Plans were also made to publish twelve pamphlets in several languages especially for the benefit of immigrants in America.[136]

At the end of 1871 the General Conference affirmed its interest in the mission work in Switzerland and other European countries and promised assistance as far as Providence allowed.[137] A resolution was adopted outlining a strategy of world mission intended to reach "the foreign born population of this land [U.S.A.], not only for their own sakes, but as one of the

129 At this time his name seems to be "Ertzenberger," a spelling used by himself and Andrews (Ertzenberger, "Letter from Bro. Ertzenberger," *RH,* Nov. 30, 1869, p. 183; [Andrews], "Europe," p. 181). The town birth records of Liestal, near Basel, show him registered at birth (1843) as "Erzenberger." The town records of the "family booklet" (a possession of every married man in Switzerland) spells it "Erzberger" — a name by which he was known in later years. In 1864 he entered a Protestant school which prepared him for ministerial work. A few years later he joined a group of Sabbatarian Adventists which had been established by Czechowski. He died in 1920.

130 See e.g., [Andrews], "Europe," p. 181; J. White, "Seventh-day Adventist Missionary Society," *RH,* June 15, 1869, p. 197. In 1872 another Swiss believer, Adémar Vuilleumier, was sent to the U.S.A. for similar reasons (Letter, Albert Vuilleumier to General Conference Committee, May 22, 1872; Announcements, *RH,* July 2, 1872, p. 24).

131 J. White, "Missionary Society," p. 197.

132 General Conference Report, *RH,* May 25, 1869, p. 173. Special reference was made to mission among Danish immigrants.

133 Smith in J. White, "Missionary Society," p. 197. The work among the French in Vermont and Canada was still considered as "the work of Foreign Missions" (Vermont State Conference Report, *RH,* Nov. 2, 1869, p. 150).

134 [J. White], "Switzerland," p. 22. In 1874 E. G. White said: "Our publications should be printed in different languages and sent to every civilized country, at any cost" ("Sacrifice," p. 2). Cf. Haskell, "Our Work," *TrM,* May 1874, p. 37.

135 General Conference Report, *RH,* March 22, 1870, p. 109. Cf. [J. White], "Switzerland," p. 22; General Conference Report, *RH,* Jan. 2, 1872, p. 20.

136 Publishing Association Committee, "Works in Other Languages," *RH,* Oct. 4, 1870, p. 125; J. White, "Publications," p. 173.

137 General Conference Report, *RH,* Jan. 2, 1872, p. 20.

most efficient means of spreading to other lands a message which is to go to many nations, kindreds, tongues, and people."[138] In referring to missionary literature in other languages, J. White pointed out in 1872 that SDA were "several years behind the opening providence of God."[139] E. G. White urged the printing of publications in other languages, "that foreign nations may be reached,"[140] and called for individuals who could translate English SDA literature so the message of warning might go "to all nations" and men and women, "as they see the light, may turn from transgression to obedience of the law of God."[141] The study of other languages was recommended to young people so that "God may use them as mediums to communicate his saving truth to those of other nations."[142] Furthermore she said that "missionaries" should be available who were "willing, if need be, to go to foreign countries to present the truth before those who sit in darkness."[143] That year literature in Danish was both published and distributed in Denmark.[144]

The General Conferences of 1873 reaffirmed the interest in mission among non-English-speaking people.[145] The demand for missionaries grew. Haskell stated that besides the crying need for qualified workers for the English-speaking population of the U.S.A. there were calls from "the Danes, Swedes, Norwegians, French, and Germans of our own land, and letters from Europe which show that there are openings in France, Spain, Italy, and in other parts of the Eastern continent."[146] In order to meet this demand the decision was made to establish a denominational school at Battle Creek, Michigan.[147] J. White remarked that it was not sufficient to work among the immigrants in the U.S.A.; men must be sent to Europe to establish the work. In response to calls from Switzerland, White urged that Andrews be sent in the autumn of 1873.[148] He was not sent, and in Europe

138 *Ibid.*, p. 21. Cf. E. G. White, "The Foreigners in America," *RH*, July 25, 1918, pp. 19, 20 (*Instruction for Effective Christian Service*, 1947, p. 200); *supra*, p. 285, n. 103.

139 J. White, "Publications," p. 173. Cf. the attitude towards Marcus Lichtenstein (E. G. White, *TC*, No. 22, pp. 99, 121, 122 [*T*, III, 192, 205, 206]).

140 *Ibid.*, p. 118 (*T*, III, 204). She also said: "Every opportunity should be improved to extend the truth to other nations. This will be attended with considerable expense, but expense should in no case hinder the performance of this work" (*ibid.*, p. 124 [*T*, III, 208]).

141 *Ibid.*, p. 124 (*T*, III, 207, 208).

142 *Ibid.*, p. 118 (*T*, III, 204).

143 *Ibid.*, No. 21, p. 142 (*T*, III, 94).

144 Godske Petersen, "A Letter from Denmark," *RH*, Feb. 4, 1873, p. 62. In 1872 the first foreign language monthly, the *Advent Tidende*, was published. It was also sent to Denmark (*ibid.*; Smith, "The Conference," *RH*, Jan. 16, 1872, p. 36).

145 General Conference Report, *RH*, March 11, 1873, p. 108; General Conference Report, *RH*, Nov. 25, 1873, p. 190.

146 Haskell, "Ministerial Lecturers," *RH*, April 1, 1873, p. 125.

147 *Ibid.* Andrews, "Our Proposed School," *RH*, April 1, 1873, p. 124. In 1901 this school was moved to Berrien Springs, Michigan. The name was changed to Emmanuel Missionary College. In 1958-60 this institution was merged with Potomac University and adopted the name Andrews University named after J. N. Andrews ("Andrews University," *SDAE*, pp. 36-42).

148 J. White, "Progress of the Cause," *RH*, Aug. 26, 1873, p. 84. A few months earlier E. G. White said that it was God's will that Smith should visit other countries as a missionary (Letter, E. G. White to Smith, No. 10, 1873).

missionary progress continued slowly in Switzerland, Italy, and France.[149] By 1873 Rev. 10:11 was at last interpreted as having world-wide significance,[150] one of the arguments being similarity between the first and the third angel's messages. J. White pointed out that the first angel's message was foreseen as going "with a loud voice" and the fulfillment had been world-wide (Rev. 14:6, 7). The third angel's message was also foreseen as going "with a loud voice" (Rev. 14:9), and analogy, he said, implied a similar world-wide scope.[151] This similarity also led to the practice of using the phrase "to every nation, and kindred, and tongue, and people" (Rev. 14:6) as an indication of the intended spread of the third angel's message. Thus E. G. White stated that "the message of solemn warning must be given to all nations, tongues, and people,"[152] and Haskell remarked that "wherever may be found worshipers of the true God, among every kindred, tongue, and people, there must this message be understood."[153]

In 1874 the SDA mission continued to expand. It was reported that in most cases, as a result of literature distribution, individuals had begun to observe the Sabbath in the Southern States of the U.S.A., Denmark, Sweden, Norway, Germany, Switzerland, Italy, France, Spain, England, Russia, Mexico and Australia.[154] In addition, calls for literature came from Scotland, Ireland, China and New Zealand[155] while publications had already been "sent" to "every missionary station on the coast of Africa."[156] Summarizing current mission outreach, Haskell stated that "publications upon present truth are called for by individuals in almost every nation under heaven where civilization exists."[157] Against such a background it is understandable that Mk. 16:15, "Go ye into all the world, and preach the gospel to every creature" began at last to be used, even being chosen as the motto of the periodical, *The True Missionary*. Like Rev. 10:11; 14:6, this

149 Albert Vuilleumier, "Switzerland," p. 86; Albert Vuilleumier, "From Switzerland and Italy," *RH*, March 17, 1874, p. 110.
150 See e.g., J. White, "Conference Address," p. 180; Butler, " 'The Permanency of the Cause,' " *RH*, July 22, 1873, p. 44; Butler, "Testimony No. 23 and Bro. White's Address," *RH*, Nov. 4, 1873, p. 164; Butler, "Nations," p. 20.
151 J. White, "Conference Address," p. 180. Cf. Smith, "The Third Angel's Message," *RH*, March 24, 1874, p. 116; *supra*, p. 281, n. 81. Cf. J. White, "Loud Voice," pp. 172, 173.
152 E. G. White, MS la, 1874. She added that "the message will convict and convert the hearers or condemn them. All will be left without excuse."
153 Haskell, "Prophesy Again," *TrM*, Aug. 1874, p. 57. Cf. Haskell, "Cause Is Onward," *RH*, May 26, 1874, p. 190.
154 Haskell and Butler quoted in the Quarterly Report of the Michigan Tract and Missionary Society, *TrM*, Jan. 1874, p. 3; Haskell, "The Work of the Tract Societies," *TrM*, Jan. 1874, p. 6; Haskell, "Our Work," p. 37; Haskell, "Cause," *RH*, May 26, 1874, p. 190; Haskell, "The Cause Is Onward," *TrM*, Aug. 1874, p. 60.
155 Haskell, "Tract Societies," p. 6; Haskell, "General Organization," *TrM*, Sept. 1874, p. 65; Smith, "The Seventh-day Adventists," *RH*, Nov. 17, 1874, p. 164 (*The Seventh-day Adventists . . .* , 1876-77, p. 19); Haskell, "The Cause Is Onward," *TrM*, Nov. 1874, p. 85; Haskell, "Among the Nations," *TrM*, Dec. 1874, p. 93.
156 Smith, "Seventh-day Adventists," p. 164 (*Seventh-day Adventists*, p. 19); Haskell, "Tract Societies," p. 6. This could be a reference to the influence of More (*ibid.; supra*, p. 287, n. 121).
157 Haskell, "Cause," *RH*, May 26, 1874, p. 190.

text was interpreted as having world-wide significance. Referring to it, E. G. White said: "We have a world-wide message,"[158] and a correspondent of the *True Missionary* said it implied a mission to "every habitable part of the globe."[159]

A large percentage of SDA still clung to a limited concept of the church's mission. Haskell complained that while many had a theoretical understanding that their mission was to warn the whole world, they had no idea that in practice this meant spreading "the truth . . . to every State and Territory in this Union, and into every part of such State or Territory" and "to every civilized nation on the globe, wherever there are honest hearts."[160] Furthermore he felt that "the last message of mercy must reach all that are in danger of the wrath of God, which is all mankind; for all are embraced in the call, 'Whosoever will, let him come' [Mk. 8:34]."[161] The most extensive view on world-wide mission in 1874 was provided by E. G. White, who stated that "the whole world . . . is God's great vineyard. The cities and villages constitute a part of that vineyard. These must be worked, and not passed by."[162] She added that the SDA message was "a world-wide message. It is to be given to all cities, to all villages; it is to be proclaimed in the highways and the byways."[163]

At last the SDA Church commissioned J. N. Andrews as its first official American-born overseas missionary. On September 15, 1874 he sailed for Europe,[164] an event in the mission progress described by Butler as being "of great interest."[165] Having arrived in Europe, Andrews described the importance of the world-wide SDA mission as "giving to the world the warning of the near approach of the Judgment, and in setting forth the sacred character of the law of God, as the rule of our lives and of the final Judgment, and the obligation of mankind to keep God's commandments."[166] This concept of mission was affirmed by E. G. White: "The light concerning

158 E. G. White, "Work for This Time," p. 9. Cf. E. G. White, "Offerings," p. 195 (*T*, III, 406). Regarding warning of individuals, see James Sawyer, "Who Will Respond to the Call?" *TrM*, Feb. 1874, p. 11.

159 M. Wood, "True Missionary Spirit," *TrM*, May 1874, p. 34.

160 Haskell, "Our Work," p. 37. E. G. White said: "But your conceptions of the work need to be greatly enlarged. Our message is to go forth in power to all parts of the world, — to Oregon, England, Australia, to the islands of the sea, to all nations, tongues, and people" (MS 1, 1874 [*SpT*, (Series A), No. 7, p. 17]).

161 Haskell, "System," *TrM*, May 1874, p. 40.

162 E. G. White, MS 1, 1874 (*T*, VII, 34, 35). Cf. Letter, E. G. White to Edson and Emma White, No. 19b, 1874. Letter, E. G. White to the Smiths, No. 25, 1874.

163 E. G. White, MS 1, 1874 (*T*, VII, 36).

164 Andrews, "Our Embarkation," *RH*, Sept. 22, 1874, p. 112. Earlier in 1874 Butler made an appeal for missionaries to Europe ("Nations," p. 21). See *supra*, p. 192, n. 208. A major reason why there was not much enthusiasm for going to Europe was that such an enterprise seemed to involve many difficulties at that time. Butler said: "It is safe to say that our young men would look upon such an undertaking with fear and almost with horror" (*ibid.*). J. White suggested that Loughborough would be the best man to go to England ("A World-Wide Mission," *RH*, Aug. 25, 1874, p. 76).

165 Butler, "Missionary to Europe," *RH*, Sept. 15, 1874, p. 100.

166 Andrews, "Meeting of Sabbath-Keepers in Neuchatel," *RH*, Nov. 24, 1874, p. 172. Cf. J. White, "Progress of the Cause," *RH*, Aug. 26, 1873, p. 84.

the binding claims of the law of Jehovah is to be presented everywhere. This is the deciding question; it will test and prove the world."[167]

During this year, however, due to a large dependence on literature distribution, the praxis of the world-wide mission concept was primarily confined to literate individuals living in areas where the influence of the Christian civilization had penetrated. It was not until many years later that a practical concern developed for people of religions other than Christian.[168]

C. Summary.

The period 1850-74 was a time of gradual expansion of the view of the missionary task. It was a period of transition from the idea of an imminent Second Advent to a realization that before Christ could return the third angel's message had to be proclaimed world-wide. The concept of "the remnant" did not interfere with the mission thrust because the event of the parousia was understood to await the accomplishment of the mission of the third angel and not the amassing of a certain quantity of believers. As the result of successful mission outreach, the shut-door concept continued to be modified. Although the emphasis shifted from the shut- to the open-door concept, the view that there was a shut door in 1844 was retained and became a part of SDA soteriology and missiology. Further developments in the sanctuary theology removed all theological obstructions against mission among non-Adventists.

It was especially Rev. 10:11 which was employed as a symbol for the SDA mission to other nations. At first many thought that this text was being adequately fulfilled when the third angel's message began to be accepted by European immigrants in North America. But expansion of SDA mission and of the understanding of Rev. 10:11 occurred when converted immigrants sent literature to relatives in Europe.

Until 1874 the missionary expansion of the SDA outside North America was conducted primarily by the distribution of literature. Growing requests for literature from many countries led to the introduction of the term

167 E. G. White, MS 1, 1874 (SpT, [Series A], No. 7, p. 17). Several years later when there was an emphasis on righteousness by faith in an attempt to proclaim the doctrines in a more Christocentric setting, she wrote in an article that "the burden of our message should be the mission and life of Jesus Christ. Let there be a dwelling upon the humiliation, self-denial, meekness, and lowliness of Christ. . . . Show to your hearers Jesus in his condenscension to save fallen man." However, in this article she also called attention to "the great testing truths that constitute the solemn message to be given to the world" and stressed that the mind should "dwell upon the great work of redemption, the soon coming of Christ, and the commandments of God" ("The Work of the Minister," RH, Sept. 11, 1888, p. 578). In another instance she united the major aspects of the SDA mission in the central theme of the third angel's message when she said that "the burden of our message should be 'the commandments of God, and the faith of Jesus' " (TM, p. 219).

168 For a survey of SDA missionary expansion outside North America and Europe, see Martin H. Kobialka, Mehr als Brot: Wesen und Werk der Adventmission (Frankfurt am Main: By the Author, 1975), pp. 57-168.

"world-wide" as designating the mandatory extent of the missionary task. The significance and extent of the mission of the third angel also came to be associated with such texts as Mt. 24:14 and Mk. 16:15, the interpretation of which was directly influenced by successful mission efforts.

Early 19th-century American Protestantism provided the immediate historical context for origins of the SDA theology of mission. At that time there was great interest in the study of the apocalyptic-eschatology of Scripture, which was generally interpreted by historicist hermeneutical principles. Such principles had been used by Protestants in the Reformation and Post-Reformation era and their tradition can be traced back to the primitive church.

A major reason for the popularity of this approach to the Scriptures was that many commentators had successfully interpreted certain historical events which occurred in the previous century as a fulfillment of symbolic prophecy. The majority of such historicists advocated a postmillennial Second Advent and cherished an optimistic view of society, seeing historical and contemporary events as signs of the times heralding the imminence of a glorious millennium on earth. To historicists who adhered to a premillennial view of Second Advent, these events were signs of the times indicating the imminence of Christ's return and the divine judgment on a sinful world. Both post- and premillennialists agreed that the prophetic time period in Dan. 8:14 was about to be fulfilled, and consequently they expected the inauguration of some important event in salvation history. For most postmillennialists the termination of this time period pointed to an important event connected with the inauguration of the millennium; to the majority of premillennialists, however, it signified the personal return of Christ.

At a time in history when the religio-political climate in the U.S.A. was favorable to the rise of new religious movements, premillennialists with William Miller as one of their major representatives were able to develop rapidly into a large interconfessional Second Advent movement. A theology of mission gradually emerged which interpreted this movement as playing an important role in salvation history. The realization of their being participants in a prophetic movement whose task it was to prepare the world for Christ's return induced an enormous sense of responsibility, missionary zeal, and enthusiasm. Within a few years their religious publications were distributed on a world-wide scope. These vigorous and often successful mission efforts could not but result in a reaction from both non-Millerite historicists and those inclined to a historical-critical approach to Scripture.

A strong controversy developed which led to the termination of this inter-confessional movement, a polarization of positions, and an inevitable separation from the established churches of those who continued to cherish Miller's convictions. Miller's followers, however, did not consider the rejection of his views by the ecclesiastical organizations as a set-back or defeat but as another sign of the times and a fulfillment of Bible prophecy.

Regarding the origin of the SDA theology of mission this study indicated that the Second Advent movement and Millerism were a logical consequence of a consistently applied historicist hermeneutic to a premillennial 19th-century understanding of symbolic prophecy. Both the predictions concerning the time of the Second Advent and the prediction about the inauguration of events related to the millennium failed. In many instances these unfulfilled expectations undoubtedly contributed to a rejection of these hermeneutical principles and stimulated a development toward a historical-critical approach to apocalyptic-eschatology.

After the Disappointment of 1844 the Millerites were forced again to investigate the validity of their hermeneutical method. Some rejected it and with the raison d'être of the Advent movement. Those who continued to affirm the validity of their interpretations arrived at two opposite explanations for the Disappointment. The opinion of the majority was that they had been mistaken in their time calculations but that the event predicted had been correctly interpreted as the Second Advent. The minority expressed the conviction that they had been mistaken with regard to the nature of the predicted event but that their time calculations as such had been correct, their mistake being an incorrect understanding of some of the apocalyptic symbols. A new understanding of this symbolism led the minority to a different concept of the nature of the event to take place at the end of the calculated time. The event was no more seen as the Second Advent, but was interpreted as the beginning of the final phase of Christ's high-priestly ministry, the great antitypical Day of Atonement. This new interpretation, according to them, affirmed the validity of their historicist hermeneutic, provided an explanation for the Disappointment, and shed new light on the significance of the Decalogue in Christ's post-1844 ministry. Those who accepted the new interpretation of Christ's sanctuary ministry were the only Adventists on whom a current agitation on the Sabbath (resulting from a thrust by Seventh Day Baptists) had any lasting effects. From this minority view the SDA theology of mission gradually developed.

Initially the SDA theology of mission had two focal points: (1) The affirmation of the validity of the Advent experience of 1844; (2) the necessity of a restoration of certain neglected Bible doctrines (particularly the Sabbath) before the occurrence of the parousia. It was especially the aspect of restoration which came to play an increasingly important role in the self-understanding of SDA. The three angels' messages of Rev. 14, which were frequently designated as the third angel's message, formed the basic structure of the theology of mission during the formative years of the SDA

Church. This basic structure consisting of three interrelated progressive proclamations in the context of Christ's final mission in heaven and on earth was considered to prepare man for the Second Advent.

Later developments beyond the scope of this study indicated a growing emphasis on non-apocalyptic motives for mission, and additional research is necessary to discover from the primary sources reasons for such a shift. The post-1874 basic structure of the theology of mission came to be interpreted in a more Christo-centric manner without, however, diminishing or denying eschatological import. Thus, for example, E. G. White, who was and still is the most authoritative author among SDA, associated the third angel's message with "the message of justification by faith,"[1] "the gospel commission,"[2] and "the gospel message."[3] In this context soteriological value was given to its reception and statements were made such as "a saving knowledge of the third angel's message"[4] and the "gospel of the third angel's message."[5] The proclamation of the third angel's message was also identified with the "work of sowing the gospel seed"[6] and "the only hope for the salvation of a perishing world."[7] From historical evidence the inevitable conclusion is that for SDA "the third angel's message is the gospel message for these last days."[8] A comparison between fundamental principles of SDA in the 1870s and those of the 1970s indicates that the basic apocalyptic-eschatological motives for mission have not changed. (See Appendix II and III.)[9]

At first the mission of restoration was seen as a mission to restore certain spiritual principles. Later the restoration aspect began to be interpreted in the context of man's spiritual and physical restoration as necessary preparation for Christ's return. Finally it led to the realization that their mission was to proclaim a message of the complete restoration of "the principles that are the foundation of the kingdom of God"[10] with the ultimate goal of restoring in man the image of God.[11] In this mission of restoration the concept of God's mission was recognized while man's function was placed in the context of a divine-human cooperation.

This study indicates that one of the most important factors in the emergence of SDA was the powerful influence of a historicist hermeneutic which allowed for an interpretation of contemporary events as signs of Christ's

1 E. G. White, "Repentance the Gift of God," *RH*, April 1, 1890, p. 193 (*Ev*, p. 190).
2 E. G. White, *T*, IX, 15.
3 Letter, E. G. White to the Kresses, No. 106, 1910 (*Ev*, p. 96).
4 E. G. White, "Warning the Cities," *RH*, April 7, 1910, p. 3 (*Ev*, p. 25).
5 E. G. White, MS 7, 1908, (*Ev*, p. 47).
6 E. G. White, MS 65, 1908 (*Ev*, p. 51).
7 Letter, E. G. White to Olson, No. 87, 1896 (*Ev*, p. 196).
8 E. G. White, *T*, VI, 241. Cf. *ibid.*, IX, 19.
9 Appendix II, Principles VI-XIII, XVII, XVIII, XXI-XXV; Appendix III, 11, 13-16, 20-22. The 1872 declaration of fundamental principles in Appendix II was also published in "Fundamental Principles," *ST*, June 4, 1874, p. 3; Smith, "The Seventh-day Adventists," *RH*, Nov. 24, 1874, p. 171 (*Seventh-day Adventists*, pp. 24-31). In 1888 they were slightly revised. See *Brief Sketch of the Seventh-day Adventists*, pp. 40-46.
10 E. G. White, *Prophets and Kings*, p. 678.
11 E. G. White, *Ed*, pp. 15, 16.

coming within a harmonious theological system. This is the reason why SDA could successfully develop after the failure of the 1844 prediction. It also indicated that their concept of truth, or present truth, at a particular moment was not a static but a dynamic reality, the underlying principle being that of progressive or unfolding revelation which brought out the fuller import and deeper meaning of the biblical text. For SDA, present truth was always in harmony with earlier truths, and was arrived at by their unfolding of these truths.[12] This concept of revelation provided a rationale for emphasizing special truths which they considered to be of utmost importance for the salvation of the present generation of mankind, even though these truths had not been advocated as being of normative value by Christians in previous centuries.

SDA did not consider themselves the only true Christians on earth and as far as their view of other ecclesiastical organizations was concerned, they in time came to realize that most of God's people were still to be found in the other Christian churches. It was E. G. White who pointed out that there were "true Christians in every church, not excepting the Roman Catholic communion. . . . God accepts their sincerity of purpose and their integrity before Him."[13] She further stated that "the greater part of the followers of Christ were to be found in the various churches professing the Protestant faith."[14] Many of these who actively participated in Christian service, she indicated, were "more advanced in the knowledge of practical work" than SDA,[15] and advised that believers in their mission zeal should avoid making sweeping denunciations but in "humility and love, present to all the truth as it is in Jesus."[16] She suggested that no "unneccessary barriers" should be created between the believers and "other denominations, especially the Catholics, so that they shall think we are their avowed enemies. We should not create a prejudice in their minds unnecessarily by making raids upon them."[17] In another instance it was stated that "among the Catholics there are many who are most conscientious Christians and who walk in the light that shines upon them, and God will work in their behalf. . . . Do not censure others; do not condemn them."[18] She also brought out that "our work is to weed out of all our discourses everything that savors retaliation and defiance and making a drive against churches and individuals, because this is not Christ's way and method."[19] The advice was given that SDA ministers "should seek to come near to the ministers of other denomina-

---

12 Cf. e.g., Smith, "The Bible Preacher," *RH,* Oct. 16, 1855, p. 62; E. G. White, *COL,* p. 127.

13 E. G. White, *GC,* p. 449. Cf. E. G. White, *T,* VI, 70.

14 E. G. White, *GC,* p. 383.

15 Letter, E. G. White to Ministers, No. 54, June 15, 1898.

16 E. G. White, "The Church Must Be Quickened," *RH,* Jan. 17, 1893, p. 33 *(SDABC,* IV, 1184).

17 E. G. White, MS 14, 1887 *(Ev,* p. 144).

18 E. G. White, *T,* IX, 243.

19 *Ibid.,* p. 244. Cf. *ibid.,* VI, 121, 122.

tions. Pray for and with these men, for whom Christ is interceding."[20] When invited to speak in other churches SDA should not make "denunciatory speeches" but "in word and deed be wise unto salvation, representing Christ to all with whom you come in contact. Let all see that your feet are shod with the preparation of the gospel of peace and good will to men."[21] E. G. White remarked that the believers should try to agree with others "on every point we can conscientiously," and to come "as near the people as possible, and then the light and truth we have may benefit them."[22] In order to facilitate witnessing to other Christians and to break down existing prejudice she proposed that it would be best to discuss "the truths of God's Word" which were of mutual interest. She stated that "here is common ground, upon which we can meet people of other denominations; and in becoming acquainted with them, we should dwell mostly upon topics in which all feel an interest, and which will not lead directly and pointedly to the subjects of disagreement."[23] If SDA had fully implemented these suggestions there would have been less isolationism, more contacts with other Christians, and a greater impact on the world in general.[24]

It has become clear that a mission consciousness in an eschatological context did not necessarily imply an immediate outreach on a world-wide scope. The basic structure of the theology of mission only slowly emerged to a view of a world-wide outreach. Thus it was not until the 1870s, when the theology of mission had sufficiently matured, that the increasing interest in the SDA message in other continents led to the sending of missionaries to areas outside of North America.

20 *Ibid.*, p. 78.
21 E. G. White, MS 6, 1902 (*Ev*, p. 563).
22 E. G. White, *T*, III, 462.
23 E. G. White, "Overcoming Prejudice," *RH*, June 13, 1912, p. 3 (*Ev*, p. 144).
24 For official reports on a number of conversations between certain predominantly European SDA and representatives of the World Council of Churches, see *So Much in Common*, pp. 98-112. For a SDA view on ecumenism, see e.g., Bert B. Beach, *Ecumenism: Boon or Bane?*, 1974.

Appendices

Appendix I *Miller's Rules of Bible Interpretation*

In studying the Bible, I have found the following rules to be of great service to myself, and now give them to the public by special request. Every rule should be well studied, in connection with the Scripture references, if the Bible student would be at all benefitted by them.

I. All Scripture is necessary, and may be understood by diligent application and study. 2 Tim. iii. 15, 16, 17.

II. Every word must have its proper bearing on the subject presented in the Bible. Matt. v. 18.

III. Scripture must be its own expositor, since it is a rule of itself. If I depend on a teacher to expound it to me, and he should guess at its meaning, or desire to have it so on account of his sectarian creed, or to be thought wise, then his *guessing, desire, creed,* or *wisdom,* is my rule, not the Bible. Ps. xix. 7-11; cxix. 97-105. Matt. xxiii. 8-10. 1 Cor. ii. 12-16. Eze. xxxiv. 18, 19. Luke xi. 52. Mal. ii. 7, 8.

IV. To understand doctrine, bring all the Scriptures together on the subject you wish to know; then let every word have its proper influence, and if you can form your theory without a contradiction, you cannot be in an error. Isa. xxviii. 7-29; xxxv. 8. Prov. xix. 27. Luke xxiv. 27, 44, 45. Rom. xvi. 26. James v. 19. 2 Pet. i. 19, 20.

V. God has revealed things to come, by visions, in figures and parables; and in this way the same things are oftentimes revealed again and again, by different visions, or in different figures and parables. If you wish to understand them, you must combine them all in one. Ps. lxxxix. 19. Hos. xii. 10. Hab. ii. 2. Acts ii. 17. 1 Cor. x. 6. Heb. ix. 9, 24. Ps. lxxviii. 2. Matt. xiii. 13, 34. Gen. xli. 1-32. Dan. ii., vii., and viii. Acts x. 9-16.

VI. Visions are always mentioned as such. 2 Cor. xii. 1.

VII. How to know when a word is used figuratively. If it makes good sense as it stands, and does no violence to the simple laws of nature, then it must be understood literally; if not, figuratively. Rev. xii. 1, 2; xvii. 3-7.

VIII. Figures always have a figurative meaning, and are used much in prophecy to represent future things, times, and events; such as *mountains,* meaning *governments; beasts,* meaning *kingdoms.*

> *Waters,* meaning *people.*
> *Lamp,* meaning *Word of God.*
> *Day,* meaning *year.*

Dan. ii. 35, 44; vii. 8, 17. Rev. xvii. 1, 15. Ps. cxix. 105. Ezek. iv. 6.

IX. To learn the true meaning of figures, trace your figurative word through your Bible, and, where you find it explained, put it on your figure, and if it makes good sense, you need look no further; if not, look again.

X. Figures sometimes have two or more different significations; as day is used in a figurative sense to represent three different periods of time.

1. Indefinite.
2. Definite, a day for a year.
3. Day for a thousand years.

Eccles. vii. 14. Ezek. iv. 6. 2 Pet. iii. 8.

XI. Parables are used as comparisons to illustrate subjects, and must be explained in the same way as figures, by the subject and Bible. Mark iv. 13.

XII. To know whether we have the true historical event for the fulfillment of a prophecy. If you find every word of the prophecy (after the figures are understood) is literally fulfilled, then you may know that your history is the true event. But if one word lacks a fulfilment, then you must look for another event, or wait its future development. For God takes care that history and prophecy doth agree, so that the true, believing children of God may never be ashamed. Ps. xxi. 5. Isa. xiv. 17-19. 1 Pet. ii. 6. Rev. xvii. 17. Acts iii. 18.

XIII. The most important rule of all is, that you must have *faith*. It must be a faith that requires a sacrifice, and, if tried, would give up the dearest object on earth, the world and all its desires, character, living, occupation, friends, home, comforts, and worldly honors. If any of these should hinder our believing any part of God's word, it would show our faith to be vain. Nor can we ever believe, so long as one of these motives lies lurking in our hearts. We must believe that God will never forfeit his word. And we can have confidence that He that takes notice of the sparrow, and numbers the hairs of our head, will guard the translation of his own word, and throw a barrier around it, and prevent those who sincerely trust in God, and put implicit confidence in his word, from erring far from the truth, though they may not understand Hebrew or Greek.

Hale, *SAM,* pp. 103-6.

In presenting to the public this synopsis of our faith, we wish to have it distinctly understood that we have no articles of faith, creed, or discipline, aside from the Bible. We do not put forth this as having any authority with our people, nor is it designed to secure uniformity among them, as a system of faith, but is a brief statement of what is, and has been, with great unanimity, held by them. We often find it necessary to meet inquiries on this subject, and sometimes to correct false statements circulated against us, and to remove erroneous impressions which have obtained with those who have not had an opportunity to become acquainted with our faith and practice. Our only object is to meet this necessity.

As Seventh-day Adventists we desire simply that our position shall be understood; and we are the more solicitous for this because there are many who call themselves Adventists who hold views with which we can have no sympathy, some of which, we think, are subversive of the plainest and most important principles set forth in the word of God.

As compared with other Adventists, Seventh-day Adventists differ from one class in believing in the unconscious state of the dead, and the final destruction of the unrepentant wicked; from another, in believing in the perpetuity of the law of God as summarily contained in the ten commandments, in the operation of the Holy Spirit in the church, and in setting no times for the advent to occur; from all, in the observance of the seventh day of the week as the Sabbath of the Lord, and in many applications of the prophetic scriptures.

With these remarks, we ask the attention of the reader to the following propositions, which aim to be a concise statement of the more prominent features of our faith.

- I -

That there is one God, a personal, spiritual being, the creator of all things, omnipotent, omniscient, and eternal, infinite in wisdom, holiness, justice, goodness, truth, and mercy; unchangeable, and everywhere present by his representative, the Holy Spirit. Ps. 139:7.

- II -

That there is one Lord Jesus Christ, the Son of the Eternal Father, the one by whom God created all things, and by whom they do consist; that he took on him the nature of the seed of Abraham for the redemption of our fallen race; that he dwelt among men full of grace and truth, lived our example, died our sacrifice, was raised for our justification, ascended on high to be our only mediator in the sanctuary in Heaven, where, with his own blood, he makes atonement for our sins; which atonement, so far from being made on the cross, which was but the offering of the sacrifice, is the very last portion of his work as priest, according to the example of the Levitical priesthood, which foreshadowed and prefigured the ministry of our Lord in Heaven. See Lev. 16; Heb. 8:4, 5; 9:6, 7; &c.

- III -

That the Holy Scriptures, of the Old and New Testaments, were given by inspiration of God, contain a full revelation of his will to man, and are the only infallible rule of faith and practice.

- IV -

That Baptism is an ordinance of the Christian church, to follow faith and repentance, an ordinance by which we commemorate the resurrection of Christ, as by this act we show our faith in his burial and resurrection, and through that, of the resurrection of all the saints at the last day; and that no other mode fitly represents these facts than that which the Scriptures prescribe, namely, immersion. Rom. 6:3-5; Col. 2:12.

- V -

That the new birth comprises the entire change necessary to fit us for the kingdom of God, and consists of two parts: first, a moral change, wrought by conversion and a Christian life; second, a physical change at the second coming of Christ, whereby, if dead, we are raised incorruptible, and if living, are changed to immortality in a moment, in the twinkling of an eye. John 3:3, 5; Luke 20:36.

- VI -

We believe that prophecy is a part of God's revelation to man; that it is included in that scripture which is profitable for instruction, 2 Tim. 3:16; that it is designed for us and our children, Deut. 29:29; that so far from being enshrouded in impenetrable mystery, it is that which especially constitutes the word of God a lamp to our feet and a light to our path, Ps. 119:105, 2 Pet. 2:19; that a blessing is pronounced upon those who study it, Rev. 1:1-3; and that, consequently, it is to be understood by the people of God sufficiently to show them their position in the world's history, and the special duties required at their hands.

- VII -

That the world's history from specified dates in the past, the rise and fall of empires, and chronological succession of events down to the setting up of God's everlasting kingdom, are outlined in numerous great chains of prophecy; and that these prophecies are now all fulfilled except the closing scenes.

- VIII -

That the doctrine of the world's conversion and temporal millennium is a fable of these last days, calculated to lull men into a state of carnal security, and cause them to be overtaken by the great day of the Lord as by a thief in the night; that the second coming of Christ is to precede, not follow, the millennium; for until the Lord appears the papal power, with all its abominations, is to continue, the wheat and tares grow together, and evil men and seducers wax worse and worse, as the word of God declares.

302

IX

That the mistake of Adventists in 1844 pertained to the nature of the event then to transpire, not to the time; that no prophetic period is given to reach to the second advent, but that the longest one, the two thousand and three hundred days of Dan. 8:14, terminated in that year, and brought us to an event called the cleansing of the sanctuary.

That the sanctuary of the new covenant is the tabernacle of God in Heaven, of which Paul speaks in Hebrews 8, and onward, of which our Lord, as great High Priest, is minister; that this sanctuary is the antitype of the Mosaic tabernacle, and that the priestly work of our Lord, connected therewith, is the antitype of the work of the Jewish priests of the former dispensation, Heb. 8:1-5, &c.; that this is the sanctuary to be cleansed at the end of the 2300 days, what is termed its cleansing being in this case, as in the type, simply the entrance of the high priest into the most holy place, to finish the round of service connected therewith, by blotting out and removing from the sanctuary the sins which had been transferred to it by means of the ministration in the first apartment, Heb. 9:22, 23; and that this work, in the antitype, commencing in 1844, occupies a brief but indefinite space, at the conclusion of which the work of mercy for the world is finished.

XI

That God's moral requirements are the same upon all men in all dispensations; that these are summarily contained in the commandments spoken by Jehovah from Sinai, engraven on the tables of stone, and deposited in the ark, which was in consequence called the "ark of the covenant," or testament. Num. 10:33, Heb. 9:4, &c.; that this law is immutable and perpetual, being a transcript of the tables deposited in the ark in the true sanctuary on high, which is also, for the same reason, called the ark of God's testament; for under the sounding of the seventh trumpet we are told that "the temple of God was opened in Heaven, and there was seen in his temple the ark of his testament." Rev. 11:19.

XII

That the fourth commandment of this law requires that we devote the seventh day of each week, commonly called Saturday, to abstinence from our own labor, and to the performance of sacred and religious duties; that this is the only weekly Sabbath known to the Bible, being the day that was set apart before paradise was lost, Gen. 2:2, 3, and which will be observed in paradise restored, Isa. 66:22, 23; that the facts upon which the Sabbath institution is based confine it to the seventh day, as they are not true of any other day; and that the terms, Jewish Sabbath and Christian Sabbath, as applied to the weekly rest-day, are names of human invention, unscriptural in fact, and false in meaning.

XIII

That as the man of sin, the papacy, has thought to change times and laws (the laws of God), Dan. 7:25, and has misled almost all Christendom in regard to the fourth commandment, we find a prophecy of a reform in this respect to be wrought among believers just before the coming of Christ. Isa. 56:1, 2, 1 Pet. 1:5, Rev. 14:12, &c.

- XIV -

That as the natural or carnal heart is at enmity with God and his law, this enmity can be subdued only by a radical transformation of the affections, the exchange of unholy for holy principles; that this transformation follows repentance and faith, is the special work of the Holy Spirit, and constitutes regeneration or conversion.

- XV -

That as all have violated the law of God, and cannot of themselves render obedience to his just requirements, we are dependent on Christ, first, for justification from our past offences, and, secondly, for grace whereby to render acceptable obedience to his holy law in time to come.

- XVI -

That the Spirit of God was promised to manifest itself in the church through certain gifts, enumerated especially in 1 Cor. 12 and Eph. 4; that these gifts are not designed to supersede, or take the place of, the Bible, which is sufficient to make us wise unto salvation, any more than the Bible can take the place of the Holy Spirit; that in specifying the various channels of its operation, that Spirit has simply made provision for its own existence and presence with the people of God to the end of time, to lead to an understanding of that word which it had inspired, to convince of sin, and work a transformation in the heart and life; and that those who deny to the Spirit its place and operation, do plainly deny that part of the Bible which assigns to it this work and position.

- XVII -

That God, in accordance with his uniform dealings with the race, sends forth a proclamation of the approach of the second advent of Christ; that this work is symbolized by the three messages of Rev. 14, the last one bringing to view the work of reform on the law of God, that his people may acquire a complete readiness for that event.

- XVIII -

That the time of the cleansing of the sanctuary (see proposition X), synchronizing with the time of the proclamation of the third message, is a time of investigative judgment, first with reference to the dead, and at the close of probation with reference to the living, to determine who of the myriads now sleeping in the dust of the earth are worthy of a part in the first resurrection, and who of its living multitudes are worthy of translation — points which must be determined before the Lord appears.

- XIX -

That the grave, whither we all tend, expressed by the Hebrew *sheol,* and the Greek *hades,* is a place of darkness in which there is no work, device, wisdom, or knowledge. Eccl. 9:10.

- XX -

That the state to which we are reduced by death is one of silence, inactivity, and entire unconsciousness. Ps. 146:4; Eccl. 9:5, 6; Dan. 12:2, &c.

304

- XXI -

That out of this prison house of the grave mankind are to be brought by a bodily resurrection; the righteous having part in the first resurrection, which takes place at the second advent of Christ, the wicked in the second resurrection, which takes place a thousand hears thereafter. Rev. 20:4-6.

- XXII -

That at the last trump, the living righteous are to be changed in a moment, in the twinkling of an eye, and with the resurrected righteous are to be caught up to meet the Lord in the air, so forever to be with the Lord.

- XXIII -

That these immortalized ones are then taken to Heaven, to the New Jerusalem, the Father's house in which there are many mansions, John 14:1-3, where they reign with Christ a thousand years, judging the world and fallen angels, that is, apportioning the punishment to be executed upon them at the close of the one thousand years; Rev. 20:4; 1 Cor. 6:2, 3; that during this time the earth lies in a desolate and chaotic condition, Jer. 4:20-27, described, as in the beginning, by the Greek term *abussos* (ἄβυσσος), bottomless pit (Septuagint of Gen. 1:2); and that here Satan is confined during the thousand years, Rev. 20:1, 2, and here finally destroyed, Rev. 20:10; Mal. 4:1; the theater of the ruin he has wrought in the universe, being appropriately made for a time his gloomy prison house, and then the place of his final execution.

- XXIV -

That at the end of the thousand years, the Lord descends with his people and the New Jerusalem, Rev. 21:2, the wicked dead are raised and come up upon the surface of the yet unrenewed earth, and gather about the city, the camp of the saints, Rev. 20:9, and fire comes down from God out of heaven and devours them. They are then consumed root and branch, Mal. 4:1, becoming as though they had not been. Obad. 15, 16. In this everlasting destruction from the presence of the Lord, 2 Thess. 1:9, the wicked meet the everlasting punishment threatened against them, Matt. 25:46. This is the perdition of ungodly men, the fire which consumes them being the fire for which "the heavens and the earth which are now" are kept in store, which shall melt even the elements with its intensity, and purge the earth from the deepest stains of the curse of sin. 2 Pet. 3:7-12.

- XXV -

That a new heaven and earth shall spring by the power of God from the ashes of the old, to be, with the New Jerusalem for its metropolis and capital, the eternal inheritance of the saints, the place where the righteous shall evermore dwell. 2 Pet. 3:13; Ps. 37:11, 29; Matt. 5:5.

A Declaration of the Fundamental Principles Taught and Practiced by the Seventh-day Adventists, 1872.

Seventh-day Adventists hold certain fundamental beliefs, the principal features of which, together with a portion of the Scriptural references upon which they are based, may be summarized as follows:

1. That the Holy Scriptures of the Old and the New Testament were given by inspiration of God, contain an all-sufficient revelation of His will to men, and are the only unerring rule of faith and practice. (2 Tim. 3:15-17.)

2. That the Godhead, or Trinity, consists of the Eternal Father, a personal, spiritual Being, omnipotent, omnipresent, omniscient, infinite in wisdom and love; the Lord Jesus Christ, the Son of the Eternal Father, through whom all things were created and through whom the salvation of the redeemed hosts will be accomplished; the Holy Spirit, the third person of the Godhead, the great regenerating power in the work of redemption. (Matt. 28:19; Isa. 44:6; 48:13; Matt. 12:32; 2 Cor. 13:14; Rev. 1:8, 11.)

3. That Jesus Christ is very God, being of the same nature and essence as the Eternal Father. While retaining His divine nature, He took upon Himself the nature of the human family, lived on the earth as a man, exemplified in His life as our example the principles of righteousness, attested His relationship to God by many mighty miracles, died for our sins on the cross, was raised from the dead, and ascended to the Father where He ever lives to make intercession for us. (John 1:1, 14; Heb. 2:9-18; 8:1, 2; 4:14-16; 7:25.)

4. That every person, in order to obtain salvation, must experience the new birth. This comprises an entire transformation of life and character by the re-creative power of God through faith in the Lord Jesus Christ. (John 3:16; Matt. 18:3; Acts 2:37-39.)

5. That baptism is an ordinance of the Christian church, the proper form being by immersion, and should follow repentance and forgiveness of sins. By its observation faith is shown in the death, burial, and resurrection of Christ. (Rom. 6:1-6; Acts 16:30-33.)

6. That the will of God as it relates to moral conduct is comprehended in His law of ten commandments. These are great moral, unchangeable precepts, binding upon all men in every age. (Ex. 20:1-17.)

7. That the fourth commandment of this unchangeable law requires the observance of the seventh-day Sabbath. This holy institution is at the same time a memorial of creation and a sign of sanctification, a sign of the believer's rest from his own works of sin, and his entrance into the rest of soul that Jesus promises to those who come to Him. (Gen. 2:1-3; Ex. 20:8-11; 31:12-17; Heb. 4:1-10.)

8. That the law of ten commandments points out sin, the penalty of which is death. The law cannot save the transgressor from his sin, nor impart power to keep him from sinning. In infinite love and mercy God provides a way whereby this may

306

be done. He furnishes a substitute, even Christ the righteous one, to die in man's stead, making "him to be sin for us, who knew no sin; that we might be made the righteousness of God in him." (2 Cor. 5:21.) We are justified, not by obedience to the law, but by the grace that is in Christ Jesus. By accepting Christ, man is reconciled to God, justified by the blood of Christ for the sins of the past, and saved from the power of sin by His indwelling life. Thus the gospel becomes "the power of God unto salvation to every one that believeth." This experience is wrought by the divine agency of the Holy Spirit, who convinces of sin and leads to the Sin Bearer, inducting believers into the new-covenant relationship, where the law of God is written on their hearts; and through the enabling power of the indwelling Christ, their lives are brought into conformity to the divine precepts. The honor and merit of this wonderful transformation belong wholly to Christ. (1 John 3:4; Rom. 7:7; 3:20; Eph. 2:8-10; 1 John 2:1, 2; Rom. 5:8-10; Gal. 2:20; Eph. 3:17; Heb. 8:8-12.)

9. That God "only hath immortality." (1 Tim. 6:16.) Mortal man possesses a nature inherently sinful and dying. Eternal life is the gift of God through faith in Christ. (Rom. 6:23.) "He that hath the Son hath life." (1 John 5:12.) Immortality is bestowed upon the righteous at the second coming of Christ, when the righteous dead are raised from the grave and the living righteous translated to meet the Lord. Then it is that those accounted faithful "put on immortality." (1 Cor. 15:51-55.)

10. That the condition of man in death is one of unconsciousness. That all men, good and evil alike, remain in the grave from death to the resurrection. (Eccl. 9:5, 6; Ps. 146:3, 4; John 5:28, 29.)

11. That there shall be a resurrection both of the just and of the unjust. The resurrection of the just will take place at the second coming of Christ; the resurrection of the unjust will take place a thousand years later, at the close of the millennium. (John 5:28, 29; 1 Thess. 4:13-18; Rev. 20:5-10.)

12. That the finally impenitent, including Satan, the author of sin, will, by the fires of the last day, be reduced to a state of nonexistence, becoming as though they had not been, thus purging the universe of God of sin and sinners. (Rom. 6:23; Mal. 4:1-3; Rev. 20:9, 10; Obadiah 16.)

13. That no prophetic period is given in the Bible to reach to the Second Advent, but that the longest one, the 2300 days of Daniel 8:14, terminating in 1844, reaches to an event called the cleansing of the sanctuary. (Dan. 8:14; 9:24, 25; Num. 14:34; Eze. 4:6.)

14. That the true sanctuary, of which the tabernacle on earth was a type, is the temple of God in heaven, of which Paul speaks in Hebrews 8 and onward, and of which the Lord Jesus, as our great high priest, is minister. The priestly work of our Lord is the antitype of the work of the Jewish priests of the former dispensation. That this heavenly sanctuary is the one to be cleansed at the end of the 2300 days of Daniel 8:14, its cleansing being, as in the type, a work of judgment, beginning with the entrance of Christ as the high priest upon the judgment phase of His ministry in the heavenly sanctuary, foreshadowed in the earthly service of cleansing the sanctuary on the Day of Atonement. This work of judgment in the heavenly sanctuary began in 1844. Its completion will close human probation. (Dan. 7:9, 10; 8:14; Heb. 8:1, 2, 5; Rev. 20:12, Num. 14:34; Eze. 4:6.)

15. That God, in the time of the judgment and in accordance with His uniform dealing with the human family in warning them of coming events vitally affecting their destiny (Amos 3:6, 7), sends forth a proclamation of the approach of the Second Advent of Christ; that this work is symbolized by the three angels of Revelation 14, and that their threefold message brings to view a work of reform to prepare a people to meet Him at His coming. (Amos 3:6, 7; 2 Cor. 5:10; Rev. 14:6-12.)

16. That the time of the cleansing of the sanctuary, synchronizing with the period of the proclamation of the message of Revelation 14, is a time of investigative judgment, first, with reference to the dead, and second, with reference to the living. This investigative judgment determines who of the myriads sleeping in the dust of the earth are worthy of a part in the first resurrection, and who of its living multitudes are worthy of translation. (1 Peter 4:17, 18; Dan. 7:9, 10; Rev. 14:6, 7; Luke 20:35.)

17. That the followers of Christ should be a godly people, not adopting the unholy maxims nor conforming to the unrighteous ways of the world; not loving its sinful pleasures nor countenancing its follies. That believers should recognize their bodies as the temple of the Holy Spirit, and that therefore they should clothe them in neat, modest, dignified apparel. Further, that in eating and drinking and in their entire course of conduct they should shape their lives as becometh followers of the meek and lowly Master. Thus the followers of Christ will be led to abstain from all intoxicating drinks, tobacco and other narcotics, and to avoid every body- and soul-defiling habit and practice. (1 Cor. 3:16, 17; 9:25; 10:31; 1 Tim. 2:9, 10; 1 John 2:6.)

18. That the divine principle of tithes and offerings for the support of the gospel is an acknowledgment of God's ownership in our lives, and that we are stewards who must render account to Him of all that He has committed to our possession. (Lev. 27:30; Mal. 3:8-12; Matt. 23:23; 1 Cor. 9:9-14; 2 Cor. 9:6-15.)

19. That God has placed in His church the gifts of the Holy Spirit, as enumerated in 1 Corinthians 12 and Ephesians 4. That these gifts operate in harmony with the divine principles of the Bible, and are given "for the perfecting of the saints, for the work of the ministry, for the edifying of the body of Christ" (Eph. 4:12). That the gift of the Spirit of prophecy is one of the identifying marks of the remnant church (1 Cor. 1:5-17; 1 Cor. 12:1-28; Rev. 12:17; 19:10; Amos 3:7; Hosea 12:10, 13). They recognize that this gift was manifested in the life and ministry of Ellen G. White.

20. That the second coming of Christ is the great hope of the church, the grand climax of the gospel and plan of salvation. His coming will be literal, personal, and visible. Many important events will be associated with His return, such as the resurrection of the dead, the destruction of the wicked, the purification of the earth, the reward of the righteous, and the establishment of His everlasting kingdom. The almost complete fulfillment of various lines of prophecy, particularly those found in the books of Daniel and the Revelation, with existing conditions in the physical, social, industrial, political, and religious worlds, indicates that Christ's coming "is near, even at the doors." The exact time of that event has not been foretold. Believers are exhorted to be ready, for "in such an hour as ye think not the Son of man" will be revealed. (Luke 21:25-27; 17:26-30; John 14:1-3; Acts 1:9-11; Rev. 1:7; Heb. 9:28; James 5:1-8; Joel 3:9-16; 2 Tim. 3:1-5; Dan. 7:27; Matt. 24:36, 44.)

21. That the millennial reign of Christ covers the period between the first and the second resurrection, during which time the saints of all ages will live with their blessed Redeemer in heaven. At the end of the millennium the Holy City with all the saints will descend to the earth. The wicked, raised in the second resurrection, will go up on the breadth of the earth with Satan at their head to compass the camp of the saints, when fire will come down from God out of heaven and devour them. In the conflagration that destroys Satan and his host the earth itself will be regenerated and cleansed from the effects of the curse. Thus the universe of God will be purified from the foul blot of sin. (Revelation 20; Zech. 14:1-4; 2 Peter 3:7-10.)

22. That God will make all things new. The earth, restored to its pristine beauty, will become forever the abode of the saints of the Lord. The promise to Abraham,

that through Christ, he and his seed should possess the earth throughout the endless ages of eternity, will be fulfilled. "The kingdom and dominion, and the greatness of the kingdom under the whole heaven, shall be given to the people of the saints of the most High, whose kingdom is an everlasting kingdom, and all dominions shall serve and obey him." Christ, the Lord, will reign supreme, "and every creature which is in heaven, and on the earth, and under the earth, and such as are in the sea," will ascribe "blessing, and honour, and glory, and power," unto "him that sitteth upon the throne, and unto the Lamb for ever and ever." (Gen. 13:14-17; Rom. 4:13; Heb. 11:8-16; Matt. 5:5; Isaiah 35; Rev. 21:1-7; Dan. 7:27; Rev. 5:13.)

Seventh-day Adventists, General Conference, *Church Manual*, rev. ed., 1971, pp. 29-36.

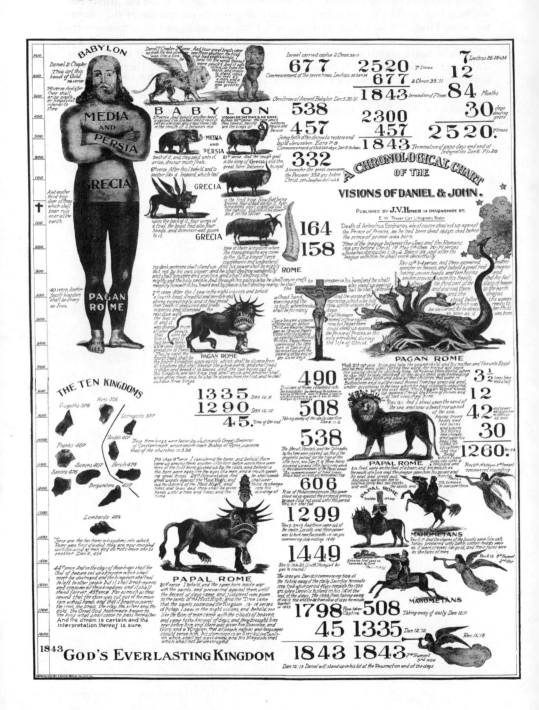

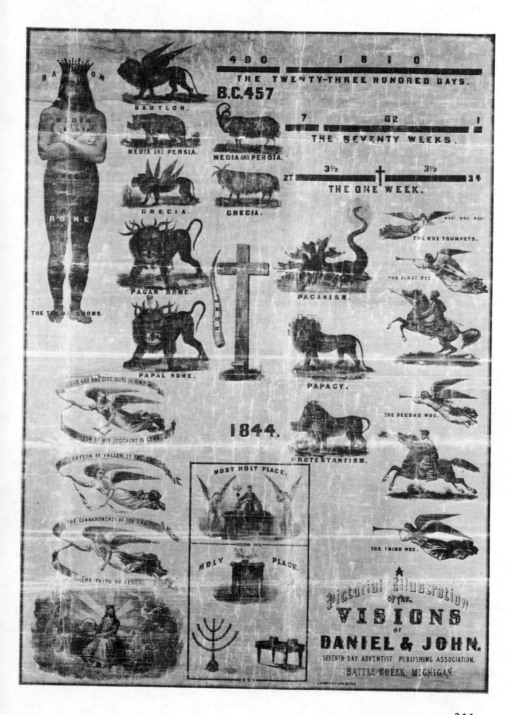

AdR	*Advent Review*
AH	*Advent Herald*
AHBA	*Advent Harbinger and Bible Advocate*
AR	*A Brief Exposition of the Angels of Revelation XIV*
ASR	*Advent Shield and Review*
AT	*Advent Testimony*
CEV	*A Sketch of the Christian Experience and Views of Ellen G. White*
COL	*Christ's Object Lessons*
"DBS"	"Dear Brethren and Sisters"
DD	*Day-Dawn*
DS	*Day-Star*
Ed	*Education*
ESH	*Evidences from Scripture and History of the Second Coming of Christ About the Year A.D. 1843 . . .*
Ev	*Evangelism As Set Forth in the Writings of Ellen G. White*
EW	*Early Writings of Ellen G. White*
FE	*Fundamentals of Christian Education . . .*
GC	*The Great Controversy . . .*
GT	*Girdle of Truth and Advent Review*
HI	*Hope of Israel*
HR	*Health Reformer*
JS	*Jubilee Standard*
LS	*Life Sketches of Ellen G. White . . .*
MC	*Midnight Cry*
MS	Manuscript
MSVT	Manuscript of an Article for the *Vermont Telegraph*
MW	*Morning Watch*
PE	*Prophetic Expositions . . .*
PFF	*Prophetic Faith of Our Fathers . . .*
PT	*Present Truth*
RH	*Second Advent Review, and Sabbath Herald,* and *Advent Review, and Sabbath Herald*
"RPA"	"Rise and Progress of Adventism"
"RSA"	"To the Remnant Scattered Abroad"
SAH	*Second Advent Harbinger*
SAM	*Second Advent Manual . . .*
SAWH	*Second Advent Way Marks and High Heaps . . .*
SCC	*The Probability of the Second Coming of Christ . . .*
SCEV	*Supplement to the Christian Experience and Views of Ellen G. White*
SDA	Seventh-Day Adventist(s)
SDABC	*The Seventh-Day Adventist Bible Commentary*
SDAE	*Seventh-day Adventist Encyclopedia*

I. Primary Sources.

    A. Published Materials.

        1. BOOKS AND PAMPHLETS.

An Address to the Baptists of the United States, on the Observance of the Sabbath: From the Seventh Day Baptist General Conference. 3rd ed. New York: n.p., 1843.

Andrews, John N. *The Commandment To Restore and Build Jerusalem.* Battle Creek, Mich.: SDA Pub. Assn., 1865.

_____. *The Sanctuary and Twenty-Three Hundred Days.* Rochester, N.Y.: James White, 1853.

_____. *Thoughts on the Sabbath and the Perpetuity of the Law of God.* Paris, Me.: J. White, 1851.

_____. *The Three Angels of Revelation XIV, 6-12.* Rochester, N.Y.: Advent Review Office, 1855.

_____. *The Three Messages of Revelation XIV, 6-12, Particularly the Third Angel's Message, and Two Horned Beast.* Battle Creek, Mich.: Review and Herald Office, 1860. [2nd ed.]. Battle Creek, Mich.: S.D.A. Pub. Assn., 1864; 3rd ed., rev., 1872; 4th ed., rev., 1876; 5th ed., rev., 1886 and 1892. (Facsimile reproduction, 5th ed., 1892. Nashville, Tenn.: Southern Pub. Assn., 1970.)

Bacon, John. *Conjectures on the Prophecies; Written in the Fore Part of the Year 1799.* Boston: David Carlisle, 1805.

Bates, Joseph. *The Autobiography of Elder Joseph Bates . . . and a Brief Account of the Great Advent Movement of 1840-44.* Battle Creek, Mich.: SDA Pub. Assn., 1868. (Facsimile reproduction. Nashville, Tenn.: Southern Pub. Assn., 1970.)

_____. *An Explanation of the Typical and Anti-Typical Sanctuary, By the Scriptures.* New Bedford, [Mass.: By the Author], 1850.

_____. *The Opening Heavens, or a Connected View of the Testimony of the Prophets and Apostles, Concerning the Opening Heavens, Compared with Astronomical Observations, and of the Present and Future Location of the New Jerusalem, the Paradise of God.* New Bedford, [Mass.: By the Author], 1846.

_____. *A Seal of the Living God. A Hundred Forty-Four Thousand, of the Servants of God Being Sealed, in 1849.* New Bedford, [Mass.: By the Author], 1849.

_____. *Second Advent Way Marks and High Heaps, or A Connected View, of the Fulfilment of Prophecy, By God's Peculiar People, from the Year 1840 to 1847.* New Bedford, [Mass.: By the Author], 1847.

_____. *The Seventh Day Sabbath, a Perpetual Sign, from the Beginning, to the Entering into the Gates of the Holy City, According to the Commandment.* New

Bedford, [Mass.: By the Author], 1846; [2nd ed., rev. and enl.], 1847.

Beecher, Lyman. *Six Sermons on the Nature, Occasions, Signs, Evils, and Remedy of Intemperance.* New York: American Tract Society, 1827.

Bliss, Sylvester. *An Exposition of the Twenty Fourth of Matthew: In Which It Is Shown To Be an Historical Prophecy, Extending to the End of Time, and Literally Fulfilled.* Boston: J. V. Himes, 1843.

——————. *Inconsistencies of Colver's Literal Fulfillment of Daniel's Prophecy.* Boston: J. V. Himes, 1843.

——————. *Memoirs of William Miller, Generally Known as a Lecturer on the Prophecies, and the Second Coming of Christ.* Boston: J. V. Himes, 1853.

——————. *Review of Morris' "Modern Chiliasm: or The Doctrine of the Personal and Immortal Reign of Jesus Christ on Earth, Commencing About A.D. 1843, As Advocated by William Miller and Others, Refuted."* Boston: J. V. Himes, 1842.

Bourdeau, Daniel T. *Sanctification: or Living Holiness.* Battle Creek, Mich.: SDA Pub. Assn., 1864. (Facsimile reproduction. Nashville, Tenn.: Southern Pub. Assn., 1970.)

Brownlee, William C. *The Roman Catholic Religion Viewed in the Light of Prophecy and History: Its Final Downfall and the Triumph of the Church of Christ.* New York: Charles K. Moore, 1843.

Bush, George. *The Millennium of the Apocalypse.* 2nd ed. Salem, Mass.: John P. Jewett, 1842.

Bush, George and Miller, William. *Reasons for Rejecting Mr. Miller's Views on the Advent, By Rev. George Bush, Professor of Hebrew and Oriental Literature in the New York City University; with Mr. Miller's Reply.* Boston: J. V. Himes, 1844.

Butler, George I. *Leadership.* [Battle Creek, Mich.: SDA Pub. Assn., 1843].

Campbell, George; Macknight, James; and Doddridge, Philip. *The Sacred Writings of the Apostles and Evangelists of Jesus Christ, Commonly Styled the New Testament.* Buffaloe, Va.: Alexander Campbell, 1826.

Carver, H. E. *Mrs. E. G. White's Claims to Divine Inspiration Examined.* Marion, Ia.: "Hope of Israel" Office, 1870.

Chase, Irah. *Remarks on the Book of Daniel, in Regard to the Four Kingdoms, Especially the Fourth; the "2300 Days"; the Seventy Weeks; and the Events Predicted in the Last Three Chapters.* Boston: Gould, Kendall and Lincoln, 1844.

Colver, Nathaniel. *The Prophecy of Daniel, Literally Fulfilled: Considered in Three Lectures.* Boston: n.p., 1843.

Cornell, Merritt E. *Facts for the Times. Extracts from the Writings of Eminent Authors, Ancient and Modern.* Battle Creek, Mich. By the Author, 1858.

——————. *Miraculous Powers. The Scripture Testimony on the Perpetuity of Spiritual Gifts. Illustrated by Narratives of Incidents and Sentiments Carefully Compiled from the Eminently Pious and Learned of Various Denominations.* Battle Creek, Mich.: SDA Pub. Assn., 1862.

——————. *The State of the Churches.* Battle Creek, Mich.: SDA Pub. Assn., [1868].

Cosmopolite [pseudonym]. *Miller Overthrown: or The False Prophet Confounded.* Boston: Abel Tompkins, 1840.

Cottrell, Roswell F. *The Bible Class: Lessons upon the Law of God, and the Faith of Jesus.* Rochester, N.Y.: Advent Review Office, 1855.

——————. *Mark of the Beast, and Seal of the Living God.* Battle Creek, Mich.: [SDA Pub. Assn., 1859].

——————. *Unity of the Church.* Battle Creek, Mich.: [SDA Pub. Assn., 1859].

Daboll, Nathan. *The New England Almanac. . . .* New London, Conn.: Bolles & Williams, 1843, 1844.

A Declaration of the Fundamental Principles Taught and Practiced By the Seventh-day Adventists. Battle Creek, Mich.: SDA Pub. Assn., 1872.

Dowling, John. *An Exposition of the Prophecies, Supposed By William Miller To Predict the Second Coming of Christ, in 1843.* Providence, [R. I.]: Geo. P. Daniels, 1840.

Dwight, Timothy. *A Discourse in Two Parts, Delivered Aug. 20, 1812, on the National Fast, in the Chapel of Yale College.* Boston: n.p., 1812.

Edson, Hiram. *An Exposition of Scripture Prophecy; Showing the Final Return of the Jews in 1850.* Canandaigua, N.Y.: [By the Author], 1849.

_____ *The Time of the End; Its Beginning, Progressive Events, and Final Termination.* Auburn, [N.Y.: By the Author], 1849.

Ferguson, James. *The Works of James Ferguson, F.R.S., Comprising Astronomy, Explained upon Sir Isaac Newton's Principles; Lectures on Select Subjects; and Essays and Treatises.* Ed. by David Brewster. Edinburgh: Sterling & Slade, 1823.

The First Report of the General Conference of Christians Expecting the Advent of the Lord Jesus Christ. Held in Boston, Oct. 14, 15, 1840. Boston: J. V. Himes, 1841.

Fitch, Charles. *"Come Out of Her, My People": A Sermon.* Rochester, N.Y.: J. V. Himes, 1843.

Fleming, Lorenzo D. *Synopsis of the Evidences of the Second Coming of Christ, About A.D. 1843.* 3rd ed. rev. Boston: J. V. Himes, 1843.

Fleming, Robert. *Apocalyptical Key.* London: G. Offor, 1793; new ed. London: W. Baynes, 1809.

Folsom, Nathaniel. *Critical and Historical Interpretation of the Prophecies of Daniel.* Boston: n.p., 1842.

Folsom, Nathaniel, and Truair, John. *A Dissertation on the Second Coming, and Kingdom of Our Blessed Lord and Savior, Jesus Christ, upon the Earth.* Cazenovia, N.Y.: n.p., 1840.

Gibbon, Edward. *The History of the Decline and Fall of the Roman Empire.* Ed. by J. B. Bury. 7 vols. London: Methuen, 1896-1900.

Graham, Sylvester. *Lectures on the Science of Human Life.* 2 vols. Boston: Marsh, Capen, Lyon & Webb, 1839.

Grant, Miles. *The True Sabbath. Which Day Shall We Keep? An Examination of Mrs. Ellen White's Visions.* Boston: Advent Christian Pub. Society, 1874.

Hale, Apollos. *Herald of the Bridegroom! in Which the Plagues That Await the Enemies of the King Eternal Are Considered; and the Appearing of Our Lord to Gather His Saints Is Shown To Be the Next Event before Us, By a Scriptural Exhibition of the Order of Events from the Fall of the Papacy Down to the Establishment of the Everlasting Kingdom.* Boston: J. V. Himes, 1843.

_____ *The Second Advent Manual: In Which the Objections to Calculating the Prophetic Times Are Considered; the Difficulties Connected with the Calculation Explained; and the Facts and Arguments on Which Mr. Miller's Calculations Rest, Are Briefly Stated and Sustained.* Boston: J. V. Himes, 1843.

Hales, William. *A New Analysis of Chronology and Geography, History and Prophecy: In Which Their Elements Are Attempted To Be Explained, Harmonized, and Vindicated, upon Scriptural and Scientific Principles. . . .* 4 vols. 2nd ed. rev. London: C. J. G. & F. Rivington, 1830.

_____ *A New Analysis of Chronology, in Which an Attempt Is Made To Explain the History and Antiquities of the Primitive Nations of the World, and the Prophecies Relating to Them, on Principles Tending To Remove the Imperfections of Preceding Systems.* 3 vols. London: By the Author, 1809-12.

Hartley, David. *Observations on Man, His Frame, His Duty, and His Expectations.* 2 vols. London: James Leake and Wm. Frederick, 1749.

[Hawthorne, Nathaniel]. *The Celestial Railroad.* [Rev. ed.] Battle Creek, Mich.: SDA Pub. Assn., [1866].

Hopkins, Samuel. *The System of Doctrines, Contained in Divine Revelation, Explained and Defended. . . .* 2 vols. 2nd ed. Boston: Lincoln & Edmonds, 1811.

—————. *A Treatise on the Millennium.* . . . Boston: Isaiah Thomas and Ebenezer T. Andrews, 1793.

Hull, Moses. *The Two Laws, and Two Covenants.* Battle Creek, Mich.: SDA Pub. Assn., 1862.

Jarvis, Samuel F. *Two Discourses on Prophecy: with An Appendix in Which Mr. Miller's Scheme Concerning Our Lord's Second Advent, Is Considered and Refuted.* New York: James A. Sparks, 1843.

Jones, Henry. *Modern Phenomena of the Heavens; or, Prophetic "Great Signs" of the Special near Approach of the "End of All Things."* New York: Piercy and Reed, July 1, 1843.

Keith, Alexander. *The Signs of the Times, As Denoted By the Fulfilment of Historical Predictions, Traced Down from the Babylonish Captivity to the Present Time.* 2 vols. New York: Jonathan Leavitt, 1832.

Kinne, Aaron. *An Explanation of the Principal Types, the Prophecies of Daniel and Hosea, the Revelation, and Other Symbolical Passages of the Holy Scriptures.* Boston: n.p., 1814.

Litch, Josiah. *Address to the Public, and Especially the Clergy, on the Near Approach of the Glorious, Everlasting Kingdom of God on Earth, As Indicated By the Word of God, the History of the World, and Signs of the Present Times.* Boston: J. V. Himes, 1842.

—————. *The Probability of the Second Coming of Christ About A.D. 1843. Shown By a Comparison of Prophecy with History, Up to the Present Time, and an Explanation of Those Prophecies Which Are Yet To Be Fulfilled.* Boston: David H. Ela, 1838.

—————. *Prophetic Expositions; or A Connected View of the Testimony of the Prophets Concerning the Kingdom of God and the Time of Its Establishment.* 2 vols. Boston: J. V. Himes, 1842.

—————. *Refutation of "Dowling's Reply to Miller," on the Second Coming of Christ in 1843.* Boston: J. V. Himes, 1842.

—————. *The Restitution, Christ's Kingdom on Earth; the Return of Israel, Together with Their Political Emancipation; the Beast, His Image and Worship: also, The Fall of Babylon, and the Instruments of Its Overthrow.* Boston: J. V. Himes, 1848.

[—————]. *The Sounding of the Seven Trumpets of Revelation VIII and IX.* Ed. by J. White. Battle Creek, Mich.: Review and Herald Office, 1859.

Loughborough, John N. *The Two-Horned Beast.* [Rochester, N.Y.: Review Office, 1854].

—————. *The Two-Horned Beast of Rev. XIII, a Symbol of the United States.* Battle Creek, Mich.: Review and Herald Office, 1857.

McCorkle, Samuel M. *Thoughts on the Millennium, with a Comment on the Revelations; also A Few Remarks on Church Government.* Nashville, Tenn.: Republican & Gazette, 1830.

Macknight, James. *A New Literal Translation, from the Original Greek, of All the Apostolic Epistles.* New ed. Philadelphia: Thomas Desilver, 1835.

Millard, D., and Badger, J., comps. *Hymns and Spiritual Songs, Original and Selected, for the Use of Christians.* 6th ed. Union Mills, N.Y.: Christian Gen. Book Assn., 1843.

Miller, William. *Dissertations on the True Inheritance of the Saints; and the Twelve Hundred and Sixty Days of Daniel and John; with An Address to the Conference of Believers in the Advent Near.* Boston: J. V. Himes, 1842.

—————. *Evidences from Scripture and History of the Second Coming of Christ About the Year A.D. 1843, and of His Personal Reign of 1000 Years.* Brandon, Vt.: Vermont Telegraph Office, 1833.

—————. *Evidences from Scripture and History of the Second Coming of Christ About* the Years 1843, Exhibited in a Course of Lectures. Troy, [N.Y.]: n.p., 1836; Troy, N.Y.: Elias Gates, 1838; Boston: B. B. Mussey, 1840; Boston: J. V. Himes, 1842.

_____. A Familiar Exposition of the Twenty-Fourth Chapter of Matthew, and the Fifth and Sixth Chapters of Hosea. Ed. by J. V. Himes. Boston: J. V. Himes, 1842.

_____. A Lecture on the Typical Sabbaths and Great Jubilee. Boston: J. V. Himes, 1842.

_____. Miller's Reply to Stuart's "Hints on the Interpretation of Prophecy." Boston: J. V. Himes, 1842.

_____. Views of the Prophecies and Prophetic Chronology, Selected from Manuscripts of William Miller; with A Memoir of His Life. Ed. by J. V. Himes. Boston: Moses A. Dow, 1841.

_____. Wm. Miller's Apology and Defense. Boston: J. V. Himes, 1845.

Pond, Enoch. A Review of the Second Advent Publications. 3rd ed. Boston: n.p., 1843.

Preble, Thomas M. A Tract, Showing That the Seventh Day Should Be Observed As the Sabbath, Instead of the First Day; "According to the Commandment." Nashua, [N.H.]: n.p., 1845.

Rush, Benjamin. An Inquiry into the Effects of Spirituous Liquors on the Human Body. Boston: Thomas and Andrews, 1790.

Seventh-day Adventists. Report of the General Conference of Seventh-day Adventists. [Battle Creek: SDA Pub. Assn., 1863].

Seventh Day Baptists. Manual of the Seventh Day Baptists; Containing an Historical Sketch of the Denomination, and Reasons for Emphasizing the Day of the Sabbath. New York: George B. Utter, 1858.

_____. Minutes of the General Conference. N.p., 1844-73.

_____. Seventh Day Baptist Anniversaries; for 1843. Containing the Minutes of the General Conference. . . . New York: J. Winchester, New World Press, 1843.

Shaw, Elijah. Christ's Second Coming. Exeter, N.H.: n.p., 1843.

Shimeal, Richard C. Age of the World As Founded on the Sacred Records. New York: n.p., 1842.

Simpson, David. A Plea for Religion and the Sacred Writings; Addressed to the Disciples of Thomas Paine, and Wavering Christians of Every Persuasion. 9th ed. London: Sereno Taylor, 1824.

Skinner, Otis A. The Theory of William Miller, Concerning the End of the World in 1843, Utterly Exploded. Boston: Thomas Whittemore, 1840.

[Smith, Uriah]. The Seventh-day Adventists: A Brief Sketch of Their Origin, Progress, and Principles. Battle Creek, Mich.: SDA Pub. Assn., 1876-77.

_____. Thoughts, Critical and Practical, on the Book of Daniel. Battle Creek, Mich.: SDA Pub. Assn., 1873.

_____. Thoughts, Critical and Practical on the Book of Revelation. Battle Creek, Mich.: SDA Pub. Assn., 1865.

_____. The 2300 Days and the Sanctuary. Rochester, N.Y.: Advent Review Office, 1854.

_____. The United States in the Light of Prophecy; or, An Exposition of Rev. 13:11-17. Battle Creek, Mich.: SDA Pub. Assn., 1872.

_____. The Visions of Mrs. E. G. White, A Manifestation of Spiritual Gifts According to the Scriptures. Battle Creek, Mich.: SDA Pub. Assn., 1868.

Snook, B. F. Review of W. G. Springer on the Sabbath, Law of God and First Day of the Week, with An Appendix on the Perpetuity of the Sabbath and Law. Battle Creek, Mich.: SDA Pub. Assn., 1860.

Snook, B. F., and Brinkerhoff, Wm. H. The Visions of E. G. White, Not of God. [Marion, Ia.: Christian Pub. Assn.], 1866.

318

Stephenson, J. M. *The Atonement*. Rochester, N.Y.: Advent Review Office, 1854.

Storrs, George. *The Bible Examiner: Containing Various Prophetic Expositions*. Boston: J. V. Himes, 1843.

Stuart, Moses. *Hints on the Interpretation of Prophecy*. Andover, Mass.: Allen, Morill & Wardwell, 1842. 2nd ed., 1842.

Trall, Russell T. *The Hygienic System*. Battle Creek, Mich.: Office of the Health Reformer, 1872.

Tyerman, L. *The Life and Times of the Rev. John Wesley, M.A., Founder of the Methodists*. 3 vols. New York: Harper, 1870-72.

Waggoner, John H. *The Atonement: An Examination of a Remedial System, in the Light of Nature and Revelation*. Battle Creek, Mich.: SDA Pub. Assn., 1868; 2nd ed., 1872.

——————. *The Nature and Obligation of the Sabbath of the Fourth Commandment: with Remarks on the Great Apostasy and Perils of the Last Days*. Battle Creek, Mich.: Review and Herald Office, 1857.

Wellcome, Isaac C. *History of the Second Advent Message and Mission, Doctrine and People*. Yarmouth, Me.: I. C. Wellcome, 1874.

White, Ellen G. *Acts of the Apostles in the Proclamation of the Gospel of Jesus Christ*. Mountain View, Cal.: Pacific Press, 1911.

——————. *An Appeal to Mothers. The Great Cause of the Physical, Mental and Moral Ruin of Many of the Children of Our Time*. Battle Creek, Mich.: SDA Pub. Assn., 1864.

——————. *The Captivity and Restoration of Israel* [*The Story of Prophets and Kings*]. Mountain View, Cal.: Pacific Press, 1917.

——————. *Child Guidance*. Nashville, Tenn.: Southern Pub. Assn., 1954.

——————. *Christ's Object Lessons*. Washington, D.C.: Review and Herald, 1900.

——————. *Counsels on Diet and Foods*. Washington, D.C.: Review and Herald, 1946.

——————. *Counsels on Sabbath School Work*. Washington, D.C.: Review and Herald, 1938.

——————. *Early Writings of Mrs. White: Experience and Views, and Spiritual Gifts*. Vol. I. 2nd ed. Battle Creek, Mich.: Review and Herald, 1882; Washington, D.C.: Review and Herald, 1945.

——————. *Education*. Mountain View, Cal.: Pacific Press, 1952.

——————. *Evangelism As Set Forth in the Writings of Ellen G. White*. Washington, D.C.: Review and Herald, 1946.

——————. *Fundamentals of Christian Education*. Nashville, Tenn.: Southern Pub. Assn., 1923.

——————. *The Great Controversy between Christ and Satan During the Christian Dispensation*. Rev. and enl. Battle Creek, Mich.: Review and Herald, 1888. Mountain View, Cal.: Pacific Press, 1950.

——————. *Life Sketches of Ellen G. White: Being a Narrative of Her Experience to 1881 As Written By Herself; with A Sketch of Her Last Sickness Compiled from Original Sources*. Mountain View, Cal.: Pacific Press, 1915.

——————. *Medical Ministry: A Treatise on Medical Missionary Work in the Gospel*. Mountain View, Cal.: Pacific Press, 1932.

——————. *The Ministry of Healing*. Mountain View, Cal.: Pacific Press, 1905.

——————. *Our High Calling*. Washington, D.C.: Review and Herald, 1961.

——————. *Selected Messages from the Writings of Ellen G. White*. 2 vols. Washington, D.C.: Review and Herald, 1958.

——————. *A Sketch of the Christian Experience and Views of Ellen G. White*. Saratoga Springs, N.Y.: J. White, 1851; 2nd ed. Battle Creek, Mich.: Review and Herald, 1882. It was also incorporated as part of *Early Writings of Mrs. White*. (See above.)

_____. *Special Testimonies for Ministers and Workers*. No. 7 (Series A). Battle Creek, Mich.: General Conference of SDA, 1897.

_____. *Spirit of Prophecy*. Vol. IV: *The Great Controversy between Christ and Satan from the Destruction of Jerusalem to the End of the Controversy*. Battle Creek, Mich.: SDA Pub. Assn., 1884. (Facsimile reproduction. Washington, D.C.: Review and Herald, 1969.)

_____. *Spiritual Gifts*. Vol. I: *The Great Controversy, between Christ and His Angels, and Satan and His Angels*. Battle Creek, Mich.: J. White, 1858. (Facsimile reproduction. Washington, D.C.: Review and Herald, 1945.)

_____. *Spiritual Gifts*. Vol. II: *My Christian Experience, Views and Labors in Connection with the Rise and Progress of the Third Angel's Message*. Battle Creek, Mich.: J. White, 1860. (Facsimile reproduction. Washington, D.C.: Review and Herald, 1945.)

_____. *Spiritual Gifts*. Vol. III: *Important Facts of Faith, in Connection with the History of Holy Men of Old*. Battle Creek, Mich.: SDA Pub. Assn., 1864. (Facsimile reproduction. Washington, D.C.: Review and Herald, 1945.)

_____. *Spiritual Gifts*. Vol. IV: *Important Facts of Faith: Laws of Health, and Testimonies Nos. 1-10*. Battle Creek, Mich.: SDA Pub. Assn., 1864. (Facsimile reproduction. Washington, D.C.: Review and Herald, 1945.)

_____. *Supplement to the Christian Experience and Views of Ellen G. White*. Rochester, N.Y.: J. White, 1854.

_____. *Testimonies for the Church*. 9 vols. Mountain View, Cal.: Pacific Press, 1948.

_____. *Testimonies to Ministers and Gospel Workers*. Mountain View, Cal.: Pacific Press, 1962.

_____. *Testimony for the Church*. Nos. 1-33. Battle Creek, Mich.: Advent Review Office, 1855-61; SDA Pub. Assn., 1862-75; Review and Herald, 1875-89.

[_____, comp.]. *Health: or How To Live*. [Nos. 1-6]. Battle Creek, Mich.: SDA Pub. Assn., 1865.

[White, James S.] *A Brief Exposition of the Angels of Revelation XIV*. [Saratoga Springs, N.Y.: By the Author, 1851].

[_____]. *The Four Universal Monarchies of the Prophecy of Daniel, and God's Everlasting Kingdom*. Rochester, N.Y.: Advent Review Office, 1855.

_____. *Life Incidents, in Connection with the Great Advent Movement, As Illustrated By the Three Angels of Revelation XIV*. Battle Creek, Mich.: SDA Pub. Assn., 1868.

_____. *Sermons on the Second Coming and Kingdom of Our Lord Jesus Christ*. Our Faith and Hope. No. 1. Battle Creek, Mich.: SDA Pub. Assn., 1870. [2nd ed., rev. and enl., 1878]. (Facsimile reproduction of 2nd ed. Nashville, Tenn.: Southern Pub. Assn., 1972.)

_____. *The Parable. Matthew XXV, 1-12*. N.p.: [By the Author, 1851].

_____. *Perpetuity of Spiritual Gifts*. Battle Creek, Mich.: SDA Pub. Assn., [1870].

[_____]. *The Prophecy of Daniel. The Four Kingdoms, the Sanctuary, and the 2300 Days*. Battle Creek, Mich.: Review and Herald Office, 1859; SDA Pub. Assn., 1863.

_____. *The Sanctuary, the 2300 Days and the Shut Door*. Oswego, [N.Y.: By the Author], 1850.

_____. *The Second Coming of Christ; or, A Brief Exposition of Matthew Twenty-Four*. [Our Faith and Hope. No. 2]. Battle Creek, Mich.: SDA Pub. Assn., 1871.

_____. *The Signs of the Times, Showing That the Second Coming of Christ Is at the Doors. Spirit Manifestations, a Foretold Sign That the Day of God's Wrath*

Hasteth Greatly. Rochester, N.Y.: Review Office, 1853.

—————. *The Sketches of the Christian Life and Public Labors of William Miller, Gathered from His Memoirs By the Late Sylvester Bliss, and from Other Sources.* Battle Creek, Mich.: SDA Pub. Assn., 1875.

—————. *The Third Angel's Message.* [Oswego, N.Y.: By the Author, 1850.]

—————, ed. *Brother Miller's Dream.* Oswego, N.Y.: [By the Author], 1850.

—————, ed. *A Solemn Appeal Relative to Solitary Vice, and the Abuses and Excesses of the Marriage Relation.* Battle Creek, Mich.: SDA Pub. Assn., 1870.

[—————, ed. and comp.] *Hymns for God's Peculiar People, That Keep the Commandments and the Faith of Jesus.* Oswego, [N.Y.: By the Author], 1849.

White, James [S.]; White, Ellen G.; and Bates, Joseph. *A Word to the "Little Flock,"* [Brunswick, Me.: J. White], 1847. (Facsimile reproduction. Washington, D.C.: Review and Herald, [1944].)

Whiting, Nathan N. *Origin, Nature, and Influence of Neology.* Boston: J. V. Himes, 1844.

2. PERIODICALS.

Advent Harbinger and Midnight Alarm. Maidenhead, Berkshire, England: Aug.-Nov. 1844.

Advent Harbinger and Bible Advocate. Rochester, N.Y.: June 1849-June 1854.

Advent Herald. Boston: 1844-55.

Advent Mirror. Boston: Jan. 1845.

Advent Review. Auburn, N.Y.: Aug. 1850-Sept. 1850; Paris, Me.: Nov. 1850.

Advent Review and Sabbath Herald. Saratoga Springs, N.Y.: Aug. 5, 1851-March 23, 1852; Rochester, N.Y.: May 6, 1852-Oct. 30, 1855; Battle Creek, Mich.: Dec. 4, 1855-Dec. 1874.

Advent Shield and Review. Boston: May 1844 and Jan. 1845.

Advent Testimony. Boston: March and April 1846.

Bible Examiner. New York: Sept. 24, 1844.

Day-Dawn. Canandaigua, N.Y.: March 19, April 2 and 16, 1847.

Day-Star. Cincinnati: Feb. 18, 1845-46.

Girdle of Truth and Advent Review, Extra. New York: Jan. 20, 1848.

Health Reformer. Battle Creek, Mich.: Aug. 1866-74.

Hope of Israel. Portland, Me.: April 17, 1845.

Jubilee Standard. New York: April 3, 17, 24, May 22-July 10, 31, Aug. 7, 1845.

Midnight Cry. New York: Nov. 17, 1842-45. (Name changed to *Morning Watch,* Jan. 2, 1845.)

Morning Watch. New York: 1845 (Merged with *Advent Herald* on Aug. 13, 1845).

Present Truth. Middletown, Conn.: July-Sept. 1849; Oswego, N.Y.: Dec. 1849-May 1850; Paris, Me.: Nov. 1850.

Sabbath Recorder. New York: 1844-47, 1870.

Second Advent Harbinger. Bristol, England: March-May 1844.

Second Advent Review, and Sabbath Herald. Paris, Me.: Nov. 1850-June 1851. (Formed by merging of *Present Truth* and *Advent Review* in Nov. 1850. Name changed to *Advent Review, and Sabbath Herald,* Aug. 5, 1851.)

Signs of the Times. Boston: March 20, 1840-44. (Name changed to *Advent Herald,* Feb. 14, 1844.)

Signs of the Times. Oakland, Cal.: June-Dec. 1874; 1876.

True Day Star. New York: Dec. 29, 1845.

True Midnight Cry. Haverhill, Mass.: Aug. 22, 1844.

True Missionary. Battle Creek, Mich.: 1874.

Voice of the Shepherd. Utica, N.Y.: March, May-Sept. 1845.

Voice of the West and Second Advent Pioneer. Buchanan, Mich.: 1864-69.
Voice of Truth and Glad Tidings of the Kingdom at Hand. Rochester, N.Y.: 1844-45.
Western Midnight Cry. Cincinnati: 1844-45. (Name changed to *Day-Star,* Feb. 18, 1845.)
World's Crisis and Second Advent Messenger. Boston: 1854-57, 1864-75.

3. ARTICLES.

Andrews, John N. "Dear Brethren and Sisters." *PT,* Dec. 1849, p. 39.
_____. "The Opening of the Temple in Heaven." *RH,* April 6, 1869, pp. 113-16.
_____. "The Perpetuity of the Law of God." *RH,* Jan. and Feb. 1851, pp. 33-37, 41-43.
_____. "The Proclamation of Rev. XIV, 9-12," *RH,* June 22, 1869, p. 204.
_____. "The Sanctuary." *RH,* Dec. 23, 1852-Feb. 3, 1853.
_____. "The Sanctuary and Its Cleansing." *RH,* Oct. 30, 1855, pp. 68, 69.
_____. "The Seven Last Plagues." *RH,* Dec. 29, 1868, p. 5.
[_____]. "The Seventh-day Adventists of Europe." *RH,* Nov. 30, 1869, p. 181.
_____. "Thoughts on Revelation XIII and XIV." *RH,* May 19, 1851, pp. 81-86.
_____. "The Three Angels of Rev. XIV, 6-12." *RH,* Feb. 6-May 1, 1855.
_____. "The Use of Tobacco a Sin Against God." *RH,* April 10, 1856, p. 5.
Arnold, David. "Daniel's Visions, the 2300 Days, and the Shut Door." *PT,* March 1850, pp. 59-63.
_____. "The Shut Door Explained." *PT,* Dec. 1849, pp. 41-46.
_____, ed. "Dream of William Miller." *RH,* Extra, c. 1851.
Bates, Joseph. "The Beast with Seven Heads." *RH,* Aug. 5, 1851, pp. 3, 4.
_____ "Duty to Our Children." *RH,* Jan. 1851, pp. 39, 40.
_____ "Incidents in My Past Life." Nos. 1-51, *YI,* Nov. 1858-May 1863.
_____ "The Laodicean Church." *RH,* Nov. 1850, pp. 7, 8.
_____ "Midnight Cry in the Past." *RH,* Dec. 1850, pp. 21-24.
_____ "Our Labor in the Philadelphia and Laodicean Churches." *RH,* Aug. 1851, pp. 13, 14.
Bliss, Sylvester. "Review of Prof. Stuart's Hints on Prophecy." Nos. I-VII. *ST,* Sept. 21-Nov. 2, 1842.
[_____]. "The End of the Prophetic Periods." *ST,* April 5, 1843, pp. 33-35.
Bourdeau, Augustin C. "Our Present Position, in the Waiting, Tarrying Time." *RH,* May 28, 1867, pp. 276-78.
Bourdeau, Daniel T. "Advantages of God's People under the Messages, and Dangers of Backsliding." *RH,* Feb. 26, 1867, pp. 133, 134.
_____. "Health." Nos. 1-10. *HR,* Aug. 1866-Aug. 1867.
_____. "Tobacco and Tea." *RH,* March 17, 1863, p. 125.
Brown, F. G. "Reasons for Withdrawing from the Church." *AH,* March 27, 1844, pp. 58, 59.
Bush, George. "Prophetic Designations of Time." *AH,* March 6, 1844, pp. 33-35.
Butler, George I. "Advent Experience." Nos. 1-10. *RH,* Feb. 10-April 11, 1885.
_____. " 'Early Writings' and 'Suppression.' " *RH,* Supplement, Aug. 14, 1883, pp. 3-5.
_____. "What Have We Been Doing for Other Nations?" *TrM,* March 1874, pp. 20, 21.
C. "Midnight Cry." *ST,* June 15, 1842, p. 84.

Canright, Dudley M. "Present Condition of the World." *RH,* April 16, 1872, pp. 137, 138.

—————. "The Three Messages of Rev. XIV, 6-13." *RH,* Jan. 1, 1867, pp. 37-39.

Case, J. F. "Tobacco." *RH,* Sept. 24, 1857, pp. 166, 167.

[Cook, J. B.] "The Doctrine of Providence." *AT,* March 1846, pp. 1-5.

[—————]. "The Necessity and Certainty of Divine Guidance." *AT,* March 1846, pp. 5-8.

Cornell, Merritt E. "The Tobacco Abomination." *RH,* May 20, 1858, pp. 1, 2.

Cottrell, Roswell F. "Babylon Might Have Been Healed." *RH,* Aug. 4, 1853, p. 46.

—————. "Closing Messages." Nos. 1-30. *RH,* Aug. 1869-April 1870.

—————. "Elijah the Prophet." *RH,* July 9, 1867, pp. 49-51.

—————. "The 'Evangelical Alliance' vs. True Christian Union." *RH,* Feb. 24, 1874, p. 85.

—————. "Extract from 'Elijah the Tishbite.'" *RH,* Oct. 1, 1861, p. 141.

—————. "The Great Revival Here." *RH,* Aug. 29, 1865, pp. 100, 101.

—————. "'I Can Do More Good.'" *RH,* May 29, 1856, pp. 44, 45.

—————. "Making Us a Name." *RH,* March 22, 1860, pp. 140, 141.

—————. "Mark of the Beast, and Seal of the Living God." *RH,* July 28, 1859, pp. 77-79.

—————. "The Present 'Revivals' in Babylon." *RH,* May 13, 1858, p. 206.

—————. "Proselytism." *RH,* July 3, 1866, p. 36.

—————. "Speaking of the Image." *RH,* Dec. 12, 1854, p. 134.

—————. "To Sabbath-Keepers Who Have Not Yet Heard the Third Angel's Message." *RH,* June 10, 1852, p. 22.

—————. "Unity of the Church." *RH,* Oct. 18, 1870, p. 141.

—————. "Unity of the Remnant Church." *RH,* March 3 and 10, 1859, pp. 116-18, 125.

[Crosier, Owen R. L.] "The Advent This Spring." *DD,* April 2, 1847, pp. 6, 7.

—————. "Inquiry — the Sanctuary, &c." *AHBA,* March 5, 1853, pp. 300, 301.

—————. "The Law of Moses." *DS,* Extra, Feb. 7, 1846.

—————. "Prophetic Day and Hour." *VT,* April 9, 1845, p. 15.

[—————]. Remarks to Weston, *DD,* March 19, 1847, p. 2.

"The Daily." *MC,* Oct. 5, 1843, pp. 52, 53.

Editorial, "Address to the Public." *AH,* Nov. 13, 1844, pp. 108-12.

—————. "The Advent Herald." *AH,* Oct. 30, 1844, pp. 92, 93.

—————. "The Advent Question." *AH,* Nov. 27, 1847, pp. 132, 133.

—————. "Behold! The Bridegroom Cometh!" *AH,* Oct. 9, 1844, pp. 77-80.

—————. "Chronology." *ST,* June 21, 1843, p. 123.

—————. "Come Out of Her, My People." *SAH,* April 2, 1844, pp. 19-21.

—————. "Does the Bible Shroud the Coming [?]" *ST,* Nov. 16, 1842, p. 68.

—————. "Elijah." *WMC,* Dec. 21, 1844, p. 27.

—————. "Fundamental Principles, on Which the Second Advent Cause Is Based." *ST,* May 3, 1843, p. 68.

—————. "The Holy Alliance." *DS,* July 1, 1845, p. 31.

—————. "Hope of Israel," *VT,* May 14, 1845, p. 56.

—————. "Hope within the Veil." *JS,* July 3, 1845, pp. 132, 133.

—————. "The Jewish Year." *AH,* March 20, 1844, pp. 52, 53.

—————. "The Jewish Year." *MC,* Oct. 11, 1844, p. 117.

—————. "The Midst of the Week." *ST,* Dec. 5, 1843, pp. 132-36.

—————. "A Mistake Corrected." *VT,* July 2, 1845, p. 368.

—————. "The New Year." *ST,* Jan. 3, 1844, p. 164.

—————. "Our Course." *ST,* Nov. 15, 1840, pp. 126, 127.

_____. "Our Duty." *ST*, Nov. 30, 1842, p. 86.

_____. "Our Health Institute." *HR*, Feb. 1872, pp. 48, 49.

_____. "Our Position." *AH*, April 24, 1844, pp. 92, 93.

_____. "Reply to Brother Turner." *ST*, July 12, 1843, pp. 148, 149.

_____. "The Sign of the Son of Man in Heaven." *ST*, Oct. 11, 1843, pp. 59, 62, 63.

_____. " 'The Time of the End.' " *ST*, Jan. 4, 1843, p. 121.

_____. "The Types." *MC*, Oct. 11, 1844, pp. 116, 117.

_____. "The World Has Had the Midnight Cry." *ST*, Sept. 20, 1843, p. 36.

Edson, Hiram. "An Appeal to the Laodicean Church." *AdR*, Extra, Sept. 1850.

_____. "Beloved Brethren, Scattered Abroad." *PT*, Dec. 1849, pp. 34-36.

_____. "The Commandments of God, and the Mark of the Beast Brought to View By the Third Angel of Rev. XIV, Considered in Connection with the Angel of Chap. VII, Having the Seal of the Living God." *RH*, Sept. 2, 16 and 30, 1852.

_____. "Daniel Standing in His Lot." *RH*, July 30, 1857, p. 101.

Elliott, Wm. B. "The Door Is Shut, and We Know It." *JS*, May 22, 1845, pp. 81, 82.

Frisbie, Joseph B. "Church Order." *RH*, Dec. 26, 1854, and Jan. 9, 1855, pp. 147, 148, 153-55.

"The General Conference" (Oct. 14-15, 1840). *ST*, Nov. 1, 1840, pp. 113-17.

Gross, H. H. "The Times and the Seasons." *WMC*, Feb. 7, 1845, pp. 50, 51.

[Hale, Apollos]. "Adventists." *AH*, March 20, 1844, p. 53.

_____. "Has the Bridegroom Come?" *AH*, Feb. 26 and March 5, 1845, pp. 17-19, 26-28.

_____. "Letter of Dr. Pond, of the Theological Institution, Bangor, Me., with Notes in Reply to His Objections against the Doctrine of the Second Advent in 1843." *ST*, Oct. 26-Nov. 16, Dec. 14, 21, 1842.

_____. "Letter to N. N. Whiting." *AH*, Oct. 16, 1844, 2nd ed., pp. 81-83.

[_____]. "The Tenth Day of the Seventh Month." *AH*, Sept. 18 and 15, 1844, pp. 52, 53, 60-62.

Hale, Apollos, and Turner, Joseph. "Has Not the Savior Come As the Bridegroom?" *Advent Mirror*, Jan. 1845.

Haskell, Stephen N. "The Cause Is Onward." *RH*, Oct. 13, 1874, p. 125.

_____. "A Few Thoughts on the Philadelphia and Laodicean Churches." *RH*, Nov. 6, 1856, p. 6.

_____. "Missionary Spirit." *TrM*, April 1874, p. 28.

_____. "Object of Missionary Work." *TrM*, April 1874, pp. 28, 29.

_____. "Our Work." *TrM*, May 1874, p. 37.

[Himes, Joshua V.] "The Closing Up of the Day of Grace." *ST*, Aug. 1, 1840, pp. 69, 70.

_____. "The Crisis Has Come!" *ST*, Aug. 3, 1842, pp. 140, 141.

_____. "Editorial Correspondence." *AH*, Sept. 18, 1844, p. 53.

Hooper, John. " 'The Second Advent.' " *ST*, June 15, 1840, pp. 44, 45.

Hotchkiss, C. B. "Termination of Prophetic Periods." *MC*, Sept. 21, 1843, pp. 38, 39.

Hutchins, A. S. "The Field Is the World." *RH*, March 26, 1857, p. 168.

"Is Antiochus Epiphanes the Hero of Daniel's Prophecy?" *ST*, Extra, Dec. 21, 1842, pp. 1-3.

[Jacobs, Enoch]. "The Door of Matt. 25:10 Is Shut." *DS*, June 24, 1845, pp. 26-28.

[_____]. "The Time." *WMC*, Nov. 29, 1844, pp. 18-20.

Litch, Josiah. "Babylon's Fall — the Sanctuary Cleansed." *ST*, July 26, 1843, pp. 165, 166.

——————. "Bro. Litch on the Seventh Month." *AH*, Oct. 16, 1844, 2nd ed., p. 81.

——————. "Events To Succeed the Second Woe." *ST*, Aug. 1, 1840, p. 70.

——————. "Fall of the Ottoman Power in Constantinople." *ST*, Aug. 1, 1840, p. 70.

——————. "The Nations." *ST*, Feb. 1, 1841, pp. 161, 162.

——————. "The Restoration of the Jews." *ST*, Aug. 15, 1840, pp. 76, 77.

[——————]. "The Rise and Progress of Adventism." *ASR*, May 1844, pp. 46-93. (Nearly all was repr. in *RH*, April 24-May 29, 1856.)

——————. "The Seven Last Plagues." *MC*, Aug. 17, 1843, pp. 205-7.

——————. "This Gospel of the Kingdom." *ST*, Nov. 15, 1843, p. 109.

——————. "The Three Wo [*sic*] Trumpets." *ST*, Sept. 7, 1842, pp. 179-82.

[——————]. "The 24th of Matthew." *MC*, Aug. 17, 1843, pp. 202, 203.

Loughborough, John N. "Report from Bro. Loughborough." *RH*, Aug. 14, 1866, pp. 84, 85.

——————. "Response." *RH*, Sept. 25, 1866, pp. 133, 134.

——————. "Thoughts on the Day of Atonement." *RH*, Aug. 15, 1865, pp. 81-83.

——————. "The Two-Horned Beast." *RH*, March 21 and 28, 1854, pp. 65-67, 73-75, 79.

Loughborough, John N.; Hull, Moses; and Cornell, Merritt E. "Conference Address." *RH*, Oct. 15, 1861, pp. 156, 157.

Marsh, Joseph. "Come Out of Babylon!" *VT*, Sept. 11, 1844, p. 127.

Matteson, John [G.]. "Godly Sorrow." *RH*, June 19, 1866, p. 21.

McLellan, J. M. "The Temple of God Is No Place for Idols." *RH*, Oct. 9, 1856, p. 182.

Miller, William. "An Address to the Second Advent Believers, Held at Portland, Me., October 12, 1841." *ST*, Nov. 1, 1841, pp. 114-17.

——————. "Bro. Miller's Letter on the Seventh Month." *MC*, Oct. 12, 1844, pp. 121, 122.

——————. "Cleansing of the Sanctuary." *ST*, April 6, 1842, pp. 1, 2.

——————. "A Dream." *AH*, Feb. 2, 1850, pp. 2, 3.

——————. "Evidence from Scripture and History of the Second Coming of Christ About the Year 1843, and of His Personal Reign of 1000 Years, First Published in 1833." *ST*, April 1-Oct. 1, 1841.

——————. "A Lecture on the Signs of the Present Time." *ST*, March 20, 1840, pp. 3-7.

——————. "Miller's Lectures — No. 1." *ST*, July 1, 1840, pp. 49-51.

——————. Miller's Letters Nos. 3, 5 and 8. *ST*, April 15, May 15, and Sept. 1, 1840, pp. 14, 15, 25, 26, 81, 82.

——————. "Mr. Miller's Review of Dowling." *ST*, Aug. 1 and 15, 1840, pp. 67, 68, 74, 75.

——————. "Synopsis of Miller's Views." *ST*, Jan. 25, 1843, pp. 145-50.

Minor, C. S. " 'The Harvest Is Past.' " *DS*, April 22, 1845, pp. 41, 42.

"Mutual Conference of Adventists at Albany." *AH*, May 14, 1845, pp. 105-8.

Nichols, Otis. "Extract of Letters." *AdR*, Sept. 1850, pp. 47, 48.

Peavey, George W. "Behold the Bridegroom Cometh!" *MC*, Oct. 3, 1844, p. 103.

——————. " 'The Hour of His Judgment Is Come.' " *JS*, June 19, 1845, pp. 113-15.

——————. "The Seventh Month." *MC*, Sept. 12, 1844, p. 75.

[——————]. " 'Unto Two Thousand and Three Hundred Days: Then Shall the Sanctuary Be Cleansed.' " *JS*, Aug. 7, 1845, p. 166.

Pierce, Stephen. "Eating Not of Faith." *RH*, March 12, 1867, pp. 157, 158.

——————. "The Use of Tobacco." *RH*, Dec. 4, 1855, p. 79.

Preble, Thomas M. "The Sabbath." *VT,* Aug. 27, 1845, pp. 432, 433.

"The Sabbath in Ireland." *RH,* Nov. 19, 1861, pp. 198, 199.

Seventh-day Adventists. General Conference Report. 1867-75. *RH,* May 28, 1867; May 26, 1868; May 25, 1869; March 22, 1870; Feb. 14, 1871; Jan. 2, 1872; March 11, Nov. 25, 1873; Aug. 25, 1874 and Aug. 26, 1875.

"The Sin of Doing Nothing." *RH,* Aug. 21, 1855, p. 32.

Smith, M. B. "Coffee — Its Effects." *RH,* Oct. 1, 1861, pp. 142, 143.

_____. "Tea — Its Effects." *RH,* May 21, 1861, pp. 5, 6.

Smith, Uriah. "The Cleansing of the Sanctuary." *RH,* Oct. 22, 1855, pp. 52, 53.

_____. "Objections to the Visions." *RH,* Jan. 21, 1862, pp. 62-64.

[_____]. "The 1335 Days." *RH,* Feb. 27, 1866, p. 100.

_____. "The Sanctuary." *RH,* March 21, 28 and April 4, 1854, pp. 69, 70, 77, 78, 84-86.

[_____]. "The Seal of the Living God." *RH,* April 24 and May 1, 1856, pp. 12, 20, 21.

_____. "The Seventh-day Adventists." *RH,* Nov. 3-24, 1874, pp. 148, 149, 156, 164, 171.

[_____]. "Synopsis of the Present Truth." Nos. 1-28. *RH,* Nov. 12, 1857-June 10, 1858.

_____. "Thoughts on the Book of Daniel." *RH,* Jan. 5-June 15, 1869; June 21, 1870-Oct. 4, 1870; Dec. 20, 1870-March 28, 1871; May 16, July 4-July 18, 1871.

_____. "Thoughts on the Revelation." *RH,* June 3, 1862-Feb. 3, 1863.

_____. "The United States in the Light of Prophecy." *RH,* Oct. 17, 1871-Feb. 13, 1872.

_____. "The Visions — Objections Answered." *RH,* June 12-July 10, 31, 1866.

Snook, B. F. "The Great Missionary Society." *RH,* July 7, 1863, p. 46.

Snow, Samuel S. "And the Door Was Shut." *JS,* April 24, 1845, pp. 52-54.

_____. "Behold He Cometh!!" *DS,* April 22, 1845, p. 41.

_____. "The Confederacy." *JS,* June 12, 1845, pp. 108, 109.

_____. "The Laodicean Church." *JS,* June 12 and 19, 1845, pp. 108, 117.

_____. "Prophetic Chronology." *AH,* Aug. 14, 1844, p. 15.

_____. "Prophetic Chronology." *MC,* Sept. 19, 1844, p. 87.

_____. "Remarks." *JS,* June 5, 1845, p. 102.

_____. No title given. *TMC,* Aug. 22, 1844, pp. 1-4.

Spaulding, Joel. "Exposition on Matt. XXIV." *ST,* Sept. 14, 1842, pp. 185-87.

Stephenson, J. M. "The Atonement." *RH,* Aug. 22, Sept. 26, Oct. 13, 17, 31-Dec. 5, 1854.

_____. "The Number of the Beast." *RH,* Nov. 29, 1853, p. 166.

Storrs, George. "Come Out of Her, My People." *MC,* Feb. 15, 1844, p. 237.

_____. "Exposition of Matthew, XXIV, Chap." *MC,* Jan. 27, 1843, pp. [12-15].

_____. "Go Ye Out to Meet Him." *Bible Examiner,* Sept. 24, 1844, pp. [1, 2].

_____. "The Lord's Chronology." *MC,* Oct. 3, 1844, p. 102.

"To the Believers Scattered Abroad." *DS,* March 25, 1845, pp. 21-24.

Vuilleumier, Albert. "Switzerland." *RH,* Aug. 26, 1873, p. 86.

Waggoner, Joseph H. "The Atonement — Part II." *RH,* Sept. 8-22, Oct. 6-Dec. 1, 1863.

_____. "The Gospel of Health." *HR,* July and Sept. 1871, pp. 11, 12, 79, 80.

_____. "Moral Duty of Preserving Health." *HR,* Feb. 1872, p. 51.

_____. "Present Truth." *RH,* Aug. 7, 1866, pp. 76, 77.

_____. " 'Suppression' and 'the Shut Door.' " *RH,* Supplement, Aug. 14, 1883, pp. 1-3.

——————. "Tobacco." *RH,* Nov. 19, 1857, pp. 12, 13.

Ward, Henry D. "Prof. Stuart's Hints on Prophecy." Nos. 1-2. *ST,* Aug. 31 and Sept. 7, 1842, pp. 175, 176, 183.

——————. "The Restoration of Israel." *ST,* Sept. 1, 1840, p. 86.

——————. "To the Conference of Christians Expecting the Lord's Appearing Convened in Boston, 30th Nov., 1841." *ST,* Jan. 1, 1842, pp. 145-47.

"The Watching Time." *MW,* Jan. 30, 1845, p. 37.

Weston, J. "The Seven Churches." *AH,* July 3, 1844, pp. 174, 175.

White, Ellen G. "Dear Brethren and Sisters." *PT,* Aug. 1849-Nov. 1850, pp. 21-24, 31, 32, 64, 86, 87.

——————. "Duty To Know Ourselves." *HR,* Aug. 1866, pp. 2, 3.

——————. "Experience and Views." *RH,* Extra, July 21, 1851, p. [2].

——————. "The First Advent of Christ." *RH,* Dec. 24, 1872, pp. 10, 11.

——————. "The Laodicean Church." *RH,* Sept. 16-30, 1873, pp. 109, 117, 125.

——————. "The Life and Mission of John." *RH,* Jan. 7, 1873, pp. 26, 27.

——————. "Mrs. Ellen G. White." *Signs of the Times,* May 4, 1876, pp. 164, 165.

——————. "The Need of Home Religion." *RH,* June 29, 1905, pp. 7, 8.

——————. "Notes of Travel." *RH,* Nov. 20 and 27, 1883, pp. 721, 722, 737, 738.

——————. "Our Late Experience." *RH,* Feb. 20, 1866, pp. 89-91.

——————. "Parents Their Own Physicians." *HR,* Oct. 1866, pp. 35-37.

——————. "Questions and Answers." *RH,* Oct. 8, 1867, pp. 260, 261.

——————. "The Science of Salvation the First of Sciences." *RH,* Dec. 1, 1891, pp. 737, 738.

——————. "Search the Scriptures." *RH,* Oct. 9, 1883, pp. 625, 626.

——————. "Serving God Fervently." *RH,* July 26, 1887, pp. 465, 466.

——————. "The Spirit of Sacrifice: An Appeal for Men and Means To Send the Truth to Other Nations." *TrM,* Jan. 1874, pp. 1, 2.

——————. "Testimony to the Church." *RH,* Nov. 26, 1861, pp. 205, 206.

——————. "Tithes and Offerings." *RH,* Aug. 25 and Dec. 15, 1874, pp. 73, 74, 194, 195.

——————. "To the Remnant Scattered Abroad." Broadside, April 6, 1846. *WLF,* pp. 14-18.

——————. "To the Saints Scattered Abroad." *RH,* Feb. 17, 1853, pp. 155, 156.

——————. "To Those Who Are Receiving the Seal of the Living God." Broadside, Jan. 31, 1849.

——————. "The Value of Bible Study." *RH,* July 17, 1888, pp. 449, 450.

——————. "A Vision." Broadside, April 7, 1847.

——————. "The Work for This Time." *TrM,* Feb. 1874, pp. 9, 10.

——————. "The Work of the Minister." *RH,* Sept. 11, 1888, pp. 577, 578.

[White, James S.] "The Angels of Rev. XIV." Nos. 1-4. *RH,* Aug. 19-Dec. 23, 1851, pp. 12, 20, 63, 64, 68-72.

[——————]. "Babylon." *RH,* June 24, 1852, pp. 28, 29.

——————. "Babylon." *RH,* March 10, 1859, pp. 122, 123.

[——————]. "Bible Hygiene." *HR,* July 1871-Sept. 1872.

[——————]. "A Brief Sketch of the Past." *RH,* May 6, 1852, p. 5.

[——————]. "Brother Miller's Dream." *PT,* May 1850, pp. 73-75.

[——————]. "Cause in Switzerland." *RH,* Jan. 11, 1870, pp. 21, 22.

——————. Comments, *RH,* Extra, July 21, 1851, p. [4].

——————. "Conference Address before the General Conference of S.D. Adventists, March 11, 1873." *RH,* May 20, 1873, pp. 180, 181, 184.

——————. "The Day of Judgment." *AdR,* Sept. 1850, pp. 49-51.

[——————]. "The Faith of Jesus." *RH,* Aug. 5 and 19, 1852, pp. 52, 53, 60, 61.

[——————]. "The Faith of Jesus." *RH,* March 7 and 14, 1854, pp. 53, 54, 60.

——————. "Health and Religion." *HR,* Feb. 1874, pp. 33-35.

——————. "Health Reform." Nos. 1-7. *HR*, Nov. 1870-May 1871.

——————. "The Judgment." *RH*, Jan. 29, 1857, pp. 100, 101.

——————. "The Laodicean Church." *RH*, Nov. 13, 1856, p. 13.

——————. "Leadership." *TC*, No. 25, 1875, pp. 181-92.

——————. "The Light of the World." *RH*, April 21, 1863, pp. 164, 165.

——————. "The Loud Voice of the Third Angel." *RH*, Oct. 20, 1859, pp. 172, 173.

——————. " 'Making Us a Name.' " *RH*, April 26, 1860, pp. 180-82.

——————. "The Mystery of God." *RH*, March 27, 1856, pp. 204, 205.

——————. "New Fields." *RH*, Oct. 6, 1859, p. 98.

——————. "The Office." *RH*, July 24, 1855, pp. 12, 13.

——————. "Our Faith and Hope; or, Reasons Why We Believe As We Do." *RH*, Nov. 16, 1869-May 24, 1870; Dec. 20, 1870-Feb. 7, 1871.

——————. "Our Present Position." *RH*, Dec. 1850 and Jan. 1851, pp. 13-15, 27-30.

[——————]. "Our Present Work." *RH*, Aug. 19, 1851, pp. 12, 13.

[——————]. "Our Tour West." *RH*, Feb. 17, 1852, pp. 93, 94.

——————. "The Parable, Matthew XXV, 1-12," *RH*, June 9, 1851, pp. 97-103.

——————. "The Philadelphia Church." *RH*, Oct. 30, 1856, p. 205.

——————. "Publications in Other Languages." *RH*, Nov. 12, 1872, p. 173.

[——————]. "Redemption." *HR*, Dec. 1872, p. 371.

[——————]. "Remarks in Kindness." *RH*, March 2, 1852, pp. 100, 101.

[——————]. "Remarks on Luke XIII, 23, 25." *RH*, May 26, 1853, p. 4.

[——————]. "Repairing the Breach in the Law of God." *PT*, Sept. 1849, pp. 25-28.

——————. "Resolution of the Seventh-Day Baptist Central Association." *RH*, Aug. 11, 1853, pp. 52, 53.

[——————]. "The Sanctuary, 2300 Days, and the Shut Door," *PT*, May 1850, pp. 75-79.

——————. "The Seven Churches." *RH*, Oct. 16, 1856, pp. 188, 189, 192.

[——————]. "The Seventh Angel; Events To Occur During His Sounding." *RH*, March 7, 1854, p. 52.

——————. "Seventh-day Adventist Missionary Society." *RH*, June 15, 1869, p. 197.

[——————]. "The Shut Door." *RH*, April 14, 1853, pp. 188, 189.

——————. "Signs of the Times." *RH*, Aug. 11-Sept. 13, 1853.

——————. "A Sketch of the Rise and Progress of the Present Truth." *RH*, Dec. 31, 1857 and Jan. 14, 1858, pp. 61, 77, 78.

——————. "The Testimony of Jesus." *RH*, Dec. 18, 1855, pp. 92, 93.

——————. "The Third Angel's Message." *PT*, April 1850, pp. 65-69.

——————. "The Third Angel's Message." *RH*, Aug. 7-Sept. 4, 1856, pp. 108, 116, 117, 132, 133, 141.

——————. "The True Missionary." *TrM*, Jan. 1874, p. 4.

——————. "Voice of the Fourth Angel." *AdR*, No. 2, Aug. 1850, pp. 5, 6.

[——————]. "Who May Hear the Truth?" *RH*, Feb. 17, 1852, p. 94.

[——————]. "The Work of the Lord." *RH*, May 6, 1852, pp. 4, 5.

Woodcock, H. B. "The True Millennium." *WMC*, Dec. 30, 1844, pp. 31, 32.

4. LETTERS.

Brown, F. G. to Editor. *DS*, April 15, 1845, p. 34.

Case, Hiram S. to J. White. *PT*, Nov. 1850, p. 85.

Catlin, N. M. to E. Jacobs. *DS*, April 15, 1845, p. 40.

Clemons, Emily C. to Editor. *DS,* April 15, 1845, pp. 34, 35.
Cook, J. B. to E. Jacobs. *DS,* June 24 and July 8, 1845, pp. 26, 36; March 7, 1846, p. 3.
Cottrell, Roswell F. to J. White. *RH,* Feb. 3, 1852, p. 87.
Crosier, Owen R. L. to E. Jacobs. *DS,* Oct. 11, 1845, pp. 50, 51; Nov. 15, 1845, p. 23; April 18, 1846, p. 31.
――――――― to J. Pearson. *HI,* April 17, 1845, p. [4].
Curtis, Eli to S. S. Snow. *JS,* June 19 and 26, 1845, pp. 115, 116, 127.
Daniels, Dexter to U. Smith. *RH,* Feb. 5, 1857, p. 110.
Drew, Lebbeus to E. Jacobs. *DS,* Jan. 10, 1846, p. 13.
Edson, Hiram to S. S. Snow. *JS,* May 29, 1845, pp. 90, 91.
Greenleaf, Wm. J. to E. Jacobs. *DS,* June 3, 1845, p. 14.
Harmon, Ellen G. to E. Jacobs. *DS,* Jan. 24, 1846, pp. 31, 32; March 14, 1846, p. 7.
Hill, B. B. to S. S. Snow. *JS,* June 5, 1845, p. 100.
Holt, George W. to Dear Brethren. *PT,* March 1850, p. 64.
Main, C. to E. Jacobs. *DS,* Aug. 25, 1845, p. 12.
Martin, Jane to E. G. White. *RH,* Dec. 16, 1862, pp. 21, 22.
Matthias, B. to Wm. Miller. *JS,* April 24, 1845, p. 56.
Miller, William to S. Bliss. *AH,* Feb. 12, 1845, pp. 2, 3.
――――――― to J. V. Himes. *ST,* May 17, 1843, p. 85; *AH,* April 10, 1844, pp. 77, 78; Nov. 27, 1844, p. 128; Dec. 11, 1844, p. 142; May 6, 1846, p. 99; Jan. 8, 1848, p. 182.
――――――― to I. E. Jones. *AH,* Dec. 25, 1844, pp. 154, 155.
――――――― to J. Marsh. *VT,* repr. in *DS,* March 11, 1845, p. 13.
Nichols, Otis to E. Jacobs. *DS,* Sept. 27, 1845, p. 34.
Peavey, George W. to S. S. Snow and B. Matthias. *JS,* April 24, 1845, p. 55.
Pickands, J. D. to E. Jacobs. *DS,* Sept. 20 and 27, 1845, pp. 25, 33.
――――――― to J. Marsh. *VT,* Feb. 12, 1845, p. 12.
――――――― to S. S. Snow. *JS,* June 19, 1845, pp. 119, 120.
Sisley, John to Brethren and Sisters. *RH,* June 2, 1861, p. 47.
Snow, Samuel S. to Brethren of the Advent Faith. *MC,* May 2, 1844, p. 353 [335].
――――――― to J. Marsh. *VT,* April 16, 1845, p. 20.
――――――― to N. Southard. *MC,* Feb. 22, June 27, 1844, pp. 243, 244, 397.
Thomas, J. H. to E. Jacobs. *WMC,* Dec. 21, 1844, p. 28.
Turner, Joseph to Editor. *HI,* Jan. 24, 1845.
――――――― to S. S. Snow. *JS,* July 10, 1845, pp. 137-39.
Wardwell, J. F. to O. R. L. Crosier. *DD,* April 16, 1847, p. 10.
White, Ellen G. to J. Bates, No. 1, April 7, 1847. *WLF,* pp. 18-20.
――――――― to Brethren and Sisters. *RH,* Jan. 10, 1856, p. 118.
――――――― to E. Curtis, No. 2, April 21, 1847. *WLF,* pp. 11, 12.
――――――― to S. N. Haskell and [G. A.] Irwin, No. 207, Dec. 15, 1899. *SDABC,* VII, 982.
――――――― to Hastings, No. 10, March 18, 1850. *SM,* II, 263.
――――――― to Charles Lee, No. 54, Oct. 24, 1874. *T,* III, 414-34.
――――――― to J. N. Loughborough, No. 2, Aug. 24, 1874. *SM,* I, 74.
White, James [S.] to E. Jacobs. *DS,* Sept. 6, 20 and Oct. 11, 1845, pp. 17, 18, 25, 26, 47; Jan. 24, 1846, p. 25.

5. CHARTS.

[Fitch, Charles, and Hale, Apollos]. A Chronological Chart of the Visions of Daniel & John. Boston: J. V. Himes, [1842].
[Rhodes, Samuel W.]. A Pictorial Illustration of the Visions of Daniel & John and Their Chronology. Dorchester, Mass.: Otis Nichols, [1850].

[White, James S.]. A Pictorial Illustration of the Visions of Daniel & John. Battle Creek, Mich.: SDA Pub. Assn., [1863].

B. Unpublished Materials.

1. LETTERS.

Bliss, Sylvester to Wm. Miller, Feb. 11, 1845.
Clayton, T. Greer to Wm. Miller, Oct. 26, 1844.
Clemons, Emily C. to Wm. Miller, Feb. 17, 1845.
Himes, Joshua V. to Wm. Miller, March 12 and 29, 1845.
Jones, I. E. to Wm. Miller, Nov. 23, 1844 and Feb. 15, 1845.
Miller, William to Andrus, Feb. 15, 1831.
_____ to E. Galusha, April 5, 1844.
_____ to T. Hendryx, Aug. 9, 1831.
_____ to J. O. Orr, Dec. 13, 1844.
_____ to T. Wrightson and Others, March 20, 1845.
Nichols, Otis to Wm. Miller, April 20, 1846.
Shipman, J. H. to Wm. Miller, Feb. 28, 1845.
Turner, Joseph to Wm. Miller, Jan. 20 and Feb. 7, 1845.
White, Ellen G. to [Abram] Barns, No. 5, Dec. 14, 1851.
_____ to J. Bates, No. 3, July 13, 1847.
_____ to [H. G.] Buck, No. 18, Jan. 19, 1861.
_____ to the Church in Hastings' House, No. 28, Nov. 7, 1850.
_____ to the [Gilbert] Collinses, No. 2, Feb. 10, 1850.
_____ to M. B. Czechowski, No. 3, c. 1864.
_____ to the [A. A.] Dodges, No. 4, July 21, 1851 and No. 5, July 5, 1853.
_____ to Friends, No. 13, Jan. 8, 1859.
_____ to Friends in Mansville, No. 7, c. 1856.
_____ to Hastings and Harriet, No. 7, July 27, 1851.
_____ to Arbella Hastings, No. 8, Aug. 4, 1850.
_____ to the [Leonard] Hastingses, No. 1, May 29, 1848 and No. 18, Jan. 11, 1850.
_____ to the [S.] Howlands, No. 8, Nov. 12, 1851.
_____ to Kellogg, No. 9, Dec. 5, 1853.
_____ to Lay, No. 1a, Jan. 11, 1872.
_____ to the Lovelands, No. 26, Nov. 1, 1850.
_____ to Morrell, No. 20, Dec. 28, 1867.
_____ to S. Pierce, No. 2, 1851 and No. 4, Dec. 3, 1857.
_____ to Sawyer, No. 8, 1863.
_____ to the Scotts, No. 5, July 6, 1863.
_____ to U. Smith, No. 10, May 14, 1873.
_____ to the U. Smiths, No. 25, May 6, 1874.
_____ to Edson and Emma White, No. 19b, April 27, 1874.
White, James [S.] to [J. C.] Bowles, Oct. 17 and Nov. 8, 1849.
_____ to Brother, July 21, 1850.
_____ to the Hastingses, Aug. 26 and Oct. 2, 1848.
Wrightson, T. to Wm. Miller, March 18, 1845.

2. OTHER MANUSCRIPTS.

Edson, Hiram. MS (Incomplete), Experience in the Advent Movement, n.d.
Miller, William. MS, Sept. 5, 1822; MS of an article for the *Vermont Telegraph*, c. 1831.

White, Ellen G. MS 3, 1849; MS 5 and 11, 1850; MS 5, 1851; MS 1, 1863; MS 4, 1866; MS 1, 1869; MS 1 and MS 1a, 1874; MS 4, 1883; MS 173, 1902; MS 19, 1910.

C. Location of the Primary Sources.

American Antiquarian Society. Worchester, Mass.
Archives of the General Conference of Seventh-day Adventists. Washington, D.C.
Ellen G. White Estate. Washington, D.C.
Ellen G. White Research Center. Andrews University. Berrien Springs, Mich.
Heritage Room, A Seventh-day Adventist Archive. Andrews University. Berrien Springs, Mich.
Library of Congress. Washington, D.C.
Massachusetts Historical Society. Boston, Mass.
Orrin Roe Jenks Memorial Collection of Adventual Materials. Aurora College, Ill.
Seventh Day Baptist Historical Society. Plainfield, N.J.

II. Secondary Sources.

A. Published Materials.

1. BOOKS AND PAMPHLETS.

Ahlstrom, Sydney E. *A Religious History of the American People.* New Haven, Conn.: Yale University Press, 1972.
Beach, Bert B. *Ecumenism: Boon or Bane?* Washington, D.C.: Review and Herald, 1974.
Berkhofer, Robert F., Jr. *Salvation and the Savage: An Analysis of Protestant Mission and American Response, 1787-1862.* [Lexington, Ky.]: University of Kentucky Press, 1965.
Billington, Ray A. *The Protestant Crusade, 1800-1860: A Study of the Origins of American Nativism.* New York: Macmillan, 1938.
Brauer, Jerald C. *Protestantism in America.* Rev. ed. London: SCM Press, 1965.
A Brief Sketch of the Origin, Progress, and Principles of the Seventh-day Adventists. Battle Creek, Mich.: Review and Herald, 1888.
Canright, Dudley M. *Seventh-day Adventism Renounced after an Experience of Twenty-Eight Years By a Prominent Minister and Writer of That Faith.* 2nd ed. New York: Fleming H. Revell, 1889.
Clark, Jerome L. *1844.* 3 vols. Vol. I: Religious Movements. Vol. II: Social Movements. Vol. III: Intellectual Movements. Nashville, Tenn.: Southern Pub. Assn., 1968.
Conley, Paul C., and Sorensen, Andrew A. *The Staggering Steeple: The Story of Alcoholism and the Churches.* Philadelphia, Pa.: Pilgrim Press, 1971.
Conradi, L. Richard. *Ist Frau E. G. White die Prophetin der Endgemeinde?* Hamburg, Germany: [By the Author, 193?].
Cross, Whitney R. *The Burned-over District: The Social and Intellectual History of Enthusiastic Religion in Western New York, 1800-1850.* Ithaca, N.Y.: Cornell University Press, 1950; New York: Harper & Row, 1965.
De Jong, James A. *As the Waters Cover the Sea: Millennial Expectations in the Rise of Anglo-American Missions, 1640-1810.* Kampen, The Netherlands: J. H. Kok, 1970.

Debo, Angie. *A History of the Indians in the United States.* Norman, Okla.: University of Oklahoma Press, 1970.

Drummond, Andrew L. *Story of American Protestantism.* Boston: Beacon Press, 1950.

Elsbree, Oliver W. *The Rise of the Missionary Spirit in America, 1790-1815.* Williamsport, Pa.: n.p., 1928.

Froom, LeRoy E. *The Conditionalist Faith of Our Fathers: The Conflict of the Ages over the Nature and Destiny of Man.* 2 vols. Washington, D.C.: Review and Herald, 1965-66.

_____. *The Prophetic Faith of Our Fathers: The Historical Development of Prophetic Interpretation.* 4 vols. Washington, D.C.: Review and Herald, 1946-54.

Gaustad, Edwin S., ed. *The Rise of Adventism: Religion and Society in Mid-Nineteenth-Century America.* New York: Harper & Row, 1974.

Haller, William. *Elect Nation: The Meaning and Relevance of Fox's Book of Martyrs.* New York: Harper & Row, 1963.

Handy, Robert T. *A Christian America: Protestant Hopes and Historical Realities.* New York: Oxford University Press, 1971.

Historical Sketches of the Foreign Missions of the Seventh-day Adventists. Basel, Switzerland: Imprimerie Polyglotte, 1886.

Horn, Siegfried H., and Wood, Lynn H. *The Chronology of Ezra 7.* 2nd ed., rev. Washington, D.C.: Review and Herald, 1970.

Hudson, Winthrop S. *Religion in America: An Historical Account of the Development of American Religious Life.* 2nd ed. New York: Charles Scribner's Sons, 1973.

Hyde, Gordon M., ed. *A Symposium on Biblical Hermeneutics.* Washington, D.C.: General Conference of SDA, 1974.

Latourette, Kenneth S. *Christianity in a Revolutionary Age: A History in the Nineteenth and Twentieth Centuries.* Vol. III: *The Nineteenth Century Outside Europe: The Americas, the Pacific, Asia, and Africa.* New York: Harper, 1961.

Lindén, Ingemar. *Biblicism Apocalyptik Utopi: Adventismes Historiska Utforming i USA samt dess Svenska Utveckling Till o. 1939.* Uppsala: University of Uppsala, 1971.

Littell, Franklin H. *From State Church to Pluralism: A Protestant Interpretation of Religion in American History.* Garden City, N.Y.: Doubleday, 1962.

Long, A. C. *Comparison of the Early Writings of Mrs. White with Later Publications.* Marion, Ia.: [Advent and Sabbath Advocate Press], 1883.

Loughborough, John N. *The Great Second Advent Movement: Its Rise and Progress.* Nashville, Tenn.: Southern Pub. Assn., 1905; repr. New York: Arno Press, 1972.

_____. *Rise and Progress of the Seventh-day Adventists with Tokens of God's Hand in the Movement and a Brief Sketch of the Advent Cause from 1831 to 1844.* Battle Creek, Mich.: General Conference Assn. of SDA, 1892.

Ludlum, David M. *Social Ferment in Vermont 1791-1850.* New York: Columbia University Press, 1939.

Mueller, Konrad F. *Die Frühgeschichte der Siebenten-tags Adventisten bis zur Gemeindegründung 1863 und ihre Bedeutung für die moderne Irenik.* Marburg, Germany: N. G. Elwert, 1969.

Neufeld, Don F., ed. *Seventh-day Adventist Encyclopedia.* Washington, D.C.: Review and Herald, 1966.

Nichol, Francis D. *Ellen G. White and Her Critics: An Answer to the Major Charges that Critics Have Brought Against Mrs. Ellen G. White.* Washington, D.C.: Review and Herald, 1951.

_____. *The Midnight Cry: A Defense of William Miller and the Millerites.* Washington, D.C.: Review and Herald, 1944.

_____, ed. *The Seventh-day Adventist Bible Commentary.* 7 vols. Washington,

D.C.: Review and Herald, 1953-57.

Olmstead, Clifton E. *History of Religion in the United States.* Englewood Cliffs, N.J.: Prentice-Hall, 1960.

Olsen, M. Ellsworth. *A History of the Origin and Progress of Seventh-day Adventists.* Washington, D.C.: Review and Herald, 1925.

Pfeffer, Leo. *Church, State, and Freedom.* Rev. ed. Boston: Beacon Press, 1967.

Robinson, D. E. *The Story of Our Health Message: The Origin, Character, and Development of Health Education in the Seventh-day Adventist Church.* 3rd ed., rev. and enl. Nashville, Tenn.: Southern Pub. Assn., 1965.

Sandeen, Ernest R. *The Roots of Fundamentalism: British and American Millenarianism 1800-1930.* Chicago: University of Chicago Press, 1970.

Seventh-day Adventists Answer Questions on Doctrine: An Explanation of Certain Major Aspects of Seventh-day Adventist Belief. Washington, D.C.: Review and Herald, 1957.

Seventh-day Adventists. General Conference. *Church Manual.* Rev. ed. [Washington, D.C.]: General Conference of Seventh-day Adventists, 1971.

Smith, Elwyn A., ed. *The Religion of the Republic.* Philadelphia, Pa.: Fortress Press, 1971.

Smith, H. Shelton; Handy, Robert T.; and Loetscher, Lefferts A. *American Christianity: An Historical Interpretation with Representative Documents.* 2 vols. New York: Charles Scribner's Sons, 1963.

Smith, Timothy L. *Revivalism and Social Reform: American Protestantism on the Eve of the Civil War.* New York: Abingdon, 1957; New York: Harper & Row, 1965.

So Much in Common: Documents of Interest in the Conversations between the World Council of Churches and the Seventh-day Adventist Church. Geneva: World Council of Churches, 1973.

Spalding, Arthur W. *Origin and History of Seventh-day Adventists.* 4 vols. Washington, D.C.: Review and Herald, 1961-62.

Spicer, William A. *Pioneer Days of the Advent Movement with Notes on Pioneer Workers and Early Experiences.* Washington, D.C.: Review and Herald, 1941.

Stokes, Anson P. *Church and State in the United States.* 3 vols. New York: Harper, 1950.

Sweet, William W. *Religion in the Development of American Culture, 1765-1840.* New York: Charles Scribner's Sons, 1952.

Toon, Peter, ed. *Puritans, the Millennium and the Future of Israel: Puritan Eschatology 1600 to 1660.* Cambridge, England: James Clarke, 1970.

Tuveson, Ernest L. *Redeemer Nation: The Idea of America's Millennial Role.* Chicago: University of Chicago Press, 1968.

Tyler, Alice F. *Freedom's Ferment: Phases of American Social History to 1860.* Minneapolis, Minn.: University of Minnesota, 1944.

Weber, Herman C., ed. *Yearbook of American Churches.* New York: Round Table Press, 1933.

Wheeler, Henry, *Methodism and the Temperance Reformation.* Cincinnati, Ohio: Walden and Stowe, 1882.

White, Arthur L. *Ellen G. White: Messenger to the Remnant.* Rev. ed. Washington, D.C.: Review and Herald, 1969.

2. PERIODICALS.

Adventist Heritage. Loma Linda, Cal.: 1974.
Church History. Chicago: June 1962.
Ecumenical Review. Geneva: April 1972.

3. ARTICLES.

Beaver, R. Pierce. "American Missionary Motivation before the Revolution." *Church History,* **XXXI** (June 1962), 218.

_____. "Missionary Motivation through Three Centuries." *Reinterpretation in American Church History.* Ed. by Jerald C. Brauer. Chicago: University of Chicago Press, 1968.

Blake, John G. "Health Reform." *Rise of Adventism.* Ed. by Edwin S. Gaustad. (See above.)

Maclear, J. F. "The Republic and the Millennium." *Religion of the Republic.* Ed. by Elwyn A. Smith. (See above.)

Sandeen, Ernest R. "Millennialism." *Rise of Adventism.* Ed. by Edwin S. Gaustad. (See above.)

B. Unpublished Materials.

1. LETTERS.

Lindén, Ingemar to the Ellen G. White Trustees, Sept. 2, 1971.

_____ to A. L. White, Sept. 3, 1971.

White, Arthur L. to I. Lindén, Oct. 21, 1971.

2. OTHER MANUSCRIPTS.

Arthur, David T. " 'Come Out of Babylon': A Story of Millerite Separatism and Denominationalism, 1840-1865." Ph.D. dissertation, University of Rochester, 1970.

Davis, Roger G. "Conscientious Cooperators: The Seventh-day Adventists and Military Service, 1860-1945," Ph.D. dissertation, George Washington University, 1970.

Dick, Everett N. "The Adventist Crisis of 1843-1844." Ph.D. dissertation, University of Wisconsin, 1930.

Frei, Jacques. "Recueil de documents concernant Michael Belina Czechowski." Wetzikon, [Switzerland], 1971.

Haddock, Robert. "A History of the Doctrine of the Sanctuary in the Advent Movement 1800-1905." B.D. thesis, Andrews University, 1970.

Harkness, Reuben E. E. "Social Origins of the Millerite Movement." Ph.D. dissertation, University of Chicago, 1927.

Rowe, David L. "Thunder and Trumpets: The Millerite Movement and Apocalyptic Thought in Upstate New York, 1800-1845." Ph.D. dissertation, University of Virginia, 1974.

White, Arthur L. "Ellen G. White and the Shut Door Question." 1971.

_____. "Memorandum Concerning Washington Morse." Jan. 21, 1975.

Indices

337

341

343

56371